The Decline of Medieval Hellenism in Asia Minor and the Process of Islamization from the Eleventh through the Fifteenth Century

Published under the auspices of the
CENTER FOR MEDIEVAL AND RENAISSANCE STUDIES
University of California, Los Angeles

Publications of the
CENTER FOR MEDIEVAL AND RENAISSANCE STUDIES, UCLA

1. Jeffrey Burton Russell: Dissent and Reform in the Early Middle Ages
2. C. D. O'Malley: Leonardo's Legacy
3. Richard H. Rouse: Serial Bibliographies for Medieval Studies
4. Speros Vryonis, Jr.: The Decline of Medieval Hellenism in Asia Minor and the Process of Islamization from the Eleventh through the Fifteenth Century

The Decline of Medieval Hellenism in Asia Minor and the Process of Islamization from the Eleventh through the Fifteenth Century

Speros Vryonis, Jr.

Berkeley   Los Angeles   London   1971

UNIVERSITY OF CALIFORNIA PRESS

University of California Press
Berkeley and Los Angeles, California
University of California Press, Ltd.
London, England
Copyright © 1971 by The Regents of the University of California
ISBN: 0-520-01597-5
Library of Congress Catalog Card Number: 75-94984
Printed in the United States of America

To my mother and to the memory of my father

Preface

The writing of this book arose from the convergence of two interests that have long intrigued me: the Hellenization of the Levant in antiquity and the centuries-long confrontation of Byzantine and Islamic societies, the joint heirs of this semi-Hellenized Levant. The decline of Byzantine Hellenism and the phenomenon of Islamization in Anatolia from the eleventh through the fifteenth century focus on that area and time within which these two interests converge for the last time. Perhaps this undertaking is inordinately ambitious, encompassing as it does a vast geographical and chronological span and cutting across three disciplines (those of the Byzantinist, Islamist, and Turkologist). Now that this work is finished the words that Helmut Ritter spoke to me in an Istanbul restaurant in 1959, and which then seemed to be a challenge, take on a different meaning. This renowned orientalist told me, simply and calmly, that it would be impossible to write a history of this great cultural transformation. My own efforts have, of necessity, been restricted to certain aspects of this huge problem. Scholarship badly needs new, detailed histories of the Seljuk, Nicaean, Trebizondine states, and of many of the Turkish emirates. There has been no comprehensive history of the Rum Seljuks since that of Gordlevski (1941),[1] of Nicaea since those of Meliarakes and Gardner in 1898 and 1912, of Trebizond since that of Miller in 1926. The archaeology of Byzantine and Seljuk Anatolia is still in its infancy, and the mere establishment of the principal events and their dates in these four centuries remains unachieved. Unwritten also is the history of Arabo-Byzantine relations and confrontations in Anatolia, though the monumental work of Marius Canard on the Hamdanids represents a substantial beginning. The story of the decline that Islamization occasioned in the Armenian, Georgian, and Syrian communities of eastern Anatolia, though absolutely essential, is yet to be written. Finally a comparative study of the folklore and folk cultures of the Anatolian Muslims and Christians would do much to fill the wide gaps in historical sources. The number and extent of these scholarly desiderata surely indicate how imperfect and insufficient the present work must be. I have concentrated

---

[1] The book of Claude Cahen, *Pre-Ottoman Turkey* (London, 1968) appeared after the completion of my own work.

on the fate and Islamization of the Greek population in Anatolia to the exclusion of the other Christian groups. There has been no attempt to present a conventional chronological history of events, but rather the approach has been topical.

It is with pleasure that I acknowledge the support of several institutions which greatly facilitated my research. The Middle East Center of Harvard University enabled me to begin the investigation as a Research Fellow of the Center in 1959–60. A grant from the Harvard Center and Dumbarton Oaks subsequently allowed me to spend a summer at Dumbarton Oaks in this early stage. The interest and sympathy of former Chancellor Franklin Murphy and the director of the UCLA library, Dr. Robert Vosper, resulted in the constitution of a respectable Byzantine collection of books and periodicals absolutely essential for research in Byzantine history, and which had previously been lacking on the UCLA campus. The UCLA Research Committee and the Center for Near Eastern Studies, by their unstinting generosity, made it possible for me to work at those institutions in the United States and abroad which would provide me with the necessary materials. Thanks to a grant of the Social Science Research Council in 1962–63, I spent one semester at Dumbarton Oaks and one semester in Greece and Turkey where I enjoyed the facilities of the Gennadius Library, the Center for Asia Minor Studies, and the kindness of the members of the history faculty of the University of Ankara. As the work neared an end, William Polk, Director of the Middle East Center, and William McNeill, chairman of the history department, invited me to spend 1966–67 at the University of Chicago where they provided me with the badly needed leisure to finish the basic writing.

I am particularly indebted to my colleagues at UCLA who in meetings of the Near Eastern Center, the Medieval and Renaissance Center, the faculty seminar of the history department, and in individual encounters contributed to the sharpening of the work's focus as well as to the improvement of its contents. Milton Anastos, Amin Banani, Andreas Tietze, Gustave von Grunebaum, and Lynn White came to my assistance in certain specialized areas, and more important listened to what must have seemed an endless outpouring of Anatolica with a patience that would easily rank them among the Byzantine saints and Muslim dervishes of Anatolia. I am also grateful to Andreas Tietze who took time from his busy schedule as chairman of the Department of Near Eastern Languages to read through the manuscript. His great knowledge and kindness saved the book from many errors. I wish to express my gratitude to Peter Charanis with whom I frequently discussed many of the problems entailed in the writing of this book, and to whose research on Byzantine ethnography I am much indebted. Thanks are also due to Osman Turan and Halil Inalcik who, with their unsurpassed expertise in things Seljuk and Ottoman, have been so kind as to discuss with me many particulars related to Byzantino-Turcica, who supplied me with copies of their writings, and who gave me encouragement. The studies of Paul Wittek and Claude Cahen have been of particular value and aid, and those of Richard Ettinghausen have been helpful in the area of art history. I wish to thank my editor, Shirley Warren, who performed admirably with a difficult manuscript and also the editors of the new *Encyclopedia of Islam* for permission to reproduce the statistical chart from the article "Anadolu," by Franz Taeschner. I have dedicated the book to my father and mother, who first imbued me with a love for the historical past, who educated me with great patience and expense, and who gave me every encouragement.

The problems of transliteration and of geographical names have been such that there is no conceivable system that would satisfy everyone. Basically I have followed the new edition of the *Encyclopedia of Islam* in the transliteration of Islamic names. The Turkish equivalents for the names of Byzantine towns and villages will frequently be found in the key to the map. Though to some my treatment of transliteration and of geographic names will seem cavalier, I shall be satisfied if I have conveyed the meaning rather than a particular philological form.

Contents

List of Illustrations

Abbreviations

Greek historians in the *Corpus Scriptorum Historiae Byzantinae* are simply listed by name and with no further identification.

AS	*Acta Sanctorum.*
Aksaray-Gençosman	M. N. Gençosman and F. N. Uzluk, *Aksarayli̇ Kerimeddin Mahmud'un müsameret-el-ahyer adli̇ Farsça tarihinin tercümesi* (Ankara, 1943).
A.B.	*Analecta Bollandiana.*
A.Ι.Σ.	Ἀνάλεκτα Ἱεροσολυμιτικῆς Σταχυολογίας, vols. I–V (Petersburg, 1891–1898).
Anna Comnena	*Anne Comnène. Alexiade, texte établi et traduit,* B. Leib, vols. I–III. (Paris, 1937–1945).
A.I.P.H.O.S.	*Annuaire de l'institut philologique et historique orientales et slaves.*
A.Π.	Ἀρχεῖον Πόντου.
B.K.	*Bedi Karthlisa.*
B.G.A.	*Bibliotheca geographorum arabicorum,* ed. J-M. de Goeje, vols. I-VIII, (Leiden, 1885–1927).
B.J.R.L.	*Bulletin of the John Rylands Library.*
B.S.O.A.S.	*Bulletin of the School of Oriental and African Studies.*
B.F.	*Byzantinische Forschungen.*
B.N.J.	*Byzantinisch-neugriechische Jahrbücher.*
B.Z.	*Byzantinische Zeitschrift.*
B.S.	*Byzantinoslavica.*
C.E.H.	*Cambridge Economic History,* ed. J. H. Clapham and E. Power (Cambridge, 1941 ff.).
Δ.Ι.Ε.Ε.Ε.	Δελτίον τῆς ἱστορικῆς καὶ ἐθνολογικῆς ἑταιρίας τῆς Ἑλλάδος.
D.T.C.	*Dictionnaire de théologie catholique* (Paris, 1903 ff.).
D.H.G.E.	*Dictionnaire d'histoire et de géographie écclesiastiques* (Paris, 1912 ff.).
Dölger, *Regesten*	F. Dölger, *Regesten der Kaiserurkunden des oströmischen Reiches* (Munich-Berlin, 1924 ff.).
D.O.P.	*Dumbarton Oaks Papers.*
E.O.	*Échos d'Orient.*
Eflaki-Huart	C. Huart, *Les saints des derviches tourneurs,* vols. I–II (Paris, 1918–1922).
EI₁	*Encyclopedia of Islam,* first edition.
EI₂	*Encyclopedia of Islam,* second edition.

E.H.R.	*English Historical Review.*
G.R.B.S.	*Greek Roman and Byzantine Studies.*
Grumel, *Regestes*	V. Grumel, *Les regestes des actes du patriarcat de Constantinople* (Chalcedon, 1932 ff.).
Ibn Bibi-Duda	H. Duda, *Die Seltschukengeschichte des Ibn Bibi* (Copenhagen, 1959).
I.A.	*Islam Ansiklopedisi.*
I.M.	*Istanbuler Mitteilungen.*
J.Ö.B.G.	*Jahrbuch der österreichischen byzantinischen Gesellschaft.*
J.A.	*Journal Asiatique.*
J.H.S.	*Journal of Hellenic Studies.*
J.A.O.S.	*Journal of the American Oriental Society.*
J.E.S.H.O.	*Journal of the Economic and Social History of the Orient.*
J.R.A.S.	*Journal of the Royal Asiatic Society.*
K.C.A.	*Körösi Csoma-archivium.*
M.B.	K. N. Sathas, Μεσαιωνικὴ Βιβλιοθήκη (Venice, 1872–1877).
Miklosich et Müller	F. Miklosich and J. Müller, *Acta et diplomata graeca medii aevi sacra et profana* (Vienna, 1860–1890).
M.X.	Μικρασιατικὰ Χρονικά.
M.A.M.A.	*Monumenta Asiae Minoris Antiqua* (London, 1928 ff.).
M.G.H.	*Monumenta Germaniae Historica.*
N.E.	Νέος Ἑλληνομνήμων.
O.C.P.	*Orientalia Christiana Periodica.*
Π.Π.	S. Lampros, Παλαιολόγεια καὶ Πελοποννησιακά, vols. I–II (Athens, 1912–1924).
P.P.T.S.	*Palestine Pilgrims' Text Society* (London, 1885–1897).
P.S.	*Palestinskii Sbornik.*
P.G.	J. P. Migne, *Patrologiae cursus completus, series graeca* (Paris, 1857 ff.).
P.O.	*Patrologia Orientalis* (Paris, 1904 ff.).
P.W.	*Real-Enzyklopädie der klassischen Altertumswissenschaft* (Stuttgart, 1893 ff.).
Π.Φ.	Ποντιακὰ Φύλλα.
Π.Ε.	Ποντιακὴ Ἑστία.
P.P.S.	*Pravoslavni Palestinskii Sbornik.*
Ramsay, *Geography*	W. Ramsay, *The Historical Geography of Asia Minor* (London, 1890).
R.H.C.	*Recueil des historiens des Croisades* (Paris, 1841 ff.).
Regel	W. Regel, *Fontes rerum byzantinarum, sumptibus academiae scientiarum rossicae* (Petrograd, 1892–1917).
R.C.E.A.	*Répertoire chronologique d'épigraphie arabe*, ed. E. Combe, J. Sauvaget, G. Wiet, (Cairo, 1931 ff.).
R.O.C.	*Revue de l'Orient chrétien.*
R.E.I.	*Revue des études islamiques.*
R.H.	*Revue historique.*
Rhalles and Potles	K. Rhalles and M. Potles, Σύνταγμα τῶν θείων καὶ ἱερῶν κανόνων, vols. I–VI (Athens, 1852–1859).
R.S.O.	*Rivista degli studi orientali.*
S.I.	*Studia Islamica.*
S.F.	*Südost-Forschungen.*
T.M.	*Türkiyat Mecmuasi.*

V.D.	*Vakïflar Dergisi.*
V.V.	*Vizantiiskii Vremennik.*
W.Z.K.M.	*Wiener Zeitschrift für die Kunde des Morgenlandes.*
Z.R.V.I.	*Zbornik Radova Vizantoloshkog Instituta.*
Z.D.M.G.	*Zeitschrift der deutschen morgenländische Gesellschaft.*
Z.B.	*Zeitschrift für Balkanologie.*
Zepos, *J.G.B.*	I. Zepos and P. Zepos, *Jus Graecoromanum*, vols. I–VIII (Athens, 1931).
Z.M.N.P.	*Zhurnal Ministerstva Narodnago Prosviescheniia.*

I. *Byzantine Asia Minor on the Eve of the Turkish Conquest*

Since the fall of North Africa, Egypt, and the Levant to the Arabs and the occupation of Italy by the Germanic peoples and of much of the Balkans by the Slavs, Byzantium had been restricted to the southern confines of the Balkan peninsula, Anatolia, the isles, and southern Italy.[1] Of these areas, Anatolia was by far the largest, most populous, and economically the most important. Unfortunately, almost nothing in the way of population statistics for Anatolia has survived, but aside from the factor of its great size, there are other indications that Asia Minor was the most populous region of the empire.[2] So long as Anatolia continued to be an integral part of the empire, Byzantium remained a strong and comparatively prosperous state. Once Anatolia slipped from Byzantine control, the empire became little more than a weak Balkan principality, competing with Serbs and Bulgars on an almost equal footing.

With the decline of medieval Hellenism in Anatolia, there arose a Turkish-Muslim society that is at the base of the Seljuk state and Ottoman Empire. This new society differed from those of the Asiatic steppe and from that of the Islamic Middle East because it arose in a Byzantine milieu. Consequently, the related Anatolian phenomena of Byzantine decline and Islamization are essential to a basic understanding of both Turkish and Byzantine societies. For the student of cultural change, the Islamization of Asia Minor has a twofold interest. Specifically it represents the last in a long series of religio-linguistic changes to which Anatolia had been subjected over the centuries. Broadly considered, the Islamization and Turkification of the Anatolians in the later Middle Ages, along with the Christianization and Hispanization of Iberia, constitute one of the last chapters in the history of cultural change in the Mediterranean basin. Since antiquity the inhabitants of the Mediterranean world had been subject to a remarkable variety of transforming cultural forces: Hellenization, Romanization, Arabization, Christianization, and Islamization. To these were now added Turkification.

---

[1] For a picture of the Byzantine world at this time, G. Ostrogorsky, "The Byzantine Empire in the World of the Seventh Century," *D.O.P.*, XIII (1955), 1–21.

[2] The evidence is discussed below.

As the subject of this book is the cultural transformation of Greek Anatolia between the eleventh and fifteenth centuries, one must begin with a descriptive analysis of Byzantine society in the peninsula on the eve of the Turkish invasions. This will entail a discussion and partial description of administrative, military, and ecclesiastical institutions, towns, rural society, demography, roads, ethnography, and religion.[3]

Administrative Institutions

Certain political, economic, and religious institutions characterized Anatolian society prior to the drastic upheavals of the eleventh century which caused serious dislocation of this society. These institutions produced an element of homogeneity in the life of the inhabitants of this immense area and at the same time integrated them effectively into a Constantinopolitan-centered organism. The system of the themes, by which the civil administration became subordinate to the thematic strategus, dominated the administrative and military activity of the Anatolians. At the time of the death of Basil II (1025), there existed in Anatolia approximately twenty-five provinces, mostly themes but including also duchies and catepanates, largely under the direct control and administration of the strategoi.[4] Though the administrative apparatus placed the provincial bureaucracy under the tutelage of the military, it also acted as a partial check on the absorption of the free peasantry by the landed magnates and thereby assured the empire of military, social, and fiscal strength. The thematic system served as a vital impetus to and support of the existence of the free peasant society, which in turn not only served as a balance to the landed aristocracy, but fought the Arabs and was a major contributor to the imperial tax collectors.[5]

The strategus, as supreme authority in the theme, was a veritable viceroy. Nothing could be done in his province, save for the assessment and collection of taxes, which were effected by agents directly under Constantinople, without his consent. His most important function was to command the army of the theme. Much has been said about the efficacy and importance of these local armies drawn from the inhabitants of the provinces, but there is little information as to their numbers. The Arab

[3] The art of eleventh-century Byzantine Anatolia is still insufficiently investigated, and education and intellectual life cannot be satisfactorily reconstructed because of the nature of the sources. Hence, there will be no attempt to include these two categories in this chapter, regrettable though this fact may be. A useful and brief sketch of Anatolian geography and its significance for the history of the area is to be found in P. Birot and J. Dresch, *La Mediterranée et le Moyen-Orient*, tome 2: *Les Balkans, l'Asie Mineure, le Moyen-Orient* (Paris, 1956), pp. 125-192.

[4] N. Skabalanovič, *Vizantiiskoe gosudarstvo i tserkov v XI. v.* (St. Petersburg, 1884), pp. 193-209. Ostregersky, *Geschichte des byzantinischen Staates*, 3d ed. (Munich, 1963), pp. 80-83, and *passim* for the literature. H. Glycatzi-Ahrweiler, *Recherches sur l'administration de l'empire byzantin aux IXe-XIe siècles* (Paris, 1960).

[5] For a cautious reevaluation and refinement of the role of the themes, W. E. Kaegi, "Some Reconsiderations on the Themes (Seventh-Ninth Centuries)," *J.Ö.B.G.*, XVI (1967), 39-53.

author Abu'l-Faradj Kudama ibn Djafar noted that the levy of the Anatolian themes in the first half of the ninth century was approximately 70,000.[6] By the tenth century, however, there is every indication that the size of Byzantine military forces must have increased markedly. The conquest of new lands in the east witnessed the creation of new provinces and army corps, whereas the intensification of the Byzantine offensive efforts similarly demanded an increase in the size of the armies. Perhaps the remarks of Leo VI, that the armies ought not be too large, is a reflection of this expansion.[7]

Beside the men the government recruited from the local soldiery, there were other sources of military personnel in the provinces. These included a

[6] H. Gelzer, *Die Genesis der byzantinischen Themenverfassung*, Abh. d. Kgl. sachs. Ges. d. Wiss., Phil.-hist. Kl., vol. XVIII, Nr. 5 (1899), pp. 97–98 (hereafter cited as Gelzer *Die Genesis*). For the breakdown of these forces which follows, A. Pertusi, *Constantino Perphirogenito De Thematibus* (Vatican, 1952), pp. 115–148.

Anatolicon	15,000
Armeniacon	9,000
Cappadocia	4,000
Charsianon	4,000
Thracesion	6,000
Opsicion	6,000
Optimaton	4,000
Bucellarion	8,000
Paphlagonia	5,000
Chaldia	4,000
Seleuceia	5,000
	70,000

The thematic army was organized in units of decreasing size, the turm, drungus, and and bandon. But because of the differences in size of the various themes, the number of turms, drungoi, and banda in a particular theme varied. A thematic army usually had, for any given theme, between two and four turms, but it would seem that the size of the turm was not regularly established and observed.

[7] *Leonis imperatoris tactica*, P.G., CVII, 709. The bandum should not have more than 400 men, the drungus not more than 3,000, the turm not more than 6,000. Michael Psellus, *Chronographie*, ed. E. Renauld (Paris, 1926–1928), I, 36 (hereafter cited as Psellus-Renauld). L. Bréhier, *Les institutions de l'empire byzantin* (Paris, 1948), p. 369. Ibn Khuradadhbih, B.G.A., VI, 111, gives the following figures: 5,000 in a turm, 1,000 in a drungus, and 200 in a bandum. Constantine Porphyrogenitus, *De Caerimoniis*, I, 651–655, 696–697. In the order of honorary precedence and size of payment the generals of the more important and powerful themes generally preceded the generals of these three themes (see below).

The catalog of the expedition to Crete in the reign of Leo VI tends to confirm the growth in the size of the thematic forces. The levies of the Cibyrrheote force amounted to 6,760, those of Samos 5,690, of Aegean 3,100. One century earlier Kudama noted that the forces of the theme of Seleuceia, amounted to only 5,000. The themes of Cibyrrheote, Seleuceia, Samos, and Aegean, were among the less important and numerous of the Anatolian provinces in the eyes of the central administration. In addition the thematic soldiery of the Cibyrrheote under Leo VI was larger than 6,760, as this does not include the two ships that the strategus of the theme sent to watch the shores of Syria, and probably other ships and personnel that had to remain to guard the shores of the theme and to cut timber for shipbuilding. This comparatively large number for such a theme as the Cibyrrheote, in contrast to the smaller figures for the ninth century, indicates that the size of the thematic armies had increased by the early tenth century. When one compares the size of the Cibyrrheote force under Leo VI with the size of the forces of the themes as reported by the Arabs in the ninth century, this conclusion seems inescapable, for the Cibyrrheote levy of Leo VI is greater than that of any of the ninth-century Anatolian themes save those of the great Anatolicon, Armeniacon, and Buccelarion.

variety of ethnic groups that the emperors settled as distinct military bodies throughout Anatolia. Theophilus, by way of example, settled 2,000 Persians in each theme (though these seem to have been incorporated into the thematic levies); Mardaites were settled around Attaleia, possibly by Justinian II; there were also bodies of Slavs and Armenians.[8] In addition the government stationed tagmata of imperial troops in certain of the Anatolian districts.[9] This superimposition of foreign bodies of soldiers in the provinces increased the military manpower of a given province considerably. With the addition of the Mardaites to the forces of the Cibyrrheote theme, the military strength of the district may have been as large as 10,000.[10]

Other large themes very probably had as large a military force, if not larger, with the consequence that the military manpower stationed in Anatolia during the tenth and early eleventh centuries must have far surpassed the 70,000 thematic levies mentioned by the Arab sources for the early ninth century. The success of Byzantine arms against the Arabs during this period is in part to be explained by the effectiveness of this Anatolian manpower, and the importance of these Anatolian forces emerges from the obvious correlation between thematic decline and the Turkish invasions in the eleventh century. The professional mercenaries who took the place of the indigenous thematic soldiers in this period of crisis were ineffective replacements and were unable to halt the Turks.

The military apparatus in Anatolia had an important role in the provincial economic life. It contributed to the local economy by paying out salaries in gold to the officers and soldiers who lived in Asia Minor, and stimulating local industry, commerce, and agriculture by its expenditures. The government was able to feed into the business life of the Anatolians a comparatively steady and significant sum of coined money in the form of the military roga. One can gain some idea as to the sums of money involved in military pay from the sources of the ninth and tenth centuries. During the reign of Leo VI the generals of the more important themes received the following cash payment:[11]

Anatolicon	40 pounds of gold
Armeniacon	40
Thracesion	40
Opsicion	30

[8] A. Vasiliev, *Byzance et les Arabes I: La dynastie d'Amorium (820–876). Édition française preparée par H. Grégoire et M. Canard* (Brussels, 1935), pp. 92–93. C. Amantos, "Μαρδαῖται," Ἑλληνικά, V (1923), 130–136. Ostrogorsky, *Geschichte*, pp. 109–110, 140. Constantine Porphyrogenitus, *De Caerimoniis*, I, 651–656.

[9] Constantine Porphyrogenitus, *De Caerimoniis*, I, 652.

[10] The Mardaites of the west in the Cretan expedition of Leo VI numbered over 5,000, *ibid.* 655.

[11] *Ibid.*, 696–697. Ibn Khuradadhbih B.G.A., VI, 111, gives the following salary range: 40, 30, 24, 12, 1, lbs. of gold. Soldiers received between eighteen and twelve solidi per year. On the pay for the lesser officers and for the soldiers, Constantine Porphyrogenitus, *De Caerimoniis*, I, 669.

Bucellarion	30
Cappadocia	20
Charsianon	20
Paphlagonia	20
Thrace	20
Macedonia	30
Chaldia	10 plus 10 from commercium
Coloneia	20
Mesopotamia	from commercium
Sebasteia	5
Lycandus	5
Seleuceia	5
Leontocome	5
Cibyrrheote	10
Samos	10
Aegean	10

The pay of the thematic soldiers in comparison with that of the officers was quite small, and yet the overall expenditure on military salaries was very substantial, as emerges from the incidental accounts of the period. In the early ninth century, the military pay chests of the themes of Armeniacon in Anatolia and of Strymon in Europe amounted to 1,300 and 1,100 pounds of gold respectively, or 93,600 and 79,200 gold solidi each.[12] On the basis of these figures it seems likely that the government paid out between 500,000 and 1,000,000 solidi annually to the soldiery of Asis Minor.[13] The soldier was also entitled to part of the spoils of war, and in many instances pensions were given to disabled soldiers and to the widows of the slain.[14]

The army and navy required supplies, armament, and provisions on their frequent expeditions. Though the government undoubtedly acquired many of the necessary items by taxes in kind on the populace, the authorities also paid out cash to artisans and merchants to provide a wide assortment of items and services. Craftsmen were hired to make weapons of every type for the armed forces, to sew the sails for the ships, to caulk the boats; merchants sold the government the cloth for the sails, rope, bronze, wax, lead, tin, oars, foodstuffs, and other necessary

[12] Theophanes, *Chronographia*, ed. C. de Boor (Leipzig, 1883–1885), I, 484, 489 (hereafter cited as Theophanes).

[13] Speros Vryonis, "An Attic Hoard of Byzantine Gold Coins (668–741) from the Thomas Whittemore Collection and the Numismatic Evidence for the Urban History of Byzantium," *Z.R.V.I.*, VIII (1963), 298–299. On the basis of these and other figures in Constantine Porphyrogenitus an estimate of 690,300 solidi was made for government military expenditures in Anatolia during the early ninth century. The Arab sources record that the Anatolian levy of 70,000 received pay of between eighteen and twelve solidi, or between 1,260,000 and 840,000 solidi. Thus the Byzantine and Arab sources tend to corroborate one another.

[14] Bréhier, *Les institutions*, p. 382. Five pounds of gold were given to the widows in the reign of Michael I.

materials.[15] The administration saw to it that salaried craftsmen specializing in the production of military weapons were maintained in the principal towns,[16] and their production was quantitatively significant.[17] The military organization of Byzantium, and the passage of armies through the provinces, thereby played a stimulating and significant role in the economic prosperity of Anatolia.[18]

Towns and Commerce

By late Roman and early Byzantine times there had developed in Anatolia a large number of thriving cities and lesser towns with a considerable commercial life and money economy.[19] The question has often arisen as to the continuity of this urban character of much of Anatolia into the middle Byzantine period. To what extent, if at all, did Anatolia continue to be the possessor of extensive urban settlements down to the period when the Turks first appeared? This question is doubly important, first in that it bears on the relative importance of the area for Byzantine civilization and strength, and second because it is closely related to the problem of Muslim urban developments in Anatolia during the later period.

Some students of the question have maintained that between the seventh and ninth centuries the polis of antiquity, and so cities generally, underwent a disastrous decline.[20] But actually there seems to have been

[15] In the outfitting of eleven ships that participated in the Cretan expedition of Constantine VII and Romanus II, the treasury paid out approximately twenty-two pounds of gold to craftsmen and merchants for services and materials, Constantine Porphyrogenitus, *De Caerimoniis*, I, 673–676.

[16] This situation existed as late as the reign of John Vatatzes in the thirteenth century. Theodore Scutariotes, M.B., VII, 506–507 (hereafter cited as Theodore Scutariotes-Sathas). *Leonis imperatoris tactica*, P.G., CVII, 1088–1093, on craftsmen in the army.

[17] In Leo's Cretan expedition there are extensive details, Constantine Porphyrogenitus, *De Caerimoniis*, I, 657–660. The strategus of Thessalonike was ordered to manufacture 20,000 arrows, 3,000 lances, and as many shields as possible. The archon of Hellas was to produce 1,000 lances; the archon of Euboea 20,000 arrows and 3,000 lances. The generals of Nicopolis and Peloponnesus were to perform in a similar manner. The protonotarius of the Thracesian theme was to collect 20,000 measures of barley; 40,000 of wheat, hardtack, and flour; 30,000 of wine; 10,000 "sphacta." He was to prepare 10,000 measures of linen cloth for Greek fire and ship caulking, and 6,000 nails for the ships, and so forth. Procopius, *Anecdota*, XXX, 5–7, records that the state post system had also provided business and cash to the inhabitants of the provinces by purchasing from them horses, fodder, and provisions for the grooms. It is not clear whether this system continued after Justinian I.

[18] Byzantine armies on the move spent considerable sums of money, Vryonis, "An Attic Hoard," p. 300. The λογιστική or accounting office of the army was in charge of moneys so spent, *Leonis imperatoris tactica*, P.G., CVII, 1092.

[19] T. R. S. Broughton, *Roman Asia Minor*, in T. Frank, *An Economic Survey of Ancient Rome*, IV (Baltimore, 1938), 903–916. The Anatolian cities were able to recover from the crisis of the third century. A. H. M. Jones, *The Greek City from Alexander to Justinian* (Oxford, 1940), pp. 85–94.

[20] The principal exponent of this theory is A. P. Každan, "Vizantiiskie goroda v VII–XI vv," *Sovetskaia Arkheologia*, XXI (1954), 164–188; *Derevnia i gorod v Vizantii IX–X vv*, (Moscow, 1960), pp. 260–270. He relies very heavily upon the numismatic evidence which, however, is unsatisfactory and unreliable. For a critique of his theory, Ostrogorsky, "Byzantine Cities in the Early Middle Ages," *D.O.P.*, XIII (1959), 47–66; Vryonis, "An Attic Hoard," p. 300, *passim*. On urban continuity see also, E. E. Lipšic, *Očerki*

no such abrupt decline or hiatus during the seventh century in Anatolia, though the Slavic invasions in the Balkans did cause a marked decline of many of the towns of the western half of the empire. This condition in the Balkans served to put in even bolder relief the economic and political importance of the continuity of towns and cities in Anatolia. It is quite possible that a number of the towns may have decreased in size by the late seventh or the eighth century,[21] or possibly have shifted their locations slightly to more strategic positions on higher ground,[22] or been "ruralized," but this does not mean that they did so to the point of becoming insignificant as an urban phenomenon. It is doubtful that Byzantium could have survived as a centralized state without a money economy and towns, and it is even more doubtful that the Greek language and Byzantine Christianity could have spread and penetrated to the extent they did in Anatolia. Obviously what had happened to the Byzantine urban settlements in the Balkans did not occur in Anatolia. The raids of the Arabs were, in spite of their frequency, transitory affairs (when one compares them to the Slavic invasions of the Balkans which not only effaced cities but also Christianity, or to the Turkish invasions).[23]

What were the characteristics of these Byzantine cities in the eleventh century? When one speaks of cities he thinks primarily in terms of autonomous municipal institutions. This is certainly the case of the town in antiquity, where there were also divisions of the citizenry according to tribes, and finally a walled enclosure. Obviously the Byzantine towns of Anatolia in the eleventh century would hardly fit such a description, at least insofar as the meager sources permit conjecture. The existence of

---

istorii vizantiiskogo obščestva i kultury VIII-pervaia polovina IX veka (Moscow-Leningrad, 1961), pp. 87 ff.; "K voprosu o gorode v Vizantii VIII–IX vv." V.V., VI (1953), 113 ff. M. J. Siuziumov, "Rol gorodov-emporiev v istorii Vizantii," V.V., VIII (1956), 26 ff.

[21] E. Kirsten, "Die byzantinische Stadt," Berichte zum XI. Internationalem Byzantinisten-Kongress (Munich, 1958), p. 14. There is even archaeological evidence for the temporary disappearance of a few towns, as for instance Corasium in southern Asia Minor during the seventh century, Každan, "Vizantiiskie goroda," 186.

[22] Kirsten, "Byzantinische Stadt," p. 28.

[23] Každan, "Vizantiiskie goroda," p. 187, is ambivalent on this point. He attributes the decline and to a certain extent the disappearance of the Byzantine towns to the disappearance of the slave method of production. He adds, however, that this was significantly accelerated by the invasions of foreign peoples.

The history of Arabo-Byzantine warfare and relations in Asia Minor is yet to be written. For the earlier period one may consult the following works. E. W. Brooks, "Byzantines and Arabs in the Time of the Early Abbassids, 750–813," E.H.R., XV (1900), 728–747; XVI (1901), 84–92; "The Arabs in Asia Minor from Arabic Sources," J.H.S., XVIII (1898), 182–208. W. Ramsay, "The War of Moslem and Christian for Possession of Asia Minor," Studies in the History and Art of the Eastern Provinces of the Roman Empire (Aberdeen 1906), pp. 281–301. J. Wellhausen, "Die Kämpfe der Araber mit den Romäern in der Zeit der Umaijaden," Nachrichten von d. kön. Ges. der Wiss. zu Göttingen, Phil.-hist. Kl. (1901), pp. 414–447. M. Canard, "Les expeditions des Arabes centre Constantinople," J.A., CVIII (1926), 61–121. H. Manandean, "Les invasions arabes en Arménie," Byzantion, XVIII (1948), 163–195. For the later period, Vasiliev, Grégoire, Canard, Byzance et les Arabes, vols. I–II (Brussels, 1935, 1950). Glycatzi-Ahrweiler, "L'Asie Mineure et les invasions arabes (VIIᵉ–IXᵉ siècles), R.H., CCXXVII, (1962), 1–32.

autonomous, independent institutions in the municipalities of antiquity had been threatened from the moment the Hellenistic monarchs had placed their epistates or representative in the polis to oversee its foreign affairs. The crisis of the third century further undermined these institutions, as is witnessed by the attempts of Diocletian to stabilize them. So in the fifth century the city, as it had evolved, at least in Asia Minor, did not preserve the city type of the Hellenistic and Roman periods. The later militarization of the provincial administration through the implementation of the thematic system consummated the end of urban autonomy, for the affairs of the town were subjected to the strategus who was appointed from Constantinople. The novel of Leo VI abolishing the remnants of urban autonomy simply put into legal language a state that had come into being previously and that had been in the process of formation for centuries.[24] Nevertheless, the populace of Byzantine towns does not seem to have been quiescent in political matters and it frequently expressed its will in riots and political outbursts, first through the demes, and later through the guilds.[25]

The "aspect" of the eleventh-century Byzantine town was characterized by institutions of a different sort. These institutions were largely thematic and ecclesiastical, both ultimately centering in Constantinople. Consequently, the city in the early eleventh century was the seat of a strategus with his immediate retinue (or of one of his subordinates) appointed by Constantinople. These officials presided over routine matters of administration and juridical business as well as over military and police affairs, though the lesser officials were local inhabitants.[26] Alongside the officials of the military administration were those of the ecclesiastical hierarchy— metropolitans and the bishops. The integration of the ecclesiastical administrative set up into that of the provincial government is not as well known as the parallelism existing between the structure of the earlier provincial administration and the structure of the hierarchical administration. The church had modeled its administration along the lines of the

---

[24] F. Dölger, "Die frühbyzantinische und byzantinisch beeinflusste Stadt," *Atti de 3° Congresso internazionale di studi sull' alto medioevo* (Spoleto, 1958), pp. 22–23. Zepos, *J.G.R.*, I, 116.

[25] On this Byzantine "demokratia" during the earlier period, G. Manoljović, "Le peuple de Constantinople," *Byzantion*, VI (1936), 617–716; Vryonis, "Byzantine Circus Factions and Islamic Futuwwa Organizations (neaniai, fityān, aḥdāth)," *B.Z.*, LVIII (1965), 46–59. A. Marciq, "La dureé du régime des partis populaires à Constantinople," and "Factions de cirque et partis populaires," *Bulletin de la classe des lettres et des sciences morales et politiques*, XXXV (1949), 63 ff., and XXXVI (1950), 396–421. For the later period, Vryonis, "Byzantine Δημοκρατία and the Guilds in the Eleventh Century," *D.O.P.*, XVII (1963), 289–314. F. Cognasso, *Partiti politici e lotte dinastiche in Bizanzio alla morte di Manuele Comneno. Reale Accademia delle scienze di Torino, 1911–12* (Turin, 1912). For a general survey, D. Xanalatos, Βυζαντινά μελετήματα. Συμβολὴ εἰς τὴν ἱστορίαν τοῦ βυζαντινοῦ λαοῦ (Athens, 1940).

[26] Ahrweiler, "L'histoire et la géographie de la région de Smyrne entre les deux occupations turques (1081–1317) particulièrement au XIIIᵉ siècle," *Travaux et Mémoires* (Paris, 1965), I, 103–104, 155 (hereafter cited as Ahrweiler, "Smyrne").

civil administration of the fourth and fifth centuries. In this manner those cities that were the centers of the provincial administration became the centers of the ecclesiastical organization. The council of Chalcedon in 451 decreed that cities or poleis would be the seats of bishops, and consequently the concept of a polis or city became inseparably associated with the presence of a bishop, and the exact reverse was also true; wherever there was a bishop there had to be a city. Justinian I restated this one century later:

> We decree that every city ... shall have ... its own and inseparable ... bishop.[27]

The episcopal powers and rule in provincial administrative organization were to remain important until the end of the Byzantine Empire and beyond. By the sixth century the bishops were participating in the elections of local urban officials, were important in city finances, and were often the recipients of imperial gifts bestowed upon the city.[28] One can say that episcopal authority became a refuge of the last vestiges of urban autonomy, though the eastern bishops, because of the authority of the centralized state, never attained the power of the western Latin bishops.[29] Not only did the bishops take some part in these strictly governmental matters, but they seem to have had charge of performing many services that today one generally, though not exclusively, connects with the state: education, care for the sick, the aged, the orphaned, and others in need. In short they cared not only for the souls of the provincials but for their bodies as well.

The Byzantine town of Asia Minor in the eleventh century was, then, characterized by the presence of the members of the ecclesiastical hierarchy (bishops or metropolitans), and by the presence of the strategus or his representatives. In addition there were other characteristics of the towns—the presence of trade or commercial activity whether with foreign states or with neighboring towns and villages. The Byzantine polis had resident a number of local craftsmen as well as merchants both indigenous and foreign. This particular aspect of the town as a center of craftsmen and merchants and of industry and commerce is not well documented. According to some scholars this basic element for the existence of towns was seriously lacking in the eighth and ninth centuries.[30] But such arguments are based largely upon the silence of the sources,

---

[27] *Cod. Iust.*, I.3.55. " πᾶσαν πόλιν ... ἔχειν ... ἀχώριστον καὶ ἴδιον ... ἐπίσκοπον θεσπίζομεν." A later list of episcopal sees uses the terms bishoprics and cities interchangeably, πόλεις ἤτοι ἐπισκοπάς. Gelzer, *Ungedruckte und ungenügend veröffentlichte Texte der Notitiae Episcopatum, Abh. der bay. Akad. der Wiss.*, LI (1901), 546 (hereafter cited as Gelzer, *Notitiae Episcopatum*). As late as the twelfth century, Balsamon remarks that only inhabited centers which are πολυάνθρωποι can have bishops. Those towns that decline in population lose their status as bishoprics.

[28] *Cod. Iust.*, I.4.18-26. E. Stein, *Histoire du Bas-Empire*, II (Paris-Brussels-Amsterdam, 1949), II, 213.

[29] Dölger, "Stadt," pp. 16, 24–25.

[30] Každan, "Vizantiiskie goroda," *passim*.

sources that are not only rare but are also Constantinople-centered. Archaeology has not yet progressed to the point where it can be of service in regard to the extent of urban life in Byzantine Anatolia during the period under consideration. If one looks at the scattered references of the tenth and eleventh centuries, however, it becomes obvious that neither trade nor commerce, neither craftsmen nor merchants, were absent from Asia Minor during this period.[31]

Ephesus was a lively harbor town with a panegyris or trade fair that yielded 100 pounds of gold in annual taxes during the reign of Constantine VI (780–797).[32] Incidental information concerning the economic activity of the city emerges from an eleventh-century hagiographical composition in which we get a glimpse of what must have been a very busy town. The monks of the monastery on Mt. Galesium near Ephesus are constantly going to the κάστρον (Ephesus) for the various needs of the monastery.[33] Books are purchased there,[34] and the monks are permitted to attend the fair,[35] though this is felt to be something of a formidable temptation for the brethren. Craftsmen and merchants of various sorts appear: a painter, a plasterer, a nauclerus, and there is also mention of a state bakery.[36] This commercial activity was of more than a local nature, as there is mention of Saracens, Jews, Russians, and Georgians.[37] These incidental bits of information indicate that eleventh-century Ephesus was no sleepy hollow but was rather a center of both local and international trade. It is

[31] The famous passage of Hudud al-'Alam, so often quoted, remarks that cities were few in Rum, V. Minorsky, *Hudud al-'Alam. The Regions of the World: a Persian Geography, 372 A.H.-982 A.D.* (London, 1937), p. 157 (hereafter cited as Hudud al-'Alam-Minorsky). But in the preceding passage, p. 156, it makes the contradictory remark that Rum has many towns and villages. The translator and commentator on the text, p. 40, remarks that the relevant passage is confused as a result of incorrect copying from other sources. A useful collection on the towns, trade, and commerce is to be found in A. Rudikov, *Očerki vizantiiskoi kultury po dannym grečeskoi agiografii* (Moscow, 1917). P. Tivčev, "Sur les cités byzantines aux XIᵉ–XIIᵉ siècles," *Byzantine-Bulgarica*, I (1962), 145–182. Because the source material is so scarce, random factual information spanning a long period of time has been gathered. There is no intention of trying to adduce urban conditions in the eleventh century by facts pertaining to earlier centuries. Rather there is an attempt to give a general, if impressionistic, picture of the towns over a period of time.

[32] F. Dvornik, *Vie de Grégoire Décapolite et les Slaves Macédoniens au IXᵉ siècle* (Paris, 1926) p. 53. Theophanes, I, 469. H. Vetters, "Zum byzantinischen Ephesos, *J.Ö.B.G.*, XV (1966), 273–288. N. Bees, " Μελετήματα σχετικὰ πρὸς τὴν μεσαιωνικὴν Ἔφεσον καὶ τὸν καλούμενον Θεολόγον," Ἀρχαιολογικὴ Ἐφημερίς pt. 2. (1953–54), pp. 263–283. A number of the texts that follow are also cited in Každan, "Vizantiiskie goroda," pp. 182–186.

[33] AS Nov. III, 532, 554, 586. The monastery, which received money from pious donors, bought many of its necessities in the shops of Ephesus.

[34] *Ibid.*, 536.

[35] *Ibid.*, 556.

[36] *Ibid.*, 537, 540, 541. This would seem to imply the continued existence of state regulated corporations in the provinces during the eleventh century.

[37] What is most interesting is that the Saracen, who has just converted to Christianity in Ephesus, receives an interpreter from the metropolitan of Ephesus so that when he goes to see St. Lazarus he will be able to converse with him. There may have been a small colony of Muslim merchants in Ephesus, for in an earlier period Ibn Khuradadhbih, *B.G.A.*, VI, 106, mentions the presence of a mosque in the city. Gelzer, *Die Genesis*, p. 83.

interesting to note that when Alexius I accorded the Venetians commercial privileges, Ephesus was one of the cities that Venetian merchants could visit.[38] Its plain was fertile, well watered, and the nearby sea was a rich fishing ground.[39]

The western Anatolian coast was dotted with natural harbors that seem to have been active maritime centers in the tenth and eleventh centuries, though possibly not on the same scale as Ephesus. The monks of Mt. Athos sailed to Smyrna to purchase necessities, and shipping constantly plied the lanes between Smyrna and Constantinople and the isles in the eleventh century.[40] Phygela served as a debarkation point to and from Crete[41] as well as a commercial center and depot for naval stores.[42] Phocaea and Strobilus were among the important ports of Anatolia in which Venetian merchants were to be allowed to trade late in the eleventh century. Miletus and Clazomenae were undoubtedly of similar importance.[43] The hinterland of these towns in the Thracesian theme produced much grain, the surplus of which was exported to regions in Phrygia, which produced only barley.[44] The towns farther north were also centers of lively trading activity. Nicomedia, a central emporium with

[38] G. F. L. Tafel and G. M. Thomas, *Urkunden zur älteren Handels-und Staatsgeschichte der Republik Venedig* (Vienna, 1856), I, 52 (hereafter cited as Tafel and Thomas, *Urkunden*).

[39] *The Pilgrimage of the Russian Abbot Daniel in the Holy Land 1106–1107 A.D.*, C. W. Wilson, *P.P.T.S.* (London, 1895), IV, 6 (hereafter cited as Daniel, *P.P.T.S.*, IV). For a general treatment see the following: O. Benndorf, *Zur Ortskunde und Stadtgeschichte von Ephesus* (Vienna, 1905), I. W. Brockhoff, *Studien zur Geschichte der Stadt Ephesus vom 4. nachchristlichen Jahrhundert bis zum ihrem Untergang an der ersten Hälfte des 15. Jahrhunderts* (Jena, 1905). J. Keil, *Ein Führer durch die Ruinenstadt und ihre Geschichte*, 5th ed. (Vienna, 1964); "Ephesus," *Oriens Christianus*, 3d series, VI (1931), 1–14. Ibn Battuta, H. A. R. Gibb, *The Travels of Ibn Battuta* (Cambridge, 1959) II, 444 (hereafter cited as Ibn Battuta-Gibb). C. Defrémery and B. R. Sanguinetti, *Voyages d'Ibn Batoutah* (Paris, 1854), II, 309 (hereafter cited as Ibn Battuta-Defrémery), noted it to be still well watered and that the vine was cultivated.

[40] "Vie de Saint Athanase l'Athonite," *A.B.*, XXV (1906), 81. AS Nov. III, 579. On the agriculture, commerce, and mining of the Smyrna region, Ahrweiler, "Smyrne, *passim*.

[41] AS Nov. III, 578. Attaliates, 223.

[42] Constantine Porphyrogenitus, *De Caerimoniis*, I, 658. The eighth-century pilgrim Willibaldus, *Hodoeporicon S. Willibaldi*, in *Itinera Hierosolymitana et Descriptiones Terrae Sanctae*, ed. T. Toller and A. Molinier (Geneva, 1880), I₂, 256, describes Phygela as "villam magnam." For some reason Každan, "Vizantiiskie goroda," p. 194, lists Phygela as one of the the "new cities" which he claims were founded in the late ninth and tenth centuries, after the decline of the "old cities." But Phygela is described as a large town in 723–726 and, of course, had existed in classical times, Strabo, XIV.i.20. For further reference, Benndorf, "Ephesus" pp. 73–75.

[43] Tafel and Thomas, *Urkunden*, I, 52, mentions both Strobilus and Phocaea. A Strobilite merchant pledges to his patron saint one-half of all his gains from maritime commerce if he comes back safely, AS Nov. III, 532–533. Strobilus also had a Jewish colony, J. Starr, *The Jews in the Byzantine Empire* (Athens, 1939), p. 228. Ahrweiler, "Smyrne," pp. 50–51, on Clazomenae as a port of call and seat of a bishopric in the eleventh century.

[44] J. Darrouzès, *Épistoliers byzantins du Xᵉ siècle* (Paris, 1960), pp. 198–199. This condition also prevailed in the thirteenth century between the Seljuk and Nicaean domains, see chapter III below.

state khans for the residence of the merchants,[45] exported livestock to the capital and served as the market for villagers in the vast rural area around the city. These ἀγρογείτονες came to town to sell their own produce, to buy what they needed,[46] and also to visit the church of the Archangel Michael. Prusa, an important market for grain and livestock, was in addition famed for its thermal baths.[47] Its neighbor, Nicaea, was an equally active commercial center and mart for local farming products.[48] The city contained granaries for the agricultural produce of the rural environs[49] and an active colony of Jewish merchants.[50] The tenth-century Theophanes Continuatus refers to Nicaea as rich and heavily populated.[51] It is pertinent that the Arab geographer al-Mukaddasi mentioned the presence of Muslims in the cities of Bithynia, some probably there for purposes of trade.[52] Though the literary references to the town are scanty, the archaeological finds indicate that in the eleventh century Pergamum was the site of some local industry,[53] and its neighbor Adramyttium was a town of more than respectable size.[54] Abydus, Cyzicus, Lampsacus, and Pylae enjoyed a certain prosperity because of

[45] Zepos, *J.G.R.*, III, 386. Constantine Porphyrogenitus, *De Caerimoniis*, I, 720.

[46] *Michaelis Pselli Scripta Minora*, ed. E. Drexl and F. Pertz (Milan, 1936, 1941), I, 333 (hereafter cited as Drexl and Pertz). " αἰτία ἐμπορία καὶ πραγματικὰ συναλλάγματα."

[47] Papadopoulos-Kerameus, *Α.Ι.Σ.*, IV, 384, 387, 397. V. Laurent. *La vie merveillsuse de S. Pierre d'Atroa 837* (Brussels, 1956), p. 109. Ibn Battuta-Gibb, II, 450, noted that the springs were still visited by the sick in his day. Ibn Battuta-Defrémery, II, 318.

[48] Much of this produce was evidently shipped to Constantinople, *Géographie d'Edrisi*, trans. P. A. Jaubert (Paris, 1840), II, 302 (hereafter cited as al-Idrisi-Jaubert).

[49] Cedrenus, II, 428. Wheat was grown in the area and fish were supplied from the lake, AS Nov. Iv, 643, 645. The fish and crustaceans were believed to cure fever and paralysis, al-Idrisi-Jaubert, II, 304. As late as the early fourteenth century Nicaea was an important silk manufacturing center, A. M. Schneider, *Römischen und byzantinischen Denkmäler aus Nicaea-Iznik* (Berlin, 1943), p. 5. Northwestern Asia Minor had remained an important area of silk production down to the early fourteenth century. Most of the silk to be found in the shops of Constantinople came from these regions. Laudanum was produced and the thermal baths of the city were still visited at this late date. F. Taeschner, *Al-Umari's Bericht über Anatolien in seinem Werke masālik al-absār fī mamālik al-amsār* (Leipzig, 1929), p. 43 (hereafter cited as al-Umari-Taeschner); E. Quatremère, "Notices de l'ouvrage qui a pour titre: Mesalek etc.," in *Notices et extraits des mss. de la bibliothèque du Roi*, XIII, (Paris, 1838), 365–366 (hereafter cited as al-Umari-Quatremère). Ibn Battuta-Gibb, II, 453, notes that the environs abounded in fruits, of which the "virgin" grapes were a speciality. Ibn Battuta-Defrémery, II, 323–324.

[50] AS Nov. IV, 642, " Νίκαια ἡ πόλις πολλοῖς μὲν βρίθει τοῖς ἄλλοις καλοῖς, τῷ δὲ πρὸς ἐμπορείαν ἔχειν εὐφυῶς ἐκκαλεῖται τοὺς ἐπιτηδεύοντας τὸ χρῆμα πρὸς ἑαυτήν. ὅθεν καί τινες Ἑβραίων φυλῆς αὐτόσε κατοικοῦντες ἐμπορείας τε χάριν καὶ τῆς ἄλλης ἀφθονίας." Thus Synnada also had a small group of Jews in the ninth century, AS Nov. IV, 629. For a survey of the history of Nicaea, J. Sölch, "Historisch-geographische Studien über bithynischen Siedlungen," *B.N.J.*, I, (1920), 263–337. A. M. Schneider and K. Karnopp, *Die Stadtmauer von Iznik* (Berlin, 1938). Schneider, "The City Walls of Nicaea," *Antiquity*, XII (1938), 438.

[51] Theophanes Continautus, 464, " πόλιν ἀρχαιόπλουτον καὶ πολύανδρον."

[52] E. Honigmann, "Un itinéraire arabe à travers le Pont," *A.E.P.H.O.S.*, IV (1936), 263 (hereafter cited as "Un itinéraire"). It is quite possible that some of them were prisoners taken in war.

[53] Každan, "Vizantiiskie goroda," p. 183. A Conze, *Stadt und Landschaft Pergamon* (1913), I, 322–324.

[54] B. Leib, *Anne Comnène, Alexiade* (Paris, 1937), III, 143 (hereafter cited as Anna Comnena), " . . . πολυανθρωποτάτη."

their favorable location along the land and maritime routes leading to Constantinople.[55] Pylae possessed ξενοδοχεῖα or Khans for the merchants,[56] and the town specialized in the export of swine, cattle, horses, and asses to Constantinople.[57] Pythia (the Turkish Yalova), embellished since the time of Justinian I with public baths and buildings, became a famous resort town that Constantinopolitans visited for the cures of the warm baths.[58] The whole region of northwest Anatolia was unusually favored, commercially, by its proximity to a large market in Constantinople, by the presence of large towns and centers of population, by numerous harbors, and by the existence of fairly rich and large villages.[59] Great numbers of merchant vessels touched at such ports of call as Cyzicus, Lampsacus, Nicomedia, Helenopolis, Abydus, Cius, Chalcedon.[60]

Attaleia remained throughout the whole period the principal naval base and commercial station that the Byzantines possessed in southern Anatolia, visited by great numbers of ships.[61] It was the most convenient harbor between the region of the Aegean and Cyprus and points eastward, and travelers and merchants voyaging between the two areas usually stopped at Attaleia.[62] It was not only an important center for the deposit of naval stores and grain but an international trading center[63] where in addition to the local merchants one could expect to see Armenians,[64]

---

[55] Tafel and Thomas, *Urkunden*, I, 52–53. Abydus was an important station for the levying of maritime tolls. It also had a Jewish colony.

[56] Constantine Porphyrogenitus, *De Caerimoniis*, I, 720.

[57] Darrouzès, *Épistoliers byzantins*, p. 209, " ἐν ἀστείῳ ἐχόντι πάντως καὶ περισπούδαστον τὸ χοίρους καὶ ὄνους, βόας τε καὶ ἵππους καὶ πρόβατα τοὺς ἐν αὐτῷ κατοικοῦντας μεθ' ὅσης οὐκ ἂν εἴποι τις ἐπιμελείας ἐκδέχεσθαι καὶ διαπερᾶν καὶ τῇ βασιλίδι παραπέμπειν τὰ θρέμματα." It was still an important commercial center in thirteenth century commerce between Bithynia and Constantinople. Nicholas Mesarites, *Neue Quellen zur Geschichte des lateinischen Kaistertums und der Kirchenunion*, ed. A. Heisenberg *Sitz. der bay. Akad. der Wiss. Philosoph.-philolog-Kl.*2 Abh. (1923), II, 39, "πολίχνιον εὐπερίγραπτον μέν, ἰσχυρὸν δὲ τὰ πολλά."

[58] Procopius, *Buildings*, V, iii, 17–20. Darrouzès, *Épistoliers byzantine*, p. 326, for the restoration of the baths by Leo VI. Leo Choerosphactes composed a poem on the baths, S. G. Mercati, "Intorno all' autore del carme εἰς τὰ ἐν Πυθίοις θερμά," *R.S.O.*, X (1923-25), 241; G. Kolias, *Léon Choirosphactes* (Athens, 1939), p. 54.

[59] See for example in Drexl and Pertz, I, 132, the description of the village of Oreine in Bithynia, which belonged to Psellus.

[60] In the early eighth century, the forces rebelling against Anastasius II were able to capitalize on this factor to raise a large fleet of merchant vessels in this area with which to oppose the emperor. Theophanes, I, 385, " συλλαμβάνονται πλεῖστα μικρά τε καὶ μεγάλα πραγματευτικά σκάφη ..." This rich area exported such items as grain, pottery, and silk, Procopius, *Anecdota*, XXII, 17. Mesarites, *Neue Quellen*, II, 44; Al-Umari-Quatrèmere, p. 366; Al-Umari-Taeschner, p. 43.

[61] AS Nov. III, 590, "... περιφανὴς καὶ ὅτι ἀγχίαλος καὶ πλῆθος ἀεὶ τῶν πανταχόθεν εἰς αὐτὴν καταιρούντων ... " K. Lanckoroński, G. Niemann, and E. Petersen, *Städte Pamphyliens und Pisidiens*, (Vienna, 1890), I.

[62] AS Nov. IV, " ἧς ἀφορμᾶν εἰώθησαν οἱ πλεῖστοι τῶν εἰς Κύπρον πορευομένων."

[63] Constantine Porphyrogenitus, *De Caerimoniis*, I, 659. Ibn Battuta-Gibb, II, 418, mentions springs of cold water and apricots that were exported to Egypt; Ibn Battuta-Defrémery, II, 259–260. Al-Idrisi-Jaubert, II, indicates that later Attaleia was built on a different site but this is perhaps a confusion with Side.

[64] AS Nov. III, 511.

Saracens,[65] Jews,[66] and Italians.[67] The Arab accounts of the ninth and tenth centuries describe the district of Attaleia as densely populated and rich in cereals. Its agricultural produce found ready markets in the less fertile regions of the Anatolian plateau.[68]

The northern Anatolian coast was the scene of similarly energetic commerce and industry. Heracleia engaged in a brisk trade with Constantinople[69] and with Cherson, which needed its grain.[70] To the northeast was Amastris, a more important commercial center. Nicetas the Paphlagonian, describing Amastris as the "eye" of Paphlagonia, relates that the "Scyths" who lived on the north coast of the Black Sea were in frequent and intense commercial relation with the inhabitants of the city.[71] Its merchants were quite active as early as the ninth century, and probably earlier.[72] The combination of local industry, trade, and the produce of the soil made Amastris one of the more prosperous towns on the Black Sea.[73] Sinope, the site of the church of St. Phocas, was important as a grain port and naval base,[74] and also as the sponsor of the great

[65] *Ibid.*, 590, " ... Σαρακηνοῖς, οἱ πολλοὶ περὶ τὴν Ἀττάλειαν τὸ τηνικάδε ἔτυχον ὄντες, ἐμπορίας χάριν κατάραντες."

[66] Z. Ankori, *Keraites in Byzantium* (New York, 1959), pp. 46-47. Starr, *The Jews* p. 26.

[67] Italians were calling at Attaleia at the end of the eleventh century, Tafel and Thomas, *Urkunden*, I, 52, but possibly earlier as well. In the period of Ibn Battuta-Gibb, II, 418, there were Latins, Jews, Greeks, and Muslims in the city.

[68] Ibn Hawkal, *B.G.A.*, II₁, 101-102. Darrouzès, *Épistoliers byzantins*, pp. 198-199, they exported wheat to the Phrygian district. The region of Synnada, by way of example, produced only barley. It was at too high an elevation for the cultivation of olive oil or the vine, and for fuel the inhabitants had to utilize animal dung, ζάρζακον, instead of wood. William of Tyre, *A History of Deeds Done beyond the Sea*, trans. and annotated by F. A. Babcock and A. C. Krey, XVI, xxvi, also comments on the fertility of the soil. X. de Planhol, *De la plaine pamphylienne aux lacs pisidiens. Nomadisme et vie paysanne* (Paris, 1958), pp. 83-85. On Side, east of Attaleia: A. M. Mansel, "Side," *P.W.*, *Supplementband* X (1965), 879-918; Mansel, *Die Ruinen von Side* (Berlin, 1963). Eyice, "L'église cruciforme byzantine de Side en Pamphylie," *Anatolia*, III (1958), 35-42; "La ville byzantine de Side en Pamphylie," *Actes de X Congrès International d'Études Byzantines 1955* (Istanbul, 1957) pp. 130-133.

[69] Nicephorus Bryennius, 93-94, records the case history of a certain Maurix who, though of humble origin, became wealthy and great from this maritime commerce.

[70] Constantine Porphyrogenitus, *De Caerimoniis*, I, 287.

[71] Nicetas of Paphlagonia, *P.G.*, CV, 421, " Ἀμάστρα, ὁ τῆς Παφλαγονίας, μᾶλλον δὲ τῆς οἰκουμένης, ὀλίγου δεῖν, ὀφθαλμός, εἰς ἣν οἵ τε τὸ βόρειον τοῦ Εὐξείνου μέρος περιοικοῦντες Σκῦθαι, καὶ οἱ πρὸς νότον δὲ κείμενοι, ὥσπερ εἴς τι κοινὸν συντρέχοντες ἐμπόριον, τὰ παρ' ἑαυτῶν τε συνεισφέρουσι, καὶ τῶν παρ' αὐτῆς ἀντιλαμβάνουσι." Eyice, "Deux anciennes églises byzantines de la citadelle d'Amasra (Paphlagonie)," *Cahiers Archéologique*, VII (1954), 97-105.

[72] When George the bishop of Amastris had to journey to Trebizond to free merchants of Amastris from jail, Vasilievsky, *Trudy* (St. Petersburg), III, 43-47.

[73] Nicetas of Paphlagonia, *P.G.*, CV, 421, " οὐδενὶ μὲν τῶν ἀπὸ γῆς ἢ θαλάσσης ἀγωγίμων σπανίζεται· πᾶσι δὲ τοῖς ἐπιτηδείοις δαψιλῶς εὐθυνουμένη, οἰκοδομησί τε λαμπροῖς καὶ τείχεσι καρτεροῖς, ναὶ δὴ καὶ λιμέσι καλοῖς καὶ οἰκήτορσι ἄνωθεν περιφανεστάτοις κεχρημένη." S. Vailhé, "Amastris," *D.H.G.E.*

[74] C. Van de Vorst, "Saint Phocas," *A.B.*, XXX (1911), 289. St. Phocas was patron saint of the merchants and seamen, who always dedicated a share of the wheat (in which they traded) to his church. N. A. Oikonomides, " Ἅγιος ὁ Φωκᾶς ὁ Σινοπεύς. Λατρεία καὶ διάδοσις αὐτῆς," Α.Π., XVII (1952), 184-219.

panegyris, or commercial fair, held on the feast day of St. Phocas.[75] Slightly to the southeast was another grain port, Amisus, which traded extensively with the Chersonese.[76] Cerasus, which participated in this maritime intercourse with the "Scyths" and the other Pontine cities, was one of the major textile centers of northern Anatolia, supplying Constantinople with linen cloth.[77]

Certainly the most important of the Anatolian cities on the Black Sea, in terms of population, wealth, commerce, and industry, was Trebizond.[78] It was situated in the vicinity of the fertile grain-producing regions of Paipert and Chaldia[79] and served as a storage center and market for the region's grain.[80] But significant as it was in the grain trade, Trebizond was more important as a commercial center in which converged trade routes coming by sea from Cherson and by land from the Caucasus, Central Asia, Syria, Constantinople, and Anatolia. There were several market fairs held each year,[81] the most important of which was the panegyris of St. Eugenius, the patron saint of Trebizond, instituted in the region of Basil I.[82] Merchants and travelers from all parts of the Middle

[75] Van de Vorst, "Saint Phocas," p. 289, " ἤδη γάρ σοι κ'ανταῦθα πανήγυρις τῶν μεγάλων.". It was also the site of an imperial treasury in the eleventh century, Anna Comnena, II, 64.

[76] Constantine Porphyrogenitus, *De Administrando Imperio*, ed. G. Moravcsik and R. Jenkins (Washington, D.C., 1967) pp. 286–287 (hereafter cited as Constantine Porphyrogenitus, *De Adm. Imp.*). G. Schlumberger, "Sceaux byzantins inédits," *Revue Numismatique*, 4th ser., IX (1905), 348-349, for the seal of a tenth-eleventh century commerciarius of Amisus.

[77] Zepos, *J.G.R.*, III, 381. The silk-garment merchants used this linen to line the so-called bombycene tunics. Al-Idrisi-Jaubert, II, 393.

[78] Papadopoulos-Kermaneus, *Sbornik v istočnikov po istorii trapezundskoi imperii* (St. Petersburg, 1897), p. 58 (hereafter cited as Papadopoulos-Kerameus, *Ist. trap. imp.*). (This is from the miracula of St. Eugenius by Joseph the metropolitan of Trebizond.) " ἤνθει μὲν γὰρ τὸ τηνικαῦτα καιροῦ ἡ Τραπεζοῦς ἥδε καὶ περίοπτος ἦν καὶ περίκλυτος, καὶ παρὰ πάσης, σχεδόν, γῆς ἐδοξάζετο· προύχοντές τε ὑπῆρχον ἐν αὐτῆ οὐκ ὀλίγοι καὶ στρατιῶται ἐπίλεκτοι, ἔμποροί τε πλεῖστοι καὶ ὄλβιοι, μοναὶ δὲ καὶ παρθενῶνες διαβεβοημέναι κατάπυκνοι καὶ πλῆθος λαοῦ οὔκουν ῥᾳδίως ἀρίθμητον." The city also had mining works in the vicinity, Papadopoulos-Kerameus, " Συμβολαὶ εἰς τὴν ἱστορίαν Τραπεζοῦντος," *V.V.*, XII (1906), 140. Chrysanthos, Ἡ ἐκκλησία Τραπεζοῦντος, Α.Π., IV–V (1936). H-G. Beck, *Kirche und theologische Literatur im byzantinischen Reich* (Munich, 1959), pp. 168–170, for bibliography. On the later period, S. Lampros, Βησσαρίωνος ἐγκώμιον εἰς Τραπεζοῦντα νῦν τὸ πρῶτον ἐκδιδόμενον κατὰ τὸν Μαρκιανὸν κώδικα (Athens, 1916).

[79] Papadopoulos-Kerameus, *Ist. trap. imp.*, p. 56, " πάνυ εὐήροτός ἐστι καὶ βαθεῖα καὶ εὔφορος . . . " For the seal of the crites of the theme in the ninth–tenth century, see A. Bryer, "A Molybdobull of the Imperial Protospatharius Constantine, Krites of the Theme of Chaldia," *A.Π.*, XXVII (1966), 244-246. See also O. Lampsides, "Nicétas èvêque inconnu de Trébizonde," *B.Z.*, LVII (1964), 380-381, for an ecclesiastical seal of the eleventh and twelfth centuries (or possibly of the tenth century). H. Antoniadis-Bibicou, *Recherches sur les douanes à Byzance. L' "octava," le "kommerkion" et les commerciaires* (Paris, 1963), *passim*.

[80] Papadopoulos-Kerameus, *Ist. trap. imp.*, pp. 49–50, 81.

[81] Mas'udi, *Les prairies d'or, texte et traduction*, C. B. de Maynard and P. de Courteille (Paris, 1914) II, 3 (hereafter cited as Mas'udi), refers to Trebizond as اسواق-markets.

[82] Papadopoulos-Kerameus, *Ist. trap. imp.*, pp. 57–59. It was officially observed by the government officials, τοῖς ἐν τέλει, until the end of the eleventh century when the Turkish invasions interrupted the celebration.

East were to be seen buying and selling goods in Trebizond and visiting the shrine of St. Eugenius for cures: Arabs, Armenians, Greeks,[83] Russians, Colchians,[84] Jews,[85] Georgians,[86] and Circassians.[87] The Trebizondines were engaged in a vast international commerce between east and west. The Kachaks, a Caucasian people, came to the city to purchase Greek brocades and other textiles.[88] The tenth-century Arab Istakhri relates that most of the Greek textiles and brocades in his day were imported into the Islamic world via Trebizond. Aside from the grain that Trebizond sent to the imperial capital on the Bosphorus, very important were the perfumes and other exotic items that entered the empire via the emporium of Trebizond. The trade of the region furnished a further source of revenue to the state by virtue of the customs duties that the *commerciarioi* levied.[89]

Bona and Oenoe were smaller towns of some commercial note, the latter as a ship building center and naval base.[90] This whole tier of Pontic towns participated in a vital commercial and industrial life, a fact reflected by such authors as Theophanes and Constantine Porphyrogenitus. The former relates that when Constantine V wished to rebuild the acqueduct of Valens in Constantinople during a severe drought, he transported craftsmen and builders from western Asia Minor and Pontus.[91] Also, the exports of grain, wine, and other commodities were not only necessary for Constantinople but were absolutely essential to the existence of the Chersonites. The latter, in return for the goods that the Greek merchants brought them, sent to Pontus such items as hides and wax which they acquired from the Patzinaks. Constantine Porphyrogenitus tells his son that in case the Chersonites should revolt, imperial agents should be sent to the coasts of the provinces of Armeniacon, Paphlagonia, and Bucellarion to take possession of the Chersonite ships, arrest the crews, and confiscate the cargoes. The merchant ships of these provinces were to be prevented from going to Cherson with their much needed

---

[83] Mas'udi, I, 3. Vasilievsky, *Trudy*, III, 43-47.

[84] Papadopoulos-Kerameus, *Ist. trap. imp.*, pp. 40, 43.

[85] Ankori, *Keraites*, pp. 122-125. The earliest mention of Jews in Byzantine Trebizond is 1188, but it is quite possible that they were to be found there earlier.

[86] Constantine Porphyrogenitus, *De Adm. Imp.*, pp. 216-217, relates that commerce flowed from Trebizond to the Georgian town of Adranoutzi. This latter is depicted as a very busy, prosperous, and extensive emporium with commerce coming to it from Trebizond, Georgia, Abasgia. Armenia, and Syria. It collected κομμέρκιον ἄπειρον, enormous customs revenue.

[87] Mas'udi, II, 45-47.

[88] *Ibid.*

[89] Istahri, *B.G.A.*, I, 188 تجتمع فيه التجّار فيدخلون بلد الروم للتجارة فما وقع من دبابيج

وبز يون وثياب الروم الى تلك النواحى فن طرابزندة. Al-Idrisi-Jaubert, II, 393. W. Heyd, *Histoire du commerce du Levant au moyen age* (Leipzig, 1923), I, 44.

[90] Al-Idrisi-Jaubert, II, 393

[91] Theophanes, I, 440. He brought 1,000 builders and 200 plasterers.

cargoes. For

if the Chersonites do not journey to Roumania and sell the hides and wax that they get by trade from the Pechenegs, they cannot live. If grain does not pass across from Aminsos and from Paphlagonia and the Bukellarioi and the flanks of the Armeniakoi, the Chersonites cannot live.[92]

Prior to the Seljuk invasions, the Byzantines possessed in eastern Anatolia a number of comparatively prosperous commercial towns. One of the most important of these and located to the southeast of Trebizond was Artze, a fairly large town[93] inhabited by numerous merchants, including not only local Syrians and Armenians but also many others.[94] The town possessed and traded in all types of goods and wares that were produced in Persia, India, and the rest of Asia.[95] Theodosiopolis in the vicinity seems to have been an important caravan town that traded with the Georgians in the early tenth century.[96] Many of its inhabitants moved to the town of Artze where commercial conditions were more favorable, but after the Turkish sack of Artze much of the populace returned to Theodosiopolis. Ani, one of the most recently acquired cities of the empire in eastern Asia Minor, was an important and very populous emporium, with great numbers of churches and grain silos.[97] At the easternmost extremity was the town of Manzikert, also recently acquired.[98] Melitene, a large commercial town[99] that had been incorporated into the empire during the reign of Romanus I, was later repeopled primarily with Jacobite

[92] Constantine Porphyrogenitus, De Adm. Imp., pp. 286–287.

[93] Attaliates, 148, refers to it variously as "πολιτείαν, μεγάλην . . . χωρόπολιν." Cedrenus, II, 577, as "κωμόπολις . . . μυρίανδρος καὶ πολὺν πλοῦτον ἔχουσα." Zonaras, III, 638, " κωμόπολις δ'ἦν τούτῳ πληθὺς δ'ἐνῴκει αὐτῷ, ἵν' οὕτως εἴποιμι, καὶ ἀριθμὸν ὑπερβαίνουσα, ἔμποροι δ'ἦσαν οἱ ἄνθρωποι καὶ πλοῦτος ἦν αὐτοῖς περιττός."

[94] Cedrenus, II, 577.

[95] Attaliates, 148, " καὶ παντοίων ὠνίων, ὅσα Περσική τε καὶ Ἰνδικὴ καὶ ἡ λοιπὴ Ἀσία φέρει, πλῆθος οὐκ εὐαρίθμητον φέρουσα." The situation was much the same in the days of Justinian I, Procopius, History of the Wars, II, xxv, " Καὶ παιδία μὲν ἐνταῦθα ἱππήλατά ἐστι, κῶμαι δὲ πολλαὶ πολυανθρωπόταται ᾤκηνται ἀγχωτάτω ἀλλήλαις καὶ πολλοὶ ἔμποροι κατ' ἐργασίαν ἐν ταύταις οἰκοῦσιν. ἔκ τε γὰρ Ἰνδῶν καὶ τῶν πλησιοχώρων Ἰβήρων πάντων τε ὡς εἰπεῖν τῶν ἐν Πέρσαις ἐθνῶν καὶ Ῥωμαίων τινῶν τὰ φορτία ἐσκομιζόμενοι ἐνταῦθα ἀλλήλοις ξυμβάλλουσι." Chronique de Matthieu d'Édesse (962–1136) avec la continuation de Grégoire le prêtre jusqu'en 1162, trans., E. Dulaurier (Paris, 1858), pp. 83–84 (hereafter cited as Matthew of Edessa), elaborates on the wealth and numerous population.

[96] Constantine Porphyrogenitus, De Adm. Imp., pp. 208, 214.

[97] Matthew of Edessa, p. 123. Attaliates, 79, " πόλις ἐστὶ μεγάλη καὶ πολυάνθρωπος."

[98] It is one of the few Byzantine towns whose personality momentarily shines through the darkness of the sourceless period. In the mid-eleventh century Toghrul attempted to take the city but after a furious siege that was unsuccessful, he decided to abandon the effort. The inhabitants of Manzikert then placed a pig on a ballista and hurled it into the sultan's camp with the cry, "Sultan! take this sow to wife and we shall give you Manzikert as dowry." Matthew of Edessa, 101–102. Al-Idrisi-Jaubert, II, 328, describes a commerce of salted fish taken from Lake Van and of clay for crockery.

[99] Matthew of Edessa, pp. 107 ff., remarks that its population was as numerous as the sands of the sea. Theophanes Continuatus, 415, 416–417, calls it in the tenth century, " . . . τὸ ἐπίσημον καὶ ἐξάκουστον καὶ πάνυ ὀχυρὸν καὶ δυνατὸν κάστρον . . . " Melitene and the surrounding towns were quite prosperous, p. 416, " πολυφόρους τε καὶ πιστάτας οὔσας καὶ οἵας πολλὰς παρέχειν προσόδους." Melitene itself brought in a

Christians[100] and to a lesser degree with Armenians and Greeks.[101] The few remarks that emerge from the sources reveal that this town was inhabited by wealthy merchants.[102] Nisibis and Edessa were comparatively populous and wealthy,[103] obviously dependent for much of their prosperity on trade with Syria.[104] Antioch, though actually not in Asia Minor, was very important in the economic life of the empire and especially in the commercial activities of the Anatolian towns. It was one of the important points at which commerce flowed between the domains of Byzantium and Islam. This trade had no doubt always existed and the wars and *razzias* only temporarily interrupted it.[105] Though much of this

---

rich revenue to the crown, " ταύτην οὖν . . . εἰς κουρατωρίαν ἀποκαταστήσας ὁ βασιλεὺς πολλὰς χιλιάδας χρυσίου καὶ ἀργυρίου ἐκεῖθεν δασμοφορεῖσθαι ἐτησίως πεποίηκεν." G. Ficker, *Erlasse des Patriarchen von Konstantinopel Alexios Studites* (Kiel, 1911), p. 28, " πόλις μὲν ἡ Μελιτηνὴ μεγάλη καὶ πολυάνθρωπος, πόλις ἀρχαῖα καὶ ἐπίσημος, ἐν καλῷ ἀέρος κειμένη καὶ χώρα ὑπ' αὐτὴν ὀλβία καὶ ἀγαθή, οὐ τοῖς ἀναγκαίοις μόνον εἰς βίον ἄλλα καὶ ταῖς περιττοῖς εἰς τέρψιν εὐθυνουμένην." But perhaps this eulogy was lifted from the legislation of Justinian, see Honigmann, "Malatya," EI₁.

[100] *Chronique de Michel le Syrien Patriarche Jacobite d'Antioch*, ed. and trans. J-B. Chabot (Paris, 1905), III, 130–131 (hereafter cited as Michel the Syrian), says that the Greeks refused to settle there and so Nicephorus Phocas asked the Syrians and their church to move to Melitene as they were accustomed to living between two peoples.

[101] Ficker, *Erlasse, passim*. Michael the Syrian, III, 136.

[102] Thus, in the eleventh century a wealthy inhabitant of Melitene, a Syrian Christian, is said to have ransomed 15,000 Christians from the Turks at five dinars a head, Michael the Syrian, III, 146. Matthew of Edessa, pp. 107–108, says it was full of gold, silver, precious stones, brocades, and people. *The Chronography of Gregory Abu'l Faraj the Son of Aaron, the Hebrew Physician commonly known as Bar Hebraeus being the First Part of his Political History of the World*, trans. E. A. W. Budge (London, 1932), I, 178 (hereafter cited as Bar Hebraeus), relates the story of the three sons of a certain Abu Imrun who were so rich that they struck the imperial gold coinage at their own expense, and, in addition, they are reported to have loaned Basil II 100 centenaria of gold. In the eleventh century these Syrian Christian merchants of Melitene were very active commercially, trading in Constantinople and in the lands under the sway of the Turks. Both the Armenians and Syrians had their own church and corporation of merchants in Constantinople. In the reign of Constantine X Ducas the walls of the city (destroyed in the tenth century by the Byzantines) were rebuilt at the expense of the wealthy Syrian inhabitants. Michael the Syrian, III, 165.

[103] Cedrenus, II, 502, relates that the yearly tax, which went to the treasury at Constantinople was fifty pounds of gold. Edessa is one of the few cities for which there are population figures. According to Sawiras ibn al-Mukaffa', *History of the Patriarchs of the Egyptian Church*, trans. and ed. A. S. Attiya and Y. Abd al-Masih, (Cairo, 1959), II, iii, 305 (hereafter cited as Sawirus ibn al-Mukaffa'), the city had, in 1071–1072, 20,000 Syrians, 8,000 Armenians, 6,000 Greeks, and 1,000 Latins, for a total of 35,000. For further discussion of the population of towns see below. Edessa was an important textile center and prior to its destruction by the Turks in the twelfth century was inhabited by silk merchants, weavers, cobblers, and tailors. Chabot, "Un épisode de l'histoire des Croisades," *Mélanges offerts à M. Gustave Schlumberger* (Paris, 1924), I, 173–174. Its inhabitants resisted the Turks valiantly.

[104] Matthew of Edessa, pp. 48, 130.

[105] Gibb, "Arab-Byzantine Relations under the Umayyad Caliphate," *D.O.P.*, IXI (1958), 230–231, G. Le Strange, *Baghdad during the Abbasid Caliphate from Contemporary Arabic and Persian Sources* (Oxford, 1924), p. 149, indicates the presence of Greeks in Baghdad. See also Yakubi, *Les pays*, trans. G. Wiet (Cario, 1937), p. 22. There is a particularly significant mention of it in the treaty concluded between the Byzantines and Hamdanids in 969–970, translated from the Arabic text by Canard, *Histoire de la dynastie des Hamdanides de Jezira et de Syrie* (Algiers, 1951), I, 835. "En ce qui concerne la dime prélevée sur (se qui vient du) pays des Rum, des douaniers de l'empereur siègeront à

trade with the Muslim east was transacted in northern and eastern Asia Minor, a considerable portion of it must have entered into and passed through southern and central Anatolia. Anazarba and Podandus in the tenth and eleventh centuries were populous and prosperous, with thickly inhabited and productive clusters of villages in their environs.[106] The highland town of Tzamandus was also wealthy and of good size.[107] Adana, Tarsus, Mopsuestia, and Seleuceia were significant towns characterized by commercial enterprise.[108] Caesareia, favored by its location on the commercial route connecting Mesopotamia-Syria with Anatolia, the seat of one of the most important Greek metropolitanates and an important point of religious pilgrimage, was the principal town of Cappadocia.[109] Nigde, Archelais, and Heracleia, though certainly not as

---

cotè des douaniers de Qargawaih et Bakjur, et sur loutes les merchandises comme or, argent, brocart grec, soie non travaillée, pierres précieuses, bijoux, perles, étoffes de soie fines (sundus), les douaniers impèriaux préléveront la dime; sur les étoffes (ordinaires), les étoffes de lin, les étoffes de soie à fleurs de diverses couleurs (buzyun), les animaux et autres merchandises, ce seront les douaniers du chambellan et de Bakjur après lui qui préléveront la dime, Après eux tous ces droits seront perçus par les douaniers impériaux." For a complete analysis of this treaty preserved in Kamal al-Din, see Canard, *Hamdanides*, pp. 833–837. Article twenty-one speaks of caravans coming from Byzantium to the domain of Islam. Canard, "Les relations politiques et sociales entre Byzance et les Arabes," *D.O.P.*, XVIII (1964), 48-55. Aside from the commercial and industrial importance of Byzantine Mesopotamia, it was also an important producer of wheat, Liudprand, *Legatio*, ed. J. Becker in *Die Werke Liudprands von Cremona*, 3d ed., *Scriptores rerum germanicarum inu sum scholarum ex Monumentis Germaniae Historicis separatim editi* (Hannover-Leipzig, 1915), p. 198.

[106] Cedrenus, II, 414-415. Zonaras, III, 502. Matthew of Edessa, p. 4. Cinnamus, 180, in the twelfth century still regards Anazarba as " πόλιν περιφανῆ. " Nicetas Choniates, 33, says of Anazarba, " κουροτρόφος οὖσα καὶ πολυάνθρωπος." Al-Idrisi-Jaubert, II, 133, Anazarba produced fruit in great abundance. M. Gough, "Anazarbus," *Anatolian Studies*, II (1952), 85-150.

Unfortunately source material is lacking here. In eastern Asia Minor information preserved by the Islamic, Syriac, and Armenian authors, who are provincial in nature, reveals incidental facts about the cities in this area. For northern and western Anatolia the saints' lives, which are also local in character, have preserved significant information. But for south and central Anatolia we have only the Byzantine chronicles, and they are concerned only with the capital.

[107] Cedrenus, II, 423, " πόλις . . . ἐν ἀποκρήμνῳ πέτρᾳ κειμένη, πολυάνθρωπος καὶ πλούτῳ περιβριθής." Zonaras, III, 54, " πολυπληθῆ πόλιν." Bardas Sclerus during his revolt was able to raise considerable sums of money from its inhabitants. Zonaras, III, 541.

[108] Nicephorus Phocas recolonized Tarsus after its conquest. Bar Hebraeus, I, 171, "And Tarsôs was (re)built, and was exceedingly prosperous, and the supply of food therein was so abundant that 12 litres of bread were sold for one zûzâ. And many of her citizens returned to Tarsôs, and some of them were baptized and became Christians; others remained in their Faith, but all their children were baptized." Scylitzes, II, 703, refers to Adana as a πόλιν. See Tafel and Thomas, *Urkunden*, I, 52, for mention of the commercial ports of southern Anatolia. Al-Idrisi-Jaubert, II, 133, refers to Adana and Tarsus as large towns with an active commerce and fine stone bazaars. He is either referring to conditions of the eleventh century or else to the period of the reconquest and reconstruction of the towns of the area under Alexius Comnenus. Seleuceia, after being rebuilt, attracted Jewish merchants from Egypt as settlers. Ankori, *Keraites*, p. 117. S. Goitein, "A Letter of Historical Importance from Seleuceia (Selefke), Cilicia, dated 21 July 1137," English summary of the article in *Tarbiz*, XXVII (1958), vii-viii.

[109] When al-Harawi, *Guide des lieux de pèlerinage*, trans. J. Sourdel-Thomine (Damascus 1957), p. 133, journeyed through Anatolia in the latter half of the twelfth century the Byzantine hippodrome and baths were still to be seen. For an account of the shrine of St. Basil, see Attaliates, 94.

large as Caesareia, also drew their livelihood from their position on the road system of southern Anatolia. West of Caesareia was the city of Iconium, the administrative, communications, religious, and commercial focal point of south-central Anatolia.[110] Chonae and Laodiceia, west of Iconium, were urban agglomerates that lived from the traffic passing along the road leading from Iconium to the Maeander River valley. Located near the sources of the river, they were possessed of well-watered and productive countrysides. The lakes were well stocked with fish, the valleys supported livestock and a host of agricultural products which included liquorice, cardamum, myrtle, figs, and other fruits.[111] Chonae, a town of respectable size, enjoyed a certain commercial prosperity as a result of the great trade fairs held at the panegyris of the Archangel Michael. Merchants traveled long distances to do business at this event, and the faithful came on pilgrimage to see the great church of the Archangel with its mosaics.[112] Laodiceia, famed for its textiles in late antiquity, doubtlessly continued to produce these materials during the Byzantine period, for when Ibn Battuta saw the city in the early fourteenth century, he observed that the Greek textile workers were still making excellent clothes and materials.[113]

Northwest of Iconium, along the road to Dorylaeum, existed a series of smaller towns that served as administrative, ecclesiastical, and military centers. These included Laodiceia Cecaumene, Tyriaeum, Philomelium, Synnada, Polybotus, Acroenus, Amorium, Caborcion, Santabaris, Nacoleia, Cotyaeum, Trocnada, and Pessinus.[114] Amorium, before its

---

[110] Attaliates, 135, " ἦν γὰρ τότε πλήθει τε καὶ μεγέθει ἀνδρῶν τε καὶ οἰκιῶν καὶ τῶν ἄλλων χρηστῶν καὶ ζηλωτῶν διαφέρουσα, καὶ ζώων παντοδαπῶν γένη τρέφουσα". W. Pfeifer, *Die Passlandschaft von Nigde. Ein Beitrag zur Siedlungs-und Wirtschaftsgeographie von Inneranatolien* (Greisen, 1957). Zonaras, III, 693, " ἀνθρώπων τε πολυπλήθειαν ἔχον καὶ πᾶσι τοῖς δοκοῦσι ἀγαθοῖς εὐθηνούμενον." As the Seljuk capital it continued to be a large town. When the members of the Third Crusade passed by the city they noted it to be larger than the city of Cologne. Al-Idrisi-Jaubert, II, 310, describes it as a beautiful city where routes converged. When Ibn Battuta-Gibb, II, 430, visited it in the first half of the fourteenth century it was still an impressive town, but it soon declined. Ibn Battuta-Defrémery, II, 281.

[111] Ansbert, ed. Chroust, *M.G.H., S.R.G., Nova Series*, V (Berlin, 1928), 75 (hereafter cited as Ansbert). Al-Umari-Quatremère, p. 355, compared the gardens of the city to those of Damascus. The markets abounded in fruits, grapes, pomegranites, and wine.

[112] Nicetas Choniates, 230, " πόλιν εὐδαίμονα καὶ μεγάλην." With the stabilization of relations between Konya and the Byzantines in the late twelfth century, the panegyris recovered and was attended by the inhabitants of Lydia, Ionia, Caria, Paphlagonia, and Iconium see chapter iii. The church, with its mosaics, was larger than the church of St. Mocius in Constantinople, Nicetas Choniates, 523–524. Theodore Scutariotes-Sathas, 388. For references to the church as a site of pilgrimage, see below.

[113] Ibn Buttuta-Gibb, II, 425. Ibn Battuta-Defrémery, II, 271–272. The tradition of textile manufacture in the region of Laodiceia was already famous in the time of the geographer Strabo, XII, 8. 16. The gold embroidery which Ibn Battuta mentions was a speciality of the craftsmen of Lydia and Phrygia in antiquity, Broughton, *Asia Minor*, p. 818.

[114] For a discussion of these smaller towns, W. Ramsay, *The Historical Geography of Asia Minor* (London, 1890) (hereafter cited as Ramsay, *Geography*), and his *The Cities and Bishoprics of Phrygia, Being an Essay of the Local History of Phrygia from the Earliest Times to the Turkish Conquest* (Oxford, 1895–97) (hereafter cited as Ramsay, *Phrygia*).

celebrated sack by the Arabs in the ninth century, was one of the larger Anatolian towns,[115] and the presence of Jews in the city during the early ninth century is possibly an indication that Amorium was the site of considerable commercial life.[116] It has been assumed that the city had all but disappeared as a result of the Arab destruction. Attaleiates, however, who is very careful in the nomenclature that he applies to cities, towns, and villages, still refers to Amorium as a πολιτεία in the eleventh century.[117] The largest and most important of the plateau towns in northwestern Anatolia was Dorylaeum. Located at the point of egress from and entrance to the plateau, its plain watered by the streams of the Bathys and Tembris, the city enjoyed the advantages that strategic location and generous nature bestowed. The fields produced rich harvests of grain and the rivers abounded in fish, the villages were densely populated and the city was embellished with stoas, fountains, and houses of illustrious citizens.[118] Between Dorylaeum and Nicaea were the lesser towns of Malagina, Pithecas, and Leucae.[119]

The northern rim of the plateau contained a number of towns, the most important of which was Ankara.[120] Slightly to the east was Saniana (a military base), and farther north were Gangra and Castamon. Euchaita, midway between the Halys and Iris rivers, was a center of commercial

[115] Vasilievsky and Nekitene, "Skazaniia 42 amoriiskikh mučenikakh i tserkovnaia služba," *Zapiski imperatorskoi akademii nauk*, ser. VIII, vol. VII, no. 2, p. 11, " πόλις μεγίστη ἐν τοῖς ἀνατολικοῖς τῆς Ῥωμαϊκῆς ἐπικρατείας μέρεσιν ... ἐπίσημός τε καὶ περιφανὴς καὶ πρώτη τῶν μετὰ τὴν βασιλεύουσαν καὶ τῶν ἀπασῶν πόλεων προκαθήμενη, τὰ μάλιστα πολυάνθρωπος καὶ πλῆθος ἀμύθητον πολιτικόν τε ..." Canard, "Ammuriya," EI₂.

[116] Theophanes Continuatus, p. 42.

[117] Attaliates, 121. Zonaras, III, 692, the Turks killed large numbers of the inhabitants when they devastated Amorium in the reign of Romanus IV. Al-Idrisi-Jaubert, II, 301, 307, speaks of it as a beautiful town with forty towers, and as a commercial center where communication routes meet, but it is difficult to ascertain the period to which he refers.

[118] Cinnamus, 294–295, " Τὸ δὲ Δορύλαιον τοῦτο ἦν μὲν ὅτε πόλις ἦν μεγάλη τε εἴπερ τις τῶν ἐν Ἀσίᾳ καὶ λόγου ἀξία πολλοῦ. αὔρα τε γὰρ τὸν χῶρον ἀπαλὴ καταπνεῖ, καὶ πεδία παρ' αὐτὴν τέταται λειότητός τε ἐπὶ πλεῖστον ἥκοντα καὶ ἀμήχανόν τι προφαίνοντα κάλλος, οὕτω μέντοι λιπαρὰ καὶ οὕτως εὔγεω, ὡς τήν τε πόαν δαψιλῆ μάλιστα ἐκδιδόναι καὶ ἀβρὸν παρέχεσθαι ἄσταχυν. ποταμὸς δὲ διὰ τοῦ τῇδε τὸ νᾶμα πέμπει καὶ ἰδέσθαι καλὸς καὶ γεύσασθαι ἡδύς. πλῆθος ἰχθύων τοσοῦτον δὲ ἐννήχεται τούτῳ, ὅσον εἰς δαψίλειαν τοῖς τῇδε ἁλιευόμενον ἐλλιπὲς οὐδαμῇ γίνεσθαι. ἐνταῦθα Μελισσηνῶν ποτε καίσαρι οἰκίαι τε ἐξῳκοδόμηνται λαμπραὶ καὶ κῶμαι πολυάνθρωποι ἦσαν θερμά τε αὐτόματα καὶ στοαὶ καὶ πλυνοί, καὶ ὅσα ἀνθρώποις ἡδονὴν φέρει, ταῦτα δὴ ὁ χῶρος ἄφθονα παρεῖχεν."

[119] Ramsay, *Geography*, pp. 202, 207.

[120] Its medieval walls alone would indicate its importance. Bryennius, 64–65, says that in one of his numerous campaigns against the Turks the brother of Alexius Comnenus was captured. In order to ransom him he was obliged to raise several thousand gold pieces. This he was able to do from the rich of Ankara and the neighboring towns by promising to repay the loan with interest, " πολλοὶ γὰρ τῶν εὐπόρων χρυσίον πεπόμφασιν αὐτῷ." On Byzantine Ankara, G. de Jerphanion, "Mélanges d'archéologie anatolienne," *Mélanges de l'Université St. Joseph*, XIII (1928), 144–293. Grégoire, "Inscriptions historiques d'Ancyre," *Byzantion*, IV (1927–28), 437–468; "Michel III et Basile le Macédonien dans les inscriptions d'Ancyre," *Byzantion*, V (1929), 327–346. P. Wittek, "Zur Geschichte Angoras im Mittelalter," *Festschrift Georg Jacob* (Leipzig, 1932), 329 ff. C. Karalevsky, "Ancyre," *D.H.G.E.*

note and evidently of some size. Its fair attracted merchants from afar with the result that the city prospered.[121] Amaseia, much as Ankara and Euchaita, was a town of importance as a result of its strategic location in the mountain passes (Psellus speaks of it as a famous city, "the city mentioned by every tongue".[122]) Its rural neighborhood, though chopped up by precipitous mountains, was nevertheless well watered and productive. Like so many other towns in northeastern Anatolia, Amaseia was located in a metalliferous region and the mines seem to have been worked in Byzantine and Seljuk times.[123] Doceia, Neocaesareia, Sebasteia, Coloneia, Nicopolis, and Argyropolis were important administrative, ecclesiastical, and commercial centers of the conventional Anatolian type.[124]

Anatolian towns were subject to ever-present and powerful currents of trade and commerce. In spite of the aridity of the historical sources, it seems quite clear that Greek, Armenian, Jewish, Russian, Chersonite, Circassian, Georgian, Muslim, and Italian merchants traversed the maritime and hinterland trade routes. Maritime commerce came to the Anatolian coastal cities along the entire Black Sea, Aegean, and Mediterranean littorals. In the north the trade followed the coastal towns ultimately reaching Constantinople in the west or Trebizond in the east. Much of this commerce must have deployed itself along the river valleys and mountain passes leading from the littoral to the towns of the plateau. The maritime commerce of the coastal towns was tied up with Constantinople, Cherson, and the Caucasus while the commerce of the Aegean coastal centers was connected with the Greek peninsula and the islands as well as with Constantinople. The sea trade of Attaleia was supplied by Egypt, Cyprus, Antioch, and the Aegean. The major land route from the east entered the various border cities from Antioch in the

---

[121] P. deLagarde and J. Bollig, *Johannis Euchaitarum metropolitae quae supersunt in cod. vaticano graeco 676* (Berlin, 1882) pp. 131–134, 207 (hereafter cited as John Mauropus-Lagarde), " . . . πολυάνθρωπον πόλιν . . ." AS Nov. IV, 54.

[122] Psellus-Renauld, II, 166, " τὸ δὲ πάσης γλώττης βοώμενον πτόλισμα." *Cecaumeni strategicon et incerti scriptoris de officiis regiis libellus* (Petropolis, 1896) p. 72 (hereafter cited as Cecaumenus), mentions the existence of an important state prison, the μαρμαρωτή. Alexius Comnenus found himself forced to rely upon the wealthy inhabitants of Amaseia in order to raise the ransom money with which to purchase Roussel from the Turks, Anna Comnena, I, 13, "τοὺς τὰ πρῶτα φέροντας καὶ χρημάτων εὐπορούντας." The rich Amaseians, however, incited the poor of the city to riot in opposition to the suggested loan. Vailhé, "Amaseia," *D.H.G.E.*

[123] Vryonis, "The Question of the Byzantine Mines," *Speculum*, XXXVII (1962), 7–8. When the Turks first invaded the area the inhabitants sought refuge in the mines, and the works were still being exploited in the thirteenth-fourteenth centuries at which time merchants from the Muslim world came to purchase the metal.

[124] When the Turks attacked Sebasteia in the eleventh century, the churches with their high domes were so numerous that the Turks at first hesitated to enter. It was at that time a city with numerous inhabitants and wealthy in gold, silver, precious stones, and brocades, Matthew of Edessa, pp. 111–112. Argryopolis, the Turkish Gümüshhane, was a mining town, and when the Danishmendids took it, according to Turkish tradition, they struck their first coins from the metal mined there. The mining traditions of the Greeks of this town were still alive in the nineteenth century, see chapter vii. Bar Hebraeus, I, 223, mentions cloth merchants in eleventh-century Doceia.

south to Trebizond in the north. Again, some of this commerce was sea borne from Trebizond to Constantinople and to other harbors, or from Antioch to Attaleia and other ports. But at the same time a good portion of this commerce found its way into the cities of the plateau via the Cilician Gates and other routes.[125]

There is evidence for the existence of well-developed local industry in the Anatolian towns. The Anatolians manufactured brocades and various textiles of linen, wool, silk, and cotton; they wove carpets, produced glassware and pottery, incense, bows, arrows, swords, shields, nails, rope, and other naval supplies; and they built ships. Certainly they must have produced many of the everyday items that they needed in their own urban and rural life. Various types of craftsmen, specialized labor, and merchants are mentioned on rare occasion in the texts and inscriptions.[126] The peninsula was a major region of the Byzantine mining industry, producing silver, copper, iron, lead, possibly some gold, marble, alum, and semiprecious stones.[127] Food production played a very

---

[125] Minorsky, "Marvazi and the Byzantines," *A.I.P.H.O.S.*, X (1950), 462–464. Caravans travel from Syria to Constantinople where they have their depots. Also Michael the Syrian, III, 185, 166–167. The routes are given in Ibn Khuradadhbih, *B.G.A.*, VI, 101 ff. On the import of Byzantine luxury items into late tenth-century Egypt, K. Röder, "Das Mīnā im Bericht über die Schätze der Fatimiden," *Z.D.M.G.*, LXXXIX (1935), 363–371.

[126] Minorsky, "Marvazi," pp. 462–464, describes the Byzantines as "gifted in crafts and skillful in the fabrication of (various) articles, textiles, carpets . . ." They are second only to the Chinese in these skills (a theme that reappears in the Mathnawi of Djalal al-Din Rumi in the thirteenth century). The Christian inscriptions from Anatolia, though, incomplete (Grégoire, *Recueil des inscriptions grecques chrétiennes d'Asie Mineure* (Paris, 1922), I, 21, 27, 91,) contain the epitaphs of marble workers from the regions of tenth-century Smyrna, eighth to tenth-century Tralles, and of a butcher from seventh and eighth century Caria. The hagiographical and other texts note various craftsmen. The anonymous author of the Hudud al-Alam-Minorsky, p. 156, describes Rum (Anatolia) as a very rich province producing great quantities of brocades, silk, textiles, carpets, stockings, trouser cords. For the export of Anatolian capets and textiles to the Turks of Central Asia, *Ibn Fadlan's Reisebericht*, ed. and trans. Z. V. Togan in *Abhandlungen für die Kunde des Morgenlandes*, vol. XXIV, pt. 3 (Leipzig) p. 64 (hereafter cited as Ibn Fadlan-Togan). See also Goitein, "The Main Industries of the Mediterranean Area as Reflected in the Records of the Cairo Geniza," *J.E.S.H.O.*, IV (1961), 175. The fact that Bokht-Isho Bar Gabriel, physician of the caliph Mutawakkil, wore gowns of Byzantine silk would indicate that Byzantine textiles were fashionable in ninth-century Baghdad, Bar Hebraeus, I, 143. The Byzantine products of the silk industry, especially brocades, mandils, and material for upholstering, were widely demanded in the Mediterranean. On carpet production in eastern Asia Minor, Canard, "Armenia," EI₂. It is of interest that Hudud al-Alam mentions Anatolia as an important center of the rug industry. The rugs of Sardes were considered to be among the finest in the ancient world. They were highly prized by the Achemenid royal court. Athenaeus, *Deipnosophistae*, XII, 514, " καὶ διῄει διὰ τῆς τούτων αὐλῆς πεζὸς ὑποτιθεμένων ψιλοταπίδων Σαρδιανῶν, ἐφ' ὧν οὐδεὶς ἄλλος ἐπέβαινεν ἢ βασιλεύς," and were associated by the Greeks with excessive luxury and effeminacy, VI, 255, ". . . κατέκειτο δ' ὑπερβάλλουσαν τρυφὺν ἐπὶ ἀργυρόποδος κλίνης ὑπεστρωμένης Σαρδιανῇ ψιλοτάπιδι τῶν πάνυ πολυτελῶν." The textile industry of Anatolia was of great renown in late antiquity. For a detailed listing of the references to the various cloths and textiles produced in late ancient Anatolia, Broughton, *Asia Minor*, pp. 817–823. See also n. 570 in chapter iii.

[127] Vryonis, "Byzantine Mines," *passim*. Ahrweiler, "Smyrne," 18–19. Y. Manandian, *O torgovle i gorodakh Armenii v sviazi s mirovoi torgovle i drevnikh vremen* (Erevan, 1954), pp. 225 ff.

important role in the commerce of the towns, the Byzantine villages being more closely connected to the towns than was the case with many areas in western Europe.[128] The towns served as markets for the produce of the peasants most important items of which were grain, fish, wine, fruit, legumes, nuts, livestock, and lumber. Each town had its group of villages, the inhabitants of which brought these products to town, very often during the big fairs held on the feast day of the saints.[129] Here the villagers sold their produce and bought the products of local or foreign industry.[130] Many of these villages were quite large and thriving.[131] Thus, parallel to the larger movements of trade, there was generated also this smaller local trade between the villages and the towns, which was just as important in some respects as the larger scale trade. In this manner the farmers and herdsmen received cash for their goods. The towns in turn were able to dispose of the villagers' produce both by sale among the townsmen and by selling it to merchants of Constantinople and other cities.

Great Landed Families

One of the critical phenomena in the history of Anatolia was the evolution of the great landed families, whose deeds permeate the chronicles and legal literature of the tenth and eleventh centuries. Possessed of vast estates and high official position in the provincial administration and military, they were largely responsible for the social and historical development in Asia Minor prior to the Seljuk invasions. Most of the families rose to power and eminence via the armies and then consolidated their position by an economic expansion that was largely, though not exclusively, based on the acquisition of great land holdings. These magnates, by virtue of their control of the provincial armies, wielded great power. Very often the exercise of the strategeia in a particular province tended to become semihereditary in a particular family, as in the case of the Phocas' and the theme of Cappadocia. Aside from control of these thematic armies, the large estates of the aristocracy enabled them to maintain large bodies of private troops. So long as the government was able to check their more extreme political and economic abuses, this

---

[128] S. Runciman, "Byzantine Trade and Industry," *Cambridge Economic History* (Cambridge, 1952), II, 86–87. Ostrogorsky, "Agrarian Conditions in the Byzantine Empire in the Middle Ages," *Cambridge Economic History* (Cambridge, 1941), I, 200. Often the chroniclers describe the main Anatolian cities in conjunction with the clusters of villages around them: Attaliates, 81, Ani had πολίχνια and ὕπαιθρα; Attaliates, 95, Antioch had its κῶμαι; Attaliates, 131, Chliat had τὰ ὑπὸ τούτου πολίχνια; Drexl and Pertz, II, 54, Euchaita had its χωρία . . . ἀγροικικά; Zonaras, III, 502, Anazarba and Pondandus had χωρία πολυάνθρωπά τε καὶ πάμφορα; Anna Comnena, II, 279, Iconium had its κωμοπόλεων; Bryennius, 58, Caesareia had its κωμοπόλεις.

[129] Zepos, *J.G.R.*, I, 271–272, regulates affairs having to do with these fairs.

[130] Drexl and Pertz, I, 133, describes this for Nicomedeia.

[131] Such for example were Cryapege near Caesareia, Attaliates, 146; Oreine, Drexl, and Pertz, I, 132.

provincial aristocracy contributed to the defense and expansion of Byzantium in the east. In the eleventh century, however, this powerful class played a crucial role in the decline of the state.[132]

Demography

Unfortunately almost nothing is known about the numbers of the population in Byzantine Anatolia and its towns, for little has survived in the way of comprehensive tax registers or population figures. The silence of the sources and the thoroughness of the cultural transformation effected by the fifteenth century have led many scholars to conclude, erroneously, that Byzantine Asia Minor was sparsely inhabited. Estimates, which are really little more than educated guesses, have been made for the size of Anatolian population in antiquity. These estimates, all based upon an assumption of commercial prosperity and urban vitality in the period of the Roman and early Byzantine Empires, vary from 8,800,000 to 13,000,000.[133] J. C. Russell has suggested that the population remained

---

[132] The following representative list of the estates and domiciles of the Anatolian magnates is drawn from a study in progress on the internal history of Byzantium in the eleventh century. I have not gone into the problem of the relation of this landlord class to the Anatolian towns.

Cappadocia	*Anatolicon*	*Paphlagonia*
Alyattes	Mesanactes	Doceianus
Ampelas	Radenus	Souanites
Goudeles	Argyrus	Theodora (wife of Theophilus)
Scepides	Botaniates	Ducas
Lecapenus	Maniaces	Curcuas
Diogenes	Musele	Comnenus
Ducas	Sclerus	Calocyres
Maleinus	Synnadenus	
Phocas	Bourtzes	*Chaldia*
Boilas	Straboromanus	Xiphilenus
	Leichudes	Gabras
Coloneia	Melissenus	
Cecaumenus	Ducas	*Mesopotamia*
	Charsianon	Palaeologus
Bithynia	Argyrus	
Maurix	Maleinus	*Iberia*
Ducas		Boilas
Maleinus	*Lycandus*	Pacurianus
	Melias	Apocapes
Cibyrrheote		
Screnarius		*Armeniacon*
Ducas		Dalassenus
Maurus		

[133] J. Beloch, *Die Bevölkerung der griechisch-römischen Welt* (Leipzig, 1886), pp. 277 ff. Broughton, *Asia Minor*, pp. 812–816. For more recent remarks on the methods of arriving at population figures in the ancient and medieval world, see H. Bengtson, *Griechische Geschichte von der Anfängen bis in die römische Kaiserzeit*, 2d ed. (Munich, 1960), p. 421. C. Roebuck, *Ionian Trade and Colonization* (New York, 1959), pp. 21–33. J. C. Russell, "Recent Advances in Medieval Demography," *Speculum*, XL (1965), 84–101; *Late Ancient and Medieval Population, Transactions of the American Philosophical Society*, vol. XLIII, no. 3 (Philadelphia, 1958), p. 81, proposes a population of 8,800,000 around the year 100 A.D., and 11,600,000 for Anatolia in the fifth century of the Christian era. The most recent survey of Byzantine demography is P. Charanis, "Observations on the Demography of the Byzantine Empire," *Thirteenth International Congress of Byzantine Studies, Oxford, 1966*, vol. XIV.

at the comparatively high figure of 8,000,000 during the middle Byzantine period but that it declined to 6,000,000 by the beginning of the thirteenth century and the Turkish period.[134]

There are indications that by the tenth and eleventh centuries the population of Anatolia was growing. That there was a certain stability in Anatolian demography emerges from the survival, en masse, of the ancient towns.[135] These towns were comparatively safe and shielded from the massive upheaval that enveloped urban society in much of the Balkans. As late as the eleventh century, such important cities as Melitene, Sebasteia, and Artze were unwalled despite the fact that they were close to the Muslim lands.[136] The trade routes (actively plied by Muslim and Christian merchants) going through the towns, and the presence of dense village clusters in the environs of the cities are also factors that would tend to support the assumption of a certain demographic vitality. The active policy of transplanting peoples to Anatolia certainly contributed to the growth of the population,[137] and there are other testimonials to an increase in population in the two centuries prior to the Seljuk invasions. The older tax system, by which the *caput* was tied to the *iugum* because of the insufficient labor force, was relaxed, and in the middle Byzantine period the system underwent a transformation by which the head tax and land tax were separated. The replacement of the reciprocal unit of the two taxes with a separate collection presupposes that the earlier scarcity of agricultural labor had disappeared, a conclusion supported by the growing land hunger of the landed magnates in the tenth century.[138]

A further indication of demographic stability and growth is the evolution of the ecclesiastical administrative structure in Asia Minor. The Byzantine requirement that each town should constitute a bishopric was observed as late as the twelfth century. The basic stipulation for the existence of a bishopric was that an inhabited area should be sufficiently populous to be considered a town. If it were too small it could not be

---

[134] Russell, "Recent Advances in Medieval Demography," p. 99. O. L. Barkan, "Essai sur les données statistiques des registres de recensement dans l'empire ottoman aux XVe et XVIe siècles," *J.E.S.H.O.*, I (1958), 20, 24, estimates the population of Anatolia in the early sixteenth century at about 5,000,000 on the basis of the tax figures. The decline of the population is, according to Barkan, due to the unsettled conditions in the provinces. With the comparative pacification and normalization that ensued in the sixteenth century, the population increased considerably.

[135] Ostrogorsky, "Byzantine Cities," pp. 61–62, reproduces a list of the more important towns that Theophanes mentions after the beginning of the seventh century for Asia Minor. Abydus, Adramyttium, Acroenus, Amaseia, Amastris, Amida, Amorium, Ankara, Antioch of Pisidia, Attaleia, Caesareia, Chalcedon, Charsianon, Chrysopolis, Cyzicus, Dorylaeum, Edessa, Ephesus, Germaniceia, Iconium, Martyropolis, Melitene, Mopsuestia, Myra, Nacoleia, Nicaea, Nicomedia, Pergamum, Perge, Prusa, Pylae, Samosata, Sardes, Sebasteia, Sebastopolis, Sinope, Smyrna, Syllaion, Synnada, Tarsus, Theodosiana, Theodosiopolis, Trebizond, Tyana.

[136] Matthew of Edessa, pp. 83–84, 111–112.

[137] For the details see below.

[138] Ostrogorsky, "Die Steuersystem in byzantinischen Altertum und Mittelalter," *Byzantion*, VI (1931), 231–234.

included on the list of episcopal seats. The canon law and the commentators make it plain that the appointment of a bishop to a place depends unequivocally and exclusively upon the " . . . πλῆθος ἀνθρώπων . . . ." Bishops are to be ordained " . . . εἰς ἐκείνας τὰς πόλεις . . . τὰς πολυανθρώπους . . . ." A bishop may never be appointed to " . . . ὀλίγην πόλιν καὶ κώμην."[139] During the course of the tenth and eleventh centuries new bishoprics appear and former bishoprics are promoted to archbishoprics or metropolitanates. The increase is due in part to the rise in population and prosperity of the Anatolian provinces as well as to new conquests in the east.[140]

The chronicles and histories of the period refer to a large number of the towns by a nomenclature that differentiates them sharpy from villages. The sources use the terms ἄστυ, πόλις, πολιτεία, μητρόπολις, κάστρον to differentiate the town from the village, κώμη, χωρίον.[141] A

[139] K. Rhalles and M. Potles, Σύνταγμα τῶν θείων καὶ ἱερῶν κανόνων (Athens, 1852–59), III, 222–223, 245–248 (hereafter cited as Rhalles and Potles).

[140] F. Miklosich et J. Müller, Acta et dipolmata graeca medii aevi sacra et profana (Vienna, 1860–90), II, 104 (hereafter cited as Miklosich et Müller). De Jerphanion makes this observation in regard to Cappadocia, Une nouvelle province de l'art byzantin: Les églises rupestres de Cappadoce (Paris, 1925–42), I₁, li–lxii; II₂, 397–400 (hereafter cited as de Jerphanion, Cappadoce). In southern Anatolia Cybistra was raised in rank to an archbishopric in the eleventh century, W. Ramsay, "Lycaonia," Jahreshefte des Österreichischen Archäologischen Instituts, VII (1904), Beiblatt, 115. For a more detailed treatment of this point see chapter iv.

[141] As early as the reign of Justinian I πόλις and κάστρον were used interchangeably, Novella CXXVIII, c. 20. These terms are used in the same manner by Constantine Porphyrogenitus, De. Adm. Imp., pp. 198, 200, where Artze is referred to as a κάστρον and πολιτείαν. Attaliates, 28, 46, 89, 90, 166, 174, 199, 201, 206, 245, 249, refers to Adana, Amaseia, Manzikert, Rhaedestus as κάστρα and πόλεις. Smyrna is called both κάστρον and πόλις, Anna Comnena, II, 117, 118, as is Ephesus, AS Nov. III, 554. Rudikov, Očerki, p. 74, has attempted to equate κάστρον only with πολίχνη instead of πόλις. Πόλισμα, πολίχνιον, and φρούριον are generally employed to designate settlements intermediate between towns and villages, which often have fortifications. But this differentiation is not as rigidly observed as that between πόλις and κώμη. Cedrenus, II, 423, 678, calls Tzamandus both πόλις and πόλισμα. Κωμόπολις and ἀγρόπολις, seem to be applied to a settlement larger than a village but scattered and not formed according to a synoicismus. These could be rather large affairs and were not restricted to essentially agrarian establishments. Important commercial emporia could have the form of a κωμόπολις. Thus Artze, though a κωμόπολις, was heavily populated and a rich center of commercial exchange of goods from Persia and India. Zonaras, III, 638, "κωμόπολις δ'ἦν τοῦτο, πληθὺς δ' ἐνῴκει αὐτῷ, ἵν' οὕτως εἴποιμι, καὶ ἀριθμὸν ὑπερβαίνουσα, ἔμποροι δ' ἦσαν οἱ ἄνθρωποι, καὶ πλοῦτος ἦν αὐτοῖς περιττός." It had no walls, however. Phrygian Laodiceia was formed of several settlements or villages scattered about the lower slopes of the mountain. It was not a centralized town with extensive walls. Nicetas Choniates, 163, "οὐκέτι οὖσαν συνοικουμένην ὡς νῦν ἑώραται, οὐδ' εὐερκέσι φραγνυμένην τείχεσι, κατὰ δὲ κώμας ἐκκεχυμένην περὶ τὰς ὑπωρείας τῶν ἐκεῖσε βουνῶν." Χωρόπολις was used to refer to an ordinary village community. Dölger, Beitäge zur byzantinischen Finanzverwaltung, besonders des 10. und 11. Jahrhundert (Leipzig-Berlin, 1927), pp. 66, 126, 134–135. The term χωρόπολις could refer to a settlement next to a town, which was separated from the town by walls. Χωρόπολις was thus possibly the equivalent of προάστειον or ραπάτιν. Constantine Porphyrogenitus, De Adm. Imp., p. 216, Adranoutzi is a κάστρον, but also has a considerable suburban area. "ὅτι τὸ κάστρον τὸ Ἀρδανούτζην ἐστὶν ὀχυρὸν πάνυ, ἔχει δὲ καὶ ραπάτιν μέγα ὡς χωρόπολιν." Honigmann, "Charsianon Kastron, Byzantion, X (1935), 148–149. Attaliates, 148, and Zonaras, III, 638, indicate that πολιτεία and χωρόπολις were interchangeable terms.

27

number of the towns are described by epithets (τοιαύτη πόλις, μεγάλη, πολυάνθρωπος, μυρίανδρος πολὺν πλοῦτον ἔχουσα, ἀνθρώπων τε πολυπλήθειαν ἔχον, πόλις περιφανής, πολυανθρωποτάτη, μεγίστη, πολύανδρος, πλῆθος λαοῦ) which indicate that the contemporary observers considered these towns to be large by the standards of the day.[142] But just how large was πολυάνθρωπος? The city of Edessa in the year 1071 was said to have 35,000 inhabitants. When the Muslim Nur al-Din captured the city three-quarters of a century later, 30,000 were killed, 16,000 enslaved, and only 1,000 escaped.[143] The total population prior to the fall of the city, 47,000, indicates that the population had increased, a phenomenon to be explained by the flight of the agrarian population to the safety of the walls over a long period of time. The city of Tralles, which was rebuilt and recolonized with 36,000 inhabitants by the Byzantines in the thirteenth century (1280), was said to be πολυάνθρωπος.[144] The number of captives taken from Anatolian towns in the twelfth century will perhaps assist in giving some idea as to the size of towns. In the mid-twelfth century, Yakub Arslan carried away 70,000 Christians from Gaihan and Albistan.[145] Of the captives that the Turks took from Melitene in the eleventh century, 15,000 were ransomed by the merchants of that city,[146] and c. 1124–25 during the course of a six-month siege of the city the inhabitants are said to have perished by the "thousands."[147]

A perusal of the texts of Bryennius, Zonaras, Attaliates, Psellus, Cedrenus, Cinnamus, Anna Comnena, Cecaumenus, Constantine Porphyrogenitus reveals approximately seventy inhabited areas referred to as towns by these various terms: Manzikert, Perkri, Chliat, Artze, Kars, Theodosiopolis, Adranoutzi, Lycandus, Tzamandus, Amaseia, Ankara, Antioch, Abydus, Lycian Adrianople, Anazarbus, Castamon, Acroenus, Dorylaeum, Gangra, Iconium, Neocaesareia, Pračana, Pounoura, Trebizond, Oenoe, Sozopolis, Adana, Amorium, Pisidian Antioch, Edessa, Nicaea, Nicomedeia, Philo-melium, Euchaita, Side, Syllaion, Synnada, Chalcedon, Podandus, Ani, Chonae, Germaniceia, Hierapolis, Melitene, Mopsuestia, Praenetus, Pylae, Sebasteia, Tarsus, Caesareia, Colonia, Ephesus, Basilaion, Matiana, Parnassus, Sinope, Argaous, Amara, Tephrice, Samosata, Zapetra, Larissa, Abara, Ticium, Chelidonium, Chrysopolis, Attaleia, Cyzicus, Cius, Smyrna, Seleuceia. This of course does not exhaust the possibilities, for the notitiae episcopatum have not been utilized.

[142] For the references to these towns and territories see the material above on Adana, Ani, Antioch, Artze, Iconium, Anazarba, Podandus, Tzamandus, Adramyttium, Amaseia, Dorylaeum, Sozopolis, Strobilus, Nicaea, Basilaion, Attaleia, Amastris, Trebizond, Melitene, Edessa, Chonae, Euchaita and Sebasteia.

[143] Sawiras ibn al-Mukaffa', II, iii, 305. Bar Hebraeus, p. 273. Chabot, "Episode de l'histoire des Crusades," pp. 176–177, when Zangi first captured the city two years earlier, in 1144, between 5,000 and 6,000 were killed and 10,000 youths and maidens were taken captive. Zangi is said to have delivered the 10,000 from captivity. Matthew of Edessa, p. 289, refers to an earthquake that killed 40,000 at Marash in the eleventh century. The sources are not to be taken literally.

[144] Pachymeres, I, 469. For the date, I. Ševcenko, Études sur la polémique entre Théodore Metochite et Nicéphore Choumnos (Brussels, 1962), pp. 137–138.

[145] Matthew of Edessa, p. 344. When the Turks sacked the city of Artze in the eleventh century, Cedrenus, II, 578, exaggeratedly reports that 150,000 of the inhabitants were slain. Bar Hebraeus, I, 426, relates that in 1256–57 the Mongol Baidju slew 7,000 in Albistan.

[146] Michael the Syrian, III, 146. In 1145, 15,000 captives were taken from Tell Arsanias.

[147] Matthew of Edessa, p. 315.

Thus Melitene was probably a town comparable in size to Edessa. There is some indication as to the size of a comopolis in the twelfth century. When the Seljuk sultan attacked the two comopoleis of Tantalus and Caria in western Asia Minor, he took away captive 5,000 of the inhabitants. This would indicate roughly 2,500 inhabitants for each of the two comopoleis. But Caria had been sacked on a previous occasion and was to suffer devastation and enslavement a third time. Thus its popuation was larger than 2,500,[148] perhaps about 5,000.[149]

The indirect evidence for an increase in the Anatolian population of the tenth and eleventh centuries and the few figures for town population would indicate that the epithet πολυάνθρωπος as applied by Byzantine sources to the cities has some numerical substance. A large city could have as many as 35,000 inhabitants, though it is likely that most of the towns were smaller. One may assume that towns had populations varying between 10,000 and 35,000.[150] Caria, which was not a full-fledged town in the twelfth century, probably had a population of about 5,000. Dorylaeum had been one of the prosperous towns of the eleventh century. As a result of its destruction during the Turkish invasions, it was inhabited by only 2,000 Turkmens in the twelfth century, a figure that the historian Cinnamus considers to be insignificant when compared with the former size of the city.[151] Though the evidence is very scant, one

[148] Nicetas Choniates, 655–657.

[149] The word κωμόπολις here may mean a large village, though it also has the meaning of a town scattered over a large area.

[150] Dölger, "Die byzantinische Stadt," p. 12, has given a similar, though slightly lower estimate of between 5,000 and 20,000. L. Torres Balbas, "Extension y demografia de las ciudades hispanomusulmans," *S.I.*, III (1955), 55–57, on the basis of area measurements, gives the following population estimates for eleventh-twelfth century Spain:

Toledo	37,000	Zaragoza	17,000
Almeria	27,000	Malago	15–20,000
Granada	26,000	Valencia	15,000
Mallorca	25,000		

Barkan, "Les données statistiques," p. 27, furnishes reliable figures for some of the Anatolian towns in the years c. 1520–1530 (based on tax registers):

Bursa	34,930	Tokat	8,354
Amid	18,942	Konya	6,127
Ankara	14,872	Sivas	5,560

Though the similar magnitudes of the Spanish figures (arrived at by area measurement) and the Ottoman figures (results of reliable tax registers from a later period) when combined with the Byzantine estimates do not necessarily prove anything, it is interesting that the size of the towns tend to range between similar extremes.

Byzantium	5–10,000 to 36,000 (perhaps 47,000)
Spain	15,000 to 37,000
Ottoman Empire	5,560 to 34,930

See also Russell, "The Population of Medieval Egypt," *Journal of the American Research Center in Egypt*, V (1966), 69–82.

[151] Cinnamus, 295. *Itinerarium Willelmi de Rubruc*, ed. A. van den Wyngaert, in *Sinica Fransiscana*, (1929), I, 327 (hereafter, cited as William of Rubruq-Wyngaert), reports that an earthquake killed more than 10,000 people in Erzindjan in the mid-thirteenth century. Ramon Muntaner, *Chronique d'Aragon, de Sicile et de Grèce*, trans. J. A. C. Buchon in *Chroniques étrangères relatives aux expéditions françaises pendant le XIIIe siècle* (Paris, 1841), p. 419, (hereafter cited as Ramon Muntaner-Buchon) relates that in the early fourteenth century (before the Turkish conquest), the peninsula of Artake (Cyzicus) had 20,000 habitations, houses, farms, etc.

must conclude on the basis of this material that not only did the population of Asia Minor increase by the tenth and eleventh centuries, but the population of the towns and province as a whole was significant in absolute terms.[152] Thus it would be incorrect to speak of Anatolia as semidesolate or depopulated on the eve of the Seljuk invasions.

Road System

The large land mass of Byzantine Anatolia was closely knit by the system of roads which the empire had largely inherited from the days of the Roman Empire. There was some readjustment of the system which occurred with the transferral of the capital to Constantinople, but aside from that the road system persisted in its principal form down to Turkish times.[153]

The organization and maintenance of the road network was essential for the Byzantines in Asia Minor inasmuch as it was the means by which this province could be more tightly integrated into the empire. It facilitated the movement of Byzantine armies and ensured areas threatened by the enemy with a more rapid defense. The roads also made easier the relative efficiency of the bureaucrats who administered the provinces and who, at the same time, remained under closer supervision of the central government as a result of these roads. Of equal importance was the accessibility of the major Anatolian towns and cities to merchants, caravans, and currents of trade as a result of this arterial network.[154] The frequent use of these highways by the armies, officials, merchants, pilgrims, and others, is copiously noted not only by the Byzantine historians and hagiographers but also in the accounts of the Arab geographers and travelers.

The major routes ran in a northwest to southeast direction, though there were smaller routes running in a north and south direction. The northwest-southeast routes generally ascended from the coastal region of northwest Anatolia at some point along the Sangarius, cut through the mountains

[152] This estimate of Anatolia's demographic condition generally coincides with the results that Russell ("Population of Medieval Egypt," pp. 81, 92–99), has attained by entirely different methods. He suggests, on the basis of the area contained by the medieval fortress, that eighth-century Ankara may have had between 25,000 and 30,000 inhabitants. We must, at any rate, think of town populations in terms of their size in late antiquity rather than in modern times. Thus the population density of Asia Minor in the eleventh century contrasts with the assertions of certain scholars that the peninsula was semidesolate on the eve of the Turkish invasions. M. Köprülü, *Les origines de l'empire ottoman* (Paris, 1935), p. 60. F. Sümer, *Oğuzlar (Türkmenler). Tarihleri-boy teşkilâtî-destanlarî* (Ankara, 1967), p. XII.

[153] Ramsay, *Geography*, p. 74. For the Seljuk and Ottoman routes, K. Erdmann, *Das anatolische Karavansaray des 13. Jahrhunderts* (Berlin, 1961), vol. *I-II*; Taeschner, *Das anatolische Wegenetz nach osmanischen Quellen* (Leipzig, 1924–26), vol. *I-II*. For a reference to the survival of the Romano-Byzantine roads in western Anatolia, in the Turkish period see *Hans Dernschwam's Tagebuch einer Reise nach Konstantinopel und Kleinasien (1553/55)*, ed. F. Babinger (Munich and Leipzig, 1923), p. 238.

[154] On the merchant khans throughout the empire, P. Koukoules, Βυζαντινῶν βίος καὶ πολιτισμός (Athens, 1941), II₁, 128–140.

separating the coastal region from the central plateau, and then traversed the plateau itself. Thus one route skirted the northern rim of the plateau going through Amaseia and Coloneia, another route cut through the central plateau region via Saniana and Sebasteia, and a third skirted the southernmost reaches of the plateau going through Iconium to the Taurus. The most important of these was the great military highway used by the emperors when marching out to meet the Arabs on the eastern borders. It led from Nicaea via Pithecas, Leucae, and Malagina to Dorylaeum where the road climbed through the mountains onto the plateau. Then it proceeded through Trocnada and Pessinus, across the Sangarius River over the Zompus Bridge, through the town of Gorbaeus to the south of Ankara, across the Halys River to the town of Saniana. Here the road forked, the branch leading to the southeast going through Mocissus and then branching again, the two branches going to the great Cappadocian center of Caesarea and to Tyana and Tarsus respectively. The other road leading from Saniana went almost directly east to the city of Sebasteia. Once more the highway branched into three routes: the northernmost leading to Nicopolis and Coloneia; the central branch going to Tephrice and Theodosiopolis; the southeast artery pushing to Melitene where it joined the road from Caesarea. A critical juncture of this highway was Saniana, for it was from this town that the three main branches went to the regions of the Taurus, Cappadocia, Melitene, Sebasteia, and Coloneia.[155]

There was a number of large military stations or camps along this highway, at which standing camps the armies of the various themes gathered and joined the emperor as he marched eastward to the borders.[156] These military bases, or *aplecta* as they were called, were often important towns located on the main highway or within easy reach and were supplied with all the necessities for provisioning troops. The tenth-century emperor Constantine VII mentions six aplecta. The first, at Malagina east of Nicaea on the banks of the Sangarius, possessed the extensive stables of the emperor, an arms depot, and storehouses with provisions for the army.[157] This was probably the mustering center for the troops of the theme of Optimaton. Dorylaeum, the gateway to the central plateau, was the

[155] Ramsay, *Geography*, pp. 199–221.

[156] G. Kolias, "Περὶ ἀπλήκτου," Ε.Ε.Β.Σ., XVII (1941), 144–184. J. B. Bury, "The ἄπληκτα of Asia Minor," Βυζαντίς, II (1911), 214–224.

[157] Constantine Porphyrogenitus, *De Caerimoniis*, I, 444–445, 459, and especially Ramsay, *Geography*, pp. 202 ff., for certain emendations of the text. Ibn Khuradadhbih, B.G.A., VI, 112–113. J. R. Sterett, *The Wolfe Expedition to Asia Minor, Papers of the American School of Classical Studies at Athens*, III (1884–85), 5, published a bronze tablet found at Ören Köy in southeast Asia Minor. The inscription on the tablet was the identification of an animal from such a stable.

Ζῶον διαφ(έρον)
τῷ θείῳ ἀρμαμέν(τῳ)
προσταχθὲν κατὰ θ(ε)ῖ(ον)
τύπον (δ)ι' ἀγγαρ(ίαν)

gathering place for the troops of the Thracesian and Opsicion themes. Ibn Khuradadhbih reveals that the emperor had constructed seven large bathing arcades over the hot springs of the city, and that each could accommodate 1,000 men, no doubt intended for use by the armies. The third aplecton, the bishopric of Kaborkeion, was slightly to the south of the highway. The troops of the Anatolic and Seleuceian themes, together with those troops under the Domestic of the Scholes, assembled at Kaborkeion, a site amply fed by the sources of the Sangarius River, and then marched to Trocnada on the military highway where they fell in with the advancing army.[158] The fourth aplecton, Saniana, was on the eastern bank of the Halys, again a well-watered spot and thus capable of accomodating large numbers of men and horses. It was here that the road forked, going on the one hand to Sebasteia, on the other to Caesareia and the Taurus mountains. If the emperor were marching to Cilicia, then the troops of all the eastern themes joined him at Saniana. But if he were marching directly east toward Melitene, only the troops of Bucellarion, Paphlagonia, and Charsianon met him at Saniana, while the troops of Cappadocia, Armeniacon, and Sebasteia met him at Caesareia, the fifth aplecton. The sixth aplecton was that of Dazimon. Here the troops of the Armeniacon were mustered, and when the emperor was marching to Sebasteia and points east, they joined him at the station of Bathys Rhyax.[159]

A second trans-Anatolian highway skirted the southern confines of the Anatolian plateau, a route often referred to as the pilgrim's route, though it was also an important military and commercial artery. It too commenced at Malagina and progressed through Dorylaeum, Polybotus, Philomelium, and Iconium to the Cilician Gates.[160] There were at least two variations of this route to Iconium: one that went via Malagina-Cotyaeum-Acroenus-Polybotus-Philomelium-Iconium and the other that traversed Malagina-Dorylaeum-Amorium-Laodiceia-Iconium. There was a third road that avoided Iconium altogether by going from Dorylaeum-Pessinus to Archelais and then south through Tyana to the Taurus. Another highway left from Nicomedia and went through Ankara, south to Archelais, Tyana, and the Taurus.[161] Nicomedia and Ankara both served as important points of departure for the roads going across the northern regions of the Anatolian plateau. One route led from Nicomedia through Gangra (or an alternate route slightly to the north of Gangra), Euchaita (on the more southerly route), Amaseia, Neocaesareia, Coloneia, and Satala. Another road ran from Ankara to Gangra, Amaseia, and so on. There were also some important roads running north and south, perhaps the most prominent being the route from the coastal city of Amisus to

[158] Ramsay, *Geography*, pp. 213–214.
[159] *Ibid.*, pp. 219–221.
[160] *Ibid.*, pp. 197 ff.
[161] *Ibid.*, pp. 197–198, and accompanying map.

Amaseia and down to Caesareia. Undoubtedly, there were similar roads leading inland from such Black Sea ports as Heracleia, Amastris, Sinope, and Trebizond. In the east, the road from Sebasteia went through Tephrice and Theodosiopolis to Manzikert, while Arabissus was similarly joined to Melitene in the east and to Germaniceia in the south via the passes of the Anti-Taurus while Germaniceia was in turn connected with Samosata.[162]

Of particular importance was the busy road from Attaleia via Cotyaeum and Malagina to Constantinople. An official of the post system, who resided in Attaleia, supplied horses and transportation for travelers going overland, or passage by ship to those going by sea. Ibn Hawkal states that while the journey took only eight days on the highway, the sea voyage, provided the winds were favorable, required fifteen days.[163] Side and other towns of Cilicia were similarly connected by traversible roads to the main highway system going through Iconium. In western Asia Minor the roads for the most part seem to have followed the coastline and the river valleys.

Anatolia was effectively served by this system of major roads, which went generally in a west to east, or west to southeast direction. This network was intersected by numerous smaller roads, entering from the coastal areas of the northwest and west, and also by a smaller number of north-south routes cutting over the plateau. That the armies frequently used these roads goes without saying. Merchants, including Jews and Arabs, seem to have followed the great networks for commercial reasons with the result that knowledge of all the major land routes appears in the texts of the Arab geographers.[164] The roads were extensively traveled by pilgrims—pilgrims who visited not only the Holy Land but also the numerous shrines of the greater and lesser Anatolian saints.[165]

[162] *Ibid.*, pp. 242–279. Honigmann, "Charsianon Kastron," p. 156.

[163] Marquart, *Osteuropäische und ostasiatische Streifzüge* (Leipzig, 1903), pp. 208–209.

[164] By way of example, al-Mukaddasi describes the journey of a Muslim who traveled from Mayaferrikin via Coloneia, Neocaesareia, across the Pontic region to the Sangarius River (Honigmann, "Un itinéraire," pp. 263–267, 268). It is of some interest that his itinerary followed the northwest route described above and that when he arrived in the region of the Bucellarion theme he remarks that there was an inn for Muslims. This was one of the Byzantine ξενοδοχεῖα, hostels, which existed for travelers. Constantine Porphyrogenitus mentions such institutions in the region of the Sangarius, at Nicomedeia, and at Pylae (*De Caerimoniis*, I, 720). But undoubtedly they existed throughout the peninsula. Al-Mukaddasi describes a second journey that led from Amid via Melitene, Tzamandus, Caesareia, Ankara, Sangarius, Nicomedeia to Constantinople (Honigmann, "Un itinéraire," p.270). It is significant that this information comes from a Muslim rather than a Byzantine source and so one is able to deduce the commercial importance of these Anatolian networks. The presence of a hospice for Muslims in the Bucellarion theme is important evidence for inferring the presence of Muslim merchants in Anatolia. The same author mentions that there were Muslims in the cities of Bithynia, Trebizond, and Ma'din an-Nuhas (Honigmann, "Un itinéraire," p. 263).

[165] Quite illustrative of this type of itinerant was St. Lazarus (d. 1054) who performed the pilgrimage both to the Holy Land and to various sanctuaries of Asia Minor. In his first journey Lazarus set out from the coastal town of Strobilus for the shrine of the Archangel Michael in Chonae. En route he fell in with a group of Cappadocian pilgrims, also

The Church

Anatolia had an elaborate ecclesiastical organization of metropolitanates, archbishoprics, and bishoprics subordinated to the patriarch of Constantinople.[166] In the earlier centuries this provincial organization of the church had followed the pattern of the imperial administrative organziation. Thus the town, or polis, became the seat of the bishopric. By the eleventh century, Asia Minor possessed approximately forty-five metropolitanates,[167] ten archbishoprics,[168] and a great number of

on their way to the shrine, and before arriving at the town, another pilgrim (a Paphlagonian monk) joined the party. After a number of distractions, Lazarus finally made his way to Palestine where he visited the various shrines and churches. He then returned to Antioch. From Cilicia he took the road going north by Mt. Argaeus to Caesarea where he prayed at the church of St. Basil. There he followed the northern route to Euchaita, the center of the cult of St. Theodore Teron, and departing from Euchaita made his way through the Anatolic theme to Chonae, once more to the church of the Archangel. The last leg of his long pilgrimage was from Chonae to Ephesus where Lazarus went to the church of St. John the Theologian (AS Nov. III, 517–518). Ephesus remained a favorite pilgrim site through its Byzantine life. In 1106–07 the Russian abbot Daniel (*P.P.T.S.*, IV, 5–6), visited the tomb of St. John and relates that on the anniversary of the latter's death a holy dust arose from the tomb, which believers gathered as a cure for diseases. He visited the cave of the Seven Sleepers, the remains of the 300 holy fathers, of St. Alexander, the tomb of Mary Magdalene, the coffin of the Apostle Timothy. He saw the image of the Holy Virgin used to refute Nestorius. Ramon Muntaner-Buchon (pp. 425, 465–466), witnessed miracles at the tomb in 1304, and remarked that the exudations of the tomb were beneficial for childbirth, fever, and when thrown on the stormy sea would calm it. After the Turks took Ephesus they traded three of the relics of his cult to Ticino Zacaria of Phocaea for grain. These included: a piece of the true cross taken by St. John himself from the place where Christ's head lay, and which was enclosed in gold and precious stones and which had hung from the neck of St. John on a golden chain; a cloth that Mary had made and given to St. John; a book of the Apocalypse written in gold letters by St. John.

In 1059 the famous Georgian monk, George the Hagiorite, accompanied by his biographer, journeyed from Antioch to Caesarea, and thence to the shrine of St. Theodore where they were graciously received by the archbishop. They then journeyed to the port of Amisus on the Black Sea and set sail for the Caucasus. P. Peeters, "Histoires monastiques gèorgiennes," *A.B.*, XXXVI–XXXVII (1917–19), 121–122. H. Delehaye, "Euchaita et la légende de S. Théodore," in *Anatolian Studies Presented to Sir William Mitchell Ramsay* (London, 1923), pp. 133–134 (hereafter cited as Delehaye, "Euchaita et S. Théodore"). For other references to these Anatolian pilgrimages, AS Nov. I, 343; F. Halkin, "Saint Antoine le Jeune et Petronas le vainqueur des Arabes en 863," *A.B.*, LXII (1944), 187–225, 218; V. Laurent, *La vie marveilleuse de Saint Pierre d'Atroa 837* (Brussels, 1956), pp. 87, 99–101.

Pilgrimages to the great shrines of Anatolia must have been commonplace. Notice that on his way to the shrine of the Archangel, Lazarus met other pilgrims from as far away as Cappadocia and Paphlagonia. These pilgrimages were not limited to the ancient and established centers, for Lazarus was himself visited by many pilgrims on Mt. Galesium, including not only Greek Christians from the vicinity, but also by a Georgian, a baptized Muslim, and by Jews. The Anatolian road system saw a certain number of Latin pilgrims on their way to the Holy Land, though most of them probably went by the sea route that skirted the western and southern coasts of the peninsula. Bréhier, *L'église et l'Orient au moyen-âge* (Paris, 1928), pp. 43–47.

[166] Some churches in southeastern Anatolia were subordinate to the patriarchate of Antioch. Beck, *Kirche und theologische Literatur*, pp. 190–196.

[167] Skabalanovič, *Gosudarstvo*, pp. 404–418. Gelzer, "Ungedruckte und wenig bekannte Bistumerverzeichnisse der orientalischen Kirche," *B.Z.*, I (1894), 253–254. Caesareia, Ephesus, Ankara, Cyzicus, Sardis, Nicomedeia, Nicaea, Chalcedon, Side, Sebasteia, Amaseia, Melitene, Tyana, Gangra, Claudiopolis, Neocaesareia, Pessinus, Myra, Stauropolis, Laodiceia, Synnada, Iconium, Antiocheia, Pisidia, Perge, Mocissus, Seleuceia,

suffragant bishoprics. In the tenth century there had been approximately 371 bishoprics subordinate to them,[169] and by the eleventh century there was a significant increase in their number[170] due largely to the expansion of the frontiers in the east.[171] The metropolitans were the ecclesiastical lords of large areas and usually of a number of towns as well as villages, over which towns were the bishops. The powers and influence of these hierarchs in their respective provinces were considerable, not only in the spiritual domain but also in the sphere of administration and in the courts.[172] It was the metropolitans and archbishops who linked the provincial administrative structure of the church to Constantinople, patriarch, and emperor. They had the right to participate in the meetings of the synod in Constantinople and also to participate in the election of the patriarch. The elaborate structure of metropolitanates-bishoprics— indeed of the whole ecclesiastical institution—was supported by extensive properties and certain cash incomes.[173] It was with these incomes that the metropolitans and bishops provided for guesthouses, poorhouses, orphanages, hospitals and to a certain extent, local education. The ecclesiastical as well as the bureaucratic, administrative personnel were recruited from the local population and Constantinople, so that the priesthood and hierarchy represented both the capital and the provinces.

Asia Minor was not only the most important Byzantine province militarily and economically, but also it was so in the religious domain. Anatolia possessed the richest, most populous metropolitanates of the empire. Their importance relative to that of the European metropolitanates is clearly reflected in the official lists, the *notitiae episcopatum*, composed for purposes of protocol, where the metropolitanates are listed in order of their rank. Of the first twenty-seven metropolitanates listed in a notitia of the eleventh century, only two were located in Europe, the remaining twenty-five were situated in Anatolia.[174] This emerges more clearly when one compares the number of bishops to be found in the two regions of the empire. In the first half of the tenth century, there were about 371 bishoprics in Asia Minor, 99 in Europe, 18 in the Aegean isles, and 16 in Calabria and Sicily.[175] Also, and most important, Asia Minor

---

Trebizond, Smyrna, Amorium, Camacha, Cotyaeum, Euchaita, Amastris, Chonae, Pompeiopolis, Attaleia, Abydus, Celesene, Coloneia, Cerasus, Nacoleia, Apameia, Basilaion, Nazianzus.

[168] Gelzer, "Bistumerverzeichnisse," pp. 254–255. Skabalanovič, *Gosudarstvo*, pp. 418–420. Miletus, Parium, Proiconnesus, Cius, Neapolis of Pisidia, Selge of Pamphylia, Mistheia of Lycaonia, Pedacthoe, Germia, Heracleia Cybistra.

[169] *Nova Tactica*, ed. H. Gelzer in *Georgii Cyprii descriptio orbis romani* (Leipzig, 1890), pp. 61–83 (hereafter cited as *Nova tactica*).

[170] De Jerphanion, *Cappadoce*, I_1, li–lxii; II_2, 397–400.

[171] Gelzer, *Notitiae Episcopatum*, pp. 576–579.

[172] Bréhier, *L'église et l'orient au moyen-âge*, pp. 526–527. Beck, *Kirche und theologische Literatur*, pp. 71–76.

[173] Bréhier, *L'église et l'orient au moyen-âge*, p. 522.

[174] Gelzer, "Bistumerverzerchnisse," p. 253.

[175] Gelzer, *Nova Tactica*, pp. 61–83.

was strewn with sanctuaries and cults of numerous saints. Some of the cults centered on the martyrs, others on the personages of later saints, and still others on the personalities of "mythical" saints. Asia Minor had been one of the earliest provinces of Christian missionary activity, intimately associated with the personality, activity, and writings of the Apostle Paul.

The cults and churches of the various Anatolian saints were famous not only among the Greek Christians but also among Latins, Georgians, Slavs, and others who visited them on the pilgrimage, and these cults were, of course, very important in the everyday life of the Byzantine inhabitants of Asia Minor. The list of the sanctuaries located in Anatolia is a long one, and some of these were especially popular.[176] In the westernmost regions the important cults included those of Tryphon at Nicaea, Polycarp at Smyrna, John the Theologian at Ephesus, Nicholas at Myra, and the Archangel Michael at Chonae. On the Black Sea coast were the shrines of Eugenius at Trebizond, Phocas at Sinope, and Hyacinthus at Amastris. The most famous of the martyrs' sanctuaries in the hinterland included those of St. Theodore at Euchaita, the Forty Martyrs at Sebasteia, Mercurius and Mamas at Caesareia, and the various shrines of St. George in the regions of Paphlagonia. Of equal importance were the churches of the fourth and fifth-century saints Basil of Caesareia, Gregory of Nyssa, Gregory of Nazianzus, and Amphilochius of Iconium, all of whom had played such an important role in determining the evolution of the Eastern church.

New sanctuaries continued to arise about the personalities of newer holy men, a fact that intensified the sanctity of Anatolia as a repository of τὰ ἅγια for the Byzantines. Ioannicius (d. 846) of Mt. Olympus in Bithynia, Michael Maleinus (d. 961) in Bithynia, Lazarus (d. 1053) on Mt. Galesium near Ephesus, Philaretus the Merciful (d. 792) of Paphlagonia, George (d. c. 802–807) of Amastris, Nicephorus (fl. tenth century) of Latmus in the district of Miletus, Paul (d. 955) in western Anatolia, Luke the Stylite (d. 979) in Chalcedon, Blasius (d. c. 911–912) of Amorium, the Forty-two Martyrs (d. 838) of Amorium, and many others were evidence of the intensity, if not the variety, of religious life in Anatolia during this period. From these holy men came a considerable portion of the monastic, hierarchical, and missionary leaders. It was an Anatolian monk, St. Nicon tou Metanoeite, who in the tenth century left Asia Minor to convert the Muslims of newly reconquered Crete and the Slavs in the Morea.[177] The great Athonite father and organizer St. Athanasius was born and educated in Trebizond. The eleventh-century professor of law and patriarch Xiphilenus was also born and partially

---

[176] For an extensive catalog of the cults of the Anatolian martyrs, Delehaye, *Les origines du culte des martyres* (Brussels, 1933), pp. 145–180.
[177] Lampros, " Ὁ βίος Νίκωνος τοῦ Μετανοεῖτε," *N.E.*, III (1906), 151–152, 200–202.

educated in Trebizond, while the illustrious twelfth-century archbishop of Athens Michael Acominatus and his brother the historian Nicetas Choniates were from Chonae. These men of Anatolia, who are so illustrative of the influence and importance of Anatolia as a spiritual reservoir of Byzantine society, are not unique.

Less spectacular, perhaps, but of equal importance was the significance of these cults for the integration of the majority of the Anatolians into a generally homogeneous society and culture. These cults were absorbed by the Byzantine church, an institution that played such a critical role in unifying the empire. Though the church tended greatly to regularize the practices attendant upon these cults in consonance with the Orthodoxy of Constantinople, many local strains were so firmly entrenched that they were simply accepted.[178] It has been repeatedly stated that the bishops and metropolitans, and the clergy in general, attempted to care for both the spiritual and physical needs of their flocks, and the local saints, in the eyes of the provincials, did much the same thing. It was this close attachment of the provincial peoples to the saints which forced the church to accept many of the anomalous practices attendant upon their cults. The principal city or town of the saint was usually identified with that in which his bones rested, though of course there would be numerous churches and shrines (to say nothing of bones) associated with that particular saint elsewhere. Usually the saint was the possessor of a special town, and the inhabitants of that town thought of the saint almost as their co-citizen, and they naturally conceived of him as being partial to this city. In such a spirit an eleventh-century citizen of Trebizond addresses St. Eugenius as φιλόπολι, φιλόπατρι.[179] One of the most important functions of the saint was to protect his city from devastating invasions of various foreign peoples, which came to be such a salient feature of Byzantine life. The *miracula* of the various saints credit them with considerable success in this respect. St. Theodore is said to have routed the Arabs, who were besieging Euchaita in 934, by appearing before the gates of the city on horseback.[180] St. Eugenius performed the same task for the Trebizondines by interceding from above and turning away and smashing the bows and swords

---

[178] This is a phenomenon that needs further study. Two examples of this phenomenon, animal sacrifice and absorption of pagan deities into the Christian cult of saints, are among those that have been studied in some detail. F. Cumont, "L'archevêché de Pédachtoé et le sacrifice du foan," *Byzantion*, VI (1931), 521–533. A. Hadjinicolaou-Morava, *Saint-Mamas* (Athens, 1953). See also M. Nilsson, *Greek Popular Religion* (New York, 1947), pp. 13–18, on the continuity of pagan practices, and on the link between the pagan cult of the heroes and the Christian cult of the saints.

[179] Papadopoulos-Kerameus, *Ist. trap. imp.*, p. 51.

[180] AS Nov. IV, 53. The eleventh-century metropolitan of Euchaita, John Mauropus-Lagarde, p. 116, describes Theodore as "τὸν ἡμέτερον ἄρχοντα καὶ τῆς περιχώρου ταύτης κληροῦχον καὶ προστάτην καὶ ἔφορον." P. 132, he is "ὁ τοῦ χριστωνύμου λαοῦ κατὰ βαρβάρων προπολεμῶν." This same phenomenon is to be observed in the miracula of the Muslim holy men of Seljuk Anatolia, as in the case of Djalal al-Din Rumi who saved Konya from the Mongols.

of the godless barbarians.[181] George of Amastris, while still living, went out of the walls of that city, gathered as many of the Christians in the neighborhood as he could, and then brought them to safety within while the Arabs were raiding the area.[182] St. Amphilochius is credited with turning away the Ismaelite army from the walls of Iconium.[183] But these saints, not always content to remain on the defensive, often took the offensive, even leading the imperial armies to victory in foreign lands. The Archangel Michael is credited with helping Heraclius defeat the Persians,[184] and John Tzimisces as a result of the victory over the Russians in the Balkans, which he attributed to the intervention of St. Theodore, rebuilt the saint's church in Euchaita.[185] The saints also figure quite prominently, at least in their miracula, in the repatriation of Christians taken prisoner by invaders. Accordingly, Saints Theodore, Nicholas, and George answer the prayers of the local inhabitants of Caria, Paphlagonia, and Euchaita who have lost relatives to the Arabs, and then secure the return of these relatives from Crete and Syria.[186] Some of the cults were particularly close to soldiers, those of the so-called military saints, Theodore, George, and Mercurius.[187]

The saints are frequently alleged to have intervened with Byzantine administrative authorities, and especially with the tax collectors, on behalf of their co-citizens.[188] The most numerous miracles and services, however, attributed to the saints are those that have to do with healing. In a period of history when knowledge of medicine had not progressed sufficiently, particularly in the more remote provinces that might be even less well equipped medically, it was to the local saint that the ill came, or sometimes they would travel long distances from their own villages and towns to the shrines of particular saints whose medical reputations were widespread. A steady column of lepers, epileptics, paralytics, and cripples marches through the countless pages of the miracula on their way to the shrines in hope of cure. The provincials also appealed to the saints to still the dreadful forces of nature. If disease came upon their livestock, if

---

[181] Papadopoulos-Kerameus, *Ist. trap. imp.*, p. 76, Eugenius is "τῆς κοινῆς ἡμῶν πόλεως ταυτησὶ καὶ πατρίδος ἐπόπτα καὶ πρόμαχε καὶ φρουρὲ καὶ προστάτα καὶ πᾶσι κοινὸν ἡμῖν ἐντρύφημα."

[182] Vasilievsky, *Trudy*, III, 38–40.

[183] Halkin, *Bibliographia Hagiographica Graeca*, 3d ed. (Brussels, 1957), I, 22.

[184] Drexl and Pertz, I, 125.

[185] Zonaras, III, 534.

[186] A. Sigalas, " Ἡ διασκευὴ τοῦ ὑπὸ τοῦ Χρυσίππου παραδεδομένων θαυμάτων τοῦ Ἁγίου Θεοδώρου," Ε.Ε.Β.Σ., I (1924), 314–315. AS Nov. IV, 78. G. Anrich, *Hagios Nikolaos. Der heilige Nikolaos in der griechischen Kirche* (Leipzig-Berlin, 1913), I, 171–173, 175–181, 189–195, 286. J. B. Aufhauser, *Miracula S. Georgii* (Leipzig, 1913), pp. 13–18.

[187] Delehaye, *Les légendes grecques des saints militaires* (Paris, 1909). S. Binon, *Documents grecs inédits relatifs à S. Mercure de* (Louvain, 1937). In one of the miracula of St. Theodore of Euchaita, a soldier of the region previous to a military expedition went into the sanctuary and prayed to St. Theodore to protect him. After the campaign the soldier returned and as an offering of thanks presented his sword to the saint. Sigalas, "Διασκευή" p. 328.

[188] Vasilievsky, *Trudy*, III, 37, 43–47.

drought or floods destroyed the crops, one invoked the saints with special prayers and invocations.[189]

The subject of religious conversion does appear in the hagiographical texts, though the accounts are not often as precise as one would desire. St. Nicholas, at least according to his *miracula*, was known as far afield as Muslim Egypt and Syria.[190] St. George τροπαιοῦχος is credited with the conversion of Muslims in Syria.[191] St. George of Amastris was responsible for the conversion to Christianity of the pagan Russ who, while raiding Amastris, broke into his sanctuary in order to steal the rich treasures they believed to be buried under his casket.[192] Indeed, one of the tenth-century Anatolian saints St. Constantine was himself a converted Jew.[193] St. Lazarus converted a village of heretics, probably Paulicians, in the vicinity of Philetis in Caria,[194] and the same hagiographer describes the conversion of a Saracen in Ephesus. The references to conversion are scattered and few in number, but there is no reason to doubt that the church, through the shrines and sanctuaries, exerted a considerable proselytizing and missioning force upon the non-Christians and heretics of Anatolia. This role of the saints and their shrines as vital integrating forces in society is more forcefully illustrated by the activities of St. Nicon in Crete and Sparta and by the mass program of conversion which John of Ephesus implemented in the sixth century.[195]

The shrines of the saints, as indeed the whole of the ecclesiastical institution, were intimately involved in the economic life of the Anatolians. The saints and their churches were the sponsors of the local fairs (some of which were of an international character) or panegyreis held on the feast days of the saints. Such were the panegyreis of St. John at Ephesus,[196]

---

[189] An especially spectacular performance in this respect was that attributed to St. Eugenius of Trebizond. On one occasion when Trebizond had had a particularly severe winter with violent storms on the sea accompanied by heavy snows, the city was without sufficient grain supplies. As the winter storms made the seas too dangerous for the grain ships, the Trebizondines were threatened with starvation. St. Eugenius, however, intervened and calmed the seas so that the ships were able to bring grain to the starving city (Papadopoulos-Kerameus, *Ist. trap. imp.*, pp. 49–50). St. Nicholas intervened to procure grain for the starving inhabitants of Myra (Anrich, *Hagios Nikolaos*, pp. 132–133).

[190] Anrich, *Hagios Nikolaos*, pp. 408–409, 415. His hagiographer reports the story of one Syrian mule merchant who wore a golden likeness of the saint on his chest as a result of having been saved by St. Nicholas when he was lost on a journey to India. In another case a Muslim fisherman from Egypt, threatened by storms while at sea, promised to become Christian if St. Nicholas would save him. As a result of the saint's intervention, the fisherman and his small boat entered the harbor of Attaleia safely, and he became a Christian.

[191] *Ibid.*, p. 415.

[192] Vasilievsky, *Trudy*, III, 65–69.

[193] AS Nov. IV, 629–630.

[194] *Ibid.*, III, 512, 543, 580.

[195] Lampros, "Βίος Νίκωνος," pp. 150–151, 200–202. John of Ephesus, *The Third Part of the Ecclesiastical History of John of Ephesus*, trans. R. Payne Smith (Oxford, 1860), *passim* (hereafter cited as John of Ephesus-Payne Smith).

[196] Theophanes, I, 469. On the ancient Greek panegyreis and their survival as a religioeconomic institution in modern times see Nilsson, *Greek Popular Religion*, pp. 97–101. For a good description of a pagan, religious-commercial panegyris in Comana during the ancient period, Strabo, XII, iii. 36.

St. Eugenius at Trebizond,[197] St. Phocas at Sinope,[198] St. Theodore at Euchaita,[199] St. George throughout the lands of Paphlagonia,[200] and Michael at Chonae.[201] These fairs were important for the church of the particular saint, and for the town and rural environs as well, by virtue of the economic activity and economic prosperity that they brought. These panegyreis attracted great numbers of people, both from the neighborhood and from far away. The Trebizondine fairs were international and attracted traders and goods from the whole of the Islamic and Indic worlds. Even farther inland, at such a town as Euchaita, John Mauropus remarks that a great host of people came to the celebration.[202] He states that it was the great fame of the shrine of St. Theodore and the panegyris that had made it into a great, prosperous, and populous city,[203] full of stoas and marketplaces.[204]

The pious from all classes of society made lavish gifts to the various saints in return for the services that the saints performed. The offering of the emperor John Tzimisces has already been mentioned. In the eleventh century John Orphanotrophus was cured of a serious illness by St. Nicholas, so he lavished gifts on the church and built a wall around the city.[205] The middle classes were equally attached to the cults of the saints. Sailors and maritime merchants pledged wheat and other items from their cargoes to saints Lazarus, Nicholas, and Phocas if they would guard them during their dangerous sea voyages and enable them to reap financial

[197] Papadopoulos-Kerameus, *Ist. trap. imp.*, pp. 57–58.

[198] Van der Vorst, "Saint Phocas," p. 289. N. Oikonomides, "῞Αγιος Φωκᾶς ὁ Σινοπεύς," pp. 184–219; "Κανὼν ᾿Ιωσὴφ τοῦ Ὑμνογράφου εἰς ῞Αγιον Φωκᾶν τὸν Σινωπέα," Α.Π., XVIII (1953), 218–240.

[199] John Mauropus-Lagarde, pp. 134, 207–208.

[200] Aufhauser, *Miracula S. Georgii*, p. 18.

[201] Lampros, Μιχαὴλ ᾿Ακομινάτου τοῦ Χωνιάτου τὰ σωζόμενα(Athens, 1879), I, 56 (hereafter cited as Michael Acominatus-Lampros).

[202] John Mauropus-Lagarde, p. 131, " . . . ἐκ παντὸς ἔθνους."

[203] *Ibid.*, p. 132, " . . . ἐξ ἐρημίας ἀβάτου πολυάνθρωπον πόλιν."

[204] He describes the brilliance of the celebration when the local people and officials have come together to chant, burn incense, pray, and, very important, to bring gifts to the saint. John Mauropus-Lagarde, pp. 134, 207. Delehaye, "Euchaita et S. Théodore," p. 130. An industry that catered to pilgrims as well as to the religious heads of the local population was the manufacture of black incense and gomphytis in the coastal towns of Macri and Myra. Daniel, *P.P.T.S.*, IV, 6–7; "Makri and all the country as far as Myra produce black incense and gomphytis. It exudes from the tree in a viscous state, and is collected with a sharp-edged piece of iron. The tree is called zyghia and resembles the alder. Another shrub, resembling the aspen, is called raka-storax. A huge worm, of the large caterpillar species, bores through the wood beneath the bark, and the worm-dust, which comes away from the shrub like wheat bran, falls to the ground, as a gum similar to that from the cherry-tree. This is gathered and mixed with produce of the first tree, and the whole is then boiled in a copper vessel. Thus it is that they produce the gomphytis incense, which is sold to the merchants in leather bottles." Strabo, XII, 7.3., says that this same product was used by Anatolians in the worship of pagan Gods! It was still an important product of the district of Attaleia in the eighteenth century, P. Lucas, *Voyage du Sieur Paul Lucas fait par ordre du roi dans la Grèce, l'Asie Mineure, la Macédoine et l'Afrique* (Amsterdam, 1714), I, 244.

[205] Cedrenus, II, 512.

profits from their commerce.[206] Merchants and craftsmen are constantly streaming through the shrines of these Anatolian saints,[207] as are also soldiers, government officials and, of course, the poor farmers and herdsmen.[208] The merchants and wealthy classes donated generously to the saints (one well-to-do family in Myra gave 100 gold pieces annually to St. Nicholas);[209] the common folk gave more modestly. In the *miracula* of St. Theodore a soldier presents his sword, a farmer gives an ox, and a poor woman is saving a chicken for the saint.[210] Gifts of such a nature were brought to the saint not only by the inhabitants of his town but very often by Christians living in another part of the empire.[211]

The saints' shrines, and indeed the church as an institution, were closely connected with the economic life of the provinces, whether as the possessors of large landed estates and serfs, or as the recipients of considerable wealth in cash and kind, or as the sponsors of the large panegyreis.[212] The presence in a town of a saint's shrine, of the bishop and his staff, were of great significance for any settled area.

One must also keep in mind that from the seventh century until the foundation of the coenobitic institutions of Mt. Athos, Asia Minor was also the basic monastic province of the empire, the monastic foundations and traditions of Anatolia going back to St. Basil of Caesaieia and his

---

[206] AS Nov. III, 532–533, a merchant promises one-half of his cargo to St. Lazarus. Anrich, *Hagios Nikolaos*, pp. 130–131, 167–170, 415. Van de Vorst, "Saint Phocas," p. 289, "μερίδα σοι μίαν οἱ ναυτιλλόμενοι . . . τιθέασι."

[207] Sigalas, "Διασκευή," pp. 312, 319, at the shrine of St. Theodore. AS Nov. III, 532–533, 537. Van de Vorst, "Saint Phocas," p. 289. Papadopoulos-Kerameus, *Ist. trap. imp.*, p. 58, at the shrine of St. Eugenius.

[208] One rather humorous anecdote from the miracula of St. George is quite illustrative of the incidental and anecdotal nature of these sources. There was a famous church of St. George in Paphlagonia known as Phatrynon. A group of young boys was playing next to the church and during the course of the games one boy continually lost. Finally he appealed to St. George promising to give him a cake (σφογγᾶτον) if the saint should help him to win. After his luck changed, the boy did not forget his vow; he promptly marched off to his mother, obtained the cake, and placed it in the church as his offering to St. George. Soon afterward four merchants passing through the city came to the church to pray. Spotting the fragrant cake, they remarked that inasmuch as St. George could not eat it, they would eat it and give the saint θυμιάματα. So they consumed the cake but then found themselves unable to get out of the church. They thus became somewhat more generous and each gave one miliaresium to the saint, but to no avail. They raised the offering to one nomisma and finally to four nomismata before the church doors opened. On departing they remarked, " Ὦ ἅγιε Γεώργιε κνιπὰ πωλεῖς τὰ σφογγάτά σου, καὶ ἡμεῖς ἐκ σοῦ ἄλλο οὐκ ἀγοράζομεν." Aufhauser, *Miracula S. Georgii*, pp. 103–107. The anecdote is of interest in showing the presence of itinerant merchants, the offerings made even by children and, finally, that the saints were shrewd businessmen.

[209] Anrich, *Hagios Nikoloas*, p. 286.

[210] Sigalas, "Διασκευή," pp. 328, 333, 317.

[211] The inhabitants of Gangra in Paphlagonia sent one pound of gold as an offering, καρποφορία, to the church of the Archangel Michael in Chonae. Aufhauser, *Miracula S, Georgii*, pp. 108–113. St. George is not at all jealous, in this particular incident, that his followers are making the gift to the patron saint of a different area. In fact, he intercedes to save both the gold and its purveyor from robbers so that they may reach Chonae safely!

[212] For the church as a legal custodian of the property of others, there is the case of the church of St. Theodore of Euchaita which served as a guardian of the dowry of a recently deceased woman. Sigalas, "Διασκευή," pp. 322–333.

institution of a monastery at Annesoi. The regions of Chalcedon, Mt. Auxentius, as well as the whole of the Opsicion theme, were important monastic centers. Mt. Olympus, Prusa, Nicaea, and the entire Propontid coast were literally strewn with these establishments. In the south, Mt. Galesium, near Ephesus, and Latmus, in the vicinity of Miletus, were the scenes of vigorous monastic life. In the district of Iconium, on the present day Kara Dağ, monastic communities thrived down to the Seljuk invasions.[213] The bishopric of Hagios Procopius (Ürgüp) was the center of the famous troglodyte monasteries, while at Trebizond and the environs were located the famous monasteries of St. Eugenius, Vazelon, and Sumela. Many of these monasteries had existed for centuries when the Seljuks first arrived in Anatolia, while many were founded from the ninth through the eleventh century. At the moment of the Turkish invasions, the monasteries were thriving.[214]

Ethnography

Perhaps the most interesting, and certainly the most perplexing problems facing the historian of Byzantine Anatolia are those that have to do with the languages, religions, and ethnic groups of the peninsula at various times. There has been considerable discussion, debate, and disagreement on all three of these items in regard to the inhabitants of Byzantine Asia Minor in the eleventh century. Some scholars have maintained that the Byzantine population of Anatolia was only lightly and superficially Hellenized and was, in fact, indifferent to the language, church, and government of Constantinople.[215] Others have asserted that the population of the peninsula in the eleventh century was the same which had inhabited Anatolia since the days of the Hetites.[216] But from the point of view of language and religion, the principal discernible elements in the culture of eleventh-century Anatolia, there is little that would lend weight to these suppositions. The dominant language of western, central, and eastern Anatolia to the confines of Cappadocia was Greek, and the dominant religion was that of the Greek or Byzantine church. In the regions of Anatolia east of Cappadocia this Greek element, though present, was very weak in comparison with the non-Greek elements. Anatolia, however, had not always possessed this predominantly Greek

---

[213] G. I. Bell and W. Ramsay, *The Thousand and One Churches* (London, 1909), p. 257.

[214] De Jerphanion, *Cappadoce*, II₂, 396–401. Beck, *Kirche und theologische Literatur*, pp. 207–212. Eyice, "Trabzon yakininda Meryam Ana (Sumela) manastiri. Arkheolojik ve tarihi değeri ile bugünkü durumu hakkinda bir araştirma," *Belleten*, XXX (1966), 243–264. G. Millet, "Les monastères et les églises de Trebizonde," *Bulletin de Correspondance Hellenique*, XIX (1895), 419–459.

[215] W. Langer and R. Blake, "The Rise of the Ottoman Turks and its Historical Background," *American Historical Review*, XXXVII (1932), 476–481.

[216] M. H. Yinanc, *Türkiye tarihi. Selçuklular devri I. Andolunun fethi* (Istanbul, 1944), pp. 162 ff. On these and related themes that momentarily appeared in Turkish historiography in the early Kemalist period and then subsided, B. Lewis, "History-writing and National Revival in Turkey," *Middle Eastern Affairs*, IV (1953), 218–227.

character. The actual process by which Greek language and Greek Christianity had come to predominate was a long one, and one that has not been documented in sufficient detail.

The process of Hellenization in terms of language and culture had begun centuries before the pre-Christian era and continued long afterward. The linguistic situation of pre-Greek Anatolia, or rather of Anatolia in the first millenium of the pre-Christian era, has been compared to that of the Caucasus in later times as "the meeting place of a host of unrelated languages." [217] It had hosted Urartians, Hetites, Phrygians, Lydians, Lycians, Carians, Cappadocians, Isaurians, Armenians, Kurds, Greeks, Jews, Cimmerians, and Persians, to name only the better known ethnic groups. These peoples brought their own languages, for most of which there are extant remains, which in some cases are sufficient to permit classification of the languages.[218] The majority of the people in western Anatolia seem to have come from Europe and the Aegean isles, whereas those in eastern Anatolia apparently came from both Europe and Asia.

Of all the languages and cultures of pre-Christian Anatolia, it was Greek that showed itself to be the most dynamic. Greek colonies came to be established on the coasts of western and southern Asia Minor as early as the Mycenaean period, seemingly for commercial purposes.[219] By 800 B.C. the Aeolians, Ionians, and Dorians had founded colonies along the western coast in considerable number, and these in turn colonized the shores of the Black Sea. This second wave of settlement was fateful not only for the coastal regions but in the long run for the hinterland of Asia Minor as well, for it was the basis of a vast process of Hellenization which was to continue as late as Byzantine times. It is interesting that the progress of Hellenization at this early stage in a sense depended less on the numbers of settlers than upon the consequences of the economic and cultural superiority that these emigrants developed in Anatolia. Their influence in classical times was centered on the coastal area, for the

---

[217] A. H. Sayce, "Languages of Asia Minor," *Anatolian Studies Presented to Sir William Mitchell Ramsay* (London, 1923), p. 396.

[218] A. Goetze, *Kulturgeschichte des alten Orients. Kleinasien*, 2d ed. (Munich, 1957), pp. 180–183, 193–194, 201–204, 202–209. D. C. Swanson, "A Select Bibliography of the Anatolian Languages," *Bulletin of the New York Public Library* (May–June, 1948), 3–26. D. Masson, "Épigraphie Asianique," *Orientalia*, nov. ser. XXIII (1954), 439–442. J. Friederich, *Kleinasiatische Sprachdenkmäler* (Berlin, 1932). M. B. Sakellariou, *La migration grecque en Ionie* (Athens, 1958), pp. 414–437. More recently Ph. J. Howink ten Cate, *The Luwian Population Groups of Lycia and Cilicia Aspera during the Hellenistic Period* (Leiden, 1961). G. Neumann, *Untersuchungen zum Weiterleben hethitischen und luwischen Sprachgutes in hellenistischer und romischer Zeit* (Wiesbaden, 1961). L. Robert, "Inscriptions inédites en langue carienne," *Hellenica*, VIII (1950), 1–38. Some rather humorous incidents have occurred in the search for the remnants of these languages in modern times. One philologist claimed to have found Hetite spoken in an Anatolian village in the twentieth century. He announced this sensational discovery and promised a forthcoming grammar of modern Hetite. But Friederich, "Angebliche-moderne Reste alte Kleinasiatischer Sprachen," *Z.D.M.G.*, LXXXVIII (1934), pointed out that the language in question was Circassian and spoken by Circassians who had fled the Russian conquest of the Caucasus.

[219] Goetze, *Kulturgeschichte des alten orients*, pp. 182–183.

geographical nature of Anatolia combined with the Persian domination of the plateau to limit Hellenization to the maritime regions.[220]

The penetration of Greek cultural influence inland continued at a slow rate, nevertheless, in the period from the sixth to the fourth century of the pre-Christian era. The Lydians had been particularly receptive to this culture, as were the fourth-century dynasts of Caria and Lycia, the inhabitants of the Cilician plain and of the regions of Paphlagonia.[221]

After the conquests of Alexander the Great and the establishment of the Epigonoi, the tempo of Hellenization greatly accelerated and henceforth Hellenism acquired the prestige of political domination and empire. The Hellenistic monarchs pushed the process through the foundation of Greek cities, while the more ambitious of the local population found their desires for advancement a stimulus to learn Greek. The indigenous urban settlements and villages of Anatolia in many places coalesced, on their own initiative, to form cities in the Greek manner. The Attalids were active in promoting Greek cities in western Asia Minor; the local kings of Hellenistic Anatolia adopted Greek as their official language and sought to imitate other cultural forms.[222] It was in the towns that Hellenization made its great progress, the process often being synonymous with urbanization. In contrast, the rural areas were far less affected and retained more of the pre-Greek culture, as reflected in languages and religious practices.[223] Urbanization continued under the Romans, so that in a sense Rome maintained the traditions of Hellenization in the peninsula.[224] The geographer Strabo, himself an inhabitant of one of these Hellenized Anatolian towns (Amaseia), comments on Hellenization by remarking that Lydian was no longer spoken in Lydia (though it survived for a while among the isolated Cibyratae), and he implies that Carian was in the process of dying,[225] the language having acquired large numbers of Greek words.[226] The degree to which Hellenism had penetrated in the towns and cities of large portions of Anatolia is reflected in the

---

[220] *Ibid.*, pp. 210–211. By the late sixth century of the pre-Christian era, Anatolia, the meeting ground of East and West, was subject to two rival processes, Hellenization and, Iranization.

[221] *Ibid.*, p. 209. Jones, *The Greek City*, pp. 1–2, 27–29.

[222] S. K. Eddy, *The King is Dead* (Lincoln, Feb., 1961), pp. 163–182.

[223] Jones, *The Greek City*, pp. 40–50.

[224] *Ibid.*, pp. 51–67.

[225] Strabo. XIII. 4. 17, "τέτταρσι δὲ γλώτταις ἐχρῶντο οἱ Κιβυρᾶται, τῇ Πισσιδικῇ, τῇ Σολύμων, τῇ Ἑλληνίδι, τῇ Λυδῶν." Thus Greek had also penetrated these more isolated areas. Strabo also remarks, "τῆς (γλώττης) Λυδῶν δὲ οὐδ' ἴχνος ἐστὶν ἐν Λυδίᾳ." On the Hellenization of Lydian names and religion consult, Robert, *Noms indigènes dans l'Asie Mineure grecoromaine* (Paris, 1963); L. Zgusta, *Anatolische Personennamen* (Prague, 1963); A. Laumonier, *Les cultes indigènes en Carie* (Paris, 1958).

[226] Strabo, XIV. 2. 28, uses the verb καρίζειν in a fashion parallel to σολοικίζειν, showing that though the Carians spoke an impure Greek, they spoke it extensively. On Carian, Robert, *Hellenica*, pp. 1–38.

comparatively large numbers of men of letters who appeared there in Hellenistic, Roman, and Byzantine times.[227] But the literary aspect of Hellenic culture was largely an urban phenomenon, and if its presence does show the degree to which many of the cities and towns had been Hellenized, it does not reflect at all on the rural areas. Even though Greek was the official as well as the literary language, it had not yet conquered the countryside.

The slower rate of Hellenization of rural Asia Minor is reflected in the survival of a number of the "Anatolian" languages as late as the sixth century of the Christian era, although even here Greek cultural influence of a type is to be seen in the rural areas and in their languages.[228] A study of the *fortleben* of these Anatolian tongues (one is not concerned here with Armenian, Georgian, Kurdish) demonstrates the losing nature of the battle they fought against the progress of Greek. The nature of the sources and the archaistic use of ethnic epithets often make it difficult to ascertain whether a linguistic or ethnic term is being used purely geographically rather than culturally. Consequently, the interpretation of what are apparently geographical terms as denoting ethnic groups has been more harmful than helpful.

One of the better known cases of linguistic continuity is that of the language spoken by the Isaurians, who played such an important part in the fifth-century history of Byzantium, and whose language seems still to have been spoken as late as the sixth century.[229] There is evidence that Cappadocian was still known and spoken in the fourth century; Gothic

[227] In Hellenistic times Perge in Pamphylia was associated with the mathematician Apollonius, Soli in Side with the philosopher Chrysippus and the poet Aratus. Mollus produced the grammarians Crates and Zenodotus. Tarsus contributed the poets Dioscurides and Dionysides and the town became one of the chief centers of philosophy, rivaled only by Alexandria. Greek poets, rhetoricians, historians, grammarians, biographers, doctors of note in the Hellenistic and Roman periods arose in such Hellenized cities as Sardes, Alabanda, Tralles, Mylasa, Nyssa, Amaseia, Nicaea, Laodiceia, Pergamum, Nicomdeia, Anazarba, Prusa, Samosata, Caesareia, Aphrodisias, Cotyaeum, Laranda, Tyana. For this summary, Jones, *The Greek City*, pp. 280–283.

[228] It has been customary to speak of these rural areas as completely unaffected by the penetration of Hellenism, as for instance Jones, *The Greek City*, p. 288. But it is not only through the linguistic medium that a group or society is influenced. Certainly linguistic change is the most striking evidence of cultural change, but the other facets of human society (law, religion, art, etc.) can be receptive to outside influence independently of linguistic considerations. It is also highly probable that in many areas where native tongues survived, the inhabitants were bilingual (Strabo, XIII. 4. 17). For modern examples one may cite certain Greek villages that speak both Greek and Arvanitika, but in which the cultural consciousness is exclusively Greek. Also there is the example of certain Anatolian towns and villages in the nineteenth and early twentieth centuries which spoke Greek and Turkish. For other examples of Anatolian bilingualism in late ancient and early Byzantine times, C. Holl, "Das Fortleben der Volkssprachen in Kleinasien im nachchristlicher Zeit," *Hermes*, XLIII (1908), 243–244. For an example of the spread of Greek, Theodoretus, *P.G.*, LXXXII, 1488D, "ὁ δὲ τῇ Ἑλλάδι χρησάμενος φωνῇ. Κίλιξ γὰρ τὸ γένος ἐτύγχανεν ὤν."

[229] On what follows, Holl, "Das Fortleben der Volkssprachen," pp. 248–254. For the economic specialization of the Isaurians, C. Mango, "Isaurian Builders," *Polychronion. Festschrift Franz Dölger zu 75. Geburtstag* (Heidelberg, 1966), pp. 358–365.

in the fourth century; and Phrygian at least into the third century.[230] But these languages were for the most part dead or moribund in the sixth century of the Christian era.[231] Of these languages spoken in Anatolia, Neo-Phrygian has received the greatest amount of scholarly attention because of the survival of the Neo-Phrygian inscriptions. Those who have proposed a more lively continuity of these Anatolian languages in western Asia Minor during the Byzantine period have concentrated on the case of Neo-Phrygian. The principal literary texts that have been brought to bear on the question are the ecclesiastical histories of Socrates and Sozomenus, the contents of which refer to events in the fifth century. Holl (and those who have followed him) has concluded as a result of two passages in these texts that Phrygian was a spoken and understood language as late as the fifth century.[232] Let us look then at these two texts on which so many scholars have relied.

Socrates mentions that the bishop of the Goths in Asia Minor, a certain Selinus, was the son of a mixed marriage.

He was a Goth from his father and a Phrygian through his mother. And because of this he taught in both languages, readily, in the church.[233]

This passage has been interpreted as meaning that Selinus addressed his congregation in both Gothic and Phrygian. But the real question is the meaning of ἀμφοτέραις ταῖς διαλέκτοις, "in both languages." Does this mean that he really spoke both Gothic and Phrygian? Or, is the word Phrygian in the text simply a reference to the fact that his mother was from the district of Phrygia? Here again one is faced with an archaistic use of a

---

[230] Holl, "Das Fortleben der Volkssprachen," p. 241, mentions Mysian and Lycaonian as possible languages in this period. But these two terms seem to be geographical rather than linguistic. Harnack, *Die Mission und Ausbreitung des Christentums*, 4th ed. (Leipzig, 1924), II, 764, n. 4, maintains that Lycaonian was actually Phrygian. Jones, *The Greek City*, p. 366, n. 43, rejects Mysian as a language. Strabo, XII. 8. 3, indicates that already by Roman times people were not sure as to what Mysian was, "μαρτυρεῖν δὲ καὶ τὴν διάλεκτον μιξολύδιον γάρ πως εἶναι καὶ μιξοφρύγιον." This indicates, in contrast to Holl, that Mysian was no longer a spoken language. See also J. G. C. Anderson, "Exploration in Galatia Cis Halym," *J.H.S.*, XIX (1899), 313–316.

[231] Holl, "Das Fortleben der Volkssprachen," pp. 243–244, drawing upon an incident in the life of St. Martha, AS Mai V, 418–419, attempts to show that "Lycaonian" was a vital language in the sixth century. This incident has to do with the cure of a man who was speechless. Upon being cured he spoke in his own tongue, "τότε τῇ ἰδίᾳ διαλέκτῳ δοξολογῶν τὸν θεὸν ἐβόα." But in effect this does not prove the vitality of "Lycaonian" (whatever tongue this may have been). The remainder of the story indicates just the opposite. The healed man felt compelled to relate the wonder to others. But as he spoke no Greek, "οὐ γὰρ ἠπίστατο τὴν Ἑλλήνων γλῶσσαν," he obtained the services of a bilingual interpreter who knew Greek in addition to "Lycaonian," "διηγεῖτο περὶ πάντων τούτων, ἑτέρου συνόντος αὐτῷ γινώσκοντος τὴν Ἑλληνικὴν φωνὴν καὶ ἑρμηνεύοντος τὰ περὶ αὐτοῦ." In his desire to communicate, the healed Lycaonian was drawn into a society where the customary linguistic medium was Greek. The translator, a bilingual, symbolizes the process by which Greek was spreading.

[232] Holl, "Das Fortleben der Volkssprachen," pp. 247–248. W. M. Calder, *M.A.M.A.*, VII, xv, xxxii. Friederich, "Phrygia," *P.W.*, pp. 868–869.

[233] Socrates, P. G., LXVII, 648, "... Σεληνᾶς ὁ τῶν Γοτθῶν ἐπίσκοπος, ἀνὴρ ἐπίμικτον ἔχων τὸ γένος. Γότθος μὲν ἦν ἐκ πατρός. Φρὺξ δὲ κατὰ μητέρα. καὶ διὰ τοῦτο ἀμφοτέραις ταῖς διαλέκτοις ἑτοίμως κατὰ τὴν ἐκκλησίαν ἐσίδασκε."

term that refers to nothing more than a geographical district. The second language to which he refers is probably Greek. That this is so, and that the passage has nothing to do with the Phrygian language, emerges from the parallel text in Sozomenus which is much more explicit as to what this second language of Selinus was. Sozomenus narrates that Selinus was able to deliver sermons "not only in their national language [Gothic], but also in that of the Greeks." [234] Both texts indicate the following. The Goths, who settled in Phrygia in the fourth century, still preserved their national tongue in the fifth, and so Selinas their bishop often addressed them in Gothic. But, as his mother was a non-Goth, an inhabitant of the district of Phrygia, he could also speak Greek, the inhabitants of Phrygia having been Hellenized in their speech. Thus, he used both languages, Greek and Gothic. This passage, then, does not prove the vigorous survival of Phrygian into the fifth century. Rather it shows the process of Hellenization at work among the Goths through intermarriage and religion.[235]

There is also the question of the body of Neo-Phrygian inscriptions. These are the latest texts of the Anatolian languages (third century of Christian era), which have survived. As of 1956 the known and published number of such inscriptions was an even 100,[236] and practically all these have been dated to the third century.[237] What is the significance of this material? Would it justify the proposition that Neo-Phrygian underwent a renaissance and that it was the living language of the people in a limited area of Anatolia? The majority of these inscriptions contain the epitaphs and names in Greek, with a curse on the would-be violators of the tomb written in Phrygian. Though a very few of the epitaphs are in Phrygian, they are usually in Greek, and in both cases the Greek alphabet of the period is employed. The curses themselves seem to be rigidly formulated with little variation.[238] Thus Neo-Phrygian survives in these third-century

---

[234] Sozomenus, P. G., LXVII, 1468, "καὶ ἐπὶ ἐκκλησίας ἱκανῷ διδάσκειν, οὐ μόνον κατὰ τὴν πάτριον αὐτῶν φωνήν, ἀλλὰ γὰρ καὶ τὴν Ἑλλήνων."

[235] Their descendants were still known as Γοτθογραῖκοι (and not as Gotho-phrygians) in the eighth century, and the geographical term is mentioned in the late eighth century; Theophanes, I, 385. "Acta Graeca SS. Davidis, Symeonis et Georgii," A.B., XVIII (1899), 256. Charanis, "On the Ethnic Composition of Byzantine Asia Minor in the Thirteenth Century," Πρόσφορα εἰς Στίλπωνα Π. Κυριακίδην (Thessalonike, 1953),141 (hereafter cited as Charanis, "Ethnic Composition,"). Amantos, "Γοτθογραῖκοι-Γοτθογραικία," Ἑλληνικά, V (1932), 256. At an earlier period the Celts had been similarly Hellenized and were called Γαλλογραῖκοι. Galatia was also called Γαλλογραικία Strabo, XII. 5. 1. Appian, Mithradates, 114. Diodorus Siculus, V. 32. 5. Ammianus Marcellinus, XXII. 9. 5. On the absorption and Hellenization of the Celtic nobility in the early Christian era Bosch, "Die Kelten in Ankara," Jahrbuch für kleinasiatischen Forschung, II (1952), 283–291. See also the remarks of L. Mitteis, Reichsrecht und Volksrecht in den ostlichen Provinzen des römischen Kaiserreichs (Hildesheim, 1963), pp. 22–24. On the use of Γραικία to designate the Byzantine Empire see the interesting study of P. Speck, "ΓΡΑΙΚΙΑ und ᾿ΑΡΜΕΝΙΑ. Das Tätigskeit eines nicht identifizierten Strategen im frühen 9. Jahrhunder," J.Ö.B.G., XVI (1967), 71–90.

[236] Calder, M.A.M.A., p. xxix.

[237] Ibid., p. ix, one is actually dated to the year 259 A.D. Calder attributes a few of the inscriptions to the end of the second century.

[238] Friederich, "Phrygia," p. 870.

monuments for the most part in fixed ritualistic, formulaic curses. One is not convinced, as a result, that Phrygian existed as a vital living language among the people. W. M. Calder, the foremost student of these inscriptions, has at one point stated that these inscriptions "represent an artificial revival of the epigraphical use of the Phrygian language by the Tekmoreian Society." [239] The powerful influence of Greek is evident in these inscriptions. Aside from the alphabet, there is the fact that most of the epitaphs are in Greek, as are most of the names. Though the number of these Neo-Phrygian inscriptions is in itself considerable (100), one should keep in mind the fact that in eastern Phrygia alone there were some 1,076 inscriptions found. Of these, 18 are in Latin, 38 in Neo-Phrygian (or Greek and Phrygian), and 1,020 in Greek.[240] Certainly some knowledge of Neo-Phrygian existed in the mid-third century. But there is some evidence for the assertion that it was artifically revived and that Greek probably was, already in the third century, decisively victorious in Phrygia.[241]

One may assume that by the sixth century the Greek language had triumphed over the various indigenous tongues of western and central Anatolia (to the regions of Cappadocia).[242] At least references to these early languages are, so far as it has been possible to ascertain, lacking in the sources. It is true, however, that in the easternmost parts of Anatolia, Armenian, Syriac, Kurdish, Georgian, Arabic, and possibly Lazic not only survived but were spoken by the overwhelming majority. Political factors in the Byzantine period contributed to the victory of the empire's language. In contrast to the Balkan peninsula, which from the sixth century and even earlier, received large numbers of migrations and settlements, Asia Minor was shielded from such large ethnic movements of peoples who might have changed the linguistic pattern, until the migrations of the Turks in the eleventh century.[243] Perhaps this was partially

[239] Calder, "Corpus inscriptionum neo-phrygiarum, III," *J.H.S.*, XLVI (1926), 22. See also his "Philadelpheia and Montanism," *B.J.R.L.*, VII (1923), 352.

[240] Calder, *B.J.R.L.*, VII, xxx.

[241] Calder suggests that the Phrygians were bilingual in the third century, "Corpus inscriptionum neo-phrygiarum, I," *J.H.S.*, XXXI (1911), 163. He also supposes that the Phrygians of Galatia had been completely Hellenized by the third century, for no Phrygian inscriptions have been found in Galatia. In *M.A.M.A.*, VII, xiv, and in *Anatolian Studies Presented to Sir William Mitchell Ramsay*, p. 76, n. 4, he speaks of a fourth-century inscription from Phrygia, in Greek, which mentions the word Phrygia. He postulates that this usage is indicative of the fact that the inhabitants of the area still felt themselves to be Phrygian. But the usage is more likely geographical, with perhaps no linguistic connotation, much in the same manner in which Socrates used the term Φρύξ. This archaistic geographical nomenclature was used throughout Byzantine history. Constantine Porphyrogenitus' use of these terms led Rambaud, *L'empire grec au dixième siècle* (Paris, 1870), pp. 252–253, to conclude that all these linguistic groups existed to the end of the empire. Strabo, XII. 8. 21, in his day already bore witness to the process in which the Phrygians were disappearing as an ethnic group, for he mentions the disappearance of a number of Phrygian tribal divisions.

[242] Jones, *The Greek City*, p. 294, and Taeschner, "Anadolu," EI₂, who have studied this problem from the Hellenic and Turkish sides, share the view that Anatolia was effectively Hellenized.

[243] Rambaud, *L'empire grec*, pp. 244–245. On the Laz, A. Bryer. "Some Notes on the Laz and Tzan." *B.K.*, XXI–XXII (1966), 174–195.

due to the fact that there was in existence a relatively strong and organized state to the east, first the Sassanid monarchy and later the caliphate, so that Anatolia had something of a buffer against the peoples of central Asia.

Though there were no large migrations of new peoples into Anatolia from the East, the Byzantine emperors over the centuries introduced non-Greek, as well as Greek, populations into their Anatolian provinces on numerous occasions.[244] The reasons for this transplanting of peoples were closely linked to state policy. In some cases the foreigners brought to Anatolia had been causing trouble for the empire in other provinces. Hence they were removed from their familiar social and ethnic environment, placed in a strange one, and subjected to Hellenization (often indirectly) and to Christianization (or in the case of heretics, to Orthodoxy). On other occasions the transferred populations were brought for military purposes, or were Christians fleeing the conquests of the Arabs. In this way the Goths were settled in Phrygia in the fourth century, the Greek Cypriots were moved to Cyzicus by Justinian II,[245] and the Mardaites were sent to Attaleia.[246] Similarly, odd groups of Armenian soldiers were settled in various parts of Asia Minor. Constantine V settled one group on the eastern borders,[247] seventh-century Pergamum possibly had an Armenian colony,[248] but the emperor Philippicus (711–713) expelled a considerable number of Armenians from Byzantine Anatolia, causing them to settle in Melitene and Fourth Armenia.[249]

The settlements of Armenians were most numerous in the easternmost regions of Byzantine Anatolia, as in the regions of Coloneia and Neocaesareia, where by the latter part of the seventh century they must have existed in considerable numbers.[250] Probably there also was settled a

---

[244] For the general practice of transplanting populations, Charanis, "The Transfer of Population as a Policy in the Byzantine Empire," *Comparative Studies in Society and History*, III (1961), 140–154 (hereafter cited as "Transfer,"). On the general ethnographic picture the same author's "Ethnic Composition," pp. 140–147; "Ethnic Changes in the Byzantine Empire in the Seventh Century," *D.O.P.*, XIII (1959), 25–36 (hereafter cited as "Ethnic Changes,"); "Slavic Element in Asia Minor in the Thirteenth Century," *Byzantium*, XVIII (1948), 69–83. Rambaud, *L'empire grec*, pp. 248 ff.

[245] Theophanes, I, 365. Charanis, "Transfer," p. 143.

[246] Constantine Porphyrogenitus, *De Caerimoniis*, I, 657, 668. It is not recorded whether the five detachments of cavalry which Justinian sent to fight on the Persian front (Procopius, *History of the Wars*, IV, xiv, 17–18), settled in Asia Minor or not. Theophanes, I, 364. Amantos, "Μαρδαῖται.," Ἑλληνικά, V (1932), 13–136.

[247] Charanis, "Transfer," p. 144, but these were later removed by the Arabs. Agapius de Menbidj, *Kitab al'Unvan. Histoire universelle* ed. and trans. A. Vasiliev, *P.O.*, VIII (1912), 531, 538.

[248] Charanis, "Ethnic Changes," p. 29. Gelzer, *Pergamon unter Byzantinern und Osmanen Abhand. der kön. preuss. Akad. der Wiss.* (Berlin, 1903), pp. 42 ff.

[249] Theophanes, I, 382.

[250] On the Armenians of Byzantium, Charanis, "The Armenians in the Byzantine Empire," *B.S.*, XXII (1961), 196–240; "Ethnic Changes," p. 29. Grégoire, "Précisions géographiques et chronologiques sur les Pauliciens," *Académie royale de Belgique, Bulletin de la classe des lettres et des sciences morales et politiques*, 5ᵉ série, XXXIII (1947), 297–298 (hereafter cited as "Précisions,").

number of Armenian soldiers in the Armeniac theme,[251] and it was customary to post Armenian contingents in various parts of western Anatolia. In an expedition against the Arabs of Crete during the reign of Leo VI, there were mustered 500 Armenians from Platanion in the theme of Anatolicon and 500 more from Priene.[252] Under Constantine VII the tagmata of the east were bolstered for another Cretan expedition by the addition of 1,000 Armenian troops,[253] whereas 600 Armenians (possibly those of Priene) were to guard the shores of the Thracesian theme.[254] All these references, however, are to scattered contingents of soldiers posted on the shores of the western Anatolian coast or on the eastern borders to fight the Muslims. Most of the large scale transplanting of Armenians from their homeland by the Byzantine emperors, at least up to the tenth century, seems to have been made to the European provinces.[255]

Other groups were sent to Anatolia, such as the several thousand Persian soldiers who deserted to Byzantium in 834 and were then settled throughout Asia Minor.[256] In the course of the seventh and eighth centuries, the emperors transplanted considerable numbers of Slavs to the northwesternmost corner of the peninsula.[257] There are references to the presence of Slavs in the seventh, eighth, ninth, and tenth centuries. The first such mention would seem to be the 5,000 Slavs who deserted to the Arab invaders of Anatolia in 665.[258] Almost a quarter of a century later, in 688, Justinian II sent the Slavs, whom he had taken prisoner in Europe, to the theme of Opsicion,[259] and in 692 he was able to raise a

---

[251] Charanis, "Ethnic Changes," p. 35.

[252] Constantine Porphyrogenitus, De Caerimoniis, I, 652, 655–657.

[253] Ibid., pp. 666–667, but it is not clear whether they were settled there, or simply assembled and paid with the τάγματα τῆς 'Ανατολῆς.

[254] Ibid., p. 666. Charanis, "Ethnic Composition," pp. 142–143.

[255] Charanis, "Ethnic Changes," p. 30.

[256] Theophanes Continuatus, 112, 124–125. Symeon Magister, 625–627, 647. Cedrenus, II, 131. Vasiliev, Byzance et les Arabes, I, 92–93, 124–126. There existed a mosque in ninth-century Ephesus (Ibn Khuradadhbih, B.G.A., VI, 106); in tenth-eleventh century Athens (G. Miles, "The Arab Mosque in Athens," Hesperia, XXV (1956), 329–344), as well as in Constantinople. These were probably for Muslim captives, merchants, and inhabitants. In the eleventh century the metropolitan of Ephesus had an interpreter for the Saracens (AS Nov., 542), and he converted a Saracen in Ephesus. Aside from the settlement of Persians in ninth century Anatolia, and the settlement of the tribe of Banu Habib (Canard, Hamdanides, I, 737–739), a Christian Arab monk is mentioned in an inscription of one of the Cappadocian troglodyte monasteries (de Jerphanion, Cappadoce, II₁, 243–244). These monasteries feature considerable pseudo-kufic decoration in their frescoes. Muslims are mentioned in the cities of Bithynia, Muslim merchants in Attaleia, Trebizond, Coloneia, Neocaesareia, Melitene, Tzamandus, Caesareia, Ankara, and Nicomedeia (Honigmann, "Un itinéraire," pp. 263–270). AS Nov. III, 590. Canard, "Quelques' 'à-côté' de l'histoire des relations entre Byzance et les Arabes," Studi orientalistici in onore de Giorgio Levi Della Vida, I (Rome, 1956), 98–119.

[257] There is an extensive literature on this subject, most recent of which are the following items. Charanis, "Transfer," pp. 143–144; Charanis, "Ethnic Changes," pp. 42–43. Ostrogorsky, Geschichte, pp. 108–109. Charanis, "Ethnic Composition," pp. 141–142; "The Slavic Element in Byzantine Asia Minor," Byzantion, XVIII (1948), 69–83, and the comments of G. Soulis, E.E.B.Σ., XIX (1949), 337–340.

[258] Charanis, "Ethnic Changes," p. 42. Theophanes, I, 348.

[259] Charanis, "Ethnic Changes," p. 42. Theophanes, I, 364.

military force of 30,000 from among them. But when he marched against the Arabs with his armies, 20,000 of these Slavs deserted to the enemy. Justinian was so infuriated that on his return he slew the remainder of the Slavs with their women and children at Leucate on the Gulf of Nicomedia.[260] The largest Slavic or Bulgaro-Slavic colonization in Asia Minor seems to have occurred during the eighth century. In the reign of Constantine V many Slavs fled the Balkans and were allowed to settle in the region of the Atarnas River not far from the Bosphorus. Nicephorus mentions that their number was 208,000.[261] Though this figure is doubtlessly exaggerated in the manner of medieval chroniclers, nevertheless after one has allowed for the exaggeration, this must have been the largest Slavic settlement in Asia Minor.[262]

That the Slavs were still to be seen as an ethnic group in this northwestern corner of Anatolia in the ninth century is recorded in Theophanes Continuatus.[263] These are the last references to major Slavic settlements in Anatolia prior to the Turkish invasions. Constantine Porphyrogenitus does mention the presence of Sthlavesianoi in the Opsicion theme in the tenth century,[264] for in his reign they furnished 220 men for the expedition to Crete.[265] Their numbers are comparatively small as revealed in this

---

[260] Theophanes, I, 366. The exact interpretation and translation of this rather important text has excited some disagreement. Some have interpreted this passage to mean that Justinian destroyed the remnants of the Slavic colony and that the colony therefore disappeared. A. Maricq, "Notes sur les Slaves dans le Péloponnèse et en Bithynie," *Byzantion*, XXII (1952), 348–349, commented that in fact Justinian did not exterminate the whole colony, for such reasoning neglects the exaggeration with which it is always necessary to reckon in narratives of this type. Therefore the testimony of Theophanes as to the complete disappearance of this Slavic settlement must be discounted as the exaggeration of a medieval chronicler. Ostrogorsky, *Geschichte*, 110, has rejected Theophanes' testimony on the extermination of this group as being an exaggeration. However he does accept the numbers of Theophanes, I, 432, of a slightly later Slavic settlement as being exact and accurate figures. Whether one interprets Theophanes literally or makes allowance for exaggeration, the Slavic settlement under Justinian II was a considerable one, but at the same time it must have been greatly depleted if not exterminated. It is possibly to the Slavs that the author of the life of St. Peter of Atroa refers by the phrase, ἐμφύλια ἔθνη, Laurent, *La vita retracta et les miracles posthumes de Saint Pierre d'Atroa* (Brussels, 1958), pp. 41–42.

[261] Theophanes, I, 432.

[262] On the exaggerated nature of the number, Charanis, "Ethnic Changes," pp. 76–78.

[263] Theophanes Continuatus, 50, refers to Thomas as of Slavic origin, though his origin is elsewhere said to have been Armenian, Charanis, "Ethnic Changes," p. 79, n. 3. This source remarks on the continued existence of a Slavic element in Asia Minor. See also P. Lemerle, "Thomas le Slave," *Travaux et Mémoires*, I (Paris, 1965), 257–297.

[264] Constantine Porphyrogenitus, *De Caerimoniis*, I, 622.

[265] *Ibid.*, p. 666, but on p. 669, he mentions that there were only 127 in the Opsicion theme. In regard to the continuity of the Slavic settlements of the seventh and eighth centuries the question has been raised whether these Sthlavesianoi were their descendants or not. It is difficult to answer this question from the text of Constantine Porphyrogenitus. It is conceivable that these tenth-century Sthlavesianoi might have been moved from Europe and posted in the Opsicion theme. The text reads " . . . οἱ Σθλαβησιανοὶ οἱ καθισθέντες εἰς τὸ Ὀψίκιον." It would seem a little strange that a tenth-century author would refer to them as καθισθέντες if in fact they had been there since the seventh and eighth centuries. Amantos, "Σκλάβοι, Σκλαβησιανοὶ καὶ βάρβαροι," Πρακτικὰ τῆς Ἀκαδημίας Ἀθηνῶν, VII (1932), 333–335.

text, for they furnished much smaller numbers of troops than the Armenians in western Anatolia. After this their presence is no longer noted, and it is quite probable that they were Christianized and Hellenized.[266]

A group about which comparatively little is known, but which was no doubt of commercial importance in Anatolia, was that of the Jews. By the time of the Roman Empire, the Diaspora of the Jews had resulted in Jewish establishments in over sixty Anatolian cities and towns.[267] From the seventh to the eleventh centuries there are references to Jews in Nicaea (tenth century), Abydus (1096), Pylae (eleventh century), Ephesus (eleventh century), Mastaura in the regions of the Maeander (eleventh century), Amorium (ninth century), Cappadocia (seventh century), Neocaesareia (eighth century), and in the border town of Zapetra (ninth century). Five more Anatolian towns are mentioned as having settlements of Jews during the twelfth and early thirteenth centuries, and it is probable that Jews had lived in some of these towns even earlier. These include Chonae (c. 1150), Strobilus (eleventh century), Seleuceia (1137), Trebizond (1180), and Gangra (1207).[268] The reference to the Jews in these Anatolian towns is quite important, especially when one recalls the Constantinopolitan nature of the Byzantine sources. It is highly probable that there were many more such towns but they simply have not been mentioned. In most cases they must have been in direct line of descent from the communities founded during the Diaspora, though a number of arrivals probably entered the empire during the late tenth century, following the Byzantine expansion to the east and the religious persecutions of the eleventh-century caliph al-Hakim.[269] These Jews were settled primarily in the towns along the great roads of Anatolia along which flowed the commerce of the empire, and it is clear that they were actively engaged in commerce and the crafts. There is, however, no indication as to their numbers.[270]

The practice of settling foreign military contingents (Mardaites, Slavs, Armenians, and Persians from the seventh through the ninth century) in Anatolia not only continued in the tenth and eleventh centuries, but the military troops settled increased in ethnic variety. It is not always clear,

[266] F. Dvornik, *Les Slaves, Byzance et Rome* (Paris, 1926), p. 103. Charanis, "Ethnic Changes," pp. 78–82. Vryonis, "St. Ioannicius the Great (754–846) and the 'Slavs' of Bithynia," *Byzantion*, XXXI (1961), 245–248.

[267] J. Juster, *Les Juifs dans l'empire romain* (Paris, 1914), I, 188–194.

[268] See the basic work of Starr, *The Jews, passim.* Ankori, *Keraites, passim.* A. Andreades, "Les Juifs et le fisc dans l'empire byzantin," *Mélanges Charles Diehl* (Paris, 1930), I, 7–29; "Οἱ Ἑβραῖοι ἐν τῷ βυζαντινῷ κράτει," Ε.Ε.Β.Σ., VII (1927), 3–23. Ahrweiler, "Smyrne," p. 20. *Chronique de Denys de Tell-Mahre,* trans. J. B. Chabot (Paris, 1895), p. 24. Beneševič, "K istorii Evreev v Vizantii VI–X v.," *Evreiskii Mysl,* II (1926), 197–224, 305–318, was not available to me.

[269] Ankori, *Keraites,* p. 167.

[270] Starr, *The Jews,* pp. 27–30. Figures are given for the Jewish communities of the Balkan lands of the empire in the twelfth century by Benjamin of Tudela. The early tax registers for Ottoman Anatolian show almost no Jewish population at all in the sixteenth century, see chapter vii.

however, if these tenth- and eleventh-century groups were permanently settled in an area, or were simply temporarily quartered in Anatolia during the period of their military service. Contingents of Russ were sent to the regions of Trebizond in the region of Romanus I,[271] and in the mid-eleventh century one tagma of Russ had their winter quarters in northeast Anatolia, as did two tagmata of Franks.[272] The eleventh-century documents list a bewildering variety of ethnic military groups in the various provinces of the empire—Russians, Kulpings, English, Normans, Germans, Bulgars, Saracens, Georgians, Armenians, Albanians, Scandinavians, and others.[273] It is very difficult to ascertain the numbers of these groups, their location, and whether they were permanent or temporary settlers.

It was, however, the eastern regions of Byzantine Anatolia which contained the majority of the non-Greek populations—Kurds, Georgians, Lazes, Syrians, and Armenians. The eastern expansion of the tenth and eleventh centuries incorporated areas into the empire which were non-Greek in speech and non-Chalcedonian. The Kurds were numerous in such regions as Amid, Mayaferrikin, Chliat, Manzikert, Ardjish, and in the regions to the northeast of Lake Van. [274] Georgians and Lazes were to be found in the southeastern districts of the Black Sea coast. Of these eastern peoples in eleventh-century Anatolia, the most important were the Syrians and the Armenians. In the tenth century the emperor Nicephorus Phocas, in an effort to revive the city of Melitene which had been incorporated as a result of the Byzantine reconquest years earlier, asked the Syrian Jacobite patriarch to repeople the areas of Melitene and Hanazit with Syrians and to establish his patriarchal seat in that area. In this manner an extensive emigration of Jacobite Syrians to these regions took place. By the eleventh century they seem to have come in considerable numbers and possessed bishoprics in a large number of the eastern and southeastern towns: Zapetra, Tell Patriq, Simnadu, Saroug, Mardin, Germaniceia (Marash), Laqabin, Hisn Mansur, Goubbos, Gaihan-Barid, Callisura, Mayefarrikin, Arabissus, Melitene, Anazarba, Tarsus, Amid, Edessa, Kaisum, Nisibis, Tell Arsanias, Claudia, Hisn Ziad, Caesareia (at least by the twelfth century if not earlier), Samosata, and Gargar. They spread as far north as the Armenian town of Erzindjan where they possessed a monastery. Active in Anatolian commerce, from which they acquired considerable wealth, the radius of their caravans comprehended the lands of the Turks in the east and in the west

[271] Papadopoulos-Kerameus, *Ist. trap. imp.*, pp. 40 ff.

[272] Cedrenus, II, 624–625. The Normans Roussel and Herve had their estates in Asia Minor. Eleventh-century Edessa had 1,000 Latins, and the Armenian adventurer Philaretus based his political activity in Cilicia on a force of 8,000 Latin mercenaries in the eleventh century.

[273] G. Rouillard and P. Collomp, *Actes de Lavra* (Paris, 1937), I, 83, 111.

[274] Minorsky, "Kurds," EI₁. For the Merwanids of Diyarbekir in the tenth and eleventh centuries, H. F. Amedroz, "The Marwānid Dynasty at Mayāfāriqīn in the Tenth and Eleventh Centuries," *J.R.A.S.* (1903), pp. 123–245.

Constantinople itself. They were also important as physicians and in the translation of the Greek texts.[275]

The most significant movement of peoples into the Anatolian provinces of the empire was, however, that which brought in the Armenians during the tenth and eleventh centuries. This transplanting of large numbers of Armenians is closely connected with the Byzantine eastern expansion and the somewhat later western movement of the Seljuks. As a result of these two converging forces, Byzantium annexed Taron (968), Taiq (1000), Vaspuracan (1021), Ani (1045–46), Kars (1064). The expansion of Byzantium into the east was accompanied by a large-scale emigration of Armenian princes, nobles, and their retinues to the lands of the empire. There had previously existed settlements of Armenians in these provinces between Tephrice and Melitene, and the Armeno-Byzantine general Melias had organized the newly formed theme of Lycandus in the early tenth century and colonized it with Armenians. As a result of the Byzantine conquest of Cilicia and northern Syria, the government brought large numbers of Armenian colonists to both regions.[276] The newer emigrants were often posited upon the older stratum of Armenian population. In the tenth century the Taronites family received estates in Celtzene;[277] the nobility of Taiq, after its absorption, acquired lands at Labaca, Arnasaciou, and Martisapao in the theme of Armeniacon (also at Ani, Tais, Tzourmere).[278] In 1021 Basil II transplanted the population of Basean to Chaldia,[279] and with the annexation of Vaspuracan, there took place a significant emigration of Armenians. When Senecherim-Hohvannes and his son David received landed possessions in Sebasteia, Larissa, Abara, Caesareia, Tzamandus, and Gabadonia in the theme of Cappadocia, they were accompanied by 14,000 men (and presumably by their families).[280] In 1045–46 Gregory Bahlavouni exchanged his lands for estates in the province of Byzantine Mesopotamia[281] and in the same year Kakig of Ani gave up his kingdom and settled within the empire, acquiring estates in the themes of Cappadocia, Lycandus, and Charsianon.[282]

[275] Michael the Syrian, III, 130–146, 160. Bar Hebraeus, I, 169–178, 204. Honigmann, "Malatiya," EI₁. Chabot, "Les évêques jacobites du VIIIᵉ au XIIIᵉ siècle d'après la chronique de Michel le Syrien," *R.O.C.*, IV (1899), 443–451, 495–511; V (1900), 605–636; VI (1901), 189–219.

[276] J. Laurent, *Byzance et les Turcs seldjoucides dans l'Asie occidentale jusqu'en 1081* (Nancy-Paris-Strasbourg, 1919), pp. 29, 71. R. Grousset, *Historie de l'Armenie des origines à 1071* (Paris, 1947), pp. 489, 522. Asolik, *Histoire universelle*, trans. F. Macler (Paris, 1869), II, 142.

[277] Cedrenus, II, 375. Grousset, *Armenie*, p. 492.

[278] Honigmann, *Die Ostgrenze des byzantinischen Reiches von 363 bis 1071 nach griechischen, arabischen, syrischen und armenischen Quellen* (Brussels, 1935), pp. 222–226. Cedrenus, II, 447–448.

[279] Grousset, *Armenie*, p. 548.

[280] Honigmann, *Ostgrenze*, p. 173. Grousset, *Armenie*, p. 553. Michael the Syrian, III, 133. Aristakes of Lazdivert, *Histoire d'Armenie*, trans. Prud'homme (Paris, 1864) pp. 32–38 (hereafter cited as Aristakes). Cedrenus, II, 464.

[281] Aristakes, pp. 32–38. Grousset, *Armenie*, p. 580. Dölger, *Regesten*, I₂, no. 873.

[282] Grousset, *Armenie*, p. 581. Cedrenus, II, 557–559. Honigmann, *Ostgrenze*, pp. 168, 175. Matthew of Edessa, p. 78.

Finally in 1064 Gagik-Abas of Kars received lands in Tzamandus, Larissa, Amaseia, and Comana.[283] Though large-scale emigrations are specifically mentioned in only two instances, it must be assumed that all these princes and nobles were accompanied by considerable numbers of followers. So extensive was the number of Armenians in this diaspora that by the middle of the eleventh century there were three Armenian military corps stationed in the cities of Sebasteia, Melitene, and Tephrice.[284] One of the principal Byzantine sources of the eleventh century Michael Attaliates remarks, "the Armenian heretics have thronged into Iberia, Mesopotamia, Lycandus, Melitene, and the neighboring places."[285] Michael the Syrian confirms this in remarking that once Senecherim-Hovhannes had been installed in Sebasteia, the Armenians "spread throughout Cappadocia, Cilicia, and Syria."[286]

Religion

As important as the ethnic configuration of eleventh-century Anatolia and, in a sense, more difficult to reconstruct, is the religious and sectarian picture of the peninsula. The history of the Byzantine church in Anatolia as well as a comprehensive history of Anatolian heresies and their significance remain to be written. Paradoxically, Anatolia was at the same time the strength of the Orthodox church during the period between the seventh and the eleventh centuries, and also the nest of a number of smaller and larger heresies. The Greek church of history is in a sense the church of Asia Minor.[287]

Christianity, brought by such distinguished preachers as Paul and John of the Apocalypse, spread to Anatolia very early, and, up to the period of the first ecumenical council, it was, next to Egypt, the Christian land κατ' ἐξοχήν. Hellenism had spread on a significant scale in Asia Minor, and in many provinces local culture, the ethnic languages, and memories of ancient independence were so weak that they offered little resistance to Christianization. The presence of the large number of Jewish communities, the mixing of Judaism and paganism in thought, the spread of Greek as a universal medium of communication were all factors that prepared the region for a new religious syncretism. Though there were significant religious cults in Anatolia, they were not serious obstacles to the penetration of Christianity.[288] The Christianity that emerged in Anatolia,

---

[283] Grousset, *Armenie*, p. 616. Matthew of Edessa, p. 126. Honigmann, *Ostgrenze*, p. 188. On the general absorption of the Armenian east, A. Akulian, *Einverleibung armenischen Territorien durch Byzanz im XI. Jahrhundert; ein Beitrag zur vorseldschuken Periode der armenische Geschichte* (1912).

[284] Laurent, *Byzance et les Turcs*, p. 33. Cedrenus, II, 626.

[285] Attaliates, 97.

[286] Michael the Syrian, III, 133.

[287] Harnack, *Die Mission*, II, 734.

[288] *Ibid.*, pp. 732–733.

however, bore the marks of the absorptive process. On the one hand, because Hellenism was the dynamic culture of the peninsula Hellenism and Christianity fused, as is evidenced in the philosophy and theology of the Cappadocian fathers. On the other hand, though paganism seems to have been effaced without too great a struggle, in disappearing it re-appeared within the church.[289] Many of the significant developments and struggles of the early church had appeared in Anatolia: the contest between the itinerant and local organization of the church, the struggle with gnosticism, the rise of monasticism, and the development of the metropolitan-episcopal structure. Asia Minor also witnessed a strong development in the cult of the relics.

In the first century of the Christian era, Christian communities arose in such towns as Perge, Pisidian Antioch, Iconium, Derbe, Lystra; in the regions of Galatia, Cappadocia, and Bithynia; in Ephesus, Colossae, Laodiceia, Phrygian Hierapolis, Smyrna, Pergamum, Sardes, Phila-delpheia, Thyateira, Troas, Tralles, Magnesia ad Maeandrum, and others.[290] A continuing expansion is observable in the second century,[291] and by the third and fourth centuries Christianity had not only won over the Hellenes and Hellenized of the towns but had begun to absorb the cults of the rural areas. All this is reflected in the complex network of bishoprics and chorespiscopates established on Anatolian soil by the church. Paganism did not completely disappear, and even when it did vanish as the accepted or dominant religion of a particular locality, it quite possibly entrenched itself in some one of the heretical or schismatic sects that arose over much of the early Christian world. Some of the sects were indigenous to Anatolia, others were imports from different areas of the empire.[292]

The most important of these early indigenous Anatolian heresies was that of Montanism. Founded in the second half of the second century by Montanus (according to tradition a converted pagan priest, and possibly even a former priest of Cybele), the heresy seems to have incorporated certain religious characteristics generally (though not exclusively) associated with the regions of Phrygia. These included a particular emphasis on the role of ecstatic prophecy, as well as the general emotional or "enthusiastic" approach to religion. The heresy apparently spread most effectively in Phrygia (it was known as the Phrygian or Cataphrygian

---

[289] *Ibid.*, pp. 734.

[290] *Ibid.*, pp. 735-736.

[291] Sinope, Philomelium, Parium, Nacoleia, Amastris (and other churches of Pontus), Hieropolis, and possibly Ankara, Otrus, Pepuza, Tymium, Apamaea, Comana, Eumenea. *Ibid.*, pp. 737-738.

[292] For an introduction to Anatolian heresies, J. Gouillard, "L'hérésie dans l'empire byzantin des origines au XII⁰ siècle," *Travaux et Mémoires*, I (Paris, 1965), 299-324; "Le synodikon de l'Orthodoxie: édition et commentaire," *Travaux et Mémoires*, II (1967), 1-316.

heresy), Lycaonia, and the environs.[293] This Phrygian heresy continued to exist for a number of centuries, though its vigor seems to have been spent early.[294] The sect is mentioned in the laws of Justinian I, and Procopius records that during the general persecution of heretics by that emperor, the Montanists of Phrygia locked themselves in their churches and set them afire, destroying both themselves and the edifices.[295] A sect that bore the name Montanist existed in the early eighth century, at which time its members refused to be converted and baptized in consonance with the decree of Leo III (721–722), and so once more they locked themselves in their religious buildings and consigned themselves to the flames.[296] The sect had by then probably become insignificant.[297]

[293] Bardy, "Montanisme," *D.T.C.*, pp. 2358–2370. Calder, in a most suggestive article, "The Epigraphy of the Anatolian Heresies," in *Anatolian Studies Presented to Sir William Ramsay* (London, 1923), 59–91 (hereafter cited as "Epigraphy,"), has described an interesting group of Greek Christian inscriptions from Phrygia which date from the late second and the third century. These inscriptions included a number that are addressed as follows, Χρειστιανοὶ Χρειστιανοῖς, Christians to Christians. According to Calder this is almost unique, for Christian tombstones revealing so openly the religious affiliation of the deceased belong to the postpersecution era. Previous to the period of toleration, with the exception of Rome, Christians did not dare to reveal so openly their religious identity. Therefore the unique appearance of these second and third century inscriptions is due to the activity of the Montanists in Phrygia. Calder repeats his ideas in "Philadelphia and Montanism," *B.J.R.L.*, VII (1923), 25–38. Grégoire, who formerly accepted this view, had more recently, *Les persécutions* (1951), p. 18, denied that these Christian epitaphs are to be attached to the Montanists. He declared them to have been the work of "phanero-chrétiens," as opposed to Crypto-Christians. Though Calder has not proved his point conclusively, one is nevertheless impressed by the striking coincidence of the dating of the inscriptions, their uniqueness in the Christian world, and their chronological coincidence with the appearance of the Montanists. He goes on to generalize ("Epigraphy," p. 64), that these inscriptions also bear witness to a sectarian struggle in central Phrygia in this period. By that time the Phrygian heretical movement had been defeated by the church in central Phrygia, an area teeming with Hellenized towns. So the heresy at the beginning of the third century turned north toward the more rural regions of the Tembris valley, an area he assumes to have been only slightly affected by Hellenism. J. G. C. Anderson, "Paganism and Christiantity in the Upper Tembris Valley," *Studies in the History and Art of the Eastern Provinces of the Empire* (Aberdeen, 1906), pp. 183–227.

[294] Two sixth-century inscriptions were found which shed some light on the hierarchical structure of the sect, Grégoire, "Du nouveau sur la hiérarchie de la secte montaniste," *Byzantion*, II (1925), 329–336. Calder and Grégoire, "Paulinus, κοινωνός de Sébaste de Phrygia," *Académie royale de Belgique, Bulletin de la classe des lettres et des sciences morales et politiques*, 5e ser., XXXVIII (1952), 162–183.

[295] *Cod. Iust.*, I. v. 20. Procopius, *Anecdota*, XI. 14. 23.

[296] Theophanes, I, 401.

[297] The use of the term Montanist survived, however, in the archaism so prevalent in Byzantine literary and intellectual monuments. It would be difficult to prove that its recurrence in later years was anything more than an archaism. It is repeated in the Ecloga of Leo III and Constantine V where Manichees and Montanists are condemned to perish by the sword, XVIII. 52 (Zepos, *J.G.R.*, II, 61), where it would seem to apply to actual conditions. In the eleventh century it is used by a scholiast to denote someone who has left Judaism. Starr, *The Jews*, pp. 177–178. For further confusion of Jews and Montanists in the eighth century, Starr, *The Jews*, p. 92. Gouillard, "L'hérésie," *Travaux et Mémoires* I, 309–310. They are mentioned in canon 95 of the Council in Trullo (692) as Phrygians. Some scholars feel that by the ninth century what remained of the sect may well have merged with the Paulicians. Charanis, "Ethnic Changes," p. 27. A. Scharf, "The Jews, the Montanists, and the Emperor Leo III," *B.Z.*, LIX (1966), 37–46, indicates that these eighth-century "Montanists" were actually a Jewish messianic sect.

The ecclesiastical authors and inscriptions of the fourth and fifth centuries mention numerous less well-known and smaller heresies that had appeared in Anatolia, in the regions of Cilicia, Pisidia, Phrygia, Paphlagonia, and Lycaonia. These included Catharioi, Encratitai, Saccophoroi, Apostatitai, Tatianoi, Hypsistarioi, Euchitai, Novatians, and others.[298] Of these the more important, the Euchitai and Novatians, were examples of nonindigenous heresies, heresies that had entered Anatolia from points farther east and west respectively. It would be a mistake to think of Byzantine Anatolia as the spawning ground of the majority of those heresies that eventually made their appearance there. The Novatian schism, begun in third-century Rome, made its way to Anatolia where its rigorist doctrines may have had some appeal to a portion of the inhabitants. Novatians are mentioned in Paphlagonia, in the towns of Cyzicus, Nicomedia, Nicaea, Cotyaeum, Ankara, and they came to be particularly strong in Phrygia and Paphlagonia, possibly due to the fact that they built on top of the remnants of much of the Montanist heresy.[299] They seem to disappear by the eighth century, at least in the sources. The Euchitai (Messalians), so-called because of the preponderant emphasis that they placed upon prayer at the expense of certain sacraments, apparently originated in the Mesopotamian region of Osrhoene, and by the second half of the fourth century entered Anatolia. During the course of the fourth and fifth centuries, the heresy appeared in Lycaonia, Pamphylia, Lycia, Cappadocia, and Pontus. But its later history is veiled in obscurity, and whether the use of the term in the eleventh century is archaistic, or due to the fact that the later sects were in some way similar to the Messalians, or due to the actual continuity of the original sect, is not clear.[300]

The great heresy of Mani also made its appearance in fourth-century Cappadocia, Paphlagonia, and Lydia.[301] Later Anastasius I and Justinian I took severe measures against the heresy, and by the eighth century the term is used to describe other similar dualistic movements, in particular that of the Paulicians.[302]

[298] For a detailed description of the inscriptions and the literary sources see Calder, "Epigraphy," *passim;* C. Bones, "What are the Heresies Combatted in the Work of Amphilochius, Metropolitan of Iconium (c. 341–345—c. 395–400) 'Regarding False Asceticism' " *The Greek Orthodox Theological Review,* IX (1963), 79–96; Holl, *Amphilochius von Ikonium in seinem Verhältnis zu den grossen Kappadoziern* (Tübingen-Leipzig, 1904), pp. 23 ff. As late as the ninth century there is mention of Nestorians (whether they refer to the fifth-century Christological heretics is not clear) in the villages at the foot of Mt. Olympus of Bithynia. Laurent, *La vie merveilleuse de Saint Pierre d'Atroa 837* (Brussels, 1956), p. 66.

[299] A. Amann, "Novatiens," *D.T.C.,* pp. 816–849.

[300] Bareille, "Euchaites," *D.T.C.,* pp. 1455–1465.

[301] E. de Stoop, *Essai sur le diffusion du Manichéisme dans l'empire romain* (Gand, 1909), pp. 63–69. He mentions the heresies of the Priscillians and Eustathians in Asia Minor.

[302] Papadopoulos-Kerameus, A.l.Σ, IV, 382, for mention of a wandering Manichee in the region of Prusa in the first half of the ninth century. G. Bardy, "Manichéisme," *D.T.C.,* pp. 1841–1895.

Thus Byzantine Anatolia had, by the time of the losses to the Arabs of Syria, Egypt, and North Africa, enjoyed a respectable history of heresy. One is struck by the number of sects and also by the continuity of heresy in certain parts of Anatolia, but opinion has varied as to the degree the Anatolian population was heretical or orthodox. It is a question that cannot be answered definitively. Certainly in the third, fourth, and fifth centuries heresies were numerous and common throughout many of the lands where Christianity was establishing itself, including Syria, Egypt, and Asia Minor, but also North Africa, Italy, and other parts of the Western world as well. One must view the presence of heresies in Asia Minor at this time partially against this background. On the other hand some of these heresies (Montanism, Novatianism, and Messalianism) seem to have persevered longer and to have left a more marked coloring on subsequent Anatolian heresies.

To what degree the presence of heresy can be related to the survival of non-Greek languages is yet one more of those "difficult" problems. The principle had been enunciated by Holl (and subsequently followed by others) that the heresies in Anatolia were toughest to eradicate in those areas where the Anatolian languages survived longest. Thus, he stated, the heretical sects found support in the local languages.[303] This is so general a statement that it glosses over many important points. First, all surviving tombstones of Anatolian heretics are in the Greek language. And yet, earlier pagan tombstones have survived which have been inscribed in Phrygian. Why then, have none of the early heretical Christian inscriptions, including those of the Montanists, been inscribed in one of the indigenous Anatolian tongues? If, in fact, Holl's dictum were strictly valid one would have expected to find epigraphical testimonial to this conjectured relation between the survival of heresy and that of indigenous languages. Obviously many of the pagan Anatolians were Greek-speaking (prior to their conversions to Christianity), and so were great numbers of Christian heretics. The process of Hellenization had been operative for a long time previous to the birth of the Christian religion. It is virtually impossible to substantiate Holl's thesis that the heretical and linguistic lines in central and western Asia Minor coincided to any significant extent.[304] It is quite possible or even probable, however, that an indigenous sect such as the Montanists, and nonindigenous sects such as the Manichaeans and Messalians, had a marked effect on the subsequent religious

[303] Holl, "Das Fortleben der Volkssprachen," p. 253.

[304] The Cappadocian speakers in the flock of St. Basil were Christianized long before the Greek-speaking population of the southern Peloponnese who were converted only in the ninth century. Constantine Porphyrogenitus, *De. Adm. Imp.*, trans. R. J. H. Jenkins, p. 237; "The inhabitants of the city of Maina are not of the race of the aforesaid Slavs, but of the ancient Romans, and even to this day they are called 'Hellenes' by the local inhabitants, because in the very ancient times they were idolaters and were worshippers of images after the fashion of the ancient Hellenes; and they were baptized and became Christians in the reign of the glorious Basil."

development in Anatolia and that they left a rich legacy which was partially incorporated by later sectaries.

Heresy in Asia Minor during the middle Byzantine period is closely linked first with the Paulicians (and to a lesser extent with the Athinganoi and Iconoclasts)[305] and then in the eleventh century above all with the Monophysites. The Paulician heresy, having entered Anatolia from Armenia, would seem to fit much more closely the patten that Holl has suggested in the relationship of national language and heresy, though even here it would be wrong to describe it as a "national" heresy, for the Armenian church fought this sect (as well as that of the Thondraki) with as much energy and violence as did the Byzantine church.[306] Further, once the heresy entered Byzantine territory it also attracted segments of the Greek population. By the mid-ninth century the sect was strongly established as a border principality in the regions of Melitene, Tephrice, Pontic Phanaroia, and Coloneia.[307] After the destruction of their state by Basil I, the Paulicians abandoned many of these regions and sought refuge farther to the east. It was not until the region of John Tzimisces that the Byzantine eastward drive incorporated sufficient numbers of them to cause further concern. At this later date many of them were transplanted to Thrace.[308]

---

[305] Starr, "An Eastern Sect, the Athinganoi," *Harvard Theological Review*, XXIX (1936), 93–106.

[306] The appearance of a considerable literature on the Paulicians in the postwar era indicates that the interest in this heretical sect has, if anything, increased. The best guide to this literature is to be found in the studies of M. Loos, "Où en est la question du mouvement paulicien?" *Izvestia na instituta za istoriia*, XIV–XV (1964), 357–371; "Gnosis und mittelalterlicher Daulismus," *Listy Filologicke*, XC (1967), 116–127; "Zur Frage des Paulikianismus und Bogomilismus," *Byzantinische Beiträge*, ed. J. Irmscher (Berlin, 1964), pp. 323–333; "Le mouvement paulicien à Byzance," *B.S.*, XXIV (1963), 258–286; XXV (1964), 52–68; "Deux contributions à l'histoire des Pauliciens. 1. A propos des sources grecques réflétant des Pauliciens," *B.S.*, XVII (1956), 19–57; 2. "Origine du nom des Pauliciens," *B.S.*, XVIII (1957), 202–217. R. M. Bartikian, *Istočnik dlia izuceniia istorii pavlikianskogo dviženia* (Erevan, 1961), reviewed by Loos in *B.S.*, XXIV (1963), 135–141. In this, and other studies ("Petr Citseliiskii i ego istoriia Pavlikian," *V.V.*, XVII [1961], 323–358; "K voprosu o pavlikianskom dviženii v pervoi polovine VIII v.," *V.V.*, VIII [1956], 127–131) he discusses among other things the Armenian sources and the reasons behind the westward movement of the Paulicians in the eighth century. See also his "Eretiki Arevordi (Syna Solntsa) v Armenii i Mesopotamii i poslanie armianskogo katolikosa Nersesa Blagodanogo," in *Ellinisticeskii Bliznii Vostok, Vizantiia i Iran* (Moscow, 1967), pp. 102–112. S. Runciman, *The Medieval Manichee* (Cambridge, 1955), places the Paulicians in the broader movement of dualistic heresies throughout the late ancient and medieval periods. Further literature includes, J. E. Lipsic, "Pavlikianskoe dviženie v Vizantii v VIII i pervoi polovine IX v.," *V.V.*, V (1952), 49–72; *Ocerki istorii vizantiiskogo obscestva i kultury (VIII-pervia polovina IX v.))* (Moscow-Leningrad, 1961), pp. 166 ff. F. Scheidweiler, "Paulikianer-probleme," *B.Z.*, XLIII (1950), 10–39. Grégoire, "Précisions," pp. 289–324; "Autour des Pauliciens," *Byzantion*, XI (1936), 610–614; "Les sources de l'histoire des Pauliciens, Pierre de Sicile est authentique et Photius un faux," *Bulletin de l'académie de Belgique*, XXII (1936), 95–114; "Pour l'histoire des églises pauliciennes," *O.C.P.*, XIII (1947), 509–514. K. Ter-Mkrttschian, *Die Paulikianer im byzantinischen Kaiserreiche und verwandte Erscheinungen in Armenien* (Leipzig, 1893).

[307] Runciman, *Manichee*, pp. 35–39. Grégoire, "Précisions," pp. 291–297.

[308] Runciman, *Manichee*, p. 44. Cedrenus, II, 382. Zonaras, III, 521–522.

The Paulician heresy had also appeared in parts of Anatolia farther to the west. In the upheavals among the members of the Paulician community, one of their leaders, a certain Joseph, moved to Chortocopaeum in the vicinity of Pisidian Antioch in the first half of the eighth century.[309] The Paulicians of western Anatolia survived as a sect for a considerable period, and they appear in the hagiographical literature of the tenth and eleventh centuries. St. Paul the Younger (d. 955) removed the most important and dangerous of these "Manichaeans" from the districts of the Cibyrrheote theme and Miletus.[310] A century later St. Lazarus of Galesium converted a village of heretics in the bishopric of Philetis (under Myra), and though the heretics are not mentioned by name, their geographical location (identical with that of the Manichaeans of St. Paul the Younger) and the fact that St. Lazarus converted a Paulician in his own monastery[311] would seem to indicate that these heretics were also Paulicians. As late as the tenth century the Paulicians were numerous in the regions of Euchaita where they seem to have caused the metropolitan considerable difficulty.[312]

The history of the Paulicians of Byzantine Anatolia becomes complicated and obscure in the eleventh and twelfth centuries with the appearance of the term "Bogomil" in the lexicography of the Greek theologians and historians. Euthymius, a monk from a Constantinopolitan monastery, records that he had been present at a trial of certain heretics in Acmonia of Phrygia sometime between 976 and 1025. He relates that these sectaries were known by two names: in the theme of the Opsicion they were called Phundagiagitai, but in the Cibyrrheote they went by the name of

---

[309] Runciman, *Manichee*, p. 35. Theophanes, I, 488, possibly indicates that they were to be found in Phrygia and Lycaonia in the early ninth century where along with the Athinganoi they appear as the befriended of Nicephorus I.

[310] I. Sirmondi, "Vita S. Pauli Iunioris," *A.B.*, XI (1892), 156, " Ἀπόδειξις τῶν εἰρημένων αἱ κατὰ τῶν μανιχαίων αὐτοῦ σπουδαί. ὧν τοὺς ἐπισημοτέρους καὶ τῷ βλάπτειν πιθανωτέρους, τῶν ὁρίων Κιβυρῥαιώτου τέ φημι καὶ Μιλήτου μακρὰν ἐκτετόπικε." The use of the word Manichee is archaistic and by this time it came to signify Paulician, Theophanes, I, 488, "τῶν δὲ Μανιχαίων, τῶν νῦν Παυλικιανῶν καλουμένων." Also, Grumel, *Registres*, I₂, 223.

[311] AS Nov. III, 512, 543. The saint's life gives a vivid picture of the heretics' hatred for the Orthodox. They are described as a numerous group with their center in one of the mountain villages.

[312] This emerges from a letter of the mid-tenth century addressed to Philotheus, metropolitan of that city (Darrouzès, *Épistoliers*, pp. 274–276). The sender of the letter, Theodore, metropolitan of Nicaea, opens by remarking that he sympathizes with the condition of Philotheus. The latter's condition, or rather that of his ecclesiastical district, is the presence of heretics, "ὅτι δέ σοι πληθὺς αἱρετιζόντων παρουσιάσαντι προσπελάσασα ..." Theodore then lists the necessary procedures for receiving into the Orthodox Church, Arians, Macedonians, Sabbatians, Novatians, Aristeroi, Tessareskaidekatitai, Apollinarians, Eunomians, Montanists, Sabellians, Jacobites, and *Paulinistai*. Without going into all of these, it would seem that Theodore is simply repeating an age old procedure without specific reference to conditions at Euchaita. However the phrase, ". . . καὶ τούτους δὴ τοὺς παυλινιστάς, περὶ ὧν σοι ὁ πλείων λόγος," indicates that Philotheus had written at length to Theodore about the Paulinistai, and it is they who have caused him concern. No doubt παυλινισταί (a fourth century sect) is an archaizing reference to παυλικιανοί, Paulicians.

Bogomils.[313] It is possible that these Phundagiagitai and Bogomils of western Anatolia were either the older Paulicians under a new name, or else they represent a mutation resulting from the grafting of Balkan Bogomilism onto the Paulician sect in a manner paralleling the relation of Paulicianism and Bogomilism in the Balkans.[314] In 1143 the Constantinopolitan synod condemned Clement of Sasima, Leontius of Balbissa, and the monk Niphon for spreading Bogomil practices in Cappadocia.[315] The terms Bogomil and Messalian, however, had come to be used as exact and interchangeable equivalents in the twelfth century so that the question is once more obscured.[316] In any case it is

[313] G. Ficker, *Die Phundagiagiten* (Leipzig, 1908), pp. 62–63. The twelfth-century metropolitan George Tornices reports the presence of heretics in Ephesus. R. Browning, "The Speeches and Letters of Georgios Tornikes, Metropolitan of Ephesos (XIIth Century)," *Actes du XII⁰ congrès international d'études byzantines* (Belgrade, 1964), II, 424.

[314] D. Obolensky, in his very useful book, *The Bogomils. A Study in Balkan Neo-Manichaeism* (Cambridge, 1948), pp. 174 ff, concludes that as the heresy appears under a Bulgarian name (Bogomil) and at a comparatively late date (976–1025), and because of the possible Bulgarian origin of one of its propagandists (John Tzurillas) the heresy was brought to Anatolia by the Bulgars in the latter half of the tenth century. He feels that this was all the more likely because of the "close" connection between Bithynia and Opsicion with the Balkan Slavs. The writings of Euthymius, Obolensky continues, describe a fusion of Paulician and Messalian teachings, a fusion that characterized Bogolimism. Thus the Bulgarian origin of the doctrines he attributes to John Tzurillas is confirmed by this double influence, Paulician and Messalian. For, he says, it was only in Thrace (inhabited by Paulicans and Messalians) that such a fusion could have taken place, and so Tzurillas must have brought these from Bulgarian lands.

This view, however, of the origins of the Bogomils and Phundagiagitai in western Anatolia encounters certain obstacles. The term *Phundagiagitai* (carriers of a sack or purse) is not of Slavic origin (though the Slavic *torbeski* appears later in the Balkans), and there is a good Anatolian precedent for this term in the so-called *saccophoroi* of the fifth century. Though the word "Bogomil" is of Slavic origin, it is possible that the term came to be applied to these Anatolian sects because of certain doctrinal similarities with the Bogomils of the Balkans. Byzantine usage of heretical nomenclature had, by this time, become quite loose. The comparatively late date (976–1025) of Euthymius' reference to the Bogomils and Phundagiagitai in western Anatolia does not necessarily prove that because of the time sequence the doctrines entered the peninsula from Bulgaria. For if the Bogomils-Phundagiagiati are in reality the Paulicians, they were present in western Anatolia much earlier. Even the argument based on the supposition that a fusion of Paulician and Messalian doctrines, which so characterized Bogomilism in the Balkans and the Bogomils and Phundagiagitai in Anatolia, could have taken place only in the Balkans is not at all certain. Not only were the Paulicians present in western Asia Minor (from the eighth through the eleventh century) but also the Messalians in Paphlagonia and Lycaonia in the first half of the eleventh century. Thus the fusion of Paulician and Messalian could have taken place in Anatolia as well as in the Balkans (Grumel, *Registres*, II₂, 263–264). Finally, to speak of "close" connections between Bulgaria and Bithynia-Opsicion in the eleventh century is to attribute to the eleventh century circumstances that may, or may not, have existed in the eighth century.

[315] Rhalles and Potles, V, 80–91. Grumel, *Registres*, I₃, 88–93. Papadopoulos-Kerameus, "Βογομιλικά," *V.V.*, II (1895), 720–723. On this see the articles of Loos and Gouillard.

[316] Rhalles and Potles, II, 531–532, speaks of the Οὐαλεντινιανοί as "οἱ εὑρεθέντες κατὰ τὸν καιρὸν τοῦ Οὐάλεντος τοῦ βασιλέως Βογόμιλοι, ἤτοι Μασσαλιανοί, καὶ Εὐχῖται, καὶ ᾽Ενθουσιασταί." VI,408, "Περὶ Μασσαλιανῶν τῶν νῦν βογομίλων." Also, V, 80. On this onomastic confusion in the tenth and eleventh centuries, H-C. Puech and A. Vaillant, *Le traité contre les Bogomiles de Cosmas le Prêtre* (Paris, 1945), p. 293. The sermon of the thirteenth-century patriarch, Germanus II, on the Holy Cross and the Bogomils does not specifically refer to Bogomils in the Nicaean Empire, *P.G.*, CXL, 621–644. Rather it is a homily on the holiness of the cross and at the same time excoriating the Bogomils because of their doctrine on the cross. Loos, "Certains aspects du Bogomilisme

probable that the Paulician tradition in Asian Minor played some role in the movements variously referred to as Messalian and Bogomil at this later date.

The most important influx of heretical Christian populations occurred in the latter part of the tenth and in the eleventh century. These were largely composed of Armenians and Syrian Monophysites, who came in to the eastern Anatolian provinces as a result of the Byzantine policies of transferring populations.[317] It is possible that the Thondraki may have come in at this time,[318] and that heretical Jewish Keraites entered Anatolia in the tenth century.[319] Attaliates remarked upon the influx of Monophysites, relating that the Byzantine districts of Iberia, Mesopotamia, and Melitene were full of them.[320] The important city of Melitene and its surrounding terrirories became the center of the Syrian Jacobites, whereas the Armenians had come as far west as Cilicia, Cappadocia, and Armeniacon. The Monophysites constituted by far the majority of the heretical population of Byzantine Anatolia in the eleventh century, and, of course, here linguistic differences coincided with heresy or religious differences.

The narrative at this point has focused on the two cardinal points of the languages and religions of Byzantine Anatolia. As these were the salient aspects of cultural differentiation, it is by their definition that the cultural character of Anatolia can best be described. Unfortunately, many of the smaller details of this cultural picture have disappeared. There is every reason to believe that in the late tenth and the early eleventh century, prior to the transplanting of the bulk of the Armenians and Syrians, Asia Minor to the eastern portions of Cappadocia, Trebizond, and to the northern confines of Cilicia was predominantly Greek-speaking and of the Chalcedonian rite. But Anatolia had not been so in late Roman and early Byzantine times. How, then, did such a cultural transformation come about? The processes operative had, to a certain degree, come into being before the foundation of the Byzantine Empire. Hellenism, either as a linguistic or institutional phenomenon, had by the time of Constantine I existed in Anatolia in one form or another for over a millenium. During the Hellenistic and Roman periods the Hellenic tradition had struck profound roots in Asia Minor and the local languages and cults were

---

byzantin des 11e et 12e siècles," *B.S.*, XXVIII (1967), 39–53, also shows reason to doubt the Bogomil affiliations of these personages.

[317] Vryonis, "Byzantium: The Social Basis of Decline in the Eleventh Century," *G.R.B.S.* II (1959), 169–173. Charanis, "The Armenians in the Byzantine Empire," *B.S.*, XXII (1961), 231–234.

[318] Bartikian, "Otvetnoe poslanie Grigoriia Magistra Pakhlavuni Siriiskomu Katolikosu," *P.S.*, VII (1962), 130–145. K. N. Yuzbashian, "Tondrakitskoe dviženie v Armenii i Pavlikiane," *Izv. Akad. Nauk. Arm. SSR*, no. 1 (1956), pp. 31–44. A-G. Ioanisian, "Dviženie Tondrakitov v Armenii (IX–XI vv.)," *Voprosy Istorii*, no. 10 (1954), pp. 100–108.

[319] Such at least is the assertion of Ankori, *Keraites, passim.*

[320] Attaliates, 97.

strongly affected. By the time of Constantine I, Anatolian city life, within the above-described geographical boundaries, was largely Greek. The native languages had either died, by the sixth century, or would soon expire.

Christianity had also made considerable progress in Anatolia by the time that Constantinople was founded. It had come to be one of the most extensively Christianized of all the Roman provinces. Again it was in the towns, apparently, that the new religion first spread and conquered. When Christianity expanded it came into contact with two general cultural milieus. First, it encountered the Hellenic or Hellenized urban population, and then, gradually, it spread to the less Hellenized, rural population. Though Hellenism had partially penetrated the rural areas, these latter remained far less affected than the towns. It was here, quite often, that the local cultural forms struggled the longest against both Hellenization and Christianization. The development of Christianity in Anatolia from the second to the sixth century reflects the product that resulted when Christianity confronted these two cultural types, the urban and the rural. In the case of the former, Hellenism and Christianity fused, producing the Cappadocian fathers, Amphilochius of Iconium, and others. In the case of the latter, though Christianity triumphed in the rural areas, the local cultural traits on some occasions reappeared within triumphant Christianity. The most spectacular example of this phenomenon may perhaps be seen in the emergence of Montanism, the greatest of the early local Anatolian heresies. One may generalize that subsequent Anatolian history is to a certain degree characterized by these two traditions right up to the eleventh century—the Hellenic tradition as typified by the Cappadocians, and the local heretical tradition exemplified by Montanism. But the point has already been made that this is a great oversimplication of the problem and stands in need of rigorous qualification. Though this Christianizing process did absorb local cultural variety, Montanism is the only really striking heresy to result from it; most of the local heresies were not so vital. Second, heresy often came into Byzantine Anatolia from the outside, and though one could argue that it prospered there because of local receptivity, it is in a sense different from the phenomenon just described. Third, there is evidence that even in the case of a supposedly local variety of "native" religious phenomenon such as Montanism, the heretics had been Hellenized linguistically.

After the removal of the imperial capital to Constantinople, Anatolia came increasingly within the focus of forces working for the transformation of the non-Greek speaking and non-Chalcedonian elements of the population. The emperors and patriarchs were most often Greek-speaking, Orthodox, and resident in a city, which though cosmopolitan and polyglot, was predominantly Greek. They formed the apex of Byzantine society, toward which the consciousness of all was focused.

In Anatolia the representatives of the government were largely Chalcedonian and most frequently Greek in tongue. Whether the Anatolian provincial served in the local military levies, or in the local administration, or went to the local courts for his business, or pursued learning and literature in educational institutions—Greek was the usual language for the relevant transactions. The language of the church in Anatolia was largely Greek. The Greek language enjoyed the prestige attendant upon any language used almost exclusively by governmental, ecclesiastical, and pedagogical institutions. It was also the usual language of commercial intercourse, and consequently the peasants coming into the urban areas to buy and sell were also exposed to Greek. Undoubtedly, the church must have contributed to the Hellenization of the rural areas, though here it is difficult to speak with certainty. From the bishoprics in the urban centers, the Greek-speaking church of Anatolia spread its organization and doctrine into the rural areas. A. H. M. Jones has gone so far as to make the seducing proposition that whereas it was the spread of the Hellenized type of urban center which Hellenized the cities and towns of Anatolia, it was the church that completed the process in the rural areas and finally presided over the extinction of some of the Anatolian tongues.[321]

The process of absorption and assimilation was constantly operative under these circumstances, though its success varied. In the long run, however, the prevalence of these general conditions favored the victorious progress of the dominant tongue and religion, Greek and Orthodoxy. There are innumerable specific instances of its success which help to give a general picture of its effect on the non-Greek non-Chalcedonians. Perhaps the most impressive recorded example of the church's success is what John the sixth-century bishop of Ephesus has described in his Ecclesiastical History. During the reign of Justinian I, John had been appointed to missionize among the pagans residing in the provinces of Asia (Ephesus), Caria, Phrygia, and Lydia. He began his Christianizing task by building four monasteries in the mountain village of Derira, which had evidently been the stronghold of the pagans. Justinian had generously supplied funds for the whole project and then provided that the new churches and monasteries be obedient to missionaries operating from Derira. The Christianization of this portion of rural Anatolia seems to have proceeded rapidly.[322]

The activity of the church in this respect is evidenced throughout Asia Minor. By the tenth and eleventh centuries there existed even among the Armenians a minority, but a significant one, which belonged to the Chalcedonian rather than to the Armenian church. These were the so-called Tzats, a group that included the Armenians, who had remained within the empire and accepted the Chalcedonian creed early, as well as

---

[321] Jones, *The Greek City*, p. 298.
[322] John of Ephesus-Payne Smith, pp. 229–233. Bar Hebraeus, I, 74.

many of the inhabitants of the districts of Tao-Khlarjeti and Meso-potamia.[323] The number of Armenian aristocrats who came to Byzantium and who appear as Chalcedonians is particularly impressive. One need mention only the families of Lecapenus, Tzimisces, Musele, Martinaces, Taronites, Tornices.

The conversionary activities of the church bore fruit among the Jews of the empire as well. The meager sources reveal converted Jews from late seventh-century Cappadocia, but the most famous example of a convert from Judaism was St. Constantine, a Jew of ninth-century Synnada.[324] Formulas by which Jews abjured Judaism and accepted Christianity have survived in a manuscript of the early eleventh century, and con-versions of Anatolian Jews to Christianity are evidenced as late as the twelfth century.[325]

During the long course of the struggle between Greeks and Arabs, considerable numbers of Muslims found their way into the Anatolian regions, sometime as prisoners of war, at other times as political refugees. The large group of Persians who fled to Anatolia in the reign of Theophilus were settled there, given Greek wives, and were baptized.[326] A well-known passage in the *De Caerimoniis* of Constantine Porphyrogenitus gives details as to the manner in which the central government imple-mented this policy of absorption through religious conversion. The text

---

[323] The fact that the Tzats were Armenian Chalcedonians seems to have been established by N. Marr, "Arkaun', Mongol'skoe nazvanie Khristian', v sviazi s' voprosom' ob Armianakh'-Khalkedonitak'," *V.V.*, XII (1906), 30–32. N. Adontz, "O proiskhoždenie Armia-Tsatov," *Ž.M.N.P.*, new series, XXXII (April, 1911), 243–245, attempted, unsuccessfully, to prove that Tzats were not Armenians but Gypsies. The subsequent studies of Peeters confirm Marr's identification of the Tzats with the Armenian Chal-cedonians. Peeters, "Sainte Sorisanik martyre en Arménie-Géorgie (14 Decembre 482–84)," *A.B.*, LIII (1935), 254–256. Here he gives a highly probable derivation of the term Tzat from the Arabic جاحد, *djahid*, a renegade. See also Peeters, "S. Grégoire, l'Illuminateur dans le Calendrier lapidaire de Naples," *A.B.*, LX (1942), 121–122; "Un témoinage autographe sur le siège d'Antioche par les Croisés en 1098," *Miscellanea historica in honorem Alberti De Meyer* (Louvain, 1946), I, 373–390; *Le Tréfonds oriental de l'hagiographie byzantine* (Brussels, 1950), pp. 162–163. I. Doens, "Nicon de la Montagne Noire," *Byzantion*, XXIV (1954), 134. As a result of the westward migrations of Armenians in Turkish times Chalcedonian Armenians were also to be found in western Anatolia. Settlements of these Chalcedonian Armenians, or Haikhrum as they are called in modern times, were to be found in the Bithynian villages of Choudion (Saradj Ustu), Ortakon, and Funduklu in the nineteenth century. According to their own traditions these Haikhrum had migrated from the Armenian district of Egin some two and one-half centuries previously, G. A. Paschalides, " Ἀρμενόφωνοι Ἕλληνες ἐν Χουδίῳ τῆς Μικρασίας," Ἑβδομάς VIII no. 45 (1891), pp. 2–3. Ecclesiastical vestments and objects from these villages are to be seen at the Benaki Museum in Athens. On the Haikhrum of nineteenth-century Kayseri, A. D. Mordtmann, *Anatolien. Skizzen und Reisebriefe aus Kleinasien* (1850–1859), ed. F. Babinger (Hanover, 1925), p. 492. G. Anastasiades. "Χάϊ-Χουρούμ (Ἀρμενόγλωσσοι Ἕλληνες)," *M.X.*, IV (1948), 37–48.

[324] AS Nov. IV, 629–631. Starr, *The Jews*, pp. 119–122.

[325] Starr, *The Jews*, pp. 173–180, 219–222. For the conversionary process as it affected the Jews of Attaleia in the twelfth century see the document in Zepos, *J.G.R.*, I, 373–375. Also, Cumont, "La conversion des Juifs byzantins au IXᵉ siècle," *Revue de l'instruction publique en Belgique*, XLVI (1903), 8–15.

[326] Cedrenus, II, 131. Symeon Magister, pp. 625–627. George Monachus, p. 793. Bar Hebraeus, I, 135.

remarks that Saracen captives settled in the various themes who should accept Christian baptism were to receive three nomismata on their baptism, six nomismata ὑπὲρ ζευγαρίου (for a yoke of oxen), and fifty-four *modia* of grain for seed and *annona*—a considerable incentive for a war prisoner to convert. But the imperial effort to assimilate these Muslims went further. Each Christian household that would take such a baptized Muslim into the family through marriage received a three-year exemption from the taxes of *kapnikon* and *synone*, and the land the convert received would be tax-free for three years.[327] A spectacular case of conversion was that of the Taghlabite tribe of the Banu Habib, a tribe that could put 10,000 to 12,000 cavalry into the field. Toward the middle of the tenth century, they and their families fled the Hamdanids, converted to Christianity, and settled in the provinces.[328]

The state and church continually subjected Christian heretics to pressure. Aside from the individual efforts of such monks as St. Lazarus in converting Paulicians,[329] or of Photius in bringing the Tessareskaidekatitai into the church,[330] there were the more systematic attempts to enforce Chalcedonian Christianity on the various nonconformists of Anatolia, attempts that the government backed with persecution. Such measures were applied, at various times, to Jews, Montanists, Paulicians, and Monophysites. Of a similar nature were the policies of Nicephorus Phocas during his reconquest of Cilicia, where all the Muslim population who wished to remain in the land might do so and retain their property by conversion to Christianity. Those who wished to remain Muslim had to depart from Cilicia.[331]

Thus the assimilative process on the religious plane was constantly in motion. Though it never achieved a complete and unqualified success, time favored it. In easternmost Anatolia it was a complete failure in the eleventh century, for here the Monophysite population was a majority and Monophysitism was too strongly associated with ethnic consciousness and linguistic differences.

The same forces that worked for Christianization (church, state, and the Greek Christian milieu of Anatolia) also worked for Hellenization on the linguistic plane. There are numerous examples of the preponderance of Greek among the population of western and central Anatolia. Catacolon Cecaumenus, whose grandfather apparently was an Armenian, wrote his *Strategicon* in Greek. Nicetas of Amnia, the grandson of St. Philaretus of

---

[327] Constantine Porphyrogenitus, *De Caerimoniis*, I, 694–695. A similar practice of tax exemption was adopted by the Seljuk sultan of Konya for his newly transplanted Greek peasants, see below, chapter iii. Bar Hebraeus, I, 144–145, 152.

[328] Canard, *Hamdanides*, I, 737–739. The ἀτζουπάδες seem to have been converts from Islam.

[329] AS Nov. III, 512, 543.

[330] C. Mango, *The Homilies of Photius, Patriarch of Constantinople* (Cambridge, 1958), pp. 279–292, they were almost certainly from Asia Minor. See Darrouzès, *Epistoliers*, pp. 274–275, for policy toward heretics in the metropolitanate of Euchaita.

[331] Bar Hebraeus, I, 171.

Armeniacon, recorded the life of his grandfather in Greek. Genesius the historian, though of Armenian ancestry, also recorded the affairs of the empire in the Greek language. Romanus Lecapenus and John Tzimisces, first generation Byzantines, were acclimatized to the Byzantine way of life and alienated from their Armenian patrimonial environment.[332] In some extreme cases Armenian aristocrats came under the literary and intellectual sway of the Greek classics. The famous Gregory Magistrus, who played a leading role in Armenian affairs during the eleventh century, translated Plato into Armenian.[333] The influence of these Greek authors is evident in the continuation of the translating activities of the Syrian Monophysites of eastern Asia Minor. Evidence, though sparse, exists also for the process of Hellenization of the Slavs of the peninsula and of the Jews.[334]

Anatolia on the eve of the Seljuk incursions constituted the most heavily populated, important, and vital province of medieval Hellenism, a province continuously subject to the integrating power of church, state, and culture emanating from the heart of the empire, Constantinople. The culture of Anatolia, however, reflected the disparate elements that had been submerged under the appearances of Hellenism and Orthodoxy. In some cases the older cultural localisms simply disappeared, but frequently they forced themselves into the cultural forms of Byzantine Anatolia. Though the peninsula was largely Hellenized in speech, there developed in the spoken Greek local variations and eventually dialects.[335] In religion, heresy remained a very vital fact in the life of the Byzantine Anatolians, as indeed of the Seljuk and Ottoman inhabitants, so that Anatolia exhibited a split religious personality—Orthodox and heterodox. It has often been asserted that this cultural variety deprived Anatolia of the social and cultural bonds of cohesion and predisposed the province to an easy conquest at the hands of the Turks. This is an inaccurate view, for all historical societies have been characterized by varying degrees of cultural variation, and the crucial question is rather the degree. One should note that though Syria, Egypt, and North Africa fell quickly before the Arabs, and the northern Balkans before the Slavs, central and western Anatolia resisted the Arabs for 400 years. The Turkish conquest, settlement, and absorption of the peninsula required another four centuries, so that it was not an accomplishment of the moment but one of gigantic proportions.

[332] Written testimony to this Hellenizing process among the Armenians appears in bilingual chrestomathies in the Egyptian papyri of the seventh century.

[333] V. Langlois, and M. Leroy, "Grégoire Magistros et les traductions arméniennes d'auteurs grecs," *A.I.P.H.O.S.*, III (1935), 263–294. Matthew of Edessa, p. 259.

[334] Vryonis, "St. Ioannicius the Great," pp. 245–248. Vasilievsky, *Trudy*, III, 65–68. On the partial Hellenization of the Jews of Mastaura T. Reinach, "Un contrat de mariage du temps de Basile le Bulgaroctone," *Mélanges offerts à M. Gustave Schlumberger* (Paris, 1924), pp. 118–132.

[335] Strabo speaks of καρίζειν and σολοικίζειν, see above. By the time that Dawkins studied Anatolian Greek it had become quite different from the Greek spoken in other regions. Most of this difference, however, was due to Turkish influence, see chapter vii.

II. *Political and Military Collapse of Byzantium in Asia Minor*

If, as we have seen in the preceding chapter, Asia Minor was the principal physical and spiritual reservoir upon which Constantinople drew, and if it had been Hellenized and Christianized to such a significant degree, how does one explain the apparent completeness and rapidity of the Byzantine political and military collapse in Asia Minor after the battle of Manzikert in 1071? Political and military decline before a foreign enemy do not necessarily stem from, and imply as their principal cause, a lack of significant ethnic and religious homogeneity, an implication historians often adumbrate in attempting to explain the decline of a state under attack by an outside foe. Though clearly facilitated by ethnic and religious pluralism, the political and military failure of Byzantium stemmed ultimately from political and military weakness. Actually, a number of far-reaching and complex events stretching over more than half a century had prepared the way for the Anatolian cataclysm of 1071, so it is not strictly accurate to speak in terms of a sudden catastrophe. Further, the Byzantine collapse in Anatolia in 1071 was not complete, for the Turkish conquest of Anatolia was a long process. In contrast to the Arab sub-jugation of the Middle East, which was comparatively rapid and brought far less upheaval, the Turkish conquest of Anatolia was much more piecemeal in nature, disruptive, and even destructive, lasting four centuries. The continued existence of Anatolia as a province of the dar al-harb is a fact that has been incisively illuminated by Paul Wittek, but the significance of this fact for the decline of Byzantine civilization and the process of Islamization in Anatolia remains to be appreciated and comprehended. The purpose of this chapter is to demonstrate that Byzantine defeat in eleventh-century Anatolia came as the culmination of a long series of complex developments, and that the process by which the Turks conquered and settled Anatolia was a long and repetitive one for large portions of the peninsula.[1] Consequently, the four centuries spanning

[1] Since a great deal has been written about the supposedly peaceful conquest of Anatolia (most recently see the paper of F. Sümer, "The Turks in Eastern Asia Minor in the Eleventh Century," *Supplementary Papers, Thirteenth International Congress of Byzantine Studies* [Oxford,

the initial Turkish appearance and the final reunification of Anatolia under one political authority constitute an epoch in the history of Anatolia characterized by wars, raids, upheavals, and chaos, interrupted by one peaceful, prosperous era (thirteenth century) and two transitional periods in which stability began to crystallize (mid-twelfth century and the consolidation of the beyliks in the mid-fourteenth century).

Events Leading to Manzikert

BYZANTINE INTERNAL DEVELOPMENTS (1025-71)

If one glances, even cursorily, at the intricate events in the internal and external history of Byzantium in the half century prior to Manzikert, he will realize that the Byzantine prostration in 1071 was the result of prolonged developments and not of a single isolated event, that is, the Turkish victory at Manzikert.[2] When one looks at the whirlwind that struck the empire in the eleventh century, he is not surprised that it collapsed before the Seljuks, but rather that it did not disappear completely from the pages of history. Instead, the empire made a partial recovery from these catastrophes and survived for three and one-half centuries. Among the developments that led to Manzikert was the vicious struggle for supreme political power in the state between bureaucrats and the military, a struggle related to the process of expansion of the landed

---

1966], pp. 141-143), it is necessary to describe at some length the actual conquest and to establish its prolonged character before proceeding to an analysis of this fact in chapter iii. There is no attempt, however, to ascertain all the political and military specifics of this four-hundred-year period as the task would be enormous and unnecessary for the purposes of this book. The mere establishment of all the dates of this long period would in itself call for a special monograph.

[2] The best statement and analysis of these events is the chapter of P. Charanis, "The Byzantine Empire in the Eleventh Century, in K. M. Setton, *A History of the Crusades* (Philadelphia, 1955), I, 177-219. Also R. J. H. Jenkins, *The Byzantine Empire on the Eve of the Crusades* (London, 1953); S. Vryonis, "Byzantium: The Social Basis of Decline in the Eleventh Century," *Greek Roman and Byzantine Studies*, II (1959), 159-175. Still of interest is C. Neumann, "La situation mondiale dans l'empire byzantin avant les Croisades," trans. Renauld and Kozlowski in *Revue de l'Orient latin*, X (1905), 57-171. Arnold J. Toynbee, *Study of History* (Oxford, 1948), IV, 72-73, 395-400, also insists that the decline of Byzantium resulted from events that occurred long before Manzikert. His assertion, however, that Byzantium declined partly as a result of its victories over the Bulgars at the end of the tenth and in the early eleventh century is yet one more of his literary mysticisms. The subject of the eleventh century was the central theme of the Thirteenth International Congress of Byzantine Studies at Oxford in 1966. But little that is new emerged from the papers dealing with the subject of Byzantine decline during this century. Relevant to Byzantine decline are, N. Svoronos, "Société et organisation intérieure dans l'empire byzantin au XIe siècle: les principaux problèmes"; H. Evert-Kappesowa, "Société et organisation intérieure au XIe siècle," pp. 121-124; E. Stanescu, "Solutions contemporaines de la crise: Un quart de siècle de réformes et contre-réformes impériales," pp. 125-129; *Supplementary Papers, Thirteenth International Congress of Byzantine Studies* (Oxford, 1966). The paper of C. Toumanoff, "The Background to Manzikert," promises much but unfortunately is nothing more than a very general survey of Transcaucasian relations with Byzantium over several centuries. It in no way explains the outcome at Manzikert and in general is the most disappointing of the papers on the eleventh century. See the very interesting article of P. Lemerle, "Le notion de décadence à propos de l'empire byzantin," in R. Brunschvig and G. von Grunebaum, *Classicisme et déclin culturel dans l'histoire de l'Islam* (Paris, 1957), pp. 263-277.

magnates by which the latter sought to absorb the free peasantry and the free landholdings. The economic difficulties of the eleventh century, though not known in sufficient detail, are nevertheless manifest in the rise of tax farming, sale of offices, debasement of the coinage, appearance of the Venetians as the merchants of the empire, and the granting of *excuseia* and *pronoia*. All these factors led to the breakdown of the Byzantine military, naval, and administrative systems in varying degrees. The empire, polyglot and multisectarian in nature, and stretching from the Danube to the Euphrates, had the double liability of nonhomogeneous populations and extensive, widely separated frontiers. Thus ethnic and religious difficulties, some of which became critical in the eleventh century, plagued Byzantium throughout this period. All were of an internal nature, having arisen within the borders of the state, but external events, equally alarming, occurred at this time. In the west, Norman adventurers laid the foundations of a new kingdom in Italy and Sicily, and the mercantile endeavors of Venice began to attain a commercial and political crescendo. Both polities were in a sense Constantinople-oriented. The Normans had set their Italian state in Byzantine ground on a Byzantine foundation, and their gaze and desires came to be fixed upon Constantinople itself. The Venetians, closely associated with the East in the past, now became so preoccupied with their commercial interests in Constantinople and in the other emporia of the empire, that they were to play a role of the first order in the decline of Byzantium during the twelfth century. Onto the northern and eastern borders were to spill the tribal hordes of the Ural-Altai in one of those many migratory waves that since the beginning of the empire had threatened to inundate the civilization of New Rome. These tribes, members of the same great linguistic family and the products of the same harsh steppe environment, made their way to Byzantium by separate routes. The Patzinaks, Uzes, and Cumans traveled across the Russian steppe and around the northern shores of the Black Sea to the Danube. The Seljuks came down into the Islamic world via Khurasan, subjugating Baghdad and a large part of the lands of the caliphate, during which process large numbers of Turkmen tribes made their way or were intentionally sent to the eastern Anatolian borders of Rum.

The most significant factor among all these developments was the convulsion of eleventh-century Byzantine society arising from the violent struggle between the representatives of the civil bureaucracy in the capital and the military magnates in the provinces. The party of the bureaucrats in the eleventh century included certain aristocratic families (such as those of Ducas and Monomachus) who came to be associated with the central administration in Constantinople and a portion of the senate. It comprehended in addition the professors and many of the graduates of the refounded University of Constantinople, people such as Psellus and

Xiphilenus who had risen to prominence in the government because of their intellectual brilliance. Finally, the bureaucratic party embraced all those who had entered the administration and risen through the ranks, such as Philocales, John Orphanotrophus, and Nicephoritzes. The basis of bureaucrat power lay in a number of items, not the least of which was the fact that the bureaucrats were located in Constantinople, the center of the empire and its political life. Here they were close to the emperor, could influence and control him, and could isolate him from the provincial militarists. In Constantinople they were in virtual control of the imperial navy and troops stationed in that area and were in possession of an impregnable city. They also presided over the vital domain of finances. Because of all this the civil administrators were possessed of real power and they were able to control the flow of internal politics for a great part of the eleventh century. The magnate-generals from the provinces were able to remove this element from power only after a long, violent, and exhausting struggle.

The generals consisted of the landed magnates in the provinces, who served as the leaders of the armies levied in Anatolia and the Balkans. Often these aristocrats belonged to families with centuries-long military traditions while others had arisen more recently, during the wars of Basil II or even later. In any case, these aristocrats were characterized by their possession of great landed estates and by a virtual monopoly of the generalships of the provincial armies. The families of Phocas, Sclerus, Maleinus, Comnenus, Melissenus, and others, dominate both the agrarian and military history of Byzantium. By virtue of this combination—great landed wealth and military prominence—the provincial aristocrats were an inordinately powerful and ambitious social group. It was this power of the provinces which eventually corroded and in effect destroyed centralized government in Byzantium and in this sense constituted a "feudalizing" element.

The political ambitions of the provincial generals had already threatened to exceed all bounds in the tenth century, but fortunately Nicephorus Phocas and John Tzimisces, though of this social class, were able as emperors to exercise a restraining hand on the political activities of the generals. In the early years of the reign of Basil II, however, the generals plunged the empire into a long civil war that almost succeeded in removing the Macedonian dynasty and in dividing the empire. Thanks to the appearance of the grim Basil, the disrupting violence of the provincial aristocracy was temporarily bridled by policies of persecution which entailed discriminatory legislation, confiscation of their great landed estates, and exile. As a result of Basil's successful opposition to the political designs of the generals, the bureaucrats were able to keep the generals from political power for thirty-two years after the death of Basil II (1025–57).

During the course of these thirty-two years, the heads of the bureau-cratic group, most important of whom were John Orphanotrophus and Constantine IX Monomachus, waged a constant war against the ambitions of the generals. The fact that Constantine VIII had died in 1028 leaving no heir save his three daughters added fuel to the struggle, and thus the contest between bureaucrats and generals centered on the question of succession. The bureaucrats attempted, successfully, to find a "bureaucrat" husband for the unfortunate empress Zoe, one who would be subordinate and obedient to those bureaucrats promoting him. On the other hand members of the military class also appeared as candidates; but because of the tight hold that the bureaucrats had on the central apparatus of administration in Constantinople, they succeeded in promoting to the position of power men who were in sympathy with the bureaucrats. The only recourse that the generals had in this struggle for political power was the provincial armies. During this thirty-two year period of civilian preponderance in the capital, the sources record thirty major rebellions, or about one every year, and the list of the generals who were exiled, executed, or blinded is a long and monotonous one. Rebellion became such a commonplace occurrence that the shrewd general Cecaumenus included in his *Strategicon* a chapter on the conduct of a prudent man during the outbreak of rebellions.[3] As the program of the bureaucrats called for the elevation to the throne of men who would be primarily obedient to the bureaucrats, obedience alone came to be the criterion of selection with the consequence that there was a series of husband-emperors of little ability and with no worthy conception of the duties of such an august office. The Byzantine state had the evil fate of experiencing as its rulers (from 1028 to 1057) emperors of the lowest caliber, for the most part ill, old, or dominated by women and the eunuchs, and concerned only with enjoying the pleasures of their office.

In 1057 the generals were able to win their first victory in the struggle with the bureaucrats when the Anatolian general Isaac Comnenus revolted. Aided by other Anatolian magnates (most important of whom were Sclerus, Bourtzes, Botaniates, Argyrus, and Cecaumenus), he brought the military forces of Anatolia against Constantinople. In spite of this impressive show of force, it is highly doubtful that the generals would have succeeded had it not been for other factors. Within the capital itself the patriarch and the guilds had sided with the generals, and of equal importance was the split in the ranks of the bureaucrats, which saw the Ducas family temporarily abandon the bureaucrats and join the generals. As the generals had been able to win only with the aid of other social groups, their victory was not complete and so their enjoyment of the political fruits was correspondingly incomplete. Upon the illness of Isaac in 1059, the representatives of the bureaucratic party, Psellus and

[3] Cecaumenus, 73–74.

Constantine Ducas, seized power and the generals were once more excluded. By 1067 a military reaction and another split in the ranks of the bureaucrats once more brought an Asia Minor general Romanus IV Diogenes to the throne. But the reign of Romanus was hamstrung, as had been that of Isaac, by the incomplete victory of the generals and by the persistence of the leading bureaucrats (Psellus and John Ducas) in the government. The results of this military-civil hatred were disastrous for the state. From the death of Basil II in 1025 down to the fateful battle of Manzikert, Byzantine society lay in the convulsive throes of civil strife between administrators and soldiers. Other segments of society, the church and the guilds in the capital, had also been drawn into the power struggle, first on one side then on the other.

The contest was characterized by a feature that usually marks all such political struggles: the determination to attain political power at all costs and in spite of all consequences. Obviously the principal weapons in the hands of the generals were the armies stationed in the provinces and so when the generals rebelled in the east or the west, all the armies of Anatolia or the Balkans would be mustered and then directed toward the capital city of the empire. It was in this manner, when Isaac Comnenus rebelled in 1057, that Anatolia was denuded of its military defenses for reasons of political interest.[4] And in 1047–48 during the rebellion of Tornices, the western armies were commanded to march on Constantinople, leaving much of the Balkans bare of troops. In this case the eastern borders were also stripped in order to bring troops to defend Constantinople against the armies of Tornices.[5] The generals were determined to use this, their only weapon, in the struggle with the bureaucrats. In so doing, however, they were simultaneously baring the frontiers in the face of growing enemy pressures and destroying these forces by pitting the armies of Anatolia against those of the Balkans.

The bureaucrats, in a sense at the mercy of the generals when it came to military affairs, defended themselves by embarking upon the dismantling of the military apparatus. This included the dismissal of competent generals, in some cases the dissolution of entire military corps, but above all the cutting off of financial support of the local, indigenous troops forming the thematic levies, who were fast being replaced by foreign mercenaries. This overall policy becomes clearly apparent with Constantine IX Monomachus during whose reign the prize moneys of the soldiers and revenues that were ostensibly marked for military expeditions were diverted to the use of others, without benefit to the state.[6] He converted the army of the province of Iberia, 50,000(?) strong and crucial for the defense against the Seljuks, from a body that owed

[4] Cedrenus, II, 625–627. H. Mädler, *Theodora, Michael Stratiotikos, Isaak Komnenos* (Plauen, 1894).

[5] Attaliates, 29. Cedrenus, II, 562.

[6] Psellus-Renauld, I, 121.

military service, into a taxpaying community. The transformation of the army into a taxpaying unit not only deprived the area of its defense but also caused many of the inhabitants to go over to the Seljuks.[7] Thus at one blow a key province in the defense of Asia Minor was deprived of its military strength during the period when the Seljuks appeared on the eastern borders. With the gradual dissolution of the provincial, indigenous armies, the emperors began to rely increasingly upon foreign mercenaries. It is true that mercenary troops had always been employed in the past by the emperors, but thematic levies had been more important. Now the mercenaries would replace the Byzantine soldiery in primary importance and the empire's armies came to be characterized more and more by the presence of these mercenary troops that included a bewildering ethnic array—Normans, English, Russians, Georgians, Alans, Armenians, Patzinaks, Turks, Arabs, and other foreign groups.

By the reign of Constantine X Ducas the depletion of the local levies and the reliance upon foreign mercenaries was to become nearly complete. Constantine ruled through the foremost representatives of the bureaucratic element, the university professors Psellus and Xiphilenus, the former in charge of the administration and the latter in charge of the church. At the end of his reign, the destruction of the armies by the bureaucrats, which was already under way during the reign of Constantine IX, had gone so far that the provincial forces were no longer feared either by the civil element of the capital or, more ominously, by the Seljuks, Patzinaks, Uzes, and Normans on the borders. This antimilitary policy of the bureaucrats was continued in all its vigor even after the battle of Manzikert, when it was obvious to all that the army was the most important factor in the survival of the empire. The accession of Michael VII Ducas to the throne (1071), a scion of the leading bureaucratic family and the pupil of Psellus, was most unfortunate in this respect. For he

busied himself continuously with the useless and unending study of eloquence and with the composition of iambics and anapests; moreover he was not proficient in this art, but being deceived and beguiled by the consul of the philosophers [Psellus], he destroyed the whole world, so to speak.[8]

With the crippling of the native military strength, the increased reliance upon the services of foreign troops brought a double liability: questionable loyalty, and far greater financial expense. The numbers of mercenary troops, if one can judge by the information that the sources relate in connection with the revolt of Isaac Comnenus in 1057, was not insignificant. Of the troops collected on the northeastern frontier by Catacolon Cecaumenus in this year, there were two *tagmata* of Franks, one *tagma* of Russians, and only two *tagmata* of Chaldians and Coloneians. In other words three-fifths of these were foreign mercenaries, as were

---

[7] Cecaumenus, p. 18. Attaliates, 44–45. Cedrenus, II, 608. Zonaras, III, 646.
[8] Scylitzes, II, 725.

also the Armenian levies of Sebasteia, Melitene, and Tephrice.[9] There were enough Normans in Anatolia by the reign of Michael VII so that the Armenian rebel Philaretus Brachamius was able to enlist the services of 8,000.[10] When Alexius Comnenus set out to halt the advance of Nicephorus Bryennius, he had in addition to his Norman troops, 2,000 Turks from Anatolia.[11] Nicephorus Palaeologus was sent to the Caucasus where he raised 6,000 Alans with which he was supposed to suppress the rebellion of Roussel,[12] and Roussel himself had perhaps something like 3,000 Normans in his service.[13] Although it is impossible to obtain anything like exact figures of the mercenaries, and even though some of the figures often reproduced may be exaggerated, they indicate that by the mid-eleventh century mercenaries had replaced or supplemented the indigenous troops of the Byzantine armies. The presence and activities of these mercenaries in eleventh-century Anatolia were to play a prominent role in the Byzantine collapse. As their only bond of loyalty to the empire was based on their salaries, any financial difficulties of the state which might delay or lessen these financial rewards would of course break the slender bond that held them to the empire. In 1057 the Norman chief Herve Frankopoulus, dissatisfied at not having obtained a promotion, retired to the theme of Armeniacon and deserted to the Turk Samuh who was then raiding the eastern borders.[14] In 1063, after having returned to the services of the emperor, he betrayed the Byzantine commander of Edessa to the enemy for which deed he was summoned to Constantinople and drowned in the Bosphorus.[15] Herve is only one example from many that would appear as events progressed. This pattern of mercenary disloyalty, rebellion, and ravaging of the very provinces that they had been hired to defend becomes a singularly constant theme in these bleak years of the empire's history.

Finally, the strife of bureaucrats and generals resulted in the summoning of Turkish invaders, each side bidding highly for the favor of Turkish chiefs and generals and for the services of their troops. On each occasion that the two factions prepared for military action, victory usually depended on success in acquiring the services of the Turkish chieftains. This pattern, however, did not come to prevail until after the battle of Manzikert.

The single most fateful development leading to the defeat of Byzantium in Anatolia was, then, this vicious contest for political power between the bureaucrats and the generals, consuming as it did the energies of the state

[9] Cedrenus, II, 625–626.
[10] Matthew of Edessa, p. 174.
[11] Bryennius, 130, 140–143. Attaliates, 288 ff.
[12] Bryennius, 83–84.
[13] Attaliates, 188.
[14] Cedrenus, II, 616–619. G. Schlumberger, "Deux chefs normands des armées byzantines au XIe siècle: sceaux de Hervé et de Roussel de Bailleul," *R.H.*, XVI (1881), 294.
[15] Matthew of Edessa, pp. 118–120.

in a destructive manner at a time when the external pressures were becoming dangerous. It resulted in the studied and intentional neglect of the indigenous armies and in the reliance upon expensive and less reliable mercenary bodies. These latter, because of their lack of loyalty and because of tardiness in their payment, did not hesitate to plunder and ravage the very lands that they had been hired to defend, or even to desert to the Turks.

Of considerable importance in the decline of the indigenous armies as well as in the socioeconomic difficulties of the state, were the growth and expansion of the landed aristocracy and the corresponding decline of the free peasant and the free landholding soldier. Though it has been customary to assign primary importance to this phenomenon in Byzantine decline, it would seem that in terms of the eleventh century and the Turkish invasions, the struggle between bureaucrats and generals was more important in the dissolution of the thematic levies. It is true, however, that this other process had been at work for a long time and entailed the weakening of peasant soldiery and of state finances. The existence of the free peasant community had been of crucial economic, military, and social importance to the state in the period of its greatness. This free village community had formed the basic financial unit for purposes of the Byzantine tax system, and it was on the basis of a portion of this land of the free communities that the thematic armies were largely supported. Finally, the existence of these free rural communities, which paid the taxes and performed military service, provided for a healthy social structure and a balance against the provincial aristocrats. This social structure was threatened and altered by the decline of the free peasantry which occurred when, for one reason or another, the peasant abandoned his land or his title to it. The crucial phase of this decline was the appearance of the powerful landowner (both ecclesiastical and lay) in the communities during the tenth and eleventh centuries. The peasants sold or gave their land to the magnates, sometimes willingly in order to escape burdens imposed by taxation, inclement weather, famine; at other times unwillingly, having been the victims of coercion by the powerful. Though the emperors realized that the diminution of the free peasant community would have disastrous results on financial and military affairs and so legislated accordingly,[16] nevertheless they were in the end unable to halt the process. The strenuous efforts of the tenth-century rulers had a certain staying effect, but with the death of Basil II and the appearance of lesser men on the throne, the dynamics of the process carried all resistance before it. The free peasantry, though it continued to exist, had been significantly weakened, and henceforth the numbers of *paroicoi* (serfs) of the state,

---

[16] Zepos, *J.G.R.*, I, 201. In the introductory paragraph of the novella attributed to Romanus(922), it is stated that the law was promulgated because "we have great concern for the public taxes and for the performance of military and civil duties."

church, and magnates increased greatly, while the numbers of the free peasantry declined.[17] The increase of the *paroicoi* was accompanied by the increase of state-granted exemptions, such as *excuseia* and *pronoia*, on behalf of the magnates.[18] Thus the free peasantry declined in a process that did not provide the state with any sufficient recompense for its loss of revenues and soldiery. Simultaneously, the magnates became more powerful and thus a greater menace to central authority. Byzantium was in the process of an evolution that, for want of a better word, must be described as "feudalization."

The economic decline and especially its causes are not sufficiently documented by the sources, yet the coinage of this period reflects with grim accuracy the hard times that had beset the Byzantines. Beginning with the reign of Michael IV (1034–41) and continuing until the reign of Alexius I (1081–1118) the solidus underwent a radical debasement, a debasement that destroyed the purity of the "dollar of the middle ages." [19] Among those developments that had the most serious economic repercussions was the above-mentioned social evolution that weakened the free peasant community and strengthened the landowning class. The former was the basis of the tax system, and the latter received vast exemptions from taxes, thus this social phenomenon brought dire economic consequences to state finance. The effect on finance by the time of Isaac Comnenus had become very serious.[20]

[17] The entire history of Byzantine social and agrarian evolution has been exposed to a vigorous and searching reconsideration by P. Lemerle in his study, "Esquisse pour une, histoire agraire de Byzance: Les sources et les problèmes," *R.H.*, CCXIX (Jan.-Mar., 1958), 32–74; (Avr.-Juin., 1958), 254–284; (Juillet-Set., 1958), 43–94. Many of his conclusions and propositions suggest important alterations in the studies of G. Ostrogorsky, especially "Agrarian Conditions in the Byzantine Empire in the Middle Ages," *Cambridge Economic History* (Cambridge, 1941), I, 194–223; *Pour l'histoire de la feodalité byzantine* (Brussels, 1954), pp. 10–13. All three studies, nevertheless, attest to the financial, military, and social significance of the free peasantry and to the importance of its decline. Ostrogorsky has, however, changed his views somewhat on the free peasantry in the monograph, "*La paysannerie byzantine* (Brussels, 1956). Most recently, N. Svoronos, "Les privilèges de l'église à l'époque des Comnènes: un rescrit inédit de Manuel Ier Comnène," *Travaux et Mémoires* (Paris, 1965), I, 357 ff. Kaegi, "Some Reconsiderations," pp. 39–53. A. Hohlweg, "Zur Frage der Pronoia in Byzanz," *B.Z.*, LX (1967), 288–308.

[18] For a brief discussion and bibliography see Charanis, "The Byzantine Empire," p. 204.

[19] P. Grierson, "Notes on the Fineness of the Byzantine Solidus," *B.Z.*, LIV (1961), 91–97, which modifies his earlier study "The Debasement of the Bezant in the Eleventh Century," *B.Z.*, XLVII (1954), 379–394.

[20] Charanis, "Economic Factors in the Decline of the Byzantine Empire," *The Journal of Economic History*, XIII (1953), 412–424. Also Attaliates, 60–62, who indicates that the effect on finances by the time of Isaac Comnenus had become ruinous. The economic decline and especially its causes in the eleventh century are not sufficiently documented. One may consult with profit the following works of R. Lopez: "Un borgne au royaume des aveugles: La position de Byzance dans l'économie européene du haut moyen age," *Association Marc Bloch de Toulouse* (1953–1955), 25–30; "Du marché temporaire à la colonie permanente. L'Évolution de la politique commerciale au moyen age," *Annales. Économies-Sociétés-Civilisations*, IV (Oct.-Dec., 1949), 389–405; "The Dollar of the Middle Ages," *The Journal of Economic History*, XI (1951), 209–234. For the sale of offices, G. Kolias, *Ämter-und Würdenkauf im früh- und mittelbyzantinischen Reich* (Athens, 1939).

There has been some discussion as to the failure of the Byzantines to develop a trading class and a commercial spirit such as developed in Italy. The proponents of this theory maintain that this oversight on the part of Byzantines (according to them it was really a congenital defect rather than an oversight) was a basic cause in its collapse and in the triumph of Venice. But if one examines the question he will see that perhaps this supposed shortcoming has been exaggerated and that it was not responsible for the collapse of the state first before the Turks and then before Venice. In fact, what little source material is at hand testifies that maritime and land commerce both on a local and international scale, as well as a merchant-artisan class, played a prominent role in Byzantine economic life,[21] and regardless of whether the commerce was carried by Greek or foreign merchants, the state collected large sums in taxes from both. There is no indication that this trade had halted in the eleventh century except insofar as disorders in the provinces might have interfered. That this supposed lack of a developed merchant class and spirit did not substantially contribute to the economic decline in the eleventh century is apparent from the state of finances at the end of Basil's reign in 1025. The fisc was in such excellent shape that the emperor left the taxes of the poor uncollected for the last two years of his reign.[22] Any government that can afford to leave taxes uncollected for a period of two years is in better than average condition. That Venice did triumph over the Byzantines is clearly illustrated by the series of treaties and events between the two states beginning with the reign of Alexius I and ending in the Fourth Crusade. But the reasons for this economic triumph are not that the inhabitants of the lagoons developed a commercial mentality whereas the coastal inhabitants of the empire did not, rather it was political events that contributed so greatly to the economic fortunes of Venice and destroyed those of Byzantium. The appearance of the Normans in Italy, the decline of the Byzantine naval and land forces, and the specter of political disaster hanging over the empire in 1081 were the determining factors that induced Alexius I to accord the first of that fateful series of chrysobulls to the Italian cities. It was the stipulations of these treaties which made Venetian fortunes, because henceforth Byzantine merchants suffered a tax discrimination to the advantage of their Venetian competitors. Venetian merchants, in fact, enjoyed the benefits of a "protective tariff," that is, they were exempt from paying the 10 percent *ad valorem* tax on the goods they carried, whereas the Greeks were forced to continue paying it. As a result, the Venetians could and did acquire almost a monopoly of the carrying trade, for they could pay more for the goods and then sell them cheaper than the Byzantine merchants. Once they acquired superiority in

[21] See chapter i for references to this trade.
[22] Cedrenus, II, 484. Psellus-Renauld, I, 19–20, relates that he had to construct underground chambers to store the excess in the treasury.

the carrying trade, the 10 percent *ad valorem* tax on all those cargoes escaped forever the coffers of the imperial treasury in Constantinople. The commercial victory of the Venetians was not due to their superior commercial spirit and to the Byzantine congenital defect in the same, but rather to that confluence of political circumstances which forced the empire to purchase the aid of the Venetian fleet at a dear price. The superiority of the Venetians lay primarily in their privileged and tax-free position in contrast to the position of their Byzantine competitors. Even so, Italian commercial supremacy and its consequences occurred after the battle of Manzikert, and so contributed neither to the socioeconomic nor to the political decline that led to Manzikert.

The extravagance of the rulers in the eleventh century came to be commonplace. The Empress Zoe, Constantine IX Monomachus, and the Paphlagonians were remarkably prodigious in exhausting the imperial coffers that Basil II had been so careful to fill.[23] Also the tax-yielding provinces in the Balkans and Anatolia were disturbed by other events above and apart from the socioeconomic developments affecting the peasant communities.[24] The numerous rebellions, the countless foreign raids (especially in the Balkans), and the depredations of the mercenaries, kept the provincial tax system out of balance. The economic decline of the eleventh century, though still imperfectly understood, played a serious role in the events leading to Manzikert. Stemming primarily from the social evolution of agrarian society and the grants of excessive immunities to the great landowners, economic conditions were further aggravated by the extravagance of the rulers, and above all by the military rebellions, Patzinak raids, and mercenary rapacity in the provinces which choked off the state tax moneys. Such financial difficulty was of course disastrous for a state that functioned primarily on the basis of a money economy.

But there were also serious external developments.

THE FIRST APPEARANCE OF THE TURKS

The first appearance of the Turkish raiders in the district of Vaspuracan (1016–17) struck terror in the Armenians who dwelt there.

In the beginning of the year 465 a calamity proclaiming the fulfillment of divine portents befell the Christian adorers of the Holy Cross. The death-breathing

---

[23] Psellus-Sewter, p. 237. "As I have often remarked, the emperors before Isaac exhausted the imperial treasures on personal whims. The public revenues were expended not on the organisation of the army, but on favors to civilians and on magnificent shows . . . they not only emptied the palace treasury, but even cut into the money contributed by the people to the public revenues . . . while the military were of course being stinted and treated harshly."

[24] On the eve of a rebellion, the Byzantine insurgents collected the taxes for themselves. The Norman bands alternatively pillaged provinces and "collected" taxes for themselves. The constant appearance of the Patzinaks and Uzes in the Balkans must have meant not only a cutting off of the taxes from Constantinople but also a serious disturbance of the tax-producing communities. It is related that after one such raid the inhabitants thought of abandoning Europe.

dragon appeared, accompanied by a destroying fire, and struck the believers in the Holy Trinity. The apostolic and prophetic books trembled, for there arrived winged serpents come to vomit fire upon Christ's faithful. I wish to describe, in this language, the first eruption of ferocious beasts covered with blood. At this period there gathered the savage nation of infidels called Turks. Setting out, they entered the province of Vaspuracan and put the Christians to the sword.... Facing the enemy, the Armenians saw these strange men, who were armed with bows and had flowing hair like women.[25]

At the time of this Turkish appearance in Vaspuracan the empire was extending its power in the East and its armies inspired fear in the hearts of its enemies from the Danube to the Euphrates. The Greek chroniclers took almost no notice of this first appearance of the Turks in Armenia; Cedrenus merely remarked that the Armenian prince Senecherim, being under pressure from his Agarene neighbors, later abandoned Vaspuracan to Basil II and settled in Cappadocia (1021) at which time the Turkish raiders appeared in the Armenian district of Nig.[26] Though the Byzantines and Armenians had seen Turkish slave troops and generals in the Arab armies and had had contact with Patzinaks and Khazars, the Turks of 1016–17 (whether or not they were affiliated with the Seljuks) were as yet unknown to them.

Nevertheless, in half a century from the first appearance of these Turks in Vaspuracan, the Seljuk nomadic raiders would have established an

---

[25] Matthew of Edessa, pp. 40–41. The English is my own rendition of Dulaurier's French translation and conveys the same sense as the Russian translation of Agadzanov-Yuzbašian. The date, however, has been altered from 467 to 465 for the reasons given by S. G. Agadzanov and K. N. Yuzbašian, "K istorii tiurskikh nabegov na Armeniiuv-XI v.," *P.S.*, XII (1965), 149. Both 465 and 467 occur in manuscripts of Matthew of Edessa, but the former is fixed by the text of Cedrenus. The confusion in the Muslim, Greek, Armenian, and Syriac sources has greatly obscured the questions of the dates of the early Turkish invasions and the affiliation of the earliest Turkish raiders with the main Seljuk group. The most satisfactory examination of these two points, date of appearance of the first Turks in Armenia and their tribal affiliations, is that of Agadzanov-Yuzbašian. According to them the first Turkish raids in Armenia were those of 1016–17 (in Vaspuracan) and 1021 (in Nig). But the Turkmens who made these raids were probably not Seljuk Turks. They represented tribesmen (as well as Turkish gulams of local military potentates) who had moved into Adharbaydjan and been received in the military forces of the Rawwadids of Tabriz and the Shaddadids of Gandja. In 1029 a group of Seljuks rebelled against Mahmud of Ghazna, were defeated, and 2,000 moved west, eventually to Adharbaydjan. They may have participated in the attack of local Muslim forces on the regions of Lake Van in 1033–34, but they definitely attacked Armenian lands in 1037–38, though Turks had raided Vaspuracan as early as 1016–17. Though the affiliation of these Turks of 1016–17 is not mentioned in Matthew, as Agadzanov-Yuzbašian rightly point out, their affiliation with the Seljuks is not necessarily excluded, for this group may have split off early and made its way westward unnoticed. Cahen has put forth the thesis that the events Matthew ascribes to 1016–17 actually took place a decade later when a group of Oghuz left Caghrï Beğ, "A propos de quelques articles de Köprülü Armağani," *J.A.*, CCXLII (1954), 275–279. I. Kafesoğlu, "Doğu Anadolu'ya ilk Selçuklu akinci (1015–21) ve tarihi ehemmiyeti," in *Fuad Köprülü Armağani* (Istanbul, 1953), pp. 259–274, has suggested that the first Seljuk attacks were those between 1015 and 1021. He has repeated this in his, *Sultan Melikşah devrinde Büyük Selçuklu Imparatorluğu* (Istanbul, 1953), pp. 2–3. See the long review of M. A. Köymen, "Büyük Selçuklu Imparatoru Melikşah devrinde bir eser münasebetiyle," *Belleten*, XVII (1953), 557–601. Cahen and Kafesoğlu have resumed the discussion in *J.A.*, CCXLIV (1956), 129–134, and again in Cahen, "Çağri-begi," EI₂.

[26] Cedrenus, II, 464.

empire reaching from Afghanistan into Anatolia, would have destroyed Byzantine power in Anatolia, and would have begun the last major ethnographical alteration of the Near East. It is obvious from the Christian sources that the Byzantines knew very little as to the origins and history of the Seljuks, but the Muslim authors seem not to have known a great deal more. What the Seljuks themselves purported to believe about their origins was not committed to writing until the latter half of the twelfth century and this work, the Malikname, has not survived.[27] These Seljuk tribes entered the Middle East via the steppe regions to the east and northeast of the Caspian Sea. This area had begun to be occupied by Turkic peoples as early as the sixth century of the Christian era and the Oghuz Turks, to whom the early Arab geographers refer, were probably their descendants. After the breakup of the great Turkic empire in Mongolia, the history of the Oghuz Turks concentrated increasingly, from the eighth and ninth centuries, on the northeastern borders of the Islamic world.[28] The Seljuks were of these Oghuz Turks. According to their traditions a certain Dudak and his son Seljuk, of the Kïnïk tribe of the Oghuz,[29] were vassals of a "Khazar" khan in the Asiatic steppe. Seljuk then broke away from the khan, established himself with a modest following in the regions of the Jaxartes River where he was converted to Islam, and henceforth fought his pagan "compatriots" as a ghazi defender of the Islamic border lands. In this region and toward the end of the tenth century, Seljuk and his followers were called in by the Samanids against the power of the Turkish Karakhanids; they were thereafter employed by the latter and so became a permanent part of the political scene in the Islamic world. But by 1025 the followers of Seljuk had split into two separate groups, the main body (under Toghrul and Caghrï) remaining in the service of the Karakhanids for a period, and a second group of 4,000 tents under Arslan which broke away and took service under the Ghaznevids in Khurasan. Henceforth these two groups had different historical experiences, but nevertheless, complementary to each other. Therefore it is of some profit to trace, briefly, their separate histories. In a sense, this second group of Arslan constituted the advance guard of the Seljuks into the Islamic world, and as they advanced, those places that they had temporarily settled, plundered, and abandoned were occupied by the larger group of Toghrul and Caghrï.

[27] Cahen has made a careful reconstruction of this work in "Le Malik-nameh et l'histoire des origines seljukides," *Oriens*, II (1949), 31–65 (hereafter cited as Cahen, "Le Malik-nameh").

[28] V. V. Barthold, *Four Studies on the History of Central Asia:* vol. III, *A History of the Turkman People* (Leiden, 1962), pp. 88–90 (hereafter cited as Barthold, *Turkman People*). Cahen, "Ghuzz," EI₂; R. N. Frye and A. M. Sayili, "Turks in the Middle East before the Seljuks," *J.A.O.S.*, LXIII (1943), 194–207.

[29] Barthold, *Turkman People*, pp. 110–111. Cahen, "Le Malik-nameh," p. 42; "Les tribus turques d'Asie occidentale pendant la période seljoukide," *W.Z.K.M.*, LI (1948–52), 179. Of the twenty-four tribes which the eleventh century author Kashgari says made up the Oghuz, the Kïnïk was the princely tribe.

The Ghaznevids first settled Arslan and his Turks in the Khurasan steppe around Sarakhs, Abivard, and Kizil Avrat (Farava), to the east of the Caspian. But no sooner were they installed than their disturbances caused the Ghaznevids to make war upon them,[30] and in the campaigns that followed, the Turkmens were defeated and scattered. One group moved to the regions of Balkhan and Dihistan to the northwest of Kizil Avrat, whereas a second group of perhaps 2,000 tents moved south to Kirman and Isfahan, and by the 1040's was raiding as far west as Mesopotamia, Kurdistan, and Armenia. As a result, by the early years of the third decade of the century, the original body of followers of Seljuk had split into the three following divisions: Balkhan, "Iraqi," and the Seljuks proper (who had remained under Toghrul and Caghrï). The first group played little role in the events that followed, whereas the Iraqi Turks served as the advance guard for the Seljuk expansion that was to follow and would in some instances join the main body of Seljuks at that time when they would appear in Iran and Mesopotamia.

It was the third group, that of Toghrul-Caghrï, which was to remake the history of the Middle East. For a while they had remained with the Karakhanids at Bukhara, but then moved on to Khwarazm near Shurkhan on the Oxus (Amu Darya) River. By 1034 they had moved into Khurasan and occupied the lands recently vacated by their tribal compatriots, those of Arslan, in the districts of Nesa, Sarakhs, Abivard, Kizil Avrat, and others. As the Ghaznevids had refused to grant these lands to the Seljuks (no doubt as a result of their experiences with the Seljuks of Arslan) Toghrul and Caghrï took them by force of arms. In this manner began the final struggle between Seljuks and Ghaznevids as to the fate of the key Muslim province of Khurasan. The issue was decided at the fateful battle of Dandanaqan in 1040. This date marks a decisive point not only for the Middle East but also for Byzantium as henceforth the Seljuks became the possessors of an established territorial state won by trial of arms.[31] This first possession of the Seljuks, Khurasan, was on the borders of the Islamic world, presenting the Seljuk princes with the temptation to enter Persia and the lands to the west. From this time the Seljuks no longer thought of the Jaxartes region, their point of departure, and did not oppose the occupation of these more northerly regions by another Turkic people, the Kipchaks. The great problem now facing the Seljuk princes was that of transforming themselves from war chiefs of nomadic tribes, who were preoccupied with pillage and with procurement

[30] Barthold, *Turkman People*, p. 104. One official had suggested, prior to their installation in Khurasan, that these Seljuks should be exterminated, or that at least their thumbs should be hacked off so that they might not draw their terrible bows. Their notoriety as foes of settled life had preceded them.

[31] B. N. Zakhoder, "Dendanekan," *Belleten*, XVIII (1954), 581–587. Spuler, "Ghaznevids," EI₂. O. Pritsek, "Die Karahaniden," *Der Islam*, XXXI (1953–54), 17–68. On the history and society of the Great Seljuks there has now appeared the comprehensive work of O. Turan, *Selçuklular tarihi ve Türk-Islami medeniyeti* (Ankara, 1965).

of pasturage for their flocks, to monarchs of sedentary, civilized Middle Eastern society. There was the alternative before Toghrul of giving free rein to the Turkmen instinct to plunder the sedentary society, or to protect it from the pillaging of the nomads. Toghrul achieved the latter by sending the Turkmen tribes westward to raid the frontiers of the Christian states of Armenia, Georgia, and Byzantium.[32] By this time (1040) there had occurred a large accretion of Turkmens to the standards of Toghrul and Caghrï, attracted by the great victories and the prospects of plundering new lands.

Toghrul's primary concern was the conquest of Persia and Mesopotamia and so it was here that he concentrated his attention and military efforts. By 1055 he had secured this conquest and enjoyed a triumphal entry into Baghdad where took place his celebrated audience with the caliph.[33] But previous to this consolidation of power in Mesopotamia-Iran, there had taken place a rapid expansion northwestward into Adharbaydjan, Transcaucasia, and Armenia, caused by the increasing number of Turkmens either fleeing Seljuk authority or else shunted northwestward by the Seljuks in an effort to save Mesopotamia-Iran from their presence. Their movements are difficult to follow but certain patterns appear. There were actual military campaigns of the sultan or his representatives in these areas in an effort to stabilize the frontiers and to maintain some kind of authority over the tribesmen in the border regions. There were also raids of the sultan's representatives which often had as their primary end the satisfaction of the tribal instincts and appetites for plunder and djihad. Finally, and most important, there were the activities of the Turkmens either in rebellion or simply not recognizing any Seljuk authority.[34]

The political conditions prevailing in these areas of new Turkish

[32] Cahen, "Le Malik-nameh," pp. 62–64. For the most detailed political and socio-economic survey of the background to the Seljuk appearance in Khurasan see Barthold, *Turkestan down to the Mongol Invasion* (London, 1928), pp. 254–304. Zakhoder, "Selçuklu devletinin kuruluşu sïrasïnda Horasan," *Belleten*, XIX (1955), 491–527. On the problem of the degree to which the Oghuz had accustomed themselves to urban life and on the character of their society one may consult, C. Brockelmann, "Mahmud al Kasghari über die Sprache und die Stamme der Türken im 11. Jahrhundert," *K.C.A.*, I (1921–25), 26–40. Houtsma, "Die Ghusenstamme," *W.Z.K.M.*, II (1888), 219–233. Ibn Fadlan-Togan, pp. 19 ff. Hudud al-Alam-Minorsky, pp. 100–101, 150, 311, 311–312. V. Gord-levski, *Izbrannyie Sochineniia* (Moscow, 1960), I, 70–95. F. Sümer, "Anadolu'ya yalnïz göcebe türkler mi geldi?" *Belleten*, XXIV (1960), 567–596. D. Theodoridis, "Turkei-turkisch nadas," *Zeitschrift für Balkanologie*, IV (1966), 146–148, has introduced a slight modification on one aspect of Sumer's study, deriving the Turkish *nadas from the Greek* νεστός. The Islamic materials on the Turkic tribes are conveniently collected and trans-lated in S. L. Volina, A. A. Romaskevič, A. Y. Yakubovski, *Materialy po istorii Turkmen i Turkmenii* (Moscow, 1939).

[33] For details, Spuler, *Iran in früh-islamischer Zeit* (Wiesbaden, 1952), pp. 124–129.

[34] Cahen, "La première pénétration turque en Asie Mineure seconde moitié du XIe siècle," *Byzantion*, XVIII (1946–48), 12–13 (hereafter cited as "Prem. Pén."); "The Turkish Invasions: The Selchukids," in *A History of the Crusades*, ed. K. Setton (Phila-delphia, 1955), I, 144–147 (hereafter cited as "Turk. Inv."); "Qutlumush et ses fils avant l'Asie Mineure," *Der Islam*, XXXIX (1964), 14–27.

expansion greatly facilitated first the Turkish penetration and then the conquest of the Seljuks in Adharbaydjan, Transcaucasia, and Armenia, for in all these areas there were numerous dynasties, both Christian and Muslim, in a state of constant war with one another.[35] Quite often the Muslims hired the services of Turks in this advance guard of raiders, but soon they acquiesced in the political domination of the succeeding waves of Turkish invaders, or submitted to the commanders of the Seljuk sultan. Thus portions of Adharbaydjan, Kurdistan, Transcaucasia, and the borders of Armenia were saturated by the newcomers, who in the end replaced many of the local dynasties. It was in this manner that the eastern frontiers of Byzantine Anatolia were eventually threatened by a deluge of Turkmens in the reign of Constantine and thereafter.

INTERRELATION OF BYZANTINE DECLINE AND
TURKISH PRESSURE (1042-71)

In the three decades between the accession of Constantine IX (1042) and the battle of Manzikert (1071), one can discern a definite pattern in the reaction of the Turkmen groups building up on the eastern borders to the deteriorating internal conditions of the empire in Anatolia and the Balkans. The raids, starting out in a somewhat cautious manner, were not frequent in the beginning. But as the condition of the empire progressively weakened each year, and as the number of Turks on the borders increased, the audacity, frequency, and extent of the raids increased considerably. One gets the impression from the Greek chronicles that, even before Manzikert took place, the Turks were raiding deep into Anatolia with little danger from Byzantine forces.

In this period of roughly thirty years, the struggle between the provincial magnate-generals and the bureaucracy did not abate but rather became more acute. The armies of Anatolia were turned against Constantinople and the bureaucrats, or they were brought to defend Constantinople against rebellious generals at the head of the armies in the Balkans, or else to combat the Patzinaks who had crossed the Danube. At the same time the indigenous provincial armies were being dissolved. It is no mere chance that the Seljuk incursions became prominent for the first time, and permanent, in the reign of the bureaucrat emperor

[35] R. Huseynnov, "La conquête de l'Azerbaijan par les Seldjoucides," *B.K.*, XIX–XX (1965), 99–109; *Siriiskie istočnik ob Azerbaidžane* (Baku, 1960), pp. 93–113, states that the basic conquest of Adharbaydjan took place after Dandanaqan (1040), but that isolated raids occurred earlier. Toğan, "Azerbaycan," *I.A.,*; *Umumi Türk tarihine giriş* (Istanbul, 1946), pp. 182–192. Minorsky, "Adharbaydjan," EI₂. Sümer, "Azerbaycanin türkleşmesi tarihine bir bakiş," *Belleten*, XXI (1957), 429–447. For Transcaucasia, Minorsky, *Studies in Caucasian History* (London, 1953); *A History of Sharvān and Darband in the 10th–11th Centuries* (Cambridge, 1958). On the Kurds see also Minorsky, "Kurds," EI₁. K. V. Zettersteen, "Marwanids," EI₁. H. F. Amedroz, "Three Arabic MSS on the History of the City of Mayyafariqin," *Journal of the Royal Asiatic Society* (1902), pp. 758–812; "The Marwanid Dynasty at Mayyafariqin in the Tenth and Eleventh Centuries," *Journal of the Royal Asiatic Society* (1903), pp. 123–154. Canard, "Dvin," EI₂.

Constantine IX Monomachus (1042–55).³⁶ Constantine's inept military policies, which led to the dissolution of the indigenous soldiery of the Iberian theme and of the region of Byzantine Mesopotamia with their accompanying conversion into tax-paying units, have already been discussed elsewhere.³⁷ These border areas, among the most vital regions in the defense of the eastern provinces, had been disturbed previously by other events.³⁸ In 1047 there had taken place the revolt of Leo Tornices, who, supported by many of the dissatisfied and idle western generals, marched on Constantinople.³⁹ Because the capital itself was without defenders, Monomachus summoned the magistrus Constantine from the eastern borders where he was waging war against Abu'l-Sewar the Shaddadid. As a result of the civil strife in the empire, he was forced to conclude peace with Abu'l-Sewar and to bring the eastern armies to Constantinople. Soon after the revolt of Tornices and the withdrawal of the magistrus Constantine, the empire's Anatolian frontiers became the object of serious Turkish raids when, in 1048, a body of Turks under Asan descended from the regions of Tabriz and proceeded to lay waste Vaspuracan. Aaron, the governor of that province, did not have sufficient forces to meet the invaders and so he summoned Cecaumenus the governor of Ani, and upon the arrival of the latter the combined forces defeated the Turks by resorting to a ruse.⁴⁰ In 1049 a larger army of Turks appeared in Vaspuracan under the Seljuk prince Ibrahim Inal, and as a result Cecaumenus and Aaron had to await the arrival of Georgian reinforcements under Liparites.⁴¹ While the Byzantines awaited reinforcements this considerable Turkish force captured and plundered the important commercial center of Artze near Erzerum. The destruction of this city marks the beginning of the sacking of many of the important urban centers in Byzantine Anatolia.⁴² On the arrival of the Georgians, the Turkish and Byzantine forces came to blows at Kapetru, but the outcome was indecisive.⁴³ The Byzantine forces had not been numerically sufficient

³⁶ Bryennius, 31–32; Zonaras, III, 641. Cedrenus, II, 609.

³⁷ Cedrenus, II, 608, enters this event just before the plague of the seventh and eighth years of the indiction, viz. 1054-55.

³⁸ Attaliates, 44–45. Cecaumenus, p. 18. Zonaras, III, 647. " ἀλλὰ καὶ χωρῶν οὐσῶν, αἱ τοῖς βασιλεῦσιν οὐ δασμοὺς συνεισέφερον, ἀλλ' ἀντὶ πάσης δασμοφορίας δυσχωρίας ἐφρούρουν καὶ τοῖς βαρβάροις τὴν εἰς τὰς Ῥωμαίοις ὑποκειμένας χώρας ἀπετείχιζον πάροδον, ἐκεῖνος φόρους ταῖς χώραις ἐπιτάξας ἐσχόλασε τὰς φρουράς. κἀντεῦθεν ἡ πρὸς τὰς Ῥωμαΐδας χώρας ῥάστη τοῖς βαρβάροις ἐγένετο πάροδος. ἐκεῖνος τοίνυν ὁ ἀνὴρ αἴτιος τοῖς ἀπαθῶς λογοζομένοις κριθήσεται τοῦ τὴν ἑῴαν μοῖραν δουρὶ κυριευθῆναι βαρβαρικῷ." In the place of the local soldiery were to be found some Frankish and Varangian mercenaries. Cedrenus, II, 606.

³⁹ Cedrenus, II, 561–566.

⁴⁰ Cedrenus, II, 573-574, implies that the Byzantine armies were not strong enough to meet the Turks in battle. It was for this reason that Cecaumenus devised the ruse and then fell upon the Turks in their disarray while they were plundering the Byzantine camp.

⁴¹ Ibid., 575, gives the exaggerated figure of 100,000.

⁴² On its wealth, population, and the Turkish booty, Cedrenus, II, 577–578; Matthew of Edessa, pp. 83–84.

⁴³ Cedrenus, II, 579, indicates that the Byzantine right and left wings drove the Turks from the field and chased them through the night until ". . . the crow of the cock."

to meet the Turkish armies in the beginning, and even after the arrival of the Georgians, they had not been able to destroy the Turkish forces. The incursions of Asan and Ibrahim, as well as the destruction of Artze, were no doubt the consequences of the revolt of the western generals which had so weakened the defenses of the eastern borders.

The Patzinak raids in the Balkans during the reign of Monomachus were a more visible and far more immediate threat to the empire, as it seemed virtually impossible to halt them. On at least two occasions the emperor removed troops from Anatolia to bolster the Balkan front. In 1050 troops were brought from the east to augment the Byzantine armies in the Patzinak campaigns,[44] but as the Patzinak ravages continued unabated, Monomachus employed eastern armies in the Balkans as late as 1053.[45] It was soon after this, in 1054, that the sultan Toghrul, appeared in the regions of Lake Van where his army spread out to raid. The cities of Paipert and Perkri were besieged and sacked, and the key city of Manzikert underwent a difficult siege.[46] It was as a result of these events, it would seem, that Monomachus subsequently transported the troops from the Macedonian theme to the east under Bryennius.[47]

In the years 1056-57 the Turkish chief Samuh appeared with 3,000 Turks in greater Armenia, where he remained for a number of years.[48] In the face of the growing number of Turks massed on the eastern frontier in Armenia, the military aristocracy of Anatolia launched a revolt that marks a turning point in the acceleration of the Turkish raids into the peninsula. Isaac Comnenus, supported by the Anatolian generals, raised the majority of the thematic, mercenary, and Armenian troops of Anatolia, and marched them toward the Bosphorus.[49] Those of the Anatolian forces which had not adhered to the rebellion, the troops of the Anatolic and

[44] Catacolon Cecaumenus and Herve Frankopoulos, and probably their troops also, had already been transferred to Thrace before 1050. Cedrenus, II, 593-594, 597.

[45] L. Bréhier, *Vie et mort* (Paris, 1947), p. 257.

[46] Attaliates, 46-47. Matthew of Edessa, pp. 98-102. Bar Hebraeus, I, 207. M. Yinanc, *Anadolu'nun fethi* (Istanbul, 1944), p. 49. Honigmann, *Ostgrenze*, p. 181.

[47] Cedrenus, II, 611. According to popular belief the Turks would be destroyed by a force similar to that of Alexander the Great which had conquered the Persians. Thus Macedonian troops and soldiers were sent. J. Laurent, *Byzance et les Turcs seljoucides dans l'Asie occidentale jusqu'en 1081* (Nancy, 1913) p. 33 (hereafter cited as Laurent, *Byzance et les Turcs*), asserts that all the western armies were in Asia Minor at the time of Toğhril's appearance in 1054. It is true that according to the text of Cedrenus, II, 611, western troops had been moved to Anatolia under Constantine IX. But no date is given in the text, and Laurent has, by erroneously placing the death of Constantine IX in 1054 (instead of 1055), made it probable that they were present when Toğhril appeared in 1054. But his account errs in two points. The text clearly states that the troops of the Macedonian theme were brought over, and not all of the troops of the west. However, Monomachus died in 1055, and it is quite probable that the Macedonians were brought over after Toğhril's appearance, for according to Attaliates, 46-47, and Matthew of Edessa, p. 99, the Byzantine defenses were under Basil Apocapes, there being no mention of Bryennius

[48] Cedrenus, II, 616. As has already been indicated above, the dissatisfied Frankish mercenaries of Armeniacon under Herve made common cause with him. *Ibid.*, 617.

[49] *Ibid.*, 627, " ... ἡ πᾶσα ἑῴα ˊΡωμαϊκὴ χεὶρ πλὴν ὀλίγων ... "

Charsianite themes, joined the western military contingents loyal to the government. The two armies, east and west, met in a sanguinary battle just outside the city of Nicaea, and though the Anatolian generals won the victory, the empire actually suffered defeat, for the soldiery of east and west were locked in a mutually destructive struggle and the number of the dead was great.[50] One chronicler states that on that day Isaac Comnenus plunged the whole Greek nation into mourning,[51] and another remarks that Isaac's revolt brought misfortune to Armenia.[52] Both were correct, for not only did the slaughter further exhaust the already depleted armies,[53] but the borders were left unguarded. This battle, in 1057, marked the departure of the traditional Byzantine armies from the Anatolian scene. On October 3, 1057, just one month after the entry of Isaac into Constantinople, a Turkish army under the emir Dinar, finding the east undefended, approached Camacha where it spread out. One column marched against Coloneia, the home of Catacolon Cecaumenus who had just raised the armies of that area for the civil war and had left his province undefended; the second column besieged Melitene, one of the great commercial centers of the eastern Anatolian regions.[54] Melitene and its population of wealthy Syrian, Armenian, and Greek merchants suffered the fate of Artze, as great numbers of the inhabitants were either killed or enslaved, and the booty the Turks took—gold, silver, and other loot—was great.[55]

In the twelve years between the death of Isaac Comnenus and the battle of Manzikert, the internal crisis of the empire became further aggravated and the Turkish tribesmen continued to saturate the border lands. Thus the financial, administrative, and military collapse of the Anatolian provinces characterized this period of slightly more than a decade. The bureaucratic fear of the armies and financial difficulties of the state caused the final disappearance of the locally levied troops as effective military units. The ethnic groups of Byzantine Anatolia—Greeks, Syrians, and Armenians—were at the throats of one another as separatist movements among the Armenians commenced, and open warfare broke out between Greeks and Armenians, Armenians and Syrians, and Greeks and Syrians. In such a situation the mercenary units began to disregard the commands of the government and to act as free agents. It was during this time of military, administrative, and fiscal anarchy that the Turks began to raid

[50] Attaliates, 55, 69. Matthew of Edessa, pp. 103–104.

[51] Attaliates, 69. On Isaac's death (1059) it was noticed that his corpse swelled with liquid. Many saw in this a divine punishment for his responsibility in the great slaughter of 1057.

[52] Aristaces, *passim*.

[53] The armies had been previously subject to extensive decimation at the hands of the Patzinaks in the Balkans, Bréhier, *Vie et mort*, p. 257.

[54] Honigmann, *Ostgrenze*, p. 184. Matthew of Edessa, pp. 107–108.

[55] Matthew of Edessa, p. 108. Bar Hebraeus, I, 212–213. Michael the Syrian, III, 158–159.

Anatolia almost without hindrance, and started the systematic pillaging of the urban hearths of Anatolian Hellenism.

For this twelve-year period, we have a firsthand witness to the military deterioration in the Byzantine armies, the historian Michael Attaliates who served as an official in the armies during many of the Anatolian campaigns and who was present at the battle of Manzikert.[56] The dismantling and demoralization of the military, well on the way in the time of Constantine IX, was largely consummated by the end of the reign of Constantine X (1067). The temporary interregnum of the generals under Isaac I had not lasted long enough to effect any significant change in this demilitarization, and when Constantine X ascended the throne in 1059 the government was once more completely in the hands of the bureaucrats. Their antimilitary sentiment set the fashion for the society of the day.

> The very soldiers themselves abandoned their weapons and military service and became advocates and devotees of legal problems and questions.[57]

The military catalogs were no longer fully maintained, the bravest and most able troops being completely withdrawn from service because of expense and fear of the generals. Even Psellus, the archbureaucrat, felt constrained to protest at the extremity of the emperor's cuts in the military budget.[58] With the appearance of the Turkish chief Samuh and the Khurasan Salar and their raiding Turks in Anatolia, Constantine X was finally obliged to send an army to halt their ravages. But, Attaliates remarks, this army was not satisfactory,

> because [it was] unarmed and uneager as a result of the deprivation of its provisions; So to speak it was the worst section [of the army], for the better soldiers were removed from military service by reason of the greater rank and salary [involved]. That which occurred was blameworthy, for nothing brave or in keeping with the former Rhomaic magnificence and strength was accomplished [by the army].[59]

The same emperor virtually handed over Ani to the Turks because the Armenian Pancratius promised to defend it without spending money on military forces. This left Ani without military defenders and caused it to

---

[56] Cedrenus' account follows that of Attaliates faithfully.

[57] Cedrenus, II, 652. Attaliates, 76–77, " τὸ δὲ φειδωλὸν καὶ ἄγαν ποριστικὸν τῶν δημοσίων χρημάτων ἔστιν οἷς καὶ οὐκ ἐν εὐπροσώποις αἰτίας, καὶ τὸ κατ' ἐξουσίαν δικαστικόν, καὶ τὸ καταφρονητικὸν τῆς στρατιωτικῆς εὐπραγίας καὶ στρατηγικῆς καὶ ἀκριτικῆς εὐπαθείας πολλῶν καὶ σχεδὸν ἁπάντων τῶν ὑπὸ Ῥωμαίοις τελούντων λυμαντικὸν ἐψηφίζοντο. ἠγείρετο γὰρ πολὺς γογγυσμὸς ... τῶν καταδρομὰς ὑφισταμένων βαρβαρικὰς διὰ τὸ μὴ κατὰ λόγον τὸν στρατιωτικὸν κατάλογον γίνεσθαι."

[58] Zonaras, III, 677. Psellus-Renauld, II, 146–147.

[59] Attaliates, 78–79, 85. He refused to send an army to halt the Uze depredations in the regions of Hellas, Macedonia, and Thrace. When the pressure of "public opinion" became too great to withstand, Constantine finally mustered a tiny force of 150 men to march out against a horde which the contemporary sources, exaggeratedly, estimate to have numbered 60,000! "Upon which everyone was amazed that the emperor should have left the capital with such a small army against such a powerful force ... and it was like the mythological expedition of Dionysus, when he marched against the Indians, with the maenads and silenoi."

fall to the Turks.[60] Shortly after Constantine Ducas's death in 1067 and during the brief regency of Eudocia, the state of the armies had become chaotic. On many occasions these tattered remnants of the military forces simply retired to the safety of walls and refused to march out and oppose the Turks.

The Turks, who were raiding the east again came against the Rhomaic armies encamped in Mesopotamia, but especially against those around Melitene. These, being in want of their salary and deprived of the provisions usually supplied them, were in an abased and deprived state.[61]

Because of this condition they refused to go out against the invaders, with the consequence that the Turks sacked the city of Caesareia.

When, to the southeast, combined Turkish and Arab forces raided the regions about Antioch, Nicephorus Botaniates tried to muster an army, but again the miserliness of the administration paralyzed these efforts. As only a portion of the salary was paid, the soldiers took it and then scattered to their homes leaving the enemy forces free to ravage the neighborhood of the city. So this time an attempt was made to levy a few raw youths.

But they were without military experience and without horses, and more or less without armour, naked and not even [provided] with daily bread.[62]

Having temporarily overthrown the bureaucrats, the general Romanus Diogenes found the armies in an even more dreadful state. Cedrenus, in pages filled with Gibbonian melancholy, describes the mustering of the armies by Romanus for his first great campaign against the Turks in 1068.

The emperor, leading an army such as did not befit the emperor of the Rhomaioi but one which the times furnished, of Macedonians and Bulgars and Cappadocians and Uzes and the other foreigners who happened to be about, in addition also of Franks and Varangians, set out hastily. All were mustered by imperial command in Phrygia, that is in the theme of the Anatolicoi, where there was to be seen the incredible [viz.] the famous champions of the Rhomaioi who had enslaved all the east and west [now] consisted of a few men. These were bent over by poverty and distress and were deprived of armour. Instead of swords and other military weapons ... they were bearing hunting spears and scythes [and this] not during a period of peace, and they were without war horse and other equipment. Inasmuch as no emperor had taken the field for many years, they were for this reason unprofitable and useless, and their salary and the customary provisions had been stripped away. They were cowardly and unwarlike and appeared to be unserviceable for anything brave. The very standards spoke out taciturnly, having a squalid appearance as if darkened by thick smoke, and they had few and poor followers. These things being observed by those present, they were filled with despondency as they reckoned how low the armies of the Rhomaioi had fallen, and by what manner and from what moneys and how long it would take to bring them back to their former condition. For the older and experienced were without horse and without armour, and the fresh detachments

---

[60] Attaliates, 79–82. M. Canard, "La campagne arménienne du sultan salgukide Alp Arslan et la prise d'Ani en 1064," *Revue des études arméniennes*, II (1965), 239–259.

[61] Cedrenus, II, 660. Attaliates, 93.

[62] Cedrenus, II, 661–663. Attaliates, 94–96.

were without military experience and unaccustomed to the military struggles. Whereas the enemy was very bold in warfare, persevering, experienced, and suitable.[63]

This is the military instrument that Romanus inherited from a quarter century of bureaucrat policies. The conditions of the armies were obvious to the Byzantine contemporary observers, and their great inferiority in terms of equipment, experience, and morale to the Turkish troops clearly noted. Romanus, however, did the best he could with the poor material at hand. He collected youths from all the regions and cities,[64] but as they were completely inexperienced, he mixed them with what veterans were at hand, expecially from the Balkan *tagmata*. Though this energetic emperor was a capable soldier, his armies were not equal to the enormous task before them and their nervousness and cowardice in the face of the Turkish enemy had by now become an almost ingrained characteristic.

The mercenaries, upon whom the Byzantines were forced to rely, began to demonstrate clearly that their loyalty depended directly on, and was proportionate to, the strength of the central and provincial governments and their pay. When the central and provincial administration became weak in this period, and as the government no longer had sufficient funds to live up to its terms of hire, the mercenaries showed themselves to be independent agents. This twelve-year period, then, witnessed an intensification of the unruly conduct of the foreign soldiery. The Muslim military leader, Amertices, who had served Byzantium, deserted to the Turks because his pay had been witheld, and then played a major role in the raids in Anatolia and around Antioch.[65] The Armenian troops had an old tradition of instability,[66] and when the Turks appeared before Sebasteia in 1059 the Armenian princes and their troops abandoned the city to its fate.[67] A decade later (1068) while Romanus Diogenes' army was before Syrian Hierapolis, the Armenian infantry caused a major crisis by threatening to rebel.[68] The rebellion of the Frankish leader Crispin in 1069 was of a major dimension. Having considered his reward from the emperor as unsatisfactory, he returned to the Armeniac theme and there raised the Latins in revolt. The tax collectors and the land were plundered, and when Samuel Alusianus (the general of the five western *tagmata* encamped in that area) took the field, Crispin defeated him and inflicted severe losses on these western forces. All this having occurred as Romanus was setting out on his second Turkish campaign, it seemed as if the whole military expedition against the Turks would have to be redirected to stay the rapacity of the Franks

[63] Cedrenus, II, 668–669.

[64] Attaliates, 104, " καὶ ἐκ πάσης χώρας καὶ πόλεως νεότητα συλλεξάμενος."

[65] *Ibid.*, 94–95. Scylitzes, II, 661. He had previously attempted to assassinate the emperor Constantine X Ducas.

[66] Zepos, *J.G.R.*, I, 247.

[67] Matthew of Edessa, pp. 111–117.

[68] Attaliates, 113. Scylitzes, II, 674.

who were ravishing the very provinces they had been hired to defend. Crispin finally made his submission, but in the end had to be imprisoned. As retaliation, the Latins then proceeded to ravage the regions of Byzantine Mesopotamia at the same time that the emperor was forced to proceed to Caesareia to meet a serious Turkish raid.[69]

On the eve of the battle of Manzikert itself, when the emperor was encamped at Cryapege, the mercenaries were busy ravaging the environs. As Romanus attempted to halt their depredations, the Germans attacked the emperor in force and the remainder of the army had to be mustered in order to put down the Germans.[70] The shortsightedness of the bureaucrats in hiring such large numbers of mercenaries at the expense of the local soldiery was dramatically manifested during this period, and their disloyalty severely hampered the defense of Anatolia against the Turks and contributed to the chaos and disruption of provincial administration.

With this paralysis of the provincial governmental structure, the hostilities of the three principal ethnic groups in eastern Byzantine Anatolia came into full play. There had been tense moments in the relations of Greeks, Syrians, and Armenians in he first hal of the eleventh century, but at that time Byzantine authority was effective in these eastern provinces and a semblance of order and regularity prevailed. The disruption of provincial administration in the reign of Constantine X, and the latter's ill-conceived religious policies, unleashed the specter of ethnic and sectarian strife from Antioch to Sebasteia and Caesareia. The state, in a policy recalling events of the sixth and seventh centuries, attempted to force ecclesiastical union and the Chalcedonian creed on both Syrians and Armenians. In 1063 all who did not accept the Chalcedonian creed in Melitene were to be expelled from the city, and one year later the Syrian patriarch was arrested and the leading Syrian clergymen were brought to Constantinople. Charged with spreading their own religious doctrines and having refused to accept Chalcedon, the Syrian ecclesiastical leader (the metropolitan of Melitene) was exiled to Macedonia. The Armenians similarly experienced considerable imperial pressure in this matter, as the Armenian catholicus and many of his bishops were summoned to Constantinople and held virtual prisoners (1060–63). Two years later (1065) they were once more ordered to appear in Constantinople, but this time the Bagratid and Ardzrouni princes were also summoned. The Armenians, like the Syrians, refused to give in at the religious discussions that followed, but unlike the Syrians they obtained permission to return to their domains in Anatolia. When Kakig, the Bagratid prince, returned to his lands in the province of Cappadocia he instigated what amounted to open warfare against the Greeks in his

[69] Attaliates, 122–125. Scylitzes, II, 678–680.
[70] Attaliates, 146–147.

vicinity. That these regions of Anatolia were thrown into a state of ethnic war seems to be confirmed by a number of incidental facts. The outrage of the Armenians was such, Matthew remarks, that Kakig intended to desert to the Turks, but he was eventually slain by the Greeks in the Taurus before he could do so.[71] Romanus had considerable trouble with the Armenians and considered the areas in which they were settled as a no-man's land that was not safe for his armies. During his eastern campaign of 1069 Romanus was obliged to halt to receive the stragglers from his army lest they perish at the hands of the Armenians in the regions of Celtzene.[72] When he made his appearance at Sebasteia, the Greek inhabitants complained to him that when Sebasteia had been sacked by the Turks (1059), the Armenians had been more violent and unpitying toward the Greeks than had the Turks themselves! So it was that Romanus ordered his troops to attack Sebasteia, a Byzantine city, and then he swore that he would destroy the Armenian faith.[73] In addition to the tension between Greeks and Armenians and between Greeks and Syrians, there was strife between the Syrians and Armenians in the region about Melitene where the Armenians raided the Syrian monasteries and roamed the countryside attacking the Syrian population. They even considered taking the famous Syrian monastery of Bar Mar Sauma.[74] The existence of these diverse ethnoreligous groups in the eastern provinces of Anatolia, and Constantine's attempt to enforce the Chalcedonian creed upon them during this period, were among the factors leading to the breakdown of Byzantine authority in these critical areas.

Against this background of ghost armies, rampaging mercenaries, and ethnic warfare in the provinces, the Turkish invaders make their appearance with greater frequency, numbers, and effectiveness. The border warfare of the Turks was loosely controlled by the sultan, who for this purpose had entrusted command of the Anatolian borders to Yakuti Beg.[75] The Turkish bands were considerably increased in number when

---

[71] Vryonis, Social Basis," 169–172. Matthew of Edessa, pp. 95–98, 152–154. Michael the Syrian, III, 161, 166–168. There is further evidence for this phenomenon in which Georgian and Armenian princes and aristocrats joined the Turks and in some cases converted to Islam. This is clear not only from the Armenian and Georgian chronicles but especially from the Turkish epic, the Danishmendname. Religious discussions between Byzantines and Armenians resumed in the twelfth century when religious passions had somewhat subsided, P. P. Tekeyan, *Controverses christologiques en Arméno-Cilicie dans la seconde moitié du XIIe siècle (1165–1198)*, Orientalia Christiana Analecta (Rome, 1939).

[72] Attaliates, 135. Scylitzes, II, 683.

[73] At least this is what Matthew of Edessa, pp. 166–167, reports.

[74] Michael the Syrian, III, 162–164. Bar Hebraeus, I, 217. On religious polemic of the Syrians with Greeks and Armenians in the twelfth century, there is the contemporary tract of Dionysius bar Salibi (d. 1171), bishop of Amid, *The Work of Dionysius Barsalibi against the Armenians*, ed. and trans. A. Mingana (Cambridge, 1931); "Barsalibi's Treatise against the Melchites," in *Woodbrooke Studies* (Cambridge, 1927), I, 2–95; "The Work of Dionysius Barsalibi against the Armenians," in *Woodbrooke Studies*, IV (Cambridge, 1931). E. Ter-Minassiantz, "Die armenische Kirche in ihren Beziehungen zu der syrischen Kirche," *Texte und Untersuchungen, Neue Folge*, XI, 4 Heft, 1–212.

[75] Yinanc, *Fethi*, p. 51.

the Turkmens of the rebel Ibrahim Inal were moved westward by the Seljuks, and then again in 1063 when Kutlumush with 50,000 Turkmens revolted against Alp Arslan in Rayy. After the defeat and death of Kutlumush, his sons were pardoned and sent to fight on the Anatolian borders.[76] The names of the raiding chiefs now begin to appear in greater numbers in the sources; Samuh in the regions of Sebasteia and else-where;[77] the Khurasan Salar in the districts of Thelkum, Nisibis, and Seveverek;[78] Amertices about southern Anatolia and Coelo-Syria.[79] But perhaps the most active of these was the emir Afsinios (Afshin) who established himself on Mt. Amanaus in 1066–67[80] and raided from Antioch[81] and Melitene[82] as far west as Chonae.[83] The emir Kumush Tekin operated in the vicinity of Thelkum and Edessa,[84] whereas Gedrigdj-Chrysoscule raided northern Anatolia before deserting to the emperor.[85] In addition to the ever-present bands on the borders, the sultans themselves made occasional appearances there, strengthening the Turkish forces.

When Constantine X Ducas ascended the throne (1059), the Turkish raids had previously devastated Armenia, the Byzantine provinces of Iberia and Mesopotamia, the regions around Coloneia, Melitene, and Chaldia, and were now to threaten the more centrally located regions of Anatolia. At least eight major urban centers were to suffer pillaging at the hands of the Turks, and others were to experience difficult sieges in the next years. The first of the important cities to be plundered was the comparatively large and wealthy town of Sebasteia, the location of the famous shrine of the Forty Martyrs. In 1059 the emir Samuh and other emirs suddenly appeared before the unwalled city, but initially they hesitated to attack mistaking the domes of the many churches for the tents of the defending army. They soon realized that the city was defense-less, and so massacred pitilessly large numbers of the inhabitants. The Turks remained in Sebasteia for eight days, reducing it to ashes and taking a great booty and many prisoners.[86] The sultan himself took the field in 1064 with a large army and appeared in Armenia.

Proud of his success, the sultan, this dragon of Persia, that year pounced upon Armenia. Instrument of divine vengeance, his wrath spread over the oriental nation, which he forced to drink the vial of his malice. The fire of death enveloped

---

[76] *Ibid.*, pp. 53, 57. Cahen, "Qutlumush et ses fils avant l'Asie Mineure," *Der Islam*, XXXIX (1964), 14–27.

[77] Matthew of Edessa, pp. 111–113. Attaliates, 78.

[78] Matthew of Edessa, pp. 115–118.

[79] Attaliates, 94–95.

[80] Matthew of Edessa, p. 156.

[81] Bar Hebraeus, I, 218.

[82] Attaliates, 107.

[83] Bar Hebraeus, I, 220., says as far as Constantinople! Yinanc, *Fethi*, p. 68.

[84] Matthew of Edessa, p. 157. Bar Hebraeus, I, 217.

[85] Matthew of Edessa, p. 162.

[86] *Ibid*, pp. 111–113.

with its flames the faithful of Christ. The land was inundated with blood, and the sword and slavery spread their ravage here.[87]

The most important Byzantine city in Armenia, Ani, was taken and many of the inhabitants put to the sword or carried off into slavery.[88]

By reason of the weakened resistance at the end of Constantine's reign, the Turks had become even bolder and so began to push their incursions farther to the west, where the larger towns which had been spared the rigors of siege for centuries now lay defenseless. The urban centers in central and western Anatolia were in a peculiar situation, for though protected from the invaders by a greater distance, they did not have even the protecting forces that the border cities possessed. With the dissolution of the larger part of the thematic armies, the more westerly provinces had little defense; the mercenaries and other available troops were kept on the eastern borders where they often let the Turks pass through unhindered, hoping to attack them in the mountain passes when they were returning from Anatolia in disarray and laden with booty. Thus once the Turks had overrun the border defenses they sacked the interior almost freely. The Turks reached the important Cappadocian city of Caesareia after having been let through by the recalcitrant troops guarding Melitene. They plundered, destroyed, and burned the city, singling out the famous shrine of St. Basil. This they looted, carrying away all the holy items of the church, and attempted to break into the structure housing the saint's remains. The church was desecrated and the inhabitants massacred.[89] In the following year the Turkmens became bolder, daring to raid, sack, and lead-off captive, the inhabitants of Neocaesareia, even though Romanus was encamped in the eastern theme of Lycandus. The ability of the enemy to sack such an important Anatolian city indicates not only how completely the system of local defense had collapsed, but also the essentially different type of military procedure followed by the Byzantines and their foes. The numerous Turkish bands might strike at any time and in any place, but the Byzantine army was usually in one or two places at any given time.[90] In the same year, while Romanus besieged the Syrian city of Hierapolis, the Turkish bands raided farther into Anatolia, and for the second time in the long history of the Christian-Muslim holy war, the famous city of Amorium was sacked by a Muslim army, and its citizens massacred.[91] Hereafter, the raiders contemptuously disregarded the emperor and his armies in Anatolia. In 1069 while Romanus was in the district of Celtzene, the Turks passed through Cappadocia pillaging it en route and continued westward in the

---

[87] Ibid., p. 122.

[88] Scylitzes, II, 653–654. Attaliates, 79–82. Matthew of Edessa, pp. 120–124.

[89] Attaliates, 93–94. Scylitzes, II, 661. The sanctuary was so strongly built that the Turks contented themselves with stripping it of its gold, pearls, and precious stones.

[90] Scylitzes, II, 684–685.

[91] Ibid., 678, " . . . λαφυραγωγίαν καὶ φόνον ἀνδρῶν ἀμύθητον."

direction of Iconium, the emperor receiving news of this only after he had arrived in Sebasteia. So he set out in an effort to catch up with the marauders, but upon arriving at Heracleous Comopolis, he was informed that the Turks had already sacked the city.[92]

One year later it was the turn of Chonae, the city sacred to the Archangel Michael. In 1070 Romanus had been forced to remain in Constantinople to keep an eye on the bureaucrats and the Ducas family, so the armies were sent out under the command of Manuel Comnenus. As Hierapolis in Syria was under a severe siege, Comnenus was forced to divide his army and to send a large portion of it to relieve the besieged city. He himself encamped with the remainder of the army at Sebasteia where he was defeated and captured by the Turkish emir Chrysoscule. No sooner had the emperor received this news in Constantinople than an even greater disaster was reported to him, the city of Chonae had been savagely pillaged by the Turks. The famed shrine of the Archangel was profaned and turned into a stable for the Turkish horses, and the raiders "filled the region with murder." The inhabitants, who were accustomed to flee to the caverns, where the river went underground in the vicinity of the sanctuary, were all drowned when the river suddenly flooded. The sack of Chonae, and especially the drowning of the fugitives in the underground caverns, were taken by Byzantine society to be an indication of God's wrath. Cedrenus relates that formerly the Greeks had interpreted the devastations and incursions of the Turks in Iberia, Mesopotamia up to Lycandus, and Melitene to be a sign of God's anger with the Armenian and Syrian heretics who inhabited this area. But when the ravages spread to the regions inhabited by the Greeks, they decided that henceforth "not only correct belief but also living the faith"[93] were necessary.

Manzikert (1071)

Accidents, evil omens, and ugly spectacles studded the beginning of Romanus' final campaign (1071) against the Turks as his armies journeyed to the eastern front. A gray dove alighted on Romanus' ship and came to the emperor's hand as the imperial vessel was crossing the Bosphorus to Asia, a sign interpreted by some to bode well, but felt by many others to be a forewarning of evils to come.[94] Upon the pitching of the imperial pavilion at Helenopolis, instead of at Neocome, the soldiers remarked

---

[92] *Ibid.*, 683–684. Attaliates, 135–137.

[93] Scylitzes, II, 686–687. Attaliates, 140–141.

[94] Attaliates, 143. The prevalence of superstition at critical points in Byzantine history is striking. Liparites had refused to fight the Turks at the appropriate moment because it fell on a day not propitious to him. Nicephorus II Phocas on his way to the conquest of Crete stopped with the fleet on the Anatolian coast at one of the many port towns. He asked the name of the port, and on being told that it was Phygela, he ordered the fleet to avoid it as the name was not propitious to the expedition (pp. 223–224). Contrary to Gibbon, who severely criticized this superstitious behavior as Byzantine, this superstitious behavior was not peculiarly Byzantine but was also characteristic of the fifth century Athenians, as witness the events surrounding the fateful Sicilian expedition.

that inasmuch as the place was called Eleinopolis (miserable city) by the rustics, this was very definitely unlucky.[95] Indeed, after the imperial tent had been raised, the central pole supporting it gave way and the tent collapsed,[96] an event too obvious in its implications to pass unnoticed. The emperor himself seems not to have been perturbed by such superstitious signs and moved on to the important military station of Dorylaeum[97] and to the theme of Anatolicon to muster the Anatolian armies. Here again the emperor's coming misfortune seemed to be announced, for the structure built to house Romanus and his retinue caught fire, and his select horses, armor, bridles, and carriages were consumed by the flames. Though some of the animals were saved, others were to be seen running wildly through the camp, living torches.[98] Romanus next crossed the Sangarius River at the Zompus Bridge in hopes of collecting the Anatolian levies. But as these had scattered to the mountaintops, caverns, and other places of refuge (because of the Turkish raids), Romanus took few of them. The expedition crossed the Halys, eventually making its way to the military station of Cryapege, and it was here that the German mercenaries attacked Romanus. The following station, Sebasteia, brought Romanus no respite, for the Greeks of the city complained against their Armenian neighbors. On the road from Sebasteia to Coloneia, Romanus and his troops were treated to the sight of the corpses of Manuel Comnenus' army that had been handled so roughly by the Turks in 1070, and this in particular was interpreted as a bad omen. Upon arrival in Erzerum, rations for two months were passed out to the army as "they were about to march through uninhabited land which had been trampled underfoot by the foreigners."[99] The march to the eastern front must have had quite a demoralizing effect on the soldiery for they had seen many frightening signs. The mercenaries had rebelled, the Greeks had complained about Armenian cruelty, and just before reaching the borderlands they had seen the corpses of their former comrades, a sight that was morbidly suggestive.

The armies continued their march to the northwestern shores and the vicinity of Lake Van, intending to take Manzikert and Chliat. The decision to divide the armies on the eve of the fateful battle was due, perhaps, to the intelligence report of Leo Diabatenus who wrote that as soon as Alp Arslan had received news of the Byzantine advance, he broke off his march on Damascus and retired to the east with such haste that his army virutally disbanded and the animals were drowned in crossing the Euphrates. The sultan had not been interested in attacking the Byzantine

[95] *Ibid.*, 144.
[96] *Ibid.*, 144. Scylitzes, II, 689.
[97] Bryennius, 35.
[98] Attaliates, 145.
[99] *Ibid.*, 148. Brosset, *Géorgie*, I, 327–328, 346, comments upon the desertion of these areas.

borders but was occupied with his schemes against the Fatimids, and for this reason the advance of Romanus had caught him by surprise.[100]

In dividing his forces, Romanus wished to reduce Manzikert (captured by the sultan in the previous year), and then to rejoin his forces before Chliat. As the body of Turkish and Daylamite defenders in Manzikert was negligable, Romanus further weakened his army by sending the majority of it, and the very best troops, to Chliat under the leadership of Joseph Tarchaniotes.[101] Manzikert fell almost without resistance.[102] The strategy of the emperor, which had called for the splitting of the armies and which had left him with the weaker portion, seemed justified on the basis of his intelligence reports. But Diabatenus failed to keep him informed of later developments, for on his way eastward Alp Arslan received the fugitives from Manzikert, who appealed to him to come to their aid. Sometime previous to Romanus' final campaign, the Turkish emir Afsinios had raided central Anatolia with such ease that he reported to the sultan that Asia Minor was defenseless.[103] Whatever the reason, the sultan hurriedly, but quietly, gathered his forces and marched on Manzikert. After having captured Manzikert, Romanus retired to his camp outside the city and planned to march to Chliat on the following day to rejoin the major portion of the army. It was at this time that the advance body of the sultan's army came upon Byzantine forces that were foraging in the vicinity of Manzikert. As yet the emperor had not realized that the sultan was present, and he believed that this was just a raiding force of Turks under some emir. The emperor sent out Nicephorus Byrennius to oppose them, but as he was soon being hard pressed by the Turkish force he sent an urgent message for reinforcements. Romanus, still unaware of the true nature of the situation, first accused Bryennius of cowardice, but eventually sent another force under Basilacius to aid him. Basilacius and his troops charged the Turks, forced them to retreat, but, in the pursuit that followed, Basilacius was captured near the enemy defenses. Bryennius, though seriously wounded, returned to the side of the emperor.[104] On the report of Basilacius' capture, the Byzantines began to fear, and this suspence

---

[100] Cahen, "La campagne de Mantzikert d'après les sources musulmanes," *Byzantion*, IX (1934), 627–628 (hereafter cited as Cahen, "Manzikert").

[101] Attaliates, 149. " ἦν δὲ τὸ ἐγχειρισθὲν ἐκείνῳ στρατιωτικὸν τὸ ἔκκριτόν τε καὶ δυσμαχώτατον, κἂν ταῖς συμπλοκαῖς καὶ τοῖς ἄλλοις πολέμοις προκινδινεῦον καὶ προσμαχόμενον, καὶ εἰς πλῆθος πολὺ προέχον τῶν ὑποκρατηθέντων τῷ βασιλεῖ."

[102] *Ibid.*, 152–153, remarks that even in this moment of victory portents of impending disaster were present. A soldier, who had taken a donkey from a Turk, was punished most severely by Romanus. In spite of the man's supplication before the icon of the Blachernitissa, the sacred vanguard of the army, the emperor disregarded his state of asylum and had his nose slit. This brought the fear of divine retribution upon many of the soldiers.

[103] Bar Hebraeus, I, 220. Cahen, "Manzikert," p. 628, does not indicate that this occurred prior to Romanus' expedition. He implies also that Alp Arslan received news of this after Romanus was already in Armenia, which is not what Bar Hebraeus says.

[104] Bryennius, 38–39, remarks that the sultan had prepared an ambush. The narrative of Bryennius, however, is not to be preferred to that of Attaliates in the details that follow. Attaliates, 154.

and fear of the unknown were spread throughout the camp by the sound and sight of the many returning troops who had been wounded by Turkish arrows. Romanus immediately marshaled his force and set out to seek the enemy, but as they had retired before the charge of Basilacius, they were nowhere in sight so the emperor returned to camp.[105]

That night while the Uze mercenaries were outside the encampment buying goods from the merchants, the Turks attacked them by riding around the camp and raining arrows upon them from horseback. The mercenaries rushed back into the enclosed camp in such disorder that those inside feared the Turks would enter the camp simultaneously and then all would be lost. It was a moonless night, and the pursuers could not be distinguished from the pursued, Attaliates remarking that to the Byzantines the Turks and Uzes looked alike. The Turks, possibly for this very same reason, did not attempt to enter but remained before the camp during the whole night, making noise and shooting their arrows. Attaliates graphically depicts the sleepless night passed by the terrorized troops in the encampment. On the following day a portion of the Uze mercenaries, under their leader Tamis, deserted to the Turks. This increased the fear of the Byzantine generals and further undermined the morale of the troops, because they now feared the remainder of the Uzes would desert.[106] The Byzantines achieved a temporary success when their archers marched out and drove the Turkish forces away from the encampment with heavy losses to the latter. Romanus himself wished to come to close quarters with the Turkish forces immediately and thus to determine the issue without further delay. He had hesitated, however, as the majority of his forces were still supposedly encamped before Chliat. Even though he sent messengers to summon them, the emperor felt that they might not arrive in time, so he decided to march out against the Turks on the next day. Unknown to him, Tarchaniotes and Roussel, with the Frank, Uze, and Byzantine troops under them, had dispersed upon hearing of the sultan's arrival, and, without bothering to inform the emperor, they had fled across the regions of Byzantine Mesopotamia to Anatolia.[107]

Unexpectedly an embassy from the sultan arrived bringing proposals for peace. As Romanus was not disposed to accept the offer, he placed stiff conditions on the opening of such discussions. Before he would consider the proposition, he informed the envoys, the sultan would have to withdraw from his present camp and let Romanus occupy it. Reasoning that the sultan was afraid and his forces weak, the emperor's counselors strengthened the emperor in his resolve and advised him to reject the sultan's peace offer. The sultan was merely stalling for time, the counselors

---

[105] Attaliates, 155–156.

[106] Their unreliability had been dramatically displayed in the time of Constantine IX when, sent to Anatolia to fight the Seljuks, they simply deserted, recrossed the Bosphorus, and returned to the Balkans.

[107] Attaliates, 158.

argued, and as soon as his forces should be augmented he would return and attack the empire, and in this the counselors succeeded in persuading Romanus. There were other factors that must have helped persuade him. The military activities had been extremely expensive, and it was not likely that the emperor could muster another such force in the near future. Then it had been difficult to catch the Turks during his four year reign, for they were always on the move, split up into small but rapidly striking bodies. He now had before him the sultan himself. There were other issues as well to be considered. Psellus and the Ducas' were constantly plotting against him in Constantinople and during the preceding year he had not been able to leave Constantinople because of this fact. So Romanus made what seemed to him the logical choice: force the issue with the enemy of the empire now, a similar opportunity would never present itself again.

On the day of battle Romanus drew up all his troops, leaving none to guard the camp. Most of his army, as mentioned above, had been sent to invest Chliat, and so the emperor needed everyone he could muster on the fighting line. Bryennius commanded the left wing, Romanus the center, Alyattes the right wing, and Andronicus Ducas was placed in the rear with a large body of *hetairoi* and *archontes*.[108] When the emperor attacked, the sultan's forces gave way and retreated, the emperor pursuing them until evening.[109] Romanus halted the pursuit, deciding to

---

[108] Bryennius, 41.

[109] Such is the account of Attaliates, 160–161. "τὸ δὲ πλεῖστον φυγή τις κατεῖχεν αὐτούς, συντεταγμένας ἰδόντας τὰς τῶν Ῥωμαίων φάλλαγγας ἐν τάξει καὶ κόσμῳ καὶ πολεμικῷ παραστήματι." Bryennius, 41, also remarks that the Turks feared to oppose the Byzantines en masse. The accounts of the defeat given by Attaliates and Bryennius are quite different. Both are reliable, but as Attaliates was an eyewitness, his account must be preferred. When Bryennius' account coincides with that of Attaliates, it can be accepted, but otherwise it must yield to the version of Attaliates. The battle of Manzikert has been thoroughly investigated from the point of view of the Muslim sources by Cahen, Manzikert," but strangely it has not been critically examined from the side of the Greek sources. Cahen's article, excellent in other respects, is confused and contains considerable error as a result of misuse of the Greek texts. His mistakes result from the mistranslation of Attaliates, and then following the mistranslation of the critical passage, he rejects Attaliates as a primary authority on the basis of this mistranslation, preferring the narrative of other historians.

Of those authors who have left us accounts of the events that took place at the fateful battle, Attaliates is the only one who was present, participated, and is, therefore, the only eyewitness whose record has survived. Although it may be true that later authors relied upon valuable archival material that is now lost, nevertheless they were removed from the events in time and place, and so did not see them. Nicephorus Bryennius, whose account Cahen prefers, was born in 1062 and therefore was only nine years of age when the battle occurred. He began writing his work probably in the latter years of the reign of Alexius Comnenus (1081–1118), so that perhaps as much as forty years had elapsed between the battle and his writing. He does give certain details that Attaliates omits, but by and large the narrative of Attaliates is longer and more detailed. Bryennius and Attaliates give two entirely different versions of the battle. Scylitzes, Zonaras, and Matthew of Edessa repeat the version of Attaliates, though Matthew is confused and adds a few details not in Attaliates. The oldest of the Muslim sources, Ibn al-Qalanisi, did not write his history of Damascus until sometime after 1145, and the remaining Muslim and Eastern Christian sources spread themselves from this time until the late thirteenth century

return to the camp (now divested of guards) lest the Turks return at night and attack it, as they had done previously. So Romanus ordered the army to retire from the pursuit and to march back to camp. The imperial standard was turned from the direction of the enemy toward the camp and

---

and even later. Thus the account of Attaliates has incontestable superiority on the basis of nearness to the event itself.

Cahen has rejected Attaliates' account of the battle on the following grounds. At one point in the battle Attaliates records that one of Romanus' personal enemies intentionally spread the false rumor that Romanus had been defeated, and that he then took his men and left the emperor on the field of action, thus precipitating the rout (Attaliates, 161–162).

"ὡς δ' οἱ πολλοὶ πληροφοροῦσιν, ὅτι τῶν ἐφεδρευόντων αὐτῷ τις, ἐξάδελφος ὢν τῷ τοῦ βασιλέως προγονῷ Μιχαήλ, προβεβουλευμένην ἔχων τὴν κατὰ τούτου ἐπιβουλήν, αὐτὸς τὸν τοιοῦτον λόγον τοῖς στρατιώταις διέσπειρε, καὶ τάχυ τοὺς οἰκείους ἀναλαβὼν (ἐμπεπίστευτο γὰρ παρὰ τῆς τοῦ βασιλέως καλοκαγαθίας οὐ μικρόν τι μέρος λαοῦ) φυγὰς εἰς τὴν παρεμβολὴν ἐπανέδραμε." Who was this ἐξάδελφος ὢν τῷ τοῦ βασιλέως προγονῷ Μιχαήλ? Cahen has taken the phrase to refer to the son of Constantine X Ducas, Michael Ducas, the future Michael VII. Cahen, then has interpreted this key passage as follows: Attaliates blamed Michael Ducas for the catastrophe at Manzikert. But in so doing, he was really attempting to blacken the character of Michael VII whom Attaliates' hero, Nicephorus III Botaniates, removed from the throne. "En fait, il est inutile de salir, avec le serviteur de Botaniate, la mémoire de Michel Dukas." (Cahen, 635.) And with this, Cahen discredits the account of Attaliates.

Let us look at the text once more: ἐξάδελφος ὢν τῷ τοῦ βασιλέως προγονῷ Μιχαήλ. The correct translation is; "Being a cousin to Michael the emperor's step-son." Therefore the man who, according to Attaliates, betrayed Romanus was a cousin of Michael Ducas and not Michael Ducas himself. Michael Ducas, so far as we know, did not leave Constantinople at this time and so was not present at the battle. Who was this cousin of Michael Ducas? The other Greek texts tell us. Nicephorus Bryennius, 41, remarks that Andronicus, the son of the Caesar John Ducas (the brother of Constantine X Ducas; thus Andronicus was the cousin of Michael Ducas) had been put in charge of the rear guard with the archontes and the hetairoi: "οὐραγεῖν δὲ ἐτέτακτο ὁ τοῦ καίσαρος υἱὸς ὁ πρόεδρος Ἀνδρόνικος τάς τε τῶν ἑταίρων τάξεις ἔχων καὶ τὰς τῶν ἀρχόντων." Bryennius adds, " οὐ πάνυ δὲ φιλίως ἔχων πρὸς βασιλέα." In other words, even Bryennius (Cahen's primary authority) knew of the instability of Andronicus Ducas. Scylitzes, II, 698, repeats Attaliates' charge that Andronicus Ducas betrayed the emperor by a premeditated plot.

"μᾶλλον δέ τις τῶν ἐφεδρευόντων αὐτῷ, Ἀνδρόνικος ὁ τοῦ Καίσαρος μὲν υἱὸς τῶν δὲ βασιλέων ἐξάδελφος, προβεβουλευμένην ἔχων τὴν ἐπιβουλὴν αὐτὸς δι' ἑαυτοῦ τὸν τοιοῦτον λόγον διέσπειρε, καὶ τοὺς περὶ αὐτὸν στρατιώτας ἀναλαβὼν ταχὺς τῇ παρεμβολῇ ἐφοίτησεν." Zonaras, III, 701, remarks that the Caesar and his sons were constantly plotting against Romanus. " ἀεὶ γὰρ ὅ τε Καῖσαρ καὶ οἱ τούτου υἱεῖς ἐφήδρευον τῷ βασιλεῖ καὶ ἀφανῶς ἐπεβούλευον." The tradition of Andronicus' desertion is echoed even in the chronicle of Michael the Syrian, III, 169, who records that Romanus and his nobles were divided and that most of them abandoned him on the field of battle. This is obviously a reference to the withdrawal of Andronicus who commanded the ἄρχοντες. See also Sawirus ibn al-Mukaffa', II, iii, 308–309.

The behavior of Andronicus during the battle is in consonance with the great tension between the Ducas family and Romanus before the battle, and their promptness in removing him from the throne afterward. In 1070 it would seem that Romanus had remained in Constantinople because of the heightened tensions between himself and the Ducas family. He arrested the Caesar on several occasions and even considered putting him to death. But he had to satisfy himself with an oath that the Caesar and his sons would never be disloyal to him (Psellus-Renauld, II, 160–161). Sometime before departing for his final Anatolian compaign in 1071, he exiled the Caesar to Bithynia (Bryennius, 43).

When properly translated, the passage in Attaliates refers not to the future emperor Michael Ducas, but to Andronicus his cousin. Therefore we must not reject Attaliates on Cahen's grounds that ostensibly the historian has distorted the facts in order to blacken the memory of Michael Ducas. Attaliates remains our most reliable source, and it is his account that deserves the greatest degree of credence.

the soldiers in the vicinity of the emperor evidently performed the movement correctly.[110] But those who were far away, upon seeing the reversal of the imperial standard, thought that the emperor had been defeated. More specifically, Andronicus Ducas intentionally spread the false rumor that the emperor had been defeated and withdrew his men from the field in haste, bringing them to the camp. The Byzantine sources state categorically that Ducas was executing a premeditated plot, for he and his family had been waiting for an opportunity to do away with their hated enemy.[111]

One must recall in this conjunction that prior to his expedition in 1071, Romanus had arrested and exiled the Caesar John Ducas, father of Andronicus. The whole episode is vaguely but definitely echoed in the later account of Michael the Syrian who remarks that Romanus and his nobles were at odds, and then that most of the nobles abandoned him in the battle.[112] This is in complete accord with the accounts of Attaliates and Bryennius, the latter of whom tells us that the *archontes* or nobles were under the command of Ducas. Given the already nervous state of the soldiers, the anarchy in the armies thus begun by the activities of Andronicus Ducas spread rapidly and the emperor was unable to halt it. The Turks on the heights, by now becoming aware of this amazing development, informed the sultan and so they came out to attack the emperor who had been abandoned on the field by much of the army. Romanus and those about him defended themselves bravely and for a long time, but as the men fled toward the encampment, the rumors began to spread among the demoralized men. According to some the emperor had defeated the Turks, but according to the others he had been killed. The terrorization was finally completed by the gradual desertion of the Cappadocians and the appearance of the imperial horses in the camp.[113] By this time the Turkish horsemen were attacking the fleeing troops, slaying, capturing, and trampling them underfoot, Romanus fighting until he was wounded in the arm and his horse shot out from under him.[114]

For the first time in the long history of the Byzantine empire, the supreme disgrace had occurred: the august and living person of the Basileus Rhomaion had fallen into the hands of barbarians.[115] In

[110] Attaliates, 161–162.

[111] *Ibid.*, 161–162. Even Bryennius, 41, remarks of Andronicus, "οὐ πάνυ δὲ φιλίως ἔχειν πρὸς βασιλέα." Though his account of the battle differs from that of Attaliates, he also remarks (42), that the rear guard immediately withdrew after the Turks made their first contact with the Greeks, "εὐθὺς δ' ἀνεχώρουν καὶ οἱ περὶ τὴν οὐραγίαν." In essence, then, Bryennius does not contradict Attaliates' charge of the treachery and withdrawal of Andronicus. He confirms it.

[112] Michael the Syrian, III, 169.

[113] Attaliates, 162.

[114] *Ibid.*, 163.

[115] In actual fact the treatment that Romanus Diogenes received at the hands of the magnanimous Alp Arslan is highly praised by all the sources, but especially by the Greek historians. On this interesting episode and the famous dialogue between the two sovereigns see Attaliates, 164–166; Cahen, "Manzikert," pp. 636–637.

reexamining the details of this most important battle, one is struck by a number of factors that, by 1071, had already enjoyed a considerable history in the empire's evolution during the eleventh century. The treachery of Andronicus Ducas was purely and simply one of the more dramatic and consequential acts in the long and bitter strife between bureaucrats and militarists.[116] Unfortunately for the empire, it was not to be the final act of this drama, and the struggle between administrators and soldiers was to have dire consequences in the decade to follow. The desertion of the Uze mercenaries under Tamis to the Turks is again another act from the same drama, that is, the demobilization of the local armies and use of hired foreigners, policy much employed by the bureaucrats as an antidote to the power of the generals.[117] The Franks of Roussel and the Uzes who were sent to Chliat simply fled on news of the sultan's approach, and Germans had attacked Romanus at Cryapege. All this was complicated by the enmity of Greeks and Armenians, so ominously forecast when Romanus had stopped at Sebasteia on his way to Manzikert. Michael the Syrian relates that the Armenian troops, as a result of religious persecution, were the first to flee and that all of them fled from the battlefield.[118]

The great victory of Alp Arslan in 1071 was due to a large degree, then, to these internal developments in the Byzantine Empire which had fused to produce the situation prevailing in the Byzantine ranks in 1071.

Initial Turkish Conquest and Occupation of Anatolia (1071–81)

Alp Arslan was apparently not interested in exploiting directly his great victory at Manzikert; it was instead the Turkmen tribes that consummated the military victory by swarming into Anatolia literally unopposed. There is no indication that they attempted to found a state when they first came. Rather they came to raid and plunder in the vast expanses of Anatolia and thus disrupted what little was left of the Byzantine administrative and military apparatus. It is true that the defeat of the Byzantine armies in 1071 had opened Anatolia to the Turks,[119] but their appearance, and finally their settlement, were greatly faciliated and

[116] Michael VII rewarded his relative with gifts of land and immunities in the regions of Miletus in the year 1073, Dölger, *Regesten*, no. 992–994.

[117] Attaliates, 158–159, who personally administered the oath to the remainder of the Uzes specifically states that they remained loyal throughout the battle. Thus Matthew of Edessa (p. 169), who asserts that all the Patzinaks and Uzes deserted, has to be corrected. Only the followers of Tamis, a minority of the whole, deserted.

[118] Michael the Syrian, III, 169; "Les troupes des Armeniens, qu'ils voulaient contraindre à adopter leur hérésie, prirent la fuite des premières et tournèrent le dos dans la bataille."

[119] On this question and on the treaties between Byzantium and the Seljuks, J. Laurent, "Byzance et les Turcs seldjoucides en Asie Mineure. Leurs traités anterieurs à Alexius Comnène," Βυζαντίς II (1911–1912), 101–126. G. Vismara, *Bisanzio e l'Islam. Per la storia dei trattati tra la Christianita orientale e le potenze musulmane* (Milan, 1950), pp. 44–45, 69–78, presents a sketch of diplomatic relations between Byzantium and the Seljuk-Ottoman Turks.

accelerated by the continuation of those very factors that had brought Byzantium to the brink at Manzikert. The strife between the generals and bureaucrats not only did not abate, but the very appearance of the Turks in Anatolia seemed to add a certain zest to the struggle as each side strove to outdo the other in purchasing Turkish military aid in a quest for power. This graphically illustrates how narrow and selfish political considerations outweighed all other factors, the Turkish danger included. By this time the true nature of the Turkish menace was apparent to all, to both bureaucrats and generals, but the desire for the imperial crown was overpowering.

The mercenaries, creating ever greater difficulties, attempted to found a new Normandy in northern Asia Minor during the chaos that enveloped Anatolia following Manzikert. Farther to the south, the Armenian princes and adventurers, secure in their mountain strongholds in the craggy Taurus area, at last had a good opportunity to throw off the hated Byantine authority and to give expression to their own separatist desires. Finally, out of all this chaos and upheaval, the Seljuk princes founded a new state in Nicaea, at the northwestern extremity of the peninsula. Simultaneously, other Muslim dynasties were arising in the political debris at the end of the century in northeastern Anatolia. Manzikert resulted in the destruction of a comparatively stable political unity in Anatolia and substituted for it a relatively unstable system of smaller quarreling states which would keep Anatolia in a more or less constant state of war and unrest, enduring until the final Ottoman reunification and political conquest of the large peninsula. In short, immediately following Manzikert, Byzantine administrative authority collapsed in Asia Minor, and in the vacuum Turks, Armenians, and Normans attempted to found states.

Alp Arslan, knowingly or unknowingly, contributed to the Turkish penetration of Rum when he released Romanus Diogenes after the latter's defeat and capture. The captivity of Romanus had enabled the Caesar John Ducas to seize control of the government in Constantinople and to promote his nephew Michael VII to the throne. Upon receipt of the news of Romanus' release, the Ducas family in the capital was faced with a serious problem and the result was a civil war in Anatolia which involved what was left of the Byzantine armies. Romanus tried vainly, first at Doceia, then in Cappadocia, and finally at Adana to alter his evil fate, but without success. In the end he was defeated and captured by the very man who had betrayed him at Manzikert, Andronicus Ducas.[120] The description of his brutal blinding, on the very Anatolian soil that he had so valiantly but vainly fought to protect, is a fitting finale to this act in the political collapse of medieval Hellenism in its foyer. Consequently, the fragmentary Byzantine armies were used to fight one another at the very

[120] Attaliates, 168–175. Bryennius, 45–55.

moment when the borders were completely open to the Turkish tribes. Still more fateful was the precedent of Romanus in appealing to the Turks for aid in the civil war,[121] a pattern that was to become firmly established in the internal strife of the next critical decade.

The bureaucrats, first under the leadership of the Caesar John and then under the notorious eunuch Nicephoritzes, were able to control the government for six years after the death of Romanus. But when the military reaction came, in 1077, it was violent and once more mobilized what was left of the armies in the west and the east in a suicidal war. At that time two generals, Nicephorus Bryennius and Nicephorus Botaniates rebelled in the Balkans and Anatolia respectively. Nicephorus Bryennius, as a reward for his suppression of the Bulgarian rebellion at Skopia which had previously broken out, was to be assassinated by the agents of Nicephoritzes. Because his brother and Basilacius were likewise slighted by the bureaucrats in the capital, they also rebelled, declared Nicephorus Bryennius emperor, and marched the western armies on Constantinople. During this rebellion in the west, the Patzinaks, finding no armies before them, raided to the very walls of Adrianople unopposed. Simultaneously, Nicephorus Botaniates, supported by the Anatolian magnates Cabasilas, Synnadenus, Goudeles, Straboromanus, Palaeologus, and Melissenus, capitalized upon the provincial dissatisfaction with the government's neglect and inability to halt the Turks, and so raised the standard of rebellion in the east.[122] It is significant that up until the time he reached Nicaea, Botaniates had been able to gather no more than 300 men with which to take Constantinople. Again one sees how complete was the breakdown that the provincial military system had suffered.[123] When news of the outbreak reached the court, Michael VII immediately hired the services of Sulayman to halt the advance of the rebel, thereby causing Botaniates to abandon the regular roads and to travel by night in order to avoid his Turkish pursuers. Even so, the Turks caught up with him before he was able to reach Nicaea. Fortunately for Botaniates, the Turkish renegade Chrysoscule, who was with him, intervened with Sulayman and was able to bribe him to abandon the emperor and to support Botaniates. Thus Sulayman changed sides, and accompanied the insurgent to the shores of the Bosphorus,[124] where he probably had his first sight of the city destined to become the center of Turkish might

---

[121] Bryennius, 57, relates that it was after the Sultan heard of Romanus' death that the Turks raided and plundered the whole of the east. The same author (99), speaks of the many ταραχαί, ἀποστασίαι, στάσεις in the east after Romanus' death. Scylitzes II, 707–709.

[122] Scylitzes II, 726. Bryennius, 117–118.

[123] Bryennius, 118, 120.

[124] Ibid., 119. Scylitzes, II, 735. The emperor Michael had negotiated not only with Sulayman but with Malik Shah as well, 1073–1074; H. Antoniades-Bibicou, "Un aspect des relations byzantino-turques en 1073–1074," Actes du XIIᵉ congrès international d'études byzantines (Belgrade, 1964), II, 15–25.

almost four centuries later. As Botaniates had been short of troops, even after incorporating the troops of Nicaea into his armies, he had embodied the Turks of Sulayman in his forces. Subsequently many of the Turks were posted as guards to hold the various cities through which Botaniates passed—Nicaea, Chalcedon, Pylae, Chrysopolis, Praenetus, Nicomedia, Ruphinianae, and Cyzicus.[125]

The civil strife in the empire did not cease with Botaniates' accession to the throne for he still had to deal with the rebellion of Bryennius in the west. Alexius Comnenus was sent to face Bryennius, but as he was drastically short of troops, he was in the end forced to rely upon 2,000 Turkish horsemen furnished by Sulayman and Mansur who at this time were still in Nicaea.[126] Once the rebellion of Bryennius was stifled, another broke out, that of Basilacius.[127] When Alexius rebelled (1081) the tattered armies of the east and west were mustered, were marched toward the Bosphorus, and for yet one more time the provinces were left unprotected. Alexius Comnenus, at the head of the western armies, succeeded in removing Botaniates from the throne, but not before the rebellion of Alexius' brother-in-law Nicephorus Melissenus complicated the chaos, now long rampant, in Anatolia. As the Turks were the military masters, he sought and obtained their alliance, opening large numbers of towns of western Anatolia to them. These cities opened their gates to Melissenus when he appeared as emperor, and then he turned them over to his Turkish allies.[128]

In the rapid disintegration that followed the battle of Manzikert and during the course of the subsequent civil war, separatist political movements began to crystallize in Asia Minor. The most spectacular of these attempts to found a state on Anatolian soil was that of the mercenary leader Roussel of Bailleul,[129] who found conditions in the peninsula ripe for his attempt to establish a new Normandy in southern climes. Of all the mercenaries in Byzantine service, the descendants of the Norsemen had the most highly developed political instinct, with traditions going back 200 years and extending to Russia, Sicily, and England. While the Turkish flood poured into the whole of Anatolia, Michael VII was forced to send Isaac Comnenus with an army in an effort to halt their ravages (1073), but en route he had occasion to punish one of the Normans for

[125] Attaliates, 263–268.
[126] Bryennius, 130.
[127] *Ibid.*, 149 ff.
[128] *Ibid.*, 158.
[129] L. Bréhier, "Les aventures d'un chef normand en Orient au XIe siècle . . . Roussel de Bailleul," *Revue des cours et conferences*, XX (1911–1912). G. Schlumberger, "Deux chefs normands des armées byzantines au XIe siécle: sceaux de Hervè et de Roussel de Bailleul," *R.H.*, XVI (1881), 289–303. K. Mekios, *Der frankische Krieger Ursel de Bailleul* (Athens, 1939). Marquis de la Force, "Les conseillers latins d'Alexius Comnène," *Byzantion*, XI (1936), 153–165. R. Janin, "Les Francs au service des Byzantins," *E.O.*, XXIX (1930), 61–72.

mistreating a local inhabitant. Roussel used this incident as a pretext to rebel, taking his 400 Normans and marching northward toward his estates in the Armeniacon. Actually the punishment of his soldier was only an excuse, for Roussel had no doubt been planning his rebellion for some time. He began to besiege, plunder, and subject the cities and towns of the regions of Galatia and Lycaonia, forcing them to pay him tribute.[130] It soon became clear in Constantinople that this was not the customary mercenary rebellion, and the emperor with his advisers feared that given the state of imperial impotence in the province Roussel would succeed in establishing a new state. The Caesar John and Nicephorus Botaniates were dispatched with military forces to put down Roussel before he could consolidate his position, but in the battle fought at the Sangarius River, Roussel and his Franks were victorious; the Byzantine army suffered a crushing defeat and the Caesar was taken captive.[131]

There seemed to be no way to stop Roussel after this victory. The Franks, upon hearing of his rebellion, had flocked to his standards to the number of 2,700 to 3,000.[132] Roussel, profiting from his victory over the Caesar, subjected all the towns in the region of the Sangarius River to his authority, and marched through Bithynia to the Bosphorus where he burned Chrysopolis. The rebellion took on even more serious overtones as Roussel proceeded to acclaim the Caesar John emperor, hoping thus to obtain the allegiance of the remaining Byzantine soldiery in Anatolia and also to collect the taxes from the cities.[133] Defenseless before the victorious progress of Roussel, Michael VII enlisted the services of the emir Artuk who had appeared in the regions of the Bithynian fortress of Metabole with a large contingent of Turks. Roussel was defeated and both he and the Caesar were captured and held for ransom. But once more Roussel escaped the imperial authorities, having been ransomed from the Turks by his wife before the imperial envoys could reach the Turkish camp. [134] Nevertheless the court had moved hastily to ransom the Caesar for fear that the Turks would utilize him as Roussel had planned to do, and thus enter the towns and collect moneys.[135] Having renounced his more grandiose scheme, Roussel withdrew to Armeniacon where he drove out the Turks, and raiding Amaseia, Neocaesareia, and other towns, forced the urban centers to pay their taxes to him. Here he hoped to found a more modest state.

The government in Constantinople was no nearer to the solution of its Norman dilemma, and so sent Nicephorus Palaeologus to the Caucasus to raise a new army of mercenaries. On his return to Pontus with a force

[130] Bryennius, 73–74.
[131] *Ibid.*, 77. Attaliates, 196.
[132] Attaliates, 188, 190.
[133] Bryennius, 77–80. Attaliates, 189.
[134] Bryennius, 81–83.
[135] *Ibid.*, 81–82. Attaliates, 190–192.

of 6,000 Alans, Nicephorus was unable to pay their salaries and consequently most of the Alans simply abandoned him and returned to their homes. Roussel easily defeated and dispersed those few who remained. The desperation of the government in this situation is reflected in the final victory that it achieved over Roussel (1074). In a last attempt the government dispatched the future emperor Alexius Comnenus to Amaseia to cope with the rebel, and he arrived there without soldiers or money! Thanks to his cunning, energy, and above all to Turkish aid, he succeeded in purchasing his enemy from the Turks by bribing the latter to betray Roussel. Though Alexius once more brought the cities under imperial control, he had succeeded only because he had appealed to a Turkish emir in the area, in this case a certain Tutuch.[136]

The rebellion of Roussel illustrates how unreliable an army based so largely on mercenary loyalty could be. Because of its own military weakness, the government had to rely first on Alan soldiers, and finally upon the Turks. But both government and rebel did not hesitate to court the Turkish emirs, thus encouraging them, revealing the weaknesses of Constantinople, and accelerating the Turkish penetration of Anatolia and the ravaging of the towns. Bryennius states that of all the upheavals, rebellions, and revolutions that took place in Anatolia after the removal of the emperor Romanus IV, that of Roussel was the cause of the greatest of all evils to the empire.[137] Bryennius has probably exaggerated very little if at all in his evaluation of the significance of this event. It resulted in the calling in of large Turkish forces as far as Bithynia, and when Alexius returned from Amaseia with his captive Roussel, he was forced to take ship at Heracleia in order to reach the capital, for the roads were swarming with Turks.[138]

Less spectacular, but with a more durable effect, were the separatist movements of the Armenian princes in the regions of Mesopotamia, the Taurus, and Cilicia.[139] The violent hatred of the Armenians for the Greeks, so vividly revealed in the vitriolic pages of Matthew of Edessa, found its satisfaction in the years immediately following Manzikert. The numerous Armenian chiefs and adventurers, taking advantage of the collapse of Byzantine authority (in which collapse they had already played an important role),[140] began to assert themselves as independent political factors. They were aided by the mountainous topography of

[136] Bryennius, 83–90. Attaliates, 199–206.
[137] Bryennius, 99. "῞Οσα μὲν οὖν ξυνέβη κατὰ τὴν ἕω μετὰ τὴν τοῦ Διογένους τοῦ βασιλέως καθαίρεσιν, καὶ ὅσαι ταραχαὶ καὶ ἀποστασίαι καὶ στάσεις ἀνήφθησάν τε καὶ αὖθις ἐσβέσθησαν, καὶ ὡς ἡ μεγίστη πασῶν τυραννίς, φημὶ δὴ τοῦ Οὐρσελίου, εἰς μέγα ἀρθεῖσα καὶ μεγίστων κακῶν αἰτία τῇ Ῥωμαίων γενομένη . . ."
[138] Ibid., 93–95.
[139] For general remarks see J. Laurent, Byzance et les Turcs, pp. 81–89; S. Der Nersessian, "The Kingdom of Cilician Armenia," in A History of the Crusades, II (Philadelphia, 1962), 631–634.
[140] Cecamenus, p. 18. Cedrenus, II, 571. Laurent, Byzance et les Turcs, p. 74.

southeastern Anatolia and also by the presence there of a large Armenian population. The ethnic character of these regions had begun to change with the Byzantine reconquest of the tenth century when Armenians colonized Cilicia. This settlement was further reinforced by the transplanting of the Armenians in the eleventh century, and finally by the flight of Armenians to Cilicia for security from the Turkish raids. In Cappadocia, Adom and Abucahl of Vaspuracan, and Kakig of Ani were now free of all Byzantine authority. Kakig carried on open warfare against the Greek inhabitants of Cappadocia, killing the Greek metropolitan of Caesareia, pillaging his rich estates, ordering his soldiers to violate the wives of the Greek aristocracy, and as a result eventually found his death at the hands of the Greek landed magnates.[141]

Independent Armenian princes were to be found in Tarsus, Lampron, Mudaresun, Andrioun, and elsewhere. It was a Byzantine official, however, Armenian by birth and Greek in religious affiliation, who coalesced these centrifugal forces to found an extensive state in the Taurus, Cilicia, and Mesopotamia. Philaretus Brachamius had held important office under Romanus IV, but in the chaos following Manzikert he set out to make himself independent in the Taurus mountains.[142] Refusing to recognize the authority of Michael VII, he began to take over many of the Byzantine cities and fortresses that had been isolated and cut off from the capital as a result of the Turkish invasions.[143] The basis of his army was a body of 8,000 Franks and various Armenians and Turks who served under him.[144] His primary motive was to establish a state at any cost and in this he did not hesitate to call in the aid of the Turkish emirs against recalcitrant Armenian princes[145] or even to apostatize to Islam.[146] In spite of the fact that both the Armenians and Greeks hated Philaretus violently,[147] he succeeded in establishing himself for a number of years in these strategic regions of Anatolia. His domains eventually came to include the regions between Romanopolis, Kharpert, and Melitene in Mesopotamia on the north; Mopsuestia, Anazarba, and Tarsus in Cilicia on the south; and Antioch in the east. Shortly after his capture of Antioch, Botaniates concluded a treaty with Philaretus by which the latter acknowledged the suzerainty of Constantinople, but in return he was officially given charge of the remnants of Byzantine forces in the southeast and received the title of *couropalates*. This was in fact to recognize his

[141] Matthew of Edessa, pp. 152–154, 183. Laurent, *Byzance et les Turcs*, p. 78, who gives good reasons for dating these events after 1071.

[142] On his career, Laurent, *Byzance et les Turcs*, pp. 81–89. Laurent, "Byzance et Antioche sous le curopalate Philarète," *Revue des Études Arméniennes*, IX (1929), 61–68; "Des Grecs aux Croisés," *Byzantion*, I (1924), 367–449.

[143] Attaliates, 301, "καὶ πόλεις βασιλικὰς εἰς ἑαυτὸν οἰκειούμενος, καὶ εἰς μῆκος ἐξαίρων τὴν ἰδίαν κατάκτησιν."

[144] Matthew of Edessa, pp. 173–174.

[145] *Ibid.*, pp. 175–176.

[146] *Ibid.*, p. 196. Bar Hebraeus, I, 231.

[147] Matthew of Edessa, p. 173. Attaliates, 301.

actual independence and to treat him much in the same manner as Byzantium had treated the sovereigns of Armenia and Georgia. He was independent and did as he pleased.[148] The Normans of Roussel had not succeeded in founding a state because they were small in number, but Philaretus and the Armenian princes had at the basis of their political separatism a whole nation, securely ensconced in the rocky heights of the Taurus. Thus the Armenians consummated the disruption of Byzantine authority in southeastern Asia Minor.

The Turks do not seem to have taken immediate advantage of Manzikert to occupy Asia Minor or to raid on any extensive scale. That this was so is clearly indicated by the course of events during the civil war between the Ducas' and Romanus IV. In the accounts of contemporaries, especially in that of Attaliates (who was in Anatolia at the time), Byzantine authority was still recognized in Trebizond, Manzikert, Erzerum, Iberia, Coloneia, Amaseia, Melissopetrium, Doceia, Tyropaeum, Podantus, the Taurus, Cilicia, Adana, and Cotyaeum. This geographical range is considerable, stretching from the Black Sea to the Mediterranean, and from Armenia to Bithynia.[149] But it was to be the last time that Byzantine armies and officials would be able to cross the Taurus passes, collect soldiers in Iberia and Cappadocia, and march all the way from Cilicia to Cotyaeum in the west unhindered and unaccompanied by Turkmens.

Following the defeat of Romanus and as a result of the voiding of the treaty between the emperor and the sultan, Alp Arslan took the opportunity to send the tribes into Asia Minor on a major scale and eventually to occupy the towns and cities. Henceforth, the Turkmens were to carry their raids into almost every corner of the vast peninsula.[150] The last attempt to halt their Anatolian inroads by meeting them in the east came early in the reign of the feeble Michael VII, when Isaac Comnenus was sent to Caesareia to halt the sacking of the towns and villages in Cappadocia. With the defection of Roussel and the Normans, Isaac was defeated and captured by the Turks near Caesareia. The victors followed up their success by scattering out to plunder; Alexius barely escaped capture at their hands while fleeing via Mt. Didymon toward the town of Gabadonia in Cappadocia.[151] Alexius, wishing to ransom his brother, made his way to Constantinople, picked up the ransom money, and returned to Ankara. Upon his return to Ankara in late evening he found the gates locked, for the Turks, who had defeated and captured his

---

[148] Attaliates, 301.

[149] *Ibid.*, 166–177. Bryennius, 46–50. Bar Hebraeus, I, 223, adds Melitene, and Matthew of Edessa, p. 170, adds Sebasteia.

[150] Attaliates, 183, " . . . θεήλατός τις ὀργὴ τὴν ἑῴαν κατέλαβεν." All the themes suffered, "δεινῶς κατελυμαίνοντο καὶ κατήκιζον ταῦτα ταῖς συνεχέσιν ἐπιδρομαῖς." Bryennius, 57, " . . . τὴν ἑῴαν πᾶσαν ἐδῃοῦντο καὶ ἐληΐζοντο." Matthew of Edessa, p. 170. Alp Arslan, upon hearing of Romanus' blinding, directed his troops to take the land of the Greeks and to shed the blood of the Christians. See n. 119 above.

[151] Bryennius, 62–63.

brother Isaac, were encamped nearby watching the city closely. Soon afterward this particular band left Asia Minor, but by now other Turks had come in, for the defeat of Isaac left the borders defenseless, and they began to take control of many of the key arterial routes stretching across Anatolia.[152] Thus when Isaac and Alexius set out from Ankara for Constantinople via the highway leading through Nicomedia, they were surprised on the road by 200 Turks at Decte.[153] This occupation of the roads and passes by the Turks, deep in Anatolia, was characteristic of the first phase of their occupation of the peninsula after Manzikert. Cities such as Ankara and Gabadonia had been bypassed, protected as they were by walls. In this manner many of the towns in this early period remained in Byzantine hands, but they suffered isolation as the Turks swarmed about them occupying the countryside, cutting them off from one another and from Constantinople and its representatives.

The events of Roussel's revolt brought the Turks into the northern regions of Armeniacon and Pontus as well as into Bithynia. Because of Roussel's victory over the Caesar and his appearance at Chrysopolis, Michael secured the aid of a large Turkish army under Artuk who happened to be raiding the eastern regions at the time. This army[154] surprised Roussel at Metabole, defeated and captured him, and after receiving ransom money returned to eastern Anatolia. But it would seem that many of these Turks remained behind to raid and that others had occupied various regions which the sources do not mention. Attaliates relates that the "Turks had scattered out into all the Rhomaic themes."[155] When Roussel returned to the Armeniac theme he found it full of Turks and proceeded to remove them.[156] Michael VII called in another Turkish army under the chieftain Tutuch[157] and Roussel's rebellion was ended. The cities of Pontus were brought under Byzantine authority again.[158] Though these towns were once more under Greek control, the countryside and the roads were no longer safe. The degree to which the Turks had penetrated can be ascertained from the narrative of Alexius' experiences when he returned from Amaseia to Constantinople with his prisoner Roussel. En route he stopped at Castamon to see his ancestral estates,

---

[152] Attaliates, 184, "οἱ δὲ Τοῦρκοι τὴν ἰδίαν ἔκτοτε κατέτρεχον ἀδεῶς."
[153] Bryennius, 66.
[154] Attaliates, 190. " . . . εἶδε τὸ στῖφος τῶν Τούρκων ἀπειροπληθὲς καὶ θαλάσσης ἀπλέτου μιμούμενον κύματα. ἦσαν γὰρ ὑπὲρ τὰς ἑκατὸν χιλιάδας οἱ βάρβαροι." Bryennius, 81, " . . . μετὰ πλείστης ὅτι δυνάμεως . . ." A. Sevim, "Artuklularĭn soyu ve Artuk Bey'in siyasĭ faaliyetleri," Belleten, XXVI (1962), 121–146: "Artukoğlu Sökmen'in siyasĭ faaliyetleri," Belleten, pp. 501–520; "Artukoğlu Ilghazi,' 'Belleten, pp. 649–691. See below, n. 189.
[155] Attaliates, 198. See the remarks of Melikoff, Danishmendname, I, 123–126. Anna Comnena, I, 10, remarks, " τῶν δὲ εἰς τὸ κατόπιν ὑπαχθέντων ὥσπερ ψάμμου ποδῶν ὑποσπασθείσης."
[156] Attaliates, 199.
[157] Bryennius, 86.
[158] Attaliates, 206–207. Bryennius, 92.

only to find them deserted, and he barely escaped capture at the hands of the Turks pillaging the area. On arriving at the Black Sea port of Heracleia the Turks attacked him once again. Consequently Alexius wished to stay in Heracleia and organize a defense against these raiders, but an imperial ship arrived ordering him to proceed to Constantinople by sea as the Anatolian roads to the west were infested with Turks.[159]

In this disastrous reign of Michael VII, Chrysopolis, across the straits from the imperial capital, became a lair of Turkish raiders.[160] The Turkmens had reached the sea in the west and north as well in the reign of Michael VII. By 1076 they had spread their ravages to the Aegean around Latrus,[161] and Trebizond was temporarily captured by the Turks sometime between 1071 and 1075.[162] Thus they spread out into the farthermost reaches of Asia Minor in the reign of Michael VII but without taking, apparently, many of the urban centers.[163] The actual seizure of the towns of central and western Asia Minor became critical in the very last years of Michael VII and during the short reign of Nicephorus III Botaniates.[164] When Botaniates revolted with the magnates of the Anatolicon, Asia Minor was going up in flames, and the Turks were everywhere.[165] Botaniates managed to reach the military station of Cotyaeum with no more than 300 troops,[166] but any further progress toward Nicaea and Constantinople seemed hopeless, as the Turks had flocked into these regions in considerable numbers.[167] Thus the rebel was forced to avoid the regular road and to travel by night in order to avoid contact with the

---

[159] Bryennius, 92–95.

[160] Attaliates, 267. " χρόνος γὰρ παρελήλυθεν ἱκανὸς ἀφ' ὅτου 'Ρωμαίους οὐκ ἔσχεν ὁ τόπος ἐκεῖνος ἐπιφανέντας τὸ σύνολον. Τούρκων γὰρ ἐπὶ τῶν ἡμέρων τοῦ Μιχαὴλ ἐγίνετο καταγώγιον . . ."

[161] Miklosich et Müller, VI, 18–19.

[162] Anna Comnena, II, 65–66.

[163] Michael the Syrian, III, 172, records that during the reign of Michael VII the Greek cities and forts lived in fear and terror. The Arabs succeeded in retaking Menbij from the Greeks only in 1075. Bar Hebraeus, I, 225.

[164] St. Christodoulos (Miklosich et Müller, VI, 19), relates that the "evil" reached its height in 1076 and following years. "ὁπηνίκα ἐκορυφώθη τὸ κακὸν καὶ πανταχοῦ ἐπετάσθη τὰ θήρατρα τῶν ἐχθρῶν." Attaliates 211, records after the revolt of Nestor, " 'Επεὶ δὲ καὶ τὴν ἑῴαν οἱ ἐκεῖσε καταναλίσκοντες ἦσαν βάρβαροι καὶ πορθοῦντες καὶ καταβάλλοντες." E. L. Vranouse, Τὰ ἁγιογραφικὰ κείμενα τοῦ ὁσίου Χριστοδούλου, ἱδρυτοῦ τῆς ἐν Πάτμῳ μονῆς. Φιλολογικὴ παράδοσις καὶ ἱστορικαὶ μαρτυρίαι (Athens, 1966).

[165] Attaliates, 213–214. " καὶ πᾶσαν τὴν ἑῴαν πολεμίοις ἀνάστατον . . . καὶ τῆς Τούρκων ἔτι ζεούσης ἐπιφορᾶς, καὶ πολέμων πανταχόθεν ἀναρριπιζομένων σφοδρῶς."

[166] The last recorded levies of troops from the eastern themes were those in the ill-fated army of the Caesar John Ducas. The ease with which Roussel defeated them shows that already these corps had all but disappeared. The troops who finally joined Botaniates in Nicaea were all mercenaries. It was in the reign of Michael VII that the Immortals and Chomatenoi were formed in a desperate makeshift effort to compensate for the lost Anatolian levies. H. Grégoire, "De Marsile à Anderna, ou l'Islam et Byzance dans l'epopée française," in *Miscellanea Giovanni Mercati* (Vatican, 1956), III, 451–452. Skabalanovič, *Gosudarstvo*, pp. 327–328.

[167] Attaliates, 269, " . . . τῶν Τούρκων τὴν ἀπὸ θαλάσσης μέχρι Νικαίας νεμομένων περίχωρον." Attaliates, 272, " . . . οἳ τὸν ἐν μέσῳ χῶρον ἀγεληδὸν περιέτρεχον."

Turks of Sulayman and Mansur.[168] In spite of these precautions the Turks caught Botaniates before he could reach Nicaea, but fortunately he was able to outbid Michael VII for Turkish services, and it was only then that the passageway to Constantinople was opened.[169] Having occupied much of the rural area of northwestern Asia Minor, Sulayman's Turks apparently had their first major introduction into the urban centers as garrisons of Botaniates. Of the towns that Botaniates so garrisoned were Pylae, Praenetus, Nicomedia, Ruphinianae, Cyzicus, Nicaea, Chalcedon, and Chrysopolis.[170] But if the Turks were not definitively introduced into all these towns at this time, certainly the reign of the new emperor was the decisive step in their occupation. The rule of Nicephorus Botaniates spelled the end of Byzantine Asia Minor as the future major recruiting ground for the armies and as the principal source of tax revenues; in fact, by the end of his reign Asia Minor was with a few exceptions in foreign hands.[171]

By 1079 the Turks had reached Melanoudium on the western coast, and the fall of Strobilus was imminent,[172] most of Ionia having been occupied.[173] The revolt of Nicephorus Melissenus finally delivered more of the central and western Anatolian towns to Turkish hands. The rebel summoned the Turkish armies and their leaders, who by now were well versed in the intricacies of Byzantine civil strife, and with their support acquired the submission of the cities. He left the Turks as his representatives to garrison these towns so that with the failure of his revolt, many of the towns of Asia, Phrygia, and Galatia were in the hands of the Turks.[174]

---

[168] Bryennius, 119. Attaliates, 239–240.

[169] Attaliates, 240. After the agreement with Botaniates, Sulayman's Turks permitted all those coming from Constantinople, in order to join Botaniates, to pass through Bithynia.

[170] *Ibid.*, 266, 268.

[171] Anna Comnena, I, 18. " Εἰς γὰρ τὸ μέρος τοῦτο ἡ βασιλεία Ῥωμαίων εἰς τοὔσχατον ἐληλύθει. τά τε γὰρ ἑῷα τῶν στρατευμάτων ἄλλο ἀλλαχοῦ διεσκέδαστο τῶν Τούρκων ὑφαπλωθέντων καὶ πάντα σχεδὸν περισχούντων, ὅσα Εὐξείνου πόντου ἐστὶ μεταξὺ καὶ Ἑλλησπόντου καὶ Αἰγαίου τε καὶ Συριακοῦ πελάγους (καὶ) Σάρου τε καὶ τῶν ἄλλων καὶ μάλιστα ὁπόσοι Παμφυλίαν τε καὶ Κίλικας παραμείβοντες εἰς τὸ πέλαγος ἐκπίπτουσι τὸ Αἰγύπτιον." Bryennius, 129, " τῆς γὰρ τῶν χρημάτων ἐπεισροῆς τῶν ἀπὸ τῆς Ἀσίας χορηγουμένων τοῖς ταμείοις ἀποφυγούσης ἐκ τοῦ τῆς Ἀσίας ἁπάσης κατακυριεῦσαι τοὺς Τούρκους."

[172] Miklosich et Müller, VI, 62, 119–120. According to the anonymous Selcukname of the late thirteenth century, *Anadolu Selcuklulari̇ Devleti Tarihi*, III, *Historie des Seljoukides d'Asie Mineure par un anonyme*, Turkish trans. by F. N. Uzluk (Ankara, 1952), p. 23, Sulayman took Iconium from the Byzantine commanders Marta and Kusta, and the neighboring fortress of Kavala from Romanus Macri. Thus he took the regions from Iconium to Nicaea. See Cahen, "Seljukides de Rum, Byzantins et Francs d'aprés le Seljukname anonyme," *A.I.P.H.O.S.*, XI (1951), 97–98.

[173] Miklosich et Müller, VI, 61.

[174] Bryennius, 158. " ὁ δὲ καὶ ἄκων τοῖς Τούρκοις ἐνεχείριζεν, ὡς συμβῆναι διὰ βραχέος καιροῦ, κἀκ τούτου τοῦ τρόπου πασῶν τῶν περὶ τὴν Ἀσίαν τε καὶ Φρυγίαν καὶ τὴν Γαλατίαν πόλεων κατακυριεῦσαι τοὺς Τούρκους."

Byzantine Counterattack (1081–1143)

Alexius Comnenus ascended the throne at a time (1081) when it seemed that the whole of Byzantine Anatolia was lost forever,[175] though in actuality the Turkish conquest seems to have bypassed a number of points. There were still Byzantine officials in Heracleia on the Black Sea, in parts of Paphlagonia and Cappadocia, in Choma, Trebizond, and in other unspecified[176] regions. There were also the Armenians in the region of the Taurus and Anti-Taurus who, though actually independent, often posed as officials of the emperor. If to contemporaries the situation appeared completely hopeless in the beginning of Alexius' reign, nevertheless the appearance of Alexius marks an important turning point in Byzantine Anatolian affairs. Things would improve, but they would do so only after further vicissitudes. The major problem on the emperor's hands in the earlier years was in the west, where the ambitious Norman adventurer Robert Guiscard was planning the conquest of Constantinople. There were, in addition, the raids of the Patzinaks in the Balkans. Because of the Norman threat, Alexius was forced to summon the Byzantine military forces from the regions of Heracleia, Paphlagonia, Cappadocia, Choma, and from other regions in the east still in the possession of the Greeks, an act that enabled the Turks to advance in these areas. Closer to the capital in the regions of Bithynia and Thynia, where Alexius had been carrying on a limited war with Sulayman of Nicaea in an effort to remove the Turks from the environs of Nicomedia, he was forced to conclude a treaty setting the boundary at the Dracon River.[177] But as Byzantium was in no position to enforce the treaty, the Turks violated it, pushing their incursions to the Propontis and Bosphorus.[178] In northern Anatolia the emir Karatekin took the city of Sinope and the neighboring towns.[179] A few years later, Anna Comnena remarks with some exaggeration, that the boundaries of the empire in the east and west were Adrianople and the Bosphorus respectively.[180] In 1085 Sulayman captured the important eastern city of Antioch.

But in that year two important events occurred which enabled Alexius

---

[175] Theodore Scutariotes-Sathas, 183. " Ότε τὴν βασιλείαν τῶν Ῥωμαίων παρέλαβεν, εὗρε τοὺς Τούρκους οὕς καὶ Πέρσας καλοῦμεν, πᾶσαν τὴν ὑφ' ἕω χώραν καταδραμόντες καὶ κατατρέχοντες καὶ τῶν μεγίστων δὲ Ἀνατολικῶν πόλεων κατεξουσιάζοντας . . ." Matthew of Edessa, p. 181. For general considerations of his situation at this time, M. Beck, "Alexios Komnenos zwischen Normanner und Türken," *Akten des XI Internationalen Byzantinistenkongresses 1958* (Munich, 1960), pp. 43–47.

[176] Anna Comnena, I, 131. When Alexius mustered the armies against Guiscard he summoned all the τοπάρχοι of Anatolia, " ὁπόσοι φρούριά τε καὶ πόλεις κατέχοντες γενναίως τοῖς Τούρκοις ἀντικαθίσταντο . . . τὸν Διαβατηνὸν τοποτηρητὴν τηνικαῦτα τῆς κατὰ Πόντον Ἡρακλείας καὶ Παφλαγονίας χρηματίζοντα καὶ τὸν Βούρτζην τοπάρχην ὄντα Καππαδοκίας καὶ Χώματος καὶ τοὺς λοιποὺς λογάδας . . ."

[177] Anna Comnena, I, 136–138. Dölger, *Regesten*, no. 1065. Vismara, *Bisanzio*, p. 47.

[178] Anna Comnena, II, 63.

[179] *Ibid.*, 64.

[180] *Ibid.*, 73.

to begin a limited offensive in northwest Asia Minor to push back the Turks from the Propontis and Bosphorus where they threatened the very life of the empire itself. In 1085 Guiscard died, relieving Alexius of any immediate pressure in the west. The same year marked the death of Sulayman in his eastern campaigns which permitted the emirs, whom he had left in charge of his domains, to establish themselves as independent chieftains. Indeed the death of Sulayman seems to mark a proliferation of these independent emirs in Anatolia, especially in the westernmost regions.[181] Abu'l-Kasim declared himself sultan in Nicaea; his brother was in control of Cappadocia;[182] consequently, it is possible that the sultanate of Nicaea retained some sort of general control over the regions stretching from Nicaea to Konya and eastward to Cappadocia. But on the western littoral a large number of emirs emerged, the most important of whom was Tzachas (assisted by his brother Galavatzes-Yalavach), who established a maritime principality that at its height came to include Smyrna, Clazomenae, Phocaea, Samos, Mitylene, and Chios, and whose ambitions included the conquest of Constantinople.[183] The emirs Tangripermes and Merak ruled Ephesus and the neighboring towns,[184] while to the north along the Propontis coast were Elchanes (at Apollonias and Cyzicus), Scaliarius and others.[185] The other major Turkish political force in Anatolia, aside from the sultanate of Nicaea, was the dynasty of the Danishmendids. Malik Danishmend, as the leader of the Holy War in northern Anatolia, succeeded in carving out a domain that threatened to eclipse the house of Kutlumush. It came to include Sivas, regions of the Kïzïl Irmak, Yeshil Irmak and Kelkit Su, Amasya, Comana, Tokat, Niksar, Chankiri, Ankara, and Malatya.[186] Farther to the west, Karatekin conquered and held for a brief period Sinope and the neighboring towns, but by 1085 these were restored to the Byzantine emperor.[187] The regions of Armenia, more accessible to the armies of Malik Shah, were governed

[181] The list of principalities in the list of Yinanc, *Fethi*, pp. 132–134 is not to be accepted without reservations, as a number of these emirates had nothing more than an ephemeral existence.

[182] Anna Comnena, II, 67. By the time of the Crusades, Cappadocia was under Hasan. Anna Comnena, III, 144.

[183] Zonaras, III, 736–737. Anna Comnena, II, 110–115, 158–161. For a detailed account of his interesting career, F. Chalandon, *Essai sur le règne d'Alexis Ier Comnène (1081–1118)* (Paris, 1900), 125–127, 147, 195–196 (hereafter cited as Chalandon, I). A. Kurat, *Caka ortazamanda Izmir ve yakïnïndaki adalarïn Türk hakimi* (Istanbul, 1936). It is quite possible that the Tzachas mentioned in the Danishmendname refers to this particular chieftain, Danishmendname Melikoff, I, 73.

[184] Anna Comnena, III, 23, 26.

[185] *Ibid.*, II, 79–81.

[186] The most recent discussion of the complex history of the founder of the Danishmendid dynasty and a complete bibliography are in Melikoff-*Danishmendname*, I, *passim*. But as to Malik's ethnic origin the report by Matthew of Edessa, p. 256, that he was an Armenian (an opinion shared by Yinanc, *Fethi*, p. 101), though plausible is improbable. Melikoff, "Danishmend," EI₂.

[187] Anna Comnena, II, 64–66. Karatekin was directly obedient to Malik Shah, in contrast to many of the other emirs.

by one of his officials, the emir Ismail.[188] A certain Baldukh established himself as emir of Samosata;[189] Alp Ilek temporarily occupied Edessa;[190] Sukman the son of Artuk also appeared in the regions of Edessa; [191] and Balas ruled Suruj in the same general area.[192] Other emirs directly under the authority of the sultans in Persia frequently made their appearance in Anatolia in an effort to bring the recalcitrant emirs under control of the great sultans.[193]

For the next decade, up until the appearance of the Crusaders, Alexius was able to make slow but definite progress in Anatolia. Soon after the death of Sulayman, the emperor recovered Sinope and the neighboring coastal regions by bribing an official of the sultan.[194] Nearer to home he destroyed (1092) the naval arsenal that the Turks were using at Cius,[195] built Cibotus to command the regions of the Gulf of Nicomedia,[196] and retook the important regions of Cyzicus, Poimamenum, and Apollonias.[197] Farther to the south Byzantine naval forces began to reduce the powerful Tzachas.[198] Now free of the Normans and setting one Turkish emir against another, Alexius was preparing to deal with the Turkish problem in a more decisive manner when news arrived that Latin armies were setting out for the East.[199] In a sense, the timing of the Crusades fitted the Turkish plans of Alexius, for if the Latin troops could be controlled, they could be harnessed to his plans to reconquer the eastern provinces. It was the knights of the First Crusade who dealt the Seljuks of Anatolia their first major setback and enabled Alexius to reconquer western Anatolia and reintegrate it into the empire. In 1097 the Turks were defeated across the length of Anatolia, being forced to retire from Nicaea, Dorylaeum, Antioch of Pisidia, Iconium, Heracleia, the regions of Caesareia, Plastentza (Comana), Marash, Tarsus, Adana, and Mopsuestia (Mamistra).[200] The Crusade of 1101 brought the Byzantines into

[188] Matthew of Edessa, p. 204. He is probably not to be confused with Ismail, brother of Malik Shah, who was active in the regions of Paipert. Anna Comnena, III, 29–30.

[189] Matthew of Edessa, p. 210.

[190] *Ibid.*, p. 211.

[191] *Ibid.*, p. 210.

[192] William of Tyre, IV, 6. He was an Ortokid. Cahen, "Balas," EI$_2$, and "Artukids," EI$_2$.

[193] Such were Monolycus, Kontogmen, Mahmud, and Buzan. Anna Comnena, III, 166. Matthew of Edessa, pp. 198, 203.

[194] Anna Comnena, II, 65–66. Gabras had recovered Trebizond earlier.

[195] *Ibid.*, 69.

[196] *Ibid.*, 71. He builds the fortress called Iron. Anna Comnena, II, 205. H. Glykatzi-Ahrweiler, "Les fortresses construites en Asie Mineure face à l'invasion seldjoukide," *Akten des XI Internationalen Byzantinisten-kongresses München 1958* (Munich, 1960), pp. 182–185.

[197] Anna Comnena, II, 80.

[198] *Ibid.*, 158–161.

[199] *Ibid.*, 205.

[200] For the details, H. Hagenmeyer, "Chronologie de la première Croisade (1094–1100)," *R.O.L.*, VI (1898), 285–293, 495–510. Runciman, "The First Crusade: Constantinople to Antioch," in *A History of the Crusades*, ed. K. Setton (Philadelphia, 1955), pp. 280–304. *Gesta Francorum et aliorum Hierosolimitanorum*, ed. and trans. L. Bréhier (Paris,

possession once more of the important city of Ankara and a portion of the Anatolian plateau in the north.[201] In the more easterly regions of the Taurus and Anti-Taurus, the appearance of the Crusaders resulted in a further weakening of Turkish power, but in these areas this worked less to the advantage of the Byzantines than to the benefit of the Armenians and Latins. Taking advantage of the expulsion of the Turks from northwest Anatolia, Alexius sent joint naval and land forces to liberate the western coast. Smyrna surrendered without resistance, following which the Byzantines reoccupied Ephesus. The Byzantine forces pushed into the adjacent hinterland and onto the western edge of the plateau, driving the Turks from Sardes, Philadelpheia, Laodiceia, Lampe, and Polybotus. Thus when Alexius set out in June of 1098 to join the Crusaders at Antioch, he was able to advance as far as Philomelium with relative ease.[202] In the years that followed, Byzantine land and naval expeditions eventually reclaimed the southern Anatolian coastline from Turks and Crusaders, the defeat of Bohemund in Europe constituting the critical event in this phase of the Byzantine reconquest. In the treaty of 1108, Alexius received the theme of Podandus, Tarsus, Adana, Mopsuestia (Mamistra), Anazarba, and all cities between the Cydnus and the Hermon rivers.[203] By the end of his reign, Alexius had been able to make serious progress in his efforts to reassert Byzantine authority in Asia Minor. The Anatolian provinces of the empire in 1118 included the province of Trebizond, all the land to the west of a line passing through Sinope, Gangra, Ankara, Amorium, Philomelium, and the whole of the southern coastline up to the duchy of Antioch.[204]

It is apparent that after a half century of uninterrupted warfare and disruption, the Turks had not succeeded in conquering the whole of the Anatolian peninsula. Rather they had secured the major portion of the central plateau and the eastern provinces leading into the regions of Adharbaydjan and the Euphrates. The Byzantine reconquest had succeeded in removing the Turks from all coastal regions and from the critical western edge of the plateau itself. This half century had, however, seen a warfare whose intensity had never been previously recorded in the annals of the peninsula. The Turkish invasions had brought an end to unified political control, and therefore an end to relatively stable political conditions, in Anatolia. These invasions resulted in the proliferation of independent political authorities on the Anatolian soil, a factor of prime

---

1924), pp. 37–65 (hereafter cited as *Gesta Francorum*). Anna Comnena, III, 8–19. Matthew of Edessa, pp. 214–215. See also the commentary of H. Hagenmeyer, *Anonymi gesta Francorum et aliorum Hierosolymitanorum* (Heidleberg, 1890), pp. 179–238.

[201] J. L. Cate, "The Crusade of 1101," *A History of the Crusades*, pp. 354–355. Anna Comnena, III, 36.

[202] Anna Comnena, III, 23–29. Chalandon, I, 195–198. Ahrweiler, "Smyrne," p. 5, proposes the date 1093–94 for the Byzantine reconquest of Smyrna.

[203] Anna Comnena, III, 134. Chalandon, I, 248.

[204] Chalandon, I, 271.

importance in the Turkification and Islamization of Anatolia, as we shall see in the next chapter.

The events of the next century were instrumental in determining the collapse of Byzantium in the greater part of Asia Minor and in eroding the political basis of Hellenism in large parts of the peninsula, for in the twelfth century parts of Anatolia continued to be the chaotic scene of unabating and often savage warfare. In the west on the mountainous edge of the Anatolian plateau, the Byzantines, Seljuks, and Turkmens waged a relentless and harsh struggle along a line stretching from the Sangarius and Dorylaeum to Cotyaeum, Choma, Philomelium, Sozopolis, and Laodiceia to Attaleia. In a conflict that observed no hard and fixed boundaries, the Greeks raided as far as Iconium, the Turks and Turkmens as far as the Aegean coast. In northern Asia Minor the Greeks, Turkmens, Seljuks, and Danishmendids fought along a similarly fluid border, a border that pivoted about the towns of Claudiopolis, Dadybra, Castamon, Gangra, Paura, Amaseia, Comana, and Oenoe. In eastern Anatolia (a region that though outside of the Greek portion of the peninsula, nevertheless would be the scene of events affecting the Byzantine position), Georgians, Saltukids of Erzerum, Menguchekids of Erzindjan-Coloneia-Tephrice, Artukids, Danishmendids, Shaddadids, Zangids, Crusaders, Ayyubids, Turkmens, Armenians, and Byzantines insured the same conditions—that the region would be one of considerable turmoil, upheaval, and desolation. In southern Anatolia, Greeks, Armenians, Turkmens, Latins, Kurds, and Arabs made their military appearances with hypnotizing monotony.[205]

Such unsettled conditions encouraged intense dynastic and civil strife inasmuch as any potential rebel could usually rely upon support from one or more of the Anatolian states. Rebellion and dynastic strife plagued Greeks, Armenians, and Turks alike. Byzantine princes, Seljuk sultans, Danishmendids, and Armenians became familiar sights at the various Anatolian courts where they passed their time in plotting the overthrow of their kinsmen with the aid of the forces of the enemy.

This proliferation of independent political authority and of dynastic

[205] The complicated history of Anatolia in this critical period has not as yet been written. The major outlines, however, have been established. Chalandon, *Les Comnènes*, II. M. Bachmann, *Die Rede des Johannes Syropoulos an dem Kaiser Isaak II Angelus (1185–95)* (Munich, 1935), pp. 55–64. F. Cognasso, "Un imperatore bizantino della decadenza: Isaaco II Angelo," *Bessarione* XIX (1915), 250–253. P. Wittek, "Deux chapitres de l'histoire des Turcs de Rum," *Byzantion*, XI (1936), 285–319; "Le sultanat de Roum," *A.I.P.H.O.S.*, VI, 688–703. Cahen, "The Turks in Iran and Anatolia before the Mongol Invasions," *A History of the Crusades* (Philadelphia, 1962) II, 661–692; "Selgukides Turcomans et Allemands au temps de la troièsime croisade," *W.Z.K.M.*, LVI (1960), 21–31; "Le Diyar Bakar au temps des premiers Urtukids," *J.A.*, CCXXVII (1935), 219–272; "Artukids," EI₂. Sümer, "Mengücükler," IA. Melikoff, "Danishmendids," EI₂. Der Nersessian, "Cilician Armenia." R. M. Bartikian, "K istorii vzaimootnoshenii mezhdu Vizantiei i kilikiiskim armianskim gosudarstvom v kontse XII v.," *V.V.*, XVII (1960), 52–56. A. Heisenberg, "Zu den armenisch-byzantinisch Beziehungen am Anfang des 3. Jahrhunderts," *Sitz. der bay. Akad. der Wiss. Phil.-hist. Kl.* (1929), VI.

strife at first favored the Byzantine designs to push forward the reconquest of Anatolia, enabling the emperors to exploit the rivalry of the sons of sultan Mas'ud and the struggle between Danishmendids and Seljuks. John Comnenus (1118–43), because of the relative weakness of the sultan of Iconium, was free to concentrate his efforts on the Danishmendids in the north and against the Cilician Armenians in the south. In 1119, 1120–21, and again in 1124 he undertook operations in western Asia Minor against the Turkmens, who, in violating the treaty between Alexius I and the Turks, had occupied Laodiceia, Sozopolis, Hieracory-phites, and other regions in the vicinity of Attaleia. He was successful in driving the Turkmens from these towns and enrolled a number of them in his own armies.[206] But his most important compaigns were those waged against the Danishmendids in the north at a time when relations between the Danishmendids and the sultan of Konya were inimical. A series of campaigns between 1130 and 1135 enabled John II to recover Gangra, Castamon, and a number of other towns and to subjugate various emirs.[207] During the years 1137 and 1138 he was busy restoring order in Cilicia where the Armenian Leo had taken many of the cities from the hands of the Greeks. Here he accomplished his goal with comparative ease as Mopsuestia, Tarsus, Adana, and Anazarba again recognized Byzantine authority.[208] By the time of his expedition against Neocaesareia in 1139–40 Greek arms were once more feared throughout Anatolia. The fear of the Muslim rulers was such that

When the emperor began to attack Neocaesareia, the fury of the Turks against the Christians increased in all the lands which they held. Whosoever mentioned the name of the emperor, even by accident, received the sword, and his children and house were taken. In this manner many perished in Melitene and in other lands, up until the emperor suddenly departed.[209]

The expedition against Neocaesareia failed, but at the same time it represents the high tide of the attempted Byzantine reconquest of Asia Minor. This failure was, however, soon partially compensated by the death of the Danishmendid ruler Malik Muhammad in 1142. With his death the Danishmendid patrimony was divided into three mutually hostile and warring states, Yaghibasan ruling at Sebasteia, Dhu'l-Nun at Caesareia, and 'Ayn al-Dawla at Albistan and Melitene. This relieved the

---

[206] Nicetas Choniates, 17–18, seems to imply this. Cinnamus, 5–6. Theodore Scutariotes-Sathas, 190–191. Theodore Prodromus, P.G., CXXXIII, 1382, speaks of a victory at Amorium. See also his poem in the edition of C. Welz, *Analecta Byzantina. Carmina inedita Theodori Prodromi et Stephani Physopalamitae* (Leipzig, 1910).

[207] Cinnamus, 13–15. Nicetas Choniates, 25–29. Michael the Syrian, III, 232–234. Theodore Scutariotes-Sathas, 195–197, 199. Kurtz, B.Z. XVI (1907), 75–83, edited a poem on the second fall of Castamon. Theodore Prodromus, P.G., CXXXIII, 1373–1383, mentions among the towns and emirs that he subdued: Alamon, Alazan, Balzon; the emirs Toghrul of Amaseia, Alpsarous of Gangra, Prachinon, Elelden, Elbegkous, Tzykes, Inales, Kallinoglu, Aitougdin, Ausararis, Chalandon, II, 82–91.

[208] Nicetas Choniates, 33–42. Cinnamus, 16–18. Theodore Scutariotes-Sathas, 197–200. Michael the Syrian, III, 245. Gregory the Priest, p. 323.

[209] Michael the Syrian, III, 249.

Byzantines from the pressure of the most powerful Turkish state in Anatolia, but the disintegration of Danishmendid rule was soon to upset the balance of power in favor of the Seljuks of Iconium.[210] In his last Anatolian campaign (1142–43), the object of which was Antioch, John paused en route to drive out the Turkmens besieging Sozopolis and to make his appearance among the other Phrygian cities in an effort to strengthen Byzantine authority in the area. It is of interest to note that the Greek inhabitants of the islands of Lake Pousgouse who recognized the sultan and who had established a satisfactory modus vivendi with the Turks refused to receive the emperor, and John was forced to take the islands by force.[211]

Byzantine Retreat (1143–1204)

With the division of the Danishmendid domains, the sultanate of Iconium gradually emerged as the major power in Asia Minor. This ascendancy of the house of Kutlumush was accompanied by a corresponding decline in Byzantium's Anatolian fortunes. The final failure of the Byzantine attempts to reconquer Anatolia and the establishment of the Seljuks as the dominant Anatolian power coincided with the reigns of Manuel Comnenus (1143–80) and Kïlïdj II Arslan (1155–92).[212] That this would be the final issue was not at all evident in the early years of the reigns of the two men, for with the death of Mas'ud and the accession of Kïlïdj Arslan, there was dynastic strife complicated by the intervention of the Danishmendid Yaghibasan.[213] Manuel, inasmuch as he inherited the situation in Anatolia from his father John, was in a much stronger position, a state of affairs reflected in the successful character of Manuel's campaigns and policies up until his distraction with and absorption in European affairs. This is brought out clearly by his early success in chasing the Turkmens from the regions of Melangeia and in the rebuilding of the fortifications with a view to making the Bithynian borders safe from their raids.[214] Much more spectacular was the campaign of 1146 when, as a result of the Turkish capture of Pracana in Cilicia and Turkish raids into the Thracesian theme, Manuel decided to attack Iconium itself. He defeated the forces of the sultan successively at Acrounos, Calograias Bounos, and Philomelium. Manuel burned the latter city and released the Greeks who had been held captive there for years. Then the imperial armies marched to the Seljuk capital itself where they desecrated the Muslim cemeteries outside the walls. The arrival of Muslim reinforcements from the Danishmendids, however, forced Manuel to lift the siege and to

---

[210] Melikoff, "Danishmendids," EI₂. Nicetas Choniates, 45–49. Cinnamus, 21. Theodore Scutariotes-Sathas, 205–207. Michael the Syrian, III, 249.

[211] Nicetas Choniates, 50–51. Cinnamus, 22. Theodore Scutariotes-Sathas, 208.

[212] F. Uspenskii, Istoriia Vizantiiskoi Imperii (Moscow-Leningrad, 1948), pp. 272 ff Chalandon, Les Comnènes, II.

[213] O. Turan, "Kïlïc Arslan," IA.

[214] Cinnamus, 36. Nicetas Choniates, 71. Chalandon, Les Comnènes, II, 247–248.

retire to Choma via the road along Lake Pousgouse. As Choma was considered to be well within the Byzantine boundaries, Manuel was startled by the unannounced presence of the tents of the Turkmens of a certain Rama. They were chased out and Manuel made his way to Bithynia, settled the Greeks from Philomelium and built the fortress of Pylae. Upon the approach of the Second Crusade, both Manuel and Mas'ud concluded a treaty (1147) by which Pracana and other places were returned to the Byzantines.[215]

The Crusaders found Anatolia difficult terrain in spite of Manuel's recent conquest of Melangeia. Even though Conrad and the Germans were able to advance as far as Melangeia without incident from the Turks, they were defeated at Bathys by the Turkish chief Mamplanes and eventually forced to retire to Nicaea. Louis VII led the French by a more westerly route toward Attaleia and thus avoided these more dangerous areas. Nevertheless, as they entered the Maeander valley and progressed toward Laodiceia, they were severely harassed by the Turks, and Attaleia itself had hostile Turkmens in the environs.[216]

In another region the Armenian Thoros had begun to enter the cities held by the Byzantines in Cilicia, having succeeded at Tarsus and Mopsuestia by 1152. Mas'ud, at the prompting of Manuel, invaded Cilicia and attacked Thoros in 1153 and again in 1154 but he was defeated, and with the death of Mas'ud in 1155, Thoros was freed from this quarter. Mas'ud's successor, Kïlïdj Arslan, went so far as to take the cities of Pannoura and Sibyla from the Byzantines in 1157,[217] but with the making of peace between Manuel and Kïlïdj Arslan in 1158, the emperor turned to Cilicia to settle accounts with Thoros. The emperor's eastern march in this year was highly successful. En route he defeated the Turkmens in Little Phrygia, and once in Cilicia he took the cities of Cistramon, Anazarba, Longinias, Tarsus, and Tili.[218]

Despite the treaty of 1158, from 1159 to 1161 Manuel was on a campaign against the Turkmens in western Asia Minor. On its return from the Cilician and Syrian campaign, Manuel's army had been attacked by the Turkmens in the neighborhood of Dorylaeum and it is no doubt as a result of this that he appeared in the valleys of the Tembris and Bathys near Cotyaeum in 1159, driving out large numbers of the nomads with

[215] Cinnamus, 38–46. Nicetas Choniates, 71–72. Chalandon, *Les Comnènes*, II, 248–258. Vismara, *Bisanzio*, p. 50. Dölger, *Regesten*, no. 1352.

[216] Nicetas Choniates, 89. Cinnamus, 81–84. William of Tyre, XVI-22, 26. Odo of Deuil, *De profectione Ludovici VII in orientem*, ed. and trans. V. G. Berry (New York, 1948), pp. 109-113 (hereafter cited as Odo of Deuil), gives a graphic description of the desolation that prevailed in much of western Asia Minor. Chalandon, Les Comnènes, II, 281–286, 300, 304, 310.

[217] Chalandon, Les Comnènes, II, 430–434. Cinnamus, 176. At the same time Yaghi-basan took Oenoe and Baura on the Black Sea from the Greeks.

[218] Cinnamus, 179–180. Nicetas Choniates, 134-135. Theodore Prodromus, *R.H.C.*, *H.G.*, II, 752, 766. Chalandon, *Les Comnènes*, II, 441 ff. Dölger, *Regesten*, no. 1422. Vismara, *Bisanzio*, p. 51.

their animals.[219] In 1160–61 setting out from Philadelpheia he plundered the regions of Sarapata Mylonos, regions considered to be the domain of the emir Solymas. But his campaign must have been ineffectual, for when he retired the Turks came in the van of the withdrawing army, captured the town of Philetas and killed and enslaved large numbers of the inhabitants of Laodiceia.[220] In late 1161, after suffering defeat at the hands of another Byzantine army, Kĭlĭdj Arslan once more concluded a peace treaty with Manuel. Inasmuch as the Byzantines were actively supporting the intrigues of his enemies, and as Kĭlĭdj Arslan had suffered defeat at the hands of Yaghibasan in 1160 and had been forced to relinquish Albistan, the sultan did not feel sufficiently secure with the new Byzantine treaty of 1161. For this reason in 1162 he made his celebrated journey to Constantinople where he was lavishly received by Manuel and here he succeeded in putting an end to the Byzantine diplomatic intrigues.[221] This date marks the turning point in the rise of the fortune of Kĭlĭdj Arslan and the reversal of Byzantine success on the Asia Minor front, for Manuel, given a false sense of security, became increasingly involved in western affairs with a consequent neglect of the Turkish problem. Kĭlĭdj Arslan was left free to deal with his brother Shahinshah and with the Danishmendids. The death of the last capable Danishmendid, Yaghibasan, in 1164, further eased his task and emboldened the sultan to conquer the regions of Albistan, Darende, Geduk, the Tohma River in 1165; four years later he took Caesareia, Tzamandus, Ankara, and Gangra.[222] Thanks to the intrigues of Nur al-Din, the Danishmendids were temporarily saved, but with the latter's death in 1174, Kĭlĭdj Arslan was freed of his last powerful rival in the east. One year later, in 1175, most of the remainder of the Danishmendid lands, including Sebasteia, Neocaesareia, Doceia, and Comana, fell to Kĭlĭdj Arslan,[223] and he seized Melitene two years later. All this, of course, meant a formidable growth in Seljuk strength and a sensible shift in the Anatolian balance of power.

The sources do not say very much about the events on the Turco-Byzantine border during this period between 1162 and 1174. There is mention of the appearance of the Turkish nomads in the cities of the Phrygian Pentapolis in search of pasture for their livestock, but evidently the emperor drove them out.[224] In the same period the Turks sacked

[219] Cinnamus, 191. Chalandon, *Les Comnènes*, II, 458–459.

[220] Cinnamus, 194–198.

[221] Nicetas Choniates, 155–156, has an interesting account of the Sultan's stay in Constantinople, including an account of the games in the hippodrome which he witnessed and the ridicule to which the guildsmen subjected him. Michael the Syrian, *R.H.C.*, *H.A.*, I, 355. Papadopoulos-Kerameus, " Εὐθυμίου Τορνίκη συγγραφαί," in *Noctes Petropolitanae*, (St. Petersburg, 1913), pp. 165–187 (hereafter Euthymius Tornices-Papadopoulos-Kerameus). Dölger, *Regesten*, nos. 1444, 1446, 1447. Vismara, *Bisanzio*, p. 51.

[222] Turan, "Kĭlĭc Arslan," 691. Michael the Syrian, III, 332. Bar Hebraeus, I, 293.

[223] Turan, "Kĭlĭc Arslan," 692. Michael the Syrian, III, 357. Bar Hebraeus, I, 303.

[224] Nicetas Choniates, 162–164. Theodore Scutariotes-Sathas, 253–254. Chalandon, *Les Comnènes*, II, 499.

Laodiceia and carried away many of the inhabitants and the livestock.[225] The most important action of the emperor during this interval was the fortification of the regions of Pergamum, Adramyttium, and Chliara in order to keep out the Turkish raiders and to protect the villages and rural populations.[226] But Manuel, once disengaged from his grandiose western schemes, soon realized that the political picture in Anatolia had changed considerably and so he decided to make a definite effort to curb Kïlïdj Arslan. The latter, stalling for time, informed Manuel that he would hand over to him a number of cities if the emperor would send an army to occupy them. The sultan, however, employed these troops for quite a different purpose, using them to subject cities that had previously resisted him. Simultaneously, the city of Amaseia, formerly held by Shahinshah and evidently ready to recognize the authority of the emperor, was forced to receive the garrison of Kïlïdj Arslan.[227] Manuel had previously decided to drive the Turkmens from the regions of Dorylaeum because of their constant raids and devastation of Byzantine soil. Dorylaeum had in the tenth and eleventh centuries been one of the important and most prosperous urban centers of Anatolia, but the Turkmens had razed it to the ground and caused it to be abandoned and deserted. When Manuel appeared in the area he drove out the nomads and rebuilt the fortifications and the town in 1175–76. Farther to the south he rebuilt the fortress town of Choma-Soublaion.[228]

In 1176 Manuel made the decision to put an end to the power of the sultanate by taking Iconium and capturing the sultan, and to this purpose he levied great numbers of troops, especially Latins and Uzes from the Danubian regions. He sent one force under his nephew Andronicus Vatatzes to take Neocaesareia and the emperor himself took the major portion of the army southward. He advanced on Iconium via Phrygia and Laodiceia, stopping at Chonae to visit the church of the Archangel Michael, and afterward moved on to Lampe and Celenae-Apameia where the Maeander River rises. Thence he proceeded to the recently rebuilt fortress of Choma-Soublaion and finally to the abandoned fortress of Myriocephalum. The emperor's progress had been orderly

[225] Nicetas Choniates, 163. Theodore Scutariotes-Sathas, 253–254. Chalandon, *Les Comnènes*, II, 499.

[226] Nicetas Choniates, 194–195. Theodore Scutariotes-Sathas, 268. Chalandon, *Les Comnènes*, II, 500–504.

[227] Cinnamus, 292–293, 296.

[228] Nicetas Choniates, 227–229. Cinnamus, 297–298. Theodore Scutariotes-Sathas, 283. Euthymius Malaces in K. Bones, " Εὐθυμίου τοῦ Μαλάκη μητροπολίτου Νέων Πατρῶν (Ὑπάτης), δύο ἐγκωμιαστικοὶ Λόγοι, νῦν τὸ πρῶτον ἐκδιδόμενοι, εἰς τὸν αὐτοκράτορα Μανουὴλ Α´ Κομνηνὸν (1143/80)," Θεολογία, XIX (1941–48), 526–529, 538–539, 546–547. Bar Hebraeus, I, 306. Chalandon, Les Comnènes, II, 503–504. P. Wirth, "Kaiser Manuel I Komnenos und die Ostgrenze: Rückeroberung und Aufbau der Festung Dorylaion," *B.Z.*, LV (1962), 21–29. Dölger, *Regesten*, no. 1520. According to Michael the Syrian, III, 369, he set out to attack the Turkmens, killing them by the thousands. In retaliation they entered Byzantine territory in the north and took away 100,000 captives, selling them on the slave markets.

but very slow, as there was a large contingent of unarmed men busy with the immense baggage train. The slowness had been enforced by the appearance of the Turkmens, "numerous as the locusts,"[229] who realized that the emperor had come to chase them from their habitats. The nomads harassed the army in groups of 5,000 to 10,000, and on the eve of the battle some 50,000 of them pillaged the emperor's camp.[230] The sultan had made considerable preparations for the conflict by recruiting large numbers of Turks from the regions of Mesopotamia and from the regions farther to the east.[231] As the Byzantine army had advanced, the sultan had withdrawn and scorched the earth, burning the villages and grassy plains and destroying anything that might be of use to the advancing Byzantine army. All the wells, cisterns, and springs were contaminated with the bodies of dead asses and dogs, so that even before the battle took place dysentery had spread throughout the whole of the imperial army.[232]

In spite of the fact that the sultan appeared to be in a favorable position to deal with the invaders, he sent an embassy to the emperor asking for peace. Manuel, ignoring the difficulties of the army and the vigorous objections of his most experienced generals, rejected the offers of peace. Upon the refusal of the emperor, the sultan occupied the pass of Tzybritze, which the Greeks were about to enter as they left Myriocephalum. The battle that ensued in the difficult mountain pass was a disaster almost of the magnitude of Manzikert. Caught and surrounded by the Turks in the narrow defiles, the Byzantine army was subjected to a frightful slaughter. A fierce sandstorm so obscured events that Greeks and Turks were not able to distinguish friend from foe, with the result that they killed indiscriminately. By evening, with the subsiding of the storm, it became obvious that the Turks had had the upper hand. The Byzantine troops were further demoralized during the course of the night by the Turks who came into the vicinity of the camp and called out to the Christian Turks to abandon the emperor before it was too late.[233] The plight of the army was such that Manuel seriously considered secret flight and the abandoning of all his troops to the mercies of the enemy. It is quite strange

---

[229] Nicetas Choniates, 230–231. Michael the Syrian, III, 371.

[230] Michael the Syrian, III, 371.

[231] Nicetas Choniates, 232, " ξυμμαχικόν ἱκανὸν ἀπό τε τῆς μέσης τῶν ποταμῶν καὶ τῶν ἄνω συμφύλων βαρβάρων." Theodore Scutariotes-Sathas, 284.

[232] Nicetas Choniates, 231–232. Theodore Scutariotes-Sathas, 284. Michael the Syrian, III, 371. H. v. Kap-Herr, *Die abendländische Politik Kaiser Manuels mit besonderer Rücksicht auf Deutschland* (Strassburg, 1881), p. 104. A. Vasiliev, "Manuel Comnenus and Henry Plantagenet," *B.Z.*, XXIX (1929–30), 237–240, translates the letter of Manuel to Henry II, on the disaster, which is preserved in the chronicle of Roger of Hoveden. *The Annals of Roger de Hoveden*, trans. H. T. Riley (London, 1853), I, 419–423. F. Dirimtekin, *Konya ve Duzbel 1146–1176* (Istanbul, 1944).

[233] Theodore Scutariotes-Sathas, 290. " Ἐπεὶ δὲ νὺξ ἐπῆλθε καὶ τὸν πόλεμον ἔπαυσεν, ἀδημονῶν ἦν ἅπας, καὶ οὐ τοῖς ζῶσι συνέταττεν ἑαυτόν, ὅτε τὸν χάρακα περιτρέχοντες οἱ βάρβαροι φωναῖς ἀνεκάλουν τοὺς ὁμοεθνεῖς, οἳ πάλαι πρὸς Ῥωμαίους προσέφυγον καὶ τὴν ὀρθόδοξον πίστιν ἐδέξαντο, παραινοῦντες ἐξελθεῖν πρὸς αὐτούς, ὡς ἅμα φωτὶ ἀπολουμένων τῶν ἐν τῷ χάρακι. Nicetas Choniates, 243.

that under such circumstances Kĭlĭdj Arslan called a halt to the battle by sending one of his officials, Gabras, to offer peace terms to the emperor. The principal demands were that the newly constructed fortifications of Dorylaeum and Choma-Soublaion should be destroyed.[234] Certainly the sultan's behavior is incongruous with the nature of his victory, but Nicetas Chroniates mentions two facts that may have had something to do with the decision to offer the emperor terms. He relates that the advisers of the sultan had been in the pay of the emperor in peacetime and that they persuaded the sultan to propose peace terms.[235] After the conclusion of the treaty when the Greeks began to withdraw, they saw the hosts of the slain, and even though the Turks had won the victory it was obvious that the numbers of the fallen on both sides had been great. As the emperor's troops withdrew they noticed that the skin had been removed from the heads of the slain and that many of the slain had had the genitalia severed. The Turks had done this so that it would not be possible to distinguish the Christian from the Muslim corpses and thus the heavy losses of the Turks would be obscured.[236] Finally, in spite of the catastrophic nature of the Byzantine defeat, considerable portions of the army and their commanders had succeeded in regrouping about the emperor. It was perhaps a combination of these reasons, as well as others, which caused the sultan to offer peace, an action that he later regretted. When Manuel retreated, the Turkmens began to harass his army and to raid the countryside in small bands, taking booty and slaying the stragglers and the wounded. The emperor protested the violation of the treaty but Kĭlĭdj Arslan replied that the Turkmens were independent of him and he was in any case unable to control them. The defeated were not able to relax their vigilance until they arrived at Chonae, safely within Byzantine territory.[237]

This battle was the single most significant event to transpire on Anatolian soil since Manzikert (1071), and it meant the end of Byzantine plans to reconquer Asia Minor. The empire suffered a sharp defeat and severe losses in its fighting strength at the time when it was on the verge of collapse. The events of 1176 must also have had a great demoralizing effect not only upon the emperor but, more important, upon the Greek

[234] The fourteenth-century anonymous history of the Seljuks, *Histoire des Seljoukides d'Asie Mineure par un anonyme*, Turkish trans. F. N. Uzluk (Ankara, 1952), p. 25, also mentions that the emperor paid 100,000 gold and 100,000 silver pieces, horses, and cloth. Dölger, *Regesten*, nos. 1522, 1524. Vismara, *Bisanzio*, pp. 52–53.

[235] Nicetas Choniates, 244–245, " παρασυρεὶς γὰρ οὗτος ταῖς τῶν μεγιστάνων αὐτοῦ ὑποθημοσύναις, οἵπερ ἀπήντλουν ἀμφοτέραις ἐκ βασιλέως κατὰ τὸν τῆς εἰρήνης καιρὸν χρήματα." Theodore Scutariotes-Sathas, 291.

[236] Nicetas Choniates, 247. " αἱ τε γὰρ φάραγγες εἰς ἰσόπεδον ἀνέβαινον, καὶ οἱ κοιλάδες εἰς κολωνοὺς ἀνηγείροντο, καὶ τὰ ἄλση τοῖς θνησιμαίοις ἐκεκάλυπτο. ἅπας δὲ κείμενος ἀποσυρεὶς ἦν τὸ δέρμα τῆς κεφαλῆς, πολλοὶ δὲ καὶ τοὺς ἰθυφάλλους ἀπεκαυλίσθησαν. ἐλέγετο δὲ τοὺς Πέρσας τοῦτο τεχνάσασθαι, ἵνα μὴ τοῦ ἀκροβύστου ὁ ἐμπερίτομος διαστέλλοιτο καὶ ἡ νίκη οὕτως εἴη ἀμφίπαλὴς καὶ ἀμφήριστος, ὡς ἐξ ἑκατέρων τῶν στρατοπέδων καταβληθέντων πολλῶν."

[237] Nicetas Choniates, 248–249. Michael the Syrian, III, 372.

inhabitants of the Anatolian regions still held by the empire. The last hope for the removal of the Turkish power had gone up in smoke. That this military action in 1176 took place so many hundreds of miles west of Manzikert was a clear demonstration of the great growth of Turkish strength in Asia Minor. Because of Manuel's preoccupation in the west with its attendant neglect of Turkish affairs, Kilïdj Arlsan had had the time and the opportunity to remove his rivals and to consolidate his kingdom. Though it is difficult to estimate the contribution of the Turkmen tribes to this victory in 1176, it seems safe to assume that the presence of large numbers of nomads in the border area served to absorb the shock of the Byzantine attack and to exhaust the Christian armies before their contact with the forces of the sultan.

The remaining three years of Manuel's reign (1177–80) saw an intensification of the Turkish raids on Byzantine territory along the borders from northern Bithynia to the Maeander districts. As Manuel refused to destroy the fortifications of Dorylaeum, the sultan sent the Atabeg with an army of 24,000 to raid the Christian lands. The Turks appeared suddenly in the Maeander valley and sacked Tralles, Phrygian Antioch, Louma, Pentacheir, as well as other towns. Finding little resistance, the raiders turned to the coastal regions, which they also plundered. The imperial troops did arrive in time to attack the Turks as they were crossing the Maeander at Hyelion and Leimmocheir and destroyed most of them.[238] On two other occasions the emperor himself appeared with the army in unsuccessful efforts to drive the Turkmens out of the regions of Panasium, Lacerion, and Charax (between Lampe and Graos Gala).[239] In northern Bithynia the emperor saved the city of Claudiopolis, besieged and suffering from famine, from almost certain capture at the hands of the Turkmens.[240] These isolated incidents indicate that the nomadic tribesmen on the borders had taken advantage of the battle of Myriocephalum to push their movements and depredations deeper into Byzantine territory. The sultan himself, free from the Byzantine threat, turned to the east, took the last important vestige of the Danishmendid heritage (Melitene) in 1177, and sometime later he destroyed the walls of Kaisum, carrying off its inhabitants into captivity.[241]

The quarter century elapsing between the death of Manuel in 1180 and the fall of Constantinople to the Latins in 1204 witnessed a rapid disintegration of central authority in the remaining Anatolian provinces and a correspondingly greater activity of the Turkish tribes. As the empire became inextricably drawn into the whirlpool of Balkan and Italian

[238] Nicetas Choniates, 250–254.
[239] *Ibid.*, 254–257. Theodore Scutariotes-Sathas, 296.
[240] Nicetas Choniates, 257–259.
[241] Michael the Syrian, III, 373–376, 388. Bar Hebraeus, I, 308. It was after these events that Kilïdj Arslan revisited Melitene and had his interesting meeting with Michael the Syrian, Michael the Syrian, III, 390–391.

affairs, control of the Anatolian districts slipped from the hands of the emperors. Rebellions mushroomed throughout the breadth and length of the area in question, and they were quite often supported by Turkmen troops who came in to plunder. Because of the Turkish support that the insurgents received and because they could readily seek refuge in enemy territory, the weak government in Constantinople was not able to protect its subjects in the area against these rebellious elements. The more frequent changes on the throne also enabled the sultans to exploit these critical moments to raid and to conquer bits of the borders.

Upon Manuel's death (1180), Kilïdj Arslan's armies captured Sozopolis, ravaging and subduing the surrounding villages; to the north Cotyaeum was sacked; and at the other extreme Attaleia was subject to a long arduous siege.[242] When in 1182 Andronicus Comnenus set out from Oenoe on the Black Sea to claim the throne in Constantinople, the military forces of Paphlagonia, Nicaea, and the Thracesian theme were withdrawn from the borders and employed in the civil war. The focal center of resistance to Andronicus was the city of Philadelpheia under the command of John Comnenus Vatatzes. Until the latter's defeat, the cities of Byzantine Asia were caught up in a civil war that proved as destructive as the ravages of the enemy.[243] After the accession of Andronicus, and as a result of his measures against the aristocracy, rebellion broke out once more in Asia Minor (1184) centering on the cities of Lopadium, Nicaea, and Prusa. The rebels put up a very determined struggle, calling in the Turks to aid them, so that after their defeat Andronicus subjected the cities to savage reprisals.[244] The disobedience of the provincial officials took an alarming turn in the same year when Isaac, the governor of Tarsus, rebelled and established himself independently at Cyprus.[245]

The chaos in the Byzantine regions of Asia Minor increased markedly during the reign of Isaac II Angelus (1185–95). With the change in succession, and as the soldiers of much of the Thracesian theme had crossed to Europe, Kilïdj Arslan sent the emir Same to invade the empire's territory. The Turks, unopposed, entered the regions of Celbianum and carried off large numbers of the inhabitants and livestock.[246] A few years later (1188–89), Theodore Mangaphas of Philadelpheia

---

[242] Nicetas Choniates, 340. Theodore Scutariotes-Sathas, 327. He took other regions also, but the names are not given.

[243] Nicetas Choniates, 340. " ὅθεν ἐμφυλίων στάσεων καὶ πολέμων αἱ 'Ασιάτιδες ἔγεμον πόλεις. καὶ ἦν τὰ ἐντεῦθεν δρώμενα πολλῷ δυσαχθέστερα τῶν ἐξ ὁμόρων συμβαινόντων ἐθνῶν, ἢ καὶ οὕτως εἰπεῖν, ᾧ χεὶρ οὐκ ἐπεξῆλθεν ἀλλόγωττος, τοῦτο ἡ ἐγχώριος ἐθέριζε δεξιά." Theodore Scutariotes-Sathas, 327–329. The sons of Vatatzes fled to Iconium. Michael the Syrian, III, 395–396.

[244] Nicetas Choniates, 359–375. Theodore Scutariotes-Sathas, 337 ff. Bréhier, *Vie et Mort*, p. 347. Dölger, *Regesten*, nos. 1558, 1559.

[245] On the decline of Byzantine authority in Cilicia, Der Nersessian, "Cilician Armenia," pp. 642–644. Nicetas Choniates, 376–379. C. Brand, *Byzantium Confronts the West, 1180–1204* (Cambridge, 1968), pp. 51–55.

[246] Nicetas Choniates, 480–481.

revolted and raised the towns of Lydia with him,[247] and though two expeditions finally succeeded in putting down the rebellion, Mangaphas was able to make his escape to the court of Ghiyath al-Din Kaykhusraw. The latter refused to furnish the rebel with an army but instead gave him permission to recruit followers from among those adventurous Turks (the Turkmens, no doubt) who were interested in booty and raiding. Having thus collected a sizable force, the Greek rebel returned to the environs of Philadelpheia, ravaging the rural populations and their livestock. Laodiceia and the districts of Caria were similarly pillaged, and at Chonae the threshing floors with the season's harvest were consigned to the flames as was also the magnificent church of the Archangel Michael. Thence he retreated to Iconium, from which city the emperor was in the end forced to purchase the rebel.[248] A new element of confusion appeared with the march of the German Crusaders under Frederick Barbarossa. Philadelpheia became the scene of conflict between Germans and Greeks, and, once in Turkish territory, the Germans had to fight the Turkmens of the border regions and finally the forces of the sultan. The greater portion of the difficulties that Barbarossa encountered during his march from Laodiceia-Konya to Laranda and Cilicia was due largely to the Turkmen tribes.[249]

The defeat of the Turks at the hands of the Crusaders and the division of the sultan's domains among his eleven heirs a few years before his death in 1192 permitted Isaac Angelus to undertake some modest actions against the enemy. He was able to drive them out of parts of northwestern Anatolia and then built the fortress of Angelocastrum to prevent further tribal instrusions. In the south the monastic documents record that the emperor restored some order and prosperity to the monastic establishments on Mt. Latrus in the theme of Mylasa and Melanoudium after they had been destroyed again by the Turks.[250] If the victories of Barbarossa and the squabbles of Kïlïdj Arslans's successors provided the Greeks a temporary respite from Turkish raids, there was no pause in the rebellions of the ambitious. The very year in which Kïlïdj Arslan died revolts broke out in the regions of the Maeander River, Paphlagonia, and

[247] He coined silver with his own image. Nicetas Choniates, 522.

[248] Nicetas Choniates, 521–524. Theodore Scutariotes-Sathas, 387–389. Dölger, *Regesten*, no. 1581. Vismara, *Bisanzio*, p. 53. Bachmann, *Die Rede*, p. 64.

[249] Nicetas Choniates, 539–542. Theodore Scutariotes-Sathas, 395–397. Ibn al-Athir, *R.H.C., H.O.*, II₁, 22–24. Ansbert, p. 73. Salimbene, ed. O. Holder-Egger, *M.G.H.*, XXXII (Hannover-Leipzig, 1905–13), 11–12 (hereafter cited as Salimbene). Gesta Federici I. *Imperatoris in expeditione sacra, ed.* O. Holder-Egger, *Scriptores Rerum Germanicarum in usum scholarum* (Hannover, 1892), pp. 86–95 (hereafter cited as Gesta Federici), Bar Hebraeus, I, 333. Bréhier, *Vie et Mort*, pp. pp. 353-354. Cahen, "Selgukides et Allemands au temps de la trosième croisade," *W.Z.K.M.*, LVI (1960), 21–31. M. von Giesebricht, *Geschichte der deutschen Kaiserzeit* VI (Leipzig, 1895), 258–278. Turan, "Kïlïc Arslan," IA, 698.

[250] Miklosich et Müller, IV, 323–329. M. Bachmann, *Die Rede*, pp. 56–58. W. Regel, *Fontes rerum byzantinarum* (Petropolis, 1917), II, 258–262, 280. H. Ahrweiler, "Choma Aggélokastron," *R.E.B.*, XXIV (1966), 278–283, distinguishes this Choma-Angelocastron from Choma-Soublaion.

Bithynia. The most spectacular of these rebellions was that of the Pseudoalexius who received a letter from the sultan of Iconium enabling him, in company with a Latin from the Maeandrian town of Armala, to raise 8,000 Turkmens from the tribes under Arsanes. These nomads, accustomed to raiding the lands of the Christians, proceeded to raid almost the whole length of the Maeander after having sacked the regions of Chonae and having completed the destruction of its great church by smashing the mosaics and altar. A number of the towns of the Maeander valley surrendered to the invaders but others resisted and so were destroyed, and because of the destruction of the harvests and the threshing floors the Pseudoalexius was nicknamed καυσαλώνης. The revolt was terminated by the death of the rebel at the hands of a priest in the town of Pissa.[251]

The rebellion of a second Pseudoalexius threw the regions of Paphlagonia into turmoil, and that of Basil Chortatzes at Tarsia near Nicomedia once more immersed Bithynia in chaos. There were numerous other rebels who made their appearance at this time but the chroniclers, weary from the recitation of such events, dispense with them in very few words.[252] The Turkish progress must have been quite vigorous if we are to believe a letter that Kïlïdj Arslan sent to Michael the Syrian. According to its contents, the sultan had taken seventy-two places from the Greeks since the beginning of Isaac's reign (1185).[253]

This pattern of rebellions, Turkmen raids, and invasions by the sultans prevailed for the next decade. A third Pseudoalexius appeared by the side of the emir of Ankara and then proceeded to subject the fortresses in the regions north of that city. The emperor Alexius III waged a two-month campaign, and as he was not able to apprehend the rebel, he burned and destroyed those fortresses that persisted in aiding Pseudoalexius.[254] The emir of Ankara, profiting from the confused state of affairs, besieged the city of Dadybra for four months and eventually forced it to surrender in 1196. By the terms of the surrender, the Greek inhabitants were forced to leave the city and were replaced by Muslim colonists.[255]

One year later relations between Iconium and Constantinople became so bad that Kaykhusraw invaded the Maeander River valley, sacked many of the towns, and took away captive the entire population of Caria and Tantalus (5,000 in all). He would have taken Phrygian Antioch as well, as he came upon it at night. It so happened, however, that a notable of the city was celebrating the marriage of his daughter and the noises of the cymbals, drums, and singing made such a din that the sultan mistook it for the martial music of the defending army and so he withdrew

[251] Nicetas Choniates, 549–553. Theodore Scutariotes-Sathas, 399–400.
[252] Nicetas Choniates, 553.
[253] Michael the Syrian, III, 394–395.
[254] Nicetas Choniates, 608–610. Dölger, Regesten, no. 1634. Vismara, Bisanzio, p. 53.
[255] Nicetas Choniates, 624–626.

129

to Philomelium where he resettled the 5,000 Greek captives.[256] The emperor sent an army under Andronicus Ducas to attack the Turks, and he succeeded in falling upon the Turkmens of Arsanes and their herds, killing many of them. Simultaneously the emperor had gone to Nicaea and Prusa in order to protect them from the Turkmens of the Bathys area.[257] Commercial difficulties once more led to a breakdown of relations with the sultan (Rukn al-Din) in 1201, because of which the sultan un-leashed new attacks on Byzantine territory. Profiting from the state of affairs, a certain Michael, a tax official in the district of Mylasa, rebelled, and though defeated, he followed the well-established pattern of seeking refuge with the sultan, now at war with the Greeks. The Turkish ruler gave him a Turkish army, which enabled the rebel to pillage the regions of the Maeander.[258]

The final collapse of Byzantine authority in western Anatolia seemed imminent. In the twenty-five years that had elapsed since the death of Manuel, effective central authority in Asia Minor had been seriously threatened. The great internal weakening of the state and the successive blows it received from the Latins and Balkan peoples made it virtually impossible to halt the gradual Turkish westward infiltration, and this progress of the nomads on the borders was greatly aided by the Byzantine rebels who arose in western Anatolia. What remained of Byzantine military forces was consumed in civil strife, the rebels most often appealing to the sultans and Turkmen chiefs for aid, and these latter very gladly assisted in a process that could only benefit them. Byzantine political domination in these regions of Anatolia seemed doomed to extinction. Either the Turkmens and the sultan would overrun all of Anatolia, or some rebel would succeed in establishing a splinter state, as Isaac Comnenus had done in Cyprus.

Political Stability and Polarization: Nicaea and Konya

The year 1204 would seem to mark the next step in the dissolution of Byzantine authority in the eastern provinces, for in this year a number of new principalities were established in what remained of Byzantine Anatolian territory. Following the conquest of Constantinople, the Latin emperor received, by the terms of the Partitio Romaniae, Byzantine Asia Minor.[259] Here he awarded fiefs to his brother Henry at Adramyttium; to Peter of Bracieus lands, "toward Iconium"; to Louis of Blois, the duchy

---

[256] Nicetas Choniates, 653–657. Theodore Scutariotes-Sathas, 420–421. The difficulties began when the sultan detained two Arab stallions that the ruler of Egypt had sent to the emperor. The latter retaliated by jailing the Greek and Turkish merchants of Konya and confiscating their goods.

[257] Nicetas Choniates, 657–658. Theodore Scutariotes-Sathas, 421, 427–428. Rukn al-Din, son of Kïlïdj Arslan, inherited Amisus and Amasra. He chased Kaykhusraw from Konya and the latter fled to Constantinople.

[258] Nicetas Choniates, 700–701. Dölger, *Regesten*, n. 1658.

[259] Tafel and Thomas, *Urkunden* I, 464–501.

of Nicaea; and to Stephen of Perche, a duchy of Philadelpheia.[260] As Theodore Lascaris had succeeded in rallying Greek forces about him in Asia Minor, the Latins were forced to make good their claims on Anatolian soil by military force. Following the centrifugal pattern of the last few decades of the twelfth century, three Greek aristocrats established themselves as independent lords in the river valleys of western Asia Minor. Theodore Mangaphas succeeded in taking control of the important urban center of Philadelpheia, whereas the father-in-law of the sultan, Manuel Maurozomes, was able to establish himself in the Maeander valley with the aid of Turkish troops, and the third, Sabbas Asidenus, carved out a small principality in the regions of Sampsun-Miletus.[261] In the south the Turks were infiltrating the districts of Lycia and Pamphylia, and in Cilicia Byzantine authority had disappeared with the emergence of the Armenian princes Rupen III (1175–87) and Leo II (d. 1219), under whom Cilician Armenia attained its independence.[262] Particularly significant in the fate of Byzantine civilization in Asia Minor was the capture of Trebizond by Alexius and David Comnenus in 1204 and the establishment of the Trebizond state.[263] But contrary to the inauspicious developments of 1204, Greek fortunes in western Asia Minor were to improve considerably.

During the course of the next decade Greek Anatolia was caught up in warfare among Latins, sultans, and some half-dozen Greek aspirants. Theodore Lascaris was hard pressed to maintain himself against all these foes simultaneously, but because of the Bulgarian attacks and defeat of the Latins in Thrace, the latter were not able to concentrate all their forces in Asia Minor. Thus Lascaris was able to push back the advance of the Comnenoi in the north and to put an end to the independence of the Greek lords in the river valleys. In 1211 he defeated and slew the sultan Ghiyath al-Din in the Maeander valley, and by so doing halted the further disintegration of Byzantine political control in Anatolia. Three years later (1214) Theodore concluded the treaty of Nymphaeum, which established a truce between Greeks and Latins. According to the terms of this treaty, the Latins were to keep northwest Mysia including the regions of Ciminas and Achyraous, and Theodore received the lands south of the Caicus valley and east of Lopadium. This included Neocastron (Chliara, Pergamum, Adramyttium), but Calamus was to be left uninhabited as a border region.[264] The Trebizondine Comnenoi lost their lands west of

---

[260] R. L. Wolff, "The Latin Empire of Constantinople, 1204–61," *A History of the Crusades*, II, 191–192.

[261] G. Ostrogorsky, *Geschichte*, p. 352. A. Gardner, *The Lascarids of Nicaea, the Story of an Empire in Exile* (London, 1912), p. 75. P. Orgels, "Sabas Asidenos, dynaste de Sampson," *Byzantion*, X (1935), 67 ff.

[262] Der Nersessian, "Cilician Armenia," pp. 643–651.

[263] Vasiliev, "The Foundation of the Empire of Trebizond, (1202–1222), *Speculum*, XI (1936), 3–37.

[264] Gardner, *Lascarids*, pp. 84–85. Ostrogorsky, *Geschichte*, p. 355. Dölger, *Regesten*, no. 1684, dates it after 1212.

Sinope to the new state at Nicaea, and eleven years later John Vatatzes further reduced the Latin holdings in Bithynia and eventually the Latins were removed from Asia Minor. The boundary between Konya and Nicaea remained fairly constant between 1211 and the removal of the capital from Nicaea to Constantinople. The border ran from a point west of Sinope in an arc that left Castamon, Cotyaeum, and Laodiceia to the Seljuks, and continued to the Gulf of Macri (Fetiye) opposite Rhodes in southwest Asia Minor.[265]

The Latin conquest of Constantinople was undoubtedly responsible for the prolonged life of Byzantine authority in Asia Minor inasmuch as it forced the Greeks to focus their energies and numbers in Nicaea. The disintegration of the maritime provinces was well underway by the end of the twelfth century, and it is quite likely that the Turkish conquest of the coastal regions might have taken place one century earlier than it actually did had it not been for the events attendant upon the Fourth Crusade. By the marshaling of their forces in Anatolia, the Byzantines halted the Turkish penetration after it had attained Attaleia (1207) in the south and Sinope (1214) in the north.

The Nicaean state guarded its borders zealously, reorganizing its defense forces. As both Seljuks and Greeks were preoccupied with other foes, the history of relations between Konya and Nicaea is a relatively quiet one. The Seljuks were interested in events of the northern, southern, and eastern Anatolian regions; the Nicaeans, in the reconquest of Constantinople. With the cessation of active warfare between Byzantines and Seljuks for a half century, the borders remained comparatively stable and Anatolia once more began to experience the blessings of peace. The Lascarids did much to revive the economic prosperity of the westernmost provinces, monastic and other ecclesiastical institutions once more bloomed, and cities were rebuilt and fortified.[266] The sultanate of Konya

---

[265] Wittek, *Das Fürstentum Mentesche. Studie zur Geschichte Westkleinasiens im 13–15 Jahr.* (Istanbul, 1934), p. 1.

[266] A. Meliarakes, Ἱστορία τοῦ βασιλείου τῆς Νικαίας καὶ τοῦ δεσποτάτου τῆς Ἠπείρου 1204–1261 (Athens, 1898). Uspensikii, *Istoriia*, pp. 536–606. Ahrweiler, "Smyrne", *passim*. Gardner, *Lascarids*, pp. 182 ff. D. Xanalatos, "Wirtschaftliche Aufbau- und Autarkiemassnahmen im 13. Jahrhundert (Nikänisches Reich 1204–1261)," *Leipziger Vierteljahrsschrift für Südosteuropa*, Jah. 3, 1939, Heft 2, 129–139. Charanis, "The Monastic Properties and the State in the Byzantine Empire," *D.O.P.*, IV (1948), 98–109. W. Heyd, *Histoire du commerce du Levant* (Leipzig, 1923), I, 304–307, 309. On the fortifications erected by the Lascarids to defend the towns and the roads, W. Müller-Wiener, "Mittelalterliche Befestigungen im südlichen Jonien," *I.M.*, XI (1961), 5–122. A. M. Schneider and W. Karnapp, *Die Stadtmauer von Iznik* (Berlin, 1938), pp. 16 ff. Schneider, *Die römischen und byzantinischen Denkmäler von Iznik-Nicaea* (Berlin, 1943), on building activity in Lascarid Nicaea. Glycatzi-Ahrweiler, "La politique agraire des empereurs de Nicée," *Byzantion*, XXVIII (1958), 51–66, 135–136. The basic history of the Empire of Trebizond has not yet been written. W. Miller, *Trebizond* (London, 1926), pp. 20–27. J. Fallmereyer, *Geschichte des Kaiserthums von Trapezunt* (Munich, 1827), pp. 101–125. The Greek journal Ἀρχεῖον Πόντου is a veritable mine of primary and secondary material. See especially the studies of O. Lampsides in this periodical, and more particularly his article, " Ἀπόψεις ἐπὶ τοῦ κράτους τῶν μεγάλων Κομνηνῶν," *A. Π.*, XXIV, (1961),

underwent an even more lively development and expansion during this half century. Most important was the conquest of ports on the Black and Mediterranean seas (Sinope, Antalya, Alaiya), the subjugation of the Saltukids and Menguchekids in the northeast, and the consolidation of the Taurus and eastern frontiers. The unification of these areas under Konya, the acquisition of seaports for the first time, and comparative internal peace and stability enabled economic life in most of Anatolia to flourish for the first time since the eleventh century. A striking testimony to this development is the extensive number of caravansarays and khans that were built during the thirteenth century. Muslim and Christian merchants frequented Asia Minor in increasing numbers, and treaties between the Italian commercial cities and both Konya and Nicaea were concluded. Seljuk art likewise experienced its short but amazing *essor* at this time.[267]

Withdrawal of the Byzantines to Constantinople and the Decline of Konya; Establishment of the Emirates and Emergence of the Ottomans.

The conditions responsible for the prosperity and comparative stability of life in Anatolia were not sufficiently long-lived. The centralization of authority at Konya and the continued residence of imperial authority at Nicaea were responsible for the seemingly calm state of affairs, but by 1261 both these circumstances had begun to change; once more much of Anatolia gradually lapsed into disorder and then anarchy. Within the Seljuk domains, it was the Udj Turkmens, concentrated along the Cilician, Trebizondine, and western borders, who destroyed the centralization of power in Konya and who, throughout the twelfth and early thirteenth centuries, had not been overly amenable to the control of the sultans. They had lived a quasi-independent existence and, when not engaged in raids on Christians, had on occasion become embroiled in the dynastic strife of the Seljuk ruling house. These nomads, or seminomads, substantially increased in number with the arrival of new Turkish tribes fleeing the Mongol conquest in Transoxiana and Khurasan. The pressure from the new invaders out of the Altai was such that the Khwarazm-shah himself, Djalal al-Din Mankobirti, attempted to flee to Asia Minor

---

14–34. Also A. Bryar, "The Littoral of the Empire of Trebizond in Two Fourteenth Century Portolano Maps," *A.II.*, XXIV (1961), 97–127, and his other studies. The Trebizondine manuscripts now in Ankara are cataloged by N. Bees, " Ποντιακὰ χειρόγραφα ἐν τῷ μουσείῳ τοῦ κάστρου τῆς ᾿Αγκύρας," *A.II.*, IX (1939), 193–248.

[267] Cahen, "The Turks in Iran and Anatolia before the Mongol Invasions," *A History of the Crusades*, II, 661–692 (hereafter cited as Cahen, " Anatolia before the Mongol"); "Le commerce anatolien au debut du XIIIe siècle," *Mélanges d'histoire du moyen age dediés à la mémoire de Louis Halphen* (Paris, 1951), 91–101. "Alaeddin," EI₂. K. Erdmann, *Der Orientalische Knüpfteppich* (Tubingen, 1955), 14–20; *Das anatolische Karavansaray des 13. Jahrhunderts* 2 vols. (Berlin, 1961). V. Gordlevski, *Izbrannye Soch.*, I, 56–61. M. Köprülü, *Les origines de l'empire ottoman* (Paris, 1935), gives an overall survey of Seljuk Anatolia at this time in chapter 11. For conditions in Cilician Armenia, Der Nersessian, "Cilician Armenia," *passim.* Canard, "Armenia," EI₂. The work of Z. Togan, *Umumi Türk tarihine giriş* (Istanbul, 1946), I, 197–210, must be read with extreme caution and reservations.

with his followers. Even though he was defeated at the battle of Yashichymen in 1230 by the Seljuks and Ayyubids, his group and other Turkmens no doubt continued to flock into Anatolia.[268]

Given the great differences in social and economic habits as well as in religious outlook of the Anatolian Turkmens and the Muslim sedentary society of Anatolia, one is not overly surprised at the course of events in the mid-thirteenth century. Out of close contact with Konya, the hostility of the Turkmens was galvanized by the religious preaching of heterodox holy men flocking into Anatolia at this time. The friction between sedentary and nomadic society came to a head for the first time in the explosive revolt of Baba Ishak c. 1239-40. He and his followers, through their preaching to the Turkmens of the regions between Amasya and the eastern Taurus, unleashed a revolt agaist Seljuk authority which attained considerable proportions before its suppression by armies with considerable numbers of Christian mercenaries. The nomads had not been sufficiently assimilated into the Seljuk system and would in the latter half of the century partition and destroy the Seljuk state.[269] Greatly weakened by this spectacular Turkmen rebellion, the Seljuks were crushed shortly thereafter by the Mongols in the battle of Köse Dag (1243), and henceforth the Anatolian sultanate became a vassal state of the Mongols.[270] Though there ensued a period of varying stability down to 1275 as a result of the appearance of capable Seljuk administrators, it was only with difficulty that the Turkmens of the Taurus and western Anatolia were subdued.[271] Seljuk-Mongol armies were forced to repress Turkmen disorders in the regions of Laranda and in the west about the plain of Dalaman Chay in 1261-62. The next great outbreak of Turkmen rebellion took place against the background of Mameluke intervention. The Mameluke sultan Baybars, encouraged by his victory over the Mongols at Ayn Djalut in 1260 and prodded on by certain Turkish Anatolian begs, invaded eastern Anatolia and defeated the Mongols at Kayseri (1277). As the position of the pervane was not clear, he was of

[268] H. Gottschalk, "Der Bericht des Ibn Nazif al Hamawi über die Schlacht von Jašyčimen," *W.Z.K.M.* LVI (1960), 55–67. Spuler, *Die Mongolen in Iran*, 2d ed. (Berlin, 1955), pp. 33–34. Cahen, "Anatolia before the Mongol," pp. 683–684, 690–691. J. A. Boyle, "Djalal al-Din Khwarazm-shah," EI₂.

[269] Though the grave significance of the Babai rising has long been recognized, the paucity of the sources has obscured many of the important details. The Karamanids, Baba Ilyas, and Hadji Bektash, of considerable importance in Anatolian history, were all connected with the leader of the movement. The most recent opinion of scholarship on the movement is embodied in the article of Cahen, "Baba'i," EI₂. Bar Hebraeus, I, 405–406. Önder, "Eine neuentdeckte Quelle zur Geschichte der Seltschuken in Anatolien," *W.Z.K.M.*, LV (1959), 83–88.

[270] Cahen, "Anatolia before the Mongol," p. 692. Spuler, *Die Mongolen*, p. 43. Dölger, *Regesten*, no. 1776 on the treaty between Vatatzes and Ghiyath al-Din Kaykhursraw in 1243.

[271] For the details, Cahen, "The Mongols," pp. 725 ff; Cahen, "Notes pour l'histoire des Turcomanes d'Asie Mineure au XIII⁰ siècle," *J.A.*, CCXXXIX (1951), 337–338, 342–345 (hereafter cited as "Notes"). For the Byzantino-Turkish treaty of 1254–55, Dölger, *Regesten*, nos. 1824–1825.

course compromised in the eyes of the Mongols, and when Baybars withdrew from Anatolia, the Mongols executed the pervane.[272] Previously (1276) the Turkmens of the Taurus had revolted and under the leadership of the Karamanids attacked and captured Konya where they placed a certain Djimri on the throne. The Turkmens of the western borders also seem to have been actively disobedient to Konya. Though the Turkmen rebellion failed and the Seljuk-Mongol forces eventually reasserted authority over the towns of the plateau, Turkmen independence was henceforth an accomplished fact. The Mongols took over direct control of the Seljuk administration in Asia Minor imposing their own fiscal institutions on those of the Seljuks. But if they continued to hold eastern Asia Minor firmly, the western regions were far more difficult to control, and in fact began to slip from the hands of the sultans at Konya. Even in central Anatolia the struggle of the Ilkhanids and Mamelukes made this a border region subject to considerable political fluctuation and military vicissitude.

The combined impact of Turkmen rebellions and Mongol conquest had destroyed the political unity of the Seljuk state and removed the possibility of a more peaceful development of the land in social and economic matters. The territorial disintegration of the state was further accelerated by the degeneration of Mongol rule in Anatolia during the late thirteenth and the early fourteenth century. The great movements of commerce across Anatolia were partially disrupted, and, henceforth, the caravans tended to touch on the easternmost fringes of Anatolia. The Mongol intrusion after 1277 was marked by the further settlement of Mongol and eastern Turkish tribes with their military chiefs in eastern Anatolia.[273]

In western Asia Minor, Byzantine rule collapsed in the half century following the recapture of Constantinople from the Latins. The shifting of the capital from Nicaea to the Bosphorus entailed neglect of what had remained of the empire's possessions in Asia Minor. The utterance of the protoasecretis Sennacherim the Evil, upon receipt of the news that Constantinople had been retaken, was prophetic: "Let no one hope for good, since the Greeks again dwell in the City."[274] The conquest of Constantinople rekindled, as was to be expected, Latin crusading fervor, and henceforth the Greek rulers were forced to defend themselves, diplomatically and militarily, against the counterattack of the Latins. The corollary to the reconquest of Constantinople was the repossession of the empire's former lands in Europe, so that the emperors were caught up in the politics and strife of Slav rulers, Greek despots, and Latin

[272] G. Wiet, "Baybars I," EI₂.
[273] Cahen, "The Mongols," pp. 727–732; "Notes," pp. 346 ff. Spuler, *Die Mongolen*, pp. 73 ff. Toğan, *Giriş*, I, 222–237. Cahen, "Sur les traces des premiers Akhis," *Fuad Köprülü Armağani* (Istanbul, 1955), pp. 81–91. On the economic decline see chapter iii as also, Spuler, *Die Mongolen*, pp. 302, 321–322, 325–326.
[274] Pachymeres, I, 149.

princes. The occupation of Constantinople also brought the empire into the focal point of the Venetian-Genoese commercial fire. The manpower and finances of the state were not equal to the demands and tasks that the repossession of Constantinople had imposed. Thus the words of Sennacherim were ominously prophetic, though to contemporaries they were meaningless.

The removal from Nicaea coincided with the period of Seljuk decline and with the resurgence of Udj Turkmen aggressions. In 1261 and 1262 the Turkmens had been temporarily defeated by Seljuk-Mongol armies and it is quite possible that rebuffed by Konya, they may have begun to infiltrate the Byzantine regions to the west. The withdrawal of the government and of considerable military forces to Constantinople were no doubt sufficient in themselves to consummate the necessary debilitation of Byzantine resistance in Asia Minor. Because of the actions and measures of the new Palaeologan dynasty, there resulted an outright alienation from Constantinople of large segments of Greek society in Bithynia and elsewhere. Michael VIII Palaeologus had usurped the imperial crown from the youth John IV Lascaris and had blinded him. The Lascaris dynasty had, by its economic and political accomplishments, by its piety and charity, become endeared to the Christians of the Nicaean state and the ruthless treatment of John IV produced a strong reaction, culminating in a rebellion that had to be repressed with cruelty. In pursuing his dynastic and economic policies Michael abolished the tax immunities of the *acrites* and attacked the privileges of the large landowners. These elements were either removed from the armies or else, alienated, they deserted to the Turks, whereas others were reemployed in Europe. The government imposed heavy taxes on the inhabitants and installed rapacious mercenaries who treated the inhabitants as enemies. The measures of Michael VIII made his dynasty unpopular in Byzantine Anatolia, and this unpopularity was manifested in religious controversies as well as in rebellions. In the struggle between Josephites and Arsenites, and in the strife over the ecclesiastical union of Lyon with the Latins, the Asia Minor populace by and large sided with the antigovernment party. The rebellion of Alexius Philanthropenus in 1296 also received a certain support from the Anatolians. The emperors in Constantinople were always wary of the presence of a successful or popular general in Anatolia, such as Philanthropenus, and were never content to leave him there for any long period.[275]

The dissolution of the local military defense and the alienation of the populace with the attendant rebellions and acts of disobedience brought anarchy and banditry to many parts of the Anatolian provinces. It also permitted the Turkmens to increase the extent of their raids. By the end of

[275] G. Arnakis, Οἱ πρῶτοι Ὀθωμανοί (Athens, 1947), pp. 37–48. Wittek, *Mentesche*, pp. 9–11, 16–17, 42. Arnakis, "Byzantium's Anatolian Provinces in the Reign of Michael Palaeologus," *Actes du XIIe congrès international des études byzantines* (Belgrade, 1964), II, 37–44. Dölger, *Regesten*, no. 2199.

Michael's reign (1282) only twenty years after his entry into Constantinople, Byzantine Anatolia was militarily defenseless and economically a shambles.[276]

The emperors made occasional efforts to halt or drive out the Turkish raiders who were beginning to settle down in Byzantine lands, but each military expedition failed for one reason or another to achieve its goal. The army, which succeeded in an extensive reassertion of imperial authority in parts of Caria in 1269, was soon recalled for service in Europe, and so the Turks reentered. Nine years later (1278) Byzantine generals attempted to clear the invaders from the Maeander valley, but the progress of the latter was such that Antioch and Caria were irretrievably lost. Michael's expedition was successful in driving the Turks across the Sangarius, but it was temporary and the land was already desolate and in ruins. The efforts of Alexius Philanthropenus in the Maeander valley in stemming the influx of the nomads were so successful that they aroused the envy and suspicion of the central authority. The result was his rebellion, supported by Greeks and Turks, and the donning of the purple. Soon after Philanthropenus was defeated, Andronicus II crossed to Asia Minor, but a frightful earthquake terminated the expedition before it made contact with the Turks.[277] Consequently, with the collapse of the Nicaean and Seljuk states, there arose a considerable number of beyliks or emirates which competed with one another in conquering the lands of the sultan and the emperor. By the first decade of the fourteenth century, one-half century after the removal of the emperor from Nicaea to Constantinople, the Turkmens had carried practically everything before them along a line stretching from the Black Sea to the Aegean. Trachia Stadia and Strobilus on the Carian coast were already Turkish in 1269; Caria and Antioch on the Maeander had fallen in 1278; in 1282 Tralles and Nyssa fell. During the first decade of the fourteenth century various Turkish emirs reached the sea as Pergamum fell in 1302; Ephesus, Thyraia, and Pyrgi were taken in 1304 despite the temporary relief brought by the appearance of the Catalans in Anatolia.[278] The main cities of Bithynia resisted for another two decades, Prusa (1326), Nicaea (1331), Nicomedia (1337). By default, the Turkmens had come in and within a half century Byzantine authority disappeared.[279]

[276] Pachymeres, I, 502–505.

[277] Wittek, *Mentesche*, pp. 26–34. Arnakis, 'Οθωμανοί, pp. 44 ff. Ahrweiler, "Smyrne," pp. 9, 151. H.-G. Beck, "Belisar-Philanthropenos. Das Belisar-Lied der Palaiologenzeit," *Serta Monacensia*, ed. H. J. Kissling and A. Schmaus (Leiden, 1952), pp. 46–52, discusses the episode of Philanthropenus and shows that he was probably the model of Belisarius in this late Byzantine epic, the poem of Belisarius. On the influx of Turkmens along the river valley, M. Treu, *Maximi Monachi Planudis Epistulae* (Amsterdam, 1960), pp. 174–175.

[278] Melikoff, "Aidinoglu," EI₂, says 1308, but see P. Lemerle, *L'Emirat d'Aydin, Byzance et l'Occident* (Paris, 1957), p. 20.

[279] Wittek, *Mentesche*, pp. 24–60. Arnakes, 'Οθωμανοί, *passim*. Lemerle, *Aydin*, pp. 14–18.

Anatolia was once more parceled into numerous independent principalities, and in the course of the two centuries between the collapse of the
Seljuk-Nicaean equilibrium and the final Ottoman conquest of Asia
Minor, over twenty principalities came into existence, approximately
half of these taking form prior to the end of the thirteenth century. Some
of these, such as the emirate of Denizli (c. 1261–1278), the Eshrefogullari
at Begshehir (second half of thirteenth century-1325), the Sahibogullari
at Karahisar between Kutahya and Akshehir, and the Pervaneogullari
about Sinope were comparatively short-lived.[280] The remainder of the
beyliks that had appeared prior to the end of the thirteenth century enjoyed a longer life-span. That of the Karamanids in the Taurus region
seems to have begun to take form by the mid-thirteenth century and after
1277 was in effect independent.[281] The Germiyanids, who had their
center at Kutahya, were perhaps independent by 1277.[282] Farther to the
west in the regions of Adramyttium and Balikesri, the descendants of the
Danishmendids founded the emirate of Karasi at the end of the thirteenth
and beginning of the fourteenth century. The Djandarogullari, having
received Castamon as a fief from the Ilkhanids in 1292, made this the core
of an extended state in 1307. The Ottomans, if indeed they were in
existence prior to the end of the century, were located on the borders of
Bithynia.[283] In the fourteenth century a number of new emirates appeared.
At the turn of the century the dynasty of the Hamidogullari established
itself in the districts of Egridir, Uluburlu, Yalvach, and Anatalya.
Sometime later the family holdings were split into two independent beyliks, one containing the more northerly region, the other containing
Anatalya and its environs.[284] Aydinoglu Muhammad Beg, an official of
the Germiyanids, founded an independent dynasty in the western riverine
regions about Izmir and Ephesus (Ayasoluk) in the very early years of the
fourteenth century. This principality became so powerful that it intervened
actively in the European affairs of the Byzantine Empire.[285] The

---

[280] Cahen, "Notes," pp. 336–340. I. H. Uzunçarṣiĭli, *Anadolu Beylikleri ve Akkoyunlu
Devletleri* (Ankara, 1937), pp. 13–14, 36–38. The Turkmens about Denizli seem to have
formed an independent principality but were crushed after the rebellion of Djimri by
the sultan. The emirate of the Eshrefogullari was suppressed by the Mongol governor
Timurtash in 1325. 'Ali Bey, "Eshrefogullari hakkinda bir kaç söz," *Tarih i osmani encümeni
mecmuasi*, no. 28 (1930), pp. 251–256. That of the Sahibogullari, which was originally a
Seljuk fief on the Byzantine frontier, seems to have been absorbed by its larger neighbors,
the Germiyanids. The Pervaneogullari, whose principality about Sinope dated from its
reconquest (from the Greeks of Trebizond) c. 1264, was eventually absorbed by the
Djandarogullari in the first half of the fourteenth century.

[281] Cahen, "Notes," pp. 340–349. Uzunçarṣiĭli, *Beylikleri*, pp. 3–8.

[282] Melikoff, "Germiyan oğullari," EI₂. Cahen, "Notes," pp. 349–354. Uzunçarṣiĭli,
Beylikleri, pp. 9–11; *Kutahya Şehri* (Istanbul, 1932).

[283] Uzunçarṣiĭli, *Beylikleri*, pp. 19–22, 23–26. Wittek, *Mentesche*, pp. 24–56. J. H.
Kramers, "Karasi," EI₁. Arnakis, 'Οθωμανοί, pp. 71 ff.

[284] X. de Planhol, "Hamid," EI₂. B. Flemming, *Landschaftsgeschichte von Pamphylien,
Pisidien und Lykien im Spätmittelalter* (Wiesbaden, 1964). Taeschner, "Anatalya," EI₂.

[285] Melikoff, "Aidinoglu," EI₂. Lemerle, *Aydin, passim*. H. Akin, "Results of Studies in
the History of the Aydin Oğullari," *Ankara Üniversitesi Dil ve Tarih-Cografya Fakültesi*

founder of Saruhan (late thirteenth or early fourteenth century), Saruhan Beg, was like Aydinoğlu originally an emir of the Germiyanids. He proceeded to establish an independent state and dynasty that came to rule Magnesia on the Hermus along with Menemen, Gordes, Demirdji, Nif, and Turgutlu.[286]

In eastern Anatolia there was a thread of continuity in Ilkhanid rule, but by the end of the fourteenth century, Mongol administration had given way to the rule of Turkmen tribal confederations. When the Mongol governor Timurtash fled to Egypt in 1327, he was replaced by Ghiyath al-Din Eretna (of Uighur origin) who succeeded in receiving official appointment from the Ilkhan Abu Sa'id. Profiting from the dynastic strife of the Ilkhanids, he eventually established himself as the independent ruler of much of central and eastern Anatolia, including Sivas, Kayseri, Nigde, Aksaray, Ankara, Develi Karahisar, Darende, Amasya, Tokat, Merzifon, Samsun, and Sharki Karahisar. The rule of his dynasty became so weak by the 1360's that his governors had usurped control of the main towns and in 1365–66 the beys revolted. In 1381–82 Burhan al-Din proclaimed himself sultan of the lands of Eretna, but was himself defeated and executed by the Akkoyunlu in 1398, the intervening eighteen years having been filled with the anarchy and strife of rebels, Ottomans, Karamanids, Mamelukes, and Akkoyunlus.[287] Other powerful Turkmen states appeared in the east during the fourteenth century. The rise of the Akkoyunlu (fourteenth century to 1502), Karakoyunlu, Dhu 'l-Kadr (1337–1522), and Ramazan was indicative of the density of the Turkmen penetration in the eastern provinces during this period.[288]

In destroying the Byzantine and Seljuk structure of Anatolia, the Turkmens further intensified the politically disunified character of this region and brought the specter of tribal raids and the unceasing warfare of petty states, putting upon the Anatolian population the heavy burden of supporting numerous governments and armies.

As the period of these conquests receded into the historical past, however, the capitals of the many emirates served as administrative, economic, and religious centers that gradually restored varying degrees of stability and prosperity, a process clearly discernible by the third and fourth decades of the fourteenth century. Nevertheless, the degree of recovery

---

Dergisi, V (1947–48), 103–108. See also E. Zachariadou," " Ἰστορικὰ στοιχεῖα σένα θαῦμα τοῦ Ἁγίου Φανουρίου," Α.Π. XXVI, (1964), 309–318. F. Thiriet, "Les relations entre la Crète et les Émirats turcs d'Asie Mineure au XIVe siècle (vers 1348–1360)," *Actes du XIIe congrès international des études byzantines* (Belgrade, 1964), II, 213–221. M. J. Manusakas. " 'Η πρώτη ἐμπορικὴ παροικία τῶν Βενετῶν στὰ Παλάτια (Μίλητο) τῆς Μ. 'Ασίας(ἕνα ἑλληνικὸ ἔγγραφο τοῦ 1355)," Δελτίον τῆς Χριστιανικῆς 'Αρχαιολογικῆς 'Εταιρείας, III (1962), 231–240.

[286] Uzunçarşılı, *Beylikleri*, pp. 31–32.

[287] *Ibid.*, pp. 48–52. Cahen, "Eretna," EI_2. J. Rypka, "Burhan al-Din," EI_2.

[288] Uzunçarşılı, *Beylikleri*, pp. 42–57. The articles, "Ak-Koyunlu," "Dhu'l Kadr," EI_2; "Akkoyunlar," "Karakoyunlular," IA.

does not seem to have been uniform or to have attained the prosperity of the preceding era of stability in the thirteenth century, for the very existence of so many principalities in a constant state of war precluded such an attainment. By the middle of the century, the Ottomans had not only consolidated their position in Bithynia but had, significantly, absorbed the neighboring emirate of Karasï on the southwest borders of the Ottoman lands. Though the primary impetus of expansion for several decades thereafter carried the house of Osman into Europe, the sultans took an active interest in Anatolian politics in the reigns of both Orhan and Murad I. When a number of the Anatolian emirs, primarily Burhan al-Din and the princes of Germiyan and Karaman, sought to exploit Ottoman involvement in Europe (1389) by territorial aggression, Bayazid I rapidly marched to the east to confront his enemies. His appearance in Anatolia shortly after the battle of Kossovo Polye marks the next important stage in the political development of Anatolia and indicates how far the Ottomans has outstripped the other Anatolian states. In his first Anatolian campaign (1389–90), Bayazid reduced the last independent Greek city in western Asia Minor, Philadelpheia (Alashehir), and annexed the principalities of Aydin, Saruhan, Menteshe, Hamid, and Germiyan. An alignment of Karamanids, Burhan al-Din, and the Djandarids temporarily halted Bayazid's further expansion in central and eastern Anatolia, but by 1397 after having defeated the western Crusaders at Nicopolis, he beat Karamanoğlu at Akchay, executed him, and annexed his lands with the city of Konya. One year later Bayazid's victorious armies occupied the regions of Djanik, the domains of Burhan al-Din, and the towns of Albistan, Malatya, Behisna, Kahta, and Divrigi.[289]

It seemed that Anatolia, now largely (though not completely) in the possession of one ruler, would finally enjoy peace. But this was not yet to be the case because Bayazid's expansion had been too rapid and the foundations of the empire were not set firmly. In the east the last great world conqueror, Timur, had turned his eyes westward, and when the Turkish emirs so recently dispossessed by Bayazid looked about for possible support, they very naturally found it at Timur's court. The relations of the two rulers progressively worsened as Timur captured and sacked Sivas in 1400, and two years later at the battle of Chubuk-ovasï near Ankara he scattered the armies of Bayazid and so thoroughly crippled the Ottomans that to contemporaries it appeared the Ottoman Empire had been forever

---

[289] H. Inalcik, "Bayazid I," EI₂. Uzunçarsïlï, *Anadolu Selcuklularï ve Anadolu beylikleri hakkïnda bir mukaddime ile Osmanlï devletinin kuruluşundan Istanbul'un fethine kadar,* 2d ed. (Ankara, 1961), pp. 246–249, 260–268, 275–278, 295–301. Melikoff, "Germiyan-ogullarï," EI₂. Flemming, *Landschaftsgeschichte, passim.* M. Berger de Xivrey, *Mémoire sur le vie et les ouvrages de l'empereur Manuel Paléologue* (Paris, 1851), pp. 52–60, translates writings of Manuel II which have to do with a part of Bayazid's campaign. The translations, however, are not always accurate.

destroyed.[290] The effect of Timur's Anatolian campaign was to unsettle Anatolian political conditions for another half century as he restored many of the Turkish emirates to their former rulers and promoted division and strife within the domains of the sons of Bayazid. After the battle of Ankara, Timur added his personal touch to the catastrophe, remaining in Anatolia for a considerable period of time and sending detachments of his army to reduce and plunder the regions of central and western Asia Minor.[291]

The reassertion of Ottoman authority in the peninsula following the Timurid holocaust was to stretch over the entire fifteenth century, though it was finally established in most of the regions by the end of the reign of Muhammad II (1481). Muhammad I laid the foundation for recovery from his base in Amasya as he removed his brother Isa from Bursa and united the European possessions with those in western Asia Minor. Some of the emirates, such as Saruhan, he annexed, while others he subjected to vassal status. His task in Anatolia was further complicated by the socioreligious movement of Badr al-Din of Samavna, whose followers threw the regions of Aydin into a state of political and religious ferment in 1416.[292] His successor Murad II extended Ottoman possessions in the south and east with the annexation of Tekeili in 1424 and more importantly with the land of Germiyan which Yakub Chelebi ceded in 1428–29.[293] Muhammad II conquered the Black Sea coastal region of Anatolia in 1460–61, taking Amastris from the Genoese, Sinope from the house of the Isfendiyaroğullarĭ, and putting an end to the empire of Trebizond.[294] The turn of the Karamanids came next when from 1465 to 1468 Muhammad occupied Konya and their lands, though the dynasty continued to be a factor in Anatolian affairs until the end of Muhammad's reign. Uzun Hasan, ruler of the Akkoyunlu tribal confederation, having allowed himself to be isolated politically by Muhammad II, eventually

[290] M.-M. Alexandra-Dersca, *La campagne de Timur en Anatolie* (Bucharest, 1942). Inalcik, "Bayazid I," EI₂. G. Roloff, "Die Schlacht bei Angora," *Historische Zeitschrift*, CLXI (1940), 244–262. Sharaf al-Din Ali-Yazdi, *The History of Timur-Bec, Known by the Name of Tamerlain the Great, Emperor of the Mongols and Tatars; Being an Historical Journal of his Conquests in Asia and Europe*, trans. Petis de la Croix (London, 1923), II, *passim* (hereafter cited as Sharaf al-Din Yazdi). Ashĭkpashazade, *Vom Hirtenzelt zur hohen Pforte*, trans. R. Kreutel (Graz, 1959), pp. 109–115 (hereafter cited as Ashĭkpashazade-Kreutel). E. Werner, *Die Geburt einer Grossmacht-die Osmanen (1300–1481)* (Berlin, 1966), pp. 170–179.

[291] Sharaf al-Din Ali Yazdi, II, 258–293. Uzunçarsĭlĭ *Fethine Kadar*, pp. 301–323.

[292] H. J. Kissling, "Badr al-Din ibn Kadi Samawna," EI₂. Wittek, "De la défaite d'Ankara à la prise de Constantinople (un demi-siècle d'histoire ottomane)," *R.E.I.*, XII (1938), 16–23. Ashĭkpshazade-Kreutel, pp. 130–132. Ashĭkpashazade, *Tevarikh-i Ali Othman*, ed. Ali Bey (Istanbul, 1332), pp. 91–93 (hereafter cited as Ashĭkpashazade-Ali).

[293] Melikoff, "Germiyan-oghullarĭ," EI₂. de Planhol, "Hamid," EI₂. Taeschner, "Antalya," EI₂.

[294] Ashĭkpashazade-Kreutel, pp. 220–226. Ashĭkpashazade-Ali, pp. 155–160. Babinger, "La date de la prise de Trebizonde par les Turcs (1461)," *R.E.B.*, VII (1950), 205–207; *Mahomet II le Conquérant et son temps (1432–1481)* (Paris, 1954), pp. 236 ff. Lampsides, " Πῶς ἡλώθη ἡ Τραπεζοῦς," *A.Π.*, XVII (1952), 15–54.

suffered a decisive defeat at Otluq Beli in 1473.[295] The reign of Muhammad II was the decisive stage in the political reunification of Anatolia under the rule of a single state, yet the Turkmen dynasties of the Akkoyunlu (1502), Dhu'l-Kadr (1522), and Ramazan (1517) survived into the early years of the sixteenth century.[296]

Conclusions

The detailed analysis of Byzantine internal history prior to the battle of Manzikert (1071) and the narration of the critical political and military events in Anatolia over four centuries have, it would seem, demonstrated two propositions:

1. The Byzantine defeat at the hands of the Turks in 1071 and the subsequent penetration of the Turkmen tribes in the following decade were in large part the result of a half century of violent internal disorders.

2. The Turkish conquest, settlement, and political unification of Anatolia was a long process, the final completion of which occurred four hundred years after the battle of Manzikert.

[295] Minorsky, "Akkoyunlu," EI₁. Babinger, *Mahomet*, pp. 373–374. Kramers, "Karaman," EI₂. J. Aubin, "Notes sur quelques documents Aq Qoyunlu," *Mélanges Louis Massignon* (Damascus, 1956), I, 123–147.

[296] Canard, "Cilicia," EI₁. J. H. Mordtmann-V. L. Menage, "Dhu'l Kadr," EI₂. The unification of Anatolia did not bring a permanent end to upheaval and disruption of settled life. The rise of the Safavis as well as other internal disturbances had repercussions for the stability and security of parts of Anatolia. M. Akdag, *Celali isyanларĭ (1550–1603)*, (Ankara, 1963); C. Orhonlu, *Osmanlĭ imparatorluğunda aşiretleri iskan teşebbüsü* (Istanbul 1963). By the seventeenth century, villages and agricultural activity had suffered from these rebellions, and the flight of some of the rural population from the land had followed. Because of this the government in Istanbul began to settle tribal groups in the deserted areas.

III. The Beginnings of Transformation

Nature of the Turkish Conquest in the Eleventh and Twelfth Centuries

Having established a general chronological structure and periodization of the Turkish conquests in the preceding chapter, the beginnings of the transformation by which Anatolia became Muslim must next be examined. This will entail discussion of three broad topics: the nature and effects of the Turkish conquests during the eleventh and twelfth centuries; the degree to which the Anatolian Christians had been integrated into Muslim society by the mid-thirteenth century; the character and results of the breakdown in the Konya-Nicaea equilibrium from the late thirteenth to the late fifteenth century.

Perhaps the single most fateful characteristic of the Turkish conquest in Anatolia was the longevity of the process, for this drawn-out period subjected Byzantine society to repeated shocks and dislocations. The Turks were not able to subdue Asia Minor quickly but achieved its complete conquest in a continuous process that lasted four centuries. Thus the conquest operated in piecemeal fashion. At certain periods it proceeded at an accelerated pace; at other times it made little progress; and on rarer occasions it was even reversed. Consequently, a significant number of towns and extensive regions were besieged, conquered, or raided on more than one occasion. In this, the Turkish subjugation of Asia Minor differed from the Arab conquest of the eastern Byzantine provinces in the seventh century wherein the regions of Syria, Palestine, and Egypt, disaffected because of religious persecutions on the part of the central government and weakened by the disbanding of the Arab client armies, fell rapidly and definitively to the Arabs in less that a decade, the issue having been decided by a few key battles. The striking difference between the rapidity of the Arab conquest and the slower progress of the Turks was due to geographic, ethnographic, and political factors. Anatolia is not only a large territory, but it is possessed of extensive mountainous areas that served as natural defenses against the invaders. In addition, the factor of religious disaffection, though present among Armenians and Syrians in easternmost Anatolia, played no comparable role in central and western

Asia Minor. Finally, Anatolia was much closer to the center of the Byzantine Empire than had been the provinces occupied by the Arabs and so was capable of greater resistance. As the state depended primarily on Anatolia for its resources and for much of its manpower, it could not and did not quietly acquiesce in the Turkish occupation. The loss of Asia Minor was tantamount to the destruction of the empire. The Byzantines, therefore, made serious efforts, in proportion to their sadly declining strength, first to reconquer and then to hold on to parts of Anatolia down to the period when Michael Palaeologus reconquered Constantinople in 1261.

Related to the long-term, piecemeal nature of the Turkish conquest was the disappearance of political unity and stability from Anatolia for significant periods of time. Prior to the appearance of the Turks, the Anatolian peninsula had enjoyed a political unity under Constantinople which had ensured comparative stability (at least for the regions west of a line running through Trebizond, Caesareia, Tarsus; but also to a certain degree for the regions to the east as far as Antioch, Melitene, and Ani). Society was obliged to support only one ruler, one administration, and one army. The invasions and prolonged period of active subjugation by the newcomers changed this situation abruptly and radically as the invasions resulted in a bewildering proliferation of political entities on Anatolian soil. This generalization should, of course, be qualified. These conditions were not as exacerbated in the first half of the thirteenth century when there was stability for much of Anatolia as the result of developments at Konya and Nicaea. But this was an isolated situation in the period between the eleventh century and the Ottoman unification of Anatolia in the fifteenth century. In the period down to the mid-thirteenth century, there arose on Anatolian soil Greek states on the Aegean and Black Sea coasts, an Armenian state in Cilicia, and a number of Turkish principalities in the central and eastern regions—Seljuk, Danishmendid, Saltukid, Menguchekid, Artukid. With the collapse in the relative and ephemeral stability of the Seljuks and Nicaea in the late thirteenth century, the appearance of the emirates throughout Anatolia brought a reversion to periods of anarchy and chaos until the emirates began to consolidate. The disappearance of political unity attendant upon the Turkish invasions not only brought considerable upheaval but often placed the Anatolian populations under the onerous burden of supporting a large array of courts, administrations, and armies.

The effects of the invasions down to the late twelfth century were most dramatically manifested in the pillaging and partial destruction of many urban and rural areas. Though no documentary materials survive which describe the process systematically, the existing chronicles give a clear overall picture of the upheaval. The most striking feature of this first period of Turkish conquest was the sacking of towns and villages in many regions of Anatolia, a number of these being pillaged on more than one occasion.[1] In some instances the sacking of a city or town entailed its complete destruction. But in the majority of cases the sacking of a city or town did not result in complete or immediate destruction, for these urban centers continued to exist, though often in a less prosperous state. The Turkish conquest was, however, accompanied by considerable destruction in terms of public buildings, houses, and churches. The Turkish epic, the Danishmendname, which gives a picture of the psychology of the conquerors, is replete with accounts of destruction of churches, monasteries, and places of habitation. The Byzantine sources characterize this period as one in which towns, churches, and buildings were destroyed by the Turks.[2] Though the Greek historians have exaggerated in speaking of complete destruction, nevertheless this exaggeration was the result of the extensive destruction to urban and rural life resulting from this one and one-half century of warfare. That there is a substantial and significant truth in this exaggeration becomes evident upon examination of the circumstances of the conquest in the various regions of the peninsula. Prior to the battle of Manzikert, the important cities of Artze, Perkri, Melitene, Sebasteia, Ani, Caesareia, Neocaesareia, Amorium, Iconium, and Chonae had been sacked by the Turks.[3]

WESTERN ANATOLIA

During the late eleventh and throughout the twelfth century, many parts of western Asia Minor were the scene of Turkish invasions, Byzantine counterattacks, and the ocasional appearance of Crusading armies. At the beginning of this period, as Alexius I succeeded to the throne (1081), western Asia Minor was largely in the grip of the invaders. When the veil of historical silence covering the events of this first Turkish conquest is lifted two decades later, the sources reveal that the coastal towns of western Anatolia were in a destroyed state.[4] The western Anatolian districts continued to experience the rigors of an unusually savage border warfare throughout much of the twelfth century.

A brief glance at the various regions of western Anatolia will clearly demonstrate the unrest that the Turkish invasions and settlement brought.

[1] See the comment of Eustathius of Thessalonike in his address to Manuel I Comnenus, *P.G.*, CXXXV, 944. " "Ω πολεμικῶν ἐκείνων σεισμῶν, οἳ τοὺς θεμελίους τῶν 'Ρωμαϊκῶν πόλεων ἦν ὅτε ὑπονομεύσαντες ἀνερρήγνυον."
[2] Theodore Scutariotes-Sathas, 169. " καὶ πάντων τῶν οἰκημάτων καὶ τῶν χωρίων καὶ αὐτῶν τῶν ἐκκλησιῶν τῶν ἐν ὅλοις τοῖς τῆς 'Ανατολῆς μέρεσιν ὑπ' αὐτῶν ἐρημωθέντων καὶ τέλεον κατατροπωθέντων καὶ εἰς τὸ μηδὲν ἀποκαταστάντων. Anna Comnena, III, 229. " 'Ηφανίζοντο μὲν πόλεις, ἐλῄζοντο δὲ χῶραι καὶ πᾶσα ἡ 'Ρωμαίων γῆ Χριστιανῶν αἵμασιν ἐμιαίνετο."
[3] For details see chapter ii.
[4] Anna Comnena, III, 23. " ... ἡ τῶν κατὰ θάλατταν διακειμένων πόλεών τε καὶ χωρῶν λεηλασία καὶ παντελὴς ἐρείπωσις." *Ibid.*, 142, refers to this destitution all the way from Smyrna to Attaleia. " ... τὸ κατὰ τὴν παραλίαν τῆς Σμύρνης καὶ μέχρις αὐτῆς 'Ατταλείας οἱ βάρβαροι τελείως ἠρίπωσαν."

The Bithynian regions were mostly in Turkish hands until the First Crusade. While the emperor was concerned with Robert Guiscard in the west, the Turks were ravaging all Bithynia and Thynia to the Bosphorus which was not as yet in their possession.[5] The second Byzantine–Norman war gave the Turks another opportunity, so that Abu'l-Kasim once more pillaged Bithynia all the way to the Bosphorus.[6] Despite the reconquest of Nicaea following the First Crusade, Bithynia continued to suffer from heavy raiding throughout the reign of Alexius.[7] In 1113 an army of between 40,000 and 50,000 from Persia devastated this and other neighboring regions (Prusa, Apollonias, Lopadium, Cyzicus, Lake Ascania),[8] and such attacks continued from the direction of Iconium in 1115–16. There is some record of further Turkmen incursions into Bithynia in the last quarter of the twelfth century when the emperor Alexius III entered the regions of Nicaea and Prusa to protect the cities from the attacks of the Turkmens encamped about the Bathys near Dorylaeum.[9] But inasmuch as the Turkmens had been settled near Dorylaeum for most of the period, it is not unlikely that they had continued their raiding expeditions into Bithynia during the reigns of John II and Manuel I.[10] The breakdown of Byzantine administrative control, especially as a result of the rebellion against Andronicus I Comnenus in 1183–84, no doubt greatly hastened the process, as the revels utilized Turkmens in their armies.[11] The appearance of the Latins in Bithynia immediately following the capture of Constantinople added to the confusion.[12] Mysia and the Propontis bore the brunt of the invasions and raids of the emirs Tzachas and Elchanes at the end of the eleventh century,[13] and though Alexius succeeded in removing both from this district, the latter years of his reign witnessed severe raids, in 1113 and again in 1115–16, by the Turkish armies from Persia.[14]

The western river valleys of the Caicus, Hermus, Cayster, and Maeander were frequently invaded and wasted. The Caicus as well as the regions north of Adramyttium were sorely vexed by incursions throughout the twelfth century, and large rural areas became depopulated.[15] The Hermus

---

[5] Anna Comnena, I, 136. Even before the accession of Alexius, Attaliates, 269, " . . . τῶν Τούρκων τὴν ἀπὸ θαλάσσης μέχρι Νικαίας νεμομένων περίχωρον."

[6] Anna Comnena, II, 63.

[7] The followers of Peter the Hermit also contributed by ravaging the area up to Nicomedia. Anna Comnena, II, 210.

[8] *Ibid.*, III, 159–169, 187 ff, 193, reports the advance of another Turkish army on Nicaea.

[9] Nicetas Choniates, 657–658.

[10] This is specifically stated for the regions of Pithecas and Melangeia during the reign of Manuel. Nicetas Choniates, 71. Cinnamus, 36, remarks that Bithynia had been very accessible to the Turks.

[11] Nicetas Choniates, 363–375. Theodore Scutariotes-Sathas, 337–340. The reprisals of Andronicus against the cities were savage.

[12] Nicetas Choniates, 796, reports that Henry " ἔκειρε τὰς πόλεις καὶ διετίθει κακῶς."

[13] Anna Comnena, II, 79, 165–166.

[14] *Ibid.*, III, 159–169, 187–188.

[15] Nicetas Choniates 195, " . . . τὴν ἔρημον . . . τὴν πρώην ἀοίκητον."

valley was in part conquered by Tzachas,[16] and in 1110–11 Hasan of Cappadocia pillaged the eastern reaches of the valley,[17] and shortly thereafter the Seljuk prince Malik Shah threatened Philadelpheia and the coastal regions.[18] The Cayster-Celbianum region was threatened by the armies of Hasan in 1110–11, again in the reign of Manuel I, and by the emir Same when Isaac II Angelus summoned the Byzantine troops of that area to Europe.[19] The towns and countryside of the fertile Maeander valley in particular suffered from Turkish raids in the late eleventh and the twelfth century. Though Alexius was able to restore some order to the Maeandrian regions, soon after his death John II Comnenus was forced to move against the Turks who were once more pillaging the valley.[20] By the reign of Manuel, the Turks seem to have raided the valley with regularity. Early in his reign Manuel I was forced to relieve the suffering towns,[21] for the Turkmens had settled at the source of the Maeander and were, apparently, raiding almost unhindered.[22] More imposing from the point of view of size was the raid of the Atabeg, with an army of 24,000, down the Maeander to the sea, which ravaged many of the towns severely.[23] Upon the death of Manuel the last semblance of vigorous defense disappeared and the Turks raided even more frequently, on occasion being brought in by Greek rebels. After his defeat in 1192, Pseudoalexius acquired 8,000 Turkmens from the emir Arsane (Arslan?) and pillaged the valley destroying the harvests.[24] Kaykhusraw, falling unexpectedly upon the middle and upper regions of the Maeander, captured a number of towns and took away the inhabitants.[25] A rebellious tax collector, Michael, obtained troops from the sultan Rukn al-Din and the towns of the Maeander were once more raided.[26] In the early thirteenth century Manuel Maurozomes, with the aid of Turkish troops, ravaged the valley towns but was driven out by Theodore Lascaris.[27]

Many of the districts and towns of Phrygia were in the center of the battleground between Muslim and Christian armies. After the defeat of the Turks by the First Crusades at Dorylaeum, the Turks retreated

[16] Anna Comnena, II, 110; III, 143.

[17] *Ibid.*, III, 144–145.

[18] *Ibid.*, 154–155.

[19] *Ibid.*, III, 144–145, 157. Cinnamus, 39–40. Nicetas Choniates, 481.

[20] Theodore Scutariotes-Sathas, 190.

[21] Nicetas Choniates, 71.

[22] On returning from the battle against the sultan, Manuel made his way to the source of the Maeander thinking himself to be safely out of Turkish territory there. But here he came upon a large encampment of Turkmens and their tents. These Turkmens, who were under a certain Rama, were in the habit of plundering the neighboring land of the Greeks. Cinnamus, 60, " καὶ ὡς κατ' ἔθος τὸ αὐτῶν τοὺς ἐκ γειτόνων 'Ρωμαίων ἤδη καὶ νῦν λῃστεύσαντες λαφύρων πλησάμενοι ἥκουσι."

[23] Nicetas Choniates, 250–252.

[24] *Ibid.*, 550–551. He came to be called καυσαλώνης. These Turkmens were habitually raiding Greek lands, " . . . οἱ λῃστεύειν τὰ 'Ρωμαίων εἰώθησαν."

[25] *Ibid.*, 655.

[26] *Ibid.*, 700–701.

[27] *Ibid.*, 827.

toward Iconium, and in an effort to scorch the earth in the path of the Crusaders, they gained entrance into the Greek towns, pillaged the houses and churches, carried off the livestock, silver, gold, and other booty, and then burned and destroyed everything that they could not carry away and that might have been of some use to the Latins. Later in his reign, the emperor Alexius I passed through the same areas and sought to destroy the Turkish encampments and to waste the area so that the Turks would not be able to use it to attack the empire. The sultan also scorched the earth about Iconium. As the region had become the border between Greek and Turkish possessions, it was slowly being turned to wasteland as a result of the frequent military campaigns and by express desire of both sides so that invaders might not find sustenance in these regions.[28] As Phrygia remained a critical frontier area in the reigns of John and Manuel, it suffered considerably from Turkish raiding,[29] but with the battle of Myriocephalum it was largely lost to the Turks. Pamphylia and Pisidia had a fate similar to that of Phrygia. After the initial recovery of the area by Alexius and John, the Turks raided and expanded into the region, until by 1204 little outside Attaleia remained Byzantine.[30] In the mid-twelfth century the fertile agricultural area of Attaleia was so unsafe because of the Turks that the inhabitants had to import their grain by sea.[31] There are indications that Lycia and Caria also saw repeated waves of incursions.[32]

Though the contemporary narratives give only a partial account of the events and situation in western Anatolia, these are sufficient to indicate that the invasions and warfare brought considerable upheaval to the western Anatolian districts of Bithynia, Mysia, Lydia, Caria, Ionia, Lycia, Phrygia, Pamphylia, and Pisidia. The majority of the raids have remained unchronicled, for the Seljuks at this time had nothing in the way of chronicles (at least chronicles that have survived), and the Byzantine historians were too concerned with the capital to note the recurring raids. It is to be assumed that the border raids of the Turkmens were constantly operative, and in fact the language of the Byzantine chronicles states this explicitly.[33] The disruption and destruction often brought by the Turkish raids to Byzantine urban and rural society in western Asia Minor were extensive, and a number of authors refer to this phenomenon in very general terms. Anna Comnena speaks of the Turkish "satraps"

[28] *Gesta Francorum*, pp. 54–55. Alexius burned Turkish settlements wherever he found them in order to protect his lands from the Turkmen raids, William of Tyre, VI, xii. Alexius had the villages of Bourtzes burned because of the Turks, and then removed all the Greeks, Anna Comnena, III, 200–203. Tudebodus, *R.H.C., O.C.*, III, 29.

[29] Theodore Scutariotes-Sathas, 190. Nicetas Choniates, 71–72. Cinnamus, 179.

[30] Theodore Scutariotes-Sathas, 190–191, 208. Nicetas Choniates, 50, 689.

[31] William of Tyre, XVI, xxvi.

[32] Miklosich et Müller, VI, 17, 19, 84, 87; IV, 323–329, where it is implied that the destruction of Latrus at the end of the eleventh was repeated again in the twelfth century.

[33] Cinnamus, 59–60. Nicetas Choniates, 551.

who at the end of the eleventh century were "plundering all,"[34] and of the "plundering and complete ruin of the cities and lands situated on the sea coast."[35] After the second Norman crisis (1107–08), Alexius devoted his attention to the cities of western Asia Minor, "reasoning that the barbarians had completely destroyed the coast from Smyrna to Attaleia itself."[36]

When the Second Crusaders came to Anatolia almost half a century later the situation had changed very little. Odo of Deuil remarks that the Turks had expelled the Greeks from a great part of "Romania," and had devastated much of it. As the Crusaders advanced south of Adramyttium they found many cities along the coastal regions in ruins and they observed that the Greeks still inhabited only those towns that had been rebuilt and girded with walls and towers.[37]

The question arises, however, as to whether such general statements that Anna Comnena and Odo of Deuil have made are historically reliable. The account of Anna Comnena in regard to the destruction of the coastal towns and to the destruction in western Asia Minor seems to be corroborated by an examination of the fate of a number of towns, villages, and areas, as well as by certain archaeological evidence.

Cyzicus fell to the Turks in the reign of Nicephorus III Botaniates, was taken a second time by the emir Elchanes in the reign of Alexius I, and then pillaged by a Turkish army from Persia in 1113.[38] Elchanes took Apollonias, and though recaptured by the Byzantines, the Turks ravaged its environs in 1113.[39] Anna Comnena relates that the environs of Lopadium suffered ravaging in the reign of Alexius I, and that shortly afterward the Turks who had taken and pillaged Cyzicus in 1113 sacked Lopadium during the same campaign.[40] The extent of the destruction of Lopadium, and perhaps by implication that of Cyzicus, Apollonias, and Cius, is indirectly revealed by the historian Cinnamus who remarks that the emperor John II had to rebuild the fort of Lopadium anew.[41] It suffered severe chastisement after its unsuccessful rebellion against Andronicus I Comnenus in 1184.[42] Poimamenum must have experienced the same

[34] Anna Comnena, III, 23.
[35] Ibid.
[36] Ibid., 142, " . . . λογιζόμενος αὖθις ὅπως τὰ κατὰ τὴν παραλίαν τῆς Σμύρνης καὶ μέχρις αὐτῆς Ἀτταλείας οἱ βάρβαροι τελείως ἠρίπωσαν." That this destruction includes the cities is specifically stated, " ἐν δεινῷ ἐποιεῖτο, εἰ μὴ καὶ τὰς πόλεις αὖθις ἐς τὴν προτέραν ἐπαναγάγοι κατάστασιν καὶ τὸν πρῴην ἀποδοίη κόσμον καὶ τοὺς ἀπανταχῇ σκεδασθέντας ἐποίκους αὐταῖς ἐπανασώσοιτο."
[37] Odo of Deuil, pp. 86–89, "Quam cum tota esset iuris Graecorum, hanc ex magna parte Turci possident, illis expulsis, aliam destruxerunt." Pp. 106–107, "Ibi multas urbes destructas invenimus . . . ." The accounts of the Third Crusade also bear testimony to destroyed towns.
[38] Anna Comnena, I, 69; II, 79–80; III, 165–166.
[39] Ibid., II, 79–80; III, 165.
[40] Ibid., III, 143, 165.
[41] Cinnamus, 38, " ἔνθα βασιλεῖ Ἰωάννῃ φρούριόν τι ἐκ καινῆς ἀνῳκοδομήθη."
[42] Nicetas Choniates, 374–375.

fate as Apollonias, having fallen to Elchanes and its environs having been wasted in 1113.[43] The environs of Abydus were devastated by Tzachas and by the Turkish invasion of 1113,[44] but there is no indication that the town itself fell. The nature of the destruction the emir Tzachas wrought is most clearly depicted in the case of Adramyttium.

> It was formerly a most populous city. At that time when Tzachas was plundering the regions of Smyrna, destroying, he also obliterated it [Adramyttium]. The sight of the obliteration of such a city [was such] that it seemed that man never dwelled in it.[45]

Shortly afterward in 1113 the Turks raided in the vicinity of Adramyttium. Indeed Adramyttium and its nearby villages suffered severely throughout the twelfth century from Turkish raids until Manuel walled the city and built fortresses in the depopulated countryside to protect the peasants.[46] Odo of Deuil remarks that the Crusaders immediately upon proceeding south of Adramyttium encountered ruined towns.[47] Chliara and Pergamum probably experienced much the same fate as Adramyttium, these regions having been devastated by at least three Turkish raids in the reign of Alexius I,[48] and they continued to be subject to pillaging in the reigns of John II and Manuel I. Before the latter fortified the cities and the countryside, the rural area had been abandoned by the inhabitants.[49] Calamus, one of the villages of the theme of Neocastron (Adramyttium, Pergamum, Chliara), was no longer inhabited by the time of the third Crusade,[50] and Meleum (located between Calamus and Philadelpheia) was in a destroyed state by the latter part of the twelfth century.[51] Tzachas took Smyrna, Clazomenae, Phocaea, and reached the Propontid regions wasting their environs,[52] and somewhat later Hasan raided Nymphaeum and the district of Smyrna.[53] Ephesus had fallen to the emir Tangripermes but was reconquered in the reign of Alexius I. Located on the convenient river route of the Cayster, it was no doubt accessible to raiding parties

[43] Anna Comnena, II, 80–81; III, 165.

[44] *Ibid.*, II, 165; III, 166.

[45] *Ibid.*, III, 143. "πόλις δὲ πρῴην μὲν ἦν πολυανθρωποτάτη· ὁπηνίκα δὲ ὁ Τζᾶχας τὰ κατὰ τὴν Σμύρνην ἐλῄζετο καὶ αὐτὴν παντελῶς ἐριπώσας ἠφάνισε. τὸν γοῦν παντελῆ ἀφανισμὸν τῆς τοιαύτης θεασάμενος πόλεως, ὡς δοκεῖν μηδὲ ἄνθρωπον κατοικῆσαι ποτε ἐν αὐτῇ."

[46] Nicetas Choniates, 194–195. Theodore Scutariotes-Sathas, 268.

[47] Odo of Deuil, p. 107. He adds that the Greeks inhabited only the fortified towns, no doubt a reference to the towns that Manuel and his predecessors had fortified.

[48] Anna Comnena, III, 144–145, 155, 166. The expeditions of Hasan, 1109–11, Malik Shah, 1111, the Turks from Persia, 1113.

[49] Nicetas Choniates, 194–195. Theodore Scutariotes, 268, "αἱ περὶ αὐτὰς χῶραι ἀοίκητοί τε ἦσαν τὸ πρίν."

[50] W. Ramsay, *The Historical Geography of Asia Minor* (London, 1890), p. 130.

[51] *Historia Peregrinorum*, ed. A. Chroust, *M.G.H.*, *S.R.G.*, nova series V (Berlin, 1928), p. 154.

[52] Anna Comnena, II, 110; III, 25. Tzachas surrendered it peacefully, but when a Syrian killed the Byzantine admiral, the sailors are reported to have slain 10,000 inhabitants.

[53] *Ibid.*, III, 145. Sardes, which had previously been in Turkish hands, would likewise have been exposed. *Ibid.*, 27.

such as those that had sought to enter the valley in 1110–11, again in the reign of Manuel Comnenus, and during the rule of Isaac II.[54] Odo of Deuil notes that in the mid-twelfth century the tomb of St. John at Ephesus was surrounded by walls to keep the "pagans" out, and that there were "ruins" in Ephesus.[55] Philadelpheia was retaken from the Turks after the recapture of Ephesus, but because of its more easterly location it was under constant pressure from the neighboring Turkmens. In 1110–11 Hasan besieged the city with 24,000 men, sending them out to plunder the villages about Celbianum, Smyrna, Nymphaeum, Chliara, and in 1111 the armies of the prince Malik Shah raided the territory around Philadelpheia as well as about Pergamum, Chliara, and Celbianum.[56] It was the scene of two rebellions and of opposition to the Third Crusade in the latter part of the twelfth century.[57] In 1176 the Atabeg and his troops took and sacked many of the Maeandrian towns including Tralles, Louma, Antioch, and Pentacheir.[58] Farther to the south the coastal towns also received rough handling. Melanoudium and the mountain regions of Latmus were sacked prior to the accession of Alexius I;[59] Strobilus was destroyed by the Turks, as Saewulf reported when he visited the site in 1103.[60] The Turks sacked the numerous monastic establishments of these regions, destroying and desecrating them, and driving out the monks. The monasteries of Latrus were once more pillaged toward the end of the twelfth century. The town of Myra suffered the fate of Strobilus and the other coastal cities.[61]

The Turks sacked Attaleia in the eleventh century, and consequently

---

[54] *Ibid.*, 144–145, 157. Cinnamus, 39–40. Nicetas Choniates, 480–481.

[55] Odo of Deuil, pp. 106–107. The abbot Daniel, who visited Ephesus in 1106–07, relates that Ephesus was located on a mountain four versts from the sea, *P.P.T.S.*, IV, 5–6. Al-Idrisi, II, 303, remarks that it was in ruins. The church was in such a dilapidated shape in the twelfth century that tessarae from the mosaic decoration were falling upon the head of the metropolitan during the liturgy, R. Browning, "The Speeches and Letters of Georgios Tornikes Metropolitan of Ephesos (XIIth Century)," *Actes du XIIᵉ Congrès international d'études byzantines* (Belgrade, 1964), II, 424.

[56] Anna Comnena, III, 27, 144, 154–157.

[57] Nicetas Choniates, 340, 521–522. Ansbert, p. 73.

[58] Nicetas Choniates, 251. " τὰς Μαιανδρικὰς ἐπιὼν πόλεις ἐδῄου οἰκτρῶς, ἐσβολὰς ἀκηρύκτους καὶ ἐφόδους ἀπροόπτους τιθέμενος. παρεστήσατο δὲ καὶ τὰς Τράλλεις . . . ὁδῷ δὲ προϊὼν καὶ τὰς παραθαλαττιδίους ἐλυμήνατο χώρας."

[59] Miklosich et Müller, VI, 16–19, 24, 30, 61–63, 87.

[60] "Ad Strovilo civitatem pulcherimam, sed a Turcis omnino devastatam," in W. Tomaschek, *Zur historischen Topographie von Kleinasien im Mittelalter, Sitz. der kaiser. Akad. der Wiss. in Wien, Phil.-Hist. Kl.*, CXXIV (1891), 39. Saewulf, *P.P.T.S.*, IV, 29.

[61] The documents in Miklosich et Müller, VI, 17–19, 24–25, 61, 84, 87; IV, 323–325, 329, give considerable information on the fate of the monastic communities. What occurred here was doubtlessly repeated in many other parts of Anatolia, as is suggested in the Danishmendname. St. Christodoulus relates that only the chrysobulls without valuable ornamentations survived the sack. All others were carried off by the Turks. In the various accounts of the translation of St. Nicholas, it is recorded that Myra had been destroyed by the Turks, *R.H.C., H.O.*, V₁, xlvi. Though some of this data is not reliable, this particular feature of the narrative seems to be confirmed by Anna Comnena's testimony of the destruction of these regions. Myra and Patara appear as destroyed towns in the fourteenth century, see below.

it was one of the cities Alexius rebuilt.[62] Because of its geographical location and Turkish pressure from the north, the city was largely isolated in terms of land communication. John Comnenus made two expeditions in the regions to the north of Attaleia in order to settle conditions there, but evidently he achieved only partial success.[63] By the time of the Second Crusade (1147), Attaleia was so hard pressed by the Turks that the inhabitants could not cultivate their fields and as has already been mentioned they had to bring grain by sea.[64] During the revolt of Andronicus Comnenus (1182) the sultan of Konya subjected the city to a severe siege.[65]

The mountainous regions to the east of the river valleys, which separate the Anatolian plateau from the coastal districts, constituted areas of almost continuous strife. This geographical district, stretching from Dorylaeum in the northwest to Iconium in the southeast came to be a no-man's land which Greeks, Turks, and Crusaders repeatedly devastated. On the northern edge of this region the Bithynian towns and countryside experienced numerous raids immediately following the battle of Manzikert. Nicomedia, recaptured by the Byzantines in the late eleventh century, was still a "lofty ruins" set among thorns and bushes in the mid-twelfth century.[66] Nicaea, while yet in the hands of the Turks, was besieged by the emir Burzuk for three months,[67] and shortly thereafter by Buzan.[68] The reconquest of the city by the Crusaders entailed some difficulties, for the unruly troops of Peter the Hermit pillaged the houses and churches en route to Nicomedia. In the north the depredations begun by the Norman mercenary Roussel terminated in the destruction of both towns by the Turks who left them desolate ruins.[69] The Turks once more laid siege to Nicaea in 1113, when they ravaged Bithynia and the Propontis.[70] In the latter half of the twelfth century the pressure of the Turks about the Bithynian region, as well as an abortive rebellion against Andronicus Comnenus, brought some hardship to Nicaea.[71] Prusa experienced practically the same history as Nicaea down to the end of the twelfth century. The fate of eastern Bithynia, however, is not at all clear, with the solitary exception of Claudiopolis which almost fell to the Turks but was

[62] Anna Comnena, III, 142. Al-Idrisi, II, 134, refers to it as the "Burnt," and remarks that it is built away from the old site, but this probably refers to Side. See A. M. Mansel, *Die Ruinen von Side* (Berlin, 1963); Mansel, "Side," *P.W., Supplementband*, X (1965), 879–918.

[63] Nicetas Choniates, 17–19, 50. Cinnamus, 7, 22. Theodore Scutariotes-Sathas, 190–191, 208.

[64] William of Tyre, XVI, xxvi.

[65] Nicetas Choniates, 340.

[66] Odo of Deuil, pp. 88–89.

[67] Anna Comnena, II, 72.

[68] *Ibid.*, II, 74. Matthew of Edessa, p. 203.

[69] Anna Comnena, II, 210. Attaliates, 267–268. In the days of Michael VII this region had become " . . . ἔρημος καὶ ἀοίκητος καὶ ἄβατος . . ." *Gesta Francorum*, pp. 6–9.

[70] Anna Comnena, III, 164.

[71] Nicetas Choniates, 363–371, 658.

saved by the appearance of the emperor Manuel.[72] The Turks had laid waste the towns of Pithecas and Malagina located on the westernmost bend of the Sangarius River so that Manuel was forced to rebuild and fortify them.[73] Both Dorylaeum and Cotyaeum on the Tembris River were also sacked by the Turks, and they became areas of Turkish settlement. Dorylaeum had lain an uninhabited ruin for a century and, with the exception of a few stones, had completely disappeared.[74] Before Manuel decided to rebuild Dorylaeum in 1175, it had been a pasturage for the flocks of the Turks.[75]

> There was a time when this Dorylaeum was one of the great cities of Asia and very noteworthy. A gentle breeze blows upon the land, and it has about it very extensive level plains of extraordinary beauty [which are] so rich and fertile that they give forth rich grass and supply ripe ears of grain. A river sends its stream through it and it is beautiful to see and sweet to taste. There is such a quantity of fish swimming in it, that no matter how much those fishing take, fish are never lacking. Here, formerly, splendid mansions were built by the Caesar Melissenus, the villages were populous, and [there were] natural hot springs, stoas and baths, and all such things as bring pleasure to men. These things did the land provide in abundance. But the Persians [Turks], when the invasion of the land of the Rhomaioi was at its height, had razed the city to the ground and made it completely destitute of people, and they obliterated everything in it, even the thin trace of its former dignity. It was such a city. Then about 2,000 Persian [Turkish] nomads were camped about it in tents as is their custom.[76]

While Manuel was rebuilding Dorylaeum, the nomads burned the area and their tents so that the Greeks would find no sustenance.[77] But the emperor's accomplishment was short-lived for Dorylaeum was evidently retaken by Kïlïdj Arslan and his son Mas'ud took possession of it.[78] After Manuel's death the sultan sacked Cotyaeum[79] and henceforth it seems to have remained in Turkish hands.[80] Farther to the southeast the Turks sacked the city of Amorium in the reign of Romanus IV,[81] and though there were Byzantine campaigns in the region of Amorium in the first half of the twelfth century,[82] it was removed from the Byzantino-Turkish frontier. Greeks and Turks fought over Cedrea, Polybotus, and Philomelium for long periods, and both Manuel Comnenus and Frederick

---

[72] *Ibid.*, 257–259.

[73] *Ibid.*, 71. Cinnamus, 36, 38.

[74] Euthymius Malaces, ed. C. Bones, " Εὐθυμίου τοῦ Μαλάκη μητροπολίτου Νέων Πατρῶν (Ὑπάτης), δύο ἐγκωμιαστικοί λόγοι, νῦν τὸ πρῶτον ἐκδιδόμενοι, εἰς τὸν αὐτοκράτορα Μανουὴλ Α′ Κομηνὸν (1143/80)," Θεολογία, XIX (1941–48), 529 (hereafter cited as Euthymius Malaces-Bones).

[75] Nicetas Choniates, 228. Theodore Scutariotes-Sathas, 283.

[76] Cinnamus, 294–295.

[77] Nicetas Choniates, 228.

[78] *Ibid.*, 689

[79] *Ibid.*, 340. " καὶ τὸ Κοτυάειον ἐξεπόρθησε."

[80] *Ibid.*, 689.

[81] Scylitzes, II, 678.

[82] Anna Comnena, III, 199–201. Theodore Prodromus, *P.G.*, CXXXIII, 1382.

Barbarossa burned Philomelium.[83] By the latter half of the twelfth century, Myriocephalum was uninhabited.[84] The towns between Limnai and the middle Maeander were especially exposed to raids by both the neighboring Turkmens and the forces of the sultan in Konya. Sozopolis, in the hands of the Turks for about half a century, was retaken by John Comnenus,[85] but the Turks besieged it soon afterward.[86] Relatively isolated, Sozopolis and the neighboring villages were taken and sacked by the sultan (during the revolution of Andronicus Comnenus when the cities of Byzantine Asia Minor were engulfed in civil strife)[87] and henceforth remained Turkish. The towns of the Pentapolis were in ruins by the end of the twelfth century;[88] Manuel found Choma-Soublaion a shambles,[89] and Lampe probably suffered extensively from the raiding of both sides.[90] Though Laodiceia and Chonae fared better than most of the cities between Limnai and the Maeander,[91] the latter city was pillaged by the Turks in 1070,[92] and both cities were certainly in Turkish hands by 1081. Laodiceia and possibly Chonae as well were reoccupied by the Byzantines at the end of the eleventh century.[93] The Turks retook Laodiceia, however, and so once more the Byzantine emperor John Comnenus had to remove them.[94] During the reign of Manuel the armies of Kïlïdj Arslan sacked the city so thoroughly, that it eventually had to be restored.[95] The environs of both Laodiceia and Chonae were ravaged by the Greek rebel Theodore Mangaphas and his Turkish troops,[96] and somewhat later the rebel Pseudoalexius ravaged the outskirts of Chonae with 8,000 Turkish troops who destroyed the church of the Archangel Michael, its famous mosaics and the altar.[97] The towns of the upper Maeander seem to have fared less well and when the Third Crusaders passed through

[83] Anna Comnena, III, 27, 199–201, 203. Nicetas Choniates, 71–72, 540. Cinnamus, 41–42. Salimbene, p. 11.

[84] Nicetas Choniates, 231.

[85] Cinnamus, 6–7. Nicetas Choniates, 18. Theodore Scutariotes-Sathas, 190–191.

[86] Cinnamus, 22.

[87] Nicetas Choniates, 340, " . . . τήν τε Σωζόπολιν πολέμου νόμῳ κατέσχε, καὶ τὰς πέριξ κωμοπόλεις ληϊσάμενος ὑφ' ἑαυτὸν ἐποιήσατο."

[88] Manuel had previously driven the Turkmens out of the area but they must have returned soon after, Theodore Scutariotes-Sathas, 253.

[89] Nicetas Choniates, 229. Cinnamus, 298.

[90] Anna Comnena, III, 27. Nicetas Choniates, 231. Theodore Scutariotes-Sathas, 296.

[91] Michael Acominatus, Μιχαὴλ 'Ακομινάτου τοῦ Χωνιάτου τὰ σωζόμενα, ed. S. Lampros (Athens, 1879), I, 52–53 (hereafter cited as Michael Acominatus-Lampros), speaks proudly of his patris, Chonae, as, " ἥ τε πόλις αὐτοῖς μόνη σχεδόν τι μεμένηκε τοῖς Πέρσαις ἀνάλωτος."

[92] Attaliates, 140–141. Cedrenus, II, 686–687.

[93] Anna Comnena, III, 27.

[94] Cinnamus, 5–6. Nicetas Choniates, 17–18. Theodore Prodromus, P.G., CXXXIII, 1382. Theodore Scutariotes-Sathas, 190–191.

[95] Nicetas Choniates, 163, " . . . τὴν κατὰ Φρυγίαν ἐκπορθεῖ Λαοδίκειαν, οὐκέτι οὖσαν συνοικουμένην ὡς νῦν ἑώραται."

[96] Ibid., 523.

[97] Ibid., 552–553. Chonae seems to have remained a vital economic and religious center as a result of its famed church and commercial fairs, Michael Acominatus-Lampros, I 56–57.

the region, they found both Hierapolis and Tripolis destroyed (1190).[98] Kaykhusraw, in raiding the towns of the Maeander, carried away the populations of Tantalus and Caria.[99] Caria had previously been sacked and part of the population enslaved by the Turkish troops under Theodore Mangaphas,[100] and Antioch ad Maeandrum was among the riverine towns that the Atabeg sacked in 1176.[101]

EASTERN ANATOLIA

Greater Armenia, the lower Pyramus district, the eastern regions of the Halys, and Cappadocia were partially convulsed by invasions and raids in this same period. The invasions were followed by struggles of Seljuks, Danishmendids, Saltukids, Menguchekids, Artukids, and Armenians, which kept eastern Anatolia in a state of war. Cappadocia was raided repeatedly in the eleventh century. In 1067 the Turks plundered and burned the city of Caesareia and sacked the celebrated shrine of St. Basil,[102] and in 1069 they once more ravaged Cappadocia.[103] Shortly after the battle of Manzikert the Turks again appeared before the remains of Caesareia and, spreading out, sacked the Cappadocian villages.[104] Though Cappadocia passed in part under the control of the Danishmendids in the late eleventh century,[105] Caesareia still lay in ruins when the First Crusaders came through the area[106] and until 1134 when the Danishmendid Muhammad rebuilt the city.[107] An eight-year period of ravages by Turkmens in Cappadocia and adjacent regions began in 1185 (or 1186–87); these raids were quite serious.[108] According to the archaeological and epigraphical evidence, the famous Byzantine troglodyte monastic communities of Cappadocia declined in the late eleventh and twelfth centuries[109] and were to revive only with the stability of the thirteenth century.

[98] Ansbert, pp. 74–75. *Historia Peregrinorum*, p. 154, ". . . a Turcis dirutam . . ."
[99] Nicetas Choniates, 655.
[100] *Ibid.*, 523.
[101] *Ibid.*, 251.
[102] Attaliates, 93–94. Cedrenus, II, 661.
[103] Attaliates, 135–137. Scylitzes, II, 683–684.
[104] Attaliates, 184. Bryennius, 58–60. Alexius Comnenus had to keep to the mountains to avoid them.
[105] Michael the Syrian, III, 173.
[106] Baldricus, *R.H.C., H.O.*, IV, 39, "venerunt quoque ad Caesaream Cappadociae quae ad solum diruta erat: ruinae tamen utcumque subsistentes quanta fuerit illa Caesarea testabantur."
[107] Bar Hebraeus, I, 258: "Then this Malik Mahammad restored Caesarea of Cappadocia, which had been destroyed for a long time, and there he dwelt." Michael the Syrian, III, 237: "Il se mit à restaurer la ville de Cesarée, en Cappadoce, qui etait ruinée depuis longtemps. Il en retrancha une partie; et il y batit des édifices avec les pierres de marbre qu'on arrachait des temples superbes. Il y habitait constamment." The city was finally incorporated into the Seljuk domains by Kïlïdj II Arslan in 1169. Michael the Syrian, III, 332. Nicetas Choniates, 159.
[108] Michael the Syrian, III, 400–402. The chronicler remarks that he is not able to record all the massacres that took place in these eight years. Bar Hebraeus, I, 321–322.
[109] De Jerphanion, *Cappadoce*, II₁, 395–400. N. and M. Thierry, *Nouvelles églises rupestres de Cappadoce* (Paris, 1963), pp. 220–222.

The regions of the upper Pyramus, or Gaihan, River likewise suffered. Al-Harawi, the Arab traveler of the late twelfth century, found the town of Arabissus in ruins[110] whereas Albistan and the regions of the upper Pyramus were very seriously depopulated by the expedition of Yakub Arslan in 1155–56.[111] Marash was able to resist the Turks in the early period but changed hands between Christians[112] and was damaged severely by an earthquake either in 1114 or 1115.[113] Muhammad the Danishmendid burned the environs of Marash and its villages in 1136–37[114] and Kïlïdj Arslan took it in 1148.[115] The regions of the Euphrates in southeastern Anatolia were similarly exposed to the vicissitudes entailed in the competition of various Turkish dynasties and in the raid of Turkish tribes, the upheaval extending as far south as Antioch.[116] Here the situation is somewhat clearer as the texts of Matthew of Edessa and Michael the Syrian take as their focal points Edessa and Melitene respectively. In 1120–21 the Artukid Ilghazi burned the villages, enslaving and massacring the populations, from Tell Bashir northward to Kaisum.[117] Shortly after 1134 Afshin pillaged the regions of Kaisum only to be followed by Mas'ud who in his first raid pillaged and took captives in the neighborhood. He returned a second time and reduced to ashes the nearby villages.[118] In 1136–37 Muhammad the Danishmendid burned the villages and monasteries of the land about the town, including the monastery of Garmir Vank.[119] In 1140–41 the inhabitants temporarily abandoned the town and so the Turks sacked and burned it.[120] Finally in 1179 Kïlïdj Arslan destroyed its walls and carried the inhabitants off into captivity.[121]

Edessa resisted the Turks for a comparatively long time, though it had been besieged and its environs ravaged on numerous occasions by the end of the eleventh century.[122] But the Turkish pressure on the regions of

[110] Al-Harawi, trans. J. Sourdel-Thomine, *Guide des lieux de pèlerinage* (Damascus, 1957), p. 135.

[111] Matthew of Edessa, p. 344.

[112] Michael the Syrian, III, 173. Anna Comnena, III, 40-41.

[113] William of Tyre, XI, xxiii. Bar Hebraeus, I, 247.

[114] Matthew of Edessa, pp. 320–321.

[115] Michael the Syrian, III, 290, at which time the church treasures were taken.

[116] *Sawirus ibn al-Mukaffa'*, II, iii, 320, speaks of disorders, captivity, and assassinations in 1077 following the occupation of the land by the Turks.

[117] Matthew of Edessa, p. 302. "From Tell Bashir to Kaisum he enslaved men and women, massacred without pity, and burned and roasted infants in great number with unparalleled barbarity. After crossing the Euphrates with considerable forces, he exterminated the population of a great number of villages; priests and monks perished by iron and fire."

[118] Michael the Syrian, III, 245–246.

[119] Matthew of Edessa, pp. 320–321.

[120] Gregory the Priest, pp. 324–325.

[121] Michael the Syrian, III, 388.

[122] It was attacked by Gumushtekin in 1066. Bar Hebraeus, I, 217. The emir Khusraw raided the area between 1081 and 1083, Matthew of Edessa, p. 185. Buzan took the city after a long siege attended by famine in 1087–88. Matthew of Edessa, p. 198. Shortly thereafter it was taken by Tutuch who restored it to Thoros. Matthew of Edessa, p. 208.

Edessa increased in the first half of the twelfth century. Kīlīdj I Arslan besieged the city in 1106–07,[123] and one year later the Turks burned its nearby villages and fortresses.[124] In 1112–13 the Turk Maudud raided the same area, but in this year it was the Franks who broke into the city and sacked it.[125] Ilghazi the Artukid raided the countryside prior to 1120–21, and Turkish forces carried out a vigorous siege of the city in 1134. In 1144–45 Zangi captured the city.[126] Shortly thereafter, however, the Armenian garrison turned the city over to the Franks, so the Turks under Nur al-Din recaptured and destroyed Edessa with the result that the inhabitants were completely removed from the city.[127]

Edessa remained a desert: a moving sight covered with a black garment, drunk with blood, infested by the very corpses of its sons and daughters! Vampires and other savage beasts ran and entered the city at night in order to feast on the flesh of the massacred, and it became the abode of jackals; for none entered there except those who dug to discover treasures. The people of Harran and the rest of its enemies excavated the churches and the houses of the nobles, saying, Bravo! Bravo! Our eye has contemplated it.[128]

The regions of Samosata, Hisn Mansur, and Nisibis are less well documented. In 1108–09 the Turks killed or enslaved the farmers about Hisn Mansur.[129] Nur al-Din of Aleppo took Nisibis in 1171 and ordered all new churches as well as those built in the reign of his father to be destroyed. The treasure of the Nestorian church of Mar Jacob and its library of 1,000 volumes were pillaged and destroyed.[130] Just to the north and east of Nisibis the Turks ravaged the regions of Gargar and Seveverek, and Balak took Gargar in 1122, deporting most of its population; he returned in 1123, burned the town, and enslaved the remainder of the

---

In 1095–96 Sukman the Artukid and Baldukh of Samosata laid siege to the city for sixty-five days, Matthew of Edessa, pp. 210–211. With the coming of the First Crusade, the inhabitants summoned Baldwin to give them relief from the steady Turkish pressure, William of Tyre, IV, ii.

[123] Matthew of Edessa, p. 264.

[124] William of Tyre, XI, vii.

[125] Matthew of Edessa, pp. 279, 283–284.

[126] Bar Hebraeus, I, 268–269. "The Turks pushed in with drawn swords, which drank the blood of old men and young men, of strong men and women, of priests and deacons, of monks and anchorites, of nuns and virgins, of children of tender years, and of bridegrooms and brides. O What a bitter history!" Michael the Syrian, III, 260–266. Chabot, "Un épisode," pp. 169–179

[127] Michael the Syrian, III, 272; 30,000 were killed, 16,000 enslaved, and only 1,000 escaped. Bar Hebraeus, I, 273. St. Narses, R.H.C., D.A., I, 238, 245–246. William of Tyre, XVI, v. Matthew of Edessa, p. 326.

[128] Michael the Syrian, III, 272. Though Edessa came to be inhabited by the latter half of the century, a considerable portion of the city remained in ruins. Ibid., 397–399, gives a cataloge of seventeen churches that were still in a ruined state in his time. He adds that there had been no priests in the town for a long time. Al-Harawi trans. Sourdel-Thomine, p. 143), a contemporary who visited Edessa, remarks that it contained old ruins.

[129] Matthew of Edessa, pp. 265–266.

[130] Michael the Syrian, III, 339–340.

population.[131] Sometime later Christian Armenians retook it and engaged in reciprocal, destructive raids with their enemies the Muslim Armenians of Seveverek.[132] First Muslims and Christians, and then Seljuks and Danishmendids, contested the city of Melitene and its neighboring villages so that for over a century this land knew no peace. It was one of the first large Byzantine towns that the Seljuks sacked when they appeared in eastern Anatolia.[133] By 1071 the Turkish raids in the environs were endemic[134] but the city held out until 1102 at which time the Danishmendids conquered it.[135] Kïlïdj I Arslan took it in 1106, and though he was kind to the inhabitants,[136] on his death the citizens were subjected to financial oppression by his successors.[137] The environs of the city continued to be raided by Turks as well as by Franks.[138] In 1124 the Danishmendid Ilghazi finally retook Melitene after a difficult six-month siege as a result of which the inhabitants perished in great numbers.[139] In 1140–41 the Turks of Melitene pillaged the neighboring monastic establishment of Zabar.[140] Shortly afterward, when John Comnenus appeared before Neocaesareia, hopes seem to have run high among the Christians of Melitene that he might succeed, with the result that the Turks put many inhabitants of Melitene to the sword.[141] The struggle between Danishmendid and Seljuk over Melitene was continuous and between 1141 and 1143 Mas'ud of Konya besieged the city.[142] Raiding Turks pillaged and burned the monastic complex of Bar Mar Sauma a few years later.[143] Kïlïdj II

[131] *Ibid.*, 205–206, he did this to chastise the Armenians who were raiding his lands. In 1062-63 the regions of Nisibis and Seveverek had been raided by the Khurasan Salar. Matthew of Edessa, pp. 115–118.

[132] Michael the Syrian, III, 244, 247. Bar Hebraeus, I, 265. Matthew of Edessa, p. 313. The Armenian rulers of Seveverek had converted to Islam to keep their domains.

[133] Matthew of Edessa, pp. 107–108. Bar Hebraeus, I, 212–213. Michael the Syrian, III, 165. Large numbers of its inhabitants were killed or enslaved. One source indicates that afterward some 15,000 prisoners were ransomed and returned to the city, Michael the Syrian, III, 146.

[134] Cedrenus, II, 660. Attaliates, 93, 107. The attempt of Constantine X Ducas to enforce ecclesiastical union on the Monphysites of Melitene in 1063, and the fact that the Armenians raided the Syrian monasteries and attacked the Syrian populations of the countryside, added to the upheaval, Michael the Syrian, III, 161–164, 166–168. Bar Hebraeus, I, 217. Matthew of Edessa, pp. 95–96, 152–154.

[135] Bar Hebraeus, I, 236. Matthew of Edessa, p. 230. In 1096–97 Kïlïdj I Arslan was besieging it when arrival of the Crusaders in Anatolia caused him to lift the siege. Michael the Syrian, III, 187. Matthew of Edessa, pp. 212–215. Danishmend wasted the countryside, destroying the crops, in 1099.

[136] Bar Hebraeus, I, 239. Michael the Syrian, III, 192.

[137] Michael the Syrian, III, 194.

[138] *Ibid.*, 205.

[139] The inhabitants suffered from three things: (1) the sword outside the wall which massacred those who fled; (2) famine; (3) The prince, who tortured the inhabitants in order to get their gold. Michael the Syrian, III, 219. Matthew of Edessa, p. 315.

[140] Michael the Syrian, III, 248. Bar Hebraeus, I, 266.

[141] Michael the Syrian, III, 249. Bar Hebraeus, I, 266; "At that time every Christian who mentioned the name of the King of the Greeks or of the Franks, even unwittingly, the Turks slew. And because of this many of the people of Melitene perished."

[142] Michael the Syrian, III, 254. Bar Hebraeus, I, 267.

[143] Michael the Syrian, III, 290–291.

Arslan destroyed the environs of the city in 1152,[144] while simultaneously on the inside of the city the inhabitants were being oppressed financially, a circumstance that was repeated in 1170.[145] Kïlïdj Arslan returned and laid siege to the city unsuccessfully in 1171. He carried off 12,000 of the rural population, which would have constituted a further serious de-population for the area had he not been forced to return them.[146] Six years later, 1177, he was successful, and Melitene once more became a Seljuk possession. During the siege many of the Christians had fled the city because of the severity of the famine, but those who remained suffered many afflictions from the ruler himself. With the success of Kïlïdj Arslan the lot of the Christians improved considerably.[147] When Sulayman conquered Antioch in 1085 he too was comparatively lenient with the city; nevertheless there was a massacre, the treasures of the church of St. Cassianus were stolen, and the church converted into a mosque.[148]

The city of Sebasteia was first sacked and reduced to ashes in 1059 when the Turks pillaged it for eight days,[149] and it capitulated to the Danishmendids in the latter part of the century (1085?)[150] Mas'ud, the sultan of Konya, destroyed it a second time in 1143,[151] and it was once more sacked when Kïlïdj II Arslan took it in c. 1173.[152] The Seljuk chieftain Ibrahim Inal destroyed the important international commercial emporium of Artze to the east in 1049–50, and the inhabitants abandoned the site for Erzerum.[153] The regions of Byzantine Armenia were partic-ularly savagely devastated in the latter half of the eleventh century. Matthew of Edessa speaks of this period as "the beginning of the ruin and destruction of the Eastern Nation."[154] The Turks captured and sacked Ani in 1064[155] and repeatedly raided the vicinity of Lake Van (Zorinak, Chliat, Manzikert).[156] Because of these disturbances Matthew of Edessa

[144] Michael the Syrian, III, 304–305. Bar Hebraeus, I, 279.

[145] Michael the Syrian, III, 336–337.

[146] *Ibid.*, 346. Bar Hebraeus, I, 296.

[147] Michael the Syrian, III, 373. Bar Hebraeus, I, 308. This is illustrated by the testi-mony of Michael the Syrian, who remarks that when Kïlïdj II Arslan came to Melitene he was kind to Michael, a fact that caused great astonishment "to the whole world."

[148] Michael the Syrian, III, 173. Bar Hebraeus, I, 229. Sawirus ibn al-Mukaffa', III, iii, 320.

[149] Matthew of Edessa, pp. 111–113, 166–167. It too, like Melitene, was caught up in the strike between Greeks and Armenians at this time.

[150] Michael the Syrian, III, 173. The Danishmendname, I, 198–200, relates that Danish-mend had to rebuild the city.

[151] Bar Hebraeus, I, 267.

[152] Nicetas Choniates, 159. Bar Hebraeus, I, 303. Michael the Syrian, III, 357, says 1175, but perhaps this refers to a possible second capture by Kïlïdj II Arslan, for Abu'l-Feda, *R.H.C., H.O.*, I, 43, says that in 1172–73 Nur al-Din forced Kïlïdj Arslan to return Sebasteia to Dhu'l-Nun, but that on the death of the latter Kïlïdj Arslan retook Sebasteia.

[153] Cedrenus, II, 577–578. Matthew of Edessa, pp. 83–84. Attaliates, 148.

[154] Matthew of Edessa, pp. 182–183, 204.

[155] Attaliates, 79–82. Matthew of Edessa, pp. 121–124. Cedrenus, II, 653–654. It was retaken from the Muslims by the Georgians in 1124–25 and in 1161, Matthew of Edessa, pp. 313–314. Ibn al-Athir, *R.H.C., H.O.*, I, 522.

[156] Matthew of Edessa, p. 208. Abu'l-Feda, *R.H.C., H.O.*, I, 5.

described the early twelfth century as a period of tribulations and massacres.[157] When Romanus IV Diogenes arrived at Erzerum in 1071, prior to the battle of Manzikert, two months' rations were distributed to the army as "they were about to march through uninhabited land which had been trampled underfoot by the foreigners."[158]

NORTHERN ANATOLIA

The regions of northern Asia Minor lay similarly exposed to the upsetting effects of the Turkish invasion during the latter half of the eleventh century. The critical period was the reign of Michael VII Ducas (1071–78). The whole of the coastal region from Heracleia to Trebizond as well as the hinterland about the Iris (Yeshil Irmak) and the lower Halys (Kïzïl Irmak) were turned into areas of frequent raiding and plundering, and were in many cases partially abandoned by the Christian population.[159] During this reign the Turks had come into northern Asia Minor in comparatively large numbers and the roads were no longer safe,[160] so that by the reign of Nicephorus III Botaniates (1078–81) most of the coastal regions were in Turkish hands.[161] Though the Byzantines were able to recover the coastal regions by 1085[162] and even some of the hinterland,[163] at least temporarily, northern Asia Minor remained a scene of continuous raiding and warfare throughout the twelfth century among Byzantines, Danishmendids, Seljuks, Georgians, Saltukids, and Menguchekids. There is very little specific information as to the fate of individual coastal areas. Both Sinope and Trebizond were taken by the Turks and retaken by the Byzantines in the late eleventh century,[164] and many of the towns must have suffered, in varying degrees, from the upheaval. Joseph, the metropolitan of Trebizond, writing at a later date on the reinstatement of the great religious and commercial celebration of Trebizond, the panegyris of St. Eugenius, remarks:

The Forgetting of the Celebration of the Birth of the Saint

At that time [eleventh century] there [were] massacres and captures of cities and collections of prisoners and there attended all those things which are grievous to life . . . . From that time the memory of the celebration became the victim of deep oblivion, and again this annual celebration forgot the city, as the necessities were lacking.[165]

[157] Matthew of Edessa, p. 239.
[158] Attaliates, 148.
[159] Michael the Syrian, III, 72. Attaliates, 199. The Greek forts and cities were in a state of terror, and Michael VII gathered people from Pontus and moved them across the sea. Danishmendname-Melikoff, I, 112.
[160] Bryennius, 86–95.
[161] Anna Comnena, I, 18. Michael the Syrian, III, 175. Heracleia, and possibly Sinope and Trebizond, were exceptions, though the latter two were occupied by the Turks for a short period.
[162] Anna Comnena, II, 64, 151.
[163] Ibid., III, 29–30.
[164] Ibid., II, 64, 66, 151.
[165] In Papadopoulos-Kerameus, Ist. trap. imp., I, 59.

This is strong testimony as to how the Turkish invasions affected the peace, security, and economic prosperity of this flourishing commercial emporium.[166] The city of Sinope underwent a similar experience for there too the great panegyris of the local saint, St. Phocas, came to a halt and his church was destroyed as a result of the Turkish invasions.[167] The formerly active maritime center of Amastris became an unimportant town in the twelfth century,[168] and though the hinterland of other coastal cities—Heracleia, Paurae, Oenoe, and Sinope—was raided by the Danishmendids, there is no systematic account of the experiences of these cities during the twelfth century.[169] By the end of the twelfth century the Turkish pressure and raids had brought the Turks into possession of the coastal town of Amisus just to the east of Paurae, presaging the fall of Sinope in the early thirteenth century.[170]

In many respects the hinterland of the Black Sea coastal regions resembled the regions of western Asia Minor between Dorylaeum-Cotyaeum and Loadiceia-Chonae. The hinterland of the northern coast consisted of rugged mountain country separating the Anatolian plateau from the seacoast. This difficult terrain is primarily accessible or traversable through the river valleys of the Halys, Iris, and Lycus, which penetrate the mountains from north to south and from west to east. It was in these riverine corridors that the military forces of Islam and Christianity contested the possession of northern Asia Minor in the eleventh and twelfth centuries, and the struggle must have been a constant one as the few tantalizing sources imply. This region remained a border area as late as the fifteenth century, and the Danishmendname gives an interesting insight into the mentality of the ghazi tribesmen who actively carried on the struggle against the Christians of northern Anatolia. Features of this poem, which reflect the general conditions of the conquest, include destruction of churches and monasteries, the repeated siege and capture of towns, proselytization, taking of booty, and so forth. Adding to the unsettled conditions was the fact that the Danishmendids, who ruled in

---

[166] There was a partial recovery in the twelfth century, but the city did not regain its old prosperity until the late thirteenth century. Al-Idrisi, II, 393. Papadopoulos-Kerameus, *Ist. trap. imp.*, I, 65.

[167] Van den Vorst, "Saint Phocas," *A.B.*, XXX (1911), 289. " ἤδη γὰρ σοι κἀνταῦθα πανήγυρις τῶν μεγάλων . . . καὶ ὁ νεὼς δὲ οὗτος ἠρείπωται πρὶν ταῖς ἐνγειτόνων βαρβάρων ἀθέων ἐπιθέσεσιν ὡς γενέσθαι κοινόν." Alexius Megas Comnenus restored the church and the panegyris.

[168] Al-Idrisi, II, 392, who also remarks that its inhabitants led a nomadic life.

[169] Cinnamus, 176. Anna Comnena, II, 64. Bona was an embarkation point for war with the Muslims, and seems to have enjoyed some prosperity in the twelfth century. Al-Idrisi, II, 393. In the twelfth century the Turks frequently raided the coast (at one point a certain Cassianus delivered many of the forts of Pontus to the Danishmendids [Michael the Syrian, III, 227]), and Michael the Syrian, III, 232, remarks that John Comnenus massacred most of the Turks in the coastal region (it is not exactly clear as to which coastal region is meant). In 1139 Malik Muhammad pillaged regions of Cassianus on the Pontus and took off the population selling it into slavery, Michael the Syrian, III, 248. Bar Hebraeus, I, 266.

[170] Nicetas Choniates, 689. Theodore Scutariotes-Sathas, 427.

this area until the latter half of the twelfth century, had to contest possession not only with the Greeks but with the Seljuks of the plateau. The valleys of the Lycus, Iris, Halys had been penetrated on numerous occasions and in considerable force by the Turks prior even to the appearance of Danishmend, as Paipert and Coloneia were raided in 1054 and 1057 respectively,[171] and Neocaesareia was sacked in 1068.[172] Amaseia and Castamon were surrounded by raiding Turkish bands when Alexius Comnenus left Amaseia with Roussel. He paused near Castamon to see the family estates but found them abandoned, the Turks pillaging, and he himself only narrowly escaped capture.[173] By the time of the Crusade of 1101, the Danishmendids had conquered Paipert, Argyropolis, Coloneia, Neocaesareia, Doceia, Comana, Amaseia, Euchaita, Pimolissa, Gangra, though Gabras of Trebizond had reconquered Paipert and Coloneia at one point,[174] and the Byzantine general Taronites continued to contest Danishmendid control in the area. The Crusaders of 1101 found the regions about Gangra-Castamon east to Amaseia partly deserted, and the earth scorched.[175] In the warfare of the twelfth century, especially in the reign of John Comnenus, the Greeks succeeded in retaking Gangra, Castamon, and numerous other fortresses for restricted periods, and so the area found itself in much the same state of continuous warfare and change of political domination as did western Anatolia.[176] In the latter half of the century the Seljuks of Konya began, gradually, to absorb the holdings of the Danishmendids as well as those of the Greeks. In 1196 the emir of Ankara besieged Dadybra for four months, bombarding the houses, polluting the water and eventually reducing it by famine. The Greek inhabitants were expelled and the city recolonized by Muslims.[177] Previously, rebellions of Byzantines had brought considerable destruction to Byzantine Paphlagonia in a manner strikingly reminiscent of the rebellions in western Asia Minor at this time.[178]

SOUTHERN ANATOLIA

Cilicia and the Taurus regions, especially, witnessed frequent political change and military occupation. As a result of the First Crusade, the

---

[171] Honigmann, *Ostgrenze*, pp. 181, 184. Cedrenus, II, 606.

[172] Cedrenus, II, 684–685. Attaliates, 105.

[173] Bryennius, 88, 93.

[174] Danishmendname-Melikoff, I, 71–72, 108–112, 251–258, 277–280, 315. Anna Comnena, III, 29–30, 76.

[175] Anna Comnena, III, 37. Albert of Achen, *R.H.C., H.O.*, IV, 564, says of the regions of Gangra, "segetes et omnia sata regionis depopulantes." Danishmendname-Melikoff, I, 96.

[176] See Chalandon, *Les Comnènes*, II, 46–47, 77–91. Nicetas Choniates, 25–26, 29, 45–48. Cinnamus, 13, 15, 21. Theodore Prodromus, *P.G.*, CXXXIII, 1373–1383. Michael the Syrian, III. 249, 234. Malik Ghazi massacred the Greeks of Castamon. E. Kurtz, "Unedierte Texte aus der Zeit des Kaisers Johannes Komnenos," XVI *B.Z.* (1907), 75–83.

[177] Nicetas Choniates, 626.

[178] *Ibid.*, 553

Turks relinquished most of Cilicia, and Byzantine garrisons reoccupied the area. Seleuceia and Corycus, however, were by then mere ruins and had to be rebuilt, and Mopsuestia-Mamistra was half destroyed.[179] Because of the conflict of interest among Byzantines, Latins, Armenians, and Muslims, the towns of the region changed hands frequently.[180] Turkish raiders carried off the population of Adana to Melitene in 1137,[181] and they sacked Pracana early in the reign of Manuel Comnenus.[182] Toward the end of the twelfth century, Turkmen groups began to follow the Pyramus valley in search of plunder and pastures. This brought a double danger to the Christians in the area, for the Turkmens were often supported by Muslim rulers such as Salah al-Din who in 1182 invaded and plundered Cilicia in support of Turkmens who had been defeated by the Armenians.[183] The regions of Laranda, Heracleia, and Anazarba were infested by Turkmens and so must have been in difficult straits.[184]

CENTRAL ANATOLIA

The three principal urban centers of the central plateau, Konya, Ankara, and Archelais, must likewise have been enveloped in disorder, though the Turkish conquest of this region was definitive earlier, so that conditions were regularized much sooner here than in other areas. The Turks pillaged the regions of Ankara soon after Manzikert,[185] and sometime later the city fell to them. Al Idrisi, writing one-half century later, remarks that it had been destroyed during the "time of troubles."[186] It continued to change hands in the twelfth century even after the Seljuks took it from the Danishmendids. Konya (Iconium) and its environs were sacked early in 1069. Though it was farther removed from the borders, the city and its suburbs and villages were attacked by both Greeks and Crusaders in the eleventh and twelfth centuries.[187] The sultan

[179] Anna Comnena, III, 45–46, 58. "πόλις γὰρ πρότερον οὖσα ἐρυμνοτάτη τὸ Κούρικον ἐν ὑστέροις ἔφθασεν ἐριπωθῆναι χρόνοις."

[180] Runciman, *A History of the Crusades*, (Cambridge, 1952), II, *passim.*

[181] The accounts of Michael the Syrian, III, 244, and Bar Hebraeus, I, 264, are contradictory in certain details.

[182] Cinnamus, 38.

[183] Bar Hebraeus, I, 310, 321, 328. Abu'l Feda, *R.H.C., H.O.*, I, 49, and Ibn al-Athir, *R.H.C., H.O.*, I, 644 say 1180–81. Sempad, *R.H.C., H.O.*, I, 628–629.

[184] This comes out clearly in some of the Latin accounts, as for example, Salimbene, p. 12, who remarks, "qui non sunt de potestate soldani."

[185] Bryennius, 64. The inhabitants feared to open the gates of the city to Alexius Comnenus because of the proximity of the Turkish encampments.

[186] Al-Idrisi, II, 312. Wittek, "Zur Geschichte Angoras im Mittelalter," *Festschrift G. Jacob* (Leipzig, 1932), p. 341. The oldest surviving Muslim inscription at Ankara is that of the mimbar of the so-called mosque of 'Ala' al-Din, 1197. This would seem to suggest a comparatively slow and late development.

[187] Anna Comnena, III, 200–204. Alexius Comnenus raided the villages, and the Christian inhabitants voluntarily followed his army back to Byzantine territory. The sultan had previously scorched the regions before the Byzantine advance. See also William of Tyre, VI, xii. Greek forces again raided the Konya area under John Comnenus. Nicetas Choniates, 42. Theodore Scutariotes-Sathas, 203. In 1155 Manuel encamped before Konya, destroying the suburbs and desecrating the Muslim cemetery, where

Rukn al-Din burned the town of Laodiceia Combusta forty kilometers north of Konya at the end of the twelfth century for having mistreated a member of the dynasty.[188] The fact that Kīlīdj II Arslan rebuilt Coloneia Archelais (Aksaray) would seem to imply, much in the same manner as Caesareia and Sebasteia, that it too had suffered devastation.[189]

This detailed, yet incomplete, survey of Anatolia during the latter part of the eleventh and the twelfth century indicates that violence, destruction, and upheaval accompanied the Turkish invasions and occupation of the peninsula. Consequently, the lament of Anna Comnena on the fate of Byzantine Anatolia constitutes something more than an empty rhetorical exercise:

> And since the succession of Diogenes the barbarians tread upon the boundaries of the empire of the Rhomaioi . . . the barbarian hand was not restricted until the reign of my father. Swords and spears were whetted against the Christians, and also battles, wars, and massacres. Cities were obliterated, lands were plundered, and the whole land of the Rhomaioi was stained by blood of Christians. Some fell piteously [the victims] of arrows and spears, others being driven away from their homes were carried off captives to the cities of Persia. Terror reigned over all and they hastened to hide in the caves, forests, mountains, and hills. Among them some cried aloud in horror at those things which they suffered, being led off to Persia; and others who yet survived (if some did remain within the Rhomaic boundaries), lamenting, cried, the one for his son, the other for his daughter. One bewailed his brother, another his cousin who had died previously, and like women shed hot tears. And there was at that time not one relationship which was without tears and without sadness.[190]

Obviously in some areas the destruction was greater; in other areas, less severe. It cannot be maintained that the Turkish conquest operated with ease and without serious disturbance of Anatolian society. On the other hand, it would be just as erroneous to assert that the destruction was complete.

---

his army slew 7,000 Muslims. Cinnamus, 45. *Histoire des Seljoukides d'Asie Mineure par un anonyme*, trans. F. Uzluk (Ankara, 1952), pp. 24–25. Frederick Barbarossa also burned the city during the Third Crusade. Nicetas Choniates, 542.

[188] Ibn Bibi-Duda, pp. 22–23.

[189] Uzluk, *Histoire des Seljoukides*, p. 25. *The Geographical Part of the Nuzhat-al-Qulub composed by Hamd-allah Mustawfi of Qazwin in 740* (1340), trans. G. Le Strange (London, 1919), p. 96, relates that Kīlīdj II Arslan rebuilt it in 1171 (hereafter cited as Qazwini-Le Strange). *The Ta'rikh-i-guzida or "Select History" of Hamdu'llah Mustawfi-i-Qazwini*, E. G. Browne (Leiden-London, 1913), p. 108.

[190] Anna Comnena, III, 229. The destructive nature of the conquest is repeated in most of the sources. Theodore Scutariotes-Sathas, 169. " 'Επὶ τούτου τοῦ βασιλέως ὁ σύμπας σχεδὸν κόσμος κατά γε γῆν καὶ θάλασσαν ὑπὸ τῶν ἀθέων βαρβάρων κατασχεθεὶς ἅπας ἠφανίσθη, καὶ ἔρημος οἰκητόρων κατέστη, πάντων χριστιανῶν ὑπ' αὐτῶν ἀναιρεθέντων, καὶ πάντων τῶν οἰκημάτων καὶ τῶν χωρίων καὶ αὐτῶν τῶν ἐκκλησιῶν τῶν ἐν ὅλοις τοῖς τῆς 'Ανατολῆς μέρεσιν ὑπ' αὐτῶν ἐρημωθέντων καὶ τέλεον καταστροπωθέντων καὶ εἰς τὸ μηδὲν ἀποκαταστάντων." Fulcher of Chartres, *R.H.C.*, *H.O.*, III, 336. "Nam Romaniam, quae terra est optima et valde fertilis bonorum omnium, invenimus nimis a Turcis vastatam et depopulatam." Matthew of Edessa, pp. 181–183. Odo of Deuil, pp. 86–88.

The cities in many areas suffered from the continuous state of warfare, for they underwent siege, capture, isolation from the countryside, a lessening of commercial activity, and often destruction. Though a great many of the cities continued to exist, as is indicated by the survival of the Byzantine urban toponymy, they survived in a sadly declined state. It was rural society that often was more disrupted and displaced in many parts of Anatolia. Here too, the toponymical evidence would seem to lend weight to this supposition.[191] Very often the village populations sought refuge from the invaders by going to the walled and fortified towns. This caused the population of some of the towns to experience a temporary rise. In 1071 the city of Edessa had a population of approximately 35,000, but 75 years later just prior to its destruction by Nur al-Din the city had 47,000 inhabitants.[192] This formidable increase is to be explained primarily in terms of the population of the environs which had settled down within the safety of the walls in fleeing the unsafe countryside.[193] At the western extreme of Anatolia the same phenomenon could be observed. The rural areas of Pergamum, Chliara, and Adramyttium suffered destruction and almost complete depopulation throughout a large portion of the late eleventh and the twelfth century, as a result of the Turkish raids. This was due to the fact that the rural population had previously lived scattered in small unprotected villages and so was an easy prey of the invaders. Until Manuel built forts throughout the rural area in which the agrarian inhabitants might seek refuge, the land was abandoned and no longer cultivated. When the emperor did build the fortifications, a rural society was re-formed and the land returned to cultivation.[194] Many of the

---

[191] Already in the twelfth century the Greek sources seem to refer to a very few rural areas by their Turkish names, Wittek, "Von der byzantinischen zur turkischen Toponymie, *Byzantion*, X (1935), 53, for a discussion of these names. Nicetas Choniates, 689. By far, however, the greatest part of the datable Turkish toponymical evidence occurs later. A detailed study of late Byzantine and early Turkish toponymy remains one of the most important tasks for the students of Anatolian history.

[192] Sawirus Ibnal-Mukaffa', II, iii, 305. Bar Hebraeus, I, 273. William of Tyre, XI, vii, trans. Babock and Krey, records the following for the year 1108; "They [Turks] took certain fortresses by storm, burned villages, and captured farmers and others engaged in cultivating the fields. No place was safe outside the circuit of the walled cities; consequently the tilling of the fields ceased, and food began to fail entirely."

[193] See the remarks above for the state of perpetual siege which was the fate of Edessa during this seventy-five year period. The city was repeatedly besieged, its rural areas and population subjected almost uninterruptedly to the sword, fire, and captivity. Buzan besieged the city in 1087–88; Sukman the Artukid in 1095–96; the emir Khusraw in 1083; Kïlïdj I Arslan in 1106–07. In 1108 the Turks burned the villages. Turkish armies raided the area until the city was finally sacked and destroyed.

[194] Theodore Scutariotes-Sathas, 268. " αἱ εἰς τὴν 'Ασίαν πόλεις, τὰ Χλίαρα, τὸ Πέργαμόν τε, καὶ 'Ατραμύτιον κακῶς ἔπασχον ὑπὸ τῶν Περσῶν· αἱ γὰρ περὶ αὐτὰς χῶραι ἀοίκητοί τε ἦσαν τὸ πρίν, καὶ ἐκ τοῦ κατὰ κώμην οἰκεῖσθαι, εἰς προνομὴν τοῖς πολεμίοις προέκειντο. καὶ αὐτὸς τοίνυν, κατωχύρωσε τείχεσι, καὶ τὰς πλησίον δὲ πεδιάδας φρουρίοις συνῴκισεν· οὕτω δὲ πλήθουσιν οἰκητόρων καὶ τοῖς κατὰ τὸν βίον πλουτοῦσι χρηστοῖς." Nicetas Choniates, 195, Manuel transformed the uninhabited to an inhabited area. " . . . εἰς οἰκήσιμον τὴν πρῴην ἀοίκητον." The period of the Comnenoi and the Lascarids seems to have witnessed an extension of the fortification works not only in the urban centers but in the rural areas as well. The towns and

Towns, Villages, Provinces Destroyed
Pillaged, Enslaved, Massacred, or Besieged

WESTERN ASIA MINOR

TOWNS AND VILLAGES	ENVIRONS OF TOWNS AND VILLAGES	PROVINCES
Cyzicus—C, C, C, X	Apollonias—P	West Anatolia—X
Apollonias—C, X	Lopadium—P	Dorylaeum-Iconium—P, E, P, E
Lopadium—X	Poimamenum—P	
Cius—C	Abydus—P, P	Thynia-Bithynia—P, P, P, P
Poimamenum—X	Adramyttium—P, P, F	Propontis and Mysia—P, P, P
Adramyttium—X	Chliara—F, P	
Calamus—X	Pergamum—F, P	Caicus, Hermus, Cayster, and Maeander, P, P, P
Meleum—X	Smyrna—P	
Smyrna—C, X	Clazomenae—P	Phrygia—P
Clazomenae—C, X	Phocaea—P	Paphlagonia—P
Phocaea—C, X	Ephesus—P, P	Pisidia—P
Sardes—C	Philadelpheia—P	Lycia—P
Nymphaeum—C	Attaleia—P	
Ephesus—C, X	Dorylaeum—P	
Philadelpheia—C	Cotyaeum—X	
Tralles—X	Sozopolis—P	
Louma—X	Lampe—P	
Pentacheir—X	Laodiceia—P	
Melanoudium—X	Chonae—P	
Latrus—X		
Strobilus—X		
Attaleia—X, B		
Nicomedia—C, X		
Nicaea—C, X, B		
Prusa—C, X, B		
Claudiopolis—B		
Pithecas—X		
Malagina—X		
Dorylaeum—X, C		
Cotyaeum—X, X		
Amorium—X		
Cedrea—C		
Polybotus—C		
Philomelium—C, X, X		
Myriocephalum—X		
Sozopolis—C, B, X		
Chonae—X, C		
Laodiceia—C, C, X		
Hierapolis—X		
Tripolis—X		
Tantalus—X, E		
Caria—X, E, X, E		
Antioch ad Maeandrum —X		
Choma-Soublaion—X		

EASTERN ASIA MINOR

Caesareia—X
Arabissus—X
Albistan—E, X
Kaisum—F, X, E, X
Edessa—B, B, X, B, X,
  E, M, M
Nisibis—X
Gargar—X, E, X, E
Melitene—X, M, E, X,
  C, X, B
Bar Mar Sauma—B, B,
  B, C
Sebasteia—X, N, E, C,
  X, X, C
Artze—X, F
Ani—X. C
Zorinak—X, M

Marash—P, C
Kaisum—S, M, E, P,
  X, X
Tell Bashir—S, M, E, P,
  X, X
Edessa—P, X, P, P
Hisn Mansur—M, E
Gargar—P
Seveverek—P
Melitene—P, P, P, X, E
Chliat—P
Perkri—P

Cappadocia—P, P, P, F
Pyramus R. —E, P
Armenia—M, E, F, P
Lake Van—P, P

NORTHERN ASIA MINOR

Sinope—X, C
Trebizond—X, C
Amisus—C
Paipert—B, C
Coloneia—B, C
Neocaesareia—X, C
Amaseia—B, C
Castamon—X, X
Doceia—C
Comana—C
Euchaita—C
Pimolissa—C
Gangra—C, X
Dadybra—C, F

Gangra—X, F
Castamon—X, F
Amaseia—X, F

SOUTHERN ASIA MINOR

Seleuceia—X
Mopsuestia—X
Corycus—X
Adana—X, E
Pracana—X

Pyramus Valley—P

CENTRAL ASIA MINOR

Iconium—X, M
Ankara—X, C, C
Coloneia Archelais—X
Laodiceia Combusta—X

Ankara—P, P
Iconium—P, P, P

Key: P = pillaged, X = sacked or destroyed, E = enslaved, C = captured,
M = massacred, B = besieged, F = flight.

population centers were not compactly settled and centered in one urban area and so had no walls to protect the inhabitants. Laodiceia in Phrygia was made up of scattered settlements at the foot of the mountains and was not defended by walls.[195] But as a result of the invasions, the settlement was concentrated into a centralized synoecism and fortified with walls. The rural populations of the area then must have retreated to the safety of the new walls. Just to the east Chonae, Sozopolis, and Baris must have seen the flocking of rural elements to the safety of the city walls throughout the twelfth century.[196] In the east the commercial center of Artze was, like many other cities, without walls and the town was scattered about over a considerable area. Consequently, the Turks destroyed it and the inhabitants fled to the protection of the walled city of Erzerum.[197] In the Georgian regions of Transcaucasia there was a similar devastation and consequent flight of local populations.[198] In the north the rural populations largely abandoned the regions about Gangra, Castamon, and Amaseia, some of them no doubt seeking refuge in the larger towns.[199] In the south the farmers deserted the Pamphylian plain and sought refuge in Attaleia (and elsewhere as well), and the countryside became the camping ground of the Turkmens who came to raid and to besiege Attaleia.[200] Thus the invasions and repeated raiding very markedly disrupted the rural society in many parts of Anatolia. The most abrupt and serious displacement must have taken place in those areas that Muslims and Christians contested for the longest periods, namely, the region between Dorylaeum and Attaleia in the west, along the boundary between Danishmendids and Greeks in the north, and in the border regions about the Taurus and the river valleys in the south and east.

---

countryside were thus defended by a coordinated group of forts and city walls. On this see the pioneering study of W. Müller-Wiener, "Mittelalterliche Befestigungen im südlichen Jonien," *I.M.*, XI (1961), 5–122.

[195] Nicetas Choniates, 163; " οὐκέτι οὖσαν συνοικουμένην ὡς νῦν ἑώραται, οὐδ' εὐερκέσι φραγνυμένην τείχεσι, κατὰ δὲ κώμας ἐκκεχυμένην περὶ τὰς ὑπωρείας τῶν ἐκεῖσε βουνῶν." *Ibid.*, 17. John Comnenus erected a wall about the city after retaking it from the Turks.

[196] The ability of all three towns to survive the Turkish conquest so long was due above all to their strong defenses and strategic locations. Cinnamus, 6; " Σωζόπολις αὕτη πόλις μέν ἐστι τῶν ἐν 'Ασίᾳ πάλαι ἐπισήμων, ἐφ' ὑψηλοῦ δέ τινος καὶ ἀποκρήμνου ἱδρυμένη χωρίου τῷ μὲν ἄλλῳ ταύτης μέρει πανταχόθεν ἄβατος γίνεται, μίαν δέ τινα κομιδῇ στενωτάτην παρέχεται εἴσοδον, ἐφ' ἣν οὔτε μηχανήν ἄν τις ἑλκῦσαι δυνήσεται οὔτε τι τῶν εἰς τειχομαχίαν εὐτρεπίσασθαι· καὶ ἀνθρώποις γὰρ ὅτι μὴ κατ' ὀλίγους πορευομένοις μόλις ἐπὶ τὴν πόλιν εἰσηγητὰ γίνεται." Ibn Bibi-Duda, p. 36, remarks that Isparta (Baris) was one of the strongest fortified towns of the area.

[197] Attaliates, 148. Cedrenus, II, 577. Zonaras, III, 638–639.

[198] Brosset, *Géorgie*, I, 330, 331, 346, 348. Also M. V. Tseretheli, "Das Leben des Koenigs der Koenige Dawith (Dawith II, 1089–1125)," *B.K.* (1957), pp. 45–73. P. M. Tarchnichvili, "La découverte d'une inscription géorgienne de l'an 1066," *B.K.* (1957), pp. 86–88. On the disarray and destruction attendant upon the Seljuk occupation of Adharbaydjan, see R. Huseynov, "La conquête de l'Azerbaidjan par les Seldjoucides," *B.K.* (1965), pp. 99–108.

[199] Anna Comnena, III, 37. Bryennius, 92–93. Danishmendname-Melikoff, I, 96. Albert of Achen, *R.H.C.*, *H.O.*, IV, 564.

[200] William of Tyre, XVI, xxvi.

DISPLACEMENT OF POPULATION

With this violent displacement of Anatolian urban and rural society, what happened to the inhabitants of the towns and the countryside? Their experiences in this period varied. As harsh as the Turkish invasions had been, they could not and did not destroy the indigenous population. On the other hand, the violence and length of the conquest and occupation did bring a partial desolation and displacement of the inhabitants. It is quite clear that a portion of the population in some areas of Anatolia simply fled in order to escape the raids. The chroniclers observed that this phenomenon occurred across the breadth and width of the peninsula. Obviously the majority of those who fled could not possibly have fled from the peninsula itself, but rather moved to the protection of the mountains, as in the regions of the Taurus, or else to the protection of strongly fortified towns such as Edessa, Melitene, Trebizond, and Tarsus, or into other lands held by Christians. But in western Anatolia, large numbers of the population fled to the islands and to Constantinople itself.[201] In the documents of the monastery of St. Christodoulus, we see the progressive withdrawal of the monks and inhabitants of Latrus to Strobilus and then to the islands in the face of the Turkish advance.[202] When after the reconquest Alexius sought to rebuild the coastal cities of the Smyrna-Attaleia region, he had to seek out the former inhabitants as they had fled from their original homes.[203] The Greek inhabitants, who had only to cross the Bosphorus to reach safety, soon evacuated the regions of Chalcedon and Chrysopolis.[204] When Alexius evacuated the Greeks from the villages around Philomelium, Cedrea, and Konya, considerable numbers must have been involved, but again one must assume that they were a minority of the population.[205] In the north there is evidence of a similar type, indicative of a partial withdrawal by the inhabitants from the districts of Castamon, Gangra, parts of Pontus, and from the area to the east of Erzerum.[206]

[201] Attaliates, 211, 267–268.
[202] Miklosich et Müller, VI, 62, 84, 87, 88.
[203] Anna Comnena, III, 142.
[204] Attaliates, 211, 267.
[205] Anna Comnena, III, 29, 201, 203. Zonaras, III, 757. William of Tyre, VI, xii. Anna gives a detailed description of this mass transplanting of unprotected Greeks. The refugees were put in the center of the bodies of troops where they would be protected from Turkish attacks. The advance was halted each time that a birth, serious illness, or a death occurred.
[206] Michael the Syrian, III, 72. Michael VII Ducas reportedly transferred people from Pontus "across the sea." Albert of Achen, R.H.C., H.O., IV, 564. Bryennius, 93. All these refer to partial and not to total withdrawals. The Danishmendname-Melikoff, II, 178, describes such flights of populations from villages and undefended areas to the mountains and walled towns.

> "Andan Rūm içine āvāz düşmişdikim Melik
> Dānişmend Nesŧōrile Şatŧātï ġèrü sïkmïş dèyü bu ḫaber
> kim Rūm içine düşdi kanda kim ṣarb yèrler varise,
> Kāfïrler anda kaçdïlar. Andan kim köylerde
> ŧururdï, anlardahï yabāna ve kimisi daḫï
> kal'elere kaçdïlardï. Temāmet Kāfïrler
> perākende olmïslardï."

A similarly great displacement of the indigenous population took place in southeast Anatolia. Matthew of Edessa describes the situation as it existed in the first year of the reign of Alexius Comnenus.

> Everywhere throughout Cilicia, up to Taurus, Marash, and Deluh and the environs, reigned agitation and trouble. For populations were precipitated into these regions en masse, coming by the thousands and crowding into them. They were like locusts, covering the surface of the land. They were more numerous, I might add seven times more numerous, than the people whom Moses led across the Red Sea; more numerous than the pebbles in the desert of Sinai. The land was inundated by these multitudes of people. Illustrious personages, nobles, chiefs, women of position, wandered in begging their bread. Our eyes witnessed this sad spectacle.[207]

The Turkish movements precipitated a veritable migration of Christians from the regions of Cappadocia, Lycandus, and elsewhere to the safety of the Taurus and Cilicia at this time.

The Turkish invasions thus induced migrations among the indigenous Christian inhabitants in varying degrees. The migrations Matthew described, as well as those of the Greeks from the coastal regions, were of considerable extent. Others were probably on a smaller scale. The sum total, however, was to produce a movement of Christians away from the central plateau regions toward the coastal regions on the north, west, and south. But again, it is to be doubted that these Christians who fled were anything more than a minority of the indigenous Christian population.

It would seem quite likely that after this first half century of invasions, the native population had, for the most part, remained in Anatolia.[208] The Greek populace of the northern coast was relatively unaffected by virtue of the failure of the Turks to conquer this region permanently. Ankara appears to have had a very small Turkish garrison in 1101 and was remitted to the Byzantines by the Crusaders, and to the east the Crusaders encountered Christians along their road (some of whom they massacred). In western Asia Minor, Alexius resettled and rebuilt many of the coastal towns, such as Adramyttium, so that there was a recolonization of the partially destroyed areas, a work that his successors John and Manuel continued. Farther inland the establishment of officials in such cities as Sardes, Philadelpheia, Choma, Lampe, and others, indicates that Greek populations still inhabited these towns.[209] The inhabitants of Laodiceia and Philadelpheia were still there when Alexius drove the Turks out,[210] and at the time that the Crusaders advanced from Nicaea to Heracleia, they found Christians inhabiting the whole area. The towns between Dorylaeum and Konya, the cities of Philomelium, Konya,

---

[207] Matthew of Edessa, p. 182.
[208] On this see the judicious remarks of J. Laurent, "Des Grecs aux Croisés," *Byzantion*, I (1924), 442–445.
[209] Anna Comnena, III, 27.
[210] *Ibid.*, III, 27, 29.

and Heracleia, were all inhabited primarily by Christians.[211] Tarsus had a largely Greek and Armenian population, with only a small Turkish garrison.[212] Marash, Antioch, Edessa, Melitene, Plastentza (Albistan), Coxon, were all inhabited by Christians.[213] Though Alexius I had removed considerable numbers of the inhabitants of the region between Philomelium and Iconium, others remained, as is witnessed by the example of Tyriaeum. The latter was inhabited by Greeks and because of its walls was able to resist the Turks, having no Turkish garrison within the walls.[214]

The mortality rate among the indigenous populations must have reached new heights during this period. It has been customary to pass over this aspect of the Turkish invasions in the period under discussion as being nothing more than an exaggeration on the part of contemporary and more recent Christian historians. There is no doubt that in all such similar historical phenomena there exists the tendency to exaggerate and discolor. But at the same time it must be kept in mind that the great Seljuk sultans of Persia made strenuous efforts to shunt the Turkmen tribes into Anatolia in order to spare their own domains from their ravages. Also, it was the Turkmen element, an element devoted to raiding and plundering, which effected a great portion of the conquests and occupation. The Muslim sources themselves testify to this characteristic of Turkish nomadic society within the domains of Islam.[215] In addition, Anatolia was now the scene of the djihad, and many of the Turks were imbued with the ghazi mentality which called for the destruction of the enemies of the faith.[216] Extensive massacre accompanied the sacking of the cities of Sebasteia, Ani, Caesareia, Neocaesareia, Amorium, Iconium, and Chonae prior to Manzikert,[217] and this became widespread in the reign of Michael VII Ducas when the Turks were free to go about Anatolia almost at will.[218] It is significant that the very chroniclers who praise individual Turkish and Arab rulers for their clemency to the Christians (such princes were Malik Danishmend, Malik Shah, Kïlïdj II Arslan) make them the

---

[211] *Gesta Francorum*, pp. 54–57.

[212] William of Tyre, III, xix. The Turks formed only the garrisons.

[213] William of Tyre, IV, i; V, xi. Matthew of Edessa, p. 209, 211. *Gesta Francorum*, pp. 60–65.

[214] Anna Comnena, III, 211–212.

[215] See for instance the account of Ibn al-Qalanisi, *Damas de 1065- a 1154*, trans. R. Le Tourneau (Damascus, 1952), p. 4, who describes the capture of Damascus by Atsiz in 1076. Also Bar Hebraeus, I, 225–226. Brosset, *Géorgie*, I, 330–331.

[216] Danishmendname-Melikoff, I, 284, and *passim*, as well as the Kitab-i Dede Korkut, the Desturname of Umur Pasha, and the Battalname for illustrations of this psychology. The Arab traveler al-Harawi, who visited Anatolia in the latter half of the twelfth century, has left us an account that clearly illustrates the importance of this ghazi mentality. Al-Harawi, trans. Sourdel-Thomine, p. 131, mentions the important shrine and tomb of al-Battal on the Byzantino-Turkish borders in northwest Anatolia, as well as the shrine of the Muslim raiders who fell at Amorium in the ninth century. The ghazis named a river after their hero al-Battal in western Anatolia.

[217] See above.

[218] Theodore Scutariotes-Sathas, 169. Attaliates, 183, 198.

exceptions to the more general rule.[219] Matthew remarks that the eleventh century was a period of great massacres and blood-shedding in Armenia.[220] The prologue to part three of his history, which deals with the events of the early twelfth century, reads:

We begin here the narration of the massacres and the tribulations which have marked this unfortunate time.[221]

In western Anatolia, Alexius Comnenus removed Greeks from the regions of Philomelium, Cedrea, and Konya precisely because he feared that they might perish at the hands of the Turks.[222] The Turkish raids into western Asia Minor, after the Byzantine reconquest, continued to be marked by mortality among the Christians.[223] This character of the Turkish conquest aroused equal ferocity on the part of Greeks, Armenians, Georgians, and Syrians against the Turks, which, as we shall see, became particularly manifest after the arrival of the Crusaders.[224] The most spectacular event to be recorded in this respect is the capture of Edessa in 1146, when the Turks put to the sword 30,000 out of a population of 47,000.[225]

The growing incidence of famine and plague no doubt increased the mortality rate. The invasions caused a displacement of rural society in many areas and consequently food production was seriously, often disastrously, affected. As much of the population fled to the towns, and as these towns were often besieged, conditions favorable to both famine and plague appeared. By the beginning of the reign of Alexius I all these factors had begun to take a toll.[226]

Toward the beginning of the year 528 [1079–80] famine desolated . . . the lands of the worshippers of the Cross, already ravaged by the ferocious and sanguinary Turkish hordes. Not one province remained protected from their devastations. Everywhere the Christians had been delivered to the sword or into bondage, interrupting thus the cultivation of the fields, so that bread was lacking. The farmers and workers had been massacred or lead off into slavery, and famine

[219] Some scholars who have based this claim of a peaceful Turkish conquest on Matthew of Edessa have noted only the passages where he praises these humane leaders. They fail to differentiate between the leaders and the Turkish tribes, as did Matthew.

[220] Matthew of Edessa, p. 204.

[221] Ibid., p. 239.

[222] Anna Comnena, III, 29.

[223] Ibid., 199–189. On the arrival of news of the raid of the Turks in the regions of Mt. Lentiana and of the plain of Cotoraicia, Alexius sped to the relief of the area, but came too late. When he arrived he found the region strewn with bodies, some of which were still breathing.

[224] Ibid., 189. In western Anatolia the armies of Alexius massacred the Turkish raiders and their families whenever the opportunity presented itself. See also Matthew of Edessa, pp. 264–265; Brosset, Géorgie, I, 359–360.

[225] The sources give sufficient indication that the continuous process of conquest in large parts of Anatolia resulted in widespread death. Anna Comnena, III, 165–166; "τοιοῦτον γὰρ τὸ βάρβαρον ἅπαν ἕτοιμον πρὸς σφαγὰς καὶ πολέμους." Also Anna Comnena, III, 188–189, 229. Matthew of Edessa, pp. 181, 204, 208, 239, 265, 274, 302. Theodore Scutariotes-Sathas, 169. Michael the Syrian, III, 249, 401–402. Bar Hebraeus, I, 321. Cinnamus, 198.

[226] Attaliates, 211–212.

extended its rigours to all places. Many provinces were depopulated; the Oriental nation [Armenians] no longer existed, and the land of the Greeks was in ruins. Nowhere was one able to procure bread.[227]

This testimony to the partial uprooting of farming populations, and also the severe sieges of the towns and their reduction by famine is repeated throughout the twelfth century. Ibn Bibi, writing in the thirteenth century, describes the process in considerable detail. The sultan 'Ala' al-Din desired to take the strongly fortified town of Amid, but because of its defensive strength it would have to be reduced over a period of three years. In the first year, according to his plans, its grain was to be burned, its livestock driven off, and the farmers and landowners were to be taken captive. During the second year the city was to be prevented from getting any supplies and provisions from the outside, and in the third year the town would be forced to surrender.[228] This general pattern of a partial disruption of agricultural production in the rural areas clearly appears here and there in the few unsatisfactory sources. The best documented area is that of Edessa, which down to its destruction in 1146, was frequently exposed to sieges and raids. The Turkish emir Buzan attacked the city in 1087–88 and subjected it to famine.[229] In 1108 Turks burned the villages about Edessa and enslaved the farming population. By this time no place outside the walls of the city was safe, and, consequently, the tilling of the fields stopped and food supplies began to dwindle.[230] Five years later Edessa experienced a severe famine as the Turks in the rural areas continued to disrupt agricultural activity, the inhabitants of Edessa now being forced to make bread from acorns and barley.[231] About 1120–21, Ilghazi the Artukid raided Edessa and destroyed what there was in the way of harvests.[232] Incomplete as the information is about rural conditions around Edessa, it gives some idea as to the partial disruption of rural society and agricultural production. In the regions immediately to the north the Turks raided the rural areas of Hisn Mansur in 1108–09 killing and enslaving the farmers.[233] Emir Ghazi the Danishmendid captured Melitene in 1124–25 in a severe siege, which produced a famine that brought death to the inhabitants "by the thousands."[234] Muhammad

[227] Matthew of Edessa, pp. 181–182. In 1108–09 Turkish invaders enslaved and massacred the farmers around Hisn Mansur. *Ibid.*, p. 265. In 1092–93 there was such a devastating plague that there were not enough priests to bury the dead. *Ibid.*, p. 202. Brosset, *Géorgie*, I, 348.

[228] Ibn Bibi-Duda, pp. 191–192.

[229] Matthew of Edessa, p. 198.

[230] William of Tyre, XI, vii.

[231] *Ibid.*, xxii.

[232] Matthew of Edessa, p. 302. Michael the Syrian, III, 246; speaks of Edessa in 1449 (c. 1137) as follows; ". . . quand Édesse était comme dans une prison, à cause des Turcs qui l'entouraient en grande nombre, et ne laissaient pas facilement ses habitants entrer ou sortir."

[233] Matthew of Edessa, p. 265.

[234] *Ibid.*, p. 315. Michael the Syrian, III, 219–220. Before Kïlïdj II Arslan took the city, Melitene was in the grip of such a famine that most of the Christian population abandoned it.

the Danishmendid burned the villages about Kaisum in 1136–37 during the period of the vintage, destroyed the gardens, and cut off the water supply.[235]

This condition prevailed in other parts of Anatolia as well, and William of Tyre remarks in regard to Attaleia:

> It possesses very rich fields, which are, nevertheless, of no advantage to the townpeople, for they are surrounded by enemies on all sides who hinder their cultivation. Therefore, the fertile soil lies fallow, since there is no one to work it . . . the grain supply is brought from overseas.[236]

The Crusaders were continuously perplexed by the difficulties of raising provisions in Anatolia, and they constantly reproached the Greeks with treachery in this respect. But the truth is that when agricultural productivity was so affected that on occasion there was not enough food for the inhabitants, it is hardly likely that these regions could easily support large foreign armies.[237] Other rural areas abandoned by the population in the face of incessant raids likewise ceased to be productive. Such were the regions of Pergamum, Adramyttium, Chliara (until Manuel recolonized them), Dorylaeum, Choma, Hierapolis, and Tripolis. Both sultans and emperors often resorted to the scorched earth policy in the border regions so that invading armies might find no sustenance.[238] The disruption of agricultural productivity was, of course, never complete in the whole province. But one must assume that during the troubled periods, and these were frequent during the eleventh and twelfth centuries, the disruption was so extensive that famine became a familiar condition. When agriculture declined there is no doubt it affected the density of population by the simple fact that there was not as much foodstuff to support the former numbers. This is, admittedly, a very general statement, but there is perhaps some truth in it for parts of Asia Minor in the eleventh and twelfth centuries.

A further contributing factor to the decline in the numbers of the Christian inhabitants was enslavement. Throughout antiquity and the Middle Ages, slaves constituted one of the most important items of wealth in the East. This was particularly true of Islamic society.[239] Since the beginning of the Arab *razzias* into the land of Rum, human booty had come to constitute a very important portion of the spoils. There is ample testimony in the contemporary accounts that this situation did not change

---

[235] Matthew of Edessa, p. 320.

[236] William of Tyre, XVI, xxvi, trans. Babock and Krey. The Second Crusaders found a scarcity of food here. X. de Planhol, *De la plaine pamphylienne aux lacs pisidiens. Nomadisme et vie paysanne* (Paris, 1958), p. 87.

[237] Fulcher of Chartres, *R.H.C., H.O.*, III, 336. Ansbert, pp. 73, 79. De Planhol, *Nomadisme*, p. 87.

[238] Anna Comnena, III, 200. Bar Hebraeus, I, 306. Michael the Syrian, III, 371. *Gesta Francorum*, pp. 54–55. Tudebodus, *R.H.C., H.O.*, III, 29. Anna Comnena, III, 37. Albert of Achen, *R.H.C., H.O.*, IV, 564.

[239] See the Qabus Nama, trans. R. Levy, *A Mirror for Princes* (New York, 1951), pp. 99–108, on the character of slaves of different ethnic origins.

when the Turks took over the direction of the djihad in Anatolia. They enslaved men, women, and children from all major urban centers[240] and from the countryside where the populations were defenseless.[241] In the earlier years before the Turkish settlements were permanently effected in Anatolia, the captives were sent to Persia and elsewhere,[242] but after the establishment of the Anatolian Turkish principalities, a portion of the enslaved were retained in Anatolia for the service of the conquerors. They were employed in the duties traditionally assigned to slaves in Islamic society: as domestic servants, as inmates of the harems, and of course many of the youths were set aside for special training for the *ghulam* bodies. These latter came to form one of the most important of the military groups of the Seljuk princes, and at the same time the sultans entrusted them with many of the highest government and military positions. It was for this purpose that the Turks, retiring from Dorylaeum in 1097, took with them the male Greek children from the towns between Dorylaeum and Konya.[243] The emir Balak acted similarly in the regions of Samosata.[244] As has already been mentioned, a portion of these Anatolian Christian slaves were sent off to Persia, and this number deported from Anatolia would decrease the Christian population in Anatolia. But as time passed most of these slaves were no doubt retained in Asia Minor. A goodly portion of these, however, and certainly most of their offspring, must have become Muslim, so that again the total effect was to decrease slightly the number of Anatolian Christians.[245]

[240] See above.

[241] Matthew of Edessa, pp. 181–182, 204, 265. Attaliates, 198. Anna Comnena, III, 166. Miklosich et Müller, VI, 61.

[242] Anna Comnena, III, 229.

[243] *Gesta Francorum*, p. 55.

[244] William of Tyre, IV, iv.

[245] The taking of Christians for the slave markets seems to have been quite extensive in the eleventh and twelfth centuries. Matthew of Edessa, pp. 181, 204, 265, 274, 302. Anna Comnena, III, 165–166, 229. William of Tyre, XI, vii. Attaliates, 198. Bar Hebraeus, I, 266. When Edessa fell, 16,000 were enslaved. Bar Hebraeus, I, 268–273; Michael the Syrian, III, 260 ff. The Turks of Nur al-Din, brought into Cilicia by Mleh the Armenian, took off 16,000 Christians and sold them at Aleppo. Michael the Syrian, III, 331. In 1176 a large Turkmen raid in the Greek provinces of western Asia Minor enslaved Greeks by the thousands. Michael the Syrian (III, 369), exaggeratedly places the number of the enslaved at 100,000, and he adds that they were sold in the slave markets as far away as Persia. In the Turkmen raids of 1185 and the following years, 26,000 inhabitants of the regions of Cappadocia, Armenia, and Mesopotamia were taken off to the slave markets. Michael the Syrian, III, 401–402; Bar Hebraeus, I, 321. These few sources seem to indicate that the slave trade was a flourishing one. In fact Asia Minor continued to be a major source of slaves for the Islamic world through the fourteenth century. See Vryonis, "Seljuk Gulams and Ottoman Devshirmes," *Der Islam*, XLI (1965), 224–252. Bertrandon de la Brocquiére, *Le voyage d'outremer*, ed. Ch. Schefer (Paris, 1892), p. 135, (hereafter Brocquiére-Schefer), describes the Ottoman slave mart in Bursa. Its extent and continuity in the Ottoman period emerge from the eyewitness account of Bartholomaeus Georgieuiz, *The Offspring of the House of Ottomanno and Offices Pertaining to the Greate Turkes, etc.*, trans. H. Goughe (London, 1570?) (hereafter Bartholomaeus Georgeuiz-Goughe), in the essay, "The Lamentable Affliction, as well of the captive Christians, as of them which live under the most grevous youke of tribute." The slave merchant followed the armies, often leading off as many as 500 slaves in chains. He also comments on the activities of the

The same outcome resulted from intermarriage between the Turks and the local population. This union between Turks and Christians had already produced a new generation of Anatolians by the early twelfth century, referred to in the Greek sources as *mixovarvaroi*, and their presence is attested to in various Turkish armies. When Alexius was campaigning against the Turks in the district of Polybotus, a number of the army of the emir Monolycus were mixovarvaroi who spoke Greek.[246] They are also mentioned in the army of the sultan of Konya.[247] Certainly the most celebrated instance of this intermarriage has to do with Danishmend and his marriage to a Christian woman.[248] A further example is the case of Tsiaous (chavush?) the Turkish official who betrayed Sinope to Alexius. His mother was a Georgian Christian and his father, a Turk.[249] The twelfth-century canonist Balsamon remarks, with disapproval, that though the Georgians were Orthodox, they were giving their daughters in marriage to Agarenes.[250] The mixovarvaroi from Anatolia are mentioned in a very interesting document in which Balsamon comments on canon eighty-four of the Council in Trullo.[251]

Though this phenomenon of intermarriage and the appearance of a new generation of mixovarvaroi is only briefly mentioned by the sources, one must assume that it was no rare or isolated occurrence. These mixovarvaroi suffered occasionally from a dichotomy of political sympathy and allegiance, but in the long run their appearance in Anatolia resulted in a process that favored the growth of the Muslim population at the expense of the Christian population, because Muslim society dominated politically and militarily. It is interesting, but unprofitable, to speculate about what would have happened to the Anatolian mixovarvaroi under different political circumstances.

To the extent that it took place in the eleventh and twelfth centuries, conversion also had the effect of decreasing the number of Christians while increasing the Muslim population. There is little in the way of source material on the subject of conversions, but there seems to be some indication that in this period conversions to Islam were numerically significant, though not as extensive as they later were to become. The Danishmendname reflects one aspect of the spirit in which the conquest of much of Anatolia was made. It attributes a strong proselytizing zeal to

---

local Christians who assist the slaves in escaping. H. Kopstein, *Zur Sklaverei im ausgehenden Byzanz* (Berlin, 1966), pp. 91–94.

[246] Anna Comnena, III, 205, " ἦσαν γὰρ καί τινες ἐν αὐτοῖς μιξοβάρβαροι ἑλληνίζοντες."

[247] *Ibid.*, 207. Such, probably, were also the troops of Tzachas who beseeched the Lord (in Greek) to save them from their Greek besiegers in Chios in 1090, *Ibid.*, II, 111.

[248] Danishmnendname-Melikoff, I, 129. See also, I, 318, 361, for other examples. E. Rossi, *Il Kitab-i-Dede Qorqut* (Vatican, 1952), pp. 32–33, 181 ff.

[249] Anna Comnena, II, 65–66.

[250] Rhalles and Potles, I, 271–272; II, 475.

[251] *Ibid.*, II, 498. For their adoption of Christian baptism see chapter vii, n. 165.

the Muslims, and conversion constitutes an ever-present and constantly repeated motif. There are conversions of individuals, bodies of soldiers, and whole towns,[252] and the conversions that occur in the poem break down into two categories: voluntary and forced. Those who convert voluntarily do so as a result of a religious vision, or for romantic reasons, or because of material advantage to be obtained.[253] In some instances the poem implies that the newly converted have apostitized to avoid paying the *haradj*, whereas in other cases they receive grants of land.[254] Conversion by the sword also occupies a prominent place in the Danishmendname. In numerous instances individuals and bodies of captured troops are given as alternatives conversion or death by the sword.[255] Among the most celebrated and detailed acts of conversion in the Danishmendname is that of the city of Sisiya-Comana. In the course of his campaigns Malik Danishmend vowed to convert the inhabitants of this city,[256] and upon capturing Sisiya-Comana, he forced the populace, at the point of the sword, to become Muslim.[257] But the new Muslims were not firm in their adopted faith, as they had been forcibly converted, and so the governor of Comana enforced Islamic practices on many who were recalcitrant in performing the ritual. He compelled the inhabitants to perform the five daily prayers, and all those who refused to go to the mosque were brought there by threat of physical violence. Those who continued to drink wine were flogged, and other violations of Islamic law similarly treated.[258] Evidently they were as lax in their political as they were in their religious duties, for upon the appearance of Christian armies, they betrayed the Turkish Muslims of the city and killed them along with the governor, destroying the mosques and replacing them with monasteries.[259] The fate of Yankoniya-Euchaita (Chorum) was similar. Malik Danishmend offered its citizens the choice of death or conversion, and accordingly they chose to become Muslims.[260] But these new Muslims too were disloyal, and soon after they plotted against Malik Danishmend.[261]

It would be extremely difficult and hazardous to insist upon the exact historicity of such details in the Danishmendname, inasmuch as it is a poetic compilation of the thirteenth and fourteenth centuries. But it is

[252] Danishmendname-Melikoff, I, 128–131.

[253] *Ibid.*, 223, 273–274, 370–371, 396, 426–427.

[254] *Ibid.*, 367–368, 396, 428.

[255] *Ibid.*, 257, 270, 280, 204–205, 275, 380. In one incident, I, 384, 5,000 accept Islam, 5,000 are put to the sword.

[256] Danishmendname-Melikoff, I, 278.

[257] *Ibid.*, 284, 380.

[258] *Ibid.*, 380.

[259] *Ibid.*, 381. They had to be brought back to the faith by show of arms as well as by miracles, *ibid.*, 316, 428–429.

[260] *Ibid.*, 414–415.

[261] *Ibid.*, 421. The city of Gangra-Mankuriya underwent a slightly different fate according to the poet. The conquered were given a choice. Some became Muslims, while those who preferred to remain Christian were permitted to do so. They were to live outside the walls and to pay the haradj, *ibid.*, 367.

quite possible, in fact probable, that the poet is here dealing with some actual historical events in the struggle between the Turks and Byzantines in the eleventh and twelfth centuries. It is true that the area was contested by both sides and towns frequently changed hands. As to religious conversions, however, one must look at the contemporary sources. Raymond of Aguliers testifies to the enforced Islamization of Greeks and Armenians living in Antioch between the Turkish conquest in 1085 and the appearance of the Crusaders in 1098.[262] Philaretus is reported to have become Muslim in order to save his domains, and members of the Comnenus and Gabras families apostatized and joined the court at Konya.[263] The Armenian rulers of Seveverek as well as some of the Georgian chieftains turned Muslim to save their lands.[264] All these isolated references to conversion might very well have constituted the exception to the rule; but once more the comments on the canon law indicate that conversion, far from being an isolated phenomenon, was quite prominent in twelfth-century Anatolia. Balsamon refers to extensive forced conversion during the century in his commentary on canon three of the synod of Ankara.

And many others who were forcibly circumcised by the Agarenes, and had done other things or suffered impieties, were received by the church after sincere confession and suitable penitence.[265]

In commenting upon canon eighty-one of St. Basil, which refers to those forced by foreigners to renounce Christianity, Balsamon again mentions extensive Islamization.

Some say that the contents of the present canon are at rest [not in use] because by the grace of God the faith has been firmly set in Orthodoxy, and the tyrants have, many years ago, been stoned by the engines of martyrdom. But today, once more, many are captured by the hands of the Agarenes, and being tortured some abjure the Orthodox faith and accept the godless faith of Muhammad. Others willingly throw themselves into the pit of unbelief. According to the present canon all these shall be healed after confession and fitting repentance.[266]

[262] Raymund of Aguilers, *R.H.C., H.O.*, III, 250–251; 288, "Sed insurgentibus, per Dei judicium, Sarracenis atque Turcis, in tanta oppressione servitutis isti Suriani fuerunt per quadrigentos et eo amplius annos, ut multi eorum compellerentur patriam et Christianam deserere legem." See also the taking of children from the districts between Dorylaeum and Konya, and farther to the east by the emir Balak.

[263] Danishmendname-Melikoff, I, 128, 286–287, 367, 380. Michael the Syrian, III, 173. Converts seem to have played an important role in the conquests of Malik Danishmend. William of Tyre, I, ix, remarks that the Turks intended to uproot Anatolian Christianity. This is certainly an exaggeration, but it is one of those exaggerations founded on a kernel of truth.

[264] Bar Hebraeus, I, 265. Michael the Syrian, III, 247. Apparently there was a considerable Armenian element that assisted in the Turkish conquest, as is attested by Matthew of Edessa and also by the Armenian names in the Danishmendname. Many of these Armenians converted to Islam. See also Brosset, *Géorgie*, I, 331, for Georgians.

[265] Rhalles and Potles, III, 27–28; " καὶ ἄλλοι πολλοὶ κατὰ βίαν περιτμηθέντες παρὰ Ἀγαρηνῶν, καὶ ἄλλα τινὰ πεποιηκότες ἢ καὶ παθόντες ἀσεβῆ, μετὰ ἐξομολόγησιν, καθαρὸν καὶ προσήκουσαν μετάνοιαν, παρὰ τῇ ἐκκλησίᾳ ἐδέχθησαν."

[266] *Ibid.*, IV, 247. " . . . λέγουσί τινες τὰ τοῦ παρόντος κανόνος σχολάσαι διὰ τὸ τὴν πίστιν τῇ τοῦ θεοῦ χάριτι ἐπὶ πέτραν ὀρθοδοξίας ἀραρότως στηρίζεσθαι, καὶ τοὺς τυράννους λιθολευστηθῆναι πετροβόλοις μαρτυρικοῖς πρὸ χρόνων πολλῶν,

Admittedly, the evidence is far from complete; nevertheless one must admit that conversion to Islam was an important and not infrequent event in twelfth-century Anatolia. Conversion was no doubt motivated by a wide variety of factors which included material benefit and conversion by the sword. The picture that emerges from the Danishmendname is thus confirmed by the few scattered references to apostasy in contemporary sources. Unfortunately, there is no way of ascertaining whether the dervish orders had begun to operate effectively and on a large scale in Asia Minor at this time.[267] It is only in the thirteenth and fourteenth centuries that the conversionary activities of these orders become manifest in the sources.

In spite of migrations, displacement, massacres, plagues, famine, and enslavement, it is highly probable that the majority of the Anatolian Christian population remained in Asia Minor fifty years after Manzikert. What, however, was the numerical relation between Christians and Turks at the end of this period? What was the density of the new Turkish population? Unfortunately, the sources continue to be unsatisfactory on these basic questions of demography and ethnography. We do not even know with certainty which of the Turkish tribes participated in this early conquest and settlement of Anatolia.[268] There has been a tendency to exaggerate the number of the original Turkish settlers,[269] but the sources

---

ἀλλὰ καὶ σήμερον πολλοὶ ταῖς τῶν ἀθέων ᾿Αγαρηνῶν χερσὶν ἁλώξιμοι γινόμενοι, καὶ βασανιζόμενοι, πὴ μὲν, τὴν ὀρθόδοξον πίστιν ἐξόμνυνται, πὴ δέ, τὴν ἄθεον θρησκείαν τοῦ Μωάμεθ διόμνυνται· ἄλλοι δὲ καὶ ἑκοντὶ ἑαυτοὺς ἐπιρρίπτουσιν εἰς τὸν τῆς ἀπιστίας βόθρον· οἱ δὴ πάντες κατὰ τὸν παρόντα κανόνα θεραπευθήσονται μετὰ ἐξομολόγησιν καὶ προσήκουσαν μετάνοιαν."

[267] The sultans in Persia took an interest in the establishment of Islam in these regions as is evidenced by the fact that the sultan sent fifty mimbars to Anatolia after its conquest, al-Bondari, *Recueil de textes rélatifs à l'histoire des Seldjoucides*, ed. T. Houtsma, (Ledien, 1889), II, 55. The Byzantines also took up the religious contest, seeking to convert the Turks, especially their chieftains, to Christianity and thus bring them under Byzantine control and influence. Anna Comnena, II, 81, remarks that Alexius wished to convert all the Muslims in Anatolia. Elchanes, Scaliarius, and other emirs of northwest Asia Minor went to Constantinople where they received baptism and became Christians. The Turko-Georgian Tsiaous was converted, as was also at an earlier period the emir Chrysoscule.

[268] On the whole question, Cahen, "Les tribus turques d'Asie occidentale pendant la période seljukide," *W.Z.K.M.*, LI (1948–52), 178, 182–186.

[269] This is particularly true of the otherwise useful monograph of Yinanc, *Fethi*, pp. 161–185. Utilizing the Siyasatname of Nizam al-Mulk, which mentions that an army of 400,000 riders drew pay under Malik Shah, Yinanc estimates that 150,000, of this army was in Anatolia. Then, allowing an average family of four for each of these riders, he arrives at the figure of 550–600,000. Then he adds another 500,000 for those who came to practice agriculture and animal husbandry, arriving at the sum total of 1,000,000 as the number of Turkish and Muslim settlers who came during this first stage. He proceeds to paint a picture of an earlier stratum of Turkish population in Anatolia which had existed as a linguistic and cultural unit for centuries prior to 1071. According to Yinanc these earlier "Turkish" inhabitants were:

    1. A group of Bulgars brought in to the districts of Tsorokh, Euphrates, and Trebizond in 530 by Justin I.

    2. Avars settled in eastern Anatolia by Justin II in 577.

seem to suggest that quite to the contrary the Turks who came at this time very definitely constituted a minority. As was previously mentioned, the historians of the Crusades note that though Turkish military forces were to be found along the routes from Nicaea to Dorylaeum, Philomelium, Konya, Heracleia, Tarsus, Marash, Edessa, Plastentza, Coxon, and Antioch, the inhabitants most often were largely Christians. The figures given for Turkish armies tend to confirm the fact that the Turks were still a small minority. Undoubtedly these armies constituted a substantial portion of the Turks in Anatolia at this very early date. There is mention of large armies in Anatolia, but these were usually armies sent from Persia, which came to raid or to bring recalcitrant emirs under control. Once they finished their business in Anatolia, these armies usually left the peninsula and returned to Persia, Iraq, or Syria. Such was the army of Artuk called in by Michael VII against Roussel which is

---

3. Avars sent by Heraclius to the borders in 620.

4. Bulgars settled in Tohum and Gaihan to fight the Arabs in 755.

5. Khazars and Ferghanid Turks in the retinue of the Greek commander who presided over the exchange of prisoners at Tarsus in 946, and who were supposedly settled in Cappadocia.

6. Bulgarian troops under Bardas in 947.

7. Patzinak troops brought to Anatolia in 1048 to fight the Seljuks.

8. Patzinaks in the army of Romanus IV at Manzikert.

Unfortunately Yinanc has lumped together a few events spanning six centuries, and even if the cases of supposedly "Turkish" settlement were accurate, they would have made no noticeable alteration in the ethnography of Anatolia. As a matter of fact, this supposed Turkish penetration of Anatolia is the figment of the imagination of a school of historiography which sprang up in Kemalist Turkey and had to struggle with a powerful nationalist sentiment. The Bulgars settled by Justin in the Euphrates region were not of any considerable size and were no doubt soon assimilated. Yinanc refers to a settlement of Avars in eastern Anatolia by Justin II in 577, and he does this on the authority of Muralt (I, 235). But this section in Muralt merely refers to an expedition of the emperor with troops from the Balkans, there being no mention of their settlement in Anatolia (Theophanes, I, 246–247). Contrary again to Yinanc's assertion, Muralt (I, 275), mentions no settlement of Avars on the eastern borders. As for the Bulgars settled in Anatolia by Constantine V in the eighth century, these were either Slavonized or fast on their way to becoming Slavs, and then once in Anatolia all evidence points to their rapid Hellenization (Vryonis, "St. Ioannicius," pp. 245–248). As for the Khazars and Ferghanids who appeared in Tarsus with the Byzantine commander in 946 to preside over the exchange of prisoners, they were certainly not settled in Cappadocia as Yinanc asserts, and they were few in number. These were part of the imperial troops stationed in Constantinople and recruited abroad (Constantine Porphyrogennitus, *De Caerimoniis*, I, 576). The Bulgarian troops of Bardas in 947 were recruited from the Balkans, and as such were Slavic-speaking and not Turkophone. As for the Patzinaks who were sent to Anatolia by Constantine IX Monomachus, they stayed only for a few days and then returned to the Balkans (Cedrenus, II, 587). (Even if they had stayed in Anatolia they would not have made any impression on Anatolian ethnography as they were only 15,000 in number). Thus the proposition that the existence of a substantial Turkish ethnic bloc in Anatolia prior to 1071 helped to pave the way for a smooth Turkish occupation is false. There is no evidence for it in historical sources. Yinanc's book is also marred by certain other fallacious racial theories concerning the existence of Hetite and Thracian tribes in eleventh-century Anatolia.

reported to have numbered, exaggeratedly, 100,000. The army of 50,000 under Burzuk which Barkyaruk sent against the sultan of Nicaea also left Anatolia. But again the numbers are probably exaggerated, for the mere appearance of a small army under Alexius caused Burzuk to discontinue the siege of Nicaea. Buzan was sent to Nicaea for similar reasons, but his army soon abandoned Asia Minor. Another such invasion of Turks from Khurasan which occurred in the later years of Alexius' reign is reported to have numbered 50,000. But Anna Comnena, who reports this figure, states in another passage that the army numbered 40,000, and so it is obvious that we are dealing with vague, inexact figures. One thing is clear, however; the numbers in the armies of the Turkish princes settled in Anatolia were far smaller than those of the armies coming from Persia. Tzachas' forces do not seem to have surpassed 8,000, and when Smyrna fell to the Byzantines there were only 2,000 Turks in the city. In the Turkish raids in the regions of Taurus between 1107 and 1110, there appeared three armies of 12,000, 6,000, and 1,500 (or 15,000), all of which the more numerous local inhabitants either destroyed or defeated. When Sulayman entered Antioch in 1085 he did so with 3,000 men. Though the forces of Hasan of Cappadocia in the battle at Heracleia against the Crusaders are said to have numbered 80,000, it is much more probable that this figure represents the total of the armies of Hasan and his allies Malik Danishmend and Kïlïdj I Arslan. That this is probably the case becomes evident from the fact that when Hasan invaded the regions of Philadelpheia, his army consisted of 24,000 troops. Thus the figures of the Turkish armies of Anatolia do not indicate that the Turks were particularly numerous.[270]

The Turks were, then, a small but powerful minority. They were in control of most of the crucial routes and roads so that they were in a position to block progress into and conquest of Asia Minor. During this first half century of occupation of Anatolia they formed a small governing and military caste and appear from time to time in the sources as the administrators and military garrisons of areas otherwise inhabited by Christians. Such was the case in Tarsus, Marash, Antioch, Smyrna, Laodiceia (in western Anatolia), Konya, Ankara, Nicaea, the regions between Dorylaeum-Konya-Heracleia, and elsewhere. There were many towns in Anatolia which, though technically under Turkish control, had no Turkish garrisons because there simply were not enough Turks to go around.[271]

[270] For these figures on the armies: Attaliates, 190. Anna Comnena, II, 68, 74; III, 18, 144, 159. Matthew of Edessa, pp. 264, 269. Michael the Syrian, III, 173. The exaggerated figures of Yazïdjïoǧlu, *Histoire des Seldjoucides d'Asie Mineure d'après Ibn Bibi. Texte turc publié d'après les mss. de Leide et de Paris*, M. Houtsma, in *Recueil de textes relatifs à l'histoire des Seldjoucides* (Leiden, 1902) III, 2 (hereafter cited as Yazïdjïoǧlu)., are not at all reliable as the author was writing four centuries after the events. Thus in contrast to Yinanc, *Fethi*, pp. 174–175, the figures on the armies do not presuppose a large settlement
[271] William of Tyre, III, xix; IV, i; V, xi. *Gesta Francorum*, pp. 54–55, 58–59, 60–61, 64–65. When Smyrna fell to Constantine Ducas there were only 2,000 Turks there. Anna

Because the conquerors were a minority, their position was often difficult. Anatolia was a vast territorial expanse, and with the appearance of the Crusaders and the Byzantine reconquest, the Turks were hard put to defend the conquest that as yet they had been unable to digest. For this reason they were forced to resort to a number of measures in an effort to safeguard their political supremacy in a land where their subjects far outnumbered them. In some regions they simply disarmed the Christians and kept them from positions of power in the government. In Tarsus, Marash, and Antioch, where the population was for the most part Christian, the latter were strictly forbidden to carry arms or to participate in government and were restricted to the exercise of agriculture and trade.[272] In other regions the Turks were often forced to make use of Christian troops and militia. There were Armenian contingents in the army of the Turkish emir Buzan, and the Armenian troops of Tutuch of Damascus played a particularly important role.[273] The Turkish garrison of Edessa at one point was largely Armenian. The mixovarvaroi came to play a significant role as a further source of military manpower for the ruling minority,[274] and so did the converts.[275] The Turks resorted to taking Christian children and converting them, acts specifically mentioned in Antioch, around Samosata, and in western Asia Minor.[276]

There are other indications that the Christian population of Asia Minor was still quite extensive in the twelfth century and even in the thirteenth century.[277] The *History of the Patriarchs of Alexandria* asserts that the majority of the subjects of the sultan Mas'ud I (1116–56) were Greeks, and there is the testimony of the thirteenth- and fourteenth-century travelers. Marco Polo noted that Anatolia possessed a considerable Christian population.

In Turcomania there are three classes of people. First there are the Turcomans; these are worshippers of Mahommet, a rude people with an uncouth language of their own. They dwell among mountains and downs where they find good pasture for their occupation is cattlekeeping. Excellent horses, known as Turquans, are reared in their country, and also very valuable mules. The other two classes are the Armenians and Greeks, who live mixt with the former in the towns and villages, occupying themselves with trade and handicrafts. They weave the finest and

---

Comnena, III, 26. Tyriaeum, though in a region of warfare and within Turkish domains, had no Turkish garrison or commander. Laodiceia, when it was reconquered by John II in the beginning of his reign had only 800 Turks, and this was considered to be a large number of Turks, Cinnamus, 6.

[272] William of Tyre, III, xix; IV, i; V, xi.

[273] Matthew of Edessa, pp. 199, 205–206, 209–210. Danishmend himself was possibly an Armenian. Matthew of Edessa, p. 256.

[274] Anna Comnena, III, 205; II, 66.

[275] As reflected in the Danishmendname.

[276] Raymund of Aguilers, *R.H.C., H.O.*, III, 250–251. Tudebodus, *R.H.C., H.O.*, III, 29. *Gesta Francorum*, 55. William of Tyre, IV, iv.

[277] O. Turan, "Les souverains seldjoukides et leurs sujets non-musulmans," *S.I.*, I (1953), 76 (hereafter cited as Turan, "Sujets non-musulmans.").

handsomest carpets in the world, and also great quantities of fine and rich silks of cramoisy and other colours, and plenty of other stuffs.[278]

Marco Polo implies that the urban classes contained a large Christian element. A contemporary of Marco Polo, and also a traveler in Anatolia, William of Rubruque, remarks rather exaggeratedly,

as for Turkey, I can inform you that not one man in ten there is a Saracen; rather are they all Armenians and Greeks.[279]

Both Sanuto and Ibn Battuta noted the presence of considerable numbers of Christians in western Asia Minor as late as the early fourteenth century.[280] The Christians were sufficiently numerous so that the single largest source of revenue in Muslim Anatolia during the latter half of the thirteenth century was the tax that they paid.[281]

The assumption of comparatively smaller numbers of Turks in twelfth-century Anatolia seems to underlie and to explain the Turkish policies of colonization. The invasions had caused a certain disruption and decline in the Christian population of the Anatolian plateau. As a result of the demographic decline, the various Turkish princes began to raid the land of one another and of the Christians and to carry away entire Christian towns and villages in order to repopulate their own domains. This phenomenon makes it evident that as of the twelfth century the invading Turks were not sufficient numerically to take up the demographic slack that they had caused. In addition the mass of the Turkmens was not yet sedentarized and therefore not productive of sufficient revenues for the state. In 1122 the emir Balak carried off the inhabitants of Gargar and

---

[278] *The Book of Ser Marco Polo the Venetian concerning the Kingdoms and Marvels of the East,* tr. and ed. by H. Yule, 3rd ed. (New York, 1903) I, 43 (hereafter cited as Marco Polo-Yule). It is interesting that Marco Polo associates not only the textile industry with the towns but the rug industry as well with the Greek and Armenian Christians. A. C. Moule and P. Pelliot, *Marco Polo, the Description of the World* (London, 1938), I, 95 (hereafter cited as Marco Polo, Moule-Pelliot).

[279] In C. Dawson, *The Mongol Mission* (New York, 1955), p. 219. William of Rubriq-Wyngaert, p. 330.

[280] Marino Sanuto, ed. C. Hopf in *Chroniques Graeco-Romanes inédits ou peu connuès* (Berlin, 1873), p. 143; "In l'Asia Minor, e ch'e maggior paese, che non e la Spagna dual quial abbiamo detto esser quatro Regni, la qual per la maggior parte e sottoposta a Turchi, per il piu li Popoli seguono il Ritto Greco e sono per il piu Greci." Ibn Battuta-Gibb, II, 415. "Why it is called after the Rum is because it used to be their land in olden times, and from it came the ancient Rum and the Yunanis. Later on it was conquered by the Muslims, but in it there are still large numbers of Christians under the protection of the Muslims, the latter being Turkmens."

[281] Karim al-Din Mahmud of Aksaray, trans. M. N. Gençosman, in *Selçuki devletleri tarihi* (Ankara, 1943), II, 230 (hereafter cited as Aksaray–Gençosman). Karim al-Din was an official in the Seljuk financial administration and so his statement merits attention. Passing reference to the tax of the dhimmis is made in Ibn Bibi-Duda, p. 104, where the sultan makes a gift of 100,000 dirhems and 5,000 dinars from the haradj that the Christians and Armenians pay. Ibn Battuta-Gibb, II, 425, the Christians of Laodiceia-Denizli pay the head tax. Eflaki, *Les saints des derviches tourneurs,* trans. C. Huart (Paris, 1918-1922), II, 235 (hereafter cited as Eflaki-Huart), the emir Tadj al-Din Motazz sent 7,000 dirhems sultani, from the capitation of Aksaray, to the Muslim leaders.

settled them at Hanazit.[282] The entire population of Adana was trans-
ferred to Melitene in 1137.[283] Shortly thereafter the ruler of Melitene
took captive the inhabitants of the villages about Kaisum and Marash.[284]
Yakub Arslan, the ruler of Cappadocia, took people from the Lycandus
district in 1155–56, and then uprooted the whole Christian population of
Albistan and Gaihan, 70,000 in number, and settled them on his lands.[285]
Kïlïdj II Arslan and his successors were also quite active in recolonizing the
Seljuk kingdom. In 1171 Kïlïdj Arslan took off 12,000 inhabitants from
the environs of Melitene, which city had successfully resisted him. But the
sultan was attacked at Caesareia and his enemies demanded that he
return not only the 12,000 from the environs of Melitene, but all those
he had transported from the lands of his brother Shahinshah and those he
had taken from the lands of Dhu'l-Nun (emir of Caesareia and Sebasteia).
Kïlïdj Arslan returned the 12,000 but retained all the others.[286] Six years
later he took away the inhabitants of Kaisum.[287] The Seljuks also found a
ready source of colonists in western Anatolia.[288] The sultan Kaykhusraw
took 5,000 Christians from Caria and Tantalus in 1197 and resettled them
about Philomelium. The great care the sultan lavished upon these
Christian colonists is illustrative of the importance the Muslim rulers
attached to repopulating their domains with Christian farmers. He had
them carefully guarded so none would escape en route, and on arrival at
Philomelium he gave them land and seed to plant. He bestowed upon them
a five-year tax immunity with the provision that afterward they should
pay the customary taxes they had paid in Byzantine territory. As a result
not one of them considered escaping, and indeed many who heard of the
tax exemption migrated to the sultan's domains because of the great
disorder that had now enveloped the Byzantine Maeandrian regions.[289]

NOMADIZATION

It is virtually impossible to estimate the extent of Muslim colonization
in Anatolian towns during the period to the end of the twelfth and the
early thirteenth century. Aside from scattered references to the colonization of such towns as Dadybra, Aksaray-Coloneia, Sinope, Caesareia,

[282] Michael the Syrian, III, 206. All those who returned to Gargar he enslaved, and he
returned to burn the villages, the olive trees, and the vineyards.
[283] Michael the Syrian, III, 245. Bar Hebraeus, I, 264.
[284] Michael the Syrian, III, 246.
[285] Matthew of Edessa, p. 344.
[286] Michael the Syrian, III, 346. Bar Hebraeus, I, 296.
[287] Michael the Syrian, III, 388.
[288] Large numbers of prisoners were taken from Laodiceia, Celbianum, and Caria,
though there is no specific reference to their resettlement on Turkish lands. Nicetas
Choniates, 163, 481, 523. Cinnamus, 198.
[289] Nicetas Choniates, 655–657. Philomelium and the environs had been severely
depopulated as a result of a century of warfare. The city was burned by both Manuel
Comnenus and Frederick Barbarossa, and a large number of Greeks had abandoned the
area for safety on Byzantine territory. Anna Comnena, III, 29, 200–203, 213–214.
Zonaras, III, 757. Cinnamus, 41–42, 63.

and Sebasteia,[290] one is reduced to hypothesis and conjecture. There is no doubt that alongside the ruling classes in the towns and villages there must have settled Islamic merchants, craftsmen, religious elements and, gradually, nomads. Thus the urban centers continued, by and large, to exist as centers of both Muslim and Christian society at the end of the twelfth century. There were also towns, such as Dadybra, where the Christian element was entirely expelled and the city colonized exclusively by Muslims. Such policies of forces expulsion and colonization doubtlessly explain the rapid disappearance of Christianity from twelfth-century Ankara and perhaps from other cities as well.

Simultaneous with the partial Muslim settlement in the towns, there was an even more significant colonization of the rural areas by the Turkmen tribes. The influx of tribal groups is one of the most important phenomena in the transformation of Anatolia, but unfortunately the court historiography of both Muslims and Greeks (hostile to the nomads) has largely neglected this phenomenon. The Turkmens are very much in evidence along the entire edge of the Anatolian plateau in the west, north, east, and south during the eleventh and twelfth centuries, and also in the following centuries. Inasmuch as the armies of Byzantium, the Crusades, and the Armenians came into contact with them, the chronicles note their presence, their activities, and on occasion give figures as to their numbers and the names of their chieftains. Most all these chronicles comment on their nomadic way of life and on the disruptive effect they had on the live of the sedentary populations in the rural areas.[291] The region in which the activities of the Turkmens appear most clearly is the Byzantine-Seljuk frontier along the western rim of the plateau.

The great Byzantine counterattack of 1097–98, following the defeat of the Turks by the First Crusaders, had the effect of pushing back the Turks from the Aegean coast and the river valleys into Phrygia and onto the Anatolian plateau. This meant that whereas the Turks had been sparsely scattered throughout western Asia Minor, they were now pushed back into a more restricted area. Therefore their concentration in Phrygia was greatly intensified and they became a more formidable barrier to Byzantine armies. The greatest Byzantine advance to the east which occurred in the reign of Alexius I reached the towns of Dorylaeum, Santabaris, Amorium, Cedrea, Polybotus, and Philomelium. But because of the greater number of Turks now concentrated in Phrygia, the Byzantines were able to go no farther in the reconquest. Though the Crusaders were able to capture Iconium and Ankara, the Turks shortly retook them,

---

[290] Nicetas Choniates, 624. Qazwini-Le Strange, pp. 95–97. Ibn Bibi-Duda, p. 62, Bar Hebraeus, I, 258. Michael the Syrian, III, 237. Danishmendname-Melikoff, I. 197–199, 200, 202.

[291] Gordlevsky, *Izbrannye Soch.*, I, 70–95, gives a sketch of the life and organization of the Turkmen tribes. For a detailed description and analysis of Turkmen nomadism in Asia Minor see below.

and in spite of the fact that Alexius successfully raided the villages of Konya, he made no further attempt to capture either of these two important cities. Another indication that the Turkish settlement was quite strong in Phrygia was that the emperor began to remove some of the Greek population and to resettle it on safer territory in western Asia Minor. The first expedition of Alexius into Phrygia (1098) brought him as far as Philomelium. But fearing the approach of a large Turkish army, he decided to take back with him many of the inhabitants of the regions of Philomelium lest they perish at the hands of the Turks.[292] He carried out even more extensive transferrals of Greek population from these and more easterly regions in the campaigns of 1116. The emperor sent Bardas Bourtzes to sack the "Villages of Bourtzes" because of the great number of Turks in the area, and to bring the Greek inhabitants with him. After defeating the Turks, Bourtzes evacuated the Greeks and then rejoined the emperor. On taking the city of Philomelium, Alexius sent out many detachments to the villages of Konya to free the Greeks who were being held prisoners by the Turks. These were recovered and all the inhabitants of the villages voluntarily left their habitats en masse, preferring to move to Byzantine territory with the army of Alexius.

And the inhabitants of these regions who were Rhomaioi followed them of their own accord fleeing from servitude to the barbarians; there were women with babies, and children, all rushing to the Emperor as if to a place of refuge. He then drew up his lines in the new formation with all the captives, women, and children enclosed in the center, and returned by the same road as he had come, and whatever places he approached, he passed through with perfect safety. And had you seen it, you would have said a living walled city was walking, when the army was marching in the new formation we have described.[293]

Anyone hearing the word "line of battle" and "phalanx" or "captives" and "booty" or again "general" and "captains," will think he is hearing about the things which every historian and poet mentions in his writings. But this battle formation was new and seemed very strange to everybody and was such as had never been seen before or handed down to posterity by any historian. For while advancing along the road to Iconium, the army marched in regular order and moved forward in time to the music of a flute. And if you had seen the whole phalanx you would have said it was remaining motionless when in motion and when halting that it was moving. For thanks to the close formation of the shields and the men standing in serried lines it looked like the immoveable mountains, and when it changed its route it moved like a very great beast, for the whole phalanx walked and turned as if directed by one mind. But after it had reached Philomelium and rescued men on all sides from the hand of the barbarians, as we have related

---

[292] Anna Comnena, III, 29; " Πτοηθεὶς δὲ μὴ ἐπικαταλαμβανόντων αὐτὸν ἤδη Τουρκικῶν ἀμυθήτων λαῶν οἱ ἔποικοι τῶν μερῶν Φιλομηλίου παρανάλωμα βαρβαρικῆς γένωνται μαχαίρας ... καὶ παραυτίκα διεκηρυκεύετο καὶ ὅτι ἕκαστος ἤ ἑκάστη προσεξελθέτω τῆς τούτων ἐλεύσεως τὰ σώματα αὐτὰ καὶ τὰ χρήματα ὁπόσα φέρειν δύνανται διασώζοντες. εἵλοντο μὲν οὖν εὐθὺς ἅπαντες συνέψεσθαι τῷ βασιλεῖ, οὐκ ἄνδρες μόνον, ἀλλὰ καὶ αὐταὶ γυναίκες ..." Zonaras, III, 757. The inhabitants of Kataphygia returned with Alexius.

[293] Anna Comnena, III, 203–204. *The Alexiad of the Princess Anna Comnena*, trans. E. A. S. Dawes (London, 1928) (hereafter cited as Anna Comnena–Dawes), p. 401.

before somewhere, and enclosed all the captives and the women too and the children and the booty in the centre it marched slowly on its return and moved forward leisurely, as it were, and at an ant's pace. Moreover since many of the women were with child and many of the men afflicted with disease, whenever a woman's time for bringing forth came, a trumpet was sounded at a nod from the emperor and made all the men stop and the whole army halted on the instant. And when he knew the child was born, a different call, not the usual one, but provocative of motion, was sounded and stirred them all up to continue the journey. And if anyone died, the same procedure took place, and the Emperor would be at the side of the dying man, and the priests were summoned to sing the hymns for the dying and administer the sacraments to the dying. And after the rites for the dead had been duly performed and not until the dead had been put in the earth and buried, was the army allowed to move even a step. And when it was the Emperor's time for lunch he invited the men and women who were labouring under illness or old age and placed the greater part of the victuals before them and invited those who lunched with him to do the same. And the meal was like a complete banquet of the gods for there were no instruments, not even flutes or drums or any disturbing music at all.[294]

The inability of the Byzantines to retake Konya and to retain Ankara, and the partial removal of the Greek population from southern Phrygia are not the only indications of the comparative density of the Turkmens in these regions. The sources refer specifically to the fact that the Turkmens were present in large numbers,[295] and in spite of the successes Alexius had obtained in pushing the Turks back onto the plateau, the Turks were still able to raid Lentiana farther to the west.[296]

The Turkmen pressure in this area was constant throughout the twelfth century. When John Comnenus succeeded his father in 1118, the cities of Phrygia, the upper Maeander, Pisidia, Pamphylia, and the Sangarius were being sorely pressed. John had to retake Laodiceia, Sozopolis, and Hieracoryphites from the Turks in Pisidia and Phrygia. Farther to the north he had to drive the nomads out of the regions of the Sangarius River, and was obliged to march into Pisidia and Paphlagonia to restore order.[297] In spite of John's preoccupation with the regions of Castamon-Gangra-Neocaesareia in the north, and Cilicia-Antioch in the south, the Turkmen elements in western Asia Minor seem to have been largely, though not completely, contained. The force of the Turkmen pressure westward, however, became almost irresistible during the reign of Manuel (1143–80). No doubt this was in part due to Manuel's preoccupation with affairs in Europe and Antioch, but also it would seem that there were other factors independent of western involvement.

[294] Anna Comnena, III, 213–214. Anna Comnena–Dawes, p. 408.
[295] Anna Comnena, III, 199–220.
[296] *Ibid.*, 169, 188–189.
[297] Nicetas Choniates, 17–18, 44, 50. He recruited many of the Turkmens for his own armies. Cinnamus, 9, describes their nomadic way of life thus; "οὔπω γὰρ γεηπονικοῖς ἐνησκημένοι ἔργοις γαλακτός τε ἀπερρόφουν καὶ κρεῶν ἐσιτοῦντο, κατὰ τοὺς Σκύθας, ἀεὶ σποράδες τε ἀνὰ τὶ πεδίον ἐνησκημένοι ταύτῃ τοῖς βουλομένοις αὐτοῖς ἐγχειρεῖν προχειρότατοι ἐγίνοντο."

Apparently, the numbers of Turkmens in Phrygia had increased, and there was a tremendous push for pasturage as well as for booty. During Manuel's reign the Turkmens reappeared in Bithynia, Mysia, the Cayster valley, western Phrygia, Lydia, and Pamphylia. At the very onset of his reign, the nomads sorely vexed Bithynia and parts of Mysia. He had to drive them out of Malagina and Pithecas at the westernmost bend of the Sangarius,[298] and he rebuilt both towns as defense outposts. Similarly he refortified the area of Adramyttium-Pergamum-Chliara.[299]

The heaviest concentration of Turkmens in northwest Anatolia was in the region of the Bathys and Tembris rivers around the sites of Dorylaeum and Cotyaeum. It was from this base that the Turkmens would march to the north and west to raid the Sangarius valley, Poimamenum, and Adramyttium. It was also here that the Turkish chief Mamplanes (Pamplanes, Balabanes, or Kaplanes?) defeated the army of the Second Crusade.[300] When Manuel returned with his army from Cilicia in 1159, the Turkmens of Cotyaeum killed the stragglers.[301] Consequently, when Manuel returned to Anatolia soon afterward to deal with the sultan, he passed before Dorylaeum to attack the Turkmens encamped there, temporarily driving them and their animals from the region.[302] The undeterred nomads, however, soon reassembled with their flocks in the same area. This is quite characteristic of the struggle that the emperors had to wage against the Turkmens in western Asia Minor, for the latter were generally unable to face organized military expeditions and hence retreated before them. Rather it was in times of peace or in periods of administrative disarray that the Turkmens were able to penetrate more easily into Byzantine territory. The solution Manuel had already utilized at Pithecas, Malagina, Adramyttium, Chliara, and Pergamum, was to build strongly fortified garrison towns. After Manuel withdrew from Dorylaeum, the Turkmens and their flocks reentered, so that Manuel decided to remove them permanently from this strategic area by rebuilding Dorylaeum. In 1175, while he rebuilt and recolonized the city (it had lain an uninhabited ruin for one century), the 2,000 Turkmens who lived in the plain with their tents and flocks attempted to prevent the work of rebuilding as it meant that they would lose their pasturage. But the army of the emperor was too large; so in the end the nomads burned their tents and fled from the plain of Dorylaeum.[303] The incident of the rebuilding of Dorylaeum is one of the clearest chapters in the long struggle between nomadism and sedentary society in Anatolia.

[298] Nicetas Choniates, 71. Cinnamus, 39–40, 36.

[299] Nicetas Choniates, 194–195. Theodore Scutariotes-Sathas, 268.

[300] Cinnamus, 81–84. William of Tyre, XVI, xxii.

[301] Cinnamus, 190–191.

[302] *Ibid.*, 191, "τὴν περιοικίδα τε πᾶσαν καταδραμὼν μυρίαν ἐκεῖθεν ἀνδρῶν καὶ ζώων ἄλλων ἥλασε πληθύν."

[303] Nicetas Choniates, 227–228. Cinnamus, 295–296. Theodore Scutariotes-Sathas, 283. Euthymius Malaces–Bones, pp. 526 ff.

The densest concentration and greatest expansion of the nomads apparently took place in the southwestern regions of Phrygia, regions that, in the reigns of Alexius and John, seem to have been in Byzantine hands. When Manuel returned from his expedition against Konya, he labored under this impression and so retired to the region where the Maeander rises, around Choma-Soublaion, in order to rest the army.[304] Since Alexius' reconquest, this had been Byzantine territory, removed from the Seljuk domains.[305] But the emperor was startled to come upon a numerous encampment of Turkmens in their tents,[306] the Turkmens being under a certain chieftain Rama who was continually raiding Greek lands.[307] After rebuilding Dorylaeum, Manuel rebuilt Choma-Soublaion at the head of the Maeander in order to have here, also, a strong outpost against nomad infiltration. But by this time the upper Maeander region had been so thoroughly penetrated by the tribesmen that Choma-Soublaion is described by a contemporary Greek author as being "in the midst of the Persian [Turkish] land."[308]

The nomads had also occupied the Phrygian Pentapolis to the north of Choma-Soublaion with their animals,[309] where they were under the authority of a certain Solymas who seems to have had his center at Sarapata Mylonos. Manuel drove the nomads out temporarily, but on his withdrawal they returned to sack Laodiceia and Philetas,[310] and there evidently followed a large migratory movement of Turkmens, "as many as are rich in flocks, and because of grassy meadows the whole race invades the borders of the Rhomaioi."[311] Thus Manuel was forced to send another expedition against the nomads. After the battle of Myriocephalum, he sent his armies to attack the Turkmens encamped in the plains of Panasium and Lacerion and at Charax between Lampe and Graos Gala, but again the results were ephemeral.[312] The concentration of Turkmens on the upper Maeander was such that they seem to have pushed farther down the Maeander. When the Second Crusaders went up the Maeander toward Laodiceia they found Turks on both banks of the river.[313] The

[304] Cinnamus, 59. "'Επεὶ δὲ περί τινα χῶρον ἐγένετο οὗ δὴ Μαίανδρος τὴν ἐκβολὴν ποιεῖται." Ibid., 298, remarks that the Maeander rises at Choma-Soublaion. "φρούριόν τι περὶ πρώτας που τοῦ Μαιάνδρου ἱδρυμένον ἐκβολὰς (Σούβλαιον ὄνομα αὐτῷ) . . ."

[305] Ibid., 59.

[306] Ibid., ". . . σκηνὰς μὲν ἐνταῦθα ἠθροῖσθαι πολλὰς ἤκουσε."

[307] Ibid., 59–60. "τούς τε οὖν Πέρσας οἵτινες εἶεν αὐτίκα συνεῖδεν ἐκ τῆς σφετέρας αὐτοὺς ὀνομάσας φυλῆς, 'Ραμάν τινα γεννεάρχην αὐτοῖς καταλέγων εἶναι, καὶ ὡς κατ' ἔθος τὸ αὐτῶν τοὺς ἐκ γειτόνων 'Ρωμαίων ἤδη καὶ νῦν λῃστεύσαντες λαφύρων πλησάμενοι ἤκουσι."

[308] Euthymius Malaces-Bones, 546. Cinnamus, 298.

[309] Nicetas Choniates, 162; "ἐνίοτε δὲ τοὺς ὡς πώεα πλατέα διεκκεχυμένους τοῖς 'Ρωμαϊκοῖς σχοινίσμασι Τούρκους ἀναστέλλων τοῖς περὶ τὴν πεντάπολιν ἐπιτίθεται."

[310] Ibid., 162–163. Cinnamus, 196–198.

[311] Theodore Scutariotes-Sathas, 254.

[312] Nicetas Choniates, 254–255. Theodore Scutariotes-Sathas, 296.

[313] Odo of Deuil, pp. 109–111.

Turkmen pressure continued farther to the south in the Pamphylian district where Attaleia was closely blockaded, and where also the remnants of the Second Crusade were attacked when they attempted to cross the Eurymedon River.[314] The reign of Manuel Comnenus bore witness to a marked progress of the nomadic westward advance. Though the nomads were temporarily halted in northwest Anatolia as a result of Manuel's fortifications on the Sangarius, in Bathys-Tembris, and in the theme of Neocastron, they succeeded in occupying the remnants of Byzantine territory in western Phrygia and began to follow the course of the Maeander and Cayster into Lydia and Caria.

During the twenty-five years following the death of Manuel, the Turks pushed farther down the Maeander and once more threatened the cities of Bithynia from their bases on the Bathys and Tembris. The sultans, henceforth comparatively free of involvement in eastern Anatolia, took a more active part in these Turkish raids. Sozopolis was taken; Cotyaeum, Tantalus, and Caria sacked; Laodiceia, Chonae, Attaleia were besieged. The growing anarchy in the Byzantine empire and withdrawal of troops from Anatolia for service in Europe greatly facilitated the Turkmen raids.[315] As the political situation and the administration within the Byzantine provinces deteriorated, rebels appeared in Asia Minor who generally called in bands of Turkmens to support them. The Turkmens took these opportunities to pillage towns and villages and to take booty and captives. For all these reasons, the penetration of the Turkmen groups was considerably eased.[316] By this time the Turkmen pressure was once more threatening Bithynia and the middle regions of the Maeander.

Though most of the details in the history of the nomads in western Anatolia at this time are lost, nevertheless many of the important features have survived in the sources. By looking at the map it is possible to see that the western push of the Turkmens really got under way only in the second half of the twelfth century. Alexius had managed to push them back to a line running roughly about Dorylaeum-Santabaris-Amorium-Cedrea-Polybotus-Philomelium. John had managed, to a large degree, to keep the Turkmens in the central and more easterly regions of Phrygia. But during the reign of Manuel, the Byzantines were less successful and the nomads pushed westward into the regions from Tripolis-Hierapolis-Laodiceia in the south, to Lacerion-Pentapolis-Panasium in the north. By the end of the century they were threatening the lower regions of the Maeander, Attaleia, and the towns of Bithynia in the north. This

---

[314] William of Tyre, XVI, xxvi. Odo of Deuil, pp. 109–113.

[315] Nicetas Choniates, 466, 480–481.

[316] *Ibid.*, 549–553. Pseudoalexius obtained 8,000 Turkmens (ποιμνίταις καὶ βουκολίοις) from the emir Arsanes. *Ibid.*, 657–658. Theodore Mangaphas too recruited an army from the Turkmens with which he ravaged the districts of Chonae, Laodiceia, and Caria. Nicetas Choniates, 523. The Maeandrian towns were similarly wasted by Michael the tax collector and Maurozomes with the aid of Turkish armies. *Ibid.*, 700–701, 827, 842–843. Bithynian rebels called in Turkish troops against Andronicus Comnenus.

expansion was due primarily to Byzantine internal decline and provincial chaos, but possibly also to an intensification in the numbers of Turkmens coming into western Anatolia.

Two factors seem to indicate that the numbers of Turkmens increased. First there is the successful expansion of the nomads in search of booty and pasture in the latter half of the century. Then there is also the fact that the sources speak of the nomads as being present in large numbers. The Byzantine historians often refer to the nomads as being present in great numbers, as for example in the case of the chieftain Rama who is said to have been encamped at the head of the Maeander with many tents.[317] In two instances the Greek sources do mention numbers: there were 2,000 Turks with their tents and animals encamped around Dorylaeum,[318] and the rebel Pseudoalexius obtained 8,000 Turkmens from Arsanes when he raided the Maeandrian towns.[319] But other sources indicate larger numbers.. Ibn al-Athir notes that the Udj Turkmen in the west were present in great numbers.[320] Michael the Syrian reveals that during Manuel's march on Myriocephalum, the Turkmens, in groups of 5,000 to 10,000, harassed the Byzantines, and when the army halted some 50,000 Turkmens pillaged the camp.[321] The Latin authors who describe Barbarossa's march through the district between Laodiceia-Sozopolis-Philomelium also indicate that the Turkmens were present in great numbers,[322] one source putting their figure at 100,000.[323]

The contemporary records say very little about Muslim urban centers in this border area during the twelfth century, and the Turks in these areas seem to be almost exclusively nomads. The Greek historians speak only of nomads and describe the salient features of nomadic society and life repeatedly.[324] The historians of Barbarossa remarked that they were "bedouins" and "bandits" who lived in their tents. They lived under one chieftain, possessed livestock, but as they had not cities or lands, they moved about from one place to another in search of pasturage and pillage.[325]

---

[317] Cinnamus, 59–60.

[318] *Ibid.*, 295.

[319] Nicetas Choniates, 551.

[320] *Ibn el-Athiri chronicon quod perfectissimum inscribitur*, ed. C. J. Tornberg (Upsala 1853), XII, 113 (hereafter cited as Ibn al-Athir, Tornberg).

[321] Michael the Syrian, III, 371.

[322] *Historia Peregrinorum*, p. 155, "Horum innumera multitudine . . ." Gesta Federici, 86, "Qui maximum et infinitum exercitum congregaverant." Gesta Federici, p. 87, "Et in maximo exercitu veniunt . . ."

[323] Salimbene, p. 11, speaks of a large "army" of Turks after the Crusaders left Philadelpheia, "infinitum et innumerabilem exercitum, plusquam centum milia, congregantes, exercitum Christianum die noctuque per IIII or ebdomadas impugnarunt." 30,000 Turks were awaiting the Crusaders at Myriocephalum. Ansbert, p. 77.

[324] Regel, II, 195, 261. Theodore Scutariotes-Sathas, 253–254, 283, 296. Nicetas Choniates, 227–228, 254–255. Eustathius of Thessalonike, *P.G.*, CXXXV, 938, 940. Cinnamus, 59–60, 191, 295.

[325] *Historia Peregrinorum*, p. 155. "Est autem consuetudo incolarum illius terre qui silvestres Turci sive Bedewini dicuntur, carere domibus et omni tempore degendo in

These nomads took up their abode in deserted or semideserted rural areas. As Byzantine power declined and the Turkmens pushed into new border regions, the population must often have fled the countryside to towns such as Sozopolis, Chonae, and Laodiceia, or to other more secure regions in the highlands. Thus many of the border towns were isolated by Turks who had occupied the plains and rural areas. With the destruction of Dorylaeum, they occupied the plains of Bathys with their tents and livestock, and no urban center existed on the spot of Dorylaeum for about one hundred years. Cotyaeum must have undergone a similar experience when the sultan sacked it after Manuel's death, and the Turkmens moved in.[326] Choma and the towns of the Pentapolis suffered the same fate. Hierapolis and Tripolis were both destroyed and deserted, and the nomads came into these regions also. Only Laodiceia and Chonae survived as Byzantine urban outposts, but they were isolated by the heavy nomadic settlements around them. It is as a result of this process of nomadization that Byzantine place names have virtually disappeared in the region between Ushak on the north, Isparta and Uluburlu in the southeast, and Chonae in the southwest.[327] The conquest of this area by the Turks was a long and destructive process that lasted for a century. The conquest involved a gradual settling down of the Turkmen bands and the withdrawal of the Byzantine populations. With the retreat of the latter and the settlement of the conquerors, new Turkish names replaced older Byzantine place names. The prolonged hostile relations of Byzantines and Turks in this part of Anatolia resulted in the destruction of Byzantine society[328] and in the nomadization of large areas. This process was repeated in parts of the northwest corner of the plateau about Cotyaeum-Dorylaeum, and in the Pamphylian plain.[329]

The appearance of the nomads on the borders is also connected with the fact that the sultans sent them there to carry on the djihad with the Christians. The role of these Udj Turkmens (Turkmens of the border as the contemporary Arab sources term them)[330] in the holy war is quite

---

tabernaculis de pascuis ad pascua se transferre cum gregibus et armentis." And, p. 156, "gens ista, gens odiosa silvestris indomita et effrena nullius est subdita ditioni; hii sunt predones qui soliti devastare terras finitimas ipsum eciam soldanum inquietare non verentur bellis frequentibus et rapinis." Gesta Federici, p. 86, "Sunt enim agrestes Turchi, qui nullo detinentur imperio et nulla loca possident, sed morantur in agris." And, p. 87, "Non habent civitates, sed morantur in agris; habent etiam caput unum, qui illos precedit, habent animalia, fructus et pugnant cum arcubus, lignis et lapidibus." Also, 95, "qui sunt homines agrestes et sine lege et ratione." See Brosset, *Géorgie*, I, *passim*, especially pp. 358–359, on their habits.

[326] Nicetas Choniates, 340.

[327] Ramsay, *The Cities and Bishoprics of Phrygia* (Oxford, 1897), II, 373.

[328] Regel, II, 259; "οὐ μόνον δ'οὕτω κακῶς διέθεντο καὶ ἠρήμωσαν ὁπόσα τούτοις ὅμορα καὶ ἀγχίθυρα." *Historia Peregrinorum*, p. 156.

[329] On this latter see de Planhol, *Nomadisme*, pp. 102–103. Ramsay, *Phrygia*, I, 301, as to why the process was not as disruptive to the Byzantine populations of Pisidia.

[330] Bar Hebraeus, I, 360, notes, ". . . 'IUG, a great country of the Turkomans which was on the border of the Greeks."

clearly illustrated in the Danishmendname and other Turkish epics dealing with the conquest.[331] The report of the twelfth-century Arab traveler al-Harawi also bears out the ghazi character of these nomadic groups. The two most important religious shrines he mentions in the Turkmen region of western Anatolia are the tomb of Abu Muhammad al-Battal located on a hill at the Byzantine-Turkish borders,[332] and the tombs of the Muslims who fell, martyrs, during the famous Arab raid on Amorium in 838. The prominence of the cult of Battal and the special sanctity of the tombs at Amorium demonstrate quite clearly the ghazi mentality and spirit that prevailed among the Turkmen tribes.[333] It was also convenient for the sultans to send these tribes to the frontiers, for they were thus removed from the central regions of the Seljuk domains. The exact relations between these frontier tribes and the sultanate in Konya are somewhat hazy. Invariably the Turkmens sided with the sultans against the Christians, but there were often occasions when the sultans were not able to control the Turkmens. The events surrounding the battle of Myriocephalum and the march of Frederick Barbarossa illustrate effectively the absence of any complete control over the tribes on the borders. The latter opposed Kïlïdj Arslan's peace treaty with Manuel and continued to raid Byzantine territory. Barbarossa, in spite of his friendly relations with the sultan, was harassed and attacked by Turkmens between Laodiceia and Konya, and then again after departing from Konya en route to Cilicia.[334]

The establishment of the nomads was of course not restricted to western Anatolia. This phenomenon is to be observed all along the edge of the Anatolian plateau. They settled along the Byzantine borders in the north where in the thirteenth century the tribe of the Chepni played an important role in the djihad with the Trebizondine Greeks.[335] They are also in evidence, where the Ağacheri are mentioned, in eastern Anatolia during the twelfth and thirteenth centuries. Their presence and activities are even better documented for the regions of the Taurus in the twelfth century. There are strong indications that their numbers and destructive behavior increased markedly at this time in southeastern Anatolia as the result of the arrival of newcomers from the Middle East, attendant upon the strife in the domains of the Great Seljuks.[336] The pattern of their

[331] On this see A. Bombaci, *Storia della letteratura turca* (Milan, 1956), pp. 209–225, 309–311.

[332] Al-Harawi, p. 131.

[333] *Ibid.*, p. 133, also mentions a mosque of al-Battal in Kayseri.

[334] Gesta Federici, p. 95. The close relationship, however, of sultanate and tribes is illustrated by the fact that Pseudoalexius had to obtain a menshur from the sultan in order to recruit troops from among the tribes. Nicetas Choniates, 551.

[335] Ibn Bibi-Duda, p. 321. Michael Panaretus, ed. O. Lampsides, Μιχαὴλ τοῦ Παναρέτου περὶ τῶν μεγάλων Κομνηνῶν," 'Α.Π., XXII (1958), 68, 78–79 (hereafter cited as Panaretus-Lampsides). Sümer, "Cepni," EI₂.

[336] C. Cahen, "Selgukides Turcomans et Allemands au temps de la troisiéme croisade," *W.Z.K.M.*, LVI (1960), 21–31. Bar Hebraeus, I, 330, on their involvement in Seljuk

establishment and raids was no doubt similar to what has been sketched for western Anatolia.[337]

The invasions, settlements, and raids of the Turkmens played a crucial role in the fate of the Anatolian peninsula. The impact of this nomadic-pastoral-warrior society, which was at the height of its heroic age, upon the stability of the highly developed sedentary society of the Byzantine Christians was one of the principal factors in the cultural transformation of Asia Minor. As of the late twelfth century, however, Byzantine society had managed to survive the initial shocks of these migration-invasions and conquests, and consequently the mechanics of this nomadic-sedentary encounter will be discussed at the end of the present chapter.

EFFECTS OF THE TURKISH CONQUEST ON ECCLESIASTICAL ADMINISTRATION IN THE ELEVENTH AND TWELFTH CENTURIES

One of the most difficult problems is to ascertain what happened to the church in this period. Ecclesiastical documents on the problems of the church in Asia Minor are sadly lacking until the period of the fourteenth century when they become comparatively plentiful. The Armenian and Syriac chronicles enable us to get a glimpse of restricted areas in eastern Anatolia, and isolated comments of Greek canon lawyers, synodal decrees, and histories give a few definite hints as to the problems that the church experienced elsewhere in Anatolia. This meager factual information must be understood and interpreted within the framework of general conditions. The first of these is the fact that large parts of Anatolia underwent a comparatively long period of upheaval. The history of the church at this time cannot be fully comprehended if this fact is not taken into account. Second, Asia Minor became, by virtue of the Turkish invasions and settlements, the *dar al-harb* between Islam and Christianity. Just as there was religious tension and antagonism between the two religions in Syria and Mesopotamia as a result of the Crusades, so frequently there was religious zeal and animosity in the relations between Christians and Muslims in

---

dynastic strife in the regions of Sebasteia. On the Ağacheri, Sümer, "Ağaç-Eriler," *Belleten*, XXVI, (1962), 521–528. Aksaray–Gençosman, p. 335, seems to refer to the Ağacheri. Ibn Bibi-Duda, p. 270, speaking of their invasions in 1254 says that the Ağacheri originated in the steppe and forest about Marash. Here they roamed the highways, destroyed caravans, and plundered the regions of Rum, Syria, and Armenia. See also, on movements in the second half of the twelfth century, O. Turan, *Selçuklular tarihi ve türk-islam medeniyeti* (Ankara, 1965), pp. 188–190.

[337] The attempts of the Armenian princes in the late twelfth century to halt the Turkmen infiltration are parallel to the efforts of the Comnenoi in the west. The nomads appear in southeast Anatolia seeking pastures and booty. Ibn al-Athir, *R H.C.*, *H.O.*, I, 644–645. Bar Hebraeus, I, 310, 321, 328. Bahram of Edessa, *R.H.C.*, *D.A.*, I, 510–511. Constable Sempad, *R.H.C.*, *D.A.*, I, 628–629. The armies of Barbarossa were harassed by the Turkmens when the former approached the Taurus regions after having left Konya. Gesta Federici, p. 95; "qui sunt homines agrestes et sine lege et ratione. Et isti fortiter nos impugnant et cum lignis et lapidibus et nocte et die, et viri et mulieres, et multos de illis occidimus, Et persequuntur nos, usque dum venimus in Armeniam." Ibn al-Athir, *R.H.C.*, *H.O.*, II₁, 23–24.

Anatolia. Nevertheless, the invaders were, formally, Muslims and as such their political and cultural outlook included the formal toleration of Christian society, if in a definitely abased state. Also extremely important was the fact that religious affiliation was most often equivalent to and interchangeable with political affiliation or loyalty. Thus the Byzantine church was suspect because it was tightly centralized in Constantinople and under the direct control of the emperor. It was, in a sense, a department of state.

There is some evidence in the sporadic chronicles that the disorders entailed considerable damage to ecclesiastical foundations throughout Anatolia. Even before the battle of Manzikert, the Turkish raids resulted in the pillaging of the famous churches of St. Basil at Caesareia and of the Archangel Michael at Chonae.[338] In the decade following 1071 the destruction of churches and the flight of the clergy became widespread.[339] Though there is no systematic account of this phenomenon, the chance references suffice to indicate that the churches were often pillaged and destroyed. The Danishmendname puts the following declaration in the mouth of the Muslim hero Danishmend: "I am Malik Danishmend Ghazi . . . the destroyer of churches and towers."[340] and the destruction and pillaging of churches and monasteries figure prominently in the poem. One might reasonably assume that this allusion to destruction of churches in the epic poem is due to the inflated imagination of the poet who is describing the holy war. But the incidental references to these phenomena in the chronicles indicate that there is some truth at the basis of the statement by the Turkish poet. The churches of St. Phocas in Sinope and St. Nicholas at Myra, both important centers of pilgrimage, were destroyed.[341] The monasteries of Mt. Latrus, Strobilus, and Melanoudium on the western coast were sacked and the monks driven out during the early invasions, so that the monastic foundations in this area were completely abandoned until the Byzantive reconquest and the extensive support of successive Byzantine emperors once more reconstituted them.[342] Greeks were forced to surround the church of St. John at Ephesus with walls to protect it from the Turks.[343] The disruption of active religious life in the Cappadocian

[338] The church of Chonae was ravaged on two more occasions in the latter half of the twelfth century when the Turkish troops of the rebels Theodore Mangaphas and Pseudo-alexius destroyed the mosaics, the altar, and then the church. Nicetas Choniates, 523–524, 552–553.

[339] Theodore Scutariotes-Sathas, 169; " . . . καὶ αὐτῶν τῶν ἐκκλησιῶν τῶν ἐν ὅλοις τοῖς τῆς Ἀνατολῆς μέρεσιν ὑπ' αὐτῶν ἐρημωθέντων καὶ τέλεον κατατροπωθέντων καὶ εἰς τὸ μηδὲν ἀποκαταστάντων. Regel, II, 259, refers to the extensive destruction of churches in the latter half of the twelfth century, " . . . καὶ σταθμοὺς ἱεροὺς ἐκκενώσαντες ἠρημώκασιν . . ."

[340] Danishmendname-Melikoff, I, 270; II, 84, "Benem Melik Danişmend-i Gazi . . . Benem yikan kélise vu burgazi."

[341] Van den Vorst, "Saint Phocas," XXX, 289; " . . . καὶ ὁ νεὼς οὗτος ἠρείπωται πρὶν ταῖς ἐνγειτόνων βαρβάρων ἀθέων ἐπιθέσεσιν ὡς γενέσθαι κοινόν."

[342] Miklosich et Müller, VI, 24–25, 62, 84, 87; IV, 323–324, 329.

[343] Odo of Deuil, p. 107.

cave-monastic communities is also indicated for the twelfth century.[344] Upon the taking of Antioch by Sulayman in 1085, many of the churches were desecrated, the priests were driven out, some of the churches were used as stables and for other unfitting purposes. William of Tyre gives one of the earliest descriptions of the destruction and defacing of religious pictures. In Antioch, he remarks, the Turks removed or covered the pictures of the saints on the walls, gouging out the eyes and mutilating the noses.[345] At the end of the eleventh century, the Turks pillaged the churches that they found on their path between Dorylaeum and Konya,[346] and similar instances appear throughout southeastern Anatolia. In 1120–21 the priests and monks of the regions between Tell-Bashir and Kaisum were put to the sword,[347] and sixteen years later the monastery of Garmir Vank around Kaisum was burned.[348] Muhammad of Caesarea is reported to have destroyed the churches c. 1134,[349] and almost twenty years later c. 1153 the emir of Caesarea issued another decree calling for destruction of churches.[350] Though the Armenians, and especially the Syrians, seem to have been treated with more consideration than were the Greek Christians, we see that both Armenian and Syrian religious foundations were subject to considerable strain and difficulty.[351] In 1140–41 and again c. 1149 Turks pillaged the monasteries of Beth Zabar.[352] Bar Mar Sauma, in the vicinity of Melitene, found itself in difficulties on more than one occasion. In the middle of the twelfth century the buildings of the monastery were burned by Turks who carried off the livestock (they were

---

[344] De Jerphanion, *Cappadoce*, II$_2$ 400. The monasteries of the eastern Christians in general suffered decline as a result of the eleventh century invasions of the Seljuks. D. Sourdel, "Dayr," EI$_2$.

[345] William of Tyre, VI, xxiii. This is confirmed for the Syrian churches, Raymund of Aguilers, *R.H.C., H.O.*, III, 288: "Quippe in tantum malitiam exserarant illa hominum genera, ut ecclesias Dei everterent et sanctorum ejus, vel imagines delerent, et quas non poterant delere per moram, oculos eorum eruebant, et sagittabant; altaria vero omnia suffodiebant. In ecclesiis autem magnis, mahumarias faciebant." The remarks of Ricoldo de Monte Crucis, "Lettres de Monte-Croce sur la prise d'Acre (1291)," ed. Rohricht in *Archives de L'Orient Latin*, II (1884), 273, indicate that the situation was the same in the late thirteenth century: "Nonne in tota Turchia et Percide et usque ad Baldactum invenimus omnes ecclesias christianorum diruptas aut stabulatas aut mescitas factas Sarracenorum? Et ubi non potueruent ecclesiam destruere vel stabulare, statim iuxta ecclesiam edificaverunt meschitam et menaram cum turri alta, ut super caput christianorum clament legem, ymmo perfidiam Machometi." For further reference to the Turkish destruction of Greek icons and religious images see the following: I. Ševčenko, "Alexius Macrembolites and his 'Dialogue between the Rich and the Poor'," *Z.R.V.I.*, VI (1960), 196.

[346] *Gesta Francorum*, pp. 54–55. Tudebodus, *R.H.C., H.O.*, III, 29.

[347] Matthew of Edessa, p. 302.

[348] *Ibid.*, p. 321.

[349] Michael the Syrian, III, 237.

[350] *Ibid.*, III, 310.

[351] On religious persecution of Syrian Christians and forced conversion see above n. 261. On the preferred status of Armenians over the other non-Muslims, Chalcocondyles, 123–124, "᾿Αρμενίους δὲ μόνους τῶν ἄλλων ἐθνῶν διαφερομένων σφίσιν ἐς τὴν θρησκείαν οὐκ ἀνδραποδίζεσθαι, ὡς ᾿Αρμενίων τινὶ προειρηκότι τὸ (γὰρ) κλέος αὐτοῦ ἐς τὴν οἰκουμένην ἐσόμενον. διὰ τοῦτο μὴ ἐπιτρέπειν ἀνδραποδίζεσθαι ᾿Αρμενίους."

[352] Michael the Syrian, III, 248, 286. Bar Hebraeus, I, 266.

afterward forced by the Turkish emir to return the livestock).[353] The Muslim rulers of Melitene in the first half of the twelfth century subjected it to oppressive tribute,[354] but its condition improved considerably in the latter half of the twelfth century thanks to the generosity of Kĭlĭdj II Arslan who completely freed it from paying tribute.[355]

Though the sources do not specifically indicate it, one must assume that in villages and towns destroyed or pillaged by the Turks the religious establishments were likewise despoiled. Such towns as Adramyttium, Attaleia, Dorylaeum, Cotyaeum, Caesareia, and Edessa were the objects of extensive destruction, and it is to be assumed that the religious foundations underwent the same fate (at least until they were, in some cases, recolonized). That this is so is indicated by the description of Edessa in 1186 by Michael the Syrian, who forty years after its savage destruction lists seventeen churches in the city which were still in a ruined state.[356]

Something is said, too, though very little, about conversion of churches into mosques.[357] Sulayman upon the conquest of Antioch transformed the church of Cassianus into a mosque. The Armenian cathedral of Ani remained a mosque until the Georgians reconquered the city in 1124–25, removed the Muslims from the structure, and once more turned it into a Christian sanctuary.[358] When the Seljuk sultan took Sinope in 1214 he converted its churches into mosques;[359] but when the Greeks of Trebizond retook it they reconverted them. The Greek interregnum in Sinope, however, was short-lived, and when once more the Turkish forces

---

[353] Michael the Syrian, III, 290–291.

[354] *Ibid.*, 286.

[355] *Ibid.*, 390 ff. Previously, in 1175, when Muhammad had seized power he wished to reward the monastery for its support by completely remitting the tribute. But the monks so feared the hatred of the Muslims that they insisted on paying 300 dinars per year. The same occurred with the monastery of Mar Domitius (*ibid.*, 363–364). Farther to the east of Melitene, the Christians suffered from the Muslim reaction to the Crusades. In 1152 an Armenian built an elaborate church at Hisn Ziad and so irritated the emir Kara Arslan that the latter had the church destroyed and the priest crucified. The emir then issued an edict that forbade the building of new churches or the repair of old ones in the whole region of Mesopotamia (*ibid.*, 307–308). When Nur al-Din of Aleppo took Nisibis in 1172 he ordered all new constructions in churches and monasteries to be destroyed. He pillaged the treasury of the Nestorian church of Mar Jacob and destroyed its library of some 1,000 volumes. He is said to have done the same thing elsewhere (*ibid.*, 339–340). In 1174 the church of the Forty Martyrs in Mardin was plundered (*ibid.*, 352), and the churches and patriarchal residence of the Jacobites at Amid were closed. Some of the churches were totally destroyed and others were used as storehouses for the prince's cotton (*ibid.*, 354–355). Nur al-Din of Mardin used the stones and columns of the churches to embellish his own residence (*ibid.*, 396).

[356] *Ibid.*, 397–398. They were the following: St. John Baptist, Great Church, Holy Apostles, St. Thomas, St. Michael, St. Cosmas (church of the mendil of Edessa), St. George, Saviour, three churches dedicated to the Mother of God, two churches of the Forty Martyrs, the Confessors (Gouria, Semouna, Habib), St. Stephan, St. Theodore, etc.

[357] *Ibid.*, 173. Ricoldo speaks of the large scale conversion of churches into mosques, see above n. 345.

[358] Matthew of Edessa, p. 313.

[359] Ibn Bibi-Duda, p. 68.

recovered the city, the churches again became mosques.[360] The example of Sinope was no doubt a familiar pattern throughout Anatolia. When the Turks took the towns, they usually took over many of the churches for their own cult or for other purposes.[361] Very frequently the Christians were forced to evacuate a town newly captured, as in the case of Dadybra, and one must assume that here too the churches passed into the hands of Muslims.[362] On the other hand, the Christians continued in the possession of many of their churches throughout Asia Minor, but it seems likely that the Muslims appropriated the larger and better churches.[363]

It has been customary to assume that the invasions did not affect the administration of the church in Anatolia, and it is often stated that the ecclesiastical institution continued to function as it had in the past, undisturbed in the possession of its bishoprics, ecclesiastical property, and immunities. This difficult question is further complicated by the fact that there were three major churches in Anatolia. Aside from the Greek church, there were also the Armenian and Syrian ecclesiastical establishments in the more easterly regions. It is quite possible that the Turkish attitude toward the ecclesiastical institutions of the latter two ethnic groups might have differed from their attitude toward the Greek church, inasmuch as the political institutions and attitudes of the Armenians and Syrians on occasion differed from those of the Greeks. Of these three groups, the Syrians possessed no political state and so the Syrian Christians did not constitute any potential threat to the Muslim invaders. The Armenians had, for the most part, lost their independence in the eleventh century, and the Armenian population dispersed from Armenia to Cappadocia and Cilicia. Both the Armenian and Syrian churches had undergone persecution at the hands of the Byzantines in the eleventh century, at which time the emperors had sought to impose ecclesiastical union upon them. As a result of this, the Syrian patriarchate had abandoned Melitene in Byzantine territory and sought refuge in Muslim lands at the city of Amid. On the other hand, the Greek church was tightly centralized in Constantinople and under the control of the emperors, who supported it and often worked through it. By reason of historical circumstances the identification of the ecclesiastical and political institutions in

---

[360] Aksaray-Gençosman, 168–169, remarks that in these places where formerly were read the Gospels, one now read the Koran, and the Muslim call to prayer replaced the church bells.

[361] *Le Destan d'Umur Pacha*, ed. and trans. I. Melikoff-Sayar (Paris, 1954), p. 47 (hereafter cited as *Destan d'Umur*). See n. 341 above. The process continued in the fourteenth century, Ashïkpashazade-Kreutel, pp. 39, 63–64, 69, 85, 215–217. Ashïkpashazade-Ali, pp. 18, 38, 42, 56, 154. F. Giese, *Die altosmanischen anonymen Chroniken* (Leipzig, 1925), p. 21 (hereafter cited as Anonymous-Giese). In the early conquest the Ottomans converted the churches of Nicaea, Nicomedia, Biğa, Amasra.

[362] Nicetas Choniates, 626.

[363] See the letters of Matthew of Ephesus, Treu, *Matthaios Metropolit von Ephesos. Ueber sein Leben und seine Schriften* (Potsdam, 1901) (hereafter cited as Matthew of Ephesus, Treu), p. 56.

Byzantium was complete, and in this the Greek church differed from the Syrian church. Because of these circumstances, it would be reasonable to assume that the Turks would have viewed the church of Constantinople in a somewhat different light. Inasmuch as the principal foe in Anatolia during the eleventh and twelfth centuries was the Byzantine Empire, its ecclesiastical establishment in Anatolia was ipso facto highly suspect. But above and beyond the association of religious and political institutions, there was the religious antagonism between Muslim and Christian which was fed by the flames of war.

In spite of the "favored status" that the Syrians and the Armenians enjoyed under the Turks, there are indications that the Turks did not favor or tolerate the ecclesiastical administration of the largely "nonpolitical" churches consistently and uninterruptedly. For in the latter half of the twelfth century, c. 1174, the Syrian patriarchal residence in Amid was closed, and many of the churches were either shut down or destroyed.[364] The Armenian church did not enjoy Turkish favor to the extent that the Syrian church did, probably because the Armenians continued to be factors in the political and military life of southeast Anatolia. By the end of the eleventh century, the Armenian church was undergoing such difficulties that the Armenian patriarch Basil appealed personally to the great sultan Malik Shah to ease the church's plight.

In the year 539 [1090–91] the patriarch of the Armenians, the lord Basil, went to the master of the world, the sultan Malik Shah, in order to convey his grievances at the persecutions of the faithful of Christ excited in many places, at the tribute imposed upon churches and clergy, and at the exactions which weighed upon monasteries and bishops. As a witness of the evils afflicting the Church, Basil had conceived of the idea of going to find the good and clement ruler of the Persians and of all Christ's faithful.

Having brought great sums of gold, silver, and brocade cloth as presents, he set out accompanied by the nobles of his house, bishops, priests, and doctors. Upon arriving in Persia at the court of the pious monarch, Basil presented himself before him and was received with the highest distinction. He obtained all which he desired. Malik Shah exempted the churches, the monasteries and priests of all payments, and having rendered as a result an edict, he bade farewell to the patriarch who was given official diplomas and covered with honors.[365]

The church had suffered for over twenty years before Malik Shah granted the charter of immunity. Matthew of Edessa also praised the emir Ismail who, as governor or Armenia, "had protected the monsteries against the vexations which the 'Persians' [Turks] imposed."[366] But both Malik Shah and Ismail passed from the scene and the former vexing conditions once more prevailed over the Armenian church. At some undetermined time in the twelfth century, the catholicus of Armenia had to seek refuge in

---

[364] Michael the Syrian, III, 354–355. The monks of Bar Mar Sauma seem to have been subject to oppressive taxation throughout the twelfth century down to the conquest of Melitene by Kïlïdj II Arslan, Ibid., passim.

[365] Matthew of Edessa, p. 201.

[366] Ibid., p. 204. It is for this reason that Matthew, p. 207, reports his death.

Cilicia with the Armenian princes, as the Turks were oppressing him in Greater Armenia.[367]

The effect of the Turkish invasions and conquest on the administrative structure of the Greek church was often seriously detrimental and in some cases an unqualified disaster. The contemporary literature on this subject is sparse and consequently most of the details in the ecclesiastical administrative picture of eleventh- and twelfth-century Anatolia are lacking. Nevertheless, thanks to the commentaries on canon law by Balsamon, the general situation prevailing in the realm of ecclesiastical administration of the Greek church in Anatolia is clearly discernible. Balsamon, writing in the latter half of the twelfth century, comments on the body of canon law in terms of the actual historical experiences of the period under discussion. Thus he differs from those commentators who consider the canons theoretically, and often without reference to contemporary historical circumstances. It is due, almost exclusively, to the writings of Balsamon that the historian can reconstruct the effects of the Turkish invasions on the ecclesiastical administration in Anatolia during this period. He not only interprets the canons in terms of historical events of his day, but he preserves important imperial documents (from the time of Alexius I Comnenus to Isaac II Angelus) on ecclesiastical matters which otherwise would have been completely lost. It is of no little interest that many of the canons Balsamon explains in his commentaries are cases that deal with barbarian invasions, conversion to Islam and heresy, flight of bishops from their seats, and other such matters. These were ever-recurrent situations in the history of the church since the third-century persecutions and the Persian-Arab invasions on Byzantine territory. These canons, dealing with such circumstances, were no doubt long familiar to Byzantine ecclesiastics before the eleventh century, and so one must not be surprised that such commentators as Zonaras and Aristenus did not attempt to explain them in terms of contemporary events. Rather it is exceptional that Balsamon illuminated them within the framework of the eleventh and twelfth centuries.

The disruption in the administration of the church in Asia Minor which the Turkish invasions caused is manifested primarily in that metropolitans and bishops often were not able to go to their churches in Anatolia, and these churches became economically impoverished. The irregularity in ecclesiastical administration of Anatolia is already evident during the reign of Alexius I Comnenus, who legislated in an effort to deal with the crisis. His *prostaxis* (decree) has survived in Balsamon's comments on canon thirty-seven of the Council in Trullo, a canon concerned with bishops and metropolitans who are not able to take over

---

[367] Michael the Syrian, III, 188. The Armenian monasteries of eastern Anatolia began to revive only in the late twelfth century. F. Macler, "Les couvents arméniens," *Revue de l'histoire des religions*, LXXIII (1916), 303.

their church seats because of barbarian invasions and occupation.[368] According to the canon all such bishops and metropolitans are none the less validly ordained bishops and metropolitans and can ordain clerics and perform as they normally would. Balsamon then explains this canon in terms of the history of the eleventh and twelfth centuries.

The present canon decrees that the bishops who have not been able to go to their appointed thrones because of barbarian attack are equally to be honored, and are to carry out all the episcopal duties . . . and are plainly to be reckoned as if they had gone to their church and been enthroned. Just so the metropolitan of Iconium, and other Anatolian metropolitans who have no churches as they are held by the barbarians, validly ordain bishops. And they carry out all the metropolitan duties, even if they were not at all able to go to their appointed churches and to be enthroned.[369]

But the inability of the metropolitans and bishops to go to their Anatolian seats because of the Turkish occupation was nothing new in Balsamon's time, for he refers the reader to an imperial *prostaxis* of 1094:

Read the prostaxis of the glorious emperor lord Alexius Comnenus delivered in the month of November of the second indiction, and which declares that those elected to Anatolian churches are hereafter to have again the egoumeneia and adelphata and officia belonging to them, which [prostaxis], word for word is as follows.

My majesty learned, my most holy lord and ecumenical patriarch, that [as] the appointments in the churches of God progress some chosen in the appointments

---

[368] Rhalles and Potles, II, 388, the canon describes in detail this situation; " Ἐπειδὴ κατὰ διαφόρους καιροὺς βαρβαρικαὶ γεγόνασι ἔφοδοι, καὶ πλεῖσται πόλεις ἐντεῦθεν ὑποχείριοι τοῖς ἀνόμοις κατέστησαν ὡς ἐντεῦθεν μὴ δυνηθῆναι τὸν τῆς τοιαύτης πόλεως πρόεδρον, μετὰ τὴν ἐπ' αὐτῷ χειροτονίαν, τὸν οἰκεῖον θρόνον καταλαβεῖν, καὶ ἐν αὐτῷ ἱερατικῇ καταστάσει ἐνιδρυθῆναι, καὶ οὕτω κατὰ τὸ κρατῆσαν ἔθος τὰς χειροτονίας, καὶ πάντα, ἃ τῷ ἐπισκόπῳ ἀνήκει, πράττειν τε καὶ μεταχειρίζεσθαι· ἡμεῖς τὸ τίμιον, καὶ σεβάσμιον τῇ ἱερωσύνῃ φυλάττοντες, καὶ μηδαμῶς πρὸς λύμην τῶν ἐκκλησιαστικῶν δικαίων τὴν ἐθνικὴν ἐπήρειαν ἐνεργεῖσθαι βουλόμενοι, τοῖς οὕτω χειροτονηθεῖσι, καὶ διὰ τὴν προκειμένην αἰτίαν ἐν τοῖς ἑαυτῶν μὴ ἐγκαταστᾶσι θρόνοις, τὸ ἀποκριμάτατον τηρεῖσθαι συνεωράκαμεν, ὥστε καὶ χειροτονίας κληρικῶν διαφόρων κανονικῶς ποιεῖν, καὶ τῇ τῆς προεδρίας αὐθεντίᾳ κατὰ τὸν ἴδιον ὅρον κεχρῆσθαι, καὶ βεβαίαν, καὶ νενομισμένην εἶναι πᾶσαν ὑπ' αὐτῶν προϊοῦσαν διοίκησιν."
The flight and expulsion of the Anatolian clergy is confirmed by the recently published documents in J. Darrouzès, *Documents inédits d'ecclésiologie byzantine* (Paris, 1966), pp. 40–41, 46–47, 226 (clergy of Pisidian Antioch and Ankara are mentioned). As the clergy cannot get to their seats they would have gone to Constantinople.
" Καὶ τίς ἂν εἴη νῦν ἄλλη Σιὼν τῶν πόλεων παρὰ ταύτην ἐν ᾗ συντρέχουσιν ἐκ πασῶν πόλεων καὶ χωρῶν καὶ ἐθνῶν καὶ διὰ τὴν τῶν πολεμίων ἔξωθεν ἔφοδον καὶ ἕτερα πολλὰ διὰ τὸ κράτος οἵ τε καταλειφθέντες ἐκ τῆς αἰχμαλωσίας καὶ οἱ ἀδιοκούμενοι;"
P.G., CXLVI, 1196–1197, in the reign of Alexius I Comnenus Nicephorus the metropolitan of Gangra was unable to go to his church (σχολάζων) because of the Turks and so he was given the metropolitanate of Amastris. Similarly the hierarch of Leontopoleos in Asia Minor had to take over the church of Arcadiopolis in Europe.
[369] Rhalles and Potles, II, 390. Zonaras, in *ibid.*, 344–345, remarks that clerics are abandoning the churches because of barbarian invasions, harsh taxes, and famine. " Τινὲς κληρικοί, διὰ βαρβάρων ἐφόδους, ἢ φορολόγων ἀπανθρωπίας, ἢ λιμὸν ἴσως τῇ χώρᾳ αὐτῶν ἐπισυμβάντα, ἢ καὶ δι' ἑτέρας αἰτίας μεταναστεύοντες, εἰς χώρας ἄλλας ἀπίασι." This is quite possibly an exigesis of canon 28 of Trullo, rather than a comment on the twelfth century.

who are abbots in monasteries and who administer, or those who carry out some other services and those who are simply monks, others in the great church of God and in other [churches] obtaining the necessities of life from officia and some other functions [leitourgeia] find it difficult to undertake the rank [zygon] of priesthood [ierosyne, archierosyne, refers here to the positions of bishop, archbishop, metropolitan] and to watch over the churches to which they have been appointed. They fear that as such churches are located in the Anatolian regions they [the appointees] shall never have the necessities, for the churches to which they have been appointed are altogether poor [without resources] and entirely inaccessible to them; and because they undertake the administration of these [churches] they would themselves be deprived of the egoumenia, oiconomiai, and other leitourgeai which belong to them, and of the simply called adelphata, or officia and certain other hyperesia.

Therefore my majesty arranging their affairs with a certain order, declares that no one of them shall be fastidious because of these things in undertaking the office [zugon] of archierosyne. For all these shall again enjoy the benefit of the egoumeneia and oiconomia belonging to them, and of other hyperesia and leitourgeia and officia and the adelphata belonging to them. Following the reason of teaching and submitting to perfect order they shall exercise authority over their incomes from these until they obtain relief and are transformed from their present ill fate to good fortune; For they are unable to enter the churches voted them, as has been said, because they (churches) are held by the most hateful enemy. However the things which my majesty has decreed are not to apply to the archonticium and to the priests and deacons and remaining clergy of the great church of God.[370]

By the reign of Alexius I Comnenus the upsetting effects of the Turkish invasions on the church's administration are clearly visible. As the churches in Anatolia are held by the Turks, the metropolitans and bishops are not able to enter them, and in addition the churches are impoverished. Those clerics who are appointed to such churches are of course condemned to remain without churches in Constantinople, and also without income, for upon appointment to such Anatolian churches they are required to relinquish their previous ecclesiastical incomes and offices. The emperor Alexius, however, realized that it was important to preserve the hierarchical structure of the church in Asia Minor for a future time, when he hoped to reconquer much of Anatolia. When this occurred, the bishops and metropolitans would take their places again and the church would be reconstituted. This is of course what happened after he reconquered the northern, western, and southern coastal regions. The reluctance to abandon the metropolitanates and bishoprics in Asia Minor was much stronger among the emperors than among the clergy, for the clergy were very often willing to give up a bishopric or metropolitanate as no longer economically

[370] *Ibid.*, 390–391. Zepos, *J.G.R.*, I, 325–326. See Rhalles and Potles, II, 322–323 on the ἐκκλησιαστικὰ ἀρχοντίκια. Ὀφφίκια generally refer to the various clerical offices under the bishop, i.e., oiconomus, saccelion, sceuophylax, chartophylax, saccelou, etc. Ἀδελφᾶτον denotes a sum of money that an outsider is entitled to receive from a monastery; it also describes a gift made to a monastery to support a monk. Ἀρχοντίκια refer to the pentades of officials which assisted in the administration of the patriarchate, H-G. Beck, *Kirche und theologische Literatur*, 98–120, 137.

viable. But the emperors frequently prolonged the existence of bishoprics and metropolitanates beyond what was canonically or actually justifiable in order to minister to the remaining Christians and also as a possible basis of Byzantine administration and reconquest in certain areas. This policy is clearly manifested not only by Alexius but especially by Manuel Comnenus, as will appear later. In order that the metropolitan and episcopal structures of Asia Minor might be maintained, Alexius decreed that in most instances clerics ordained to Anatolian seats were to retain their incomes from previous offices so that they might have the necessities, until conditions improved and they should be enabled to proceed to their churches in Asia Minor.

Euthymius Tornices, in a florid eulogy addressed to Manuel Comnenus, refers to the removal of the hierarchs from the churches in Anatolia.

> You persuade the barbarians to free the Christians from acts of violence, to give them extensive land to express freely their piety, and to receive the spiritual guardians [*poliouchous*] of each city. And it seemed [that] you escort the churches of God again and carefully select the grooms that they might not outrage the wedding ceremonies. You do not wed new widows, as the command of the apostles desires, but those who are long widowed and consumed by love for their grooms. Now the churches of the east are once more clad in white, having shed the darkness of their widow's garments, and they embrace their grooms, sing the nuptial song, and the children are comforted.[371]

Thus the testimony of Tornices confirms what Balsamon says about the difficulties of the Anatolian churches. But as Alexius Comnenus had anticipated, there were times when bishops and metropolitans could take up residence in their churches, and Tornices refers to such an occasion when the Turks have yielded to the demands of Manuel Comnenus.[372] Though one is not to assume that these hierarchs were permanently and uninterruptedly barred from their churches in the eleventh and twelfth centuries, it is fairly clear that because of conditions in Anatolia and the enmity between Byzantium and the Turks, the clerics were hindered more often than not. Thus the *terminus technicus* σχολάζων begins to appear frequently in the ecclesiastical literature, and the commentators are called upon to define the term.

All agreed that the σχολάζων is he who is unable to go to the church over which he was appointed because the godless foreigners or heretics have taken it, perhaps destroyed it, and do not permit the bishop to put foot in it. [373]

---

[371] Euthymius Tornices-Papadopoulos-Kerameus, pp. 182–183.

[372] Balsamon, in Rhalles and Potles, III, 156, confirms the fact that the twelfth-century sultans on occasion permitted some of the metropolitans and bishops to come to Anatolia to their churches.

[373] Rhalles and Potles, III, 156; " καὶ ἤρεσε πᾶσι, σχολάζοντα εἶναι τὸν μὴ δυνάμενον ἀπελθεῖν εἰς ἣν ἐπεκηρύχθη ἐκκλησίαν, διὰ τὸ ὑπὸ ἐθνῶν ἀθέων ἢ αἱρετικῶν ταύτην κατέχεσθαι, ἴσως δὲ κοινωθῆναι, καὶ μὴ παραχωρεῖσθαι τὸν ἀρχιερέα πόδα βαλεῖν ἐν αὐτῇ." It is thus defined elsewhere, *ibid.*, II, 147: " ὅταν τις σχολάζων, δηλονότι μὴ ἔχων παροικίαν, ὡς ὑπὸ ἐθνῶν κατεχομένην."

It is significant that the bishop who is without his church, the σχολάζων, is equated with the bishop who cannot enter his diocese because the enemy either possesses his church or has destroyed it.

The exclusion of such large numbers of bishops and metropolitans not only brought difficulties for the Christians in Anatolia, but it also caused administrative difficulties for the church in Constantinople inasmuch as the bishoprics and metropolitanates were not abolished.[374] There were two alternatives open to hierarchs who found themselves unable to take over their churches in Anatolia. They either came to Constantinople or else they were transferred to seats that were vacant and were either in Byzantine territory or at least accessible. Evidently hierarchs from all the Byzantine provinces were wont to come to Constantinople and often without permission from the patriarch. Thus both Alexius I and Manuel I decreed that all such bishops and metropolitans were to stay in their dioceses and to leave Constantinople.[375] But all the Anatolian churchmen were exempt from this prohibition, notes Balsamon in commenting on the relevant canon, seventeen, of Sardica.

Thus let it be noted, that the Anatolian bishops who do not have seats because their churches are held by foreigners are not to be ejected from the queen of cities.[376]

In Constantinople they received support until they or their successors were able to go on to Anatolia.[377] The presence of a disproportionately large number of Anatolian metropolitans at the meetings of the patriarchal synod in Constantinople is due to the fact that so many of them were unable to get to their churches.[378] A bishop or metropolitan who was σχολάζων, that is, without his church because of the Turkish occupation, did not necessarily remain in Constantinople. There were occasions when it was possible for a metropolitan who was not able to enter his church in Turkish territory to be permitted to take up residence in one of his bishoprics that was in Byzantine territory.

It seems to me that if such a metropolitan wishes to migrate to one of his bishoprics because the foreigners occupy his original church, he must be appointed there by imperial prostaxis and synodal decision. This happened with the metropolitan of Neocaesareia, having instead of his seat his bishopric of Oenoe, and with the

---

[374] *Ibid.*, II, 390–391; III, 245–246. If a bishop is unable to go to a bishopric because the vacant bishopric is held by the foreigners, his ordination shall be delayed. Rhalles and Potles, II, 275: εἰ δέ, φασί, διά τινα περίστασιν ἀπαραίτητον κωλύεται ἡ τοῦ ἐπισκόπου προχείρισις, (τυχὸν γὰρ ἡ χηρεύουσα πόλις ἐπισκόπου ὑπὸ ἐθνῶν ἑάλω, καὶ οὐκ ἔστι ῥᾷον ἀπελθεῖν ἐκεῖσέ τινα), πάντως ὑπερτεθείη καὶ ἡ χειροτονία."

[375] *Ibid.*, I, 149–153; II, 157.

[376] *Ibid.*, III, 274–275; "Ὥστε σημείωσαι, ὅτι οὐκ ὀφείλουσιν ἀπὸ τῆς βασιλευούσης τῶν πόλεων ἐκβάλλεσθαι οἱ ἀνατολικοὶ ἐπίσκοποι οἱ μὴ ἔχοντες καθίσματα, ὡς τῶν ἐκκλησιῶν αὐτῶν κατεχομένων παρὰ τῶν ἐθνῶν·"

[377] *Ibid.*, II, 157; III, 245–246. Zepos, *J.G.R.*, I, 361.

[378] Grumel, *Regestes*, I, iii, *passim*.

metropolitan of Pisidian Antioch who received Sozopolis as a seat. And [it happened] with many others.[379]

But transferral (μετάθεσις) of clerics most often was not restricted to churches within the same metropolitan jurisdiction, for many of the Anatolian metropolitanates were completely within the Turkish dominion. The metropolitan of Ankara was transferred to Cerasus; Nicephorus, metropolitan of Gangra, as a σχολάζων received the metropolitanate of Amastris; the hierarch of Leontopolis, also σχολάζων, received Arcadiopolis.[380] The cleric Eustathius was elected by the Constantinopolitan synod as metropolitan of Myra, but before his actual ordination he was transferred to Thessalonike,[381] for Myra was in regions held by the Turks.[382] Balsamon implies that this condition applied throughout the districts of Helenopontus, Paphlagonia, and possibly also in Phrygia Capatiane and Second Cappadocia.[383] Doubtless the transferral of bishops and metropolitans was a widespread phenomenon in the eleventh and twelfth centuries.

In his remarks on the thirty-fourth of the Apostolic canons, Balsamon confirms that the bishops and metropolitans had largely abandoned the towns. "Because of the foreign invasions many cities remain bishopless."[384] The presence of so many vacant ecclesiastical seats (σχολάζουσαι, χηρεύουσαι) in Anatolia required adjustments in the operation of the hierarchy. One such rearrangement involved the joining of a vacant seat to one occupied by another hierarch.

[379] Rhalles and Potles, III, 486. This text illustrates very clearly the proposition that in the twelfth century the clergy were most frequently unable to take up their positions in churches within the domains of the Muslims. Pisidian Antioch was well within the limits of Turkish control, but Sozopolis was in Byzantine hands (though near the Turkish borders). So also Oenoe was in Byzantine hands, while across the border Neocaesareia was in the hands of the enemy. Balsamon relates that many other clerics had to flee the churches in towns held by the Turks and took up residence across the borders in bishoprics on Byzantine territory.

[380] Ibid., V, 394.

[381] Ibid., 428–429.

[382] Ibid., II, 23–25. If a bishop was elected to a bishopric but was not able to go there because the occupation of the foreigners prevented him from so doing, his ordination was to be delayed. Thus Eustathius, elected to the church of Myra but unable to go there because of the Turkish occupation, was not ordained metropolitan of Myra. Evidently the throne of Thessalonike fell vacant and so he was transferred there.

[383] Ibid., I, 57. Balsamon is commenting on chapter 20 of Photius' Nomocanon concerning these regions. Chapter 20 of the Nomocanon reads: " 'Ο Ἑλενόποντος δύο ἔχει μητροπολίτας, ὡς ἡ κη΄. νεαρά· καὶ ἡ Παφλαγονία διαφόρους, ὡς ἡ κθ΄. νεαρά· καὶ ἡ Φρυγία Καπατιανή, καὶ ἡ β΄. Καππαδοκία. Οὔτε δὲ δύο πόλεων δύναταί τις εἶναι ἐπίσκοπος, ἐξήρηται ὁ Τομέως, αὐτὸς γὰρ καὶ τῶν λοιπῶν ἐκκλησιῶν Σκυθίας προνοεῖ· καὶ ἡ Λεοντόπολις Ἰσαυρίας ὑπὸ τὸν ἐπίσκοπόν ἐστι Ἰσαυροπόλεως, ὡς βιβ. α΄. τοῦ κώδικος τίτ. γ΄. διατ. λε΄. οὔτε δὲ ἡγούμενος γίνεται δύο μοναστηρίων, ὡς διάτ. λθ΄. τοῦ αὐτοῦ τίτλου." Balsamon's scholion is most significant: " 'Η κη΄. νεαρὰ κεῖται εἰς βιβλίον τῶν βασιλικῶν ς΄. τίτ. ιβ΄. κεφ. α΄. ἥτις ἐνταῦθα οὐκ ἐτέθη παρ' ἡμῶν διὰ τὸ μεγάλως ἀλλοιωθῆναι τὴν τῶν ἐν ταύτῃ δηλουμένων χωρῶν κατάστασιν ὑπὸ τῶν ἀθέων βαρβάρων, καὶ διὰ τοῦτο ἀπρακτῆσαι τὰ τῆς νεαρᾶς. Καὶ ἡ κθ΄. νεαρὰ ἐγράφη εἰς βιβλίον τῶν βασιλικῶν ς΄. τίτ. ιγ΄. κεφ. α΄. ἐνταῦθα δὲ οὐκ ἐτέθη διὰ τὴν αὐτὴν αἰτίαν."

[384] Ibid., II, 46, ". . . πολλαὶ πόλεις διὰ τὴν τῶν ἐθνῶν ἐπιδρομὴν ἀνεπισκόπητοι. . ."

It has been permitted, it would seem, by the present canon [second canon of the second ecumenical council of Constantinople] . . . that there be joined to some churches other churches held by the foreigners. Presently the synod in Constantinople gave to the metropolitan of Nazianzus the church of Ankara, and to various other metropolitans other such churches.[385]

Again the language of Balsamon implies that this was a common phenomenon. It is probable that the metropolitans were not able to call their synods of bishops frequently, a situation the eighth canon of the council in Trullo foresaw, and which decreed that in case of barbarian invasions the metropolitan need call only one synod per year.[386] But there must have been many instances when even the modest demands of this canon could not be met.

The church in Asia Minor must have suffered the loss of much of its properties and revenues as a result of the Turkish occupation. This assumption is based on a very limited number of contemporary references to the loss of ecclesiastical possessions. But the reliability of these few references is in a sense strengthened by two considerations. First is the fact that when ecclesiastical documents begin to appear in significant numbers in the fourteenth century, the pattern of Turkish confiscation of church property is very clearly discernible. This by itself, of course, does not prove that the phenomenon occurred earlier, but it does strengthen the probability of such an assumption, and it is entirely consistent with the few scattered references to this phenomenon in the eleventh and twelfth centuries. Second, one must assume that the Turks on frequent occasions appropriated church property, as they had conquered much of Anatolia, by the sword. This too appears in the documentation of the fourteenth century.

In his *prostaxis* of 1094, Alexius Comnenus had remarked that hierarchs appointed to Anatolian churches had been reluctant to accept such appointments.

They fear that as such churches are located in the Anatolian regions they [the appointees] shall never have the necessities, for the churches to which they have been appointed are altogether poor and entirely inaccessible to them.[387]

In 1173 Michael the metropolitan of Ankara petitioned the synod in Constantinople to transfer him to the metropolitanate of Cerasus in Byzantine territory. The reasons that he gave to the synod are interesting indeed.

Il ait hérité du siège d'Ancyre, il est destitué de tout moyen de vivre, du fait que les Perses (Turcs) occupent depuis longtemps cette metropole.[388]

---

[385] *Ibid*, 172.

[386] *Ibid.*, 324.

[387] Zepos, *J.G.R.*, I, 326. Rhalles and Potles, II, 390–391.

[388] Grumel, *Regestes*, I, iii, 156: "Léon metropolite d'Amasée (XII siècle)," *Études Byzantines*, III (1945), 168. On the text edited by Msgr. Athenagoras, 'Ορθοδοξία, V (1930), 543–545, see the remarks of Grumel. There is some difficulty as to whether

A further reflection of the church's poverty is the decision of the synod (between 1170 and 1178)[389] justifying the transferral of bishops and the grants of *epidosis* on the basis of penury. Bishops who are in possession of impoverished churches may, with the assent of their ecclesiastical superior, be transferred to another bishopric. A bishop in economic difficulties may receive from his metropolitan certain rights over a second bishopric. This grant is an *epidosis*, which empowers the bishop to enjoy all episcopal rights over the second bishopric save that of sitting in the synthronon of the sanctuary. In other words when there are two poor bishoprics within a metropolitan jurisdiction, the metropolitan may unite these temporarily under one bishop (provided that one of the seats is vacant), thus attempting to make one stable economic unit out of two destitute bishoprics.[390]

One must conclude, then, that the loss of church property to the conquerors, which was so clearly discernible a phenomenon throughout the fourteenth century, was equally important in the eleventh and twelfth centuries. Though one cannot assume that this amounted to a general and complete confiscation, nevertheless it was so serious that many churches could no longer support their hierarchs.[391] This pauperization of the church was a great blow to the social fabric of Byzantine life in Anatolia, for the church provided most of the charitable and educational services for the Christians. In addition, the inability of the metropolitans and bishops to sit in their churches regularly, either because of poverty or because of Turkish interference, meant that the Christian communities were often deprived of their Christian leadership.

What was the reaction in Constantinople to the upsetting of the ecclesiastical structure in Asia Minor arising from the new realities imposed by the Turkish conquest? Mention has already been made of the appearance of epidosis as well as the formal transferral (*metathesis*) of bishops to other churches. The continual appearance in the eleventh and

---

Michael ever went to Ankara; "Car le dit prelat ni n'a été intronisé dans la metropole d'Ancyre, ni n'y a eu dans les offices proclamation de son nom, puisque aucun chrétien, dit-on, ne s'y trouve."

[389] The chronological attribution is that of Grumel, *Regestes*, I, iii, 168.

[390] Rhalles and Potles, III, 223, comments that bishops are not to be appointed where circumstances do not warrant it, especially when there is insufficient income, because ". . . οὐκ ἔσται πρὸς τιμὴν τοῦ θεοῦ τὸ πεζῇ βαδίζειν ἀρχιερέα διὰ πενίαν καὶ στερεῖσθαι τῶν ἀναγκαίων." And he comments specifically that this applies to the churches of Asia Minor.

[391] In contrast to the churches within Turkish domains, the churches in Byzantine territory were rebuilt and the monastic communities flourished throughout the twelfth and thirteenth centuries. Miklosich et Müller, I and II, *passim*. Pachymeres, II, 642–650 on impoverization of the church. For tax immunities given by the Byzantine government to clergy and monasteries, Zepos, *J.G.R.*, I, 366, 427. It was because of this that Manuel I dispensed land and privileges to the church, Svoronos, "Les privilèges de l'Église à l'époque des Comnènes: un rescrit inédit de Manuel Ier Comnène," *Travaux et Mémoires*, I (Paris, 1965), 325–392.

twelfth centuries of clergymen as official holders of Anatolian metropolitanates and bishoprics regardless of whether or not they could effectively administer these churches indicates that there was no general abandoning of these churches in the official administrative literature of the church. Some scholars have characterized this as merely a manifestation of the church's fossilized archaism and its conservative attachment to forms of the past. The continuity of metropolitanates and bishoprics in the official literature, however, was due to something more than archaistic ecclesiastical practice and sentiment. The maintenance of the metropolitan skeletal structure as nearly intact as possible, even if the holder of the church had to sit idle most of the time in Constantinople, was a primary concern of the emperors. This is evident in the religious legislation of both Alexius I Comnenus and Manuel Comnenus. Alexius ruled that all these Anatolian positions should continue to be filled, regardless of the impossibility of the physical appearance of the clerics in Anatolia.[392] Manuel also ruled that the appointment of the Anatolian clerics should continue in spite of the fact that the Muslims did not permit them to enter their churches.[393] Manuel decreed this "so that the recovery of the Christians in these churches might not be forbidden."[394] It is interesting that during his reign Manuel finally obtained consent from the Turks that many of these clerics should be permitted to return to their churches.[395] Thus the emperors made strenuous efforts to maintain the episcopal structure, and they did so for very good reasons. Given the central importance of religion in the society of that time, the hierarchical structure served as an important element of Byzantine administration and of Byzantine influence. In addition, the bishops and metropolitans were indispensable to the organized life of the Christian communities. It was they who maintained Christian discipline and the faith among the communities, not to mention their importance in education and charity. Thus their presence in Anatolia was of extreme importance to the emperors.

Behold! the souls of the Orthodox are in danger, especially of the more simple minded. The head of the Orthodox is the holy clergy. So long as the priesthood is in a sound state, its whole body and members are worthily directed. But if on the other hand this [clergy] falls ill, the whole body is disposed to complete destruction. Behold, accordingly, Christianity is endangered as the ecclesiastical situation declines daily; God is angry and the depraved, evil daemon, who continually envies the good, rejoices .... What excuse shall we emperors and arch-priests make on the day of judgment to God the demiourge and creator, if in receiving Christian people we hand them over to satan?[396]

[392] Zepos, *J.G.R.*, I, 325, 326.
[393] Rhalles and Potles, III, 246.
[394] *Ibid.*, 246, "ὡς μηδὲ ἀπαγορεύων τὴν εἰς ταύτας ἀποκατάστασιν τῶν χριστιανῶν."
[395] Euthymius Tornices Papadopoulos-Kerameus, pp. 182–183. This is perhaps to be dated between 1162 (date of Kïlïdj Arslan's stay in Constantinople) and 1176 (battle of Myriocephalum).
[396] Zepos, *J.G.R.*, I, 351–352.

Accordingly it is the duty of the Christian emperor and priests to care for the souls of the Christians. It is exactly for this reason that Alexius' grandson Manuel ordered that the clergy were to take their places in Asia Minor whenever circumstances permitted. The clergy were to preside over the "recovery of the Christians."[397]

The emperors insisted upon the maintenance of the elaborate administrative structure of the church in Anatolia in spite of the fact that it was anachronistic for certain areas of Anatolia (as for instance in Ankara where few Christians remained by the late twelfth century). The church, or at least the metropolitans, bishops, and even the canon lawyers, seems to have preferred to reform the ecclesiastical institution in conformity with a more conservative reality. Canon law specifically prescribed that bishops were to be ordained only in towns, and that no village was entitled to a bishop.[398] Thus Balsamon relates that this canon was being applied in Anatolia during his own day.

It dishonors both God and the episcopate to appoint a bishop over a few people, as a result of which it [episcopate] becomes contemptible.[399] Much less is it to the honor of God for a hierarch to walk on foot because of penury and deprivation of the necessities. As a result the appointment of bishops to Anatolian churches in which are found altogether moderate numbers of Christians, is not sound. Today those officials appointed by the bishops are *periodeutai*. These go about and watch over the mistakes of the soul and put the faithful in order.[400]

Balsamon acknowledges that the official episcopal structure has been affected and where the numbers of Christians are few, the bishops have been replaced by the *periodeutai* (itinerants). This was the customary practice of the church which, it is therefore evident, did attempt to adjust to the Anatolian realities. The principle was further elaborated and refined by Balsamon in his comments on the sixth canon of Sardica which states that bishops are not to be appointed to villages or in very small towns. The commentator reiterates that the basis for assigning a bishop or creating a bishopric is τὸ πολυάνθρωπον, the density of population, and not old tradition that formerly entitled it to possess a bishop.

[397] The same sentiment is expressed in the more copious literature of the fourteenth century.

[398] Canon 57 of the synod of Laodiceia, Rhalles and Potles, III, 222. " Ὅτι οὐ δεῖ ἐν ταῖς κώμαις καὶ ἐν ταῖς χώραις καθίστασθαι ἐπισκόπους, ἀλλὰ περιοδευτάς." Canon 6 of the synod of Sardice, *ibid.*, III, 243: " μὴ ἐξεῖναι δὲ ἁπλῶς καθιστᾶν ἐπίσκοπον ἐν κώμῃ τινὶ ἢ βραχείᾳ πόλει, ἢ τινι καὶ εἷς μόνος πρεσβύτερος ἐπαρκεῖ· οὐκ ἀναγκαῖον γὰρ ἐπισκόπους ἐκεῖσε καθίστασθαι, ἵνα μὴ κατευτελίζηται τὸ τοῦ ἐπισκόπου ὄνομα καὶ ἡ αὐθεντία."

[399] Density of population is the principal and only criterion for establishing a bishopric and for maintaining it. Rhalles and Potles, III, 246: " εἰπόν τινες, μὴ ὀφείλειν τοῦτο γενέσθαι εἰς εὐτελεῖς πάντη κώμας ἢ πόλεις, διὰ τὸ προψηφίζεσθαι εἰς ταύτας ἀρχιερεῖς ὅταν ἦσαν ὑπὸ λαοῦ εὐθυνόμεναι, ἀλλὰ τὴν αἰτίαν τῆς προβλήσεως τοῦ ἀρχιερέως εἶναι τὸ πολυάνθρωπον τῆς χώρας, οὐχὶ τὸ παλαιὸν προνόμιον."

[400] Rhalles and Potles, III, 223. On the periodeutai or itinerants, H-G. Beck, *Kirche und theologische Literatur*, pp. 103 ff.

And they added the remark that a bishop was not to be appointed to a city which had declined from populous to a state of depopulation because of foreign invasions, or for some other turn of events; but (bishops are to be appointed) only in the populous cities, even if formerly they had not bishops. Moreover, our god-crowned, mighty and holy emperor was frequently asked if it was necessary to appoint [bishops] to those churches in Anatolia which were held by the Agarenes. He declared that they should be appointed to them and he bestowed by public ordinance, upon those who would be appointed, *solemnia* [gifts] for the necessities of life, until they should depart for their churches. But he did not in any manner consent that bishops be appointed to small villages, but rather he was angered with those so ordained.[401]

Balsamon seems to indicate that the ecclesiastical structure was in a state of flux and that though the emperor insisted upon the appointment of bishops to Anatolian towns, they were not to be appointed to villages or to towns that had declined as a result of the invasions. This reflects on both the decline of urban centers and the slow retrenchment of the structure of bishoprics. This, then, was the solution of the emperors. The episcopal structure was to continue in those towns where Christians still remained. Even if they were small in number, such towns were to receive bishops. But if the town has been reduced to negligible size, then bishops were no longer to be appointed as it amounted to dishonoring God. In the towns that had declined because of the Turkish invasions, the itinerants or περιοδευταί were to replace the bishops.

Of importance in any attempt to describe such a change as had occurred in Anatolia during the eleventh and twelfth centuries is the treatment of the conquered by the conquerors, and also the attitudes of the Christian subjects toward their Muslim rulers. Did the Christians, who possibly constituted a majority of the population in the Turkish-held lands, welcome the Turks, and was their status more or less favorable than it had been under Byzantium?

One theory holds that the Christians largely welcomed the Turks. The adherents of this particular school maintain that the Turks were welcomed first of all because Byzantine taxation in Anatolia was oppressive.[402] The population, they continue, had remained largely unhellenized, and so the Anatolian soil was the habitat of tribes "belonging" to the Hetites, Thracians, and Christian Turks.[403] All these peoples, because they had preserved their linguistic and cultural identity and because of Byzantine taxation, welcomed the Turks and aided in the conquest.[404] In support of this theory, its adherents had been able to bring to bear some sources that undeniably attest to the magnanimity of individual Turkish princes and sultans toward the Christians. The generosity of Alp

---

[401] Rhalles and Potles, III, 246–247. Ducange quotes Sudas in defining σολέμνια. " ἡ παρὰ βασιλέως ἀναφαίρετος δωρεὰ διδομένη ταῖς ἐκκλησίαις."

[402] Yinanc, *Fethi*, p. 174.

[403] *Ibid.*, pp. 162–164.

[404] Ramsay, *Phrygia*, I, 301.

Arslan toward Romanus IV is unanimously attested not only by the Muslim historians but by the Christian historians as well. Michael the Syrian and Matthew of Edessa both praise Muslim rulers who intervened on behalf of the Christians. Sulayman treated Antioch kindly; Malik Shah granted certain exemptions to the Armenian church; the emir Ismail, governor of Armenia, made efforts to heal the ravages perpetrated upon Armenia; the Arab Sharif al-Dawla did everything he could to protect the Christians in his kingdom; Malik Danishmend seems to have displayed considerable concern for the Christians of Melitene and of other regions in his principality; both Danishmend and Kïlïdj Arslan were mourned at their deaths by the Christians who felt that they had lost their protectors.[405] This theory, maintaining that the Christian attitude was favorable to the Turks, seems to receive further confirmation from the fact that Christians often participated in and cooperated with the Turkish conquest. Tzachas could never have built his fleet and sailed the Aegean without the aid of the anonymous Smyrniote who undertook the construction of the ships. The naval arsenal temporarily erected at Cius under the orders of Abu'l-Kasim must also have been the work of local Christians. Philaretus courted Turkish aid and approval, going so far as to apostatize in order to preserve his possessions. Reference has already been made to the presence of Christian, especially Armenian, contingents in the Turkish armies. In addition to these there were present bodies of Paulician soldiery in the armies opposing the Crusaders. There must have been numerous other incidents of such Christian participation in the Turkish conquest which have gone unrecorded.[406]

Thus the participation of a portion of the Anatolian Christians in the Turkish conquests is evident. Equally evident is the fact that a number of Muslim sultans and governors were considerate to the Christians and as a result Christian opinion was favorable to these individuals. But it is a gross exaggeration to maintain, as some have, that the entire Anatolian population, or even the majority of it, rejoiced, acquiesced, and joined in the Turkish conquest. The Greek, Armenian, and Georgian populations (and it is fantastic to speak of Hetites, Thracians, and other ancient ethnic entities long extinct) seem to have disliked and feared their Turkmen conquerors.[407] The Syrian Christians about Melitene were not as ill

---

[405] Matthew of Edessa, pp. 188, 190, 196, 201, 204, 207, 256.

[406] Anna Comnena, II, 110, 69. Matthew of Edessa, p. 195. *Gesta Francorum*, pp. 102–103. It is a pronounced theme in the Danishmendname.

[407] Islamic society itself had considerable dislike for the Turkmens, and Nizam al-Mulk devoted a short chapter to this subject in his book on government. *The Book of Government or Rules for Kings*, trans. H. Darke (London, 1960), p. 105; "Although there has arisen a certain amount of aversion to the Turkmens, and they are very numerous, still they have a longstanding claim upon the dynasty, because at its inception they served well and suffered much, and also they are attached by ties of kinship. So it is fitting that about a thousand of their sons should be enrolled and maintained in the same way as pages of the palace. When they are in continuous employment they will learn the use of arms and become trained in service. Then they will settle down with other people and with growing devotion

disposed to the Turks for the reason that they had received ill-treatment at the hands of both Armenians and Greeks. But the pages of Michael the Syrian and Bar Hebraeus, as well as the history of Melitene up to its conquest by the benevolent Kïlïdj II Arslan, indicate that they, too, frequently found Turkish rule not to their liking.

An examination of the contemporary accounts of the conditions of the Christians in Anatolia will reveal that more frequently than not the disadvantages of Turkish rule far outweighed the advantages. There is mention of general oppression of the Christian Anatolians in various parts throughout the peninsula. They were largely, though not completely, excluded from government and the armies, in both of which the Anatolians had been complete masters under the Byzantine administration.[408] Their children were taken away and converted on occasion.[409] Churches were plundered, devastated,[410] and frequently used as mosques.[411] The pillaging, enslavement, and massacre that the Turkmen raids brought would have been unwelcome to sedentary society anywhere. It was just because of all this that Christian authors saw fit to praise those individual Turkish sultans and officials who made efforts to protect the inhabitants of Anatolia

---

serve as pages, and the dislike which is generally felt for them on account of their nature will disappear." A. Lambton, *Landlord and Peasant in Persia; A Story of Land Tenure and Land Revenues Administration* (London-New York, 1953), p. 56. See V. Barthold, *Turkestan down to the Mongol Invasion* (London, 1928), pp. 309–310, for a commentary on the above and also on the difficulties that the Turkmens caused in sedentary Islamic society. Also the *Qabus Nama*, trans. Levy, p. 103; "Without any doubt, what is fine in the Turks is present in a superlative degree, but so also is what is ugly in them. Their faults in general are that they are blunt-witted, ignorant, boastful, turbulent, discontented and without a sense of justice. Without any excuse they will create trouble and utter foul language, and at night they are poor-hearted. Their merit is that they are brave, free from pretence, open in enmity and zealous in any task allotted them. For the [domestic] establishment there is no better race." Also Hudud al-Alam-Minorsky, p. 100. The Muslim urban society of the Anatolia frequently expressed a dislike for and aversion to the Turkmen nomads. C. Cahen in von Gruenbaum, *Unity and Variety in Muslim Civilization* (Chicago-London, 1955), p. 330, on use of the word "Turk" for the barbarous and unbearable Turkmen frontier population. Aksaray-Gençosman, p. 342, says of them that they are "bloodthirsty, dogs, hungry for booty, but that they immediately flee upon the appearance of a strong foe." Ibn Bibi-Duda, p. 308. Togan, *Umumi Türk tarihine giriş* (Istanbul, 1946), p. 205.

[408] William of Tyre, III, xix; IV, i; V, xi. J. Laurent, "Des Grecs aux Croisés," *Byzantion*, I (1924), 443.

[409] William of Tyre, IV, iv. *Gesta Francorum*, pp. 54–55.

[410] William of Tyre, VI, xxiii; trans. E. A. Babcock and A. C. Krey, I, 296, remarks on the state of the churches in Antioch when the Crusaders entered. "The sacriligious race of Turks had desecrated the venerable places; they had driven out the ministers of divine worship and put the churches to profane uses. Some of the sacred edifices had been used as stables for horses and other beasts of burden, and in other pursuits unbefitting the sanctuary. . . . The pictures of the revered saints had been erased from the very walls—symbols which supplied the place of books and reading to the humble worshippers of God and aroused devotion in the minds of the simple people, so praiseworthy for their devout piety. On these the Turks had spent their rage as if on living persons; they had gouged out eyes, mutilated noses, and daubed the pictures with mud and filth. They had thrown down the altars and defiled the sanctuary of God with their impious acts." On the destruction of churches see also, Miklosich et Müller, VI, 87. Theodore Scutariotes-Sathas, 169. See above nn. 338–361.

[411] Danishmendname-Melikoff, *passim*. Ibn Bibi-Duda, p. 68.

from the violence of the Turkmens. Indeed one must be careful to distinguish between the acts of benevolent rulers and the deeds of their Muslim subjects. As was previously mentioned, the Arab Sharif al-Dawla was praised for protecting the Christians of his domains, but he accomplished this by punishing his own Muslim subjects.[412] Similarly Kīlīdj I Arslan, who is lauded for his kindness to Christians,[413] was succeeded in Melitene by the Turk Il Arslan (early twelfth century); the latter oppressed the inhabitants of the city with financial exactions and thus reversed the policy of his predecessor.[414] Even the matter of religious toleration has been somewhat exaggerated, for though the sultans seem to have been, on the whole, religiously tolerant, often this tolerance was not shared by all the Muslim subjects of the sultans and forced conversions and martyrdoms were not unknown. When Malik Shah granted the Armenian patriarch Basil diplomas of immunity for the Armenian church from Turkish exactions in 1090–91, it was because Basil had protested against the violence and heavy exactions of the Turks in these areas during the preceding twenty years.[415] After the deaths of Malik Shah and Ismail, however, the former vexations once more reappeared and eventually the Armenian catholicus was constrained to flee to the Armenian princes of Cilicia.[416] It is clear that the very authors who praise Malik Shah and others as the clement protectors of the Christians make it quite obvious that the element against which the sultans had to protect the Christians was the Muslims themselves.

It is also evident that, in this period at least, the Christians continued to suffer at the hands of the conquerors in spite of the isolated measures of Malik Shah, Kīlīdj Arslan, and Malik Danishmend. The great hardship brought upon the Christian churches of Anatolia has already been described above.[417] Certainly many of the Orthodox (Chalcedonian) churches no longer enjoyed the comparative prosperity and peace they had known under Byzantine authority.[418]

Given the nature of the Turkish conquest and rule during this period (eleventh and twelfth centuries) one would not expect the Christians to be well disposed to the Turks as a whole, though one should be careful to

---

[412] Matthew of Edessa, p. 190.

[413] Ibid., p. 290.

[414] Michael the Syrian, III, 194.

[415] Matthew of Edessa, p. 201. The same happened in Georgia, Brosset, Géorgie, I, 348–349.

[416] Matthew of Edessa, pp. 204, 207. Michael the Syrian, III, 188.

[417] Zepos, J.G.R., I, pp. 325–326, "ἅτε τῶν μὲν ἐν αἷς ἐπεψηφίσθησαν ἐκκλησιῶν πάντη τυγχανουσῶν ἀπόρων καὶ ἀπροσβάτων αὐτοῖς παντελῶς ... τῶν ψηφισθεισῶν αὐτοῖς ἐκκλησιῶν ὡς εἴρηται ἀβάτων οὐσῶν τούτοις ὡς ὑπὸ τῶν ἐχθίστων κατεχομένων ἐχθρῶν." Dölger, Regesten, II, no. 1172.

[418] The religious difficulties between Byzantines and Armenians had resulted in situations that were at times unfelicitous for these churches in eastern Anatolia. But conditions were not as oppressive as they became during the late eleventh and the twelfth centuries, during the Turkish invasions and occupations. Thus by contrast, Syrian monastic life flourished in Byzantine Anatolia, Michael the Syrian, III, 124 ff., 135, 145 ff.

distinguish between the rulers and sedentary Muslim society on the one hand, and the Turkmens on the other. There were exceptions, of course, and there were also the facts of reality. The Turks were military and political masters and one simply had to make the best of it. But by and large the Christians were not completely satisfied with their new rulers, a fact illuminated by the events of the late eleventh and the twelfth century. The march of the Crusaders across the whole length of Anatolia and the Byzantine reconquest of western Anatolia and of the northern and southern littorals would have been impossible had the populations favored the Turks. Both Latins and Byzantines were aided by a population that had suffered from the Turks. When the Crusaders passed through Anatolia they were aided and received by Christians at almost every step. The Christians about Konya gave them intelligence on the areas to the east;[419] the Greeks and Armenians of Tarsus were glad to be rid of the Turks and welcomed the westerners into the city,[420] as did the inhabitants of other towns. Plastentza, which had just repulsed a Turkish siege, voluntarily opened its gates to receive the Latins.[421] Similarly the inhabitants of Coxon and Marash were relieved to see the Christian armies, as it meant a respite from the Turks.[422] The situation at Antioch at this time is of particular interest. Because of the large Christian population in the city and because of its animosity toward the Turks, the latter began to fear that the inhabitants could not be trusted with the Crusading armies on the other side of the walls. The Turks planned, therefore, to massacre the Christians in order to be safe from their treachery. But as they did not do so quickly enough, a Christian of Antioch betrayed the city to the Crusaders.[423] After the fall of the city, the local Christians helped the Crusaders to seek out and slay the Muslims within Antioch, and the Turkish emir Yagh Siyan was recognized and slain by the Armenians as he fled.[424] Previous to the fall of the city, the neighboring Armenians and Syrians set ambushes for relieving Turkish forces and did so again when the Turks fled Antioch.[425]

In the west of Anatolia, Alexius received the sympathy of much of the local population as he drove the Turks out. He too benefited from the intelligence activities of the population[426] and when Ducas' army appeared, the citizens of Laodiceia opened the gates of the town and came out to greet him. As Alexius retreated from Philomelium in 1098, many of the

[419] *Gesta Francorum*, pp. 56–57.

[420] *Ibid.*, pp. 58–59.

[421] *Ibid.*, pp. 60–61.

[422] *Ibid.*, pp. 62–65. William of Tyre, IV, i. It is true, however, that the Christians of Anatolia also suffered from the Crusaders on occasion, as witness the massacre of Greeks by the Crusaders of 1101 in northern Anatolia. Anna Comnena, III, 19–22.

[423] William of Tyre, V, xi. Anna Comnena, III, 19–22.

[424] William of Tyre, V, xxii–xxiii.

[425] *Gesta Francorum*, pp. 86–87, 156–159.

[426] Anna Comnena, II, 68. A Greek inhabitant of the regions of Nicaea came to warn Taticius of the approach of the army of Burzuk.

Greek inhabitants of the region left their homes, preferring to relocate within imperial territory.[427] During the course of his last campaign in the regions, the Greek inhabitants of the villages about Cedrea and of the regions about Konya voluntarily abandoned their homes and preferred to follow Alexius to safer habitations within the Byzantine state.[428] The general migration and flight of portions of the population before the progress of the invaders further emphasizes this point. The sentiments of a significant portion of the Christian population, even in eastern Anatolia, were well disposed to Byzantium and so the Christians were suspect in the eyes of the Turks.

When the emperor [John II Comnenus] began to attack Neocaesareia, the fury of the Turks against the Christians was increased in all the lands which they held. Whosoever mentioned the name of the emperor, even by accident, encountered the sword, and his children and house where taken. In this manner many perished in Melitene and in other lands, up until the emperor suddenly departed.[429]

It is sufficiently clear that a large portion of the Christians in Anatolia during the century after the battle of Manzikert saw a definite worsening of their conditions. As the Turkish conquest caused this upheaval, one would not expect to see the Christians favorably disposed to the conquerors. So when Christian armies appeared once more in Anatolia, the inhabitants often took the opportunity to express their dissatisfaction with Turkish rule. Indeed the hostility of Christians and Muslims in Anatolia is clear in the events of the thirteenth century when the Anatolina Christians sided with the Mongols (before their conversion to Islam), and often the Muslims sympathized with the Egyptian Mamelukes. It was for this reason that in 1277 Baybars massacred the Christians of Caesareia but not the Muslims. The same polarity of religious tension is observable during Timur's invasion of Asia Minor.[430] But as time passed and the possibilities of Byzantine reconquest faded, some of the Christian populations began to find a place for themselves in the new arrangement. Thus the Greeks of the islands in the lake of Pousgouse resisted the armies of John Comnenus. The Greeks of Tantalus and Caria who had been resettled about Philomelium-Akshehir were very happy in the Seljuk domains. Though they had been taken away from their original homes by force, the

---

[427] *Ibid.*, III, 29.

[428] *Ibid.*, 203; " Συνείποντο δὲ τούτοις αὐθαιρέτως καὶ οἱ αὐτόχθονες τῶν τοιούτων χωρῶν Ῥωμαῖοι φεύγοντες τὰς τῶν βαρβάρων χείρας, γυναῖκές τε ὁμοῦ μετὰ τῶν νεογνῶν καὶ ἄνδρες αὐτοὶ καὶ παῖδες."

[429] Michael the Syrian, III, 249.

[430] The infidelity of Christians and newly converted Muslims is a very frequent theme in the Danishmendname. See also the taunt of the Turks to the Greek cities on the approach of the Crusaders. They spread the false information that they had destroyed the Christian army and that therefore the Greeks could never hope to see Christian armies before their walls again, *Gesta Francorum*, p. 55. See Spuler, *Die Mongolen in Iran*, 2d ed. (Berlin, 1955), pp. 204–224, on this Muslim-Christian hatred in Anatolia during the strife between Mamelukes and Mongols.

generosity of the sultan in giving them lands and a five-year tax immunity contrasted so sharply with the anarchy enveloping Byzantine Anatolia in the late twelfth century that the Greeks were content to remain in their new homes.

Recolonization and Reconstruction

It is true that the war between Muslim and Christian did not cease in Anatolia during the thirteenth century, but the situation had by that time become much more stabilized. Commerce and agriculture again attained a satisfactory level of prosperity as merchants, craftsmen, and farmers found conditions favorable both in the Seljuk state of Konya and the Christian states of Nicaea, Trebizond, and Cilicia. But this stability did not come about abruptly and solely from the efforts of the Christian and Seljuk monarchs of the thirteenth century. The activities of these princes were extensive in the thirteenth century, but the process of recolonization and reconstruction of large areas of Anatolia had gone on throughout much of the twelfth century.

The course of reconstruction is more visible for western Anatolia prior to the thirteenth century as a result of the testimony of the Greek historians. When the Turks first appeared in Asia Minor during the eleventh century, the fortifications of many towns had long been neglected because they were no longer necessary. Accordingly, with the appearance of the new peril, the walls of Melitene were rebuilt during the reign of Constantine X Ducas (1059–67);[431] Romanus IV Diogenes rebuilt the fortifications of Sozopolis in 1069–70 when the Turks had begun to penetrate Phrygia,[432] and he did the same at Erzerum,[433] in the regions of the Halys River, and intended to rebuild the walls of Manzikert.[434] The anarchy and civil strife that followed Manzikert no doubt so absorbed the Byzantines that the strengthening of the fortifications in Anatolia were probably neglected. When Alexius I ascended the throne, and particularly after the reconquest of the Aegean and Mediterranean littoral regions, he inaugurated a policy of recolonization in Byzantine Anatolia which was to be continued by John II, Manuel I, and Isaac II. Because the empire was once more consumed by internal strife and institutional decay toward the end of the twelfth century, this reconstruction of Anatolia was neglected, and the Greek provinces lapsed into anarchy, the populace suffering from tax oppression, rebellions, and Turkish raids. The Lascarids, however, renewed the Comnenian policy and once more the provinces were relieved and experienced a revival of prosperity that lasted past the middle of the thirteenth century.

[431] Michael the Syrian, III, 165–166.
[432] M.A.M.A., IV, 57–58.
[433] Attaliates, 148. Scylitzes, II, 691.
[434] Attaliates, 153.

The first measures that Alexius undertook were for defense against further Turkish encroachment in Bithynia. He built the fortresses of Cibotus and Sidera in order to protect what pitifully little remained of Byzantine territory on the Sea of Marmara.[435] After the removal of the Turks from the Anatolian coasts, Alexius turned to the enormous task of once more raising the many towns that had been left in shambles. Adramyttium, Attaleia, and many of the coastal towns from Smyrna to Attaleia were rebuilt,[436] and the cities of Corycus and Seleuceia in Cilicia were also reconstructed.[437] Alexius' successor John girded Laodiceia with walls,[438] rebuilt Lopadium in the area of the Rhyndacus[439] and Achyraous farther to the south.[440] The tempo of rebuilding seems to have increased markedly with the appearance of the energetic Manuel.[441] In an effort to make Bithynia safe from the Turkish invaders, he rebuilt the towns and forts of Malagina (Melangeia), Pithecas, Pylae,[442] and Arcla-Damalis.[443] Farther south he fortified the regions of Pergamum-Chliara-Adramyttium,[444] and in Phrygia he reconstructed the towns of Dorylaeum and Choma-Soublaion.[445] Though Isaac Angelus did build the town of Angelocastrum,[446] this was an exception and the disintegration of the Byzantine administration in the last quarter of the twelfth century entailed the neglect of the Comnenian policies in Asia Minor.

The rebuilding of destroyed and deserted towns meant of course that the emperors had to resettle them with inhabitants. In many cases the inhabitants had disappeared, either completely or partly, as a result of the Turkish invasions. Towns such as Dorylaeum, Choma-Soublaion, Malagina, Pithecas, Adramyttium, and in fact the towns of the whole littoral of the Aegean from Smyrna to Attaleia had been largely abandoned by the Greeks, so Alexius and his successors had to bring in populations. In the case of the Aegean coast, Alexius was able to recall many of the original inhabitants and to resettle them in this area. Very often the Greek refugees from lands still in Turkish hands were utilized to repopulate these areas. Such were the large numbers of Greeks who fled

---

[435] Anna Comnena, II, 71, 205–206. Glycatzi-Ahrweiler, "Les fortresses construites en Asie Mineure face à l'invasion seldjucide," *Akten des XI. internationalen Byzantinistenkongresses München 1958* (Munich, 1960), pp. 182–189.

[436] Anna Comnena, III, 142–143.

[437] *Ibid.*, 45–46.

[438] Nicetas Choniates, 17. Theodore Scutariotes-Sathas, 190.

[439] Nicetas Choniates, 28. Cinnamus, 38.

[440] Nicetas Choniates, 44.

[441] Regel, I, 127. Cinnamus, 36, " . . . πλείους ἀνοικισαμένου πόλεις." Eustathius of Thessalonike, *P.G.*, CXXXV, 994; " ἀλλὰ νῦν ἡμῖν ἐπ' ἀσφαλοῦς αἱ πόλεις ἵδρυνται, ὅσαι μὲν κατέπεσον, ἀναστᾶσαι εἰς ἀριθμόν· ὅσαι δὲ φόβον εἶχον τοῦ πεσεῖν, ἐρεισθεῖσαι καὶ καταστᾶσαι εἰς ἀσφαλές· μυρίαι δὲ καὶ ἐκ καινῆς πυργωθεῖσαι, ὅπου καίριον."

[442] Nicetas Choniates, 71. Cinnamus, 36, 38, 63. Pylae was still a strong fortification in the thirteenth century. Nicholas Mesarites-Heisenberg, II, 39.

[443] Nicetas Choniates, 268.

[444] *Ibid.*, 194–195.

[445] *Ibid.*, 227–229. Cinnamus, 294–295, 297–298.

[446] Regel, II, 261.

the regions of Philomelium, Bourtzes, Iconium, and Neocaesareia.[447] Foreign groups were also employed: John settled a number of Serbs around Nicomedia as farmers and soldiers;[448] there were Armenians in the Troad;[449] the town of Pegae was inhabited by Latins.[450] By the thirteenth century there were Greeks from Crete,[451] Latins, and Cumans who were settled as soldiers and as holders of *pronoias*.[452] As important as the military settlers were the farmers, and the colonization of the Serbs about Nicomedia was in part motivated by the desire to bring the land under cultivation again so that taxes would be produced for the treasury. Manuel undertook an even more extensive colonization of the rural districts in the theme of Neocastron (Adramyttium-Pergamum-Chliara), as a result of which the deserted land was recolonized, cultivated, and produced handsome revenues for the treasury.[453] This recolonization, of course, extended into the ecclesiastical realm, as bishops and metropolitans once more returned to their churches in western Anatolia. The monastic communities of Mt. Latmus and of the Maeander district revived and by the twelfth and thirteenth centuries were once more flourishing centers of monastic life.[454] The care the Comnenoi lavished on the ecclesiastical establishment in Asia Minor has been described above.

The anarchy and rebellions that manifested themselves in the Byzantine Anatolian provinces during the last quarter of the twelfth and the early thirteenth century threatened to undo much of the Comnenian achievement in Anatolia. Nicetas Choniates remarks that on occasion these rebels ravaged the countryside even worse than the Turkmen raiders.[455] By contrast, the Greeks forcibly transplanted from Tantalus and Caria to the regions of Philomelium by the sultan were given such security that they preferred the Turkish rule to that of their own emperors. Indeed the situation around the Maeander had become unsafe because of the

[447] Anna Comnena, III, 29, 199–204. Zonaras, 757. Cinnamus, 21, 63.

[448] Nicetas Choniates, 23. Theodore Scutariotes-Sathas, 193.

[449] Nicetas Choniates, 795–796.

[450] Ansbert, p. 72. Theodore Scutariotes-Sathas, 431. It is impossible to say with certainty whether these two settlements were the result of the recolonization of the Comnenoi, but it would seem highly probable.

[451] Pachymeres, II, 209.

[452] On these pronoia, Ostrogorsky, *Pour l'histoire de la féodalité byzantine* (Brussels, 1954), pp. 40–41. Glykatzi-Ahrweiler, "La politique agraire des empereurs de Nicée," *Byzantion*, XXVIII (1958), 51–66; "Note additionnelle sur la politique agraire des empereurs de Nicée," *Byzantion*, XXVIII (1958), 135–136. Nicephorus Gregoras, I, 37.

[453] Nicetas Choniates, 194–195.

[454] Miklosich et Müller, IV, 323–325, 329. Pachymeres, I, 310–311; " ἄλλη γὰρ Παλαιστίνη ὁ χῶρος ὁ περὶ Μαίανδρον ἦν, οὐ βοσκημάτων καὶ μόνον αὐξῆσαι ἀγέλας καὶ ποίμνια, οὐδ' ἀνδρῶν φορὰν ἐνεγκεῖν ἀγαθός, ἀλλὰ καὶ μοναχῶν οὐρανοπολιτῶν ἐπιγείων συστῆσαι πληθύας ἄριστος, παρὰ τοσοῦτον ἐπ' ἄλλοις τὰ πρωτεῖα φέρων πρὸς Παλαιστίνην παρ' ὅσον ἑνὶ καὶ μεγίστῳ ἡττᾶτο, τῷ τὰς διατριβὰς ἐκεῖσε γενέσθαι τοῦ Χριστοῦ καὶ θεοῦ."

[455] Nicetas Choniates, 701. When Michael the tax collector of Mylassa rebelled with an army of Turkish troops, " τὰς Μαιανδρικὰς πόλεις πολυτρόπως ἐσίνετο, χείρων τῶν ἀλλοφύλων καὶ νηλεέστερος ἀνδροφόνος δεικνύμενος." Also *ibid.*, 549–553, 827.

empire's inability to keep out the Turkish raids or to restrain the rebels and financial oppressors.[456] The labor of the Comnenoi had been so effectively executed, however, that this quarter century of decline could not undo it. In fact the Lascarid revival in western Anatolia was possible precisely because the emperors had reconstructed a healthy society in western Asia Minor during the twelfth century. The Byzantine rulers, forced by political circumstances to flee to Anatolia, once more dedicated their energies and attentions to improving the conditions of urban and rural society in the western confines of the peninsula during much of the thirteenth century. This work, renewed by the Lascarids, once more reached an impressive climax in the reign of John Vatatzes as his eulogizers amply note.

Who shall enumerate all those things which he has provided in each city throughout the East and the western land, not only in those which are very great and famous but in those as well which by virtue of their smallness and obscurity are fittingly called fortresses and not cities. He acted in behalf of their care and safety, fortifying them with constructions; he built tower after tower, parapet after parapet, and erected wall after wall. In addition he stored away all sorts of weapons; bows, arrows, shields, armours, engines for hurling stones and as many other machines as there are for defence against attacking enemies. And in the big cities there were also salaried men, skilled in the [making] of the various weapons, who manufacture so many bows, arrows, and other weapons each year. These were stored in public buildings in great number in order that when there should be need of them the defenders would have them in plenty. And he set aside lands from which the produce should be collected and stored in granaries, or store-houses, by the thousands and tens of thousands of *medimnoi* not only of barley and wheat, but also of the other grains and necessities, saving them for a time of barrenness and need . . . . And there were to be seen entire buildings filled in this manner, with grain, wine, oil, and with the other necessities from the earth, and in addition the towers of the cities were heavy with wheat, barley, and millet. In Lydian Magnesia, where most of the merchandizes were stored, what might not one have sought of those things which men desire and having found it enjoyed it? Not only of those things which are to be found in our lands, but also of as many things (as are to be found) anywhere in the *oicumene*, in Egypt, I say, and India and elsewhere? And he brought together in the cities libraries of books of all the arts and sciences.[457]

---

[456] *Ibid.*, 657.

[457] Theodore Scutariotes-Sathas, 506–507. Pachymeres, I, 134. He fortified Tripolis and stocked it with grain and arms, Pachymeres, II, 433. Theodore Lascaris, N. Festa, *Theodori Ducae Lascaris epistulae* (Florence, 1898), pp. 107–108 (hereafter cited as Theodore Lascaris-Festa), speaks of the rebuilding of the walls of Pergamum in his day; " τὰς νῦν ἀνοικοδομάς . . . ἀνεγείρονται δὲ καὶ τείχη χαλκῶν οὐρανῶν ποικίλην ἔχοντα. ποταμὸς δὲ μέσον διέρχεται ἀψίδεσι προμηκεστέροις καταγεφυρούμενος." A. Heisenberg, "Kaiser Johannes Batatzes der Barmherzige. Eine mittelgriechische Legende," *B.Z.*, XIV (1905), 160–233. Theodore Lascaris mentions the presence of cylindrical towers on each side of the great theater. See further on the rebuilding of Theodore I Lascaris, Nicephorus Gregoras, I, 24, " πλείστας δ' ἀνώρθωσε πόλεις καλλίσταις οἰκοδομαῖς καὶ πολλοῖς ἀναλώμασιν· " Festa, "A propos d'une biographie de St. Jean le Miséricordieux," *V.V.*, XIII (1906), 1–35. Euthymius Malaces-Papadopoulos-Kerameus, pp. 106 ff. When Tralles was rebuilt in 1280 by Andronicus Palaeologus, an inscription was found during the actual work which indicated that it had been rebuilt on a previous occasion, possibly in the period of the Lascarids or of the Comnenoi, Pachymeres, I,

The tax system was once more applied in a just manner, the land was freed from the raids of the enemy, and the provinces prospered. Not only did the produce of the soil and industry increase, but the raising of livestock—horses, cattle, sheep, and camels—thrived. By the end of the reign of Vatatzes, Christian society had so recovered that the emperor was able to extend his generosity from the cities, monasteries, and churches of his own domains to the churches in Constantinople, Mt. Athos, Athens, Thessalonike, Sinai, Jerusalem, Antioch, and Alexandria.[458] The Lascarids continued the policy of recolonization which the Comnenoi had commenced, bringing in new populations from the Balkans and the islands.

A recent archaeological survey of the fortifications in the regions between Ephesus and Miletus confirms the evidence of the texts for this building activity in the period of the Comnenoi and Lascarids. Not only were the towns girded with new fortifications as a result of the Turkish invasions, but close networks of small defense outposts protected the roads connecting the towns.[459] The town of Miletus and the Miletus-Mylasa road were fortified first in the early Comnenian period, a second time in the late twelfth century, and again in the period of the Lascarids.[460] Priene and the regions of Mt. Mycale were similarly strengthened in the early Comnenian era and again under the Lascarids.[461] The coastal regions of Anaia and Ephesus were also fortified.[462] One may assume that an archaeological survey of other western Anatolian regions would bring similar results inasmuch as the texts indicate that the emperors were actively rebuilding and refortifying throughout their domains. This archaeological evidence is important proof not only of imperial activity but also of the danger and disruption that the Turkish invasions threatened.

The Seljuks and Danishmendids began similarly to rebuild and to recolonize their domains. But the height of Seljuk activity came only with the beginning of the thirteenth century, when it seems to burst forth brilliantly. In the earlier period building activity in Muslim Asia Minor seems to have been more extensive in the eastern section. Malik Danishmend is said to have rebuilt Sebasteia soon after he conquered it,[463]

469–470. Though the sources are fragmentary, there is no doubt that cities such as Nicaea, Nicomedia, Prusa, etc., all were embellished. On the rebuilding of the walls of Smyrna see the hexametric inscriptions. Grégoire, *Recueil des inscriptions grecques chrétiennes d'Asie Mineure* (Paris, 1922), pp. 22-23.

[458] Theodore Scutariotes-Sathas, 508-509. His coinage was also good.

[459] This is the situation which Nicetas Choniates describes for the rural regions of Adramyttium, Pergamum, Chliara.

[460] Müller-Wiener, "Mittelalterliche Befestigungen im südlichen Jonien," *I.M.*, XI (1961), 29–36.

[461] *Ibid.*, pp. 46–65.

[462] *Ibid.*, pp. 67–77, 99 ff. See also his study, "Die Stadtbefestigungen von Izmir, Siǧacĭk und Çandarlĭ," *I.M.*, XII (1962), 59–114.

[463] Danishmendname-Melikoff, I, 198–202.

and another Danishmendid emir rebuilt Caesareia, about 1134,[464] whereas the earliest surviving Muslim inscription of Neocaesareia dates from the mid-twelfth century,[465] and those of Ankara from the late twelfth century.[466] The Seljuks rebuilt Aksaray in 1155 (1171?)[467] and colonized Dadybra in the latter part of the century.[468] Konya had become so large and prosperous by the end of the same century that the historians of the Third Crusade remarked it to be as large as the German city of Cologne.[469] The rebuilding and colonization (indicated above) was no doubt extensive by the end of the twelfth century,[470] but the great period is the thirteenth century, from which time not only most of the inscriptions but also most of the Seljuk mosques, medresses, fountains, and caravansarays survive.[471] Indeed the art of Seljuk Anatolia constitutes one of the remarkable chapters in the annals of Muslim art. It is significant in this respect that the Greek monastic establishments in the troglodyte regions of Seljuk Cappadocia likewise experienced their final essor in the thirteenth century, after the drastic decline of the late eleventh and the twelfth century.[472]

By the last half of the twelfth century, conditions had become sufficiently stabilized so that Greek and Muslim merchants traveled between Constantinople and Konya,[473] and commercial relations, though of a

[464] Michael the Syrian, III, 237. Bar Hebraeus, I, 258.

[465] Uzunçarşılı, *Tokat, Niksar, Zile, Turhal, Pazar, Amasya vilayeti, kaza ve nahiye merkezlerindeki kitabeleri* (Istanbul, 1927), pp. 59 ff.

[466] M. Ghalib, *Ankara* (Istanbul, 1928), p. 4. Wittek, "Zur Geschichte Angoras im Mittelalter," *Festschrift Georg Jacob*, pp. 329–354.

[467] *Histoire des Seljoukides d'Asie Mineure par un anonyme*, trans. F. Uzluk (Ankara, 1952), p. 25. Qazwini-Le Strange, p. 96, says in 1171.

[468] Nicetas Choniates, 626.

[469] Ibn Bidi-Duda, pp. 110–111. Qazwini-Le Strange, p. 97.

[470] Al-Harawi, trans. Sourdel-Thomine, pp. 131–134, 143, notes the presence of Muslim religious buildings in Amorium, Seyid Ghazi, Konya, Kayseri, Divrikği, and Edessa. On colonization see above.

[471] Qazwini-Le Strange, pp. 95–98, 'Ala' al-Din rebuilt Erzindjan, Amasya, parts of Konya; Ibn Bib-Duda, pp. 64–68, 106–109, 146–147, on walls of Sinope, sultan's palace at Qubadabad, Alaiya; Aksaray Gençosman, pp. 155, 167–169, on walls of Sinope, the saray at Gargarum. K. Erdmann, *Das anatolische Karavansaray des 13. Jahrhunderts*, vols. I–II (Berlin, 1961); Erdmann, "Zur turkischen Baukunst seldschukischer und osmanischer Zeit," *I.M.*, VIII (1958), 1–39; Erdmann, "Seraybauten des dreizehnten und vierzehnten Jahrhunderts in Anatolien," *Ars Orientalis*, III (1959), 77–94. E. Akurgal, C. Mango, R. Ettinghausen, *Treasures of Turkey* (Geneva, 1966), pp. 133–171. M. K. Özergin, "Anadolu'da kervansarayları," *Tarih Dergisi*, XV (1965), 141–170. Turan, "Selçuk Kervansarayları," *Belleten*, X (1946), 471–496. Z. Oral, "Kubad Abad cinileri," *Belleten*, XVII (1953), 209–222. K. Otto-Dorn and M. Önder," Bericht über die Grabung in Kobadabad (Oktober 1965)," *Archäologischer Anzeiger*, Heft 2 (1966), pp. 170–183. S. Lloyd and D. Rice, *Alanya ('Ala'iyya)* (London, 1958). On colonization of farming populations in the twelfth century, see above in this chapter. This policy continued in the thirteenth century, see for example, Ibn Bib-Duda, pp. 179–180. 'Ala' al-Din gave seed and cattle in the area of Chliat and so the farmers returned to the land. See also K. Otto-Dorn, "Islamische Denkmäler Kilikiens," *Jahrbuch für Kleinasiatische Forschung*, II (1952), 113–126. S. Ögel, *Anadolu Selcukları'nın taş tezyinati* (Ankara, 1966). Turan, "Selçuklular zamanında Sivas şehri," *Ankara Üniversitesi Dil ve Tarih-Cografya Fakültesi Dergisi*, IX (1951), 447–457.

[472] De Jerphanion, *Cappadoce*, II₂, 396–397.

[473] Nicetas Choniates, 653–654, speaks of objects sent by the sultan of Egypt to

troubled sort, existed between the Greeks and Turks of Konya-Chonae and Lake Pousgouse-Konya. Muslim merchants from Konya visited the commercial panegyris of the Archangel Michael in Chonae, as did Greeks from various provinces.[474] In the thirteenth century Anatolia once more attained the commercial prosperity that it had experienced in Byzantine times. The Lascarid state stimulated the growth of a national textile industry by favoring Greek clothes over those being brought by Italian merchants. Italian traders and vessels visited Greek ports,[475] goods from India, Egypt, and elsewhere came to the depots in Magnesia,[476] and agricultural produce found a ready market in the less prosperous agricultural domains of the Seljuks. In the north the great commercial fairs of St. Eugenius at Trebizond were renewed at the end of the thirteenth or in the early fourteenth century and brought great prosperity.[477] The transformation of the Seljuk domains by the development of commerce is strikingly manifested in the appearance of the series of caravansarays across Anatolia in the thirteenth century. These khans were built, for the most part, along the trade routes starting in the regions of Malatya and Albistan and stretching westward through Caesareia, Aksaray, Konya, Beğshehir, then northwest in the general direction of Bithynia and Constantinople via Akshehir, Afyon Karahisar, Kutahya, and Eskishehir.[478] It is not insignificant that among the earliest of these khans were Argĭt Khan (before 1201–02) between Konya and Akshehir; Altun A-ba Khan (c. 1200) west of Konya; Kurucheshme Khan (between 1207–10) on the Konya-Beğshehir road; Deve Khan at Seyid Ghazi (c. 1207–08); and

Constantinople via Konya. John Tzetzes remarks upon the presence of Turks in Constantinople. Vryonis, "Byzantine Δημοκρατία and the Guilds in the Eleventh Century," *D.O.P.*, XVII (1963), 291.

[474] Michael Acominatus-Lampros, I, 56; " "Ελκει γὰρ, οὐ μέγα εἰπεῖν, τὰς περιοικίδας ἁπάσας πόλεις, ἀλλ᾽ ἔτι γε δὴ καὶ τοὺς ἐξ ὑπερορίων Λυδούς τε καὶ ᾽Ιωνας καὶ Κᾶρας καὶ Παμφύλους καὶ Λυκίους, πρὸς δὲ καὶ βαρβάρους ᾽Ικονιεῖς ἕνεκά γε τοῦ ἀποδοῦναι καὶ πρίασθαι." Commercial relations also existed between the Greeks of the islands in Lake Pousgousae and Iconium. Nicetas Choniates, 50; " οἱ καὶ διὰ λέμβων καὶ ἀκατίων τοῖς ᾽Ικονιεῦσι Τούρκοις ἐπιμιγνύμενοι οὐ μόνον τὴν πρὸς ἀλλήλους φιλίαν ἐντεῦθεν ἐκράτυναν, ἀλλὰ καὶ τοῖς ἐπιτηδεύμασιν αὐτῶν ἐν πλείοσι προσεσχήκασιν."

[475] There is also evidence for the manufacture of and a lively trade in pottery. Nicholas Mesarites, Heisenberg, II, 44, " σκεύη ὀστράκινα οἰνηρὰ καὶ ὕλην ἐκ φορυτοῦ . . ." Ashĭpashazade-Ali, pp. 11–12, notes that Christians of northwest Asia Minor made and sold beautiful pottery in the early fourteenth century. Ashĭkpashazade-Kreutel, p. 32. Neshri-Köymen, I, 89.

[476] Theodore Scutariotes-Sathas, 507. The income of the treasury was abundant as a result of the state of agriculture and foreign commerce, and not as a result of financial oppression, Pachymeres, I, 68, " τὸν μὲν γὰρ ἐκ γεωπονίας συνῆγον, τὸν δ᾽ ἐξ ἀλλοδαπῆς συνέλεγον." Pachymeres, I, 70, when he fell ill, Vatatzes ordered that 36 pure gold nomismata be given to each of the poor.

[477] Papadopoulos-Kerameus, *Trebizond*, p. 65. Nicephorus Gregoras, I, 42–43, this reliance upon Nicaean grain caused Turkish cash to flow into western Asia Minor. S. Lampros, Βησσαρίωνος ἐγκώμιον εἰς Τραπεζοῦντα νῦν τὸ πρῶτον ἐκδιδόμενον κατὰ τὸν Μαρκιανὸν κώδικα (Athens, 1916), pp. 20, 45 (hereafter cited as Bessarion-Lampros).

[478] See the map in K. Erdmann, *Das anatolische Karavansaray des 13. Jahrhunderts*, I (Berlin, 1961).

Egret Khan (first decade of thirteenth century), for these were built along the routes leading from Konya to the Byzantine frontiers.[479] This coincides chronologically with the notice in Nicetas Choniates that merchants of Konya were in Constantinople at the end of the twelfth century.[480] As the Seljuks conquered regions on the Black Sea and the Mediterranean, the caravansaray system stretched north toward Samsun and Sinope, and south toward Attaleia. After the fall of Chonae and Laodiceia, khans were eventually built almost to Laodiceia. Henceforth merchants and merchandise entered Turkish Anatolia from Egypt, the Middle East, the Crimea, and the Latin and Byzantine West in much the same manner goods had entered Anatolia in Byzantine times. The extent of this commerce is indicated by an incident of the late thirteenth century when the Turkmen tribes and bandits were already beginning to displace the lines of communication. In 1276, 300 Turkmen horsemen attacked a caravan of Christian merchants from Cilicia at Heracleia. Of the Christians, some eighty were killed, and one of them was robbed of 120,000 Tyrian dinars.[481]

Integration of the Christians into Muslim Society (1071–1276)

By the third quarter of the thirteenth century a large portion of Byzantine society in Anatolia had lived under Turkish rule for two centuries, with the consequence that the Greek Christian element had been integrated into a new Anatolian Islamic society. Further, within this Greek Christian element, a significant portion had been culturally transformed, but the process of this transformation was not, as of the thirteenth century, decisive. One must also keep in mind that the maritime regions of western and northern Anatolia were still largely in the hands of Christian political entities and this served to support and strengthen the Christian element in these regions. Nevertheless, a major geographical portion of Anatolia had been under the control of Konya for the better part of two centuries, or at least under Turkish control, and much of Christian society had been subjected to the vicissitudes of war and invasions and to political subjugation. This considerable dislocation greatly facilitated the process of cultural transformation. The Muslim religion had the undeniable prestige and advantage of being the religion of the conquerors, whereas Christianity became the religion of the defeated. It was the traditional Islamic administrative, religious, economic institutions and forms that received official sanction and financial support, and as the Seljuk administration, the Islamic mosques, medresses, zawiyas, and caravansarays spread throughout the Seljuk lands, these institutions began gradually to remodel Anatolian society on Islamic

[479] *Ibid., passim.*
[480] Nicetas Choniates, 653–654. This further indicates that commerce began to revive in the late twelfth century.
[481] Bar Hebraeus, I. 454. This was silver rather than gold, see below.

patterns. The whole complex of these institutions was built, supported, and nourished by the wealth the conquerors had taken from the defeated Christians.

The latter were integrated into Islamic society according to the traditional patterns. As *dhimmis* they had to pay a tax on the produce of their land or on the profit from their shops, and also they had to pay the *djizye* or poll tax.[482] There is some evidence that Christians on *wakf* lands were required to pay one-fifth of the produce of the land to the pious foundations, and they also had to perform *corvee*. This one-fifth would appear to be a heavy burden.[483]

It is very difficult to ascertain to what degree the restrictions that, according to tradition, the Umayyad caliph Umar had imposed on Christians and Jews, were applied by the Turks in Anatolia in the earlier period.[484] There seems to be no doubt that from the beginning of the fourteenth century certain restrictions attributed to Umar were being applied to the Christians of Anatolia in regard to dress. Karim al-Din Mahmud, a contemporary of the event he describes, relates that the Mongol governor of Anatolia, Timurtash, found the clothing and hats of the Jews and Christians to be indistinguishable from those of the Muslims. He announced that the non-Muslims should wear conical hats with yellow turbans so that they could be distinguished from the faithful, for, he continued, it would exalt Islam and abase the infidel. Karim al-Din noted that the Mongol governor was thus conforming to the advice the great sheikh Ibn Arabi had given the sultan Kaykaus I (1211-20). Ibn'Arabi has advised the sultan to remove the bells of the churches, to remove irreligiosity, and to glorify Islam and humble the kafirs. By way of pious example he related in his letter what the caliph Umar was purported to have ordained. In cities of a foreign religion the infidels were to build neither churches nor monasteries nor dwellings for celibate priests, nor were they to rebuild ruined churches. Every Muslim was to be entitled to three nights lodging and nourishment in the churches. The infidels should not harbor spies or bear hatred for the Muslims, but should show respect to Muslims and offer them a place to sit in their assemblies if they should so desire. Infidels were forbidden to resemble the Muslims in their

---

[482] In general see Abel, "L'ètranger dans l'Islam classique," *Recueils de la Société Jean Bodin*, IX (1958), 331–351. Turan, "Subjets non-musulmans," and A. Fattal, *Le statut legal des non-musulmans en pays d'Islam* (Beirut, 1958). A. Papadake, " Οἱ περιηγηταὶ καὶ ὁ Ἑλληνισμὸς τῆς Μικρᾶς Ἀσίας κατὰ τὸν 14ον καὶ 15ον αἰῶνα μ. χ.," Ἀφιέρωμα εἰς Κ. Ι. Ἄμαντον (Athens, 1940), pp. 381–392. An element of continuity of the Byzantine tradition in certain matters is implied in the following facts. The Greeks transplanted from Tantalus and Caria to Philomelium (Akshehir) were eventually to pay a tax to the treasury which should amount to no more than the tax which they had formerly paid to the treasury in Constantinople, Nicetas Choniates, 657, ". . . φόρον οὐχ ὑπερβαίνοντα τὸν ὅρον, ὡς εἴθισται Ῥωμαίοις."

[483] Turan, "Celaleddin Karatay, vakïflarï ve vàfkiyeleri," *Belleten*, XII (1948), 67 (hereafter cited as Turan, "Karatay").

[484] *Ibid.*, "Sujets non-musulmans," pp. 92–95, has conveniently collected the references to this subject.

costumes and clothing, in their hats, turbans, shoes, and coiffures. They were not to teach the Koran to their children or to take Muslim names or patronymics. They were forbidden to ride saddled horses, to gird themselves with swords, or to carry anything having to do with swords. They were not allowed to engrave seals in Arabic or to sell wine. Wherever they might go they were always to wear their peculiar clothing, their waists gird with a *zunnar*. In funerals they were not to lament in loud voice or to parade the corpse of the dead before Muslims, and the bells were to be struck very softly. Reading in the church service was also to be performed in a low voice. Such was the nature of the advice al-'Arabi gave to the sultan Kaykaus I, and that many years later Timurtash applied, at least in part. Karim al-Din informs the reader that it is absolutely essential to follow the advice al-'Arabi has given.[485]

When Ibn Battuta visited the city of Denizli (Laodiceia ad Maeandrum) in the first half of the fourteenth century, he noted that the distinguishing mark in Greek dress was a tall pointed hat, of either red or white cloth.[486] Toward the end of the fourteenth century Schiltberger narrates that the Christians of Anatolia wore a blue kerchief and the Jews a yellow one on the head.[487] Thus it would seem plausible that many of the so-called Umaric restrictions were in force throughout the fourteenth century. That Timurtash enforced the law in the early years of the century would seem to imply that prior to his governorship the clothing provisions were not in force (or else had lapsed) for parts of Anatolia and for varying periods of time. The imposition of the "Umaric" restrictions prior to that time seems to have been lax and irregular in many respects. The letter of Ibn'Arabi might be interpreted in two ways. It might be construed to mean that inasmuch as Christians were not subjected to the Umaric restrictions, he wrote to the sultan advising him to apply them. Or, it might be a letter in which the traditional duties of the Muslim ruler were outlined by a Muslim theoretician without any specific reference to actual conditions. Or, there is still a third possibility. As a result of the considerable Christian element and influence in the court at times in the

---

[485] Aksaray Gençosman, pp. 354-355. It was in 1212 that the sultan of Rum had written to al-'Arabi (who after passing through Konya had gone to Baghdad) to ask him as to how he should treat his many Christian subjects. The harsh counsel that al-'Arabi gave amounted to heavy oppression. The text is in Ibn'Arabi's Futuhat, IV, 710, and M. Asin Palacios, *El Islam cristianizado. Estudio del "Sufism" a traver de las obras de Abenarabi de Murcia* (Madrid, 1931), pp. 93-94, gives a Spanish translation.

[486] Ibn Battuta-Gibb, II, 425. He says that the Greek women wore capacious turbans. But the turban was not peculiarly Turkish, as it was worn earlier in Byzantium. See for this the representations in the murals of the Cappadocian cave-churches, de Jerphanion, *Cappadoce, passim*.

[487] Turan, "Sujets non-musulmans," p. 95. J. Schiltberger, *Reisen des Johannes Schiltberger aus München in Europa, Asia und Afrika von 1394 bis 1427*, ed. K. F. Neumann, *mit Zusätzen von Fallmereyer und Hammer-Purgstall* (Munich, 1859), p. 131 (hereafter cited as Schiltberger-Neumann). *The Bondage and Travels of J. Schiltberger, a Native of Bavaria, in Europe, Asia and Africa 1396–1427*, The Hakluyt Society (London, 1879), 74 (hereafter cited as Schiltberger-Hakluyt).

twelfth and thirteenth centuries, the restrictions might have been removed during periods when these elements were influential. As far as the bearing of arms is concerned, the Christians seem to have been disarmed in many areas.[488] But on the other hand, the presence of local, unconverted Greeks and Armenians in the Seljuk armies of the eleventh and thirteenth centuries indicates that this proscription against the carrying of arms was not uniformly applied.[489] It is true that the sultan of the Great Seljuks, Malik Shah, issued a decree ordering the Christians to wear clothing that would distinguish them from the faithful.[490] There are indications, also, that such laws were enforced in twelfth-century eastern Anatolia. Nur al-Din Mahmud made the Christians wear a *zunnar* and they were not to let their hair grow long; Jews were to attach a red cloth to the shoulder.[491] There are also incidents of the destruction of a newly built church at Bargahish in 1152, and the execution of the priest who built it (he was crucified on the day of the Feast of the Cross).[492] The emir Kara Arslan then issued an edict forbidding the building of new churches or the repair of old ones.[493] But as there are no contemporary local sources for central Anatolia during the twelfth century, and as the Muslim sources of the thirteenth century are not concerned with the Christian population, it is very difficult to say what the situation was here. In keeping with the idea of separating the Muslims and infidels, the practice of isolating them in distinct quarters of the towns is noticeable in the fourteenth century. Ibn Buttuta, when he visited the city of Antalya, found five major quarters in the town—those of the Jews, the foreign Christian merchants, the Greeks, the emir and his officials and mamelukes, and finally the

---

[488] William of Tyre, III, xix.

[489] Matthew of Edessa, pp. 199, 205–206, 209–210. Ibn Bibi-Duda, *passim*. The monastery of Bar Mar Sauma had fifty armed monks for protection against bandits in 1273, Bar Hebraeus, I, 450. Nicephorus Gregoras, I, 58.

[490] Turan, "Sujets non-musulmans," p. 92.

[491] Michael the Syrian, III, 342. Turan, "Sujets non-musulmans," p. 93.

[492] Michael the Syrian, III, 307–308.

[493] In this period, c. 1135, the emir of Caesareia issued an edict for the destruction of the churches (Michael the Syrian, III, 310). When Nur al-Din took Nisibis (*ibid.*, pp. 339–340), he ordered all new constructions in churches and monasteries to be destroyed. He pillaged the treasury of the Nestorian church of Mar Jacob destroying its library of 1,000 volumes, and is said to have carried out similar measures elsewhere. He sent his agents to destroy all the constructions made in the reigns of his father and brother, and this they did except where the Christians were able to save the churches by paying bribes. This incident indicates the irregularity and lack of uniformity in the application of the regulations. In an effort to please his Muslim subjects, he wrote to the caliph proposing that all those who refused to convert should be destroyed, but the caliph refused his consent (*ibid.*, pp. 343–344). Though the church of Mar Thomas in Mardin was converted into a mosque, the Christians of Melitene were allowed to rebuild a church (*ibid.*, pp. 347, 348). In 1147 the churches of Amid and the patriarchal residence were closed. Some of the churches were totally destroyed, others used as storehouses (*ibid.*, pp. 354–355). Seventeen churches were still in a destroyed state as of 1186 in Edessa (*ibid.*, pp. 397–398). There is an incident wherein a Seljuk official attempted to halt an Armenian religious festival in Erzindjan in the thirteenth century which involved the raising of crosses and the striking of church bells. But the Mongol envoy of Hulagu halted the intervention, Turan, "Sujets non-musulmans," p. 94.

Muslims. The same sort of arrangement existed in the town of Garadai Bolu.[494] In other towns the Christians were sometimes completely expelled, as at Dadybra in the late twelfth century,[495] and at Ephesus immediately after the conquest in the early fourteenth century.[496] It is quite probable that the restriction of various religious groups to separate quarters was practiced throughout the whole period, and indeed the practice was customary among the Byzantines as well as among the Muslims. By the late twelfth and the thirteenth century, the principal institution of the Greek Christians, the Orthodox church, in parts of Asia Minor had become somewhat more stabilized and began to profit from the prosperity and regularity now prevalent in Seljuk society. This seems to explain the fact that the Cappadocian cave churches and monasteries experienced their final bloom in the thirteenth century.[497]

The absorptive process was symbolized at the highest level by inter-marriage between Greek Christian aristocracy and Seljuk Muslim royalty. Kïlïdj II Arslan had a Christian wife, the mother of the sultan Ghiyath al-Din I Kaykhusraw.[498] The latter sultan himself married a Greek woman of the aristocratic family of Maurozomes,[499] whereas 'Ala' al-Din I Kaykubad took the daughter of the Christian governor of Kalonoros-Alaiya, Kir Farid, into his harem.[500] The Christian element in the family of the sultans was intensified in the middle of the thirteenth century when at least two of the sons of Ghiyath al-Din II Kaykhusraw had Christian mothers; 'Izz al-Din's mother was a Greek[501] and the mother of 'Ala' al-Din Kaykubad was Georgian.[502] Though the mother of their brother, Rukn al-Din Kïlïdj Arslan IV, seems to have been a Turk,[503] he had a Christian wife.[504] This history of intermarriage of the Seljuk sultans with Christian women is incomplete, but the process is discernible among

[494] Ibn Battuta-Gibb, II, 418, 460.

[495] Nicetas Choniates, 626. Some were allowed to settle in the environs of the city, but outside the walls.

[496] The surviving population was removed and transplanted elsewhere. The Christians seem to have been largely excluded from the refounded town of Alaiya in the thirteenth century and possibly at Aksaray in 1155, Turan, "Kïlïc Arslan," I.A.

[497] De Jerphanion, Cappadoce, II₂, 400. The sporadic references to the presence of the metropolitans of Konya in their church indicate the same thing. Pachymeres, I, 26. Papadopoulos-Kerameus, A.I.Σ., I, 464–466. Reference also to the metropolitan of Melitene in 1226–1227. Papadopoulos-Kerameus, A.I.Σ., IV, 114–118. The hierarch of Pisidia helped 'Izz al-Din escape to Greek lands. Pachymeres, I, 131.

[498] Nicetas Choniates, 689–690.

[499] Ibn Bibi-Duda, pp. 37–38.

[500] Ibid., pp. 108, 330.

[501] Ibid., p. 204, gives her name as Barduliya. William of Rubricq-Wyngaert, p. 330, refers to her as a concubine and gives the name of her son as Pacaster (possibly 'Izz al-Din). On his Greek uncles Kir Kedid and Kir Hayi, Ibn Bidi-Duda, pp. 265, 284; Aksaray-Gençosman, 136. Pachymeres, I, 131, describes his mother in the following words, "... γηραιᾷ μητρί, Χριστιανῇ εἰς τὰ μάλιστα οὔσῃ."

[502] Ibn Bibi-Duda, pp. 204, 278. William of Rubricq-Wyngaert, p. 330. Bar Hebraeus, I, 403, says she was converted to Islam.

[503] William of Rubriq-Wyngaert, p. 330. Ibn Bibi-Duda, p. 204, would seem possibly to contradict this but the text is unclear.

[504] Ibn Bibi-Duda, p. 313. Guzalia or Rozalia.

the Ottoman sultans while they were still resident in Bithynia, as well as among the Karamanid and Dulgadiroğullari dynasties and the Turkish princes who had close relation to the Greek state of Trebizond.[505] There is occasional reference to intermarriage in the ranks of the Muslim and Christian aristocracy. Tadj al-Din Husayn, son of Sahib Fahr al-Din Ali, married a daughter of Kirhane (Kiryani?) the Greek uncle of 'Izz al-Din Kaykaus II;[506] John Comnenus, the nephew of the emperor John II Comnenus, took to wife a daughter of the sultan and turned Muslim;[507] in the thirteenth century the Pervane's son wed an illegitimate daughter of Hetum the king of Armenia.[508] Presumably this phenomenon of intermarriage among the upper classes was more widespread than the sources reveal. Reference has already been made to intermarriage among the lower classes of Anatolian society. There is every reason to suppose that intermarriage took place rather extensively from the very beginning of the Turkish occupation of Anatolia and for several centuries thereafter. Anna Comnena speaks of the offspring of such unions as mixovarvaroi, and the twelfth-century Balsamon refers to their curious practices.[509] When the Greek historian Nicephorus Gregoras passed through Bithynia en route to Nicaea in the middle of the fourteenth century, just one generation after the conquest of Nicaea, he observed that the population consisted of Greeks, mixovarvaroi (Graeco-Turks), and Turks.[510] Thus intermarriage

[505] By way of example Orhan contracted a marriage alliance for his son with the daughter of the Byzantine emperor. Nicephorus Gregoras, III, 504. On marriage alliances between the Comnenoi of Trebizond and the Turkish princes of northern Anatolia, see Panaretus-Lampsides, pp. 70, 72, 74. Rossi, Il "Kitab-i Dede Qorqut" racconti epico-cavallereschi dei Turchi Oguz tradotti e annotati con "facsimile" del ms. vat. turco 102 (Vatican, 1952), p. 32. Bombaci, Storia, p. 222. I. Melikoff, "Georgiens, Turcomans et Trébizonde: Notes sur le 'Livre de Dede Korkut'," B.K., XVII–XVIII (1964), 21–22.

[506] Aksaray-Gençosman, pp. 167–168.

[507] Nicetas Choniates, 48–49, 72.

[508] Bar Hebraeus, I, 447, 450.

[509] See above, and chapter vii.

[510] Nicephorus Gregoras, III, 509, " ἔνθα δὴ πάντες συνήεσαν Βιθυνοί, ὅσοι τε τῶν βαρβάρων καὶ ὁμοφύλων αὐτῷ, καὶ ὅσοι μιξοβάρβαροι, καὶ πρός γε ὅσους τῶν ὁμοφύλων ὄντας ἡμῖν . . ." Intermarriage between Christians and Turks was a very widespread phenomenon in both Asia Minor and the Balkans, a fact for which we have considerably testimony. The Muslim author Abu'l-Fida, R.H.C., H.O., I, 180, was shocked to learn that Muslim women were marrying Christian men in the city of Melitene during the early fourteenth century. Ashïkpashazade-Ali, pp. 41–42, further remarks on this intermarriage in fourteenth-century Bithynia. When Orhan took Nicaea he gave the Greek widows to the Turkish soldiery who took them to wife. Ashïkpashazade-Kreutel, p. 68. The Catalan chronicler Ramon Muntaner, Chronique du très magnifique seigneur Ramon Muntaner, trans. J. A. C. Buchon, in Chroniques étrangères relatives aux expéditions françaises, pendant le XIII⁰ siècle (Paris, 1841), p. 418 (hereafter cited as Muntaner-Buchon) remarks on a phenomenon not unknown in later centuries. If a Turk wishes to take for a wife a Christian woman, even if she be of the most notable family in the town, her relatives must give her to the Turk. When a male child is born of this union it must be raised as a Muslim and circumcised. If it is a daughter then she may eventually choose between the two religions. For a detailed case of a parallel situation in late-sixteenth century Macedonia, see I. Basdrabelles, Ἱστορικὰ Ἀρχεῖα Μακεδονίας, Β' Ἀρχεῖον Βεροίας-Ναούσης, 1598–1886 (Thessalonike, 1954), pp. 2–3. When Evliya Chelebi visited Tabriz in the seventeenth century, its Muslim leaders flung an interesting reproach at the Turks. "You take Infidel girls as women, because you say that the man plants the

of Muslims and Christians at every level of society played a very important role in the integration and absorption of the Greek Christian element, into Muslim society.

When the Seljuks occupied Anatolia they came into possession of a land that had been the habitat and principal base of the Byzantine (Greek and Armenian) landed aristocracy. Of critical importance for the fate of Byzantine society was the reaction of this landed aristocracy toward the new state of affairs. There would seem to be no doubt that many of the representatives of this class fled the Turkish conquests and were resettled in western Anatolia or in the European provinces of the Byzantine empire.[511] The appearance, however, of a number of the representatives of these Anatolian aristocratic families in the services of the Turks during the centuries of Seljuk and Ottoman rule indicates that a significant portion of the Greek aristocracy came to a mutually profitable understanding with the Turks. The secular leaders of Greek Christian society either fled Muslim Anatolia or they accommodated themselves to the conquerors, thus setting an example for all classes of Byzantine society. Of the aristocrats who remained in Muslim Anatolia, many maintained their Christian faith for a considerable period of time, while

---

seed, and that is very well; but you also give your own daughters to Moslims, who were first infidels and afterwards converted; now if this new Moslim relapses into his former error, what then becomes of the children, who though their mother be a true descendant of the Prophet, may become Apostates and fly into the land of the Infidels?" *Evliya Efendi, Narrative of Travels in Europe, Asia, and Africa, in the Seventeenth Century* (London, 1850), II, 140-141. The mixed ethnic origin of many fourteenth-century Turks was observed by the traveler Ludolph, *Ludolphus de Sudheim, De itinere terre sancte*, ed. G. A. Neumann, *Archives de L'Orient Latin*, Vol. II (1884), *Documents*, pp. 375-376 (hereafter cited as Ludolph of Suchem-Neumann); "De ritu Turcorum. Turci eciam sunt homines fortes in armis et optimi sagittarii, quorum terra est Minor Asya, quam olim Grecis proelio abstulerunt. Et sunt christiani ad legem Magumeti se habentes ex parte. Isti bene dant filiam christiano et accipiunt mulieres de christianis, sed si filius nascitur, sequitur legem patris et si filia nascitur, sequitur legem matris." These mixed marriages produced offspring in both Greek and Turkish societies which seem to have constituted special categories. V. Menage, "Some Notes on the Devshrime," *B.S.O.A.S.*, XXIX (1966), 64-78, has indicated that this class of half-breeds received the name of igdish in Asia Minor. They were variously designated in Byzantine society. Raymund of Aguilers, *R.H.C., H.O.*, III, 246, "Turcopoli enim dicuntur, qui vel nutriti apud Turcos, vel de matre christiana patre Turco procreantur." The μιξοβάρβαροι who were raised in Christian lands were raised as good Byzantines. Among the most spectacular examples of these "half-breeds" on the Muslim side were Badr al-Din of Simavna and Balim Sultan. The former had a Greek mother, married a Christian slave in Egypt, and his son married an Armeno-Greek Christian woman. Balim Sultan, the second founder of the Bektashi order also had a Greek mother. See chapter v.

[511] This is spelled out in detail in the case of the Georgio-Byzantine soldier magnate Gregory Pacurianus. Originally his estates were in eastern Anatolia in the regions of Ani, Taiq, and Tzourmere. But with the Seljuk invasions, he seems to have left the east and received extensive lands in the themes of Philippopolis, Serres, Boleron, and Thessalonike. L. Petit, "Typikon de Grégoire Pacourianos pour le monastère de Petritzos (Bačkovo) en Bulgarie," *V.V.*, vol. XI (1904), suppl. I, pp. 54-56. The Comnenoi abandoned their family estates at Castamon. Bryennius, 93. The family of Bourtzes left their land holdings at Laptocome near Cedrea. Anna Comnena, III, 200-202. The presence of many of these aristocrats in Constantinople, western Anatolia, and Europe indicates that large numbers of the aristocracy fled.

others apostatized to Islam early. These Christians found their way into Seljuk service in a variety of ways. Some no doubt remained in Anatolia during the process of the conquest and came to terms with the conquerors.[512] Others surrendered the towns or fortifications that they had been entrusted to defend, and in return received lands and posts under the Turks. Kir Farid, the governor of Kalonoros-Alaiya delivered the town to the sultan 'Ala' al-Din Kaykubad I in return for which he was given the emirate of Akshehir and possession of several villages.[513] Cassianus, a Greek governor in the Pontine regions, similarly delivered his forts to the Danishmendids in return for a position within the domains of the latter.[514] More frequently mentioned by the contemporary historians were the cases wherein Greeks fled the wrath of the emperors, or simply rebelled, and so sought refuge with the Turkish sultans and princes.[515] Of these latter, some remained in Turkish service only temporarily,[516] while others, such as John Comnenus and members of the Gabras family, settled permanently on Seljuk territory. The former, as mentioned above, deserted to the Turks as a result of a quarrel with his

---

[512] References to such families are scattered in disparate sources. There is mention of the Xerus family in thirteenth-century Konya. Papadopoulos-Kerameus, A.I.Σ., I, 464–466. There is the sarcophagus (dated 1301) of a certain Avraam son of Nicholas in the Konya museum today. N. Bees, *Die Inschriftenaufzeichnung des Kodex Sinaiticus Graecus 508 (976) und die Maria Spilaötissa Klosterkirche bei Sille (Lykaonien). Mit Exkursen zur Geschichte der Seldschukiden-Türken* (Berlin, 1922), pp. 77–78. This phenomenon is prominently illuminated in the Danishmendname, where a large number of aristocrats siding with the Turks bear Armenian names. Armenian aristocrats appear in Turkish service elsewhere as well. Mekhitar the Patrician was in the armies of the sultan in 1095–96. Matthew of Edessa, p. 210. Philaretus became a Muslim in order to save his domains in the eleventh century. Matthew of Edessa, pp. 195–196. Boghousag, the Armenian ruler of Sevevereg, apostatized and thus his family retained control of Severek in the twelfth century. Bar Hebraeus, I, 265. Michael the Syrian, III, 247. The governor of Sinope after its conquest by the Seljuks was the Armenian Hetum. Papadopoulos-Kerameus, *Ist. trap. imp.* pp. 117–118. The same occurred in Georgia. Brosset, *Géorgie*, I, 331. The Georgian prince Aghsarthan apostatized, joined the Turks and was given lands.

[513] Ibn Bibi-Duda, pp. 107–108. There is mention of a village of Kir Farid in the wakf of Karatay. Turan, "Karatay," p. 142.

[514] Michael the Syrian, III, 227.

[515] The same phenomenon, whereby the Turks sought refuge with the emperors, is also discernible. Ghiyath al-Din I Khaykhusraw had fled to Constantinople for a period. Acropolites, I, 14. Aksaray-Gençosman, p. 128. Ibn Bibi-Duda, pp. 37–38, 43, 330–331. Theodore Scutariotes-Sathas, 454, relates that he was baptized and adopted by Alexius! 'Izz al-Din fled to the Greeks twice. Pachymeres, I, 131–132, 174, 237–238. Acropolites, I, 143–144. Aksaray-Gençosman, pp. 136–137, 145, 158–159, 162–164. On the fate of his family in Constantinople, see Pachymeres, II, 610–613. There was a steady stream of Turks to Constantinople from the eleventh century. See below chapter vi.

[516] Such were—Isaac Comnenus brother of the emperor John II Comnenus: Nicetas Choniates, 42–43, 48–49, 72; Bar Hebraeus, I, 255; Michael the Syrian, III, 230–231. Michael Palaeologus: Acropolites, I, 134; Theodore Scutariotes-Sathas, 527. Theodore Cotys: Pachymeres, I, 485. Andronicus Comnenus: Nicetas Choniates, 185, 294; Cinnamus, 251. Andronicus Nestongus in the thirteenth century: Acropolites, I, 37; Theodore Scutariotes-Sathas, 470. Manuel and Alexius Vatatzes: Nicetas Choniates, 341–342. The emperor Alexius III Angelus: Theodore Scutariotes-Sathas, 454–457; Acropolites, I, 14. Rebels had recourse to Turkish aid in the eleventh and twelfth centuries, Nicephorus Botaniates, Nicephorus Melissenus, Theodore Mangaphas, the two Pseudoalexii, Maurzomes, etc.

uncle the emperor John II Comnenus,[517] turned Muslim, and married the daughter of the sultan.[518] The Gabras family had a more interesting history, for members of this family were intimately associated with the defense of Trebizond and its environs against the Turkish invasions of the eleventh century. A Gabras was even martyred for his faith in this connection.[519] But as the family became all powerful in Trebizond during the reign of Alexius I, the emperor held the clan in suspicion. Therefore it is not at all surprising to find that members of the family turn up in Seljuk service in the twelfth century. Cinnamus relates that during one of Manuel Comnenus' early Turkish campaigns a certain Gabras, who held a high position in the sultan's armies, was slain. He was a Greek but had been raised among the Turks and had been promoted to an emirate.[520] The family retained its prominence until the end of the reign of Kïlïdj II Arslan. It was a Gabras in the sultan's court who arranged the terms of peace with Manuel Comnenus after the battle of Myriocephalum in 1176.[521] This Gabras was probably the sultan's amir-i-hadjib, Ihtiyar al-Din Hasan ibn Gabras.[522] As a result of the civil war Gabras had stirred up between Kïlïdj Arslan and the sultan's son who was governing Sebasteia, the sultan dismissed Gabras from his service. The latter collected his sons, kinsmen, servants, and two hundred horsemen and retired to the plain of Kanyukh. The sultan's son sent the Turkmens to attack him, and so they killed both Gabras and his sons. Bar Hebraeus has preserved some interesting details of this incident.

And they hacked him limb from limb, and hung him on the points of spears, and carried him round about Sebasteia on the day of the Festival of the Cross.[523]

Because of this combination of circumstances, a number of Greek Christians as well as Greek renegades appeared side by side with Turks,

[517] The emperor had forced his nephew to give his horse to a Latin. Nicetas Choniates, 48–49.

[518] The emperor Manuel saw his widow when he besieged Konya. *Ibid.*, p. 72.

[519] On this see Papadopoulos-Kerameus, " Συμβολαὶ εἰς τὴν ἱστορίαν Τραπεζοῦντος," *V.V.*, XII (1906), 132–137. Zonaras, III, 739.

[520] Cinnamus, 56; " ἦν δέ τις ἐν τῇ βαρβάρων στρατιᾷ εἰς Ῥωμαίους μὲν ἀναφέρων τὸ γένος, ἐν δὲ Πέρσαις καὶ τραφεὶς καὶ αὐξηθεὶς τύχῃ τινὶ σατραπείαν κατ' ἐκεῖνο καιροῦ παρ' αὐτοῖς διεῖπε· Γαβρᾶς αὐτῷ ἐπίκλησις ἦν· "

[521] Nicetas Choniates, 245; " ὁ δέ γε σουλτάνος πέμπει πρὸς βασιλέα Γαβρᾶν τὰ πρῶτα παρ' αὐτῷ τετιμημένον τὰ μέγιστα." 246; He greeted Manuel in the Turkish manner, " . . . Γαβρᾶς βαθεῖαν καὶ βαρβαρικὴν ἀπονέμει τιμὴν καὶ προσκύνησιν."

[522] ʿImād ed-dīn el-kātib el-isfahānī, *Conquête de la Syrie et de la Palestine de Salêh ed-Dîn,* ed. C. de Landberg (Leiden, 1888), p. 451. For the history of the family's Turkish service, Cahen, "Une famille byzantine au service des Seldjuqides d'Asie Mineure," in *Polychronion. Festschrift Franz Dölger zum 75. Geburtstag,* ed. P. Wirth (Heidelberg, 1966), pp. 145–149.

[523] Bar Hebraeus, I, 330. The full name of Gabras indicates that he was a Muslim, but the outraging of his corpse on a Christian feast day might be taken to indicate that his conversion was recent or else that the children of renegades carried some odium in the eyes of the Muslims. On this point see also the reproach flung against Zahir al-Dawla, the Georgian renegade, by ibn Muzaffar al-Din on the eve of the battle of Köse Dağ. Ibn Bibi-Duda, pp. 226–227.

Arabs, and Persians in the Turkish court, administration, and army. It is very difficult to evaluate their role and influence as the source material is far from adequate. There can be no doubt that this group of Greek Christians and renegades played an important role in bridging the gap between the conquerors and the conquered, and they may have had some role in initiating the conquerors into the customs and usages of Anatolian society. But here, again, it is very difficult to arrive at any detailed answers not only because of the nature of the sources but also in the course of time the imprint of Islamic society which came to predominate in Anatolian society has served to camouflage whatever might have existed in this respect.[524]

A number of Greeks appear with the title emir: a Gabras held this title in the early twelfth century,[525] as did Maurozomes who was later elevated to the highest position of the realm in the thirteenth century;[526] the latter's son held an undetermined position at the Seljuk court.[527] The presence of an emir Constantine in Iskilib and of an Asad al-Dawla Constantine in Kayseri are recorded in wakfs of the thirteenth century.[528] The document concerning the pious foundation of Shams al-Din Altun Aba records the names of Greek aristocrats whose lands were in the district of Konya. Two of these, interestingly enough, carried Byzantine titles: the patricius Michael son of Maurus,[529] and the son of the patricius Ioanes.[530] There is reference in the same document to a Greek Christian emir.[531] An emir Tornik of Tokat, who may be of the Byzantine family Tornices, is mentioned in the thirteenth century;[532] Kir Farid held the emirate of Akshehir.[533] In the court itself Ihtiyar al-din Hasan ibn Gabras was amir-i-hadjib under Kïlïdj II Arslan.[534] In the following century Kir Kedid the Greek uncle of 'Izz al-Din II Kaykaus was sharabsalar,[535] and though his other

---

[524] The same accommodation occurred during the Ottoman conquest. E. Frances, "La feodalité byzantine et la conquête turque," *Studia et acta orientalia*, IV (1962), 69–90.

[525] Cinnamus, 56, refers to σατραπεία, possibly an emirate.

[526] Ibn Bibi-Duda, pp. 117–120.

[527] *Ibid.*, p. 38.

[528] A. Temir, *Kırşehir Emiri Caca Oğlu Nur el-Din'in 1272 tarihli Arapça-Mogolça vakfiyesi* (Ankara, 1959), p. 123 (hereafter cited as Temir, *Cacaoğlu*). Turan, "Karatay," p. 111.

[529] Turan, "Semseddin Altun-Aba, vakfiyesi ve hayatı," *Belleten*. XI (1947), 227 (hereafter cited as Turan, "Semseddin,"). لى ارض لبطريق ميخائل بن ماروس القونوى الرومى

[530] *Ibid.*, p. 227. الى مشجرة لبكس بن بطريق ليانوس الرومى السلبوار .

[531] *Ibid.*, p. 233. لى ارض لزمره خاتون بنت الامير برمونى القونويه الرومیه المسيحية الصايفة .

There is also mention of the property of another Greek, الى بيوتالتوديوس بن يان بن المان القونوى الرومى المسيحى الفلاح .

[532] Ibn Bibi-Duda, p. 36. According to Duda this is the name of the Byzantine family of Tornikes.

[533] *Ibid.*, pp. 107–108. The title Kir is the Greek κῦρ, but Farid suggests either the Armenian Vartan or its Byzantine form Bardas.

[534] Bar Hebraues, I, 330.

[535] Ibn Bibi-Duda, p. 284. Prominent Greeks of course joined the Ottoman court in the fourteenth and fifteenth centuries. Such were Maurozomes, Mikail Köse, Markos, etc. Arnakes, Οἱ πρῶτοι 'Οθωμανοί (Athens, 1947), p. 89.

uncle played a prominent role, there is no indication as to his official position. There was apparently a Greek bureau in the sultan's chancellery as one might very well expect, given the importance of foreign and domestic relations with Greek-speaking elements. The officials in this secretariat were known by the Byzantine title of *notaran*, and it was this group who drew up the terms of treaty between the sultan and the ruler of Trebizond when Sinope was conquered in 1214.[536] This Greek bureau, or at least Greek scribes, was maintained not only in the Seljuk administration but also among some of the emirates that succeeded to the Seljuk state.[537] A few examples of the documents emanating from this Greek bureau of the Seljuks have survived and are concerned with the regulation of commercial relations between Cyprus and Anatolia.[538] Greeks also appear, on occasion, as ambassadors of the sultans. In commercial relations with Cyprus, the Seljuk ambassador was a certain Kyr Alexius,[539] and preparatory to Kïlïdj Arslan's famous visit to Constantinople in the twelfth century, he sent his Christian chancellor, Christopher, to arrange the matter.[540] There is mention of a Greek tax official and lawyer, Papa Michael, at Melitene in 1190, who was responsible for levying of taxes,[541] and of two Greek musicians at the sultan's court.[542]

[536] Ibn Bibi-Duda, p. 67. The Tetrevangelion in the Gennadius Library, MS Gr. 1.5, is signed by John Meleteniotes, prontonotarius, of Caesarea. The title protonotarius is yet another piece of evidence of the survival of Byzantine institutions within the Seljuk domains.

[537] A Greek document from the emirate of Aydin has recently been published by E. A. Zachariadou, " Μία ἑλληνόγλωσση συνθήκη τοῦ Χηδὴρ ᾿Αϊδίνογλου," *B.Z.*, LV. (1962), 254–265. For the Greek scribes of Muhammad II, and the early Ottomans, see S. Lampros, " ῾Η ῾Ελληνικὴ ὡς ἐπίσημος γλῶσσα τῶν Σουλτάνων," *N.E.*, V (1908), 39–78. A Bombaci, "Nuovi Firmani greci di Maometi II," *B.Z.*, XLVII (1954), 298–319. Chalcocondyles, 501. Inalcik, "Ottoman Methods of Conquest," *S.I.*, II (1954), 111. Greek was among the languages used in the Ottoman administration in the sixteenth century, Bartholomaeus Georgieuiz, Marshe, under "Iaziti." "Iaziti are divers scribes in the courtes of the turkishe princes howbeit they use sondrye languages and letters. For in Turkeye they speake and writte withe their propre spech and letters. In Grece and Italye with the tounge and letters of the Grecians. But in Pannonia and Moldavia are accustomed in writing the language and letters of the Rascians."

[538] Lampros, " ῾Η ῾Ελληνική," *passim*. The documents are entirely in Greek save for the word sultan which is inscribed in Arabic at the beginning of the documents. For a commentary on these see also Turan, *Türkiye Selçuklularï hakkïnda resmi vesikalar* (Ankara, 1958), pp. 109–114.

[539] Lampros, " ῾Η ῾Ελληνική," p. 48.

[540] Runciman, *A History of the Crusades* (Cambridge, 1952), II, 356–357.

[541] Bar Hebraeus, I, 334. The same author (p. 427), mentions the presence of prominent Greek "lawyers" in Melitene during the thirteenth century. Greek (as well as Armenian and Jewish) tax farmers appear prominently in the Ottoman documents of the fifteenth century. N. Beldiceanu, *Les actes des premiers sultans dans les manuscrits turcs de la Bibliothèque Nationale à Paris* (Paris, 1960), pp. 113, 146. R. Anhegger, H. Inalcik, *Kānūnnāme-i sultānī ber mūceb-i 'örf-i 'osmānī. II Mehmed ve II Bayezid devirlerine ait yasaknāme ve kānūnnāmeler* (Ankara, 1956), pp. 73–74. M. Gökbilgin, *XV–XVI. asirlarda Edirne ve Pasa Livasï. Vakïflar-Mülkler-Mukataalar* (Istanbul, 1952), *passim*. Greek tax farmers are mentioned in the Taurus passes in the first half of the fifteenth century, Brocquière-Schefer, p. 104.

[542] Pachymeres, I, 129–130, 454, gives their story. They were originally musicians from Rhodes who went to the court of the sultan. Here they seem to have functioned as court musicians for a while, but from this position they rose to great prominence as advisors

Byzantines also make their appearance as military officers in the sultan's armies.[543] The emir Maurozomes played a significant role in the expeditions against Cilician Armenia in the early thirteenth century;[544] Ibn Bibi reveals the presence of five brothers from the empire of Nicaea, the Awlad-i-Ferdahli, in a Syrian expedition of the sultan;[545] the leader of the "Frankish" mercenaries defending Erzerum against the Mongol Baidju was a certain Istankus;[546] Michael Palaeologus served as *kondistabl* in charge of Christian troops of the sultan after he had fled the kingdom of the Lascarids.[547] There are also indications that the Seljuk rulers frequently employed Christian troops, those specifically mentioned being Greeks, Franks, Georgians, Armenians, Russians, and Germans.[548] There was a body of 3,000 Franks and Greeks in the sultan's army at Köse Dağ in 1243.[549] The Greek troops were drawn from two principal sources: from the Byzantine lands and from the sultan's domains. When 'Izz al-Din II Kaykaus first fled the Mongol invasions he sought refuge in the lands of the Lascarids, but after the Mongol withdrawal he recruited an army of 400 Greeks from the Byzantine ruler and retook Konya.[550] Upon the worsening of conditions in Bithynia in the latter half of the thirteenth century, the acrites sought service with the Turks.[551] On the other hand, it seems to have been customary to recruit military units for the Seljuk armies from among the Greek Christian subjects of the sultan, and it is quite possible these soldiers were eventually converted to Islam.[552]

---

to the sultan. With the Mongol difficulties of 'Izz al-Din, the two musicians returned to Greek lands and served under the emperor. One became paracoimomenus and the other grand hetaireiarch. *Ibid.*, p. 129; " οἱ Βασιλικοὶ δ' οὗτοι ἦσαν, ἄνδρες ἐκ 'Ρόδου μὲν ἀνέκαθεν ὄντες, ἐκ θυμελικῆς δ' ἐπιτηδεύσεως τῷ σουλτὰν προσωκειώμενοι, οὐ μὴν δὲ ἀλλὰ καὶ ὡς εὖ ἔχοντες τοῦ φρονεῖν τὰ πρῶτα φέροντες ἐν ἐκείνῳ, βρύοντες δὲ καὶ χρυσῷ πολλῷ, ὅσος ἦν ἐν ἐκπώμασι καὶ ὅσος κατειργασμένος εἰς Χαλυφικὸν νόμισμα." *Ibid.*, p. 454, states they had also learned to read Arab letters.

[543] Ibn Bibi-Duda, pp. 97, 329, speaks of Greek, Frankish, and Russian officers.

[544] *Ibid.*, p, 140.

[545] *Ibid.*, p. 123. It was a member of the Ferdahla family who finally put an end to the rebellion of the Babai. *Ibid.*, p. 219.

[546] *Ibid.*, p. 223.

[547] Acropolites, I, 137.

[548] Bar Hebraeus, I, 400, 402. Ibn Bibi-Duda, pp. 333–334. Matthew of Edessa, pp. 199, 205–206, 209, mentions Armenians in the armies of Buzan, Tutuch, and in the Turkish garrison of Edessa, at the end of the eleventh century. *Gesta Francorum*, pp. 102–103, Armenians were to be found in the armies opposing the First Crusade.

[549] Ibn Bibi-Duda, p. 227.

[550] Acropolites, I, 143–145. In return for this aid, he turned Laodiceia over to the emperor. Aksaray-Gençosman, p. 145, remarks that 'Izz al-Din went to Constantinople and obtained 3,000 "Firenk" troops. But he is guilty of several errors. First of all, he sought refuge at Sardes in Lascarid domains and not in Constantinople. Second, Aksaray seems to apply the term Frank to Greeks as well as to Latins. Thus he refers to Maurozomes as a Frank, and to the Nicaean realm as the land of the Franks, pp. 128–129.

[551] Pachymeres, I, 19–20.

[552] Nicephorus Gregoras, I, 58; " ἐπεὶ γὰρ ἦσαν ὑπ' αὐτῷ πάλαι δεδουλωμένοι 'Ρωμαίων συχνοί, τούτους εἰς μοῖραν καταλέξας στρατοῦ ..." Mention has already been made of the Graeco-Turks in the armies of the sultans, see above. The classic example of Greek soldiers converted to Islam is that of Mikail Köse. Ashïkpashazade-Ali, pp. 11–16,

Because Byzantine Anatolia had been a comparatively well-developed area where commerce, industry, and agriculture flourished, one is not surprised that the Greek, Syrian, and Armenian elements are occasionally and significantly mentioned in the economic life of Anatolia. As the Seljuk state developed and progressed in the later twelfth and the thirteenth century, those elements of Christian agrarian, commercial, and artisanal population which had remained in Anatolia took an increasingly active part in the expanding economic life of the Muslim portion of the peninsula. It is this state of affairs that the account of Marco Polo reflects in the thirteenth century.

The other two classes are the Armenians and Greeks, who live mixt with the former (Turkmens) in towns and villages, occupying themselves with trades and handicrafts.[553]

In spite of the fact that sources for the economic life of Christians in Muslim Anatolia are lacking, there are scattered mentions that these elements were actively assimilated into the economic life of Seljuk Anatolia in the late twelfth, and the thirteenth and fourteenth centuries, and indeed were among the basic elements in it. During the twelfth century the Greek merchants of Konya plied the roads from the Seljuk to the Byzantine capital;[554] the Greek traders of Lake Pousgouse had close economic ties with Konya,[555] and they were also probably active in the trade between Konya and Chonae during the great panegyris of the Archangel Michael.[556] Christian caravans traveled between Konya and Cilicia as late as 1276.[557]

There is evidence that side by side with Muslim architects there were active certain Christian architects and architects who though Muslims were converts. Perhaps the best known of these Christian architects was the Greek from Konya, Kaloyan al-Qunewi, who worked on the Ilgin Khan in 1267–68 and who three years later built the Gök Medresse of Sivas (1271).[558] In 1222 the Greek architect Thyrianus built the mosque

---

23–29; Ashïkpashazade-Kreutel, pp. 31–37, 46–53. The Danishmendname is full of such examples. At Gallipoli (Inalcik, "Gelibolu," EI₂), the classes of rowers, arbaletiers, and shipbuilders included many Greeks in the fifteenth century, but by 1519 they were all Muslims. Either these Greeks were removed, or more probably they were converted. On the Greek martolos in the Ottoman armies after the conquest of Trebizond in the fifteenth century, see Gökbilgin, "XVI. yüzyil başlarïnda Trabzon livasï ve doğu Karadeniz bölgesi," *Belleten*, XXVI (1962), 293–338.'

[553] Marco Polo, Yule, I, 43. Marco Polo, Moule-Pelliot, I, 95.

[554] Nicetas Choniates, 653–654.

[555] *Ibid.*, p. 50.

[556] Michael Acominatus, Lampros, I, 56.

[557] Bar Hebraeus, I, 454. The wealthiest inhabitant of Divriği in the thirteenth century was a Christian. Aksaray-Gençosman, p. 318. There is some architectural evidence for the activity of the Syrian and Armenian merchants in the Hekim Khan built at the expense of one of the Syrian inhabitants of Melitene in 1219. Erdmann, *Karavansaray*, I, 63–67. It has inscriptions in Arabic, Syriac, and Armenian.

[558] Erdmann, *Karavansary*, I, 199. H. Edhem, *Qayseri şehri* (Istanbul, 1915), p. 105. Ferit-Mesut, *Selçuk veziri Sahip Ata ile oğullarï* (Istanbul, 1934), pp. 82 ff. Uzuncarşïli,

in the village of Nidir Köy near Akshehir;[559] a certain Sebastus took part
in the rebuilding of the walls of Sinope in 1215 after its conquest from the
Greeks;[560] Djalal al-din Rumi employed a Greek architect to build a
chimney in his house.[561] A story in the semilegendary composition known as
the Vilayetname of Hadji Bektash centers on the figure of a Greek
architect, Nikomedianous, who supposedly was prominent in the court of
the Ottoman sultan Orhan I.[562] In the building inscriptions of many of the
mosques, khans, turbes, and other such buildings, architects' names
appear which indicate that they were converts to Islam. Such was the
famous Keluk ibn Abdullah (possibly of Armenian origin) who built the
Indje Minare, the Nalindji Turbe, and the mosque near the gate of
Laranda in Konya.[563] Greek masons make their appearance in the anecdotes told of Djalal al-din Rumi by Eflaki; Greek workers paved his

Sivas Şehri (Istanbul, 1928), p. 117. *R.C.E.A.*, XII, 164–165. The inscription reads
كالويان أستاد كالويان القونوى عمل. The name كالويان is the Greek name Καλοϊάνης "Good John."
A Gabriel, *Monuments turcs d'Anatolie* (Paris, 1934), identifies كالويان with Καλοϊάνης, but
then hesitates as to the ethnic origin of this architect.

[559] I. H. Konyalï, *Nasreddin Hocanïn Şehri Akşehir* (Istanbul, 1945), p. 549, implies that
Thyrianus was the engraver of the inscription rather than the architect. But the text
reads عمل ثر يانوس. The word عمل is the usual one employed to indicate the architect who
constructed a building. Had he been the engraver of the inscription one would have
expected the word كتب.
This village still had Christian inhabitants in the fifteenth century. *Ibid.*, pp. 540 ff.
It was in the area resettled with Greek colonists by the sultan at the end of the twelfth
century.

[560] Mayer, *Islamic Architects and Their Works* (Geneva 1956), p. 119, says that the original
inscription reads "Syqstus," but Wittek suggested Sefastus-Sebastus. So Mayer has adopted
the reading Sebastus. However, *R.C.E.A.*, X, 116, reads سيقيتوس or Siqetus of Caesareia.
Ismail *Hakki Afyon Karahisar kitabeleri* (Istanbul, 1929), p. 211, n. 3. Bees, *Inschriftenaufzeichnung des todex sinaiticus Graecus*, pp. 53–54, for the Greek inscription commemorating
the rebuilding of the walls of Sinope in 1215 by the Turks. Christian architects from
Edessa built certain gates in the Cairo walls in 1087–1091, Mayer, *Architects*, p. 133.

[561] Eflaki-Huart, II, 2.

[562] E. Gross, *Das Vilayet-name des Haggi Bektash. Ein türkisches Derwischevangelium*
(Leipzig, 1927), pp. 151–152. There is a considerable element, it would seem, of anachronism in this account. But even so, the presence in the story of a prominent Greek
architect in Turkish service is significant. He is said to have built the turbe of Hadji
Bektash. See chapter v for references to Christian architects in dervish literature.

[563] *R.C.E.A.*, XII, 22–24. Mayer, *Architects*, p. 77, gives a full bibliography on this
figure. Though of Armenian origin the name ibn Abdullah indicates that he was converted
to Islam. See Mayer, *Architects*, 69, on another Armenian architect, of the late twelfth
century. For other architects with the name ibn Abdullah, Erdmann, *Karavansaray*, I,
73–74; Mayer, *Architects*, pp. 55, 56, 64, 73, 126, 132. The point as to the possibilities of
Byzantine influence on Ottoman and Seljuk architecture has been discussed by various
authors. Gabriel, "Bursa'da Murad I camii ve osmanlï mimarisinin menşei meselesi,"
V.D., II (1942), 37–43 (a French translation is appended on pp. 49–57); *Une capitale
turque Brousse*, vol. I (Bursa, 1958); *Monuments turcs d'Anatolie*, vols. I–II (Paris, 1931, 1934).
Erdmann, "Zur türkischen Baukunst seldschukischer und osmanischer Zeit," *I.M.*,
VIII (1958), 6–7, notes that the Seljuks of Rum broke with many of the older traditional,
Muslim architectural forms. They created new types of medresses, imarets, caravansarays,
sarays, and mosques. This was due, he says, to the fact that they settled in a non-Muslim
area where they came into relations with Byzantium, lived in a symbiotic relationship
with their Christian subjects, came into contact with a different art, etc. He points out
that the court of 'Ala' al-Din I Kaykubad had many similarities with the court of

terrace,[564] and in another incident Rumi explains the desirability of using Greek rather than Turkish masons.[565] Greek painters were still active, as is evident by the famous Kaloyani and 'Ayn al-Dawla Rumi, both of whom were intimates of the circle of Djalal al-Din Rumi, and of the royal court.[566] 'Ayn al-Dawla (converted to Islam by Rumi) was described by Eflaki as a second Manes. Gurdji Khatun, the sultan's wife, had him paint several portraits of Djalal al-Din Rumi so that she might have his likeness even when she was journeying far from Konya. The tradition of

---

Frederick II in Palermo. Taeschner, "Beiträge zur frühosmanischen Epigraphik und Archeologie," *Der Islam*, XX (1932), 117. H. Wilde, *Brusa eine Entwickelungsstädte turkischer Architektur in Kleinasien unter den ersten Osmanen* (Berlin, 1909). On specific examples of Byzantine architectural influences: J. M. Rogers, "The Cifte Minare Medrese at Erzerum and the Gök Medrese at Sivas. A Contribution to the History of Style in the Seljuk Architecture of Thirteenth Century Turkey," *A.St.*, XV (1965), 76. "Annual Report," *A.St.*, XV (1965), 12, on the Byzantine round arch, masonry, and construction in Iznik and Bursa. D. Kuban, *Anadolu-Turk mimarisinin kaynak ve sorunlarĭ* (Istanbul, 1965).

[564] Eflaki-Huart, II, 275–276.

[565] *Ibid.*, 208. On the Christian masons in nineteenth-century Anatolia, W. Ramsay, *The Cities and Bishoprics of Phrygia* (Oxford, 1895), I, 302. No one has as yet undertaken a systematic study of the stone masons' markings of the Seljuk buildings. Many of these marks are identical with Greek letters and might possibly suggest that Greek stone masons may have been employed in construction work along with the Muslim masons. Such seem to be the following: ΜΠΔΕΑΝΚΧ ΙΒΥΖΛΧΟ, Erdmann, *Karavansary*, I, *passim*. Gabriel, *Monuments*, *passim*. R. Nour, "Tamga ou tag, marque au fer chaud sur les chevaux à Sinope," *J.A.*, CCXII (1928), 148–151, notes that some of these mason markings bear a resemblance to the horse brands, and he suggests that the horse brands are in some cases from central Asia, in other cases from the Christian population of Asia Minor. They are strikingly similar to Byzantine shorthand notation in some cases, E. Granstrem, "O nekotoroykh oformleniia vizantiiskikh rukopisei," *Trudy dvedzati piatogo meždunarodnogo kongresa vostokovedov* (Moscow, 1960), p. 526.

[566] Eflaki-Huart, I, 333–334; II, 69. R. Ettinghausen, *Turkish Miniatures* (New York, 1965), pp. 8–9, on the Byzantine affiliations of the miniatures in MS Bibliothèque Nationale Persan 174, executed in Aksaray in 1271 and dedicated to the Seljuk sultan. Also E. Blochet, *Les enluminures des manuscrits orientaux de la Bibliothèque Nationale* (Paris, 1926), pls. 18, 19; *Musulman Painting XIIth–XVIIth Century* (London, 1929), pl. xxxiv. Pls. lv and lvi from the MS of Rashid al-Din's history have angels done in the Byzantine manner. Bar Hebraeus mentions a Greek painter who went to Tabriz to decorate the chapel of a Byzantine princess who had married the local Muslim lord. Bar Hebraeus then hired the Greek painter to decorate Syriac churches. F. Babinger, "Mehmed's II. Heirat mit Sitt-Chatun (1449)," *Der Islam*, XXIX (1950), 230–231, and plate 7 reproduces a portrait of Sitt Khatun (wife of Muhammad II) done by a Greek painter. It is in a Greek manuscript of Ptolemy's Geography probably sent by Malik Arslan Dhu'l-Kadroglu (1454–1465) to his brother-in-law Muhammad II. The manuscript, which originally contained a picture of Malik Arslan as well, is Cod. Marc. Gr. 516. Timur, as a result of his Anatolian campaigns, transported numerous Greek, Armenian, and Turkish silversmiths, masons, and gunsmiths from Anatolia to Samarqand, Gonzales de Clavijo, tr. Le Strange, *Embassy to Tamerlane 1403–1406* (London, 1928), p. 288 (hereafter cited as de Clavijo-Le Strange). The vitality and influence of Byzantine painting during the twelfth and thirteenth centuries is perhaps best understood as a phenomenon that penetrated both Europe and parts of the Near East. On this artistic penetration of Byzantium see: R. Ettinghausen, *Arab Painting* (London, 1962), pp. 59–80. K. Weitzmann, "Various Aspects of Byzantine Influence on the Latin Countries from the Sixth to the Twelfth Centuries," *D.O.P.*, XX (1966), 1–24; "Icon Painting in the Crusader Kingdom," *D.O.P.*, XX (1966), 49–83. E. Kitzinger, "The Byzantine Contribution to Western Art of the Twelfth and Thirteenth Centuries," *D.O.P.*, XX (1966), 25–47.

icon painting survived among the Greek Christians of Asia Minor until relatively recent times.[567]

The presence of Greek court musicians in thirteenth-century Konya has already been mentioned. Though Greeks do make their appearance as physicians to the sultans and aristocracy,[568] the Syrians of Edessa and Melitene seem to have been more important in that field.[569] The Greeks, Armenians, and Syrians continued to figure prominently in the Anatolian textile industry, much as they had done in Byzantine times, Marco Polo remarks that the Greeks and Armenians:

weave the finest and handsomest carpets in the world, and also a great quantity of fine and rich silks of cramoisy and other colours, and plenty of other stuffs.[570]

When Ibn Battuta visited Laodiceia-Denizli he observed:

And it has splendid gardens, perennial streams, and gushing springs. Its bazaars are very fine, and in them are manufactured cotton fabrics edged with gold embroidery, unequalled in their kind, and longlived on account of the excellence of their cotton and strength of their spun thread. Those fabrics are known from the name of the city [as ladhiqi]. Most of the artisans there are Greek women who are subject to the Muslims and who pay dues to the sultan, including the jizya, and other taxes.[571]

The Christian weavers of thirteenth-century Melitene figure in the pages of Bar Hebraeus.[572] Byzantine Anatolia continued to be an important silk and textile region throughout the thirteenth and the early fourteenth century until the Turkish conquest, and its craftsmen may have had some

---

[567] A number of Karamanli icons, with Turkish inscriptions in the Greek alphabet, were brought to Greece after the exchange of populations in 1923. For the continuity of painting in the Cappadocian cave churches, de Jérphanion, *Cappadoce, passim.*

[568] Such was Taronites in the reign of Orhan I, Arnakes, 'Οθωμανοί, pp. 18, 89, and possibly Basil who lanced a dangerous boil on the neck of the sultan 'Ala' al-Din I Kaykubad, Ibn Bibi-Duda, p. 128.

[569] Hasnon of Edessa treated various of the Seljuk emirs. Bar Hebraeus, I, 391–392. His disciple Isa left Melitene for Cilicia, *ibid.,* 409–410. When another Syrian, Rabbon Simeon, became the physician of Hulagu, the lot of the Syrian Christians improved considerably, *ibid.,* 437. Ibn Battuta-Gibb, II, 443, mentions the presence of a Jewish physician at the court of the sultan of Birgi.

[570] Marco Polo, Yule, I, 43. Also quoted in F. Sarre and H. Trenkwald, *Altorientalische Teppiche* (Vienna-Leipzig, 1928), II, 17, n. 17; "l'altre genti (in Turchomania) sono Armeni e Greci que stanno nelle citta e castelli e vivono dei mercantie e arte, e quivi si lavorano tapedi oltimi de li piu belli del mondo." It would seem that the Christians, along with the Turkmens, were active in the famous rug industry of thirteenth-century Anatolia. The tradition of rug-making in Greek and Armenian Anatolia was well known to the pre-Turkish Muslim world, see Ettinghausen, "Kali," EI₁ supplement. Greek textiles and Armenian carpets were known and highly esteemed in Turkic central Asia during the tenth century, Ibn Fadlan-Togan, p. 64. Manandian, *Gorodakh,* pp. 228–229.

[571] Ibn Battuta-Gibb, II, 425. On the ancient textile industry and guilds of Laodiceia, Broughton, *Asia Minor,* pp. 819–820. Ashïkpashazade-Ali, p. 56, during the ceremonies celebrating the marriage alliance of the Ottomans and Germiyanids linens were sent from Denizli (Laodiceia) and clothes from Philadelpheia. Ashïkpashazade-Kreutel, p. 87.

[572] Bar Hebraeus, I, 408, the Armenians of Erzindjan were famous for the fabrics that they made. For the Christian textile workers and silk merchants of twelfth-century Edessa, Chabot, "Un épisode," pp. 173–174.

part in the textile industry that arose there under the Ottomans.[573] The traditions of mining and metalwork seem to have continued among both the Armenians and Greeks as Anatolia had been a significant source of metals during the ancient and Byzantine periods, and continued to be so in Seljuk times. The Armenians of Erzindjan mined copper and manufactured utensils from the metal.[574] The Greek mining communities of Anatolia were quite active in Ottoman times,[575] and according to one tradition, a Greek goldsmith of Trebizond taught the craft of jewelry making to the sultan Selim I.[576] It was the Greeks who introduced the Turks to maritime life, an influence that was long-lived. It is everywhere discernible, from the first Turkish fleet that was built by Greek Smyrniotes in the eleventh century down to the establishment of the first Ottoman naval arsenal in Europe in the fourteenth century.[577]

A substantial element of the farming population, indeed the majority, in the Seljuk domains of the twelfth and thirteenth centuries consisted of Christians. The program of recolonization of the Turkish lands with Christian farmers was especially important in the twelfth century. In the thirteenth century the properties of large landowning as well as of peasant Christians are mentioned in the *wakf* documents where property boundaries are being defined, and it is interesting that these documents quite frequently refer to the vineyards of these Christians.[578] In fact Cappadocian and Cilician wine enjoyed considerable renown in the latter half of the thirteenth century,[579] as did evidently the wine produced by the Christian villagers of the Beğshehir district in the fifteenth

---

[573] Nicephorus Gregoras, I, 43, Vatatzes stimulated the local textile industry by prohibiting imports of Latin textiles. *Victoria and Albert Museum, Brief Guide to the Turkish Woven Fabrics* (London, 1950), on the role of Christian textile workers. The tradition remained a lively one among the Anatolian Christians in modern times. For this see the signed and dated pieces on display in the Benaki Museum in Athens, as well as the Karamanli MS T671–1919 in the Victoria and Albert Museum, a handbook in Karamanli for brocade workers. M. Schneider, *Die römischen und byzantinischen Denkmäler von Iznik-Nicaea* (Berlin, 1943), p. 5. The Turks in Anatolia manifested a definite taste for Byzantine luxury textiles from the very beginning (Attaliates, 277). The emirs of Kutlumush received Byzantine textiles from Nicephorus Botaniates. In the reign of Alexius III Angelus the emir of Ankara demanded as part of the terms of the treaty with Alexius 40 silk garments of those prepared in the Theban workshops for the emperor himself; " . . . Σηρικοῖς τεσσαράκοντα νήμασιν, ἅπερ ἐκ Θηβῶν ἑπταπύλων βασιλεῖ κεχορήγηται," Nicetas Choniates, 608–609. The gold and silk tissue of the sultan Kaykubad I in Lyon is done in a modified Byzantine style, see Van Falke, *Kunstgeschichte der Seidenweberei* (Berlin, 1922), I, fig. 162. Inalcik, "Hariri," *EI₂*.

[574] Ibn Battuta-Gibb, II, 437.

[575] Vryonis, "The Question of the Byzantine Mines," *Speculum*, XXXVII (1962), 10. R. M. Dawkins, *Modern Greek in Asia Minor* (Cambridge, 1916), pp. 6, 8.

[576] Mayer, *Isalamic Metalworkers and their Works* (Geneva, 1959), p. 16, the sultan Sulayman is said to have learned the craft of the goldsmith in Trebizond from the Greek goldsmith Constantine. Evliya Chelebi-von Hammer, II, 48.

[577] Inalcik, "Gelibolu," *EI₂*. Bar Hebraeus, I, 450, on the Greek sailors of Armenian Cilicia. See chapter vii for greater detail.

[578] Temir, *Cacaoğlu*, pp. 108, 109, 125. Ibn Battuta-Gibb, II, 456, relates that the Christians of Kainuk produced saffron.

[579] Burchard of Sion, *A Description of the Holy Land*, P.P.T.S. XII (London, 1896), 101 (hereafter cited as Burchard of Sion, *P.P.T.S.*).

century.[580] Greeks were extensively employed in domestic slavery and there is some indication of the use of Greeks in commercial slavery.[581]

In the sphere of government and the military, Christian elements were absorbed directly, though on a smaller numerical scale, by the institution first of the Seljuk gulams and later of the Ottoman devshirmes. This involved the employment of converted slaves in the armies, bureaucracy, and the court of the various Muslim states of Anatolia. The use of gulams-devshirmes by the Seljuks and Ottomans resulted from the fact that they inherited the traditional Islamic forms of government[582] and, further, from the fact that Christian youths were plentifully available to them in Anatolia, whether from their own domains or from the neighboring lands of the Greeks and Armenians.[583] There are indications that the Turks recruited male children and youths from the Anatolian Christians through-out the long period between the eleventh and seventeenth centuries. In the late eleventh century the Turks took the male children from the Greek towns between Dorylaeum-Konya,[584] and in the same period Baldukh, the emir of Samosata, had also taken children of the Christian inhabitants of the city.[585] After the conquest of Antioch (1085), the Turks were short of manpower and so made use of Armenian and Greek youths whom they forcibly converted to Islam.[586] By the thirteenth century, the methods of recruitment for the system, which now appear more clearly in the contemporary accounts, were the traditional ones. The principal

---

[580] Babinger, *Mahomet*, p. 399. See also the remarks of de Planhol, *Nomadisme*, p. 120, and the sixteenth-century traveler Hans Dernschwam.

[581] Eflaki Huart, I, 286; II, 67. Matthew of Ephesus-Treu, p. 56, says they were present in great number among the Turks and Jews of Ephesus. Ibn Battuta-Gibb, II, 425–426, comments on the use of Greek slave girls in prostitution at Laodicea. "They buy beautiful Greek slave-girls and put them out to prostitution, and each girl has to pay a regular due to her master. I heard it said there that the girls go into the bath-houses along with the men, and anyone who wishes to indulge in depravity does so in the bath-house and nobody tries to stop him. I was told that the qadi in the city himself owns slave-girls [employed] in this way." For other evidences of the immorality of the Turkish cadis, Anonymous-Giese, pp. 35–36. Prisoners taken from the Greek army of Trebizond in 1214 were put to work in the Zaradhane, Ibn Bibi-Duda, p. 65. Uzunçarṣïlï, *Osmanlï devleti teṣkilatïna medhal* (Istanbul, 1941), p. 89 (hereafter cited as Uzunçarṣïlï *Medhal*) on the Zaradhane.

[582] On the development of slave government and slave armies in the Islamic world, Uzunçarṣïlï *Medhal*. B. Papoulia, *Ursprung und Wesen der "Knabenlese" im osmanischen Reich* (Munich, 1963), and my review in *Balkan Studies*, V (1964), 145–153.

[583] This is not to say that the Seljuk gulams were raised exclusively from these groups, though in Ottoman times the devshirmes were taken originally only from Christians.

[584] *Gesta Francorum*, pp. 54–55. Tudebodus, *R.C.H.*, *H.O.*, III, 29, "Adjuc quoque et Christianorum filios secum tolerabant . . . " Tudebodus, p. 26, mentions "Angulani" in the armies of the Turks opposing the Crusaders in western Asia Minor.

[585] William of Tyre, IV, iv.

[586] Raymund of Aguilers, *R.H.C.*, *H.O.*, III, 250–251; "Quoniam Turci ante annos quatuordecim Antiochiae obtinuerant, atque Armenios juvenes et Graecos quasi pro penuria domesticorum turcaverant, et uxores eis dederant." See also Turcare in Ducange, where he quotes again from Raymund; "Quidam de Turcatis, qui erat in civitate, per Boimundum principibus mandavit nostris etc." Raymund, p. 288; "Si qui autem, per gratiam Dei, contempsissent, cogebantur tradere pulchros parvulos suos ad circumciden-dum vel ad Turcandum."

source of youths seems to have been the "domain of war"[587] because the Seljuks were engaged in extensive war and raiding against the Greeks of Trebizond and Nicaea,[588] against the Armenians of Cilicia,[589] against the Georgians in the Caucasus,[590] and against the inhabitants of the Crimea.[591] The sultans exercised their right to claim one-fifth of the spoils according to the law of *ghanimat* during these raids and expeditions.[592] But gulams were also acquired through gift,[593] possibly through purchase, through voluntary apostasy of renegades, and through the taking of hostages from other states. The latter was the case during the reign of 'Ala' al-Din I Kaykubad when, after the capture of Sugdaia in the Crimea, the sons of the notables were taken as hostages.[594] In the fourteenth century the Turkmen raiders on Byzantine territory in western Anatolia were taking away the children of the Greek Christians,[595] whereas in eastern Anatolia, Sivas served as an important slave market where youths could be purchased.[596] A petition of 1456 addressed by the Greeks of western Anatolia to the Knights Hospitalers of Rhodes indicates that the Turks were still taking away the children of the Christians.

We, your poor slaves . . . who do dwell in Turcia . . . inform your lordship that we are heavily vexed by the Turk, and that they take away our children and make Muslims of them. . . . For this reason we beseech your lordship to take council that the most holy pope might send his ships to take us and our wives and children away from here, for we are suffering greatly from the Turk. [Do this] lest we lose our children, and let us come to your domains to live and die there as your subjects. But if you leave us here we shall lose our children and you shall answer to God for it.[597]

[587] Ibn Bibi-Duda, p. 60.

[588] *Ibid.*, p. 63. After the fall of Antalya the sultan took off the families of the Christians as captives.

[589] *Ibid.*, p. 238.

[590] *Ibid.*, pp. 176–178.

[591] *Ibid.*, p. 139.

[592] *Ibid.*, p. 220. After the suppression of the Babai revolt, the wives, children, and possessions of the rebels were distributed to the troops after one-fifth was set aside for the state treasury. This might imply that Turkmens were also taken into the ranks of the gulams. *Ibid.*, p. 46, the sultan claimed one-fifth of the booty taken after the conquest of Antalya in 1207.

[593] *Ibid.*, p. 320. The begs of the borders sent slaves as gifts to the sultan. Also *ibid.*, pp. 114, 121.

[594] Ibn Bibi-Duda, p. 139. Turan, "L'Islamisation dans la Turquie du moyen age," S.I., X (1959), 147–150 (hereafter cited as Turan, "Islamisation,"); *Türkiye Selçuklularī hakkīnda vesikalar* (Ankara, 1958), p. 178; and Uzunçarşīlī-*Medhal*, pp. 115–116, have suggested that there was even a form of child tribute in Seljuk Anatolia which was parallel to the Ottoman devshirme and that these igdish formed special corps. V. Menage, "Some Notes on the Devshirme," *B.S.O.A.S.*, XXIX (1966), 65, however, gives evidence for considering the igdish as sons of gulams. These igdish, as offspring of mixed marriages were not unlike the *Tourkopouloi and mixovarvaroi* of the Byzantine sources.

[595] Taeschner, *Al-Umari's Bericht über Anatolien in seinem Werke masālik al-absār fī mamalik al-amsār* (Leipzig, 1929), p. 44 (hereafter cited as al-Umari Taeschner). Abùl Fida, *Géographie d'Aboulfida*, trans. S. Guyard (Paris, 1840), pp. 379–381.

[596] Uzunçarşīlī *Medhal* p. 442. Ibn Bibi-Duda, p. 59.

[597] Miklosich et Müller, III, 291. John Cananus, *P.G.*, CLVI, 73, on circumcision of children. Vryonis, "Isidore Glabas and the Turkish devshirme," Speculum, XXXI

With the conquest of Trebizond by Muhammad II in 1461 considerable numbers of Greek youths were taken for the Janissary corps and palace service,[598] and in the same period a number of male children were taken from the town of New Phocaea in western Anatolia.[599] By the sixteenth and seventeenth centuries, the Ottoman devshirme seems to have been levied rather extensively in Anatolia and the list of regions in which children were taken is impressive: Trebizond, Marash, Bursa, Lefke, Iznik, Kayseri, Tokat, Mihalich, Egirdir, Gemlik, Kodjaili, Bolu, Kastamonu, Chorum, Samsun, Sinope, Amasya, Malatya, Karahisar, Arapkir, Djemiskezek, Djizre, Sivas, Erzerum, Diyarbakir, Kemah, Bayburt, Nigde, Beğshehir, Karaman, Zulkadriye, Biledjik, Batum, Sis, Kutahya, and Manyas.[600]

These youths were taken out of their familiar cultural and family environment, converted to Islam, often educated in special institutions, and then enrolled in special military bodies or else employed in the court and bureaucracy. This system of slave administration and slave soldiery apparently experienced an unbroken continuity in Anatolia from the first appearance of the Turks well into the Ottoman period itself.[601] It is difficult to give the number of Christians who were taken into the system and thus Islamized. Obviously the number was comparatively small at any given time, but the system must have had some affect on the conversion of Christians over the period of several centuries.[602] We are told that after the capture of the city of Chliat in about 1231 a troop of 1,000 royal gulams was left to settle the affairs of the city,[603] and in another instance there is mention of 500 serhenk.[604] When Trebizond fell 800 Greek youths were taken,[605] and 100 were levied from New Phocaea.[606]

(1956), 441–442. For an interesting text demonstrating the fear of the devshirme, B. Papoulia, "Die Vita des Heiligen Philotheos vom Athos," *S.F.*, XXII (1963), 259–280.

[598] G. Zoras, " Ἡ ἅλωσις τῆς Κωνσταντινουπόλεως καὶ ἡ βασιλεία Μωάμεθ Β' τοῦ κατακτητοῦ, E.E.B.Σ., XXII (1952), 276.

[599] Babinger, *Mahomet*, p. 164, Ducas, p. 334.

[600] See the Ottoman documents in Uzunçarşili, *Osmanli devleti teşkilatindan kapukulu ocaklari* (Ankara, 1943), I, 20, 95–96, 102, 104, 106, 107, 115, 126, 127, 320, 438. Vryonis, "Seljuk Gulams and Ottoman Devshirmes," *Der Islam*, XLI (1965), 224–252. Menage, "Devshirme," EI₂; "Sidelights on the Devshirme from Idris and Sa'ddudin," B.S.O.A.S., XVIII (1956), 181–183. Inalcik, "Ghulam," EI₂. A. Vakalapoulos, " Προβλήματα τῆς ἱστορίας τοῦ παιδομαζώματος," Ἑλληνικά, XIII (1954), 274–293. Wittek, "Devshirme and Shari'a," *B.S.O.A.S.*, XVII (1955), 271–278. J. Palmer, "The Origin of the Janissaries," *Bulletin of the John Rylands Library*, XXXV (1953), 448–481. Papoulia, *Knabenlese passim*.

[601] Vryonis, "Gulams," *passim*.

[602] Papoulia, "Vita," 274; " Οἴμοι! πόσοι ἐκ τοῦ ἡμετέρου γένους ἐγένοντο τέκνα τοῦ ἀντιχρίστου." Sa'd al-Din, writing in the late sixteenth century, remarks that the devshirme had brought 200,000 men to Islam, "not to speak of the salves brought from the dar-al-harb, whose number nobody knows." Menage, "Sidelights on the devshirme," p. 183.

[603] Ibn Bibi-Duda, p. 180.

[604] Uzunçarşili *Medhal*, p. 93.

[605] Zoras, " Ἅλωσις," p. 276.

[606] Babinger, *Mahomet*, p. 164. Ducas, p. 334.

Among the more famous of the thirteenth-century gulams of Greek origin were Djalai al-Din Karatay ibn Abdullah, Amin al-Din Mikail, and Shams al-Din Hass Oguz. The name of Karatay occupies a prominent place in the pages of Ibn Bibi, Karim al-Din Mahmud, and Eflaki, who relate that though he was a Greek page by origin he was gifted with extraordinary talents. He held, at various times throughout the reigns of 'Ala' al-Din I Kaykubad and his successors, the important posts of na'ib, amir-i davet, amir-i tasthane, and hizanedar-i hass. As one of the four pillars of the state, he played an important role in deciding upon the succession to the sultanate and appointment of viziers and other officials. His title, atabeğ, indicates that he was a tutor to princes, and his closeness to and familiarity with the sultans comes out in certain incidental details. He was devoutly pious (the famed sheikh Suhrawardi initiated him as a murid, and he was an intimate of the circle of Djalal al-Din Rumi), an ascetic (he is said to have abstained from the eating of meat and from marital joys), and a liberal patron of Muslim institutions and architecture, having commissioned the building of the famed medresse in Konya and the caravansaray 50 kilometers east of Kayseri.[607] Another important official of gulam origin was Amin al-Din Mikail, who functioned as na'ib al-hadra under the sultan Rukn al-Din in the latter half of the thirteenth century. Though tantalizingly little has survived in contemporary accounts of his activities, it is sufficient to indicate that he played a very important role in Seljuk financial administration. He was of Greek origin, a Muslim, and a slave of Sa'd al-Din Abu Bakr al-Mustawfi al-Ardabili. Amin al-Din was responsible for reforming the financial apparatus of the Seljuk state in Anatolia by introducing the *siyaqat* system, and was famed generally for his great knowledge. As na'ib he perished defending Konya against Djimri and the Karamanid Turkmens in 1278.[608] Another product of the gulam system in the thirteenth century was Shams al-Din Hass Oguz. Ibn Bibi says of him that be was a slave of Greek descent, that he had a brilliant literary style, and that he was possessed of a calligraphic hand the product of which sparkled like a jeweled necklace.[609]

These gulams and devshirmes were fully integrated into the life of Muslim Anatolia, as is witnessed by their tremendous contribution to the military, administrative, religious, and cultural life of Anatolia. Though often of non-Muslim origin, they were fully absorbed; and over the period

---

[607] The literature on his career, as well as that on the careers of his two brothers Kamal al-Din Rumtash ibn Abdullah and Sayf al-Din Karasunqur, is extensive. Ibn Bibi-Duda, pp. 103, 128, 197, 239, 269, 337, 341. Aksaray-Gençosman, p. 133. Eflaki-Huart, I, 94–95, 192, 199, 208, 209; II, 38, 203, 204. Bar Nebraeus, I, 413, 422. Turan, "Karatay," pp. 17–172. Erdmann, *Karavansaray*, I, 117–125.

[608] Ibn Bibi-Duda, pp. 311–313, 345.

[609] *Ibid.*, 229, 239–244, 336–338. He composed a literary piece which had as subject the harp and wine.

of many centuries, they contributed to the quantitative and qualitative strengthening of the Muslim element at the expense of the Christian element.

Equilibrium of Konya and Nicaea Destroyed

With the breakdown of stability in Konya and Nicaea during the second half of the thirteenth century, conditions in Anatolia once more deteriorated and Anatolia became a congeries of small successor states until the final reunification of Anatolia by the Ottomans in the fifteenth century.[610] Conditions were similar to and in some areas perhaps as bad as those of the late eleventh and the early twelfth century. This general background is again significant for the understanding of the fate of the Greek Christian and in fact for all the Christian elements in Asia Minor.

After transferral of the Byzantine capital to Constantinople, Michael VIII Palaeologus first neglected and then penalized the Nicaean domains, with a consequent corrosion of the militarily and socially cohesive factors of the Greek state in Asia Minor. The church, the aristocracy, the army, and many of the inhabitants were in turn abandoned and alienated. The disintegration of the indigenous military forces, the rapacity of such mercenary bodies as the Catalans and Alans, and the rebellions and desertions of the troops laid bare to the Turkmen emirs the regions of western Asia Minor which the Lascarids had done so much to resuscitate.[611]

The sultanate of Konya, weakened by the Babai revolt and the defeat it suffered at the hands of the Mongols in 1243, underwent a decline that was gradual at first but accelerated toward the end of the thirteenth century. By then, ineffectual Mongol governors and a large number of Turkish emirs had destroyed the authority of this kingdom. These emirates, established on the lands of the Seljuk kingdom and on the Byzantine borders, gradually turned on the central Anatolian regions and on those of western, maritime Asia Minor. In this period, remarks Karim al-Din Mahmud, thorns replaced the rose in the gardens of excellence and prosperity, and the period of justice and security in the kindgom came to an end.[612] The disintegration was manifested not only in dynastic strife and division of the kingdom into two realms,[613] but also in the widespread

---

[610] See chapter ii.

[611] Arnakes, 'Οθωμανοί, passim; "Byzantium's Anatolian Provinces during the Reign of Michael Paleologus," Actes du XII congrès international d'études byzantines (Belgrade, 1964), II, 37–44.

[612] Aksaray-Gençosman, pp. 175–176. See Cahen, "Mongols," for a clear dilineation of the process. He states that the Turkmen periphery turned upon central Anatolia and destroyed it.

[613] This was especially striking in the period of the two brothers, 'Izz al-Din II Kaykaus and Rukn al-Din Kīlīdj Arslan IV, Aksaray-Gençosman, pp. 135, 145. Ibn Bibi-Duda, pp. 264–268, 257, 276–278.

rebellions of government officials.[614] The appearance of Khwarazmian, Mongol, and Mameluke armies increased the disarray in the Seljuk realm, presenting the occasion for intrigues and further disorders. Beginning with the rebellion of the Babais, the Anatolian Turkmens exercised constant pressure on Seljuk control from all the border areas—from the Taurus in the south, Melitene and Marash in the east, Amasya in the north, and the regions of Laodiceia-Denizli in the west. The Turkmen element was strongly reinforced throughout the thirteenth century by other groups entering Anatolia, the newcomers including Turkmens, Mongols, and Khwarazmians.[615]

Though the combined forces of the sultans and Mongols were temporarily successful in suppressing the rebellions of the tribesmen in Denizli and Karaman in the mid-thirteenth century, the success in 1276 of the Karamanids and Djimri in taking Konya demonstrated how far the power and authority of the Seljuks had declined.[616] Henceforth, "the satans were unleashed," remarked both Karim al-Din Mahmud and Ibn Bibi.[617] The collapse of the fiscal apparatus of the Seljuks in the peninsula, the financial oppression of the inhabitants, and a partial but serious disruption of commercial activity characterized the last half of the century. Karim al-Din, who was a financial official and therefore well acquainted with the situation, gives ample detail of this aspect. He narrates that the tax system was disrupted and in such a state of confusion by 1285 that the treasury was exhausted of the revenues that had accumulated in the preceding fifty years.[618] There was an increase in the number of needless officials and, he says, the people fell from one thief to another.[619] He gives the case history of a certain Sahib Fahr al-Din of Kazwin who brought a whole host of adventurers hoping to make their fortunes to Anatolia[620] and gave them positions and tax

[614] These included, in the reign of 'Izz al-Din II Kaykaus, the rebellions of Saraf al-Din Erzindjani about Niksar (Ibn Bibi-Duda, pp. 248–250); of the begs Zayn al-Hadj and Bunsuz in southern Anatolia (Aksaray-Gençosman, pp. 159–160). Following this latter rising there were disturbances in northern Anatolia from Chankiri and Castamon to Amasya (Aksaray-Gençosman, p. 162). The rebellion of the sons of Hatir in 1276 at Nigde caused considerable anarchy (Ibn Bibi-Duda, pp. 300–301). For other rebellions, both of Turks and Mongols, Aksaray-Gençosman, pp. 291–293, 298, 300, 309, 328.

[615] Togan, Giriş, pp. 225–226, describes the settlement of Mongol groups in districts of Konya, Karaman, Diyarbekir, Amasya, Choruh, Niksar, Tokat, Ankara, Kayseri. Cahen, "Turks in Iran and Asia Minor before Mongol," Crusades, II, 690–691; Cahen, "Mongols," p. 729. On some of the Turkmen tribes in thirteenth-century Anatolia, Sümer, "Ağaç-eriler," Belleten, XXVI (1962), 521–528; "Cepni," EI₂. Ibn Bibi-Duda, pp. 172, 333, 181–184, 201–202, 211–212, on the Khwarazmians. Aksaray-Gençosman, pp. 280–281, on Mongols.

[616] Cahen, "Notes pour l'histoire des Turcomans d'Asie Mineure au XIIIᵉ siècle," J.A., CCXXXIX (1951), 335–354.

[617] Ibn Bibi-Duda, p. 308. Aksaray-Gençosman, pp. 197, 194, for the remarks of a contemporary that Anatolia was full of rebels.

[618] Aksaray-Gençosman, pp. 223–224.

[619] Ibid., pp. 246–248.

[620] He brought them from Tebriz, Hamadan, Iraq, Isfahan, Haskan, Khurasan, Kerch, Elan, Merand, Nahchivan, Tiflis.

farms. In some cases the tax of a province was increased tenfold, and Fahr al-Din greatly proliferated the number of tax farms with disastrous results.[621] As the extent of tax farming and the rate of taxation increased, the populations were crushed under the burden, and there are indications that in many areas an unsettling effect on both rural and urban society resulted. Karim al-Din states that such burdensome taxation occurred at Aksaray, Tokat, Devele Karahisar, Castamon, Chankiri, Kayseri, in the regions between Amasya-Samsun, Nigde, Kirshehir, Sivas, Konya, Eyuphisar, Divriği, and Niksar.[622] In the districts between Amasya and Samsun the farmers were so ground down by the taxes and *corvees* that Kamal al-Din of Tiflis imposed, they simply fled their lands, the crops were not planted, and, consequently, it was impossible to fill the grain siloes.[623] Kamal al-Din then went to Aksaray and burdened the citizens with such onerous taxes that the inhabitants took their possessions and fled the city.[624] Another tax farmer, Mustawfi Sharaf al-Din Osman, went to Nigde to collect the taxes and set out to plunder the crops of the inhabitants with the result that the people "lost their peace and security."[625] From there he moved on to Kirshehir which he "pillaged" so extensively that the religious sheikhs had to pawn the tekkes in order to raise money to pay the taxes.[626] As a consequence of the heavy exactions and the disruption attendant upon the rebellions of both the tribes and officials, the tax system broke down and it was impossible to raise the revenues that were necessary for support of the armies by the end of the century. The wealth of certain regions had been destroyed, and the soil was no longer sown with seed. Also the destruction of villages in some areas further crippled the finances, for, as Karim al-Din apostrophized, "how could the haradj be collected from a destroyed village?"[627] The sultan 'Ala' al-Din III Kaykubad enacted such fiscal oppression that finances were thrown into confusion and many villagers fled their homes.[628]

There are indications that not only agricultural and some urban activity were affected but also the international commerce coming into the peninsula. Though commerce and caravans no doubt continued to enter

[621] Aksaray-Gençosman, pp. 227–230. Some were so ignorant, remarks Aksaray, that even though the largest revenue was the djizye, they did not know what the word meant.

[622] *Ibid.*, pp. 206, 252–257, 271–277, 293–297, 318–319, 328, 335–336, 340.

[623] *Ibid.*, p. 273.

[624] *Ibid.*, p. 275, he was so furious that he contemplated plundering the crops.

[625] *Ibid.*, p. 276, remarks that in order to improve his own clothing he denuded thousands.

[626] *Ibid.*, p. 276, the implications of this passage are important for the fate of the ecclesiastical property of the Christians. It tends to corroborate the Greek sources, see chapter iv. F. Köprülü, "L'Institution du vakouf. Sa nature juridique et son évolution historique," *V.D.*, vol. II (1942), partie française, pp. 27, 30, on decline of Seljuk wakf foundations during the Mongol invasions.

[627] Aksaray-Gençosman, p. 291.

[628] *Ibid.*, pp. 318–319, the property of both Muslims and Christians was confiscated. The richest man in Divriği, a Christian, was beaten with a polo stick and was threatened with burning in an effort to obtain his wealth. The financial decline is reflected in the geographical work of Hamd-Allah Mustawfi of Kazwin (1340), see below.

Anatolia, it would seem that displacement of the Mongol empire and the deteriorating conditions within Anatolia produced a significant decrease in the extent of this commercial activity.[629] The Khwarazmian tribes halted the Syrian caravans in 1239–40.[630] In 1256 the Ağacheri of Marash roamed the highways plundering and destroying the caravans in Anatolia, Armenia, and Syria,[631] and similarly the Karamanids began to interfere with the caravans in southern Anatolia.[632] The Turkmens had become so bold around Melitene in 1256–57 that the city could not import anything. Because the countryside had become desolate, famine forced the inhabitants to sell their children to the Ağacheri.[633] In the strife between Rukn al-Din IV Kïlïdj Arslan and his brother, the former attacked and killed all the merchants he found in the 'Ala' al-Din caravansaray outside of Aksaray.[634] The Turkmen brigands from Aintab harassed and robbed the caravans from Claudia in southeast Anatolia as far north as Amaseia and Castamon.[635] The period from 1276 to 1278 must also have been a particularly severe one for the merchants. When the Karamanids revolted in 1276, they once more cut the roads and preyed on commerce,[636] and though the rebellion was defeated, the tribes continued to cut communication routes and did not cease to commit acts of brigandage on the highways.[637]

The rebels frequently utilized the merchant khans as fortresses because of their defensive strength. Thus about 1304 a Turkmen used the Alaiya Khan for such a purpose;[638] in the same khan the rebel Memres had defended himself against the Karamanids who destroyed two of the structure's towers. Consequently, the road between Konya and Aksaray was completely closed for two years until the towers were rebuilt.[639] Further to the south, in 1300, Turkmens had taken over the fort of Saraf Hisar and the road between Nigde and Eyuphisar was unsafe for a two-year interval.[640] The bandit Ibn Budin in a similar manner rendered

---

[629] Cahen, "Mongols," pp. 720–731.

[630] Ibn Bibi-Duda, p. 211.

[631] *Ibid.*, p. 270. M. Mellink, "Archaeology in Asia Minor: Addenda," *American Journal of Archaeology*, LXX (1966), 280, on archaeological evidence suggesting destruction in the area of Samosata about the middle of the thirteenth century.

[632] Ibn Bibi-Duda, p. 308.

[633] Bar Hebraeus, I, 427. By way of illustrating this rapacity, *ibid.*, p. 426, relates that from one village near Hisn Mansur the Turkmens took off 7,000 bulls, cows, asses, 45,000 sheep and goats.

[634] Ibn Bibi-Duda, p. 267.

[635] Bar Hebraeus, I, 450. Eflaki-Huart, II, 380.

[636] Ibn Bibi-Duda, pp. 308–310. A Christian caravan departing from Cilicia was attacked and destroyed by three hundred mounted Turkmens near Heracleia, Bar Hebraeus, I, 454. Eflaki-Huart, II, 10, reports an incident where a merchant recently robbed by the Turkmens of the borders confronts Muhammad, their leader, in the presence of Djalal al-Din Rumi. See also the robbing of Michael Palaeologus, who, in process of fleeing to the sultan from Nicaea, fell into the hands of the Turkmens. Theodore Scutariotes-Sathas, 527. The Crusaders who encountered them between Laodiceia and Konya referred to them as "predones."

[637] Aksaray-Gençosman, p. 211.

[638] *Ibid.*, p. 332.

[639] *Ibid.*, p. 336.

[640] *Ibid.*, p. 298.

unsafe to travelers the district between Nigde and Sivas.[641] The effects of rebellions and Turkmen banditry on commerce seem to have been abetted on occasion by government measures. When the vizier Saraf al-Din attempted to put into circulation a type of paper money or exchange that would replace metallic coin, buying and selling came to a halt in Anatolia and all the commercial caravans from Syria turned back.[642] Though the situation in Anatolia must have improved in the fourteenth century as the emirates crystallized, there are indications that in the first half of the century travel was not always free of such dangers in Turkmen country, and Ibn Buttuta's journey is partly illustrative of this point. The emir of Gül Hisar furnished Ibn Battuta with an armed body to escort him to Denizli inasmuch as the region was infested with brigands. Once in Denizli, Ibn Battuta had to stay there for some time because of the unsafe roads. When a caravan was finally organized, he went with it to Tavas. Here they were not permitted to enter until morning and only after the commander of the castle had gone out with his troops to examine the countryside to see if it was safe. He adds that the local inhabitants brought their livestock into the fortress every night for fear that the Turkmens might steal their animals. Ibn Battuta remarks that once he and his party made their way north of Magnesia ad Sipylum, they were in constant fear of being robbed, inasmuch as they were in Turkmen country again.[643]

Though commerce and travel were not completely disrupted, obviously conditions were far less felicitous than they had been in the first half of the thirteenth century.[644]

This decline in the economic fortunes of Muslim Anatolia during the late thirteenth and early fourteenth century, set forth in such detail by a financial official of the Seljuk state (Karim al-Din Mahmud of Aksaray), is seemingly confirmed by another fiscal authority, Hamd-Allah Mustawfi al-Kazwini. Kazwini, an official in the government of the Ilkhanid Mongols, has reported the annual revenues of the various provinces of the empire toward the end of Abu Sa'id's reign (c. 1335–36), and in many cases compares the sums with those the provinces paid in earlier times. His figures for Rum (eastern and central Anatolia with the western Udj districts), Greater Armenia, and Georgia are immediately relevant.

---

[641] *Ibid.*, p. 298.

[642] *Ibid.*, pp. 283–284. On the introduction of paper money, K. Jahn, "Das iranische Papiergeld," *Archiv Orientalni*, X (1938), 308–340. Spuler, *Die Mongolen*, pp. 301–302.

[643] Ibn Battuta-Gibb, II, 427–428, 448.

[644] This state in the late thirteenth and the early fourteenth century of Anatolia is also reflected in the synodal acta of the Greek church, see chapter iv. With this period the brief revival of the Greek Cappadocian cave churches comes to an end, de Jerphanion, *Cappadoce*, II , 400. M. Akdağ, "Osmanli imparatorluğunun kuruluş ve inkisafi devrinde Türkiye'nin iktisadi vaziyeti," *Belleten*, XIII (1949), 570, interprets the low prices as an indication of the scarcity of money and an economic crisis.

Its [Rum's] revenues at the present day amount to 3,300,000 dinars,[645] as has been set down in the registers; but during the times of the Seljuks they were in excess of 15,000,000 dinars of the present currency . . . .[646]

Its [Greater Armenia's] revenues in former days amounted to near 2,000,000 dinars of the present currency; but now the total sum paid is only 390,000 dinars. . . .[647]

The revenues in the times of their native kings [of Georgia] amounted to near 5,000,000 dinars of the present currency; but in our times the government only obtains 1,202,000 dinars.[648]

In each of the three districts the revenues in Kazwini's day were less than 25 percent of what they once had been.

Official inscriptions from Ani, Ankara, and Kirshehir, all of which seemingly date from the reign of the Ilkhanid Abu Sa'id (1316–35), bear further and undeniable testimony to Anatolian economic decline and to fiscal oppression that it brought the peasantry and the city dwellers.[649] These inscriptions, embodying the contents of imperial *yarliqs*, declare that the inhabitants are to be freed from a variety of arbitrary and illegal taxes that had hitherto oppressed the people. The violence that had accompanied the enforcement of these illegal taxes, reads one inscription, had caused farmers to flee their villages and townsmen to abandon the cities. This is strongly reminiscent of the process Karim al-Din of Aksaray described for the late thirteenth century and indicates that the attrition of fiscal mismanagement was a long-term phenomenon. An inscription from Nigde (1469–70) in the lands of the Karamanids repeats the familiar prohibition of "illegal taxes," a sure indication of the vitality of tax oppression.[650]

In western Anatolia the events of the thirteenth century had resulted in an increase in the number of Turkmens on the borders, and with the neglect of the Byzantine provinces after 1261, the Turkmen push became inexorable. They were to be found in large numbers in Paphlagonia,

[645] These were silver, and not gold, dinars. On this point and their declining value, W. Barthold and W. Hinz, "Die persische Inschrift an der Mauer der Manučehr-Moschee zu Ani," *Z.D.M.G.*, CI (1951), 251–253.

[646] Kazwini-Le Strange, p. 95.

[647] *Ibid.*, p. 100.

[648] *Ibid.*, p. 94. Also Hinz, "Das Rechnungswesen orientalischer Reichsfinanzämter im Mittelalter," *Der Islam*, XXIX (1950), 131–134.

[649] For the texts, translations of, and commentaries on these important inscriptions, Hinz, "Steuerinschriften aus dem mittelalterlichen vorderen Orient," *Belleten*, XIII (1949), 745–769 (hereafter cited as Hinz-Steuerinschriften,"). Barthold and Hinz, "Inschrift," pp. 241–269. The study of Toğan, "Mogollar devrinde Anadolu'nun iktisadi vaziyeti," *Turk hukuk ve iktisat tarihi mecmuasï*, I (1931), 1–42, should be qualified by the conclusions of Hinz. See also, Toğan, "Reşideddin'in mektuplarïnda Anadolu'nun iktisadi ve medeni hayatïna ait kayïtlar," *Iktisat fakültesi mecmuasï*, XV (1953), 33–50. For the background to Mongol fiscal practices, Spuler, *Die Mongolen*, pp. 297–326, esp. p. 302 on the debasement of the silver coinage in Anatolia.

[650] Hinz, "Steuerinschriften," pp. 755–756. The inscriptions mention fifteen taxes illegally levied; sumare-i kobcur, hazr-i galle, sahnegi, tabkur, matrah-i sabun, taxes on flax seed, mohair, saltpeter, cook shops, building stone, sheep, qalan, nämäri, tarh, trnagir.

Pamphylia,[651] and Phrygia.[652] When the defense of the Greeks had degenerated sufficiently, the tribes under various chieftains overran most of Byzantine Anatolia in a quarter of a century. In fact to one Greek historian it seemed as if all the emirs had formed an alliance and then divided the spoils among themselves accordingly.[653] The raiders came, in the beginning, for booty. But as the Byzantine armies were disbanded or transferred to Europe, the raiders settled on the land until they finally reached the Aegean coastline.[654] What was the nature of this final Turkish conquest and settlement and what effect did it have on the Christian population? An examination of the actual facts reveals that this second conquest of western Asia Minor was in many ways similar to the earlier conquest at the end of the eleventh century. That is to say, it was often accompanied by violent displacement of rural and urban populations, enslavement, and destruction.

Byzantine attempts to defend western Anatolia in the three-quarters of a century following their reoccupation of Constantinople were few and halfhearted. In 1269 the despot John was forced to clear the regions of the Maeander, Tralles, the Cayster, and Magedon. A few years later the emperor sent his son Andronicus to clear the Turks from Tralles, and in 1296 Alexius Philanthropenus achieved a few temporary successes in the regions around Miletus. All these efforts were ephemeral at best, however, as the recurrent Turkish raids had by 1304 reached Ephesus and Caria, and most of the regions between the Maeander and Cayster were also in the hands of the Turkmens.[655] The areas of the Cayster, Caicus, and Mysia experienced a similar history. Turkish infiltration and settlement of Bithynia took a little longer inasmuch as the region was closer to Constantinople and was possessed of large fortified towns. The Turkish occupation took the form of repeated pillaging expeditions. On occasion the Turks remained in an area until they were forced to withdraw by expeditions such as that of the despot John in the Maeander-Cayster regions in 1269.[656] More dramatic perhaps was the retreat of the Turks before the Catalan forces or the successes of Philanthropenus near the mouth of the

[651] Nicephorus Gregoras, I, 138.

[652] Abu'l-Fida quotes the thirteenth-century Arab author Ibn Said to the effect that in the thirteenth century there were 200,000 Turkmens with their tents in the regions of Laodiceia. Turan, *Selçuklular tarihi ve turk-islam medeniyeti* (Ankara, 1965), p. 215. This exaggerated figure is very difficult to evaluate, but that the tribsemen had settled there in great numbers is further confirmed in the letters of Planudes, *Maximi Planudis epistulae*, ed. M. Treu (Amsterdam, 1960), *passim* (hereafter cited as Planudes-Treu).

[653] Nicephorus Gregoras, I, 214.

[654] For the details see Wittek, *Mentesche, passim*. Lemerle, *Aydin, passim*. Arnakis, Ὀθωμάνοί, *passim*. Ahrweiler, "Smyrne," *passim*. On the destructive aspects of the Ottoman conquests, D. Angelov, "Certains aspects de la conquête des peuples balkaniques par les Turcs," *B.S.* XVII (1956), 220–275.

[655] Pachymeres, I, 219–220, 468–469; II, 210–212, 589.

[656] *Ibid.*, I, 219–220.

Maeander.[657] But as such defensive armies were operative over short periods of time, the Turkmens pushed back in very quickly and resumed their conquests and settlement. The strongly fortified towns constituted a somewhat more serious challenge to the invaders, and here the Christians were in a better position to resist the invaders than they were in the open countryside. But these fortified centers of resistance also fell as a result of the Turkish blockades that cut off the towns from the agricultural countryside, and also as a result of the growing despair among the inhabitants who found that resistance was useless.

Extensive destruction in some areas once more characterized the conquest. The valleys of the Maeander, of the Cayster, and the regions of Magedon were repeatedly and savagely devastated,[658] as were the towns of Priene, Miletus, Caria, Antiocheia, Melanoudium.[659] Tralles had also been destroyed, so the emperor sent his son who decided to rebuild and recolonize the uninhabited town.[660] When the city was finally finished, Andronicus brought together 36,000 colonists in order to repeople the city.[661] But soon after, in 1282, Menteshe besieged the town and as a result of the severe blockade the citizens were reduced to such famine that they began to drink horse blood. The besieged repeatedly offered to surrender the city but the Turks refused, and when the latter finally entered, the slaughter of the inhabitants and the destruction of the city were extensive.[662] Nysa, just to the east of Tralles,[663] Tripolis, farther to the east, and the surrounding forts had been similarly reduced by blockade and starvation.[664] The Turkish advance and the siege of the fortified regions were so successful that by the end of the thirteenth and beginning of the fourteenth centuries, the Maeandrian and Caystrian regions were entirely in Turkish hands. The emir Sassan reduced Thyraia by starvation,[665] and when in 1304 Ephesus fell, many of the inhabitants were

---

[657] *Ibid.*, II, 210–212. On this brief but brilliant episode see the letters of Maximus Planudes, Planudes-Treu, pp. 74–75, 96–99, 120, 125–129, 135–141, 144, 150–155, 163, 166, 169, 174–178.

[658] Pachymeres, I, 219–220, 310–311.

[659] *Ibid.*, 468–469: " τὰ γὰρ κατὰ Μαίανδρον καὶ Καρίαν καὶ ᾿Αντιόχειαν ἤδη καὶ τετελευτήκει, τὰ δὲ τούτων καὶ ἐνδοτέρω δεινῶς ἐξησθένει καὶ τοῦ ἰατρεύνοτος ἔχρηζον, καὶ ἡλίσκοντο μὲν τὰ κατὰ Κάϋστρον καὶ Πριήνην, ἡλίσκοντο δ᾿ ἤδη καὶ τὰ κατὰ Μίλητον, καὶ Μαγεδὼν καὶ τὰ πρόσχωρα κατὰ πολὴν τοῦ κωλύσοντος ἐρημίαν ἐξηφανίζοντο,"

[660] *Ibid.*, 469, " ... εἶδε καὶ πόλιν μεγίστην τὰς Τράλλεις ... καί οἱ λογισμὸς ἐπήει ἀνεγείρειν πεσοῦσαν καὶ τοὺς ἐξῳκηκότας ἐκεῖθεν σὺν ἄλλοις πλείστοις οἰκίζειν."

[661] *Ibid.*, 470.

[662] *Ibid.*, 470, " εἵμαρτο γὰρ κἀντεῦθεν καὶ μυριοστύας ὅλας ὀλέσθαι τῶν ἐκεῖ κατοικησάντων." *Ibid.*, 473–474. " καὶ τὴν πρὶν ἐν χρησμοῖς κειμένην περιφανέσι καὶ γ᾿ ἐλπίσιν ἀπηωρημένην χρησταῖς εἰς χοῦν καταβάλλουσι, καὶ πλῆθος ἐκεῖνο πᾶν οὐ ῥαδίως ἀριθμητὸν ἔργον μαχαίρας ποιοῦνται."Nicephorus Gregoras, I, 142. Those who surrendered were not less than 20,000. They were taken away and so harsh was their lot that they rejoiced for those who had been slain as they thereby escaped the hardships of enslavement.

[663] Pachymeres, I, 474.

[664] *Ibid.*, II, 433–436.

[665] *Ibid.*, 589, " λιμῷ πολυημέρῳ τοὺς ἐκεῖ παραστησαμένου."

251

slaughtered; the remainder were transported to Thyraia out of fear that they might betray the city.[666] The city of Magnesia on the Maeander was still, in the fifteenth century, a complete ruin.[667]

The lands north of the Cayster as far as Caicus experienced a comparable fate, and by the end of the thirteenth century the regions of Neocastron and Abala lay desolate.[668] The districts between Magnesia on the Hermus and Philadelpheia were subjected to repeated raids and sieges.[669] In Mysia the Maryandian and Mossynian regions were so obliterated as to necessitate a "Maryandian lamentor" to bewail the destruction in a fitting manner.[670] By the early fourteenth century only the towns and forts had survived the Turkish plundering forays in Mysia as well as in Bithynia.

The situation in the east constantly declined and worsened so that daily reports upon worse reports came to the emperor . . . . There was between us and the enemies only this narrow sea. The enemies attacked without restraint, laying waste all the lands, the most beautiful churches and monasteries, and some of the fortresses, and they burned the most beautiful of these. They revelled daily in murdering and in dreadful enslavements such as had never been heard of. The inland regions of Bithynia, Mysia, Phrygia, Lydia, and enchanted Asia, except only for the fortified towns, came to an end.[671]

The invaders destroyed Croulla and Catoicia and the inhabitants were put to the sword or enslaved.[672] The regions of Scamander, Ida, Assus, and Pegae were desolated,[673] and Cenchrae was reduced by blockade. When the Turks entered the latter town they killed the majority of the inhabitants, pillaged the town, and then intentionally destroyed it by fire.[674]

The collapse of Byzantine rule in Bithynia and Paphlagonia was accelerated and facilitated by the religious and factional strife among the Byzantines there, some of whom went over to the side of the Turks.[675]

[666] Ibid., " μετῳκίζοντο δὲ καὶ οἱ πλείους τῶν πολιτῶν ἐπὶ τὸ τῶν Θυραίων φρούριον, δέει τοῦ μή τι παθεῖν ἐκ δόλου τοὺς Πέρσας ἄχαρι ἐπιθεμένων ἐκείνων, ἣν καιρὸς διδοίη. ἄλλους δὲ πλείστους ἔργον μαχαίρας ἐποίουν ἀνοικτὶ σφάττοντες."

[667] Papadopoulos-Kerameus, " Μαγνησεία ἡ ὑπὸ Σιπύλῳ καὶ αἱ Μητροπόλεις Ἐφέσου καὶ Σμύρνης ; " Δ.Ι.Ε.Ε., II (1885), 653, " Δύο δὲ οὐσῶν καὶ τῆς μιᾶς ἀφανισθείσης παντελῶς."

[668] Pachymeres, I, 311; II, 210; " τῶν γοῦν ἄκρων κακουμένων, ὡς μὴ μόνον τῶν κατὰ Μαίανδρον καὶ τὰ τῷ ζυγῷ ἐκείνῳ προσήκοντα ἀλλ' ἤδη καὶ τῶν ἐντὸς ἐξαφανιζομένων ἐξ ἐπιδρομῶν συχνῶν τῶν Περσῶν."

[669] Ibid., II, 314-319, 421, 442, speaks of the slaughter of inhabitants. Ibid., 430-405, the inhabitants of Sardes were forced to divide the city with the Turks. The two groups lived in separate sections of the town, separated by walls. Eventually the Greeks summoned Byzantine troops, with the aid of which they ejected the Turks.

[670] Ibid., I, 311; " ὅσα τε ἐν Μαρυανδηνοῖς τε καὶ Μόσυσι . . . ἐπὶ τοσοῦτον ἠφάνιστο ὥστε καὶ Μαρυανδηνοῦ θρηνητῆρος χρῄζειν ἀξίως τἀκεῖ θρηνήσοντος."

[671] Ibid., II, 338.

[672] Ibid., 413, 414: " καὶ τότε οἱ μὲν ὑποστάντες ἐσφάττοντο, γύναια δὲ καὶ παιδάρια πλῆθος μυρίον πρὸς τὸ φρούριον φεύγοντα ἄγρα ἦν ἑτοίμη τοῖς προκαταλαβοῦσι . . . ἔπειτα πῦρ ἐναύσαντες οἱ ἐχθροὶ τὰ ἐκεῖ κάλλη εἰς τέλος ἠμάθυναν."

[673] Ibid., 415, 437-438.

[674] Ibid., 444-445; " ἐντεῦθεν ἐκ πολλῆς ἀδείας οἱ Πέρσαι περικαθίσαντες ἐνδείᾳ ὕδατος αἱροῦσι τὸ φρούριον, καὶ τοὺς μὲν ὀλίγων ἀποδράντων ἔργον μαχαίρας ποιοῦσι, τὰ δ' ἐκεῖσε σκυλεύσαντες πῦρ ἐνιᾶσι καὶ τὸ πᾶν ἀφανίζουσι."

[675] Ibid., I, 221-223.

The latter finally wasted and overran the countryside, eventually cutting off the cities and blockading them. Thus such towns as Cromna, Amastris, Tium, Heracleia, and Nicomedia were accessible only by sea.[676] The Sangarius valley was left desolate.[677] In 1301 Osman devastated the Bithynian regions of Nicomedia, Prusa, Nicaea, and these cities were soon isolated from the countryside so that for the next two or three decades they lived in a state of siege.[678] Belocome, Angelocome, Anagourda, Platanea, Melangeia, Apameia, and their environs were left desolated.[679]

Just as in the late eleventh and the twelfth century, the Christian population had often sought refuge in the face of the Turkish invasions, so in the late thirteenth and the fourteenth century there is ample evidence that important segments of the populace fled before the Turks. Very often rural populations abandoned their unprotected villages for the temporary security of the walled towns and fortresses. But as safety was not assured even there, the Greeks frequently abandoned the towns for the islands off the western coast or for Constantinople and other European regions of the empire.[680] Though this partial and forced withdrawal of an important segment of the Greek population from Anatolia is not documented in great detail, there is, nevertheless, sufficient testimony as to this displacement of population, indicating that it was important in some areas. It is impossible to say what portion of the indigenous population it affected. The Maeandrian districts were severely depopulated by the invasions.

Whence the Maeander was emptied not only of people in most of the extensive lands, but also of the very monks. For the land about the Maeander was another Palestine. It was very good not only for the increase of flocks and herds of animals, and for nourishing men, but excellent for assembling earthdwelling, heavenly citizen-monks . . . . And thus after a little the Maeander regions became desolate as the inhabitants withdrew deeper because of the attacks of the foreigners.[681]

Evidently the city of Tralles had been completely deserted before Andronicus rebuilt it. With the second capture and destruction in 1282,

---

[676] *Ibid.*, 311–312.

[677] *Ibid.*, 311.

[678] *Ibid.*, II, 335–337, 597, 637. Arnakes, 'Οθωμανοί, pp. 133 ff.

[679] Pachymeres, II, 413. I. Sakellion, " Συνοδικαὶ διαγνώσεις τῆς ΙΔ' ἑκατονταετηρίδος," Δ.Ι.Ε.Ε.Ε., III (1889), 413–424.

[680] Pachymeres, II, 402: " καὶ διὰ τοῦτο τῶν μὲν φονευομένων τῶν δ' ἀπανισταμένων, τῶν μὲν εἰς πόλεις καὶ φρούρια τῶν δ' εἰς νήσους, ἄλλων δὲ καὶ εἰς τὰ κατ' ἀντιπεραίαν ἀσφαλῆ, ὅπου ἂν καὶ σωθεῖεν, βλεπόντων καὶ ὁρμώντων, τῶν δ' ἐντὸς καὶ λίαν ἐνδεῶς ἐχόντων τῶν ἀναγκαίων διὰ τὴν τῶν ἐξωτερικῶν ἐξαπώλειαν." For removal of military bodies to Europe, *ibid.*, 407–408 On the flight of population to the isles, E. Zachariadou, " Συμβολὴ στὴν ἱστορία τοῦ νοτιοανατολικοῦ Αἰγαίου (μὲ ἀφορμὴ τὰ πατμιακὰ φιρμάνια τῶν ἐτῶν 1454–1522," Σύμμεικτα, Βασιλικὸν "Ιδρυμα 'Ερευνῶν, I (1966), 192–193.

[681] Pachymeres, I, 310–311. The implication is that the areas of Neocastron, Abala, Cayster, Magedon, and Caria were also affected by this depopulation. Halkin, "Manuscrits galésiotes, *Scriptorium*, vol. XV, pt. 2 (1961), pp. 221–227, on sacking of the libraries in the early fourteenth century.

its inhabitants who had survived, some 20,000, were taken off into slavery.[682] The regions of Magedon were left desolate as well.[683] When the expedition of 1302 against the Turks failed and the emperor withdrew to the walls of Magnesia on the Hermus, the Turks came in and began to put the inhabitants in the environs to the swords, those who survived fleeing to the isles and to the European shores.[684] When the emperor decided to leave Magnesia, many of the inhabitants decided to flee. Those who survived the rigors of the flight made their way to Pergamum, Adramyttium and Lampsacus, and most crossed the Hellespont.[685] A few years later the rural areas of Magnesia and the Hermus seem to have become largely deserted. A small portion of the population had sought refuge in the towns but the majority had crossed to the islands and Europe.[686]

Cyzicus, Pegae, Assus, and Cenchrae had also become points of refuge for the uprooted populations in Mysia.[687] When the pressure of the conquerors became too great on Assus, the inhabitants and refugees completely abandoned it and crossed over to the island of Mitylene.[688] Many who fled the Scamandrian region had sought safety at Cenchrae, but here the Christians were less fortunate than at Assus for the Turks reduced the town and put most of the inhabitants to death.[689] The

---

[682] Nicephorus Gregoras, I, 142.

[683] Pachymeres, I, 311, 468.

[684] Ibid., II, 314; " καὶ ὁ λαὸς μὲν κατεσφάττετο ὁ δ' ἀπανίστατο φθάνων, καὶ οἱ μὲν πρὸς νήσους τὰς ἐγγιζούσας οἱ δὲ πρὸς τὴν δύσιν διαπεραιούμενοι διεσώζοντο."

[685] Ibid., 318–319; " καὶ τὸ πρᾶγμα ποταμῶν ἔδοξεν ῥεῦμα." The parents of St. Philotheus fled Elateia opposite Lesbos and settled in Europe, " διὰ τὸν φόβον τῶν Ἀγαρηνῶν . . ." Papoulia, "Die Vita des Heiligen Philotheos von Athos," S.F., XXII (1963) 274.

[686] Pachymeres, II, 441–442. "οὐδεὶς οὖν ἐν χώραις ὑπελείπετο, ἀλλ' ὀλίγοι μὲν ταῖς πόλεσι παρεβύοντο, καὶ οὗτοι ἐκ τοῦ παρείκοντος, οἱ πλείους δὲ σοφώτερόν τι ποιοῦντες οἱ μὲν εἰς νήσους οἱ δ' εἰς ἀντιπεραίαν ὥρμων, καὶ τὰ αὐτῶν μακρόθεν ἑώρων, προσπελάζειν οὐ τολμῶντες οὐδ' ἐς βραχύ. οἱ δὲ τολμῶντες διὰ τὴν ἀνάγκην τῆς ἀπορίας αὐτόθεν πάσχοντες τὰ δεινὰ κατεμάνθανον, καὶ προμηθεῖς τοῦ ζῆν ἐποίουν τοὺς ἄλλους αὐτοὶ πίπτοντες· οὐ γὰρ ὡς πολεμίους σφᾶς οἱ Πέρσαι, ἀλλ' ὡς κλῶπας ὧν αὐτοὶ διὰ σπαθῆς ἐκτήσαντο, ἀνὰ χείρας πεσόντας ἐτιμωροῦντο καὶ ἀνηλεῶς ἔσφαττον." For other references to the flight of population from Asia Minor to the islands and Europe, as well as to the relocation of Anatolian military bodies in Macedonia see the following. Ahrweiler, "Smyrne," p. 28. Dölger, Aus den Schatzkammern des Heiligen Berges (Munich, 1948), I, 57–58, and Lemerle, Actes de Kutlumus (Paris, 1945), pp. 89–91, on the lands of the soldiers from Clazomenae who were resettled around Serres. Also Pachymeres, II, 407–408; ". . . στρατιώτας βασιλικῶν ἀλλαγίων, οἳ δὴ καὶ ἀνατολίηθεν ἀποικισθέντες ἐξ ὑπογύου διὰ τὴν καταδρομὴν τῶν Περσῶν αὐταῖς γυναιξὶ καὶ τέκνοις ἤλυον κατὰ δύσιν." On the desertion of the land: Pachymeres, I, 401; II, 314; William of Adam, R.H.C., D.A., II, 537; "Sunt eciam castra circumquaque pulcerrima et fortia, cum fossatis magnis et turribus, sed omni habitatore carentia."

[687] Pachymeres, II, 390; "καὶ τὸ Περσικὸν πολλαχόθεν ἐπεισβαλόντες τοὺς μὲν ἔργον καθιστᾶσι μαχαίρας, ὅσοι δέ γε καὶ ἴσχυσαν ἐκφευγεῖν, τῷ τῆς Κυζίκου ἐπετειχισμῷ ἄρτι τότε συστάντι παρὰ τοῦ ἐν αὐτῇ προέδρου Νίφωνος . . . φέροντες ἑαυτοὺς καὶ γυναῖκας καὶ τέκνα καὶ ζῶα καὶ ὕπαρξιν ἐγκατέκλεισαν." 415; " . . . καὶ Πηγαὶ παραθαλασσία πόλις τῶν δυσχερῶν ἐπειράθη. τῶν γὰρ ἔξω πάντων συγκλεισθέντων ἐντός, ὅσοι καὶ τὸ ξίφος ἔφυγον." The inhabitants of Ida and Scamander fled to Assos. Ibid., 438; "ὡς δὲ πᾶσαν τὴν ἐκεῖ χῶραν προκαταλαβόντων τὴν Ἴδην Περσῶν ἐρημοῦσθαι τῶν οἰκητόρων ξυνέβαινε."

[688] Ibid., 438, "καὶ κενὸν ἐντεῦθεν τὸ φρούριον καταλέλειπτο."

[689] Ibid., 443–445.

Sangarius valley experienced a considerable depopulation,[690] as did Bithynia in the quarter-century following the battle of Baphaeum, 1301.

> You saw at that time a pitiful sight, namely those who were carrying away their possessions and crossing over to the city [Constantinople], who had despaired of their salvation. And the straits received a throng of people and animals daily who had not been freed without the greatest of tragedies. There was no one who did not lament the privation of the members of his family, one recalling her husband, another her son or daughter, another a brother and sister, and another some name of a relation.[691]

Constantinople received such great numbers of these refugees that the city was soon oppressed by famine and attacked by the plague.[692] The town of Pegae, similarly swollen by the refugees and suffering from blockade by the enemy, was also struck by famine and a devastating plague.[693]

Famine and plague must have been common occurrences in most of western Anatolia at this time. Consequently the Turkish conquest and occupation produced considerable upheaval in the late thirteenth and early fourteenth century. In many areas, towns and villages were destroyed or abandoned (or partially so), and often the inhabitants fled to the large towns, to the isles, to Constantinople, or were taken captive by the Turks. The partial diminution of the indigenous population plus the settlement of the Turks resulted in a drastic demographic change. In a passage that strikingly recalls the words that Anna Comnena used to describe the destruction of coastal Anatolia in the late eleventh century, George Pachymeres wrote of the late thirteenth century:

> And thus in a short time the [Turks], attacking the land of the Rhomaioi, transformed it into another desert encompassing the length and width of the land from the Black Sea to the sea by Rhodes.[694]

Just what the proportion was between Greeks and Turks in early fourteenth-century Anatolia is difficult to say. The Arab traveler Ibn Battuta relates that Greeks were still to be found in large numbers in western Anatolia.[695] The conditions of this troubled period, however, brought upheaval to a large portion of the towns and countryside.

[690] *Ibid.*, I, 311, "σὺν οἷς καὶ ἔτι τὰ ἔνδον Σαγγάρεως, ἐπὶ τοσοῦτον ἠφάνιστο . . ." *Ibid.*, 313, ". . . τὰς τῶν χωρῶν πέραν τοῦ Σαγγάρεως ἐρημώσεις."

[691] *Ibid.*, II, 335.

[692] *Ibid.*, 412; "πεπλήθει δὲ τῶν ἀγρομένων ἡ πόλις, καὶ ἐστενοχωρεῖτο τοῖς πανταχοῦ κειμένοις εἰκῆ τε καὶ ὑπαιθρίοις, πνοῇ ζῆν καὶ μόνῃ πιστευομένοις. λιμὸς γὰρ ἐντεῦθεν καί γε λοιμὸς ἀθλίους διεμεριζέτην." Muntaner-Buchon, p. 420, relates that the refugees in Constantinople were roaming the streets, destitute and starving. Of these Greeks, the Almugavares gave food to 2,000 with the result that this group followed the Almugavares throughout the city. Papadopoulos-Kerameus, "*Zhitiia dvukh' vselenskikh' patriarkhov' XIV v. Svv. Ahanasiia I i Isidora I* (St. Petersburg, 1905), pp. 33–34, the patriarch personally doled out wheat and wine to the destitute refugees.

[693] Pachymeres, II, 415; "ἐντίκτει νόσον λοιμώδη τὸ συνεπτύχθαι λιμῷ καὶ κακοπαθείαις. ἔτι δὲ καὶ τῇ νόσῳ ἐς ἑκατοστύας ἔπιπτον."

[694] *Ibid.*, 232.

[695] Ibn Battuta Gibb, II, 415; "Why it is called after the Rum is because it used to be their land in older times, and from it came the ancient Rum and the Yunanis (Greeks).

In eastern Anatolia as early as 1235 Edessa had been sacked first by the sultan 'Ala' al-Din and then by Kamil of Egypt, the latter having taken off the artisan population to Egypt.[696] A few years later, about 1241–42, the Mongols razed Erzerum, killed most of the population, and enslaved the youths.[697] Both Kayseri and Erzindjan suffered the same fate in 1243—destruction, massacre, enslavement.[698] The Mongol invasions and Turkmen raids of the next decades obliterated the villages and environs of Melitene and reduced the area to a desert, so that the inhabitants of the city perished like animals in the bazaars.[699] In 1256–57 Baidju proceeded from Erzerum to Aksaray burning towns and devastating the provinces,[700] killing 7,000 of the inhabitants of Albistan and carrying off the young men and women.[701] The Mameluke armies, often followed by pillaging Turkmen bands, wrought such destruction in Cilicia during the late thirteenth century that the Christians fortified the coastal islands and began to take refuge there. In 1266 they burned and despoiled Sis, Mopsuestia, Ayas, and Adana.[702] A decade later Ayas, Mopsuestia, Tarsus, and Sis were once more burned, and the Greek and Armenian monasteries as far west as Corycus were reduced by fire.[703] The Mongols plundered Aksaray c. 1277, killing and enslaving 6,000 of the inhabitants,[704] and the rebel Djimri ruthlessly plundered Konya and its environs in 1276.[705] The sparse documentation from Trebizond indicates that plague and invasions also

---

Later on it was conquered by the Muslims, but in it there are still large numbers of Christians under the protection of the Muslims, these latter being Turkmens." Marino Sanudo Torsello, *Istoria del regno di Romania*, ed. in C. Hopf, *Chroniques Greco-Romanes inédites ou peu connues* (Berlin, 1873), p. 142; "In l'Asia Minor, e ch'è maggior Paese, che non à la Spagna, della qual abbiamo detto esser quarto Regni, la qual per la maggior parte à sottoposta a Turchi, per il piu li Popoli seguono il Ritto Greco e sono per il piu Greci. Anco l'Armenia, che si chiamava anticamente Cilicia, è abitata da Greci. In la Mesopotamia è gran quantita di Greci e solevano esser molto piu al tempo del passaggio di Piero Eremita e Goffredo di Buglione, il cui fratello Balduino fu Conte in Mesopotamia, e si chiamva Conte de Roas."

[696] Bar Hebraeus, I, 401.

[697] *Ibid.*, 406. Ibn Bibi-Duda, pp. 223–224.

[698] Bar Hebraeus, I, 406–409. Ibn Bibi-Duda, pp. 230–231.

[699] Bar Hebraeus, I, 409, also 419–420, 426. Not only did the Turkmens carry away all the livestock from the rural area of Hisn Mansur, but they also sacked the Christian monasteries of Madik, Masye, and Mar Dimat.

[700] Aksaray-Gençosman, p. 136.

[701] Bar Hebraeus, I, 426.

[702] Canard, "Cilicia," EI₂, lists devastating Mameluke raids in Cilicia for the years 1266, 1275, 1283, 1297, 1303, 1315, 1320, 1322, 1335, 1337, etc. Brocquière (Brocquière-Schefer, *passim*), who traveled in Cilicia in the first half of the fifteenth century describes a region which has still not recovered from Mameluke and Turkmen depredations. The Turkmen nomads have settled on the land and the Christians have retreated to the fortresses, mountains, and to the islands. The decline of Genoese commerce in Cilicia dates from the later thirteenth century, C. Desimoni, "Actes passés en 1271, 1274 et 1279 à l'Asias (Petite Armenie)," *Archives de l'orient latin*, I (1881), 435.

[703] Bar Hebraeus, I, 456, 452–453. 60,000 were killed and many enslaved. The raids of Turkmens and Mamelukes continued throughout the century, *ibid.*, 460, 465.

[704] Aksaray-Gençosman, p. 208. Mongol armies plundered the districts of Konya, Ermenak, and Laranda. Aksaray-Gençosman, p. 209.

[705] Ibn Bibi-Duda, pp. 312–316.

caused a certain depopulation and movement of the inhabitants to more secure areas.[706]

This upheaval, however, was never complete, and many areas recuperated in the course of the fourteenth century, though one must assume that Anatolian conditions did not again attain the stability and prosperity of the early thirteenth century. Traces of this less fortunate period were still visible in the fourteenth century. Ibn Battuta remarked that in 1333 Erzerum was still mostly in ruins as a result of the feud between two groups of Turkmens;[707] Izmir too was largely a ruined town;[708] the site of Ephesus was abandoned for the neighboring heights, and the Christian population was removed. Pergamum was a shambles, as was Iznik which was uninhabited.[709] The emperor Manuel Palaeologus, who had occasion to visit Anatolia while performing military service in the army of the sultan Bayazid, observed that many of the older Byzantine towns of northern Anatolia were uninhabited and destroyed.[710] In the south Ludolph of Suchem observed about 1350 that both Patara and Myra were ruined as a result of the Turkish invasions and a century later Arnold von Harff found the same conditions at Laranda.[711] One must conclude, then, that though the events of the late thirteenth and the early fourteenth century were not complete and unqualified disasters in the long run for many of the Anatolian towns, they were serious enough

---

[706] Panaretus-Lampsides, pp. 63, 64, 66, 68, 74, 77. The plague, which seems to have visited the inhabitants regularly, is recorded in 1341, 1348, 1362, 1382. The monastic documents, though very fragmentary, illuminate the process by which the Turkmen raids and invasions, by enslavement, led to gradual depopulation in certain areas, T. Uspensky and V. Beneševič, *Vazelonskie Akty* (Leningrad, 1927), pp. 7, 17, 39, 40, 57–58, 76, 78. For further indications of the desolation that the Turks wrought, Bessarion-Lampros, pp. 35, 40.

[707] Ibn Battuta-Gibb, II, 437.

[708] Ibn Battuta-Gibb, II, 445. Ludolph of Suchem-Neumann, 332. F. Deycks, *Ludolphi rectoris ecclesiae parochialis in Suchem de itinere terrae sanctae liber* (Stuttgart, 1851), pp. 24–25 (hereafter cited as Ludolph of Suchem-Deycks).

[709] Ibn Battuta-Gibb, II, 448, 453.

[710] Manuel Palaeologus, *Lettres de l'empereur Manuel Paléologue* ed. E. Legrand (Amsterdam, 1962), p. 22 (hereafter cited as Manuel Palaeologus-Legrand), "Τὸ δὲ πεδίον ἐν ᾧ νῦν ἐσμεν εἶχε μέν τινα προσηγορίαν πάντως, ὅτε εὐτύχει ὑπὸ Ῥωμαίων πατούμενόν τε καὶ δεσποζόμενον· νῦν δὲ ζητούντι ταύτην μαθεῖν, λύκου πτερά, ὅ φασιν, ἀτεχνῶς μοι συμβαίνει ζητεῖν, τῇ τοῦ διδάξαντος ἐρημίᾳ. Πόλεις δὲ ἰδεῖν μέν ἐστιν ἐνταῦθα πολλάς, οὔκουν δ᾽, οἷς μάλιστα κοσμοῦνται πόλεις καὶ ὧν χωρὶς οὐκ ἂν κυρίως καλοῖντο πόλεις, περιεχούσας ἀνθρώπους. Αἱ δὲ πλείους καὶ κεῖνται θέαμα τούτοις ἐλεινόν." Ibid., p. 23, " Ἀκούεις τὴν Πομπηίου, τὴν καλὴν καὶ θαυμαστὴν καὶ μεγάλην, μᾶλλον δὲ τὴν ποτε τοιαύτην οὖσαν (νῦν γὰρ μόγις που λείψανα ταύτης φαίνεται)."

[711] Ludolph of Suchem-Deycks, pp. 26–27. Ludolph of Suchem-Stewart, p. 33. Arnold von Harff, *Die Pilgerfahrt des Ritters Arnold von Harff von Cöln durch Italien, Syrien, Arabien, Aethiopien, Nubien, Palästina, die Türkei, Frankreich und Spanien, wie er sie in den Jahren 1496 bis 1499 vollendet, beschrieben und durch zeichnungen erlautert hat*, ed. E. von Groote (Cologne, 1860), p. 202 (hereafter cited as Arnold von Harff-Groote), "Item van Kukro zo Larantaiij daichreyss, eyn zo brochen stat." *The Pilgrimage of Arnold von Harff Knight from Cologne, through Italy, Syria, Egypt, Arabia, Ethiopia, Nubia, Palestine, Turkey, France and Spain, which he accomplished in the years 1496 to 1499*, trans. M. Letts (London, 1946), p. 237 (hereafter cited as von Harff-Letts), See also Kazwini-Le Strange, pp. 96–98, on decline of Ermenak, Bayburt, Avnik, Abashkir, Kir, and Baqih.

to lessen the former prosperity and stability of Anatolia, to cause a marked displacement of the native Christian element in many areas, and to bring about the final decline or destruction of some towns and villages. This displacement of Christian population which arose from plague, famine, massacre, enslavement, and migration, along with the arrival of new Turkic and Mongol groups in Anatolia, resulted in an important demographic and ethnic alteration of the Anatolian population. But as has already been mentioned, it is very difficult to say anything about numbers or proportions. It is surely true that this late thirteenth- and fourteenth-century period is the period of final, critical change in the ethnic and religious configuration of Anatolia. The continuing process of conquest and reconquest had considerable effect on the indigenous population.[712]

The Nomads

Though the final conquest and reunification of Anatolia were the accomplishment of a complex and highly organized state, the principal cause of the upheavals from the late thirteenth through the fifteenth century (as of the eleventh and twelfth centuries) was the reactivation of the independence of the tribal groups. The very nature of their economy, society, and culture was such that tribal interests and conduct were frequently inimical to those of sedentary society. To be sure the periodic invasions of Mongols, Mamelukes, and others contributed to the unsettling of Anatolia, but the nomads often utilized these invasions to throw off the restraints to which one or another state had subjected them. Since the role of the Turkmens was important in the Anatolian cultural mutation, it is of the greatest interest to examine their polity in some detail and to understand how this peculiar polity might have had a disrupting effect on Byzantine society. It is true that eventually many of the nomads settled on the land, and that even those who did not settle on the land eventually came to a modus vivendi with the sedentary population. But until all this was regularized and Anatolia attained stability, the nomadic element contributed greatly to the attrition that Byzantine society underwent. In addition, as conditions in some Anatolian villages became

---

[712] We have an eyewitness as to the effect of these conditions on the Christian churches in Anatolia by the end of the thirteenth century, Ricoldus de Monte Crucis, "Lettres de Monte-Croce sur la prise d'Acre (1291)," ed. R. Röhricht in Archives de L'Orient Latin, II (1884), 273 (hereafter cited as Ricoldus de Monte Crucis, Röhricht), "Certe, credo, quod nosti, quod presens eram in Sebaste, civitate Turchie, quando postquam receperunt nova de dolorosa captione Tripolitana, ligaverunt crucem cum ymagine crucifixi ad caudam equi et traxerunt per totam civitatem per cenum, incipientes a loco fratrum et christianorum et hoc in die dominica ad maiorem contumeliam christianorum et Christi . . . . Nonne in tota Turchia et Percide et usque ad Baldactum invenimus omnes ecclesias christianorum diruptas aut stabulatas aut mescitas factas Sarracenorum? Et ubi non potueruent ecclesiam destruere vel stabulare, statim iuxta ecclesiam edificaverunt meschitam et menaram cum turri alta, ut super caput christianorum clament legem, ymmo perfidiam Machometi."

Partial List of Towns and Villages
Destroyed, Pillaged, Enslaved, or Massacred

WESTERN ASIA MINOR	EASTERN ASIA MINOR	SOUTHERN ASIA MINOR	NORTHERN ASIA MINOR
Tralles	Edessa	Mopsuestia	Pompeiopolis
Priene	Kayseri	Tarsus	Tokat
Miletus	Erzindjan	Ayas	Kemah
Caria	Albistan	Adana	
Antioch	Aksaray	Corycus	
Melanoudium	Erzerum	Patara	
Nysa	Sebasteia	Myra	
Tripolis	Alaskert	Laranda	
Thyraia	Ani	Eregli	
Ephesus	Malatya	Selefke	
Magnesia ad Hermum			
Croulla			
Catoicia			
Cenchrae			
Belocome			
Angelocome			
Anagourda			
Platanea			
Melangeia			
Assus			
Bursa			
Nicaea			
Apameia			
Smyrna			
Uluburlu			
Egridir			
Konya			
Koladna			
Karahisar			
Aynegöl			
Kopruhisar			
Akhisar			
Biğa			
Kevele			

marginal to their continued existence because of the economic crises and rebellions in the sixteenth and seventeenth centuries, a number of villages were abandoned. Consequently, the Ottoman government forced more tribal groups to settle and to abandon nomadism with the result that the older village population of the countryside underwent almost constant corrosion followed by the imposition of Turkmen groups on the soil.[713] This continued the process of Turkification and Islamization by elements that were closer to the original Turkish culture than even the older Muslim villagers.

There is sufficient source material to attempt here a composite sketch of the nomadic society that entered Anatolia in an almost continuous process during the four or five centuries following the battle of Manzikert, and to illustrate those features that contributed to this upheaval. It is not at all surprising that the details of Anatolian tribal life which emerge here and there in the contemporary sources agree with the general descriptions of Turco-Mongol society in Central Asia, which such authorities as Ibn Fadlan, al-Marwazi, and William of Rubruque have preserved. Obviously, there were differences among the various Turkic groups in central Asia, but one should recall that the settlement of Anatolia was not exclusively the work of any one tribal group or subgroup. Beside the Oghuz or Turkmen followers of the Seljuks, there were also Kipchaks, Patzinaks, Mongols, Chagatays from Timur's horde, Khwarazmians, and others.[714]

If any single feature can be said to characterize Turkmen institutions,

---

[713] M. Akdağ, *Celali isyanları* (*1550–1603*) (Ankara, 1962). C. Orhonlu, *Osmanlı imparatorluğunda aşiretleri iskan teşebbüsü* (*1691–1696*) (Istanbul, 1963).

[714] A. von Gabain, "Steppe und Stadt im Leben der ältesten Turken," *Der Islam*, XXIX (1950), 30–62, points out the hostility of settled and nomad Turks in Central Asia. W. König, *Die Achal-Teke. Zur Wirtschaft und Gesellschaft einer Turkmenen-Gruppe im XIX Jahrhundert* (Berlin, 1962), studies the Teke, who belonged to the Salor, one of the twentyfour tribes mentioned by Kashgari. A branch of the Teke came to Asia Minor in the period of the conquests. The Teke that König has studied occupied the Achal-Tekin oasis of central Asia in the eighteenth and nineteenth centuries. For general considerations of nomads in the Islamic world, H. von Wissmann, "Bauer, Nomade und Stadt im islamischen Orient," *in Die Welt des Islam und die Gegenwart*, ed. R. Paret (Stuttgart, 1961), pp. 22–63. Barkan, "Les déportations comme méthode de peuplement et de colonisation dans l'empire ottoman," *Revue de la faculté des sciences économiques de l'Université d'Istanbul*, II (1949–50), 81, gives a list of Anatolian place names derived from Turkmen "boys" and which indicate that all twentyfour "boys" of the Oghuz Turks participated in the settlement of Anatolia.

Kayï	36	Charïklï	20	Eymur	106	Yüregir
Bayat	40	Beğdili	10	Alayundlu	25	Bechenek
Yazir	44	Karkïn	34	Igdish	17	Düğer
Yaber	15	Bayïndïr	29	Bugduz	6	Alkaevli
Dodurga	13	Chavuldur	51	Yïva	35	Karaevli
Avshar	54	Sakïr	28			Chepni

See also de Planhol, "Geography, Politics and Nomadism in Anatolia," *International Social Journal*, XI (1959), 525–531.

one would have to say that it was mobility.[715] Their military, social, and cultural institutions were formed on the common axis of mobility, for mobility was the key to survival. It was by virtue of this quality that the nomad fled or struck the enemy and obtained the economic wherewithal for existence, whether in the practice of transhumant pastoralism and marginal agriculture or in raids for booty. Movement, either between summer and winter quarters or to wage war, entailed a mass movement not only of the men but of their womenfolk, children, livestock, carts, and tents. One fourteenth-century observer remarked:

It is the habit of the Turks and Tartars to take their wives, their little ones, and all their property with them in their army whithersoever they march.[716]

Nomad armies on the move constituted a nation on the move with the consequence that their families, economy, and houses were all "portable," that is to say that they had "movable" institutions. At first glance one might surmise that this mobile aspect of nomad institutional life implies a smallness of numbers in terms of the size of the nomad groups. Actually the numbers of various tribal groups both inside and outside Anatolia indicate that the amount of people involved in tribal movements could attain tens of thousands and on rare occasion even hundreds of thousands, though of course smaller numbers were more usual. Nevertheless, it is remarkable that such large movements could be carried out successfully. The most spectacular, in terms of numbers, of such tribal agglomerations (where figures have survived) are those of the Tatars about Tana in southern Russia said to have numbered 300,000 in the first half of the fifteenth century, and the Chagatay horde of Timur of 20,000 tents.[717] The numbers of the Anatolian groups seem to have been much smaller, though it is impossible to say anything about the size of the original invading groups.[718] This is no doubt a reflection of the fact that when the tribes came in they broke up into smaller groups as they found pasturages or settled permanently on the land. But occasionally there is mention of large tribal groups, usually in Cilicia, eastern Anatolia, and the Udj land

[715] Theodore Metochites, *Miscellanea philosophica et historica* ed. C. G. Müller and T. Kiessling (Leipzig, 1821), pp. 725 ff (hereafter cited as Metochites-*Miscellanea*). It is to be seen in their nomenclature. In Danishmendname-Melikoff, II, 22, they are *gokçünçi*, and in later Turkish *yürük*, *göçebe*. In Greek they are νομάδες, and in Latin *bedewini*. Barkan, "Déportations," *passim.*, discusses their mobility as a factor in Ottoman policies of colonization in the Balkans.

[716] Ludolph of Suchem-Deycks, p. 29. Ludolph of Suchem-Steward, p. 37.

[717] *Travels of Joseph Barbaro*, in works issued by the Hakluyt Society (London, 1873), p. 16 (hereafter cited as Barbaro-Hakluyt). De Clavijo-Le Strange, pp. 233–234.

[718] The following figures are reported in contemporary sources: 5,000 raiders in the Taurus, 1187 (Bar Habraeus, I, 328); 12,000 raiders, 1107–1108 (Matthew of Edessa, p. 264); 6,000 raiders, 1108–1109 (Matthew of Edessa, p. 265); 2,000 raiders in Dorylaeum, 1175 (Cinnamus, 295); 8,000 raiders of Pseudoalexius in western Anatolia (Nicetas Choniates, 551); 3,000 cavalry and 2,000 infantry killed by Catalans at Artake, 1303 (Muntaner-Buchon, 419); 8,000 cavalry of Chindi in lesser Armenia. (*Narrative of the Most Noble Vincento d'Allessandri, Ambassador to the King of Persia for the Most Illustrious Republic of Venice*, Hakluyt Society (London, 1873), p. 228 (hereafter cited as Alessandri-Hakluyt).

on the western rim of the Anatolian plateau between Dorylaeum and the hinterland of Antalya. In this latter district the tribal groups seem to have been quite densely settled and they retained their tribal structure in a vigorous state. In 1176, 50,000 of these tribesmen attacked Manuel I on his way to Myriocephalum[719] and a few years later (1189) the Crusaders of Frederick Barbarossa were savagely attacked by what must have been a great tribal mustering, for according to one source the assembled tribesmen (with their families probably) numbered 100,000.[720] An Arab source of the thirteenth century lists the tribal population of this Udj at 200,000.[721] Large tribal confederations also appeared in east and southeast Anatolia from the thirteenth through the fifteenth century. The Dhu'l-Kadroghlu could put 30,000 men and 30,000 women in the field in the first half of the fifteenth century.[722] Brocquiere saw one chieftain in Cilicia who could furnish 2,000 horsemen for military service, and Kara Yusuf in eastern Anatolia could muster 10,000.[723] The size of these latter tribal confederations of easter Anatolia (Akkoyunlu, Karakoyunlu, Dhu'l-Kadroghlu) is perhaps indicated by the following incident. On one of his Anatolian campaigns, Timur came upon a large Akkoyunlu group (men, women, and children) which he took "captive" and forcibly transplanted to the regions of Samarqand. This group numbered between 50,000 and 60,000 souls.[724] Though one cannot insist upon the reliability of such figures, nevertheless they are a consistent indication of the fact that tribal groups and confederations were occasionally quite large.[725]

[719] Michael the Syrian, III, 371.

[720] Salimbene, 11. They were all under one chief.

[721] Turan, *Selçuklular tarihi ve Türk-Islam medeniyeti* (Ankara, 1965), p. 215. It was this buildup of Turkmens on the plateau rim which resulted in the final Turkish conquest of western Asia Minor when the Byzantine defenses disintegrated from within. The figures reproduced by al-Umari are indicative of these large numbers, but the armies of the emirates by the second quarter of the fourteenth century were already the armies of sedentary princes and so their forces were no longer exclusively composed of tribesmen.

[722] Brocquière-Schefer, pp. 82, 118. In one place Brocquière contradicts himself by saying that the number of women was 100,000!

[723] Brocquière-Schefer, p. 93. De Clavijo Le Strange, p. 320. The Karamanids mustered a force of 20,000 in the thirteenth century. Aksaray-Gençosman, pp. 159–160.

[724] De Clavijo-Le Strange, pp. 134, 173–174. When de Clavijo journeyed in the district of Samarqand he saw pyramids of their skulls. Inasmuch as the Akkoyunlu had decided to return to Anatolia, Timur had them massacred and then used their skulls interspersed with layers of brick to erect these pyramids.

[725] For the numbers of nomads in the early Ottoman tax registers in the province of Anadolu, Barkan, "Essai sur les données statistiques des registres de recensement dans l'empire ottoman aux XVe et XVIe siècles," *J.E.S.H.O.*, I (1957), table no. 5 on p. 30. The province of Anadolu included Anatolia west of a line running from Sinope to Alaiya and had the following taxable hearths. (Column A represents 1520–35; column B represents 1570–80)

Sedentary Muslims		Nomads		Christians		Jews		Total	
A	B	A	B	A	B	A	B	A	B
388,397	535,495	77,268	116,219	8,511	20,264	271	534	474,447	672,512

Taxable nomad hearths were 16.29 percent of the total in 1520–35, and 17.28 percent

This great mobility in large numbers was a crucial factor in the dislocation of Byzantine rural society, for large foreign bodies were suddenly interposed in Anatolia. The mechanics of their mobility, autarky, and autonomy are not so clearly delineated, but certain details of this large ethnic invasion-migration nevertheless emerge. It was precisely this magnitude that differentiated the Turkmens from the Arab invaders of Anatolia. The former constituted migratory conquests, the latter small-scale *razzias* for booty or else occasional military expeditions in the trains of which no settlers were brought. There are numerous references to the presence of women, children, and livestock in the Turkmen armies at war in Anatolia,[726] but the most informative description of such a tribal-nation on the march is that of Uzun Hasan's followers in the latter half of the fifteenth century. A Western ambassador, the Italian Barbaro, was present at the mustering of the Akkoyunlu leader's host as it set out from Tabriz, and he has given a detailed account of it. A great area was covered by the assembled horses that, touching each other's head, comprehended thirty "miles" in circuit. Order was insured not only by the discipline of each individual but also by agents of the ruler who made a reckoning of the captains and the host and made sure that all was arranged properly. The assembly plain contained the following bodies[727] as shown on p. 264.

Uzun Hasan obviously had troops (slaves) who were traditional in Islamic statecraft and therefore not reflective of tribal practices. But the essentially tribal character of this mustering is evident in the presence of the livestock, women, and children. The women played an important role in the march, their faces covered with mufflers of horsehair to shield

---

of the total in 1570–80. On the proportion in the Balkans during the early sixteenth century, Barkan, "Déportations," pp. 129–131.

Sedentary Muslims	Nomads	Christians	Jews	Total
156,565	37,435	832,707	4,134	c.1,031,799

Taxable nomad hearths were about 19.3 percent of the Muslim population and about 3.6 percent of the total Balkan population.

[726] Planudes-Treu, p. 175. Muntaner-Buchon, p. 419. *Historia Peregrinorum*, p. 155. *Gesta Federici*, pp. 87, 95. Brosset, *Géorgie*, I, 358–359, for Georgia. Panaretus-Lampsides, pp. 78–79. Ibn Bibi-Duda, pp. 219–220. Obviously there were numerous occasions when the Turkmens raided unaccompanied by their families and flocks. Planudes-Treu, pp. 166–167, states that they left them in a recently captured Byzantine fort; Turks and Tourkopouloi left their families in care of the Catalans. Muntaner-Buchon, p. 454. Muntaner-Buchon, p. 449, remarks that the Alans move and war like the Tatars, i.e., with all their belongings and families, and do not live in cities. The early Arabs warred and moved about similarly, Ibn Khaldun, *The Muqaddimah. An Introduction to History*, trans. F. Rosenthal (London, 1958) II, 67 (hereafter cited as Ibn Khaldun), "When they [Arab bedouins in Umayyad period] went on raids or went to war, they travelled with all their camels, their nomad households [*hilal*], and their dependent women and children, as is still the case with the Arabs [bedouins] at this time. Their armies, therefore, consisted of many nomad households, and the distance between the encampments was great . . . . This was why Abd al-Malik used to need drivers to keep the people together and make them follow him."

[727] Barbaro-Hakluyt, pp. 66–67.

6,000	pavillions	5,000	carriage horses
30,000	camels	2,000	asses
5,000	cargo mules	20,000	service horses
2,000	mules	100	hunting leopards
20,000	cattle (small)	200	falcons
11,000	cattle (great)	3,000	greyhounds
		50	goshawks
15,000	soldiers of the sword		
2,000	slaves, etc., with swords		
1,000	archers	3,000	footmen of villeins and bows
. . . .	*		
25,000	good horsemen in all		
10,000	women of the best and middle sort		
5,000	women servants		
6,000	boys and girls under 12 yrs.		
5,000	children		

their faces from the sun. The infants were carried at the pommel of the
saddle on the horses the women rode. In what must have been an extraordinary feat of dexterity, the female rider with her left hand held the
cradle of the baby in place and also the horse reins, while with the right
hand she urged the horse on, with a whip attached to the little finger.
She also had to give suckle to her infant during the course of her trips.
Older children rode in covered litters carried atop the horses. In this long
train of humanity were present tailors, shoemakers, smiths, saddlers,
fletchers, victuallers, and apothecaries.[728] Parallel, and equally spectacular, are the descriptions that de Clavijo, the Spanish ambassador,
gave of the marshaling of the Turkic Chagatays in the early fifteenth
century.

When Timur calls his people to war all assemble and march with him, surrounded
by their flocks and herds, thus carrying along their possessions with them, in
company with their wives and children. These last follow the host, and in the
lands which they invade their flocks, namely and particularly the sheep camels and
horses, serve to ration the horde. Thus marching at the head of his people Timur
has accomplished great deeds and gained many victories, for the [Tartars] are a
very valiant folk, fine horsemen, very skillful at shooting with the bow, and
exceedingly hardy. In camp should they have victuals in plenty they eat their fill:
if they have lack, milk and meat without baked bread suffices them, and for a
long season they can thus march with or without halting to prepare bread stuffs,
living on [the meat and milk of] their flocks and herds. They suffer cold and heat
and hunger and thirst more patiently than any other nation in the whole world . . . .
You are to understand farther that none of these Chagatays, when on the march
with the host, ever separate from their women and children or from their herds
and flocks. These all march with them as they go to war, migrating from one place
to the next. When thus on the way the women who have small children carry them

[728] *Ibid.*, pp. 64–68. *A Short Narrative of the Life and Acts of the King Ussun Cassano by
Giovan Maria Angiolello*, Hakluyt Society (London, 1873), 94 (hereafter cited as Angiolello-
Hakluyt), is a reworked and later version of this author.

along in little craddles which, as the woman rides on horseback, she lays on the saddle bow in front. Such cradles are conveniently supported by broad straps which pass round the body, and thus the children are carried along. Indeed the women appear to ride as comfortably and lightly thus burdened with their offspring as though they were free of them. The poorer folk have to load their families, with their tents, on their camels, but the children then are worse off than those who travel with their mothers on horse-back, for the camel goes with a much rougher step than the horse.[729]

One must assume that the hosts of Timur and Uzun Hasan differed in some ways and in size from the tribes of Anatolia, but basically the type of organization was the same.

The weapons and military tactics of the Turkmens were well suited to the mobile character of their society. Though they utilized infantry, the sword, and the spear, the Turkmens preferred the mounted archer and the majority of their military forces usually must have consisted of archers on horseback. This made of the tribesmen difficult and dangerous foes who were nearby and yet far-off, enabling them to slay their foes from a distance, often without coming into close contact with them. Though the Greeks began to adjust to this type of hit and run warfare, which relied very heavily upon ruses and ambushes, the Franks, because of their heavy

---

[729] De Clavijo-Le Strange, pp. 191, 196. The same orderly arrangement attended the assembly of the tribes on more peaceful occasions, as in preparation for a feast of celebration which de Clavijo witnessed.

"In the plain here Timur recently had ordered tents to be pitched for his accommodation, and where his wives might come, for he had commanded the assembling of the great Horde, which hitherto and until now had been out in camp in the pastures beyond the orchard lands round and about the city. The whole of the Horde was now to come in, each clan taking up its appointed place: and we now saw them here, pitching the tents, their women folk accompanying them. This was done in order that all [these Chagatays] might have their share in the festivities which were going forward for the celebration of certain royal marriages now about to be declared. From their custom as soon as the camp of his Highness thus had been pitched all these folk of the Horde exactly knew where each clan had its place. From the greatest to the humblest each man knew his allotted position, and took it up, without confusion in most orderly fashion. Thus in the course of the next three or four days we saw near twenty-thousand tents pitched in regular streets to encircle the royal camp, and daily more clans came in from the outlying districts. Throughout the Horde thus encamped we saw the butchers and cooks who passed to and fro selling their roast and boiled meats, while others purveyed barley and fruit, while bakers with their ovens alight were kneading the dough and making bread for sale. Thus every craft and art needful for supply was to be found dispersed throughout the camp and each trade was in its appointed street of the great Horde. And more than this was to be found fully prepared; for there were baths and bathers established in the camp, who pitching their tents had built wooden cabins adjacent each with its iron bath that is supplied with hot water, heated in the caldrons which, with all the furniture necessary to their craft, they have there. Thus all was duly ordered and each man knew his place to go to beforehand." *Ibid.*, pp. 233–234.

Ibid., p. 290, also relates that when he departed for the campaign against Bayazid he planned to be away from Samarqand for seven years with the result that it was announced that all those who so desired might take their families with them to the war. For a description of the Mongol army, *The History of the World-Conqueror by 'Ala-ad-Din' Ata-Malik Juvaini, translated from the Text of Mirza Muhammad Qazvini* by J. A. Boyle (Manchester, 1958), I, 29–32 (hereafter cited as Juvaini-Boyle). See also Gordlevski, *Izbrannye Soch.*, I, 79, for further description of Timur's army, and p. 88, for the tribal institutions such as the kurultai.

armor and reliance upon shock combat, never did adapt to the nomadic military tactics[730]. The nomads were most effective, of course, when they were accompanied by the armies of the sultans, as at Manzikert and Myriocephalum, or when the military defenses of the enemy were in a decayed state. But more frequently they carried out military raids and banditry, on their own, for booty at the expense of their settled neighbors.[731] The total involvement of all adult tribal members in their migratory and military movements is also reflected in the military role of the Turkmen women. The fifteenth-century Ottoman historian Ashïkpashazade speaks of the *bahdjyan-i Rum*, the women of Anatolia, as one of the four groups of travelers (along with Abdals, Akhis, and Ghazis) sojourning in Anatolia. This possibly refers to the Turkmen women, who assumed along with their maternal tasks, military duties. The Dulgadiroğullarï in east Anatolia are said to have had 30,000 such women-soldiers at their command,[732] and the subject is so frequently mentioned by observers[733] and poets[734] that one assumes it to have been a regular aspect of Turkmen organization and life.

The political thought and action of the tribesmen were characterized by a certain independence and insubordination, at least in Anatolia, during much of the Seljuk and early Ottoman periods. Though originally "loyal" to the princes of the ruling Seljuk tribe (Kïnïk), their rebellious

[730] *Chronique de la principauté française d'Achaie*, ed. J. A. C. Buchon (Paris, 1841), p. 24 (hereafter cited as Chronique d'Achaie-Buchon). Varying opinions on Turkmen horses and archery may be seen in the following: Marco Polo-Yule, I, 43. Brocquière-Schefer, p. 83, *passim*. For the influence of Turkish cavalry and archery on the Trebizondine Greeks, de Clavijo-Le Strange, p. 115, who relates that the Pontus Greeks used the Turkish short stirrups and also Turkish arms. Brocquière, trans. T. Wright in *Early Travels in Palestine* (London, 1847), p. 339 (hereafter cited as Brocquière-Wright), describes a Turkish military exercise that the Greeks of Constantinople adopted. "In the front of St. Sophia is a large and handsome square, surrounded with walls like a palace, where games were performed in ancient times [the hippodrome]. I saw the brother of the emperor, the despot of the Morea, exercising himself there, with a score of other horsemen. Each had a bow, and they galloped along the inclosure, throwing their hats before them, which, when they had passed, they shot at; and he who with his arrow pierced his hat, or was nearest to it, was esteemed the most expert. This exercise they had adopted from the Turks, and it was one of which they were endeavouring to make themselves masters." On the Turkish practice of branding horses, Riza Nur, "Tamga." It is also quite probable that independent military developments among the Greeks influenced the arms and tactics of the Turks. Bodies of yoemen archers, τζαγγρατόρες had developed throughout Byzantine Anatolia from the twelfth century. On the probable Frankish origin of the τζάγγρα and its passage to the Turks via the Greeks, see below chapter vii. Gökbilgin, *Rumeli'de Yürükler, Tatarlar ve Evlad-i Fatihan* (Istanbul, 1957), p. 31, on the arms of the Yürüks in the fifteenth and sixteenth centuries.

[731] See above, chapter ii. *A Narrative of Travels in Persia by Caterino Zeno*, Hakluyt Society (London, 1873), p. 22 (hereafter cited as Zeno-Hakluyt), for an example of these devastations.

[732] Brocquière-Schefer, pp. 82, 118.

[733] Zeno-Hakluyt, p. 59. Ludolph of Suchem-Stewart, p. 37. De Clavijo-Le Strange, p. 297, reports the active participation of the soldiers' wives in one of Timur's campaigns.

[734] F. Iz, "Dede Korkut," EI₂. The twelfth-century geographer al-Marwazi relates the Amazons to Turkmen women-soldiers. Minorsky, *Sharaf al-Zaman Tahir Marwazi on China, the Turks and Arabs* (London, 1942), pp. 38, 122 (hereafter cited as al-Marwazi-Minorksy).

actions against the tribal chieftains who became monarchs are in evidence as early as the reigns of Toghrul Beg and Alp Arslan, and throughout the twelfth century in Iran.[735] Once their leaders in Asia Minor settled down in the cities and became monarchs of sedentary society, the same splitting between the sultans and the tribesmen appears. The fickle character of their political loyalty was evident as late as the fifteenth century.

They live in the open plain, and have a chief whom they obey; but they frequently change their situation, when they carry their houses with them. In this case, they are accustomed to submit themselves to the lord on whose lands they fix, and even to assist him with their arms, should he be at war. But should they quit his domains, and pass over to those of his enemy, they serve him in his turn against the other; and they are not thought the worse of for this, as it is their custom, and they are wanderers.[736]

Their begs, though theoretically loyal, frequently acted independently of the sultans, on occasion rebelling, disregarding general policies of the sultans, and even momentarily joining the Byzantines.[737] Their insubordination reached spectacular proportions in the rebellions of the Babai and of the Karamanids in the thirteenth century and culminated in the disappearance of the Seljuk state and the appearance of the emirates.[738] Throughout the period one sees Turkmen groups joining the Byzantines—Alexius I, John II, and Manuel I obtained the services of the Turkmens against the sultans—and in the late thirteenth century Turkmens joined the Greek general Philanthropenus.

The Turkmen tribal economy, as other phases of tribal life, was a "portable" one, consisting of pastoralism and raiding. The "means of production" in both cases, their animals and bows, were efficiently suited to their mobile existence. The primary Turkmen source of economic sustenance lay in their great herds of camels, horses, mules, asses, sheep, and goats.

Almost all the inhabitants [of Turcomania-Armenia] are Turcomans or Arabs, and their profession is breeding cattle, such as camels, goats, cows, and sheep. The goats are, for the most part, white, and the handsomest I have ever seen, not having, like those of Syria, hanging ears; and their hair is soft, of some length and curling. Their sheep have thick and broad tails. They also feed wild asses, which they tame; these much resemble stags in their hair, ears, and head, and have, like them, cloven feet. I know not if they have the same cry, for I never heard them. They are large, handsome, and go with other beasts, but I have never seen them

---

[735] Turan, *Selcuklular tarihi*, p. 188.

[736] Brocquière-Wright, p. 316.

[737] On this primary loyalty to their begs, rather than to the sultan, Brocquière-Schefer, p. 92. *Gesta Federici*, p. 87. Both Manuel I Comnenus and Frederick Barbarossa complained to Kĭlĭdj II Arslan that the Turkmens were not observing the treaties that the respective states had concluded with Konya. The Seljuk sultan replied that he was powerless to control the nomads. On the other hand when the Greek rebel Pseudoalexius wanted to collect Turkmen troops he had to get a μουσούριον, or menshur, from the sultan to do so. Nicetas Choniates, 551.

[738] The establishment of the emirates transformed the tribal begs into sedentary monarchs and so the process of sedentarization of a portion of the tribes was consummated.

mounted. For the carriage of merchandize they use the buffalo and ox, as we do the horse.[739]

Their livestock, a primary food source that furnished the nomads with a constant year-round source of meat, yogurt, milk, butter, cheese (and therefore a high protein diet necessary for their strenuous life), wool, and leather, was also a source of fuel and income. They sold their livestock and its produce to townsmen in those areas where the two groups had attained a symbiotic relationship.[740] Like many pastoral nomads, the Turks of Anatolia must occasionally have practiced some type of marginal agriculture though there is no detail forthcoming on this aspect of their economic activities.[741]

Warfare, pillage, and banditry were far more important in Anatolian nomadic economy than this marginal agriculture and, as a source of income, second only to their flocks. As brave and agile horsemen they "gave" their services to the sultans in return for rights to pasture land, official positions, and subsidies, They sold such services to the Greeks and Catalans as well, and their campaigns, whether in the armies of sultans or emperors, or independent, were the opportunities for economic enrichment.[742] These military actions were a principal source of slaves (taken from the Christian inhabitants of Anatolia) for the merchants who, in

[739] Brocquiére-Wright, p. 313.

[740] Barbaro-Hakluyt, pp. 19–20, describes the commerce of the Tatar herders in South Russia. One transaction involved the sale of 4,000 horses to Persians. The individual who dealt with the herder picked out what he wanted from the herd and the owner brought each horse with an instrument still in use in Central Asia today. It was a long staff with a collar on it which the Tatar slipped over the horse's head. For other references to their livestock, Schiltberger-Hakluyt, pp. 19, 123. Schiltberger-Neumann, p. 70. Ludolph of Suchem-Stewart, p. 30. Brosset, *Géorgie*, I, 358–359. Ibn Fadlan-Togan, pp. 23–24, gives a very interesting description of Oghuz pastoral economy and its integration into the commercial life of central Asia in the tenth century. The large caravans going through the region toward China (Ibn Fadlan's caravan consisted of 3,000 horses and 5,000 men!) hired horses and even borrowed money from the Oghuz nomads, and then on their trip back they returned the animals and money. The Oghuz were in turn housed by the recipients of these horses and money when the former went to the city of the latter [Gurgan] for business.

[741] Cinnamus, 9, refers to nomads in western Asia Minor who in the twelfth century practiced no agriculture whatever. Also Marco Polo-Moule and Pelliot, I, 95. Agricultural economy seems to have played a greater role in the economic organization of both the Tatars in the Tana basin and Chagatays in Iran. According to Barbaro-Hakluyt, pp. 21–22, all those of the Tana horde who wished to sow made their preparations in February and in the following month they took their carts, cattle, and seed and journeyed two days distance from the main camp of the horde. After they sowed they returned to the horde and did not return to their fields until harvest time. Inasmuch as the earth was very rich in these regions the Tatars had good crops. The farming of the Chagatays is very interesting indeed, de Clavijo-Le Strange, p. 190; "These Chagatays with whom we were thus guests are a nomad folk living in tents and booths, for indeed they possess no other more permanent habitations, both summer and winter living in the open. In summer they pass to the plains beside the river, where they sow their crops of corn and cotton, and tend the melon beds: and their melons I opine are the very best and biggest that may be found in the whole world. They also raise crops of millet, a grain which forms their chief food, and which they eat boiled in sour milk."

[742] One need only glance at the behavior of the Turkmen mercenaries utilized by Greek rebels in late twelfth-century Anatolia or by Cantacuzenus in the Balkans during the fourteenth century.

purveying this commodity to much of the Middle East, were ever present on the Udj frontiers. A few incidents, from among a great host, will suffice to demonstrate the extent of this slave trade and its importance in nomad economy. In 1186 Turkmen raiders in Cilicia took away 26,000 Armenians whom they sold on the slave market.[743] After the fall of Tralles in 1282, the 20,000 who survived the massacre were taken off into slavery.[744] Western Anatolia in the late thirteenth and the early fourteenth century was the center of a flourishing trade in Christian slaves. Matthew, metropolitan of Ephesus in this period, was depressed by the size of this commerce:

> Also distressing is the multitude of prisoners, some of whom are miserably enslaved to the Ismaelites and others to the Jews .... And the prisoners brought back to this new enslavement are numbered by the thousands; those [prisoners] arising from the enslavement of Rhomaioi through the capture of their lands and cities from all times by comparison would be found to be smaller or [at most] equal.[745]

The Arab historians and geographers relate that the Turkmens especially singled out the Greek children for enslavement, and further that the numbers of slaves available were so great that, "one saw ... arriving daily those merchants who indulged in this trade."[746] Banditry remained a profitable source of revenue for the nomads throughout the Seljuk and well into the Ottoman period. In the late thirteenth and the early fourteenth century, the tribesmen were so bold as to seize even the caravansarays and thus the caravans suffered incessantly from their harassment.[747] Banditry was one of the principal bases in the rise of more than one nomadic chieftain (such was the case in the rise of the Karamanid dynasty[748] and of the Timurids).[749]

Other economic activities that the tribesmen practised in their rural environment were hunting (usually with falcons or in large parties that encircled the wild beasts),[750] woodcutting, and the making of charcoal.[751]

---

[743] Bar Hebraeus, I, 321.

[744] Nicephorus Gregoras, I, 142.

[745] Matthew of Ephesus-Treu, p. 56.

[746] Al-Umari-Taeschner, p. 44. Abul-Fida, *Géographie d'Aboulfeda* (Paris, 1940), pp. 379, 381. Ibn Battuta-Gibb, II, 444, 445, 446, 449, acquired a number of young Greek slaves when he traveled through western Anatolia. For other references to this "slave" economy in different periods and places, Brosset, *Géorgie*, I, 346, 348. Sharaf al-Din Yazdi, II, 282. Planudes-Treu, p. 137, refers to exchange of prisoners and slaves by Turks and Greeks. Anna Comnena, III, 203, remarks that Alexius I freed all the Greek prisoners held by the Turks in the vicinity of Iconium. See Brocquière-Schefer, p. 135 on the slave market of Bursa.

[747] See chapters ii and iii above. W. Eberhard, "Nomads and Farmers in southeastern Turkey, Problems of Settlement," *Oriens*, VI (1953), 33, 40–41, on the role of banditry in pastoral nomadism and on its existence in the later Ottoman period.

[748] Ibn Bibi-Duda, pp. 308–309.

[749] De Clavijo-Le Strange, pp. 137, 210–211.

[750] Brocquière-Schefer, p. 93. Barbaro-Hakluyt, p. 19, Tana Tatars hunt with a falcon that they hold on the gloved hand, using a wooden crutch to support this hand. They shoot at geese flocks with an unfeathered arrow that turns about and breaks all in its

Though certain of the crafts were exercised by the nomads, for example, that of the smith, the one craft they seem to have developed highly was rug-weaving.[752] The character of nomad economy is further reflected in the fact that they frequently paid "taxes" to the Seljuks and early Ottomans in camels, horses, cows, sheep, and slaves,[753] and with the imposition of the Mongol tax system in thirteenth-century Anatolia, they no doubt paid the *kobcur* or animal tax.[754]

The economy of the nomad, at least the productive part of it which was not related to banditry and warfare, could and did lend itself to symbiosis with the towns and villages[755] in times of peace after Anatolia was stabilized. The flesh, milk products, hides, and wool of their flocks were marketable in the towns, as were also their rugs, though by the thirteenth century (and possibly even earlier), the manufacturing of the rugs was centered in the towns rather than in the countryside.[756] But until this symbiotic equilibrium came into being, the nomadism of the Turkmens was disruptive, as the rural populations found themselves forced to abandon many of their fields in the plains to the nomads, and those of the local populace who themselves had large flocks were forced to abandon the pasturages that were too far from the security of town walls.[757] The military sector of nomad economy was, of course, even more severe on the economic patterns of rural and urban society. It continued as an important

---

path of flight. C. Dawson, *The Mongol Mission. Narratives and Letters of the Franciscan Missionaries in Mongolia and China in the Thirteenth and Fourteenth Century* (New York, 1955), pp. 100–101. "When they want to hunt wild animals they gather together in a great crowd and surround the district in which they know the animals to be, and gradually they close in until between them they shut in the animals in a circle and then they shoot at them with their arrows." William of Rubricq-Wyngaert, p. 181. On this type of hunt as a "war exercise" among the Seljuk and Ottoman sultans, Gordlevski, *Izbrannye Soch.*, I, 82–83.

[751] Ibn Bibi-Duda, p. 308.

[752] Cahen, "Le commerce anatolien au debut du XIIIe siècle," *Mélanges d'histoire du moyen age dediés à la mémoire de Louis Halphen* (Paris, 1951), pp. 91–101. The Tatar and Chagatay hosts apparently possessed greater development and specialization in this respect for craftsmen and merchants in numbers were present in these hordes. But the highly specialized crafts, such as that of the armorers from Besh Köy, were practised not by the nomads themselves but by sedentary elements that lived in separate villages, Barbaro-Hakluyt, pp. 18, 66–67. For interesting comments on the economic habits of nomad Turks in nineteenth-century Lycia, and for pictures of their tools, see E. Petersen, F. von Luschan, *Reisen in Lykien Milyas und Kibyratis* (Vienna, 1889), II, 218–220.

[753] Ibn Bibi-Duda, pp. 97–98. Schiltberger-Neumann, p. 70. Schiltberger-Hakluyt, pp. 19, 123, the Turkmens of Adana (not Attaleia) paid 10,000 camels to Bayazid I. De Clavijo-Le Strange, p. 181, the Alavi Kurd nomads (400 tents) paid Timur 3,000 camels annually.

[754] On the kobcur see the literature in nn. 649–650.

[755] Brosset, I, 359.

[756] See above. The vitality of this Christian rug industry seems to be implied in Ibn Fadlan-Togan, p. 64. The royal pavilion of the king of the Volga Bulgars was strewn not with Turkmen rugs but with Armenian carpets and with Byzantine cloths in the tenth century.

[757] Ibn Battuta-Gibb, II, 428, in the early fourteenth century, the inhabitants of Tavas had been forced to keep their livestock within the town walls at night as a result of the occupation of the countryside by the Turkmens and because of their banditry.

hindrance to local sedentary economy even after tribal and peasant societies had settled down according to the new rules imposed by the interposition of the nomads on the land.[758] Inasmuch as the peasant economy was more productive, richer, and more important in the foundation of both the Seljuk and Ottoman kingdoms, the sultans tried to redress the economic balance between nomadism and farming in favor of the latter.[759] The nomad economy was sufficient to sustain the sparse life of the errant Turkmens, but it was completely unsuitable for the sustenance of a complicated, civilized, world state.

The religious life and practices of the tribes were as complex and varied as the origins of the different tribes themselves.[760] Though the Seljuk and Ottoman sultans were formally Sunni, the tribesmen retained the basic substructure of much of their shamanistic inheritance at the level of volksreligion. This seems to have been no less true of the Mongols and Tatars who settled in Asia Minor than of the Seljuk Turks.[761] When

[758] Even here, a change in agricultural patterns which called for winter cultivation of peasant land in the plains meant that the Turkmens were not free to quarter their flocks there in the winter. For specific examples of this, Eberhard, "Nomads and Farmers," pp. 37–38, 41. In the Chukurova plain by late Ottoman times, the Armenians and other settled peoples were in a nomad-sedentary relationship with the Turkmens of the Aydinli group. The latter went with their flocks to the summer pastures on the Kayseri plateau, and descended the Taurus mountain passes in October to the Chukurova plain around Kozan (Sis) to winter there. Here, inasmuch as the crops had been harvested and the trees were losing their leaves, the settled population were willing to allow the Turkmens to pasture their herds on the fields. Theoretically they would thus fertilize the fields, though one must remember that nomads very often gathered the manure to be used as winter fuel and so very often even here the nomad economy was at odds with that of the farmers. But, Eberhard suggests, this pattern was no longer viable when winter crops were introduced. For instance the introduction of extensive rice farming and of cotton meant that winter wheat would have to be planted and thus the farmer's land would no longer be available to the flocks of the nomads.

J. R. Sterrett, "The Wolfe Expedition to Asia Minor," *Papers of the American School of Classical Studies at Athens*, III (Boston, 1888), 280, describes an incident that he witnessed in southern Anatolia during the late nineteenth century and illustrates the fact that even in modern Anatolia the economic interests of pastoral nomads and sedentary agriculturalists often clashed. "The plain of Ilan Ovasu was thickly studded with the tents of Yuruk nomads from the Pamphylian plain, and their flocks were overrunning all the fields to the intense disgust of the hardworking stationary villagers."

[759] See above the section on recolonization.

[760] The accounts of Ibn Fadlan-Togan, pp. 20, 36, and of al-Marwazi-Minorsky, pp. 29 ff., are particularly important for a picture of this variety among the Turco-Mongol peoples in Central Asia. They mention cults of tribal totems (serpent, fish, crane), as well as phallus worship.

[761] The Tatars of Keul Khan, settled around Erzindjan, retained their idols after conversion to Islam, Vilayetname-Gross, pp. 71–73. According to E. Esin, *Turkish Miniature Painting* (Tokyo, 1960), p. 5, a Buddha image was excavated at Afyon Karahisar but she gives no further details. Ricoldus de Monte Crucis in *Peregrinatores medii aevi quatuor*, J. C. M. Laurent (Leipzig, 1873), p. 117 (hereafter Ricoldus-Laurent), gives a description of the religion of the Mongols who settled in eastern Anatolia during the late thirteenth century; "Et sciendum, quod Tartari quosdam homines super omnes de mundo honorant: boxitas, scilicet quosdam pontifices ydolorum. Et sunt indiani homines, valde sapientes et bene ordinati et valde graues in moribus. Hii communiter sciunt artes magicas, et innituntur consilio et auxilio demonum, et ostendunt multa prestigia, et predicunt quedam futura. Nam et unus maior inter eos dicebatur volare, sed secundam veritatem repertum est, quod non volauit, sed ambulabat, iuxta terram et eam non tangebat, et quando videbatur sedere, nulla re solida sustenabatur. Aliqui

the Turkmens adopted Islam, the folk character of tribal religion in Anatolia and its superstitious religiosity, the military instincts of the Turkmens, and, of course, their rural-transhumant orientation resulted in a religious transmutation that, in the beginning, changed only the external appearances of their religious life. The tribal *babas* or religious chiefs were the direct descendants of the older tribal shamans in Central Asia,[762] representing a fusion of the tribal shaman with the itinerant, Kalandar-type Muslim dervish who wandered throughout Anatolia preaching unorthodox tenets to the tribesmen.[763] If the folk character of

---

eorum dicunt esse trecentos sexaginta quinque deos. Aliqui dicunt esse centum comanos deorum. Est autem cumanus decem milia. Omnes tamen concordant, quod deus principalis est unus." See the remarks of Ugo Monneret de Villard, *Il libro della peregrinazione nelle parti d'Oriente di Frate Ricoldo da Montecroce* (Rome, 1948), pp. 47–54. William of Rubruque-Dawson, pp. 95–96. "Over the head of the master there is always an idol like a doll or little image of felt which they call the master's brother, and a similar one over the head of the mistress, and this they call the mistress' brother; they are fastened on to the wall. Higher up between these two is a thin little one which is, as it were, the guardian of the whole house. The mistress of the house places on her right side, at the foot of the couch, in a prominent position, a goat-skin stuffed with wool or other material, and next to it a tiny image turned towards her attendants and the women. By the entrance on the women's side is still another idol with a cow's udder for the women who milk cows, for this is the women's job. On the other side of the door towards the men is another image with a mare's udder for the men who milk the mares.

When they have foregathered for a drink they first sprinkle with the drink the idol over the master's head, then all the other idols in turn; after this an attendant goes out of the house with a cup and some drinks; he sprinkles thrice towards the south, genuflecting each time; this is in honour of fire; next towards the east in honour of the air, and after that to the west in honour of water; they cast it to the north for the dead. When the master is holding his cup in his hand and is about to drink, before he does so he first pours some out on the earth as its share. If he drinks while seated on a horse, before he drinks he pours some over the neck or mane of the horse." William of Rubriq-Wyngaert, pp. 174–175.

Barbaro-Hakluyt, pp. 8–9, also refers to the idols of the Mongols (of rag or wood, which they carried about on their carts with them) prior to their conversion to Islam.

[762] William of Rubriq-Wyngaert, pp. 205–208; William of Rubriq-Dawson, pp. 182–186, gives a description of the role of these "cham" at the Mongol court. They were in charge of the idols kept in the chariots, told the future, and advised the Mongol leaders when to declare war, fight battles, and so forth. On the baba-shaman, see below chapter v, n. 40. The dede or baba of the Tahtadji which Lschan, *Reisen*, II, 199, describes must have been a descendant of this tradition.

[763] Barbaro-Hakluyt, pp. 48–49. When in 1471 the Venetian ambassador to the court of Uzun Hasan traveled through southeast Anatolia (Cilicia) to Mardin there was a company of such dervishes who performed their religious dances and ceremonies at every station and lodge on the itinerary. Upon reaching Mardin, a Kalandar (Carandola) came and preached to Barbaro. He was clean shaven, dressed in a goat skin, and so forth. Very often these wandering dervishes founded villages near the Turkmens whence their religious preaching and influence spread quickly among the tribesmen. Such was the history of the spread of the religious propaganda of Baba Ishaq from the village that he founded near Amasya. Ibn Bibi-Duda, pp. 216–218. De Clavijo-Le Strange, pp. 139–140, visited such a village of dervishes in eastern Anatolia, "On Sunday we went on coming to a place called Delilarkent a name which signified the "Village of the Madmen," for those who inhabit this place are all hermits of the Moslem creed (being Dervishes) who here have the name of Kashish (or priests). The Moslem peasants from all the country round come in pilgrimage hither to visit these holy men, and forsooth those who are sick regain their health. These Dervishes have a chief to whom all pay much respect for they hold him to be a saint. When Timur lately passed through this place he took up his lodging living with this chief Dervish while he stayed here. All the Moslem people of the country round give alms abundantly to these pious men and this their chief is

Turkmen religion found its Muslim equivalent in the heterodox wandering Sufis, Turkmen martial ardor was well suited to the Ghazi life and the tradition of the holy war against the Christians. By association with the religious war on the boundaries against the Greeks and Armenians, the warlike practices and proclivities for plunder of the Turkmens were not only satisfactorily accommodated but even religiously justified, and this to the mutual benefit and satisfaction of tribal begs and sultans.[764] Thus the religious customs that they preserved from their pre-Islamic past, as well as the particular Islamic forms they adopted, contributed to the disruptive effect that the Turkmens had on Anatolian sedentary society. As tribal warriors dedicated to the djihad, the full brunt of their military activity was borne by the Greek and Armenian populations in the villages and to a lesser degree by those in the towns. A particularly striking element of religious continuity among the Turkmens in Anatolia and the Balkans was human sacrifice, a practice going back to the shamanist stage of their religious development in Central Asia.[765] As heterodox Muslims, many

---

the lord of that village, being too the master of those who embrace the religious life. The common people here consider all of them as saints. These dervishes shave their beards and their heads and go almost naked. They pass through the street, whether in the cold or the heat, eating as they go, and all the clothing they wear is bits of rag of the torn stuffs that they can pick up. As they walk along night and day with their tambourines they chant hymns. Over the gate of their hermitage is seen a banner of black woollen tassels with a moon-shaped ornament above: below this are arranged in a row the horns of deer and goats and rams, and further it is their custom to carry about with them these horns as trophies when they walk through the streets; and all the houses of the dervishes have these horns set over them for a sign." See von der Osten, *Discoveries in Anatolia 1930–31, The Oriental Institute of the University of Chicago, Oriental Institute Communications,* XIV (1933), 97–98, for an example of the survival of this type of rural religious sanctuary in twentieth-century Anatolia at Sisli.

[764] This interpenetration and transformation of the warlike mentality of the tribes by Islamic mysticism is manifested literarily in the Turkish epics of the Danishmendname, Kitab-i Dede Korkut, and the Battalname, where the Turkish poets incorporate many of the themes of the older Ghazi-Acrites traditions, as for instance in the Danishmendname where Malik Danishmend is made out to be a descendant of the Arab hero Seyid Battal. See Danishmendname-Melikoff, I, 41 ff,; Rossi, *Dede Qorqut*, pp. 25–27, 31 ff., 65–66, 74–75. The genre of epic poetry flourished during this heroic era of the tribes in Anatolia. Brocquière-Schefer, p. 97, refers to the love that the Turks had for the recitations of this poetry by the ozan. The dervish order of the Kazaruni apparently played an important role in exciting the tribes to the djihad in Anatolia, Danishmendname-Melikoff, I, 140, 343, 344 on the 10,000 marabouts.

[765] Ricoldo-Laurent, p. 114. The military character of these pre-Islamic practices survived in burial customs. The warrior's horse was closely associated with the burial of the slain tribesman, Gordlevski, *Izbrannye Soch.*, I, 86–87. William of Rubriq-Wyngaert, pp. 186–187; William of Rubriq-Dawson, p. 73, reports that the Cumans in the thirteenth century hung sixteen horsetails at the grave of the dead. Ibn Fadlan-Togan, pp. 27, 138–140, notes that they decked the dead man with his bow, sacrificed horses at the grave and ate them, and that a horse was buried with him so that in the next world he would have a mount to ride and a mare to furnish milk.

The survival of human sacrifice in the cult of the dead is attested among Ottoman Turks from the fourteenth to the sixteenth centuries. The emperor John Cantacuzene reports in the fourteenth century a version of this practice wherein slain Turkish warriors are buried with those enemies whom they have slain. If none can be found, Christian slaves are purchased and sacrificed at the grave in the belief that they will be the servants of the dead warrior in the next world, John Cantacuzene, *P.G.*, CLIV, 545. See also

of the tribesmen were a constant source of difficulty for the sultans. The Turkmens of the Karamanids, Babai, and the Udj begs destroyed the Seljuk sultanate, while the Kïzïlbash of Anatolia openly supported the Safavids and forced the Ottoman sultans to adopt a policy of partial extermination.

Very little is known about the family life and practices of the Anatolian tribes between the eleventh and fifteenth centuries, and certainly nothing that would have a bearing on their impact upon contemporary society. One would assume that the family order remained under the influences of pre-Islamic traditions, but that Islamic practices would gradually assert themselves. Polygamy among the nomads was known, both in the steppe and in Anatolia, but it is not possible to say how extensive it was.[766] The payment of the bride price was also characteristic of the tenth-century Oghuz and the thirteenth-century Mongols,[767] and the marriage of the widows to their husband's oldest son (the widows other than the mother of this eldest son) seems to have been a very widespread practice based on shamanistic beliefs.[768]

---

chapter vi. Murad II bought 600 Greek slaves in the Peloponnese and sacrificed them to his deceased father. Chalcocondyles, p. 348, "μετὰ δὲ ὠνησάμενος ἀνδράποδα ἐς ἐξακόσια θυσίαν ἀνῆγε τῷ ἑαυτοῦ πατρί, ἐξιλεούμενος τῷ φόνῳ τῶν ἀνδρῶν τούτων." This custom seems to have survived in the sixteenth century, Bartholomaeus Georgieuiz-Goughe, in the chapter entitled "What is assigned to be done by the Testamentes of the Turkes, as welle of menne as women." "But the women geve monye unto soultyers, for to kill a certaine number of Christians. They make account that by so doynge, it will greatlye profite the health of their soules." Ibn Fadlan-Togan, pp. 24–25, 236–237. In central Asia the Turks killed those near whom their comrade had died. Schiltberger-Neumann, p. 130. For human sacrifice among the Turks and Mongols of Central Asia, J.-P. Roux, *La mort chez les peuples altaïques anciens et médiévaux* (Paris, 1963), pp. 62, 107–108, 111, 117–118, 121, 123, 169–172. M. Eliade, *Le chamanisme et les téchniques archaïques de l'extase* (Paris, 1951), *passim*. A. Inan, *Tarihte ve bugün şamanizm. Materyallarï ve araştïrmalar* (Ankara, 1954), pp. 176–200. Mummification of the dead, another shamanist practice from Central Asia, is attested in thirteenth-century Anatolia, Turan, "Semseddin," pp. 208–211.

[766] Danishmendname-Melikoff, I, 206. L. Krader, *Social Organization of the Mongol-Turkic Pastoral Nomads* (The Hague, 1963), pp. 22–23, and *passim*. John of Pian de Carpini-Wyngaert, p. 50, notes the existence of polygamy among the thirteenth-century Mongols. Gordlevski, *Izbrannye Soch.*, I, 85.

[767] Ibn Fadlan-Togan, pp. 22, 128–129.

[768] *Ibid.*, pp. 22, 129–131. William of Rubriq-Dawson, p. 104. "As for their marriages, you must know that no one there has a wife unless he buys her, which means that sometimes girls are quite grown up before they marry, for their parents always keep them until they sell them. They observe the first and second degrees of consanguinity, but observe no degrees of affinity; they have two sisters at the same time or one after the other. No widow among them marries, the reason being that they believe that all those who serve them in this life will serve them in the next, and so of a widow they believe that she will always return after death to her first husband. This gives rise to a shameful custom among them whereby a son sometimes takes to wife all his father's wives, except his own mother; for the "orda" of a father and mother always falls to the youngest son and so he himself has to provide for all his father's wives who come to him with his father's effects; and then, if he so wishes, he uses them as wives, for he does not consider an injury has been done to him if they return to his father after death." William of Rubriq-Wyngaert, pp. 184–185. The marriage custom whereby the son takes the wives of the father (his own mother excepted) is the extension of the shaman belief that the man will be served in the next life by those who have served him in this

The domicile, diet, and clothing of the Turkmens were all a function and reflection of their itinerant life and economy. The tents were usually of wool or felt, round or long in shape. If round they were supported by concentric staves of wood; if they were oblong the wooden supports were of a different type.[769] Some of the dwellings were collapsible and when the time came for the nomads to move on, the tents were simply dismantled and loaded upon the backs of the animals.[770] Observers note, however, the existence of another type of dwelling (as for instance among the Tatars of Tana), not collapsible, carried about on a large cart drawn by oxen.[771] Brocquière saw large encampments of Turkmens, on the plain of the Gulf of Ayas, whose tents could each house fourteen to sixteen individuals.[772] On occasion the nomads who had to winter in the severe climes of eastern Anatolia or Central Asia went underground "like moles."[773] Their clothing was no doubt made of materials such as hides and wool, derived from their flocks, along with stuffs that they procured from merchants in the towns.[774]

The Turkmen diet consisted primarily of meat, milk, cream, yogurt, and butter, which were readily available from their flocks,[775] but it was

---

life. Ibn Fadlan-Togan, pp. 21, 25, 127–128, remarks upon Oghuz women that in spite of the fact that they do not veil themselves or hide their "shame," they are chaste; well they might have been for the penalty in cases of adultery, as in cases of homosexuality, was ferocious.

[769] See the plates in Petersen and von Luschan, *Reisen*, vols. I, II.

[770] John of Pian de Carpini-Wyngaert, p. 35.

[771] William of Rubriq-Dawson, p. 94. "They make these houses so large that sometimes they are thirty feet across; for I myself once measured the width between the wheel tracks of a cart, and it was twenty feet, and when the house was on the cart it stuck out at least five feet beyond the wheels on each side. I have counted to one cart twenty-two oxen drawing one house, eleven in a row across the width of the cart, and the other eleven in front of them. The axle of the cart was as big as the mast of a ship, and a man stood at the door of the house on the cart, driving the oxen." William of Rubriq-Wyngaert, pp. 172–173.

[772] Brocquière-Schefer, p. 89. For the palatial, luxurious tents of Timur and his nobles see the detailed description of de Clavijo-Le Strange, pp. 237–242.

[773] Ricoldus de Monte Crucis-Laurent, p. 114; "Armeniam autem transeuntes intrauimus in Turchiam, et inuenimus Thurchimanos, homines bestiales, qui sunt Sarraceni et habitant communiter sub terra ad modum talparum." Al-Marwazi-Minorsky, p. 32, notes the same practice among the Kīmak. He also describes, p. 33, an instance of portable defense walls among the Turkish tribes of Tulas and Lu'r, "It is their custom, when going forth in any direction, that every horseman carries with him twenty tamarisk pegs two cubits long. When they come to their encampment, they all plant their pegs in the ground surrounding the site, and lean their bucklers against them: in this way in less than an hour round the encampment a wall is made which cannot be pierced."

[774] Ibn Bibi-Duda, p. 311, describes the Karamanid Turks as clothed in red caps, black kilims and charuqa (shoes). Ibn Fadlan-Togan, p. 16, on heavy clothing worn in the steppe. William of Rubriq-Wyngaert, pp. 179–183. John of Pian de Carpini-Wyngaert, pp. 33–34; Ibn Battuta-Gibb, II, *passim*. Anna Comnena, III, 143 on black as a color of mourning. Ibn Fadlan-Togan, p. 21. Zeno-Hakluyt, p. 13; Brocquière-Schefer, p. 83; Von Luschan, *Reisen*, II, *passim*, on the question of the veiling of women.

[775] Brocquière-Schefer, p. 89. Cinnamus, 9. Ludolph of Suchem-Stewart, p. 30. De Clavijo-Le Strange, pp. 122, 223–224. On the idols and cult of milk production, William of Rubriq-Wyngaert, pp. 174–175.

supplemented by millet or other grain (which they themselves planted or else procured from villagers),[776] honey, fruit, and eggs.[777] The making of bread was adapted to itinerant life, with rather infelicitous results, if one is to believe those Westerners who tasted it. The oven of the Greeks and Armenians is conspicuous by its absence, its replacement being a portable arrangement.

That day, accompanied by the Armenian, we once more lodged with the Turcomans, who again served us with milk. It was here I saw women make those thin cakes [of bread] I spoke of. This is their manner of making them; they have a small round table, very smooth, on which they throw some flour, and mix it with water to a paste, softer than that for bread. This paste they divide into round pieces, which they flatten as much as possible, with a wooden roller of a smaller diameter than an egg, until they make them as thin as I have mentioned. During this operation they have a convex plate of iron placed on a tripod, and heated by a gentle fire underneath, on which they spread the cake and instantly turn it, so that they make two of their cakes sooner than a waferman can make one wafer.[778]

The tablecloth upon which they spread their meal was likewise designed for mobility and convenience, and served as both a cloth and pantry within which remnants of the meal were stored until the next sitting.

I had, when eating, a table-cloth, like the rich men of the country. These cloths are four feet in diameter, and round, having strings attached to them, so that they may be drawn up like a purse. When they are used they are spread

---

[776] William of Rubriq-Wyngaert, p. 175. De Clavijo-Le Strange, pp. 190–191, remarks that boiled millet in sour cream was a staple of the Chagatays. The diet of these latter included not only meat, milk, and sour cream, but rice, melons, and millet, the latter three of which they themselves cultivated in the summer.

[777] De Clavijo-Le Strange, p. 122, describes a dish made of clotted cream, eggs, and honey in bowls of milk, eaten in eastern Anatolia. De Clavijo-Le Strange, pp. 190–191, and Brocquière-Schefer, p. 89, on grapes. It is interesting that whenever wine is desired, the travelers invariably repaired to the houses or inns of Greeks. Also, the steady diet of flesh that travelers had to consume in Turkmen territory was a cause of dissatisfaction for these travelers. It was relieved only in towns and villages where the cuisine was not that of the nomads.

[778] Brocquière-Wright, p. 315. De Clavijo-Le Strange, pp. 121–122, noted the same method of preparing bread among the Turks who had settled down in the villages of eastern Anatolia by the fifteenth century. "Their bread in these villages was indeed of very bad quality, being made after a strange fashion. They take a little flour, knead it and make pan-cakes of the same. They then take a frying-pan set it on the fire and when it has got hot throw the thin cake of dough into it, which as soon as it is heated and baked through they remove. This was the only bread that they supplied to us in these villages." On Greek loan words in Turkish having to do with baking, ovens, and bread, see chapter vii below. This nomadic method of making "bread" is described as late as the eighteenth century by the French traveler Lucas, *Voyage du Sieur Paul Lucas fait par ordre du roi dans la Grèce, l'Asie Mineure, La Macédoine et l'Afrique* (Amsterdam, 1714), I, 257. "Ils portent sur leurs chevaux quelques sacs de farine lorsq'ils veulent faire du pain, ils en delaïent un peu dans de l'eau. Leur pâte faite ainsi, ils l'applatissent fort mince, à peu près comme une pièce de quinze fols: ensuite ils font un trou dans la terre, y allument du feu, mettent dessus une plaque de fer ronde, de l'épaisseur d'une cuirasse; & enfin lorsque cette plaque est échaufée, ils y étendent leur pâte, qui y cuit ou plûtôt s'y sèche."

out; and, when the meal is over, they are drawn up with all that remains within them, without their losing a crumb of bread or a raisin.[779]

Brocquière gives a vivid description of the nomad, at his meal, which clearly underlines the complete dependence of the cuisine upon the presuppositions of the organization of their mobile life, complete with ruins in the background.

At the foot of the mountains, near the road and close to the sea-shore, are the ruins of a strong castle, defended on the land side by a marsh, so that it could only be approached by sea, or by a narrow causeway across the marsh. It was inhabited, but the Turcomans had posted themselves hard by. They occupied one hundred and twenty tents, some of felt, others of white and blue cotton, all very handsome, and capable of containing, with ease, from fifteen to sixteen persons. These are their houses, and, as we do in ours, they perform in them all their household business, except making fires. We halted among them; they placed before us one of the table-cloths before-mentioned, in which there remained fragments of bread, cheese, and grapes. They then brought us a dozen of thin cakes of bread, with a large jug of curdled milk, called by them yogort. The cakes are a foot broad, round, and thinner than wafers; they fold them up as grocers do their papers for spices, and eat them filled with the curdled milk.[780]

The physiognomy of the tribesmen evidently set them off as sharply from the indigenous population as did their peculiar society. It is quite probable that fusion with other groups such as the Kurds, or later with Christians and converts, gradually altered the physical type in many areas and introduced further physical variety among them.[781] But

[779] Brocquière-Wright, p. 308. Variants of this "table-cloth" are to be observed among most of the Turco-Mongol peoples of the medieval period. De Clavijo-Le Strange, p. 121, describes it in eastern Anatolia: "Next they would produce a leather mat for a table-cloth, as might be with us a round of [Cordovan] leather such as we call Guadamcir, and this with them is known as a Sofra, and on this they would place bread." It was also used by the Chagatays of Timur. De Clavijo-Le Strange, pp. 223–224. William of Rubriq-Dawson, p. 98, refers to captargac of the Mongols, "that is, a square bag which they carry to put all such things in: in this they also keep bones when they have not the time to give them a good gnaw, so that later they may gnaw them and no food be wasted." Bartholomaeus Georgieuiz-Marshe, describes it as it was employed in the sixteenth-century Ottoman Empire, "The Maner of the turkische tables, and how they seat at meat. Their table having to name Tsophra is made of leather: it is spread abrode and drawn together in forme of a purse."

[780] Brocquière-Wright, p. 314, See de Clavijo-Le Strange, p. 124, for a description of eating habits.

[781] Such are the conclusions of von Luschan, Reisen, II, 198–226, on the basis of the examination and cranial measurement of settled Christians and Muslims on the one hand, and of nomads on the other. The dangers, however, of reliance upon anthropometric considerations alone are amply demonstrated by von Luschan's conclusions in the case of the origin of the Tahtadjis. On the basis of their cranial measurements he concludes that they are descendants of a pre-Greek, pre-Turkish Semitic population (related to the Phoenicians). Their religious practices, however, their babas, and their life in tents are all evidence for Turkmen origin, as are also the partial survival among them of clearly discernible central Asiatic facial types (see especially the plates). Von Luschan's study is nevertheless interesting and valuable, and has been repeated, without the fascinating plates, in "Die Tachtadschy und andere Ueberreste der alten Bevölkerung Lykiens," Archiv für Anthropologie, XIX (1891), 31–53. I am not competent to enter the complexities of physical anthropology nor to attempt to evaluate the specific factors, aside from ethnic mixture, which effect change in cranial and other physical proportions. A considerable attention and effort have been expended on the anthropometry of the

Byzantine historians of the eleventh and twelfth centuries imply that the facial configuration of the Turkmens differed greatly from that of the Greeks.[782] The central Asiatic facial type, which must have been the dominant one, is clearly apparent in the description that Brocquière gives of the Ottoman sultan Murad II, whom he saw in Adrianople.

In the first place, as I have seen him frequently, I shall say that he is a little, short, thick man, with the physiognomy of a Tartar. He has a broad and brown face, high cheek bones, a round beard, a great and crooked nose, with little eyes.[783]

Though they may not have been large in physical stature by the standards of northern Europe, their rigorous life and high protein diet preconditioned them to endure great hardships and physical distress, beyond those the farming and city populace could bear.[784]

---

ancient inhabitants of Anatolia by the Turkish scholars S. A. Kansu and M. S. Senyürek. For the period under consideration there is very little material available however. S. A. Kansu, "Selçuk Türkleri hakkïnda antropolojik ilk bir tetkik ve neticeleri," *Ikinci Türk Tarih Kongresi* (Istanbul, 1943), pp. 440–456. E. F. Schmidt, *Anatolia through the Ages. Oriental Institute Communications*, no. 11 (Chicago, 1931), p. 148. A. Inan published a study on the basis of examination of 64,000 modern Turks, *L'Anatolie, le pays de la 'race' turque. Recherches sur les caractères anthropologiques des populations de la Turquie* (Geneva 1939). K. Güngür. *Cenubî Anadolu türklerinin etno-anthropolojik tetkiki* (Ankara, 1941).

[782] Attaliates, 156–157. The Byzantine mercenary Uzes, from the Balkans, looked so much like the Seljuk Turks that the Byzantines could not distinguish the one from the other. Nicetas Choniates, 247, remarks that the Turks at the battle of Myriocephalum removed the facial skin of the fallen on both sides lest the Greeks learn how many Turks had been slain. This again, is an explicit testimonial to the fact that the facial types of Greek and Turks at this early period (as in contrast to later times) were sharply distinguishable.

[783] Brocquière-Wright, p. 346. John of Pian de Carpini-Dawson, pp. 6–7. "In appearance the Tartars are quite different from all other men, for they are broader than other people between the eyes and across the cheek-bones. Their cheeks also are rather prominent above their jaws; they have a flat and small nose, their eyes are little and their eyelids raised up to the eyebrows. For the most part, but with a few exceptions, they are slender above the waist; almost all are of medium height. Hardly any of them grow beards, although some have a little hair on the upper lip and chin and this they do not trim. On the top of the head they have a tonsure like clerics, and as a general rule all shave from one ear to the other to the breadth of three fingers, and this shaving joins on to the aforesaid tonsure. Above the forehead also they all likewise shave to two fingers' breadth, but the hair between this shaving and the tonsure they allow to grow until it reaches their eyebrows, and, cutting more from each side of the forehead than in the middle, they make the hair in the middle long; the rest of their hair they allow to grow like women, and they make it into two braids which they bind, one behind each ear. They also have small feet." John Pian de Carpini-Wyngaert, pp. 32–33. For a variation of this tonsorial arrangement among Anatolian Yuruks in the late nineteenth century, see Fig. 97 and Pl. XXXVII in von Luschan, *Reisen*, II. Beauty being a matter of subjective evaluation one is not surprised to see widely varying reactions to this physical type. To Brocquière-Wright, pp. 315–316, the Turkmens were handsome. To de Clavijo-Le Strange, p. 196, the Chagatays were ugly. See also the *Qabus Name*-Levy, p. 103, whose author says that the Turks were possessed of a facial appearance which, though unattractive in each individual feature, was nevertheless handsome in its totality. The Greeks used the epithet κυνοκέφαλοι, dog-headed, to describe them. Pachymeres, I, 134. Miniatures in thirteenth-century Arab illuminated manuscripts show that the artists were sharply aware of the different facial type of the new Turko-Mongol ruling class. R. Ettinghausen, *Arab Painting* (Skira, 1962), p. 163.

[784] Brocquière-Schefer, p. 97. Ricoldus de Monte Crucis-Laurent, p. 114.

The Turkmen groups who came into Anatolia thus constituted a nomadic society with a particular blend of military, economic, and religious characteristics which made the Turkmen presence a source of misfortune to the sedentary populations. This is evident in the complex process by which the nomads settled in Anatolia, its effect, the dislike the sedentary populace had for the nomads, and finally in the measures governments took in the face of Turkmen unruliness. At the time of the conquests in Anatolia, northern Syria, and Georgia, the tribesmen "submitted lands by cruel destruction and pillage" according to one medieval source.[785] Thus they occupied lands they often ruined and that had been partially abandoned by the Christians, who either fled, were killed or enslaved, or retreated to the hills and towns.[786] The tribe succeeded in effecting a permanent settlement in Anatolia when and if it could secure a winter base after its summer raid. Until it could acquire and defend a winter base in Anatolia, the tribe usually left Asia Minor at the end of the summer raiding season.[787] It is clear, however, that tribes acquired rights of settlement not only by conquest but often they obtained such rights from a ruler who "rented" the land to them in return for regular military service, or else settled them on the Udj (boundaries) as defenders of the state's boundaries.[788] Once located, the tribes usually established a semiannual transhumant pattern between their summer *yayla* in the mountains and their winter base in the plains. It is interesting that as

---

[785] Michael the Syrian, III, 170–171.

[786] Michael the Syrian, III, 170–171. Brosset, *Géorgie*, I, 346. Brocquière-Schefer, pp. 93–94, *passim*. During the invasion of Asia Minor the tribal chiefs of Timur's Chagatays took an oath not to leave even a plant or shrub standing. Sharaf al-Din Yazdi, II, 243–244. To contemporaries, both Muslim and Christian, the ferocious Turkmens were thought to be the instrument by which God had punished the sinful Christians or Muslims. Eflaki-Huart, II, 208–209, reports a conversation of Djalal al-Din Rumi in which the constructive, sedentary qualities of Greek Christians are contrasted with those of the destructive Turkmens. "C'est une histoire bien connue qu'un jour le chéïkh Çalâh-ed-dîn, pour bâtir (les murs de) son jardin, avait loué à gages des ouvriers turcs. 'Éfendi (c'est à dire Seigneur) Çalâh-ed-dîn, dit le Maître, pour cette construction, ce sont des ouvriers grecs qu'il faut prendre; pour la démolition, au contraire, les ouvriers turcs sont nécessaires; car la construction du monde est spéciale aux Grecs, et la démolition de ce même monde est reservée aux Turcs. Dieu, quand il a créé l'univers, a tout d'abord créé les infidèles insouciants; il leur a donné une longue vie et une force considérable, de manière que, à la façon des ouvriers à gages, ils s'efforcent, sans le savoir, de construire le monde terrestre; ils ont élevé de nombreuses villes, fortresses sur les sommets des montagnes, localités sur les hauteurs des collines, de manière qu'après des siècles écoulés, ces constructions servent de modèles aux hommes des derniers temps; or, la prédestination divine a disposé les choses de telle sorte que petit à petit ces constructions deviennent des ruines; il a alors créé le peuple des Turcs pour démolir, sans respect ni pitié, toutes les constructions qu'ils voyaient; ils l'ont fait et le font encore; ils le feront de jour en jour jusqu'à la résurrection. Finalement, la destruction de la ville de Qonya aura lieu par la main des Turcs injustes et impitoyables.' Le fait est que cela arriva comme il l'avait dit." The association of the Turks with destruction and the events announcing the end of the world are well-known themes in Islamic literature. Maqdisi, *Livre de création*, ed. and trans. Huart, II, 154. Eflaki-Huart, II, 418–419. Gordlevski, *Izbrannye Soch.*, I, 89.

[787] Brosset, *Géorgie*, I, 346–348.

[788] Schiltberger-Neumann, p. 65. Schiltberger-Hakluyt, p. 14. De Clavijo-Le Strange, p. 181.

Christian villages were abandoned or ruined the Turkmens often occupied them and made of them their camping ground in the winter.[789] Of course the majority of these tribes eventually settled down and abandoned their nomadism. According to the Ottoman tax registers of the sixteenth and seventeenth centuries, there is an indication that the seden-tary and nomad population of western Anatolia was apparently about 83 percent sedentary to 17 percent nomad, though it is impossible to say what proportion of this sedentary population was of nomadic origin, what proportion of converted Greeks and Armenians, and what proportion of original sedentary Muslim population. When the central government was sufficiently powerful, Turkmen groups were constrained to adopt sedentary life, and no doubt there were many instances of Turkmen voluntary settlements in towns and villages.[790] The vast extent

[789] Brosset, *Géorgie*, I, 358–359. Hayton, *R.H.C., D.A.*, II, 133. Michael the Syrian, *R.H.C., D.A.*, I, 321. De Clavijo-Le Strange, p. 108. Ibn Battuta-Gibb, II, 417. *Oriental Institute Communications*, nos. 14, 52–54. Al-Marwazi-Minorksy, p. 33, notes this latter type of transhumance among certain Turks of Central Asia who go to deserts in the summer and to the cities in the winter. Gordlevki, *Izbrannye Soch.*, I, 74, on the Turkmen dislike of the city.

[790] For the proportion of sedentary to nomad see n. 725 above. On the sedentarization of nomads, a topic still in need of much investigation, see the following: Eberhard, "Nomads," pp. 32–49, investigates the governmental policy of settling the nomads in the ninteenth century. C. Orhonlu, *Osmanlï imparatorluğun'un aşiretleri iskân teşebbüsü (1691–1696)* (Istanbul, 1963), describes the process by which the Ottoman government recolonized the abandoned villages in the regions of Belih Riv, Edessa, Menbj, Hama, Humus, Adana, Iskenderum in the east; the regions of Sungurlu and Yozgat east of Ankara; and the districts about Sandïklï, Isparta, and Borlu west of Konya. See also W. Ruben, "Anadolu'nun yerleşme tarihi ile ilgili görüşler. Kochisar'ïn Tuz Gölü batïsïndaki step köylerinde 1946 Eylülünde yapïlan bir araştïrma gezisinin sonuclari," *Ankara Üniversitesi dil ve tarih-coğrafya fakültesi dergisi*, V (1947), 353–391. B. Boran, "Toplumsal yapï araştïrmalarï," *Ankara Üniversitesi dil ve tarih-coğrafya fakültesi, felsefe enst., sosyoloji serisi*, no. 3 (Ankara, 1945), studies villages resulting from recent settlement of tribes. For the settlement of Turkmen tribes in the Balkans as part of Ottoman policy, Ashïkpashazade-Ali, pp. 84, 111–112. Ashïkpashazade-Kreutel, pp. 108, 155. Gökbilgin, "Rumeli'nin iskanïnda ve Türkleşmesinde Yürükler," *III. Türk Tarih Kurumu Kongresi*, 1943 (Ankara 1948), pp. 107–116; *Rumeli'de Yürükler ve Tatarlar ve Evlad-i Fatihan* (Istanbul, 1957).

Of interest for the yet unwritten history of the tribes in Ottoman Anatolia are the following: Wittek, Osmanli imparatorluğunda türk aşiretlerinin rölü," *Istanbul Üniversitesi edebiyat fakültesi tarih dergisi*, XIII (1963), 257–268 (trans. from *Mélanges Georges Smets, Les éditions de la Libraire Encyclopédique*, (Brussels, 1952). A. Refik, *Anadoluda türk aşiretleri 966–1200* (Istanbul, 1930). F. Demirtaş, "Osmanlï devrinde Anadolu'da Kayïlar," *Belleten*, XII (1948), 575–615 (On Kayï groups in districts of Konya, Ankara, and Menteşe in the fifteenth- and sixteenth centuries); "Bozulus hakkïnda," *Ankara Üniversitesi dil ve tarih-cografya fakültesi dergisi*, VII (1949), 29–60 (describes tribal groups and life of the sixteenth century); "Osmanlï devrinde Anadolu'da Kayïlar," *Belleten*, XII (1948), 575–615; "Anadoluda oğuz boylarï," *Ankara Üniversitesi dil ve tarih-coğrafya fakültesi dergisi*, VII (1949), 321–385. Sümer, "Yïva Oğuz boyuna daîr," *T.M.*, IX (1951), 156–168; "Ağaç-eriler," *Belleten*, XXVI (1962), 521–528; "XVI asïrda Anadolu, Suriye ve Irak'ta yaşayan Türk aşiretlerine umumî bir bakïs," *Iktisat fakültesi mecmuasï*, XI (1952), 509–522; "Anadolu'da yaşayan bazi Uçoklu Oğuz boylarïna mensup teşek-küller," *Iktisat fakültesi mecmuasï*, XI (1949–50), 437–508. Ali Zira (Yalgïn), *Cenupta Türkmen oymaklarï* 4 vols. (Istanbul, 1931–37). A. A. Candar, "Kayïnïn bölüntleri," *Hakimiyeti milliye* (Ankara, 1934), no. 4473 (on the settlement of Kayï from Kars to Çanakkale and from Urfa to Manisa). M. Koyman, *Konya* (1963), no. 2, pp. 121–123, on tribes about Konya. Köprülü, "Oğuz etnolojisine ait tarihî notlar," *T.M.*, I (1925), 185–211.

of tribal settlement in Anatolia is apparent not only from the historical sources but from the very rural toponymy itself, which is largely Turkish.[791] The very intrusion and physical presence of the tribesmen, their families and livestock in Anatolia, their status as pastoral military conquerors, and their continuing raids and banditry constituted a very serious disturbance to the sedentary, and especially to the Christian, groups.[792] The two most important effects of the Turkmen settlements in Asia Minor between the eleventh and fifteenth centuries were first the linguistic Turkification of Anatolia, and second, the partial nomadization of extensive areas. As they settled in the countryside, their language predominated in those areas where the Greeks and Armenians had withdrawn, and, even in those regions where the Christian groups remained, Turkish eventually prevailed as the language of the conquerors. In the cities where the Byzantino-Islamic urban traditions remained powerful, urban society survived. But when in 1276–78 the Turkmens of

---

More recently there has appeared an important and comprehensive literature. Sümer, *Oğuzlar* (*Türkmenler*). *Tarihleri-boy teşkilâtĭ-destanlarĭ* (Ankara, 1967). de Planhol, "Nomadism," 525–531. D. E. Eremeev, "Proizhoždenie Iuriukov i Turkmen Turtsii i osnovniie etapy ikh istorii. Etničeskie protsessy i sostav naseleniia v stranakh perednei Azii," *Trudy Inst. Etnogr.*, LXXXIII (Moscow-Leningrad, 1963), 24–70. W. D. Hütteroth, "Bergnomaden und Yaylabauern im mittleren kurdischen Taurus," *Marburger geogr. Schriften*, XI (1959). A. D. Novičev, "Turetskie kočevniki v XV–XVIII vv.," *XXV Meždunar. Kongr. Vostokoved.*, *Doklady Delegatsii SSSR* (Moscow, 1960), pp. 1–11; "Les nomades turcs du XVe au XVIIIe siècle," *Trudy dvedtsati piatogo meždunarodnogo kongressa vostokovedov* (Moscow, 1963), II, 413–420, *Istoriia Turtsii I. Epokha feodalizma* (XI–XVIII v.) (Leningrad, 1963). S. E. Tolybekov, "O patriarkhal'no-feodal'nykh otnošeniiakh u kočevnykh narodov," *Voprosy Istorii*, I (1955), 75–83. Hütteroth, *Ländliche Siedlungen im südlichen Inneranatolien in den letzten vierhundert Jahren* (Gottingen, 1968).

[791] *Türkiye'de meskun yerler kilavuzu*, vols. I–II (Ankara, 1946). *Köylerimiz. Köy kanun tatbik olunan ve olunmayan köy isimlerini alfabe sirasile göstir* (Istanbul, 1933). Gordlevski, *Izbrannye Soch.*, I, 73. I. R. Işitman, "Köy adlar üzerinde bir inceleme," *Türk dili belleten*, ser 3. no. 1/3 (Ankara, 1945), pp. 51–52. Nihal (Ahmed Naci), "Anadoluda Türklere ait yer isimleri," *T.M.*, II (1928), 243–259. De Planhol, *Nomadism passim*.

For the eleventh through fifteenth centuries, the sources (Ashĭkpashazade, Anonymous Giese, Muntaner, Planudes, Mahmud of Aksaray, Bar Hebraeus, al-Athir, Nicetas Choniates, Vilayetname of Hadji Bektash, Brocquière, Michael the Syrian, Panaretus, Ibn Bibi, de Clavijo, Barbaro), specifically record Turkmen settlements in the following places; Between Gül Hisar-Denizli and Denizli-Tavas, in the regions of Samsun, Menteshe, Magnesium ad Sipylum, Karahisar, Choma-Soublaion, Pentapolis, Karahisar, Artake, Menemen, Maeander, Udj borders of the west, Kutahya, Lacerion-Panasium, Dorylaeum, Lampe-Graos Gala, Bursa, Saruhan, Chorum-Ankara, Sivas-Kayseri, Tao Khlarjeti, Georgia, the southern borders of Trebizond, Erzerum, Erzindjan, Amasya, Laranda, Nigde, Kufrusund, Marash, Antioch, Gulf of Ayas, Misse, Adana-Tarsus, Eregli, Pamphylia, Pisidia. Among the tribes and confederations which they mention are the Agacheri, Chepni, Akkoyunlu, Karakoyunlu, Kara Ağach, Ad?, Semud?, Chagatay, Khwarazm, Kipchak, Karaman, Dhu'l-kadroghlu, Ramazanoghlu, Qoinari, Chapanli (Chepni?), Kĭzĭl Kodjaoghullarĭ. See also the list of Karayazĭdjĭoghlu reproduced and discussed in Gordlevski, *Izbrannye, Soch.*, I, 80–82.

[792] Brosset, *Géorgie*, I, 346. Acropolites, I, 136. Michael the Syrian, III, 158–159, Bar Hebraeus, I, 212–213. Ricoldus de Monte Crucis-Laurent, p. 114. Ibn Battuta-Gibb, II, 424, 427–428, 448. Aksaray-Gençosman, p. 211. Ashĭkpashazade-Ali, pp. 111–112. Ashĭkpashazade-Kreutel, p. 155. Ibn Bibi-Duda, p. 270. De Planhol, *Nomadism*, pp. 115–118, and *passim*. on the severe nomad harassment of village life in the district of Pamphylia and Pisidia during the Ottoman period and on the gradual disappearance of sedentary settlement in many regions that in Byzantine times had been thickly settled.

the Karamanids rebelled and entered the city of Konya one of their acts was to banish Persian and to proclaim the exclusive use of Turkish in the government and administration.[793] It was only one event among many by which Greek, Armenian, and Persian began to recede before the triumphant advance of Turkish in the fourteenth century, and by the fifteenth century not only was Asia Minor largely Turkish-speaking (including many of the Greeks and Armenians who had remained Christian) but Turkish epic poetry and literature had undergone a considerable development.[794] When the Turks settled in towns and villages and intermarried with the converted Greeks and Armenians, their position as rulers and the official use of Turkish produced a gradual retreat of Greek and Armenian to isolated areas of non-Turkish settlement, or to a few areas in which Christians remained compact, as in the Trebizondine coastal district.

Extensive regions, though it is impossible to say how extensive, reverted from agriculture to nomadism, that is to say that pastoral nomadization occurred in Anatolia between the eleventh and fifteenth centuries. Raids for booty, enslavement of the farmers for the slave trade, and animal husbandry signified unfelicitous agricultural conditions.[795] Many contemporary sources reveal the insecurity of agricultural life in the frequently troubled periods between the eleventh and fifteenth centuries. Ricoldus de Monte Crucis observed that Greek farmers did not dare to go out from the towns and fortresses to till their fields or to gather wood without a caparisoned horse, for the Turkmens would slay them upon sight.[796] Thus farming, besides the rigors of cold and drought, was subjected to a further serious debility: the insecurity of the farmer's person.

These rude nomads inspired both fear and intense dislike among the Muslims and Christians who lived in the Anatolian towns and villages.

---

[793] Ibn Bibi-Duda, p. 313, 345. See the remarks of Brocquière-Schefer, pp. 100–101, on Turkish north of Antakya and in the regions of Cilicia. Arnold von Harff-von Groote, p. 201, reports that even the Armenian Christians in his day were Turkophone, reserving the use of Armenian for their religious services alone. "Item deser Armeniani spraichen gemeynlich sarrascheynische spraich. dan in yeren gotlichen ampten bruychen sy eyne eygen spraiche . . ." Arnold von Harff-Letts, p. 235.

[794] A. Bombaci, *Storia*, pp. 261–314. M. Mansuroğlu, "The Rise and Development of Written Turkish of Anatolia," *Oriens* VII (1954), 250–264; "Anadolu metinleri (XIII. asir: 1. Seyyad Hamza, 2. Dehani, 3. Ibtidaname)," *T.M.*, VII–VIII (1940–42), 95–104. *Sultan Veled'in turkce manzumeleri* (Istanbul, 1958). Taeschner, *Der anatolische Dichter Nasiri (1300) und seine Futuvvetname* (Leipzig, 1944). A. Gölpinarli, *Yunus Emre hayatĭ* (Istanbul, 1936); Gölpinarli, *Yunus Emre ve tasavvuf* (Istanbul, 1961). E. Rossi, *Dedi Qorqut*. Danishmendname-Melikoff, I.

[795] Regel, II, 261. Ansbert, pp. 155–156. Gesta Federici, pp. 86–87.

[796] Ricoldus de Monte Crucis-Laurent, p. 114; "Inuenimus autem firmiter per fide dignos, quod Greci illi ita timent Thurcimannos, quod non audent exire de ciuitatibus nec de castris eorum, nisi portent secum capistrum paratum, quo ligentur. Dicunt enim, quod Thurcimannus statim eum occidit, nisi inueniat ei capistrum paratum. Et ideo quando exeunt ad seminandum vel ad siluam vel ad huiusmodi opus, unusquisque portat suum capistrum, quo ligetur." One sees the same retreat of the farming population before the Turkmens elsewhere as well, Ibn Battuta-Gibb, II, 428. Nicetas Choniates, 194–195. Matthew of Edessa, pp. 181–182, and *passim*.

The Greeks referred to the Turkmens by such epithets as dog-heads (κυνοκέφαλοι), cannibals (ἀνθρωποφάγοι), and wolves.[797] Muslim administrative and court officials (such as Ibn Bibi and Karim al-Din of Aksaray), religious men in the towns (Djalal al-Din Rumi, Eflaki, Sultan Walad), and the town dwellers themselves have left indelible traces in contemporary literature and historical deed of the hatred they felt for the nomads. The Turkmens were "satans" who dissolved the security of the times—God's vehicle of destruction for an errant and sinful society. When the tribes under the direction of the Karamanids attacked Konya in the mid-thirteenth century, they were defeated on the plain of Kavala. Their begs were then paraded through the streets of Konya, where they were exposed to the insults and tortures the inhabitants inflicted upon them. Their bodies were placed on a tree before the gate to the citadel and archers from the towers of the saray used their bodies in displays of marksmanship. Some years later in a second attempt, the Karamanid Turkmens succeeded in entering and temporarily holding Konya. But upon news that a Mongol relief army was approaching, Djimri and the Turkmens hastily left Konya, because had the citizens, with the assistance of the Mongols, caught them, they would not have allowed a single tribesman to leave the city alive.[798]

It was for all these reasons that Turkish sultans and Christian rulers built walls around their towns, forts in the rural areas, strengthened frontier defenses, and recolonized their lands repeatedly. Against the nomads they undertook a variety of measures; expeditions and massacres, forced sedentarization, recruitment in state armies, transfer of sedentary populations from the scenes of nomad raids, and even transfer of the nomads themselves.[799]

The traumatic impact of Turkmen settlement is described in greatest detail for northeast Anatolia and Georgia during the last quarter of the eleventh and first quarter of the twelfth century. The nomads began to raid the region during the reign of the Iberian king George II (1072–89). The Turks streamed in, sacking and enslaving the regions of Asis-Phorni, Khlardjeti to the sea, Chawcheth, Adchara, Samtzhe, Karthli, Argoueth, Samokalako, and Dchqondid. In the beginning the Turks remained in these areas only until the first snows and then departed laden with booty and slaves. Only those Christians survived who succeeded in fleeing to the mountain forests and to secure fortresses. The following year the

[797] Pachymeres, I, 134. Regel, II, 258–259. Theodore Prodromus, *P.G.*, CXXXIII, 1380. Eustathius of Thessalonike, *P.G.*, CXXXV, 941. Euthymius Tornices-Papadopoulos-Kerameus, pp. 182–183.

[798] Eflaki-Huart, II, 208–209, 418–419. Aksaray-Gençosman, pp. 159–160, 197. Ibn Bibi-Duda, pp. 308, 317.

[799] Planudes-Treu, pp. 97, 136, 141, 150–152, 163, 166, 174–176, 178. Brosset, *Géorgie*, I, 358–366, 370, 374. Ashïpashazade-Ali, pp. 111–112. Ashïkpashazade-Kreutel, p. 155. For greater detail see the earlier part of this chapter. Eustathius of Thessalonike, *P.G.*, CXXXV, 938.

nomads appeared and terrorized the land from spring until the beginning of winter so that the farmers who remained neither sowed nor harvested. The Georgian chronicler relates that the land was no longer inhabited by men but only by animals and wild beasts. The churches suffered fire and became the stables for the Turkmen horses, priests were immolated, virgins violated, young men forcibly circumcised, and children enslaved. By the reign of David II (1089–1125) the Turkmen raiders were no longer leaving Georgia and northeast Asia Minor at the onset of winter, but had effected settlements in those regions they had wasted. In the district of Somketh, for instance, the Turkmens had settled their tents, women and children, horses, sheep, mules, and camels. At the beginning of winter (October) they moved into the river valleys of the Gatchian district and settled along the banks of the Mtcouar and of the Ior (all the way from Tiflis to Barda). Here they found ample water and forest and led a "sweet life" in hunting and giving themselves up to rest and to trade with the towns they had captured. But they also continued to raid their Christian neighbors from this winter camp, taking booty and prisoners. In the spring they began to ascend the mountains of Somketh and Ararat with their families and flocks. Henceforth they conducted their raids from the summer *yayla*. Thus the series of events leading from the first Turkmen raids upon a sedentary district to its disruption, and finally to the physical interposition of a Turkmen settlement in the disrupted province is complete. The Turkmen kernels thus inserted in these areas became centers for further disruption of life in the area.

The dynamics of such an arrangement could culminate in the complete conquest of an area if a strong leader or state did not make systematic and long-term efforts to halt the process. The economic cohesion and strength of the sedentary society were sapped by the Turkmen settlements and raids, as agriculture and commerce were seriously crippled by the raids of the nomads. Conversely, the ruination of the countryside did not harm the nomads but quite to the contrary resulted in their economic enrichment—booty, prisoners for the slave markets, and the lands of the inhabitants. The reign of David II was a turning point in Turkmen successes in Georgia, for he waged a relentless and cruel war against the Turkmens in Georgia and northeast Asia Minor. He gradually reconquered the towns, and in 1116 attacked the Turkmen tents in Khlarjeti and along the Tsorokh River where he massacred the Turkmen warriors, taking as booty their women, livestock, and baggage. By 1121 he had so decimated the Turkmens wintering on the banks of the Mtcouar that they appealed to the Seljuk sultan for aid. But the tide had turned against the Turkmens and by the time of his death, David had conquered Tiflis and Ani and extirpated the Turkmen settlements from most of his lands. The half century of warfare between sedentary society and nomadism, however, had left this part of Georgia a semiinhabited ruin. When Dimitri I

(1125–54) succeeded to the throne there were inhabitants only in the citadels and towns of Hereth, Somkheth, Tachir, Djawakeheth, and Artahan. Thus both David and Dimitri had not only to rebuild the towns, villages, churches, roads, and bridges, but above all to repeople the desolate regions. It is interesting that among the colonists whom David brought were 40,000 Kipchaks and their families, who contributed greatly to the repopulation of deserted areas, and who eventually received Christianity.[800]

What happened in Georgia and this eastern reach of Anatolia in regard to nomadization was repeated throughout Asia Minor at various times between the eleventh and fifteenth centuries. It is superfluous to say that the efforts of the Comnenoi and Lascarids to extirpate the nomads never attained the success the Georgian monarchs achieved.

Conclusions

Four centuries of Turkish conquest and settlement transpired between the battle of Manzikert and the death of Muhammad II and the ultimate reunification of much of Anatolia. From the late eleventh to the mid-twelfth century, the Turkish conquest was destructive and brought great upheaval. This was followed in the late twelfth century by a period of consolidation and stability which culminated in the remarkable economic prosperity and cultural bloom of the mid-thirteenth century. But in the late thirteenth century, Anatolia reverted to tribal anarchy with consequent renewal of the destructive patterns of upheaval that characterized the late eleventh and first half of the twelfth century. The emergence of the beyliks saw an improvement of conditions in Anatolia, especially in the Bithynian domains of the Ottomans, during the fourteenth century. Until the elimination of all these petty principalities by the Ottoman sultans, however, Anatolia remained a battleground of tribal confederations and sedentary Turkish governments.

With the exception of the felicitous period during which the Nicean empire and the Seljuk sultanate revived Anatolian society, the Turkish conquests and settlements subjected Byzantine institutions to a long series of severe shocks. These repeated blows fatally dislocated Byzantine society in Asia Minor. Inasmuch as the state apparatus was Muslim, the Christian community could not at any given time recoup its previous losses. Once property, churches, and people were lost to Islam, they could never be reclaimed, for according to Islamic law and historical tradition "once Muslim always Muslim." Since the state was Muslim, this principle was always enforced. Thus, in spite of the stability and prosperity that characterized Anatolia in the first half of the thirteenth century, the Christians could do little about recovering all the ground that had been

---

[800] Brosset, *Géorgie*, I, 346, 381. P. M. Tarchnichvili, "Inscription," pp. 86–88. M. Tseretheli, "Das Leben des Königs der Könige Davith (Davith II 1089–1125)," *B.K.*, no. 26–27 (1957), pp. 45–73.

lost consequent to the decimating events of the late eleventh and the early twelfth century. Similarly, the Ottoman unification of Anatolia brought greater security and uniformity of conditions for the Christians, but it was of no avail in restoring the Christian communities to that position they had occupied in the thirteenth century. These repeated shocks so corroded the unifying bonds of the Byzantine establishment that it was left defenseless and naked before the assimilating forces of Islam.

⌐The destructive character of the Turkish conquest and settlement, which contributed so greatly to the violent dislocation of Byzantine society, was largely (though not exclusively) due to the nomadic Turkmen tribes.⌐Entering Anatolia as unruly conquerors inspired by djihad and their instinct for plunder, and settling upon the land in compact groups, they were long a bane to the settled Christian populations.

The fourteenth-century author Demetrius Cydones gives a succinct account of the effects of the Turkish conquests in Anatolia at the moment when the conquerors were embarking upon their early European adventure.

They took from us all the lands which we enjoyed from the Hellespont eastward to the mountains of Armenia. The cities they rased to the ground, pillaged the religious sanctuaries, broke open the graves, and filled all with blood and corpses. They outraged the souls of the inhabitants, forcing them to deny God and giving to them their own [i.e., the Turks'] defiled mysteries. They [the Turks] abused their [Christians'] souls, alas, with wanton outrage! Denuding them of all property and their freedom, they left the [Christians as] weak images of slaves, exploiting the remaining strength of the wretched ones for their own prosperity."[801]

[801] Demetrius Cydones, *P.G.*, CLIV, 964–968. Reprinted in A. Vakalopoulos, Πηγὲς τῆς ἱστορίας τοῦ νέου ἑλληνισμοῦ (Thessalonike, 1965), pp. 91–93. L. Petit, X. A. Siderides, M. Jugie, *Oeuvres complètes de Gennade Scholarios* (Paris, 1928), I, 178–179 (hereafter cited as Scholarius-*Oeuvres*). Scholarius relates that large numbers of Byzantine villages and towns in Asia and Europe were sacked and that mere ruins now indicated that they had once existed, even their names having disappeared. All this is the punishment that God has meted out to the Christians for having merely observed, and not lived, their Christianity. " ἢ πόθεν ἄλλοθεν οἴεσθαι χριστιανοῖς τὰς τηλικαύτας ἐπελθεῖν συμφοράς, καὶ πόλεις ἐν 'Ασίᾳ τε καὶ Εὐρώπῃ τῇ πρὸς ἡμῖν ὑπὲρ τρισχιλίας καὶ κώμας ἀναριθμήτους ὑπὸ τῶν ἀσεβῶν πορθηθείσας τὰ ἔσχατα πεπονθέναι καὶ τῶν μὲν μηδὲ τοὔνομα μένειν λοιπόν, τὰς δὲ μηδὲν ἐρειπίῳ διενηνοχέναι λειψάνοις μόνοις γνωριζομένας." Also Alexius Macrembolites, I. Ševčenko, "Alexios Makrembolites and his 'Dialogue between the Rich and the Poor," *Z.R.V.I.*, VI (1960), 195; "Have we not been delivered to the sons of Agar as sheep for the slaughter? Have they not invaded our whole land and laid it waste? Do they not dwell in our illustrious and honored cities, do they not treat as slaves their inhabitants, refined and sheltered from misery in the past? Have we not been scattered all over the earth as captives; after innumerable slaughters, is its expanse not pitifully strewn with our bones? Have our bodies not been thrown out as food to the birds of the sky and to the animals of the earth? Not long ago the survivors among us were routed by disorder and confusion and consumed. For this reason, have not our cities and our countryside been devastated and abandoned by their inhabitants?"

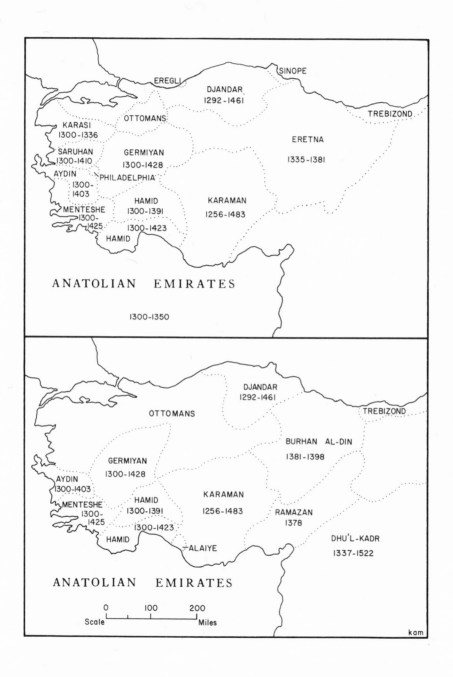

ANATOLIAN EMIRATES

1300-1350

Top map labels:

EREGLI
SINOPE
DJANDAR
1292-1461
TREBIZOND
OTTOMANS
KARASI
1300-1336
ERETNA
1335-1381
SARUHAN
1300-1410
GERMIYAN
1300-1428
AYDIN
1300-1403
PHILADELPHIA
MENTESHE
1300-1425
HAMID
1300-1391
KARAMAN
1256-1483
1300-1423
HAMID

Bottom map labels:

DJANDAR
1292-1461
OTTOMANS
TREBIZOND
BURHAN AL-DIN
1381-1398
GERMIYAN
1300-1428
AYDIN
1300-1403
MENTESHE
1300-1425
HAMID
1300-1391
KARAMAN
1256-1483
RAMAZAN
1378
1300-1423
HAMID
ALAIYE
DHU'L-KADR
1337-1522

ANATOLIAN EMIRATES

0   100   200
Scale |___|___|___| Miles

kam

IV. Decline of the Church in the Fourteenth Century

What effect did the Turkish invasions and settlement have on the structure of the church during the upheavals of the late thirteenth and the fourteenth century?

The two principal forces that had molded the formal cultural life of the Greek population in Byzantine Anatolia had been the Byzantine go ernment and the Orthodox church. The Turkish conquests had removed the former from Asia Minor and thus one of the cultural forces at the base of Anatolian Hellenism was no longer present. This was at once the most apparent and dramatic effect of the Turkish settlement. Less apparent, but no less crucial, is the effect that the Turkish invasions had on the structure of the Greek church during this long period. For with the removal of the political forces that shaped and nurtured Byzantine society, the continuity and direction of this Greek Christian community henceforth resided in the Greek church almost exclusively.

The history of the church in that portion of Anatolia conquered by the Turks in the late eleventh and the twelfth century was marked by decline. The Turkish conquerors deprived the various metropolitanates and bishoprics of their property and frequently of leadership. Thus the churches in Turkish Anatolia, in contrast to the churches of Byzantine Anatolia, suffered a sharp decline during this early period. The fate of the churches in the Anatolian domains of the Comnenoi was quite different. They were rebuilt, recolonized, and once more attained the flourishing state that had prevailed prior to the Turkish invasions. When the political tension between Greek and Turk was polarized and stabilized in Nicaea and Konya during the early thirteenth century, the Greek church in Turkish Anatolia was able to consolidate the portion that had remained after the troubles of the eleventh and twelfth centuries. The Greek church in the thirteenth century (in Anatolia) consisted, therefore, of two different but functioning parts: the revivified and flourishing ecclesiastical districts of northern and western Asia Minor; the greatly diminished but stabilized churches of central and eastern Anatolia. The reconquests of Alexius and John Comnenus had saved the church structure in northern and western Anatolia; the stability the sultans had imposed on the plateau had kept the church from completely disappearing in central and eastern Anatolia.

The question, and it is crucial, one must next examine is the effect on the church of the renewed Turkish invasions and upheavals during the late thirteenth and the fourteenth century which upset the stability and prosperity of thirteenth-century Asia Minor.

The Acta

One of the most important bodies of source material in examining the decline of Christian Hellenism in certain areas of Asia Minor and its replacement by Turkish Islam is that known as the patriarchal acta. These acta are, for the most part, decisions issued by the patriarch in session with the synod and are concerned with matters of ecclesiastical administration and discipline. Hence, these decisions are specific answers to pressing problems of the moment, and as such are a very reliable and valuable source for contemporary church history. Unfortunately, they have not come down intact (probably only a very small portion has survived), so that this body of documents is not numerically all-inclusive and comprehensive. Does this mean, then, that the picture they give is substantially lacking and incorrect, and further, that the validity of conclusions based on them is affected? This question can definitely be answered in the negative if one makes certain limitations as to the chronological period to which they apply. Most of the documents fall in the fourteenth century, though they overlap both the thirteenth and fifteenth centuries, and within this period of the fourteenth century they are of such a quantity (140 acta covering almost every general area of Asia Minor and 50 metropolitanates), that it may be safely assumed these documents give an accurate overall picture of the conditions of the Orthodox church at this time. In establishing the general condition of the church during this period, one can ascertain the state and fate of Christian Hellenism in Asia Minor.[1]

Let us proceed to examine what this body of approximately 140 acta reveals as to the fate of 50 Anatolian metropolitanates in the fourteenth century. These acta frequently speak of the granting of one metropolitanate (or bishopric) to another one κατὰ λόγον ἐπιδόσεως (by reason of sustenance).[2] This occurred when a metropolitanate became vacant due to the death of the metropolitan, and instead of appointing a new metropolitan to succeed the defunct one, the vacant metropolitanate was merely turned over to another metropolitan who held it κατὰ λόγον ἐπιδόσεως. This entitled him to all the rights and revenues of the metropolitan of that particular district, except that he could not be enthroned

---

[1] These patriarchal documents were published by Mikolsich and Müller in 1860–62 and have thus been known to the scholarly world for a rather long time. They were subsequently the basis of a most significant monograph by A. Waechter, *Der Verfall des Griechentums in Kleinasien in XIV Jahrhunderts* (Leipzig, 1903).

[2] For such grants in the twelfth century see chapter iii.

on the metropolitan throne. This grant κατὰ λόγον ἐπιδόσεως was given quite frequently in Asia Minor (and to a much lesser extent in Europe) because, as the texts inform us, the great majority of the metropolitanates had suffered serious impoverization and hence needed financial and material assistance to continue to function. The church supplied this aid simply by turning over to a particular needy metropolitan an even more impoverished and decimated church whose metropolitan had died or whose seat could not be filled because of the troubled times in Asia Minor. In addition to indicating that a particular metropolitanate is having economic hard times, these grants often indicate (and specifically state) that there has been a decrease in the number of the faithful in the metropolitan district. It is important to note that this type of grant maintained the legal existence of a metropolitanate that had been severely reduced in wealth and numbers, but also it generally indicated that Christians in a given metropolitanate continued to exist, though often in reduced numbers. When, however, the metropolitan seat disappeared from the notitia episcopatum (the formal list or catalog of the ecclesiastical hierarchy) or was united to another metropolitanate permanently, it indicated a sharp decline and significant disappearance of Christians.[3] In the section that follows, these grants will be considered as a source for the decline and disappearance of various churches in Asia Minor.

In eastern Asia Minor the metropolitan seat of Melitene found itself in great economic need

because his [the metropolitan's] church has long ago passed under the barbarians and up to the present is surrounded and ruled by them.[4]

Hence in 1318–19 the synod bestowed upon the metropolitan Theodosius of Melitene, κατὰ λόγον ἐπιδόσεως, the metropolitan seat of Celtzene (Erzindjan) since the latter "had been deprived of the consecrated seat by the foreigners."[5] The document goes on to say that there is no property left in the region of Celtzene in which the metropolitan can reside except the monastery of Ci. Formerly, Celtzene, along with Cortzene and Taron, had twenty-two suffragant bishoprics. Now it had only one significant possession left, the monastery of Ci. The last metropolitan of Melitene is mentioned in the year 1329,[6] and though both Melitene and Celtzene are mentioned thereafter in the fourteenth century, the seats are vacant, and by the fifteenth century they disappear from the list of metropolitanates.[7]

[3] Waechter, *Verfall*, pp. 2–4.
[4] Miklosich et Müller, I, 82.
[5] *Ibid.*, 83.
[6] *Ibid.*, 146.
[7] H. Gelzer, *Ungedruckte und ungenügend veröffentlichte Texte der Notitiae episcopatum, ein Beitrag zur byzantinischen Kirchen- und Verwaltungsgeschichte. Abhand. der phil. philolog. Cl. der kön. bayer. Akad. der Wiss.*, XXI (1901), 628–629 (hereafter cited as Gelzer, *Ungedruckte Texte*).

Therefore the complete decay and practical disappearance of the Greek Christian community of these two ecclesiastical seats seem to have been consummated in the course of the fourteenth century. It would be useful to consider in somewhat more detail the synodal decision of 1318–19 by which Melitene received Celtzene κατὰ λόγον ἐπιδόσεως, for this document is similar to the majority of the documents, and it also describes, simply but adequately, the factors underlying the nature of such a grant. The patriarch begins by saying that it is necessary to preserve the old order of bishoprics and metropolitanates, but

> since the disorder of affairs [which has come about because of sin] has overturned and confused the ecclesiastical order in not a few cities and lands, the protectors . . . of the church . . . have decreed a second course, so to speak, in order that those who are for whatever reason without ecclesiastical seats . . . or perhaps have only a small segment of their flock remaining so that they are not able to govern because of the lack of necessities or to give to others, [they] will receive as succour other churches.[8]

The ἀνωμαλία (disorder) and σύγχυσις (confusion) of which he speaks are, of course, references to the disintegration of Seljuk and Byzantine rule in Asia Minor and the chaos that ensued in the late thirteenth and the fourteenth century. It is this that has overturned the order and arrangement of the church and caused its great poverty. These two points are of the first order of importance and they constantly recur in the administrative literature.

In Trebizond the Christian community lived under far more favorable conditions, for here it enjoyed the protection of the secular arm of the Trebizondine empire. The domains of the empire were comparatively secure against the Turkish invaders and thus its church was also secure. So much greater was the security of the church here than in the lands held by the Turks that on occasion the seat of the metropolitanate of Amaseia was shifted to its suffragant bishopric of Limnia,[9] which, though a subordinate of Amaseia, happened to be within the political boundaries of the Trebizondine state and hence enjoyed protection against the Turks. Thus in the face of a devastating Turkish invasion (1317) during which the metropolitan underwent great danger, the patriarch gave permission to the metropolitan to shift his seat to Limnia. In 1384 the bishop of Limnia temporarily took over the administration of Amaseia because the metropolitan could not enter the area.[10] Though the church of Trebizond was considerably reduced as a result of the conquest of Muhammad II, it continued as a comparatively strong metropolitanate until the twentieth century.

Many of the Greek communities in the Byzantine provinces of Cappadocia and Lycaonia on the Anatolian plateau had declined considerably

[8] Miklosich et Müller, I, 81–82.
[9] *Ibid.*, 70.
[10] *Ibid.*, II, 66.

by the beginning of the fourteenth century. Caesareia (1327) received the metropolitanates of Sebasteia, Iconium, Mocissus, and Euchaita κατὰ λόγον ἐπιδόσεως and in 1370 received Nazianzus.[11] In the same year (1370), Caesareia was also to assume the administration of Tyana and Mocissus in case they became bereft of metropolitans.[12] All these grants of ἐπίδοσις are an indication of decline, and one must remember that Caesareia had been the first in rank, and glory (πρωτόθρονος) of the Orthodox church prior to the Turkish invasions. Though it continued to function as a metropolitan seat until the twentieth century, it seems to have been considerably reduced by the end of the fourteenth century. The information from Cappadocia and Lycaonia is impressive evidence for the history of the Anatolian church when one considers that an area that had once included five powerful metropolitanates and twenty-nine bishoprics was now united in the hands of one cleric. This would not be so striking if the bestowal had been of a temporary nature, as the author of the document had hoped it might be. But when in 1365 a new metropolitan of Caesareia was named, he again received the administration of Mocissus, Sebasteia, Iconium, and Nazianzus, and in addition the metropolitanate of Tyana.[13] Euchaita however is not mentioned, and it is probable that there were few Christians left there. As regards Sebasteia, Mocissus, and Tyana, their situation may have improved somewhat during the course of the fourteenth century before worsening again. Thus in 1384 and 1387 metropolitans of Sebasteia were again named, in 1369 and 1370 a metropolitan of Mocissus, and in 1369 a metropolitan of Tyana.[14] After this time Mocissus and Tyana fail to appear in the acta and their communities seem to have declined completely. Consequently they do not appear in the fifteenth-century list of the metropolitanates. Iconium, in contrast, continues to be mentioned in the acta of the last half of the fourteenth century, survives in the fifteenth century notitia, and indeed continued as the seat of a metropolitan until the twentieth century. But the acta reflect very unsettled conditions in the discipline of the church here.[15] Nazianzus is not heard of after 1370 when it was placed under the administration of Caesareia.[16] By this time the Greek community had fully declined, and Nazianzus does not reappear in the notitia of the fifteenth century.

Amaseia, farther to the north, managed somehow to survive the fourteenth century as the seat of a metropolitan. Nevertheless, the small community was surrounded by Muslims (μέσον ἀλλοφύλων οἰκοῦσιν ἐθνῶν) and was subjected to economic hard times, oppression, and periodic

[11] Ibid., I, 143 ff., 536.
[12] Ibid., I, 537.
[13] Ibid., I, 468. Waechter, Verfall, p. 14.
[14] Miklosich et Müller, I, 505, 537; II, 65, 78. Waechter, Verfall, pp. 14–15.
[15] Miklosich et Müller, II, 1, 46, 48, 89, 160, 167, 175. This question will receive greater attention at another point.
[16] Ibid., I, 536.

absence of the metropolitan. The church appears in the notitia of the fifteenth century and still existed in the early twentieth century.[17] A synodal decision of 1315 records that the bishop of Sinope (a suffragant of the metropolitan of Amaseia) has been driven out of the city.[18] Gangra to the west of Amaseia was one of the cities which long resisted the Turks. There is, however, but one significant synodal decision (1400–01) which deals with Gangra, and according to this document the patriarch has appointed the presbyter George Contophe metropolitan of Gangra in answer to a petition of the inhabitants of Gangra asking for a new shepherd. They asked for a metropolitan because the "foreigners" were oppressing them on all sides, and they were in danger concerning their religion. In addition to all this, many had evidently become Muslims.[19] By the mid-fifteenth century, the community had either disappeared or become so insignificant that Gangra is dropped from the notitia.[20]

The two coastal metropolitanates of Amastris and Pontoheracleia were still under Byzantine control as late as 1340 and hence were partially shielded from the shock of Turkish occupation. But by 1387 a synodal decree reveals a picture of Amastris suffering economically and in a state of general decline.[21] This shows that the community was dying out, and though a metropolitan is named in 1400, Amastris disappears from the notitia in the fifteenth century.[22]

Claudiopolis had ceased as a metropolitan seat even earlier. In the notitia of Andronicus II (end of the thirteenth century), it was replaced by its bishopric Pontoheracleia so that the community here must have been well on its way to disappearing by the early fourteenth century.[23] Though Pontoheracleia was Byzantine in 1346, there were signs of its decline in the early fourteenth century. In 1360 it was finally captured by the Turks,[24] and in a synodal decision of 1387 Pontoheracleia is given to the metropolitan of Amastris, whose church is also declining rapidly, for the following reason:

It is in no way just to leave without a metropolitan the remnant of the Christians captured by barbaric invasions in the most holy metropolitanate of Pontoheracleia. For such are in need of spiritual supervision and its consecration, since as human

---

[17] Waechter, *Verfall*, pp. 17–20. Miklosich et Müller, I, 35.

[18] Miklosich et Müller, I, 34–35. On the other hand, its position on the coast facilitated contact with the Greek cities of Constantinople and Trebizond, and Ibn Battuta-Gibb (II, 466), recorded that there were eleven villages of Greeks living just outside of the city. In the beginning of the fifteenth century a Greek merchant who had visited Sinope and Amisus in order to trade could find no commercial activity there because the whole area had been wasted by Timur's troops, Miklosich et Müller, II, 547.

[19] Miklosich et Müller, II, 491.

[20] Waechter, *Verfall*, pp. 20–22.

[21] Miklosich et Müller, II, 102–103.

[22] *Ibid.*, II, 370–372. Waechter, *Verfall*, pp. 22–23.

[23] Gelzer, *Ungedruckte Texte*, p. 497; " ιθ ὁ Ποντοηρακλείας· αὕτη ἐπισκοπὴ ἦν τοῦ Κλαυδιουπόλεως, καὶ διὰ τὸ ὑπὸ ἐθνῶν ἐκείνην κατασχεθῆναι, ἐτιμήθη αὕτη χάριν ἐκείνης εἰς μητρόπολιν καὶ θρόνον ις, νῦν δὲ ιθ γέγονεν." Waechter, *Verfall*, p. 23.

[24] Waechter, *Verfall*, pp. 25–26.

beings they are led astray by the deception of life and care little for the heavenly and immortal rewards. In addition, living in the midst of foreigners and association with them are the greatest hindrance to salvation. Since it seems impossible for them to have a valid metropolitan, for the church had previously disintegrated and the ones there are not sufficient for his aid and support . . .[25]

By the fifteenth century Pontoheracleia has dropped from the notitia.

Though there is little in the patriarchal documents about Ankara, a metropolitan is named in 1400;[26] it continues to appear in the fifteenth-century notitia (but its Greek Christian congregation must have been small), and Ankara was still the seat of a metropolitanate in the twentieth century.[27] Pessinus and Amorium are not mentioned in the patriarchal documents of the fourteenth century, but they do appear in the ecthesis of Andronicus III as independent metropolitanates. Thus their ruin was probably consummated during the early fourteenth century, and so they are absent from the fifteenth-century notitia.[28] The sources reveal very little about the metropolitanate of Pisidia, but what little they do say is in consonance with the overall picture of decline. Despite the diminution of the community, the district still possessed sufficient Christian population to warrant the continued existence of Pisidia as a metropolitanate in the fifteenth and later centuries.[29]

The information for the metropolitan seats of Side, Perge, and Attaleia in Pamphylia is somewhat more detailed for the period 1315–1400, and so one can trace the decline of the Greeks in this area. The documentation of this region presents exactly the same state of affairs as the less detailed information presents for the other metropolitanates described in the preceding paragraph.[30] The uninterrupted decline of the Christian community is reflected in a synodal decision of 1397.

> Since it [Side] was captured long ago there has been a scarcity of the faithful and poverty of the ecclesiastical things in it [property]. And because of these things it is not at all possible to ordain a legitimate metropolitan there.[31]

The patriarch has decided to unite it with the metropolitanate of Attaleia, "for it also, because of the above reasons, has not been able to have a

---

[25] Miklosich et Müller, II, 102–103.

[26] Ibid., 312.

[27] Waechter, Verfall, p. 26. Gelzer, Ungedruckte Texte, p. 628. H-G. Beck, Kirche und theologische Literatur im byzantinischen Reich (Munich, 1959), pp. 162–163. For the unfavorable conditions of the Christians in twelfth-century Ankara, see chapter iii above. When Manuel II Palaeologus visited Ankara in the late fourteenth century, it was predominantly Muslim, E. Trapp, Manuel II. Palaeologos. Dialoge mit einem "Perser" (Vienna, 1966), p. 5; "τότε τοίνυν ἐν ᾿Αγκύρᾳ, τῇ ποτε μὲν εὐγενεῖ, νῦν δ᾿ οὐκέτι ἀσέβειαν πλουτούσῃ."

[28] Waechter, Verfall, p. 27.

[29] Ibid., pp. 27–29. Gelzer, Ungedruckte Texte, 628. Vakalopoulos, ῾Ιστορία., II₁, on decline in Pisidia.

[30] Miklosich et Müller, I, 34, 182.

[31] Ibid., II, 276, and also 285.

legitimate shepherd."[32] The two seats were now united under the metropolitan Theophylactus whose title was metropolitan of Attaleia and proedrus of Side. But in a decision of 1400, Theophylactus of Attaleia-Perge and proedrus of Side, is awarded the rich metropolitanate of Sugdaia and Phyllon κατὰ λόγον ἐπιδόσεως for he had had to leave his church in southern Anatolia.[33] One may conclude that henceforth the church disappears, and in fact Side is absent from the fifteenth-century episcopal list. In this instance the texts once more speak of the oppression of the church and of the decline in the number of the faithful. The following details further emphasize the unsettled nature of conditions. There are mentions of metropolitans of Side in 1357, 1360, 1369, 1372,[34] but in between these dates appear metropolitans of other cities as τὸν τόπον ἐπέχοντες of Side (about 1365 the prelate of Pontoheracleia, in 1371 that of Larissa.[35] Now an ecclesiastical seat was held by another cleric as ὁ τόπον ἐπέχων generally because that particular seat was vacant and inaccessible. The fact that it was held in the above cases by European clerics or by metropolitans ordained to the seat but who remained in Constantinople indicates quite clearly that it was impossible for anyone to go there, hence the synod did whatever little was possible to administer it from Europe. Finally, in the fourteenth-century ecthesis of Andronicus III, the metropolitanates of Athens and Monemvasia took the place of Side in the hierarchical rank.[36]

The metropolitanates of Perge and Attaleia suffered a fate similar to that of the church of Side, but unfortunately we are less well informed, as the sources concerning them come from the end of the fourteenth century. A decision of 1387 announces the appointment of a new metropolitanate and then proceeds to describe the sad conditions of the metropolitanate. The patriarch writes of the new metropolitan of Attaleia that he "suffers and is in difficulty."[37] and that the community has all but disappeared.[38] As a result the patriarch attempted to give him, κατὰ λόγον ἐπιδόσεως, the metropolitanate of Rhodes and the church of Cos. The situation of Attaleia was so bad that in 1394 it was given to the metropolitan of Myra κατὰ λόγον ἐπιδόσεως, and in 1397, as we have seen, it was united with Side into one metropolitanate.[39] By 1400 the situation had so worsened that the metropolitan of Attaleia-Perge and proedrus of Side was appointed to the metropolitanate of Sugdaia. Consequently, by 1400 these three seats were completely desolate, and it would seem that Turkish oppression (θηριωδία and ἀγριότης) had played its role in this

[32] *Ibid.*, 277.
[33] *Ibid.*, 390.
[34] *Ibid.*, I, 367, 399 ff., 511, 594.
[35] *Ibid.*, 471, 587.
[36] Waechter, *Verfall*, pp. 30–31. Gelzer, *Ungedruckte Texte*, p. 607.
[37] Miklosich et Müller, II, 94, " καὶ πάσχει καὶ στενοχωρεῖται."
[38] *Ibid.*, 93.
[39] *Ibid.*, 205–206.

respect. All this is confirmed by the notitia of the fifteenth century, from which these three churches vanish.[40] The decline of Myra was somewhat less spectacular than that of its neighbors. In a decision of 1387 the patriarch speaks of it as comparatively better off than Attaleia.

> It is not at all good that one church grow and have many revenues, villages, and lands, and that another should be completely impoverished.[41]

But its greater prosperity was due to the fact that it held the islands of Rhodes and Cos κατὰ λόγον ἐπιδόσεως, and indeed the metropolitanate of Myra vanished from the notitia of the fifteenth century.[42]

The acta mentioning Stauropolis (also called Caria and Aphrodisias) in Caria all come from the last half of the fourteenth century. Between 1356 and 1361 Stauropolis lost its metropolitan,[43] for in that latter year it was being temporarily administered by the metropolitan of Bizye as ὁ τόπον ἐπέχων.[44] In 1365 and 1368 Stauropolis was still without a metropolitan and under the administration of the metropolitan of Bizye.[45] Conditions were evidently so unpropitious that it had not been possible to send a prelate to the area, and certainly the community must have been declining steadily (if it existed at all). In 1369 a metropolitan of the community reappears in the acta as the recipient of the churches of Miletus and Antioch ad Maeandrum, κατὰ λόγον ἐπιδόσεως.[46] This confirms the declining condition of Stauropolis. But Antioch and Miletus were probably in a worse state and therefore the patriarch had to provide the metropolitan of Stauropolis with further support. So in 1387 he conferred Rhodes, Cos, and the Cyclades on the metropolitan.[47] The metropolitan of Myra, however, contested these islands and so the metropolitan of Stauropolis finally received them (κατὰ λόγον ἐπιδόσεως) only on the death of the metropolitan of Myra in about 1394.[48] This evidently delayed the final disappearance of the metropolitanate, for a metropolitan is again mentioned in 1399, but the church is completely abandoned in the notitia of the fifteenth century.[49]

The metropolitanates of Hierapolis, Laodiceia, and Chonae, separated from Stauropolis by the Salbakus and Cadmus mountains, were located in a restricted area. Therefore this region must have been thickly settled

---

[40] Waechter, *Verfall*, p. 33. The Turkish traveler Evliya Chelebi makes interesting observations on the culture of the Attaliote Christians during the seventeenth century, see chapter vii below.

[41] Miklosich et Müller, II, 95.

[42] Waechter, *Verfall*, p. 34. Gelzer, *Ungedruckte Texte*, p. 639.

[43] Miklosich et Müller, I, 362.

[44] *Ibid.*, 429.

[45] *Ibid.*, 471, 500.

[46] *Ibid.*, 511.

[47] *Ibid.*, II, 106–108.

[48] *Ibid.*, 197–199.

[49] Waechter, *Verfall*, pp. 34–37. Gelzer, *Ungedruckte Texte*, pp. 628–630. Miklosich et Müller, II, 469.

and rich in pre-Turkish times in order to have been able to support three metropolitanates in such a comparatively small area. The decline of these communities occurred somewhat later than that of the communities in eastern Asia Minor. But in the latter half of the fourteenth century, the customary bestowals κατὰ λόγον ἐπιδόσεως appear in the acta, indicating a diminution of the Christian communities. In 1370 the metropolitan of Cotyaeum received the churches of Hierapolis, Chonae, and Synnada;[50] in 1384 Chonae, Cotyaeum, and the patriarchal possessions of Coula and Colida were placed under Laodiceia.[51] One year later (1385) Philadelpheia received the churches of Synnada and Hierapolis,[52] and in 1394 Coula, Colida, Synnada, and the bishopric of Synnada.[53] But the metropolitan seats of Hierapolis, Laodiceia, Synnada, and Cotyaeum then disappear from the episcopal catalog in the fifteenth century.[54] The church of Miletus is last mentioned in 1369[55] in which year it, along with Antioch ad Maeandrum, went to the church of Stauropolis κατὰ λόγον ἐπιδόσεως. Both are missing from the notitia of the fifteenth century.[56]

In the days before the Seljuk invasions, Ephesus had been one of the largest, richest, and most powerful of the metropolitanates, hence its decline was very striking. As a result of its ancient prominence, the church in Constantinople made extraordinary efforts to keep it from vanishing completely. Consequently the church seems to have been occupied in an irregular manner up to 1393. In the years 1400 and 1401 the metropolitan of Gothia is mentioned as τὸν τόπον τοῦ Ἐφέσου ἐπέχων.[57] A metropolitan was, however, reappointed to the seat and Ephesus retained its old place and rank in the notitia of the fifteenth century.

In spite of this conservatism, the Christian community was in a seriously depleted state, for when the Turks took Ephesus in 1304 all those whom they did not put to the sword were transplanted to another town.[58] In a pronouncement of 1368 the patriarch united the metropolitanate of Pyrgion with that of Ephesus "forever." The document states that actually Pyrgion had been given to the metropolitan of Ephesus κατὰ λόγον ἐπιδόσεως three years previously. But as he had not been able, up to the present, to reenter his church, he had not been able to visit the church of Pyrgium.[59] Even with the union of Pyrgion with Ephesus, the situation had so declined in Ephesus that by 1387 the small community could not even support a poor priest, for all had been destroyed by the

[50] Miklosich et Müller, I, 539.
[51] Ibid., II, 88.
[52] Ibid., 87.
[53] Ibid., 209–210.
[54] Waechter, Verfall, pp. 37–38. Gelzer, Ungedruckte Texte, pp. 628–629.
[55] Miklosich et Müller, I, 510. It is previously mentioned in 1365, Ibid., 471, 476, 489.
[56] Ibid., 510–511. Gelzer, Ungedruckte Texte, pp. 628–629.
[57] Miklosich et Müller, II, 312, 519, 514. Waechter, Verfall, p. 40. On the irregularity of occupancy in the first half of the fourteenth century see below.
[58] Pachymeres, II, 589.
[59] Miklosich et Müller, I, 498.

Turks. So in addition to Pyrgion, Ephesus received Pergamum, Clazo-menae, New Phocaea

not only because it is not now possible to consecrate metropolitans there, but also because this is customary and has occurred often in many churches, which having been raised in prosperous times from bishoprics to archbishoprics or metropolitanates . . . again with the decline of affairs were demoted to bishoprics.[60]

Ephesus suffered at the time of the Timurid invasion, but nevertheless survived in the notitia of the fifteenth century.[61] Pergamum and Pyrgion declined quickly in the fourteenth century and so are absent from the fifteenth-century catalog of the hierarchs.[62]

Sardes declined rapidly after the Turkish conquest in the early four-teenth century. In 1343 it was still the seat of a metropolitanate, and the seat continued to exist down to 1369.[63] But in this year the metropolitan of Philadelpheia is bestowed forever with the rank and title of Sardes, for Sardes had long been nothing more than a field of ruins.

Time . . . alters and changes all and . . . causes prosperity to progress towards extinction . . . . The great metropolis of Sardes . . . had for so long attained such glory and fame . . . and its most beautiful order and culture, so that it was num-bered among the first and the greatest metropolitanates . . . and at the tip of the tongues of all, as a pleasing delight and ornament of those many cities that are in Asia. But [time] brought her to such degradation, by consent of God that is, and so disposed her affairs as not to preserve even the outline or some small trace of a city, transferring it from a garden of luxury into a plain of destruction and extinction.[64]

Philadelpheia remained Byzantine until the Ottoman conquest in 1391 and thus continued to be a strong ecclesiastical center. It continues in the notitia of the fifteenth century.[65]

Smyrna was conquered by Aydin early in the fourteenth century and when in 1318 a metropolitan was appointed to Smyrna he was given Chios[66] and was instructed to

lead back to fear of God those who have been led astray and to take in hand those who have been perverted.[67]

In 1343 the Latins took Smyrna from the Turks and the position of the Christians seems to have been eased,[68] for previously, between 1329–1339,

[60] *Ibid.*, II, 105.

[61] Waechter, *Verfall*, p. 42. Gelzer, *Ungedruckte Texte*, p. 628.

[62] Miklosich et Müller, II, 105. Waechter, *Verfall*, p. 44. Pyrgium is last mentioned as an independent metropolitanate in 1316 (Miklosich et Müller, I, 65), and then disappears from the acta until 1387, when along with Pergamum it is made a bishopric under Ephesus.

[63] Miklosich et Müller, I, 237.

[64] *Ibid.*, 509.

[65] *Ibid.*, II, 209–210, it received Coula, Colida, and Synnada in 1394.

[66] The latter is without leadership because of the 'ανωμαλία and σύγχυσις. *Ibid.*, I, 93, reflects the spread of disorder to the islands following the erection of the emirates and the appearance of piracy.

[67] *Ibid.*, 92.

[68] Nicephorus Gregoras, II, 689. Cantacuzene, II, 420.

Matthew the metropolitan of Ephesus had been forced to remain in Europe. Though in 1347 the metropolitan of Philadelpheia was ordered to look after Smyrna and Phocaea,[69] in 1363 a metropolitan of Smyrna appears in the acta.[70] The decision states that the Christians in Smyrna are "many and without number." That it was comparatively well-off is confirmed by a document of 1387 concerning a dispute between Smyrna and Ephesus over Pergamum, Phocaea, and Clazomenae. Pergamum, Clazomenae and New Phocaea were given to Ephesus because it was more impoverished, whereas the relatively more prosperous Smyrna was given only Old Phocaea.[71] Though a metropolitan of Smyrna does not appear in the acta after 1389,[72] the church survived the conquests of Timur and appears in the fifteenth-century catalog of metropolitans.[73]

Among the metropolitanates of Abydus, Pegae, and Cyzicus in the Hellespontine regions, only Cyzicus outlived the storm of the fourteenth century. Abydus, which is not mentioned in the acta, does occur as late as the so-called ecthesis of Andronicus III (mid-fourteenth century), but after this time, it is not heard of again. It had long since been filled with bellicose Turks preparing to attack Europe, and the Greeks, being close to Thrace, must have largely fled.[74] The church of Parium was united to Pegae in the early fourteenth century because of the latter's need, and in 1354 the metropolitan of Pegae received the metropolitanate of Sozopolis as further economic support. The document that grants this epidosis in 1354 gives a picture of Pegae as having all but vanished. It then disappears from the acta and notitia after being mentioned in the ecthesis of Andronicus III.[75]

Cyzicus, whose metropolitan was the ἔξαρχος πάσης Ἑλλησπόντου, was more important because of its strategic commercial location. In 1324 it was one of the three Anatolian ecclesiastical seats which was able to contribute a temporary annual subsidy to the needy patriarchate. This shows its comparative wealth, though it was soon to undergo hard times in the fourteenth century. After the Ottoman conquest, Cyzicus had so declined that in 1347 the metropolitan of Cyzicus was given Ganus κατὰ λόγον ἐπιδόσεως.[76] In the years 1370 and 1372[77] the seat was without a metropolitan, and it was not until 1381 that a metropolitan reappeared.[78] Possibly this was due to financial difficulties. With the

[69] Miklosich et Müller, I, 256.

[70] *Ibid.*, 445. He is reprimanded for remaining in Thessalonike and not proceeding to Smyrna. The patriarch declares that if it is not possible to enter Smyrna he must take up his seat in the monastery of Croitzus in Phocaea.

[71] *Ibid.*, II, 103 ff.

[72] *Ibid.*, 138.

[73] Gelzer, *Ungedruckte Texte*, p. 629. Ducas, pp. 72–76.

[74] Beck, *Kirche und theologische Literatur*, p. 153. Gelzer, *Ungedruckte Texte*, p. 608. Waechter, *Verfall*, pp. 48–49.

[75] Pachymeres, II, 415. Gelzer, *Ungedruckte Texte*, p. 607. Miklosich et Müller, I, 330.

[76] Miklosich et Müller, I, 261.

[77] *Ibid.*, 531, 594.

[78] *Ibid.*, II, 24.

appointment of a new metropolitan in 1387 it was necessary to bestow upon him, κατὰ λόγον ἐπιδόσεως, the declining seat of Chalcedon, its possessions in Constantinople, and certain patriarchal possessions in Bithynia and Hellespont.[79] In spite of this serious decline, Cyzicus survived and appears in the catalog of the fifteenth century.[80]

The period between 1261 and 1337 was a very turbulent one for the Christian inhabitants of Bithynia.[81] Pachymeres and Gregoras give a vivid description of the wasting of the area and of the flight of its population behind the gates of the larger cities and across the sea to Thrace. But even inside the cities siege, famine, and slaughter all were experienced. With the completion and consolidation of the conquests in Bithynia by Orhan, the conditions of the Christians were stabilized, both in the cities and the countryside, and the clergy, upon the payments of money, eventually came to a modus vivendi with the conquerors.[82] Apamaea declined early, passing to the administration of the metropolitan of Prusa in 1318.[83] In the ecthesis of Andronicus III it was replaced by the churches of Litvon and Caucasion, and thus the church seems to have been abandoned.[84]

A synodal proceeding of 1318 describes Prusa as hard pressed,[85] a reflection of the growing Ottoman military pressure and sieges of the larger Bithynian cities. It was in response to this that the church of Prusa had received the administration of Apamaea and the patriarchal monastery of Hosius Eustratius within Prusa.[86] Apparently, the plight of Prusa in the half century following its conquest was severe, as in 1327 and again in 1331 the metropolitan of the city appears as proedrus of the church of Bizye in Europe and a legitimate metropolitan appears only in 1347.[87] A further indication of the difficulties of the church is the fact that from 1347 to 1386 no metropolitan of Prusa is mentioned.[88] Inasmuch as Prusa was close to Constantinople, it is highly probable that had there been a regular metropolitan he would have showed up at some of the meetings of the synod in Constantinople and would have signed the proceedings. In 1386 the metropolitan of Prusa administered the church of Cotyaeum;[89] and in 1401, the church of Nicomedia.[90] Though Prusa

---

[79] *Ibid.*, 108–110.

[80] Gelzer, *Ungedruckte Texte*, p. 628.

[81] For a detailed description see Pachymeres, I, 311; II, 335–336. Nicephorus Gregoras, I, 214.

[82] Waechter, *Verfall*, p. 54.

[83] Miklosich et Müller, I, 80–81.

[84] Gelzer, *Ungedruckte Texte*, p. 608.

[85] Miklosich et Müller, I, 80.

[86] *Ibid.*, 80–81.

[87] *Ibid.*, 144, 164, 270.

[88] *Ibid.*, II, 90.

[89] *Ibid.*

[90] *Ibid.*, 561.

survived the fourteenth-century crisis and appears in the fifteenth-century notitia, it suffered a great decline.[91]

Nicodemia, taken in 1337 by the Ottomans, also suffered the severe ordeals of continuous sieges.[92] From 1327 to 1356 no metropolitan of Nicomedia appears in the acta. In 1356 the metropolitan of Selymbria held the church of Nicomedia as ὁ τόπον ἐπέχων,[93] while it was thus held in 1381–83 and perhaps until 1385 by the metropolitan of Ungro-Vlachia.[94] These facts demonstrate the uncertainty of the conditions under which the Christians of the area lived even after the early Ottoman conquest. Nicomedia continues, however, as the seat of a much reduced metropolitanate in the notitia of the fifteenth century.[95]

Nicaea finally fell in 1331. But the surrounding areas of Belocome, Angelocome, Anagourda, Platanea, and Melangeia had previously fallen to the Turks and had become semidesolate.[96] Nicephorus Gregoras describes the effect of the conquest on the Christians.

The barbarians settled on the shores of Bithynia fearlessly and imposed the heaviest taxes on the remaining small towns. They did not, for a while, drive the people and towns to complete destruction, for they were able to pay them easily in the shortest time. However, they [Turks] did not cease to make frequent attacks and to capture the majority of the miserable ones both on land and sea.[97]

An act of the Constantinopolitan synod (1381) explicitly states that Nicaea, the seat of the first ecumenical council and capital of the Lascarid empire, is to receive Prusa as an epidosis because of its declined state.[98] The area suffered further devastation at the beginning of the fifteenth century, when Timur's general Sevindjik appeared plundering and destroying in the regions of Nicaea and Cius. Nicaea, however, survived as a metropolitanate in the notitia of the fifteenth century.[99]

In the church of Chalcedon decline is apparent from the early fourteenth century, and it seems to have been largely destroyed through the raids of the Turks. About the year 1316 the metropolitan received the church of Maeroneia (in the Balkans), and he kept it until 1327.[100] Then the

---

[91] Waechter, *Verfall*, pp. 54–55. Gelzer, *Ungedruckte Texte*, p. 628.

[92] Pachymeres, II, 412–413, the surrounding towns are emptied.

[93] Miklosich et Müller, I, 362.

[94] *Ibid.*, II, 37–38, 43, 46, 48, 51. Waechter, *Verfall*, p. 56.

[95] Gelzer, *Ungedruckte Texte*, p. 628.

[96] Pachymeres, II, 413.

[97] Nicephorus Gregoras, I, 458. This indicates a certain depopulation and confusion in certain areas of Bithynia and also fiscal oppression by the Turks. Both of these factors appear in the acta for other areas of Asia Minor. There were additional forces at work which resulted in a great diminution of the Christian population. See below, and chapter v.

[98] Miklosich et Müller, II, 25. In 1386 we find an independant metropolitan of Prusa, Waechter, *Verfall*, p. 58, and a metropolitan is named for Nicaea in 1395, Miklosich et Müller, II, 237. The ruin and poverty of Nicaea are described by Ibn Battuta-Gibb, II, 452–453.

[99] Waechter, *Verfall*, p. 58. Gelzer, *Ungedruckte Texte*, p. 628. Ducas, p. 72.

[100] Miklosich et Müller, I, 45.

metropolitanate disappears from the acta for twenty-seven years until 1354.[101] In 1387 the metropolitan of Cyzicus received the metropolitanate of Chalcedon, the document mentioning that, "The city of Chalcedon was destroyed many years ago and has very few inhabitants so that they have no need of a bishop."[102]

This is reiterated in a proceeding of 1389 which declares that though the previous patriarch (Philotheus) had ruled there should never again be a metropolitan of Chalcedon, a metropolitan is once more to be appointed. He is, however, to have none of the former rights in Chalcedon and is to remain in Constantinople "just as all the other metropolitans who come here because . . . of necessity."[103]

These administrative documents, emanating from the patriarchal synod, indicate that twenty-seven Anatolian metropolitanates ceased to exist at some time in the fourteenth or fifteenth century: Melitene, Celtzene, Mocissus, Tyana, Nazianzus, Gangra, Amastris, Pontoheracleia, Amorium, Pessinus, Side, Myra, Perge, Attaleia, Stauropolis, Hierapolis, Laodiceia, Synnada, Cotyaeum, Antioch ad Maeandrum, Miletus, Pergamum, Pyrgion, Sardes, Pegae, Abydus, and Apameia. A second group of documents, the notitiae episcopatum, not only corroborate the synodal acta but supplement them by recording the disappearance of still other Anatolian metropolitanates and bishoprics.

The Notitiae Episcopatum

The so-called notitiae episcopatum constitute a second source for reconstructing the number of metropolitanates and bishoprics and their position in the church hierarchy. These notitiae are lists of the metropolitanates, bishoprics, and archbishoprics, which were composed for purposes of protocol and were used in synods, court, and other official functions. The notitiae define clearly the positions and rank of the participant. The same sort of function was performed for the members of the Byzantine military and administrative organization by such a document as the Cleterologion of Philotheus. These lists reflect the formal changes in the makeup of the episcopacy. They give the alterations either through elevations or demotions of certain ecclesiastical seats, and also the disappearance of old and appearance of new metropolitanates or bishoprics as a result of political decline or expansion.

How are these notitiae to be used by the historian? There are three fundamental rules that must be observed: (1) these documents are, by nature, extremely conservative and tend to preserve the old order of metropolitanates and bishoprics (quite often they may mention a metropolitanate or bishopric that has either declined or disappeared); (2) we

[101] *Ibid.*, 144, 338.
[102] *Ibid.*, II, 109.
[103] *Ibid.*, 133.

find ecclesiastical sees that are not mentioned in the notitiae because of their short life;(3) when a metropolitanate is no longer mentioned in the notitiae, it is probably correct to assume either its disappearance or sharp decline as a Christian center. Of these three points, we must consider only the first and third for our purposes. We may proceed to evaluate the notitiae on this basis. If metropolitanates cease to be mentioned in these documents, it means that they have ceased to function as important Christian centers in Asia Minor, and this disappearance from the lists is doubly significant inasmuch as traditional Byzantine conservatism was reluctant to abandon the established pattern. Second, if metropolitanates continue to be mentioned in Asia Minor in the notitiae of the twelfth through the fifteenth century, we must evaluate and control the notitiae by what we know of the actual history of the area and of the period.[104]

Notitiae	Total metro-politans	Metro-politans in Anatolia	Metro-politans in Europe	Total bishops	Bishops in Anatolia	Bishops in Europe
Leo VI[105]	51	32	19	515	373	142
Nea Tactica[106]	54	35	19	503	370	133
Tzimsces[107]	56	37	19			
Skabalanovič[108]	81	46	35			
Philippicus 1477[109]	82	47	35			
Isaac II[110]	93	52	41			
c. 1204[111]	85	48	37	611	421	190
Andronicus II[112]	112	56	56			
Andronicus III[113]	108	54	54			
Notitia of 15th c[114]	72	17	54	118	3	115

[104] Beck, *Kirche und theologische Literatur*, p. 148.

[105] Gelzer, *Ungedruckte Texte*, pp. 549–567. On the dates of the various parts see Grumel, *Registre*, 598.

[106] *Georgii Cyprii descriptio orbis Romani*, ed. H. Gelzer (Leipzig, 1890), pp. 57–83 (hereafter cited as Nea Tactica).

[107] Gelzer, *Ungedruckte Texte*, pp. 569–572.

[108] Skabalanovič, *Gosudarstvo*, pp. 401–424.

[109] Gelzer, "Ungedruckte und wenig bekannte Bistumerverzeichnisse der orientalischen Kirche," *B.Z.*, I (1892), 253–257.

[110] Gelzer, *Analecta Byzantina, Index lectionum Jenensis* 1891 bis 1892 (Jena, 1892).

[111] V. Beneševič, "Monumenta Vaticana ad ius canonicum pertinentia," *Studi Bizantini* II (1927), 131–155.

[112] Gelzer, *Ungedruckte Texte*, pp. 595–606.

[113] *Ibid.*, pp. 606–610.

[114] *Ibid.*, pp. 613–637.

The notitiae that are going to be considered are ten in number and they range, chronologically, from the tenth to the fifteenth century. In each one shall be noted, first, the total number of metropolitanates; second, the number in Asia Minor; third, the number in the European provinces; fourth, the total number of bishoprics (where given); fifth, the number in Asia Minor; sixth, the number in the European provinces.

What do the statistics from these notitiae say, and, more important, what can be elicited from them? The basic notitia is that attributed to Leo VI for it is the model for those that followed. It lists 51 metropolitanates, of which 32 are in Asia Minor and 19 in the European provinces of the empire. Of the 515 bishoprics, 373 are in Asia Minor and only 142 are in the European portion of the empire. The far larger numbers of metropolitanates and bishoprics in Asia Minor reflect the comparatively greater importance, size, and wealth of the church in Anatolia. This is further reflected by the order of precedence of the various metropolitan seats in the notitia. In the list that follows, the number of bishoprics in each is listed by the side of the metropolitanate.[115]

1. Caesareia—15	27. Corinth—7
2. Ephesus—34	28. Athens—10
3. Heracleia—15	29. Mocissus—4
4. Ankara—8	30. Seleuceia—22
5. Cyzicus—12	31. Calabria—12
6. Sardes—21	32. Patras—4
7. Nicomedia—10	33. Trebizond—7
8. Nicaea—6	34. Larissa—10
9. Chalcedon—0	35. Naupactus—8
10. Side—16	36. Philippopolis—10
11. Sebasteia—4	37. Trajanopolis—7
12. Amaseia—5	38. Rhodes—10
13. Sicily—13	39. Philippi—6
14. Tyana—3	40. Adrianople—11
15. Gangra—3	41. Hierapolis—9
16. Thessalonike—5	42. Dyrrachium—4
17. Claudiopolis—5	43. Smyrna—4
18. Neocaesareia—3	44. Catana—0
19. Pessinus—7	45. Amorium—5
20. Myra—33	46. Camachus—8
21. Stauroplis or Caria—26	47. Cotyaeum—3
22. Laodiceia—22	48. Hagia Severina—4
23. Synnada—22	49. Mitylene—5
24. Iconium—15	50. New Patras—1
25. Antioch (Maeander)—21	51. Euchaita—4
26. Perge or Sylaion—18	

Not only are there more metropolitan seats in Asia Minor, but they are generally larger and their districts more heavily populated than the

[115] *Ibid.*, pp. 550–559.

metropolitanates of Europe, as is indicated by the greater number of bishoprics subordinate to each. The largest metropolitanate in Europe is that of Heracleia with fifteen subordinate bishoprics. Adrianople has ten, and a city such as Thessalonike only five. On the other hand Ephesus boasts thirty-four; Myra, thirty-three; Seleuceia, twenty-two; Sardes, twenty-one; Antioch on the Maeander, twenty-one; Stauropolis, twenty-six, and so on. Of the first twenty-six metropolitan seats that appear in the list only three (Heracleia, Sicily, Thessalonike) are in Europe, while twenty-three out of the twenty-six are in Asia Minor! This raises the next problem. Is order of rank determined by size, by the tradition of precedence which was established at an earlier date by the church, or by a combination of both? In short, does order of rank tell us anything about the comparative size of the population? It would seem that the order of rank depended, originally, on the tradition of the forming church and the position of the city in the provincial administration of the empire. Thus it must often have happened that the traditions of the forming church were connected with urban centers of respectable size. These metropolitan seats would have had to retain a certain population in order to keep their ecclesiastical importance over the centuries. That the eccleciastical provinces of Asia Minor possessed a larger population than did the European ecclesiastical provinces is demonstrated by the greater number of bishoprics which the richer Asia Minor metropolitanates possessed. The Nea Tactica and the notitia attributed to the reign of John Tzimisces attest to much the same state of affairs. In this last mentioned notitia, there are almost twice as many metropolitanates in Asia Minor (37) as in Europe (19). The notitiae of the eleventh century show a remarkable rise in the metropolitanates both in Asia Minor but especially in Europe. Of a total of eighty-two, forty-seven are in Asia Minor and thirty-five in Europe. Though there has been a trememdous increase in the number of European metropolitanates, the number in Europe does not attain that in Asia Minor. The increase in numbers, both in Europe and Asia Minor, is largely due to the expansion of the empire in the tenth and eleventh centuries in eastern Asia Minor, the Balkans, and Crete. Also, however, a number of new metropolitan sees appear in nonborder districts, both in Asia Minor and Europe. Why is this so? Is it possibly due to an increase in population, or is it merely parallel to the cutting up of the provincial themes into a larger number of smaller districts? It is very difficult to say what the reason is for the increase in the number of this type of metropolitanate, but the remarks of the canon lawyer Balsamon suggest that this expansion is partially connected with population expansion.

This trend, that is the increase in the number of metropolitanates both in Europe and Asia Minor, continues through the twelfth and thirteenth centuries and even into the fourteenth century; in fact it reaches a high point in the notitia that appeared in the reign of Andronicus II and only begins to decline slightly in the notitia of the reign of Andronicus III. This is particularly disturbing, for we well know the bad state of conditions in the Asia Minor church from the twelfth century and in the European provinces from the time of the Fourth Crusade. We should expect to see a decrease in the number of metroplitanates in both areas, or at best that the number of these seats should remain the same in keeping with traditional Byzantine conservatism. Thus in the notitia from the reign of Andronicus II there are 112 metropolitanates distributed evenly between Asia Minor (56) and Europe (56). But though the appearance of such a large number of metropolitanates in Asia Minor would tend to vitiate this list as an indicator of the church's situation in Asia Minor, it is qualified by an interesting factor. Many of the old, prominent Anatolian metropolitanates begin to sink lower in the order of precedence. Thus Side, Sebasteia, Amaseia, Melitene, Tyana, and Gangra, for instance, slip down three places in the hierarchical order. Conversely, Thessalonike in Europe jumps from sixteenth to eleventh place.[116] The trend is obvious. Certain European provinces now begin to rise in the order of honor, and many of the Anatolian churches begin to slip to lower ranks. This is, of course, what one would expect in Asia Minor. This is further reflected in the fact that for the first time the number of European metropolitanates equals the number in Asia Minor. The notitiae had continued to focus on that of Leo VI as the ideal form, and the Comnenoi and Angeloi had merely patched up the old diatyposis of Leo VI without altering it basically. Though by the time of the Palaeologoi, most of Asia Minor and much of Europe had been lost, the emperors still held on to the old forms, and concessions were still made to the past. But now one begins to see the impact of the losses of the church starting gradually to manifest themselves in the notitia of Andronicus II. The important cities of the empire such as Thessalonike, Adrianople, and Monemvasia in Europe, and Philadelpheia, Prusa, and Pergamum in northwest Anatolia (still Byzantine territory) maintain and improve their position in the hierarchy. On the other hand, many of the old Asia Minor seats, in some cases nothing more than a pile of stones and ruins, went down a few places in rank. Thus the old traditional form of the notitiae has begun to break down, and the formula of τὰ ἀρχαῖα κρατείτω begins to give ground slowly but perceptibly, before the great destruction that the church had suffered since the end of the eleventh century.[117]

With the fifteenth century, the crying dissonance between sacerdotal pretense and reality of the situation finally disappears from the notitiae. An episcopal list of the late fifteenth century lists seventy-one (or

[116] *Ibid.*, pp. 597–601.
[117] *Ibid.*, p. 613.

seventy-two?)[118] metropolitanates under the patriarch of Constantinople of which only seventeen are in Anatolia and fifty-four are in Europe! There are seven archbishoprics in Europe, but merely one in Asia Minor. Of a very large number of bishoprics, only three are in Anatolia! This ecclesiastical document reflects with startling clarity and brevity uncommon in the long tradition of ecclesiastical literature the complete collapse of Hellenism in Asia Minor. The author of the notitia, after cataloging the existing metropolitanates and archbishoprics, includes a lament on the sad state of the church in Anatolia.

What a frightful decline! Read all [of the following] and you shall greatly lament.

There were also other metropolitanates, archbishoprics, and bishoprics as appears written in the diatyposis of the emperor lord Leo the Wise, and in that of the emperor lord Andronicus the second, of the Palaeologoi, which emperor honored and raised some of the thrones from lesser to greater [ones], and other great ones he demoted to lesser thrones, having authority as emperor [to do so]. Of these, many were made desolate and were completely obliterated by those who rule us.

And neither is a metropolitan to be found in the metropolitanates, nor an archbishop in the archbishoprics, nor a bishop in the bishoprics, nor priest in church, nor monk in monastery or pious foundation or cell, nor other Christian layman in castle or land . . . .

Fifty-one metropolitanates, eighteen archbishoprics, and four hundred and seventy-eight bishoprics are desolate. In the diatyposis of the said emperor lord Leo the Wise are ninety metropolitanates.

In the [diatyposis] of the above mentioned emperor lord Andronicus the second, of the Palaeologoi, are one hundred twelve [metropolitanates] and twenty-five archbishoprics.

And not only were those metropolitanates, archbishoprics, bishoprics, the monasteries and churches obliterated; But also the provinces of the three patriarchs of Alexandria, Antioch, and Jerusalem. Neither will you find a single metropolitan there, nor other Christian, layman or clergy.

But on the thrones of those patriarchates you will find barely a few priests, monks, and laymen. Because the churches of their provinces have been obliterated completely and Christ's people, that is the Christians, have been utterly destroyed.[119]

---

[118] *Ibid.*, p. 629, the Greek text lists 71 metropolitan seats whereas the numbering erroneously lists 72.

[119] *Ibid.*, pp. 630–631. The following seats appear in this document as still existing in Asia Minor:

Metropolitanates		Archbishoprics	Bishoprics	
Neocaesareia	Pisidia	Chalcedon	Proiconnesus	Apollonias (of Nicomedia)
Trebizond	Ephesus	Prusa		Kanin (of Trebizond)
Caesareia	Philadelpheia	Nicomedia		Opheos (of Trebizond)
Iconium	Smyrna	Nicaea		
Amaseia	Cerasus	Rizaion		
Ankara	Cyzicus			

The reference to 90 metropolitanates in the time of Leo VI is erroneous and it probably refers to the eleventh and twelfth centuries. A document of the seventeenth century (Gelzer, *Ungedruckte Texte*, pp. 637–641), records that at least 430 bishoprics had disappeared from Asia Minor in the past.

It is rather obvious that the notitiae have a number of interesting things to say about Asia Minor. First of all they make it possible to trace, in rough general lines, the decline of the church in Asia Minor through the changes in the order of precedence which occur by the time of Andronicus II, and also by the disappearance of many of the Anatolian metropolitanates from the notitia of the fifteenth century. In the time of the notitia attributed to Leo VI there were thirty-two metropolitan and three hundred seventy-three episcopal seats in Asia Minor. The notitia of the fifteenth century records only seventeen Anatolian metropolitanates in contrast to fifty-four for Europe, and only three Anatolian bishoprics. These statistics speak for themselves, indicating that up to the late eleventh century the metropolitanates of Asia Minor were far and away the most important of those under the church of Constantinople. This is obviously reflected in the greater number and superior rank of these metropolitanates in the notitiae. But to what is this superiority due? As has been indicated above, it is more than a mere matter of conservative hierarchical tradition. It is to a large extent the reflection of the fact that for a long time Asia Minor was the political, economic, as well as the ecclesiastical center of gravity of the Byzantine Empire.[120] Actually the peninsula remained the most important province of the empire until the Seljuk conquests of the eleventh century. The large number of metropolitanates in Anatolia reflects more than certain pious traditions in the administrative structure of the church. It reflects the fact that Asia Minor was, of the two major portions of the empire, the more heavily populated, and the more economically prosperous. This explains why it could support twice as many bishoprics as could the European provinces. One might, rather questionably, argue that Asia Minor had more metropolitanates because of its position in the early formation of the church. But the fact that there were in the time of John Tzimisces only 133 bishoprics in Europe and 370 in Anatolia simply reflects the greater population and economic power of these eastern provinces to sustain the larger ecclesiastical structure such a number of bishoprics entailed. This general line of argument is to a certain extent borne out and supported by a consideration of the thematic structure of the provinces.

The administrative hierarchy of the government also reflects the greater importance of Anatolia as a military recruiting ground and tax reservoir. Just as for the ecclesiastical hierarchy we have the notitiae that show the relative importance of the metropolitanates, so for the overall hierarchical structure of the empire's institutions we have similar documents, the Cleterologium of Philotheus (c. 899–900)[121] and the Tacticon Beneševič of the tenth century.[122] These two documents list the order of appearance

[120] Beck, *Kirche und theologische Literatur*, p. 173.

[121] J. B. Bury, *Imperial Administrative System in the Ninth Century* (London, 1911).

[122] Beneševič, "Die byzantinischen Ranglisten," *B.N.J.*, V (1926), 97–167; VI (1928), 143–145.

in which the officials of the empire shall appear at official functions. In these documents the superiority of the eastern provinces over those of the west is clearly marked and displayed in a number of particulars. In the Cleterologium of Philotheus the order and sequence of the generals is as follows:[123]

Anatolicon	Nicopolis
Armeniacon	Cibyrrheote
Thracesian	Hellas
Opsicion	Sicily
Bucellarion	Strymon
Cappadocia	Cephallenia
Charsianon	Thessalonike
Coloneia	Dyrrachium
Paphlagonia	Samos
Thrace	Aegean
Macedonia	Dalmatia
Chaldia	Cherson
Peloponessus	

The first nine thematic officials in order of rank are in charge of themes in Asia Minor. Their higher position is further illustrated by the fact that they received a fixed salary in gold paid directly from Constantinople, while the European thematic generals (Thrace and Macedonia excepted) had to raise their salaries in their own provinces. The salary scale for the eastern generals (including Thrace and Macedonia) was as follows.[124]

Class I	Anatolicon, Armeniacon, Thracesian	40 lbs. gold
Class II	Opsicion, Bucellarion, Macedonia	30 lbs. gold
Class III	Cappadocia, Charsianon, Paphlagonia,	
	Thrace, Coloneia	20 lbs. gold
Class IV	Cibyrrheote, Samos, Aegean	10 lbs. gold
Chaldia	received customs dues plus 10 lbs. gold	
Mesopotamia	received customs dues	

Thus the details of the thematic structure seem to support the contention that Asia Minor was more important from the point of view of population.

Though it is not possible to say anything as to numbers when speaking of populations, nevertheless the conclusion that the Byzantine population of Asia Minor was substantially greater than that of the European provinces both in the tenth and the eleventh centuries is an important fact to which reference has already been made in chapter i.

This consideration of the episcopal lists and the fourteenth-century patriarchal decisions results, at this point, in three important conclusions: (1) the numerical and economic center of gravity of the Greek

[123] Bury, *Ninth Century*, p. 40. The Tacticon Uspenski gives even greater importance to the Asiatic themes.

[124] *Ibid.* For a slightly later period see the details in Constantine Porphyrogenitus, De Caerimoniis, I, 696–697. This also tends to emphasize the importance of the Asiatic themes.

church in the tenth and eleventh centuries lay in Asia Minor; (2) by the early fourteenth century the ecclesiastical structure and communities of Anatolia are undergoing (or have already undergone) a fateful and decisive crisis; (3) when Anatolia is once more largely under one rule (Ottoman) in the late fifteenth century, the Greek communities and ecclesiastical structure have been largely obliterated. The vast extent of Greek Christianity in tenth- and eleventh-century Anatolia and the degree to which it was effaced by the fifteenth century indicate that there has occurred a transformation of vast proportions. In contemplating the nature of the process by which Asia Minor was Islamized, one can no longer explain the phenomenon by positing a sparse, superficially Greek population suddenly overwhelmed by hordes of invaders who were in numbers greatly superior to the peninsula's inhabitants.

Acta: Upheaval

The decisions of the patriarchal synod are important not only because they reveal clearly the decline and collapse of Greek Christianity through-out most of Asia Minor but also because they describe critical factors and details that caused and accompanied the disappearance of the church.

One of the first items that strikes the reader of the documents is the use of certain phrases describing the general situation in Anatolia during the fourteenth century. In no less than twenty-six acta there is overwhelming reference to confusion, invasions, upheaval, turbulence, difficulties, straits, captivity, destruction, and attacks of foreigners, which have enveloped portions of Asia Minor and the church in that area.[125] By way of example, during the years from 1315 to 1318 eleven documents refer to such times in Anatolia, very often giving specific references to the localities in such widely scattered areas as Sinope, Amaseia, Pontoheracleia, Melitene, Leontopolis, Sylaion, Myra, Side, Pisidia, Nymphaeum, Prusa, and Smyrna.[126] These acta reflect a highly unsettled state of affairs and there is a very definite correlation of such documentary testimony with the emergence of the beyliks, their continuous warfate, and the raids and wars of wandering tribes.[127] This period of upheaval was in large measure

[125] On the meaning of σύγχυσις, P. Lemerle, Actes de Kutlumus (Paris, 1945), under σύγχυσις, in the index. For such terminology see the documents in Miklosich et Müller, I, 3–4, 34, 36–37, 37, 40, 69–70, 80, 88, 127, 143, 242, 330; II, 46, 61, 104, 133, 109, 197.

[126] Though references to such troubled times occur less frequently during the middle of the century, by the end of the century they again appear frequently. The remainder of the documents speak of highly unsettled conditions in the areas of Euchaita, Iconium, Mocissus, Nazianzus, Pegae, Sardes, Attaleia, Perge, Pontoheracleia, Ephesus, Smyrna, Chalcedon, Stauropolis, Sinope, and Amisus.

[127] This troubled and unsettled state is reflected by the fourteenth century traveler Ibn Battuta (Ibn Battuta-Gibb, II, passim). The road to Laodiceia (Denizli) was infested with certain robbers whom he calls Germiyan and who possessed the town of Cotyaeum (Kutahya). To this Muslim traveler the Germiyanids (one of the most powerful of the Turkmen principalities) appear as little more than robbers who infest the roads of the countryside. The uncertain state of affairs is again reflected in the account of his journey to Tavas (Tabai). He and his companions were not allowed to pass through the city's

responsible for the final destruction of the ecclesiastical structure in Anatolia.[128] It would also seem, though this is admittedly a difficult subject upon which to generalize, that the various begs were frequently less tolerant toward the Christians than had been the Seljuk sultans. We have already seen the mixed cultural milieu of the court at Konya, its strong Persian flavor, and its tolerance in all matters. The beyliks on the other hand were associated more with the ghazi traditions as interpreted by the Turkmen tribes.

The patriarchal acta therefore furnish further striking confirmation of the highly disruptive character of the Turkish conquest, a characteristic already established from chronicler and other contemporary literature in chapters ii and iii.

Acta: Impoverization

This σύγχυσις of the fourteenth century affected the church and Christians of Asia Minor in various ways. One of the more important effects was the church's loss of property and income. This is a factor that, up to the present, has not been sufficiently appreciated in discussing the disappearance of Christianity in Anatolia. It is one of the more important criteria by which the historian can measure the effects of the Turkish invasions and migrations into Anatolia vis-à-vis the church. This impoverization of the Greek church indicates the continuation, or at least the renewal, of a trend already clearly visible in the eleventh and twelfth centuries.

The poverty of the church is reflected in the quarrels that erupted between the patriarch Athanasius I (1289–93, 1304–10) and his metropolitans and bishops in the reign of Andronicus II.[129] Many of the hierarchs had left their churches and were to be found attending the synod in Constantinople. The patriarch made vigorous efforts to force them out of Constantinople and back to their churches.[130] If, however,

---

gates until after a thorough investigation satisfied the local authorities that Ibn Battuta and his company were not bandits. Farther to the north he indicates that the beg of Balïkesri, his host, was simply a robber baron. The famous Byzantine urban and ecclesiastical centers of Nicaea, Smyrna, and Pergamum he describes as being nothing more than ruins. He reports that the formerly prosperous town of Erzerum in eastern Anatolia was largely in ruins as a result of warfare between two Turkish tribes. Incomplete though his report is, it gives one a partial picture of the disruption generally prevalent in parts of Asia Minor as a result of the turbulence of the Turkish beyliks and tribes. The letters of Manuel Palaeologus, ed. E. Legrand, *Lettres de l'empereur Manuel Paléologue* (Amsterdam, 1962), *passim*, reflect the same conditions.

[128] This state of affairs had already commenced in the latter half of the thirteenth century, when the power of the Rum Seljuks had declined.

[129] Pachymeres, II, 518. On this remarkable figure see the life edited by Papadopoulos-Kerameus, *Zhitiia dvukh vselenskikh patriarkhov XIV v Svv. Athanasiia I Isidora I* (St. Petersburg, 1905). His unpublished correspondence (Cod. Vat. Gr. 2219) contains valuable material on the historical events of the day, and especially on the fate of the church and ecclesiastical administration.

[130] Pachymeres, II, 643, "... μέσον τῆς συνόδου τῶν ἡγουμένων (μετὰ τούτων γὰρ τὰς συνόδους ἐποίει). Nicephorus Gregoras, I, 181–182. Athanasius disregarded, or

it were possible for the metropolitans in the Balkans to return to their comparatively freer and more prosperous churches, it was literally impossible for many of the Anatolian churchmen.[131] The basic causes of the quarrel between Athanasius and the metropolitans, which finally led to the patriarch's abdication in 1310, were economic. The metropolitans had lost their incomes and staff of officials as a result of the Turkish conquest.[132] Athanasius insisted, nevertheless, that they take part in all the various ecclesiastical celebrations of Constantinople in their official garments while at the same time he made no economic provisions for their maintenance. Because of this they complained to the emperor Andronicus and beseeched him to intervene so that they might receive a subsidy. The patriarch consented to dole out six to eight nomismata per year for each of the metropolitans.[133] Not only was this insufficient in terms of economic necessities, but Athanasius then refused to give the money. The dissatisfaction of the metropolitans with the austerities of the monk-patriarch led to the latter's abdication.[134]

In 1315 the synod bestowed the revenues of certain metropolitan seats on the church of Constantinople because the patriarchate was having very difficult financial problems.

Formerly the mother of the church, that is the great church of God, had not a few revenues, and gave splendidly. . . . But the confusion and malaise of affairs and the alteration and transition of time and hostile movement have touched the incomes of the church and led to difficulties in and lessening of the revenues.[135]

---

rather regarded with suspicion the metropolitans. Pachymeres, II,642 ; "Οἱ δὲ τῆς ἐκκλησίας πρωτεύοντες, καὶ ὡς ἤδη προείπομεν, ὑφορώμενοι, οἱ δὲ ἐν οὐδενὶ λογίζομενοι."

[131] This parallels the conditions of the σχολάζοντες from the Balkans and Anatolia in the eleventh and twelfth centuries, see chapter iii above. The Comnenoi therefore differentiated between the two groups of clergymen, permitting the Anatolian metropolitans to remain in Constantinople but excluding the Balkan hierarchs from Constantinople.

[132] Pachymeres, II, 647; "ἡ δὲ ἁγιωσύνη οἶδεν ὅτι ποιεῖ, ὅτι καὶ ἐὰν καί τι ἐναπολειφθὲν ᾗ τῶν ἡμετέρων οἰκονομιῶν ἀπὸ τῶν ἐχθρῶν, καὶ αὐτὸ περισυνάγει ὁ τῶν σῶν δικαίων ἔφορος." Ibid., 642; " καὶ οἱ ἔχοντες οἰκονομίας ταύτας ἀποστερούμενοι καὶ αὐτῶν ὀφφικίων . . . ἀλλὰ καὶ τῶν προσόδων ἀποστερούμενοι." On the loss of their officials, ibid., 645.

[133] The text refers to Οἱ δὲ τῆς ἐκκλησίας πρωτεύοντες, which I take to refer to the metropolitans rather than to the officials of the patriarch, the μεγάλη πεντάς. Ibid., II, 644–645, also seems to refer to metropolitans. In either case, whether the document refers to the metropolitans or ὀφφίκια of the patriarch, it demonstrates the dire economic straits of the church attendant upon the Turkish conquest and the disruption of ecclesiastical discipline therefrom. How meager, and therefore insufficient, the six nomismata would have been for the maintenance of the metropolitan and his administrative officials can be seen through a comparison with the dole of 36 nomismata that John IV Vatatzes gave to the poor in the thirteenth century, at a time when the nomisma had a higher gold content, ibid., I, 70.

[134] Nicephorus Gregoras, I, 258–259. His enemies surreptitiously removed the patriarch's footstool, and painted upon it a figure of Andronicus with a bridle in his mouth, being led by Athanasius as if the latter were a charioteer. Then they returned the stool and promptly accused the patriarch of slandering the emperor.

[135] Miklosich et Müller, I, 3–4, and further reflected in 1384, ibid., II, 61–64.

It is true that hard times are mentioned specifically in connection with the patriarchate, but many of its revenues had formerly come from patriarchal property in Anatolia, which was now afflicted by the "confusion and malaise of affairs." A synodal act of 1318 describes again the overall poverty of the church.

Since the malaise of affairs, brought about through sins, upset and confused the church's order ... in not a few cities and lands ... those who for whatever manner of necessity are assembled in idleness [away] from the churches which they lead, or perhaps some small remnant of their flock having remained, they are not able to guide themselves because of the lack of necessities therein, such are they, nor to furnish others; they will receive aid by addition of another church.[136]

As the church became increasingly poorer, the archbishoprics were put under the metropolitanates, so that at least one viable economic entity would result. This situation is expressed in a decision of 1368.

And this happened in other churches, the archbishoprics being united to the metropolitanates, because they were not able to be by themselves as a result of pressing need.[137]

Things had become very bad by the last quarter of the fourteenth century and a synodal proceeding of 1387 reports that,

not only was it impossible to support a metropolitan or bishop, but not even a priest of the needy and poor.[138]

The great poverty of the church in Asia Minor is clear in a pronouncement of 1324, some sixty-three years prior to the above-mentioned document. The patriarchate in Constantinople had appealed to the synod to provide it with revenue, as it had suffered the loss of its own. Again it speaks of the difficult and troubled times that had caused the church to be dispossessed of its formerly great income. The synod voted that those archbishoprics and metropolitanates that were prospering should help with annual contributions assessed as shown on table on following page. Of thirty-three contributing metropolitanates and archbishoprics only three (Cyzicus, Proiconessus, and Lopadium) were in Asia Minor. Of the 3,208 hyperpera leveled annually, only 296, or slightly more than 9 percent, came from Asia Minor. And this list was composed in 1324, before Cyzicus, and in all likelihood Proiconessus and Lopadium as well, had become completely poverty-stricken.[139]

A perusal of the synodal decisions regarding various Anatolian metropolitan seats establishes beyond doubt the grinding poverty of the church which has resulted from Turkish policies and, of course, confirms the impression that emerges from the more general statements about the economic conditions of the church at large.

[136] *Ibid.*, I, 81–82.
[137] *Ibid.*, 499.
[138] *Ibid.*, II, 104.
[139] *Ibid.*, I, 126–128. By 1347, therefore after the Turkish conquest, Cyzicus was in a dire economic state, *ibid.*, 261.

Heracleia	200	Methymna	50
Cyzicus	200	Brysis	50
Thessalonike	200	Rosion	36
Adrianople	100	Bizye	100
Berrhoia	100	Meroneia	36
Monemvasia	800	*Proiconessus*	72
Philippopolis	150	Garelle	24
Trajanopolis	70	Dercus	24
Serres	150	Arcadiopolis	24
Philippi	100	Lemnus	50
Mitylene	100	*Lopadium*	24
Didymoteichus	100	Cypsela	16
Old Patras	40	Xantheia	36
Lacedaemon	60	Medeia	50
Melenicon	36	Drama	24
Ainus	100	Ganus	50
Madytus	36		

ATTALEIA

A synodal act of 1387 states that the local Turks have greatly impoverished the church in the district of Attaleia.

The most holy metropolitan of Perge and Attaleia . . . found . . . that the dominion and authority of the ruling foreigners seized and possessed all the property of his church and in addition demanded from him the heaviest annual taxes.[140]

This district had already become so poor that it could not support two metropolitanates, and it had become necessary to unite the two seats into one. By 1387 the situation had become such that the newly sent metropolitan had to write to the patriarch that he needed financial assistance if he were to remain and to function properly.[141] The circumstances there had already become pressing at least some thirty years earlier—about 1357—so that it had been necessary to assign to it properties from another metropolitan seat,

because without these villages there is no church, and it is not at all possible for a metropolitan to inhabit it without them.[142]

This state of affairs continued, and in 1397 Attaleia was once more united to another metropolitan seat, this time to that of Side, for it was too poor to support its own metropolitan.

Since it had been captured long ago . . . there resulted a lack of ecclesiastical properties in it.[143]

STAUROPOLIS

The metropolitan seat of Stauropolis received a number of grants κατὰ λόγον ἐπιδόσεως because of its poverty. In 1369 it acquired the

[140] *Ibid.*, II, 92.

[141] *Ibid.*, 93.

[142] *Ibid.*, 95.

[143] *Ibid.*, 276. This applies to both Side and Attaleia. In a slightly later document, *ibid.*, 285, the two metropolitanates are described as ἄποροι.

metropolitanates of Miletus and Antioch ad Maeandrum in the form of such a grant.[144] But as these two seats had dwindled away, in 1387 the metropolitan of Stauropolis was to receive the metropolitanate of Rhodes with Cos and the Cyclades so that his "despondency and sadness"[145] might be dispelled. Again in about 1393 he received the same grant, with certain reservations,

for his own church, as a result of the continuing and successive captivities, had arrived at a scarcity of provisions and was greatly impoverished.[146]

SIDE

When the newly appointed metropolitan arrived in Side (c. 1315) the church was in such bad economic state that he was given the vacant neighboring metropolitanate of Sylaion and the archbishopric of Leontopolis to administer, for these latter churches were also much reduced.[147] In 1369 the metropolitan of Side received the seat of Rhodes and Cyclades as epidosis in order to bolster his economic status,[148] but by the end of the century, Side's situation was hopeless.

Its conquest long before ... created a poverty of ecclesiastical properties, and because of these things it was impossible to ordain a legitimate metropolitan there.[149]

In 1397,

since this same Side alone and its dependencies were not judged by the synod to be sufficient for the support and administration of a metropolitan and his retinue ... this Side and Attaleia, both churches being penniless, were united.[150]

PERGE

In 1387 Perge had been united with Attaleia in an effort to make one viable economic unit out of the two poor metropolitanates, for the Turks "had taken and possessed all the property of his church, and in addition demanded the heaviest taxes of him."[151]

PYRGION

The metropolitanate of Pyrgion also declined sharply and in 1365 and 1368 was given first as epidosis and then united with Ephesus in an attempt to bolster this more important seat.[152] In 1387 it was finally

---

[144] *Ibid.*, I, 511.

[145] *Ibid.*, II, 106.

[146] *Ibid.*, 197.

[147] *Ibid.*, I, 34 ;"ὡς τῶν τοιούτων ἐκκλησιῶν ἐν στενότητι καὶ ὀλιγότητι τοῦ χριστιανικοῦ λαοῦ γεγονυιῶν."

[148] *Ibid.*, 511.

[149] *Ibid.*, II, 276.

[150] *Ibid.*, 285.

[151] *Ibid.*, 92.

[152] *Ibid.*, I, 497–499.

demoted to the status of bishopric and put under Ephesus because "it is no longer possible to ordain a metropolitan there."[153]

EPHESUS

In 1368, as we have seen above, the synod put the metropolitanate of Pyrgion under the administration of Ephesus,

caring for the church of Ephesus so that it might have partial administration and aid, since all of its properties were removed [having been captured by the barbarians] and it is not able to provide for the necessities of its metropolitan. And this also happened in other churches, the archbishoprics being joined to the metropolitanates, as they were not able to exist by themselves, because of the poverty. . . . According to the practice in these matters and because of the fame of the metropolitan throne of Ephesus and the poverty and difficulty which confronted it, the church of Pyrgion was joined to it.[154]

By 1387 the economic decline of this ecclesiastical seat had become so pressing that the metropolitan asked to have all the old bishoprics that had formerly been under the jurisdiction of Ephesus returned to him.

He said [the metropolitan of Ephesus]: "His metropolitanate formerly boasted of much prosperity, when the affairs of the Rhomaioi were in bloom and great, and there was peace throughout the oicumene. And she had a host of lands and properties not easily numbered. She had a great synod of bishops under her, superior alike to all the metropolitanates in the east and in the west by the great number of her bishoprics and the greatness of her jurisdiction. As a result of this some of the bishoprics were removed and raised to metropolitanates, and were promoted to independence to be under the patriarchal throne. And if the affairs of the Rhomaioi were well and prosperity was present in the cities so that each of the churches could have its own metropolitan, he [the metropolitan of Ephesus] was willing to agree with what had been formerly decided and not to seek to alter the decisions of the fathers. But since every city and land perished at the hands of the foreigners, and was completely obliterated, and some are not even recognizeable by some few remnants, having very few Christian inhabitants, and not only are they unable to support a metropolitan or bishop, but not even a priest of the impoverished and needy.[155]

So the synod awarded the metropolitan of Ephesus the cities of Pyrgion, Pergamum, New Phocaea, and Clazomenae, all of which had at one time been subordinate to Ephesus.

PRUSA

In 1318 the synod and patriarch bestowed upon the metropolitan of Prusa certain administrative rights over the metropolitanate of Cyzicus and the patriarchal monastery of Hosius Eustratius in Prusa "so that he might not be destitute of the necessities, having been driven to this [state] by the malaise of affairs."[156] In 1381 Prusa was temporarily turned over

[153] *Ibid.*, II, 105.
[154] *Ibid.*, I, 499.
[155] *Ibid.*, II, 104.
[156] *Ibid.*, I, 80.

to Nicaea as an epidosis in an attempt to bolster the latter's economic predicament.[157] Five years later (1386) the metropolitan of Prusa was made exarch of Cotyaeum in an attempt to give further economic support to the former.[158]

COTYAEUM

Its record is again one of poverty. In 1370 it was given the churches of Synnada, Hierapolis, and Chonae as epidosis in an effort to provide it with sustenance.[159] But in 1384 it was placed under the metropolitan of Laodiceia,[160] and in 1386 under Prusa,[161] which shows that it had been given up as beyond redemption.

CHONAE

This church was so poor that no attempts were made to buttress it, rather it was given as epidosis to Cotyaeum in 1370,[162] to the metropolitan of Laodiceia in 1385,[163] and again in 1394.[164]

SMYRNA

About 1318 Smyrna, because of its subjugation by the Turks, had become impoverished, so the patriarch and the synod bestowed upon the titular holder of the seat the bishopric of Chios as epidosis "so that he might not be deprived of the necessities."[165]

CHALCEDON

The patriarch provides for all those metropolitans who have not a sufficiency of the necessities, reads a decision of about 1316. "Such a one is the most holy metropolitan of Chalcedon . . . for the sustenance belonging to him is lacking."[166] So he received as epidosis the archbishopric of Maeroneia. By 1387 there was little left of the church structure of Chalcedon. "The city of Chalcedon was obliterated many years before and there are few inhabitants so there is no need of a bishop."[167] Consequently it was given as epidosis to the needy metropolitan of Cyzicus.

CYZICUS

Cyzicus, one of the richest of the Anatolian metropolitanates early in the fourteenth century, declined greatly during the course of the century.

[157] *Ibid.*, II, 25.
[158] *Ibid.*, 90.
[159] *Ibid.*, I, 539.
[160] *Ibid.*, II, 88.
[161] *Ibid.*, 90.
[162] *Ibid.*, I, 539.
[163] *Ibid.*, II, 88.
[164] *Ibid.*, 210.
[165] *Ibid.*, I, 92.
[166] *Ibid.*, 45.
[167] *Ibid.*, II, 109.

In 1324 it was one of the three metropolitan seats in all of Asia Minor which was able to give an annual contribution to the patriarchate. The sum that it was assessed for this purpose, 200 hyperpera, was far greater than that assessed upon Lopadium and Proiconessus, the other two Asiatic churches that contributed. Also, while not nearly as great as the 800 hyperpera assessed on Monemvasia, yet it was equal to the 200 assessed on Thessalonike.[168] But by 1347, after the completion of the Ottoman conquest of Bithynia, this seat too was beset by hard times. As the metropolitan was "toiling in lack of the necessities" the patriarch and synod bestowed upon him the epidosis of Ganus in Europe.[169] In 1387 the newly appointed metropolitan of Cyzicus received as economic sustenance the epidosis of the metropolitanate of Chalcedon, the patriarchal rights in Hyrtacium, and the possessions of the church of Chalcedon in Constantinople. He was also to have and administer all the patriarchal possession in the Hellespontine region and in all of Bithynia, "however many of them there might be."[170]

AMASEIA

Amaseia also suffered greatly from the beginning of this period.

Time, which always effects its work transforming and destroying that which exists everywhere, placed the most holy metropolitanate of Amaseia in an obliterated state, having found her famous and great. She was wholly wasted and destroyed by the invasion of the foreigners as a result of the sacred judgement of God. . . . So that she is now poverty-stricken to those who observe or consider her, even if in the beginning she was illustrious as a metropolitanate.[171]

The newly appointed metropolitan of Amaseia is to sit, for the time being, at his bishopric Limnia, rather than at Amaseia. One of the reasons for this is the fact that Amaseia is poverty-stricken, but also because the Turks will not permit the prelate to enter. In 1371 the metropolitan received the epidosis of Neocaesareia.[172]

PONTOHERACLEIA

By about 1317 Pontoheracleia was among those churches suffering economically.

It has happened that some of our most holy metropolitans have been brought to not the least penury and deprivation of the necessities and have been cut off from practically all revenues of their churches by the evil of the times. Our humility has decided to move a helping hand as is most proper. . . . And if great penury setting in violently restrains their wishes and affairs mortally, this is of no small harm to the flock.[173]

[168] *Ibid.*, I, 127–128.
[169] *Ibid.*, 261.
[170] *Ibid.*, 110–111, implies that the situation was so bad that even the patriarch was not sure of what was left of patriarchal properties in Bithynia.
[171] *Ibid.*, I, 69.
[172] *Ibid.*, 551.
[173] *Ibid.*, 74.

A certain economic minimum is necessary to the metropolitan,

for how shall he not be reckoned as of a brass voice, by those who hear, according to the holy apostle, him who only in words speaks the praises of charity?[174]

The answer is obvious—the people cannot be properly shepherded without economic means. By 1387 the situation in Pontoheracleia was hopeless.

It was not possible, it seems, for them [Christians] to have their own metropolitan since the church had previously been destroyed and they who survived were too few for his aid and support.[175]

As it was too poor to support a metropolitan, it was given as an epidosis to Amastris in an effort to salvage one of the two churches.

LAODICEIA

Gifts in the form of administrative rights and epidosis were employed in an effort to prop up the sagging economy of this metropolitan seat. In 1384 it received administrative rights over the metropolitanates of Chonae and Cotyaeum, and over the patriarchal possessions of Coula and Colida.[176] In 1394 it was deprived of all these save Chonae.[177]

HIERAPOLIS AND SYNNADA

By the second half of the century both of these metropolitanates were too poor to be independent, so they were given to other churches in an attempt to bolster the latter. Thus in 1370 they were given as epidosis to Cotyaeum.[178] Fifteen years later (1385) both Synnada and Hierapolis were given to the metropolitan of Philadelpheia to administer.[179]

PEGAE

The turmoil enveloping northwestern Asia Minor had not left Pegae unaffected.

Since the affairs of the most holy metropolitanate of Pegae have come to nothing as a result of the increasing malaise of affairs and the attack of the enemies (by permission of God because of the multitude of sins), and it is not recognizeable even from a few remnants, the metropolitan appointed to it happened to be lacking the very necessities of livelihood.[180]

Consequently he is given the metropolitanate of Sozopolis as epidosis in 1354.

[174] *Ibid.*, 74.
[175] *Ibid.*, II, 103.
[176] *Ibid.*, 88.
[177] *Ibid.*, 209–210.
[178] *Ibid.*, I, 539.
[179] *Ibid.*, II, 87. In this general area Pisidia also underwent economic difficulties and so in 1369 received the archbishopric of Mystheum as an epidosis, *ibid.*, I, 509.
[180] *Ibid.*, 330.

MELITENE AND CELTZENE

By 1318 both the churches of Melitene and Celtzene (Celtzene more so than Melitene) were having great difficulties. Because of this, Theodosius, the metropolitan of Melitene, received the metropolitanate of Celtzene as epidosis, "for he was not rich in the necessities as his church had come under the barbarians long ago."[181] Celtzene itself

had long ago been deprived of its metropolitan seat by the foreigners . . . and Celtzene did not have another property which was worthy for the habitation of a metropolitan. The said most holy metropolitan of Melitene shall have as his seat the subordinate monastery of the Immaculate Mistress and Mother of God . . . of Ci.[182]

Additionally he received the right to administer the patriarchal properties in Neocaesareia, Camacha, Celtzene, and Melitene.[183] Obviously the properties of the church in eastern Anatolia were vanishing very rapidly by the early fourteenth century.

AMASTRIS

In 1387 the penurious metropolitan of Amastris received the wasted metropolitanate of Pontoheracleia as epidosis in hopes that it would provide him with sufficient revenues,

because of the breakdown and destruction of his church, which those coming from there report to us; and he is without the very necessities and asked aid from us many times.[184]

NICAEA

Nicaea, site of two ecumenical councils of the Christian Church and seat of the Byzantine Empire for better than half of the thirteenth century, was in a very bad state, a fact upon which Ibn Battuta had already remarked shortly after its conquest by the Ottomans. In 1381 the metropolitan of Nicaea received the church of Prusa as an epidosis

since the metropolitanate of Nicaea does not have enough to furnish him with the necessities because it had been captured and utterly destroyed by the foreigners many years previously.[185]

But the state of poverty is most humorously, if piteously, revealed in a letter of the patriarch Anthony IV to the metropolitan of Nicaea dated 1395. The metropolitan of Nicaea had asked to borrow a modius of grain and wine from the monastery of Rhomaniotissa. Then when the impoverished monks, themselves lacking supplies, asked the metropolitan to return them, he refused and in anger closed their church![186]

[181] *Ibid.*, 82.
[182] *Ibid.*, 83.
[183] *Ibid.*, 83–84.
[184] *Ibid.*, II, 103.
[185] *Ibid.*, 25.
[186] *Ibid.*, 237.

ADRIANOPLE

Even during the period of the early Ottoman conquests, the church suffered the loss of its property, as we have seen in Bithynia in the cases of Cyzicus, Nicaea, and Prusa. This is most clearly illustrated in their conquest and settlement of a European metropolitanate, that of Adrianople, and consequently a detailed examination of what happened in Adrianople will shed light on what happened in Bithynia as well. The acta demonstrate that the effect of the Turkish conquest and settlement crushed the Church's organization in that city. In a synodal document of 1380, it is stated that the metropolitan seat of Adrianople

was seized years before by the hand of the barbarian, with God's permission, and the greater portion of it, also, was taken away captive, especially the better class with its own shepherd and teacher; the remainder (of the populace) was kept there and has remained without a leader until the present. Nor was that protector of the church able to return to this queen of cities [Constantinople] so that he even passed away there [in captivity].[187]

A new metropolitan is finally appointed but the document does not say whether he was able to enter the city of Adrianople. Another of the synodal proceedings, issued in 1389, gives more specific details as to the difficulties that the church was experiencing in Adrianople. It seems that as of 1389 the metropolitan had not yet been able to enter Adrianople. The document mentions that the metropolitan is in Constantinople taking part in the proceedings of the synod itself, as was the custom of many of the ecclesiastics who had been displaced from their seats because of the troubled times. He is actually presenting a petition to the patriarch in which he laments the condition of the church in Adrianople.

His most holy metropolitanate formerly boasted of many and great good things within the empire of the Rhomaioi, and it was so prosperous that it was able to provide for the many poor people and to furnish them generously with the necessities. But by permission of God, this city was also wasted by the Turks, as every city and land of ours was, and those inhabititing the city became captives. Shortly thereafter Christians returned and settled in the city, but the metropolitanate [here his residence in the city] and all the famous churches were taken by the foreigners, as were also all lands and properties and yearly revenues so that it is not [now] known if ever they existed. Not even cells remain for the dwelling and rest of the metropolitan. Now he asked of the synod for the most holy bishopric of Agathapolis, which is under him and which is without its own shepherd, so

---

[187] *Ibid.*, 18–19. K. Amantos, "Zu den Bischofslisten als historischer Quellen," *Akten des XI. internationalen Byzantinisten-Kongress München 1958* (Munich, 1960), pp. 21–23. V. Laurent, "La liste épiscopale du synodicon de la métropole d'Adrinople," *E.O.,* XXXVIII (1939), 1–34. For the difficult chronology of the capture of Adrianople, I. Beldiceanu-Steinherr, "La conquête d'Adrinople par les Turcs: La pénétration turque en Thrace et la valeur des chroniques ottomanes," in *Travaux et Mémoires,* I, 431–461. The author indicates that the initial conquest (between 1365 and 1369) was the accomplishment of emirate (non-Ottoman) Turks. The first Ottoman to take possession of Adrianople was Murad I, in 1376–77 or 1377.

that he might have for his own relief the said bishopric of Agathopolis which is under the Rhomaioi and near the sea.[188]

It had already been decreed by the Patriarch Macarius, years before, that Agathopolis could not become a metropoiltanate in place of Adrianople, but was to be reserved for the temporary relief of the metropolitan of Adrianople for so long as Adrianople was held by the Turks. As soon as Adrianople should become Greek again, the metropolitan would proceed to Adrianople and a bishop would finally be reappointed to Agathopolis.

The conditions of the above twenty-three ecclesiastical seats in Asia Minor and of Adrianople enable us to make some very important generalizations. First of all, the invasions and attacks of the Turkish beyliks and tribes deprived the metropolitanates of much of their lands and incomes. This is an important factor in the decline of the Christian communities and population of Anatolia. It becomes obvious from the synodal acta that a metropolitan could not perform his functions and services, and provide for his retinue and flock under such conditions as were imposed by the conquests. The hierarchical organization required money or income to function. Throughout the latter period of Byzantine history the church had begun to take over many of the functions of the state in the provinces, such as, for instance, judicial functions. It had also to provide for the various charitable institutions, for which the church had been, it is true, largely responsible even before the Turkish conquests. This was the case with the orphanages, schools, care of the old, needy, sick, and so forth. As the Byzantine state was no longer present, the burden fell even more heavily upon the church, and it became the only source of such functions. The seizure of so much of its property by the Turks and the assessment of heavy taxes were disastrous to the church's hierarchical structure and undermined, or at least severely limited, many of its most important social duties. Thus it could no longer perform those strictly

---

[188] Miklosich et Müller, II, 130. The fate of these properties is amply documented by M. T. Gökbilgin, *XV–XVI. asïrlarda Edirne ve Paşa Livasï vakïflar-mülkler-mukataalar* (Istanbul, 1952). They were given to Turkish religious and military foundations and institutions. This is paralleled by what happened to the churches in Constantinople after the fall of the city to the Turks in 1453.

In 1401 the patriarchal synod attempted to appoint the bishop of Melaneia as metropolitan of Adrianople, Miklosich et Müller, II, 561–562. As of about 1428, however, it would seem that a metropolitan had not entered Adrianople. Laurent, "Adrinople," 27. There are indications that the effects of the Turkish conquest and occupation of much of the Balkans in the late fourteenth and the fifteenth century were similarly very disruptive. In 1384 Isidore, metropolitan of Thessalonike, fled the city from fear of the Turks. Miklosich et Müller, II, 85–86. The metropolitan of Serres was enslaved and then ransomed by the Turks (between c. 1383 and 1387). Miklosich et Müller, II, 77–78. Ostrogorsky, "La prise de Serrès par les Turcs," *Byzantion*, XXXV (1965), 302–319. After the Turkish conquest of Trajanopolis the metropolitan had to be transferred to Lacedaemon, c. 1365. Miklosich et Müller, I, 465–468. See also Miklosich et Müller, I, 558. The archbishop of Maeroneia can no longer go to his church because of the invasions of the Turks which have destroyed everything, so he is transferred to Messembria, Miklosich et Müller, I, 593–594.

material functions upon which so many in the Christian community were dependent. Very often the metropolitanates and bishoprics were deprived of the actual leadership of the metropolitan and bishop because the poverty of the area could no longer support them and their retinues. This loss of leadership will be discussed next. But returning to the impact of poverty, in the words of the acta themselves:

How shall he not be reckoned as of a brass voice . . . he who only in words speaks the praises of charity?[189]

Acta: Ecclesiastical Discipline

ABSENTEE METROPOLITANS AND ARCHBISHOPS

The Turkish conquest and occupation affected the church in other ways as well. One can judge the effect of this conquest in Anatolia in the general area of what might be called ecclesiastical discipline. The successful and efficient functioning of any social and religious institution depends upon a number of factors—the philosophy upon which the institution is founded, its environment, the allegiance and obedience of the members who constitute the institution, and their success in inspiring one another to allegiance and obedience. This latter factor is what is here meant by discipline, and for the immediate discussion it will be limited to the members of the clergy, from metropolitans to the lowly monks. Previous to the Turkish conquest in Asia Minor, the state had always closely supported the church in the enforcement of ecclesiastical discipline. This was true whether it was a matter of applying the contents of canon law to a humble priest, the forceful deposition of a recalcitrant metropolitan, or the implementation of synodal decisions in matters of heresy. The examples of such behavior on the part of the state in Byzantine history are too numerous and too well known to need any detailed mention here. With the conquests, however, the supporting arm of the state was, for the most part, removed from the enforcement of ecclesiastical discipline; in addition, certain other complicating features appeared to hinder and lessen the enforcement of ecclesiastical order. More specifically the maintenance of church order in the provinces centered on the metropolitans, archbishops, and bishops who now inherited all the allegiance of the Christian community (with certain exceptions that increased with time). Formerly these had been shared by the church with the Byzantine state, but under the new conditions it was the churchmen who furnished the leadership to the communities.

The removal, for one reason or another, of these prelates from their seats in Asia Minor constituted a serious blow to the church for it not only

[189] Miklosich et Müller, I, 74. The poverty of many of the metropolitanates not discussed above is reflected in the granting of these metropolitanates to other poor churches; Neocaesareia, Ankara, Gangra, Apameia, Prusa, Pergamum, Miletus, Antioch, Stauropolis, Pisidia, Sebasteia. *Ibid.*, I, 359; II, 88.

deprived the communities of their leaders but also removed the principal
enforcers of ecclesiastical order. The various communities deeply felt the
loss of their leaders and repeatedly sent petitions to the patriarch in
Constantinople asking that metropolitans and bishops be sent them.
Generally speaking, the acta describe two categories of metropolitanates
and archbishoprics; those whose holders were prevented by the Turks
from actually entering their ecclesiastical seats or who were prevented
from getting to their destination because the roads leading there were
unsafe for travel; and in the second category were those who, already
located in their provincial residences, were driven out by the Turks.[190]

The Christians of Amaseia were particularly hard hit as regards
metropolitan absenteeism in the first quarter of the fourteenth century.
About 1315 they appealed to the patriarch for assistance and the patriarch's answer to this petition has been preserved in one of the synodal
acta.

To those who have been chosen to lead a people and to be keepers of [their]
souls let this be a manifest token that they shall give spiritual aid not only to those
under them who are nearby, but especially to those living far away in the midst of
foreign nations and who are menaced with spiritual danger there; because there
is strong necessity to seek out the portion which is currently in danger of being
destroyed and to work at and assure its salvation. Such happen to be they who are
spiritually subordinate to the most holy metropolitanate of Amaseia. They sent
a letter to our humility stating distinctly that their church had been deprived of a
legitimate metropolitan for a long time . . . . Thus they asked for a metropolitan,
since the evil of the dominating Persian tyranny prevailed overwhelmingly so
that he who would be metropolitan was not able to take his post there easily or
in any way whatever.[191]

The situation was no better two years later (1317).

For quite some time the Christian community there . . . were without a metropolitan and deprived of a spiritual shepherd and his teaching and aid . . . . [So]
we ordained the most reverend holy monk Kyr Callistus, being possessed of virtue
and the other attributes necessary in a metropolitan, metropolitan of Amaseia.
But . . . it is not now possible for him whom we have accepted by ordination to

---

[190] I exclude from the discussion those churches that were too small and poor to warrant
the presence of a higher ecclesiastical authority. Certainly a contributing factor to
Turkish reluctance to receive the metropolitans and bishops was the Constantinopolitan-
centered character of the ecclesiastical administration and its close association with the
state. This intimate relationship of church and state was also characteristic of the Ottoman
state. In addition there was the predisposition of some clerics to the more pleasant life
in Constantinople. On this see the letters of the patriarch Athanasius, *P.G.*, CXLII,
473–477, 516–528, and the unedited letters analyzed by R. Guillaume, "La correspondance inédite d'Athanase, patriarche de Constantinople (1289–1293, 1304–1310),"
Mélanges Charles Diehl (Paris, 1930), I, 131–132. Athanasius, while aware of the difficulties
in the Anatolian church, was unrelenting in his efforts to send the hierarchs back to the
Anatolian Christian communities. As has been indicated above, however, the synodal acta
make it clear that it was impossible for many of these clergymen to return to their
Anatolian seats. The patriarch was anxious to return these hierarchs to Asia Minor not
only because of their idleness and intrigues in Constantinople, but also because of the
great dangers to which the Anatolian Christians were exposed, *P.G.*, CXLII, 518.

[191] Miklosich et Müller, I, 35–36.

go there and spiritually to look over his church there because of the mentioned invasion and attack of the godless ones.[192]

As the newly appointed metropolitan was not able to enter his seat in Amaseia because of the difficulties presented by the Turkish occupation, he was to take up residence in one of his subordinate bishoprics, Limnia. Since Limnia was within the boundaries of the empire of Trebizond, the synodal decree goes on to say, the church there was protected and ecclesiastics could come, go, and remain without interference from the Turks. The metropolitan of Amaseia was to remain there until conditions improved and the Turks would permit him to enter Amaseia. This case is exactly parallel to the previously discussed affair of the metropolitan of Adrianople who had to reside in the subordinate bishopric of Agathopolis in Byzantine territory until such time as Adrianople should become Byzantine again and he would be able to enter the city.

The metropolitan seat of Side was vacant in 1315:

It has been a long time since there was a metropolitan in the metropolitanate of Side, and the reason is that the terrible [state of affairs] prevailed to such an extent, and the road leading there became unsafe as the result of the attacks of the foreign peoples.[193]

Pisidia was without a metropolitan for a period previous to 1315 and then again in 1345. A synodal decree dated 1345 describes the situation very clearly.

The most holy metropolitanate of Pisidia has been without the shepherding and visitation of a metropolitan for many years, and the most holy metropolitan who had received the [metropolitanate] was hindered from staying in his church by the supervening foreign rule. After his death, the members of that church asked for a legitimate metropolitan; they asked for this many times [even when he had been alive], but the times, because of the foreign violence prevailing in the area, did not permit that a legitimate metropolitan from another area should be placed in that church. For this had been permitted the metropolitan of Side, but he also was not able to make his way there, and to take the post.[194]

As a result the bishop of Sozopolis, a bishopric subordinate to Pisidia, was appointed to assume direction of affairs of the metropolitanate. Conditions were so difficult that not only could the appointed metropolitan not enter from Constantinople, but even the metropolitan of Side had been unable to go from his own provincial seat to assume care of the community because of the Turks.

In 1315 the metropolitanate of Syllaion and the archbishopric of Leontopolis

---

[192] *Ibid.*, 69–70. The document specifies that the Turks would not allow a metropolitan to enter, " . . . καὶ τὸ τοῦ κατάρχοντος ἔθνους ἐκεῖσε μάλιστα δυσπαράδεκτον."

[193] *Ibid.*, 34. This is repeated, *ibid.*, 39, in regard to Side and Syllaion; " ἅτε δὴ γνησίων ἀρχιερέων ἐκ μακροῦ χηρευούσας, ὡς παρὰ τῶν ἀθέων ἐθνῶν κατακυριευθείσας."

[194] *Ibid.*, 242.

had been without legitimate metropolitans [and archbishops] for a long time, as they had been conquered by the godless foreigner.[195]

The bishop of Sinope had been appointed to direct the affairs of Leontopolis, but it was impossible for him to do this as he could not overcome the "foreign vexations"[196] to make his way there.

The metropolitan of Smyrna (c. 1318) was unable to enter his newly conquered seat because of the Turks, so he was awarded the bishopric of Chios

for so long as the foreigners there [Smyrna] were not driven away and pushed out by the aid of God.[197]

He was given the bishopric of Chios as an epidosis

so that the enemy might not make the reproach that the disappearance of the throne from the catalogue of the metropolitans was like the amputation of a member and like some disorder.[198]

The metropolitan of Ephesus was unable to enter his metropolitanate from 1315 to 1339 and again from 1365 to 1368.[199] At the eastern end of Anatolia the metropolitan of Caesareia received as epidosis (1327) the ecclesiastical seats of Sebasteia, Euchaita, Iconium, Mocissus, and Nazianzus because

they have been without legitimate metropolitans [and archbishop] for a long time as a result of the . . . prevailing confusion and malaise arising from the attack of the godless enemies. And therefore the Christian community under them is deprived of visitation, care, and sanctification by a metropolitan.[200]

In 1387 the metropolitan of Attaleia and Perge had

to brave troubled seas and even such toil, as threatened him with death, on behalf of the command of Christ,[201]

to reach his congregation in Anatolia. The metropolitan of Attaleia and Perge received the rich metropolitanate of Sugdaia and Phyllon as an epidosis (1400),

because he had come here [Constantinople] having been driven out of his church as a result of the beastliness and savagery of the leaders there who are infidels.[202]

---

[195] *Ibid.*, 39.
[196] *Ibid.*, 40, " δυσχερείαις τε ἐθνικαῖς . . ."
[197] *Ibid.*, 92.
[198] *Ibid.*, 92.
[199] *Ibid.*, 498. Matthew of Ephesus-Treu, pp. 3–4. Miklosich et Müller, I, 50–51. Ahrweiler, "Smyrne," 43–44, 82.
[200] Miklosich et Müller, I, 143. Such provisions were again made in 1370, *ibid.*, I, 537. This situation prevailed in the churches of eastern Anatolia much earlier. For example, the metropolitan of Mocissus received the church of Proiconessus, in western Asia Minor, as epidosis in the latter thirteenth century, Pachymeres, I, 286.
[201] Miklosich et Müller, II, 92.
[202] *Ibid.*, 390; " ἐκ τῆς λαχούσης αὐτὸν ἐκκλησίας τὰ ἐνταῦθα καταλαβὼν διὰ τὴν ἐκεῖσε τῶν ἀρχόντων ἀσεβῶν ὄντων θηριωδίαν καὶ ἀγριότητα."

The Turks had thus forced the metropolitan out of his seat, and the prelate had been fortunate enough to receive another ecclesiastical seat. Many such clerics, however, were not so fortunate, and once they were forced to leave their metropolitan seats in the provinces, they were forced to remain in Constantinople with the patriarch, idle, taking part only in the meetings of the synod and waiting either for the opportunity to reenter their provincial churches or to receive some other church as an epidosis.[203]

In 1315 the bishop of Sinope was forced out of his allotted bishopric and appointed to administer the metropolitanate of Side which had likewise been without a spiritual leader for a long period of time because of "troubled conditions." So the patriarch attempted to settle two problems with the same solution. If he could possibly seat the bishop of Sinope, who had been forced out of his bishopric, in the vacant seat of Side, the bishop would have employment and income, and the community of Side would have spiritual leadership. This was, of course, the customary solution.[204] But more often the displaced clergy were reseated in a European province, as this was much easier to effect. The number of acta dealing with these phenomena of μετάθεσις (transferral) and the σχολάζων (the churchless hierarch) are quite numerous. Such was the case, for instance, of the archbishop of Nymphaeum who in 1316 as a result of

having sustained much suffering and having been banished from his allotted [seat] because of the spiteful abuse [of the Turks] arising from our sins, and is [now] idle . . . was appointed to administer the archbishopric of Dercus in Europe.[205]

Finally, the correspondence of the metropolitan Theophanes (d. 1381) reveals that he was not able to proceed to Nicaea to assume his pastoral duties there.[206]

DISPUTES OVER JURISDICTION AND PROPERTY

One of the effects of confusion and upheaval, as we saw, was the loss of property which resulted in a great economic decline of the church in Asia Minor. This further complicated the problem of order and discipline in the church, for the stricken metropolitans and bishops, now feeling the grave economic strain, began increasingly to enter into disputes with each other over possession of property, income, and titles. This general trend is best chronicled in the acta concerning the metropolitan seat of Ephesus, which date 1342, 1343, 1368, and 1387. All four documents attest to the desire and activities of the various metropolitans of Ephesus to extend their jurisdiction and so acquire greater income, and to avoid

---

[203] See also *ibid.*, I, 82, dated 1318.

[204] *Ibid.*, 34.

[205] *Ibid.*, 51.

[206] Theophanes Nicaenus, *P.G.*, CL, 321, 300–302. The three letters of Theophanes to his unshepherded flock are significant for the information that they give on the fate of Christianity in Bithynia. See also Theophanes Nicaenus (d. 1381). *Sermo in Santissimam Deiparam* (Rome, 1935).

loss of property to other indigent metropolitans. In 1342 the patriarch intervened against the attempt of the metropolitan of Ephesus to ordain a bishop in the metropolitanate of Pyrgion and thus bring it directly under his own jurisdiction.

The most holy church of Pyrgion was found promoted from bishopric to metropolitanate long ago . . . . But recently, however, a bishop has been ordained over it by the metropolitan now administering the most holy metropolitanate of Ephesus. He should refrain from it [Pyrgion] and not attempt such a thing there because formerly it had been subordinate to his church, for it has been transferred under our most holy great church of God and has been put with her other metropolitanates. And if originally it had been part of his church [of Ephesus], if one would wish to examine [the matter], also most of the metropolitanates he would find [originally] subordinate to other churches. But, however, they remain in the rank and honor which they received afterwards by imperial order and synodal decree, for to promote lower churches to higher rank is an imperial prerogative.[207]

Thus the attempt of the metropolitan of Ephesus to subordinate the metropolitanate of Pyrgion within his own jurisdiction by appointing his bishop there was momentarily thwarted by patriarchical intervention.

Nevertheless, the tension between the metropolitanates of Pyrgion and Ephesus continued. In 1343 the patriarch and synod tried a case brought by the metropolitan of Ephesus (Matthew) against the metropolitan of Pyrgion, in which the former accused the latter of homicide and of swearing a false oath. The accused metropolitan denied the charges and the patriarch appointed the metropolitan of Laodiceia to conduct an investigation. His findings were of interest to the synod and show very clearly what the motives of the metropolitan's accusations were. The prelate of Laodiceia wrote a detailed report that cleared the metropolitan of Pyrgion of both charges. Included in his dispatch to the patriarch were several letters written by the metropolitan of Ephesus himself. In one of these the metropolitan of Ephesus had written, falsely, that the accused (metropolitan of Pyrgion) had been removed after an investigation by the synod and the patriarch, and he claimed the priests of Pyrgion as his own. But the investigation now carried out by the prelate of Laodiceia showed that the man, whom the metropolitan had been accused of flaying and hanging, had actually died of an illness. It was further ascertained that though he had actually sworn the false oath, he had been forced to do so by Umur Beg in order to save twenty-five Christians from death at his hands.[208] The metropolitan of Ephesus had merely manufactured and distorted the charges in an attempt to subordinate the seat of Pyrgion as a bishopric under the jurisdiction of Ephesus.

In 1368 the metropolitan of Ephesus was finally successful in getting control of the church of Pyrgion. He had previously requested and

[207] Miklosich et Müller, I, 228–229.
[208] Ibid., 235–237.

obtained it as his own bishopric, but Pyrgion was again raised to the status of metropolitan seat. In 1365 he was again given it, this time as an epidosis. But in 1368 the patriarch and synod, because of the poverty of Ephesus, invested the metropolitan of Ephesus and his successors with the two metropolitan seats forever.[209] By 1387 the metropolitan of Ephesus was feeling the economic strain so acutely that he complained to the patriarch and petitioned that all the bishoprics that had originlly been subordinate to Ephesus should now be returned. This included former bishoprics which had in past times been promoted to metropolitanates and also a number of bishoprics which were as of 1387 being held by other metropolitans. In his petition he states that so long as the affairs of the empire had prospered, his ecclesiastical seat had not demanded the return of these seats. But with the great disaster and poverty besetting his church, he was now in pressing need of them. The synod then decreed that the metropolitanates of Pyrgion and Pergamum, formally bishoprics of Ephesus, should be demoted to the rank of bishopric and that they should again be subordinate to Ephesus. Also the two bishoprics of Clazomenae and New Phocaea held by Smyrna were to be returned to Ephesus, their original metropolitanate. In short it was decreed that Ephesus should once more possess all the bishoprics that had at one time been subordinate to her.[210]

The metropolitan of Myra seems to have been no less vociferous in voicing his claims and rights to certain properties. In 1387 an extended dispute between him and the metropolitan of Attaleia-Perge came before the patriarch and synod for adjudication. When the newly appointed metropolitan of Attaleia-Perge had arrived in his province, he found that the few properties that the Turks had not taken were being held by the metropolitan of Myra. Though these properties had in the past belonged to Myra, they had been turned over some years past to the metropolitan of Attaleia so that the metropolitan could administer his church. The newly arrived metropolitan, finding the economic situation in Attaleia impossible, immediately wrote to the patriarch for assistance. Though the patriarch wrote to the metropolitan of Myra, the latter did nothing about the matter and simply continued to hold these properties (i.e., Phoinix, Bathys Potamos, Oricante, and Stenon) as his own. Consequently, the metropolitan of Attaleia-Perge, yielding to his poverty, was forced to return to Constantinople, for

it was no longer at all possible for him or any other metropolitan to remain there . . . [as] he had no other church under him in this area.[211]

[209] *Ibid.*, 497–500. Also II, 96.

[210] *Ibid.*, II, 103–106. For further quarrels over property rights and revenues between Ephesus and Smyrna, *ibid.*, 96, in the year 1387, and Papadopoulos-Kerameus, " Μαγνησία ἡ ὑπὸ Σιπύλῳ καὶ αἱ μητροπόλεις 'Εφέσου καὶ Σμύρνης ; " Δ.Ι.Ε.Ε.Ε., II (1885), 650–660.

[211] Miklosich et Müller, II, 93.

The patriarch, desiring that both metropolitans should have some revenue, permitted Myra to keep the disputed properties since they originally belonged to this ecclesiastical seat. The metropolitanate of Rhodes, however, which the prelate of Myra held as an epidosis, was to be transferred to the metropolitan of Attaleia-Perge as an epidosis. In the synodal decision the patriarch gives Myra the opportunity to chose between the properties that he has just reclaimed from Attaleia-Perge, or else the epidosis of Rhodes with Cos and the Cyclades.

> For it will thus be possible for both churches to stand and to be shepherded and for their metropolitans to have the necessities of life. We have judged it to be unjust . . . for so much to have been bestowed on one and for the other to have been deprived of the very necessities so that he might not even have one [piece] of land there.[212]

The metropolitan of Myra seems to have been somewhat reluctant to relinquish either group of properties, and a letter from the patriarch admonishes him that he simply could not retain everything.[213]

About 1393–94 the metropolitan of Stauropolis addressed a petition to the patriarch Anthony, which shows how uncertain titles and claims to lands were and how hotly the various provincial ecclesiastics contested them. Many years previous to this petition, in the time of the patriarch Philotheus, the metropolitan of Stauropolis had received the metropolitan seat of Rhodes as an epidosis because of the great poverty of his own ecclesiastical district. Some time later the metropolitan of Myra, Matthew, also received the same grant from the patriarch Neilus, so that the metropolitan of Stauropolis was then deprived of his income. The latter, justifiably outraged by this act (epidosis was generally given for the period of the holder's life), retired to Constantinople and cried out against the injustice in strong language. Consequently, Neilus attempted to offer partial compensation in the form of a synodal letter that made the metropolitan of Stauropolis the next holder of the epidosis of Rhodes. His possession of Rhodes would be effected when any one of the following three conditions should previal; if the metropolitan of Myra should die before him; if the metropolitan of Myra were transferred to another seat; or if the said metropolitan should willingly turn Rhodes over to him. Eventually, the metropolitan of Stauropolis received Rhodes by virtue of having outlived his rival. But he felt so uneasy and insecure in his tenure that he appealed to the new patriarch, Anthony, to confirm his possession of Rhodes.[214] These documents give some idea of the great struggle and competition over property and income which had arisen from the difficulties and impoverishment of the church in southwest Anatolia.

[212] *Ibid.*, 94.
[213] *Ibid.*, 94–95.
[214] *Ibid.*, 197–198.

This indigence was reflected not only in the quarrels among the metropolitans over property, but also often within the metropolitanates between the metropolitan and his subordinate clergy. In 1394, by way of example, the patriarch threatened the metropolitan of Chalcedon with excommunication if he did not return the property of Bollas, which he had unjustly acquired, to the monks of the monastery of Acapniotes (in Thessalonike).[215] In 1395 the patriarch gave a decision on another such case between the metropolitan of Nicaea and the monks from the monastery of Rhomaniotissa (in Cius) in his jurisdiction. Two monks from the monastery came before the patriarch and the synod in Constantinople and charged that

Some time previously you [metropolitan of Nicaea] asked and received from their monastery a loan of the one modius of grain and wine, and that which you had borrowed now being demanded by them, since they were in need of them (being poor and impoverished monks and being in need of the necessities), not only have you not returned these things to them, but you sent and closed the church of the monastery and these things you did on great Thursday. You hindered them from the communion of blessings and their church remained closed even to the queen of days, the brilliant [day] of the resurrection of Christ.[216]

The fact that a dispute over such a trifling amount as one modius of grain and wine should have reached the patriarchal synod speaks fluently, if somewhat gloomily, to the indigent state of the metropolitans and their clergy.

Poverty had also struck the other Orthodox patriarchates, as is so vividly reflected in the lament included in the fifteenth-century notitia, and their metropolitans and bishops were also undergoing similar experiences.[217] Thus in 1361 Philotheus, the patriarch of Constantinople, wrote a letter to the patriarch of Antioch complaining that the latter's metropolitans were entering the domains of the church of Constantinople and collecting fees and claiming jurisdiction where in fact they had no right to do so.

We suffer greatly all the time, and the many and heavy afflictions which have occurred previously I set aside for the present. I now speak of those things which the metropolitan of Tyre did. He goes about within my territory [enoria] and functions as priest, ordaining, collecting money, and performing every illegality. It is necessary that you judge him there canonically, or if you are not able to do this, give leave and permission so that we might do it. And what of the [metropolitan] of Germanipolis? He took over two of our churches, that of Attaleia and Syllaion, by the authority of the emir in the area, and he holds these as their "legitimate" metropolitan.[218]

[215] *Ibid.*, 200–202.

[216] *Ibid.*, 237.

[217] Pachymeres, II, 123. " ἐπεὶ τὰ κατὰ Συρίαν ἠφάνιστο." Chrysostomus, Archbishop of Athens, " Ἡ κατάστασις τῆς Ὀρθοδόξου Ἐκκλησίας Ἀντιοχείας κατὰ τὸν ΙΔ´ καὶ ΙΕ´ αἰῶνα," Ε.Ε.Β.Σ., XIII (1937), 123–142.

[218] Miklosich et Müller, I, 412, also I, 511–512. It may be that the emirs preferred metropolitans from Antioch because those of Constantinople were still connected with a Christian state.

In both cases the patriarch asked that either the patriarch of Antioch intervene to halt the violations the latter's metropolitans were committing in Anatolia or else to give him leave to do so himself. It appears, however, that both patriarchs were powerless to act, and this was probably due to the fact that they were unable to enforce ecclesiastical discipline in Turkish lands where the Greek emperors had no authority, especially since the erring metropolitans had the support of the local Turkish authorities.

RECOURSE TO TURKS

This brings us to another aspect and reflection of the decline of ecclesiastical discipline. As conditions worsened, poverty increased, and metropolitans and bishops came to occupy their seats less and less regularly, a new phenomenon entered into the decline of discipline. Clerics began, increasingly, to resort to the local Turkish authorities, an action severely proscribed and prohibited by the church under pain of excommunication. When things were not going their way in some dispute, particularly over property and jurisdiction, the clerics often made a mutually beneficial arrangement with the local Turkish begs. At other times the Turkish beg would force his will on the local clerics in a unilateral manner.

The dispute between the metropolitans of Ephesus and Pyrgion occurring in 1343 is an example of such behavior. The metropolitan of Ephesus, in his desire to reunite the seat of Pyrgion with his own, slandered that metropolitan to Umur Beg. He sent him a letter in which he addressed the Turk as his good son and considered himself the "father" of the emir, and advised him to expel the metropolitan of Pyrgion from his seat.[219] Further, it would seem, the metropolitan of Pyrgion was forced to swear a false oath because of the violence and force which he had suffered from the emir.[220]

The case of Dorotheus, metropolitan of Peritheorium, is a striking example of this type of conduct (though his seat was in Europe). The details are interestingly set forth in a document of 1381. He was imprisoned by the emperor for some unknown reason, but managed to effect his escape from prison and then made his way to the Turks in Asia Minor.

He went to the Turks, received forces there and then asserted tyrannical authority over the church of Peritheorium. And previously we wrote of these things [to those] there, that the Christians should in no way receive him for he went to the Turks. We wrote him twice and thrice both in Anatolia and Peritheorium in order that he should come here and be judged by the synod, but he did not wish to do so in any way. He made an agreement with the Turks that as many prisoners as should flee to Peritheorium, he would turn them over to the Turks. And he did this often, in accordance with his agreement.[221]

[219] *Ibid.*, 236.
[220] *Ibid.*, 237.
[221] *Ibid.*, II, 38. For a similar case of returning prisoners to the Turks, Miklosich et Müller, I, 592–593. It would have been difficult, however, for the Christians to have

The patriarch goes on to say that Dorotheus' presence before the synod is not necessary for the final judgment because the holy canons rule that,

"if some bishop utilizes secular authorities and through these takes control of a church, let him be removed and exiled." And he did not simply have recourse to secular Christian authorities, but going over to the impious ones and receiving a force, he took over the church, as is known and agreed by all; so there is no necessity for [his] appearance or proof. For he said, openly and in front of everyone, that he had the Turks as his own emperors, patriarchs, and protectors.[222]

He is removed from his seat, and if he continues to err with the Turks, he will be excommunicated.

In 1387 when the metropolitan of Attaleia-Perge assumed his duties in his ecclesiastical district, he found that those properties the Turks had not seized they had given to the metropolitan of Myra on the latter's petition. Here we would seem to have an example of both emir and metropolitan sharing in the spoliation of a second metropolitan seat.[223] In the dispute of the two metropolitans, the patriarch beseeches the prelates not to take their disputes to the Turkish emir.[224]

The complaint of the monks of the monastery of Acapnius (1394) that the metropolitan of Chalcedon had taken their property of Bollas also bears on the problem of recourse to Turkish authority. The metropolitan wrote a letter to the patriarch answering the charge by stating that though the property had formerly belonged to these monks, the Turks had taken it away from them and given it to the metropolitan. The patriarch then begins to explain that this is not a valid method of transferring title to property.

I do not know how it escapes your holiness, a good man and teacher, as you say, of the politeia of God, that you do these same things to your own brothers which the Turks [do] . . . . If you desire to learn how evilly you act in these affairs, read the canon "on greediness" of St. Gregory the Thaumaturge, which he expounded in the time of the barbarian invasion and captivity, so that you might learn what he says concerning those who take alien properties. He anathematizes such persons.[225]

The patriarch warns the metropolitan of Chalcedon:

If you ignore the present synodic admonition of our humility and you persevere in these things and wrong your brothers, we shall consider you and all your retinue as having recourse to foreign authority and [as] openly unjust, and as excommunicated and removed . . . . If you ignore this they [the monks] shall have permission to consider you as publicans and foreigners.[226]

---

done otherwise. On the severe punishments inflicted upon prisoners who attempted to escape, *ibid.*, I, 592–593, and Bartholomaeus Geurgieuitz-Kidrić, *passim*.

[222] Miklosich et Müller, II, 38.

[223] *Ibid.*, 92.

[224] *Ibid.*, 95; "καὶ εἰρηνεύετε πρὸς ἀλλήλους, ὡς ἀδελφοὶ καὶ ἀρχιερεῖς καὶ τῆς εἰρήνης διδάσκαλοι, καὶ μήτε αὐτὸς διενοχλείτω τῇ σῇ ἱερότητι πρὸς τὸν ἀμηρᾶν, μήτε σὺ αὐτῷ, ἀναξία γάρ εἰσι τοιαῦτα τοῦ καθ' ἡμᾶς τάγματος καὶ τῆς ἀρχιερωσύνης."

[225] *Ibid.*, 200–201.

[226] *Ibid.*, 200.

The same question arose in 1389 when certain clerics from the church in Russia were summoned before the Constantinopolitan synod in an effort to settle a serious and complicated dispute. But these clerics, fearing the judgment of the synod, crossed into Anatolia and sought aid from the Turks. Thus the patriarchal agents sent after them were prevented from returning them to Constantinople.[227]

DISCIPLINE AND ORTHODOXY OF THE CLERGY

On a general level the breakdown of discipline was reflected in other ways. Struggles and strife in matters of doctrine in Constantinople were likely to be reflected in some of the provinces. Thus the contest between the adherents of Barlaam and Palamas seems to have spread into some of the churches of Asia Minor. The metropolitan of Ephesus was condemned as a heretical Barlaamite in 1351, and it would seem that Cyril the metropolitan of Side (c. 1360) was strongly suspected of being tainted with this heresy.[228] The church in northwest Asia Minor had suffered division and strife in the thirteenth century while it was still under Byzantine control, as a result of the pro-Latin policy of the emperor Michael Palaeologus and of the opposition between Josephites and Arsenites arising from dynastic politics.[229]

The synodal acta furnish a limited but significant number of cases that describe in great detail the decay of discipline in specific churches of Anatolia. One such case which is particularly intriguing involves the church of Iconium. The incident is of interest because it is in connection with the city of Iconium (Konya) that the activities of the proselytizing Mawlawi dervishes will be discussed. In 1379–80 the monks of a particular monastery in this district brought charges against the metropolitan stating that he had blasphemed God, cursed the protectors and leaders of the church and also the holy fathers. As the canons state that clerics who see their bishop falling into heresy have the right to abstain from communion with him, the monks had closed their church. At the particular moment that the monks brought their complaints before the synod, the patriarchal seat was vacant and consequently the synod had no right to examine all the charges and the validity of his priesthood. Instead, the assembled metropolitans embarked upon a partial investigation, limiting it to three points. The first charge was that the metropolitan of Iconium had made light of the monks' fasting and other spiritual accomplishments, adjudging these exercises false and valueless, and he also blasphemed St. Macarius. Second, he was charged with breaking a holy altar in order to use the wood for other purposes. Third,

---

[227] *Ibid.*, 125 and I, 356–363, for a detailed case in which the metropolitan of Alania appealed to the khan of the Crimean Tatars against an unfavorable decision of the patriarch.

[228] *Ibid.*, I, 408, 405–406. Matthew of Ephesus-Treu, p. 10.

[229] Arnakes, 'Οθωμανοί, pp. 43–45.

he had, his accusers alleged, introduced a certain heretic (Niphon by name) into the church of the monks on Palm Sunday and had given him a palm leaf and candle. On the feast day of Lights he permitted this enemy of the church to participate in the liturgy by allowing him to read a homily of St. Gregory the Theologian. At this point the monks were outraged and demanded that the metropolitan remove the heretic from the church, but the metropolitan refused. The synod found the metropolitan guilty and removed from his control all the monasteries, since he was permitting heretics to enter them. When, with the appointment of the new patriarch Neilus, the case was reopened, it was further ascertained that the metropolitan had struck the leader of the monks, Gregory, while the latter was assisting behind the altar in the services of Easter week. Finally, the patriarch removed the errant metropolitan from office. Unfortunately, this is one of the very few detailed cases concerning the church of Iconium in the fourteenth century which has survived; nevertheless, it does present a glimpse into the declining state of ecclesiastical discipline there.[230]

The most illustrative and detailed instance of this disorder in the array of the church on a personalized and individual level is that concerning the monk Paul Tagaris, who first appears in the synodal acta in 1370. At this time the patriarch has ordered the metropolitans of Caesareia and Mocissus to proceed to Iconium where they are to investigate all priests, deacons, and readers ordained by that "sinful monk, or rather that pseudo-monk and son of the devil Tagaris."[231] He had entered the seat of Iconium passing himself off as the metropolitan and consequently succeeded in deceiving many. The appointed metropolitans were to examine the clergy and were to remove from office all those ordained by Tagaris, even though they may have acted in good faith. They were not to be restored until a legitimate metropolitan of Iconium was appointed to office. In the meantime the metropolitan of Mocissus was to appoint and ordain clerics if and when they should be needed.[232]

Tagaris next appears in a decision of the synod dated 1384, in which it appears that he has continued in his erring ways. The "son of perdition," finding the metropolitan seat of Amaseia vacant, ordained the presbyter Joseph as bishop of Limnia (a suffragant bishopric of Amaseia). Consequently, Macárius, the metropolitan of Sebasteia, has been ordered by the patriarch and synod to go to these areas and examine and reordain those falsely ordained by Tagaris, including Joseph.[233]

Justice, however, finally catches up with the protagonist as does his conscience, very conveniently, sometime around 1391, and a considerable portion of his confession and repentance has survived. His confession

[230] Miklosich et Müller, II, 1–7.
[231] *Ibid.*, I, 537.
[232] *Ibid.*, 538.
[233] *Ibid.*, II, 64–65.

includes a number of fascinating details both as to his actual sins and his origins. He mentions that his father had won glory for himself in fighting the foes of the empire and as a result married a lady of the imperial family.[234] At the age of fifteen, Tagaris had married, but soon after left his wife to go to Palestine and become a monk. Then he returned to Constantinople and was at first prone to settle in a monastery and "be on the side of the good." He says, however, that shortly after his arrival in the capital city he changed to the "side of hypocrisy." He found an icon, and hoping to earn a livelihood from it, he announced to all that it was of the type that worked miracles. His family, however, was scandalized and soon other clergymen intervened and removed the icon from his possession. Tagaris was outraged and having no recourse against this confiscation, he set out for Palestine where he soon became a confidant of Lazarus the patriarch of Jerusalem. When, however, the latter was driven out by the Muslims, a new aspirant to the throne appeared who threatened Tagaris with death. As a result, Tagaris proceeded to Antioch where, he says,

Satan entered into me again and there was nothing illegal or unlawful which he did not force me to carry out for shameful gain. I trampled under foot the enoria of the ecumenical patriarch; bishops who had done no evil were thrust out of their own bishoprics, and in their places were brought in other dissolutes . . . [who] gave money and received bishoprics from a presbyter.[235]

The next step in his career of charlatanry was the assumption of the title of Patriarch of Jerusalem and the continuing false ordination of metropolitans and bishops. He did not bestow these offices on him worthy of them but on him who gave the most money,

no matter how full of evil he was, or how wealthy he was in illegality, and most unworthy of it, for to me he was the most fitting and holy of all. And if someone had become bishop under one of the patriarchs, I brought him down . . . as he brought obstacles to my tyranny, by buying his office with money, or else I disposed myself evilly toward him and slandered him to the local emir . . . . Who would be capable of enumerating the illegal and uncanonical ordinations of priests at my hands only so that I might make money? For the love of money which had seized my soul and the desire for wealth moved me to work every evil. . . . So that he was deemed worthy [of office] who gave more or said he would give more.[236]

---

[234] *Ibid.*, 225. Cantacuzene, I, 91, 343; II, 591, gives the history of the rise to power of the Tagaris family. Of obscure origin, a member of the family gained fame and social prominence in the wars against the Turks about Philadelpheia in the fourteenth century. A Manuel Tagaris took part in the disastrous battle of Pelecanum (1329). George Tagaris went on an embassy to the Turks of Saruhan, c. 1346.

[235] Miklosich et Müller, II, 226.

[236] *Ibid.*, 227. It is significant that he resorted to arrangements with Muslim emirs to overcome the resistance of the validly ordained metropolitans in any given district. He thereby forced the local metropolitan or bishop to split his jurisdiction into two parts, one for the *locum tenens* and one for Tagaris. " εἴ που δέ τις ἐπίσκοπος παρὰ τῶν πατριαρχικῶν τινος γεγονὼς . . . ὡς ἐκεῖνον δυσχεραίνοντα τὴν ἐμὴν τυραννίδα, χρήμασιν ἐξωνήσασθαι τὴν ἑαυτοῦ τιμήν, ἢ πρὸς τὸν τοῦ τόπου ἀμηρᾶν διαβάλλων αὐτὸν κακῶς διετίθουν, ὡς ἀναγκασθέντα τὴν οὐσίαν δίχα διελεῖν καὶ τῆς μιᾶς μερίδος ποιῆσαι κύριον."

Feeling that the "office" of patriarch of Jerusalem was too restricted for his talents "I decided to go through the whole ecumene, so that I might amass more wealth."[237] Thereafter he set out for the "Persian" borders and soon came to Georgia where he found that three men were disputing the royal throne. Having convinced them that only he could settle the dispute, he awarded the throne to the one who promised the most money, and he relates "I obtained not a little wealth thus."[238]

Not unexpectedly he soon became bishop of Tabriz and was on the way to Trebizond when justice finally began to catch up with him. He was served with a patriarchal letter in which the patriarch referred to a certain evil metropolitan of Tyre as the forerunner of antichrist and to Tagaris as his violent follower, and in so doing left no doubt as to what he intended to do with them when the opportunity presented itself. Tagaris, now in fear of his personal safety, decided to seek refuge with the Roman pope. Consequently, he crossed over to the land of the Tatars and gave eleven pearls to the leader for guides and soldiers to escort him as far as Hungary.[239] Once in Hungary he began to fear for his soul, he tells the patriarch in his confession, but dissuaded by the dangers of the road back through the land of the Tatars, he went on to Rome. Here he performed the Latin confession of faith to the pope who named him patriarch of Constantinople and dressed him in the appropriate garb. He compounded his sins, he tells the synod, by sitting down to meal with Latins and eating meat.[240] This is the end of the more interesting part of Tagaris' confession. Its implications as to the state of ecclesiastical discipline, and its indications of the troubles of the church in Anatolia and the church's inability to enforce discipline there are all too self-evident for any further comment.[241]

The difficulties and poverty that the Turkish occupation of Anatolia imposed were such that the metropolitans and bishops often refused to go to their appointed churches and take up their duties, or often they deserted their churches so that the patriarchs frequently forced the metropolitans to swear oaths not to abandon their seats because of the various difficulties and obstructions. It becomes apparent that service *in partibus infidelium* was not by any manner of means an ordinary or simple task. A number of the clerics often abandoned their metropolitanates and sought churches in less critical areas of Asia Minor, or more often they

---

[237] *Ibid.*

[238] *Ibid.*

[239] *Ibid.*, 228.

[240] *Ibid.*, 229.

[241] G. Hill, *A History of Cyprus* (Cambridge, 1942), II, 435, has dismissed the "career" of Tagaris as a historical fabrication put forth by the monk himself. Hill did not know the synodal documents that dealt with the case but relied upon the account in *Chronicum Karoli Sexti*, ed. and trans. M. L. Bellaquet, *Chronique du religieux de Saint-Denys contenant le regne de Charles VI, de 1380 à 1422* (Paris, 1839), I, 636–643. This Latin chronicle supplements the Greek accounts (which tell of Tagaris' wanderings in the East) by recounting the monk's exploits in France and Italy.

sought to be transferred to Constantinople or some other church in the European provinces.[242] This problem is clearly brought out in an oath signed about 1338 by Cyril the metropolitan of Side.

Those who are elected by the holy and universal church of God to be his metropolitans, and those others who are sent to the Christians dwelling under an impious foreign nation must turn this over in [their] minds; that they have taken up the apostolic struggle, and have been ordered to run the course of Christ's revered disciples and apostles, to whom . . . was also said, "Behold, I send you out as sheep in the midst of the wolves." And since I am by God's judgment elected by the holy church of God, and I was chosen for the church of Side which the impious foreign hand has received to rule, there is suspicion that being ordained I shall not go there, or going there I might return again to this the queen of cities for comfort and relief from the hardships at hand; I make the present written promise in this to our most holy lord the ecumenical patriarch and to the most holy, sacred synod, and say and assure that I [shall] not have leave after my ordination . . . to remain here and find an excuse for idleness and put off my departure; nor after having gone to that church to which I was elected, to return here having abandoned the flock which was entrusted to me, except [by reason] of great necessity and want.[243]

In 1363 the patriarch and synod order the metropolitan of Smyrna to leave Thessalonike and to proceed to Smyrna where he was to care for the "many and numberless Christians who are there."[244]

Most holy metropolitan of Smyrna . . . grace and peace of God be with your holiness. Your holiness knew previously that not just once, but twice, and thrice, and many times we informed you that throwing off all and every type of excuse you should go to the church which you received . . . having been promoted to metropolitan, to the area and jurisdiction of your most holy metropolitanate, and according to canonical duty perform all those things in need of metropolitan supervision and consecration there; for the Christians awaiting your presence in this area are many.[245]

The patriarch orders him to leave the city of Thessalonike where he has been seeking rest and to go occupy his seat in Asia Minor, for the Smyrniotes are continuously sending petitions to the patriarch for a metropolitan. If he does not conform with this order, he will be removed from office and replaced by another metropolitan.[246]

The newly appointed metropolitan of Mocissus, guilty of abandoning his previous seat, was forced in 1370 to swear an oath not to abandon his new church.

I the humble metropolitan of Mocissus, Ioannicius, swear in the presence of our most holy lord the ecumenical patriarch, and of the holy and sacred synod, that I shall not appear to abandon my church and go elsewhere, as I did this formerly [when] I was bishop of Nyssa. But I shall be found in my church teaching

[242] Guilland, "Athanase," pp. 130–132.
[243] Miklosich et Müller, I, 182.
[244] *Ibid.*, 447.
[245] *Ibid.*, 445.
[246] *Ibid.*, 446.

the flock of Christ entrusted to me with as much strength as I have. If I should ever appear to abandon my church and be found elsewhere, another metropolitan shall be ordained by my most holy lord the ecumenical patriarch and the great sacred synod in my church.[247]

In 1385 the metropolitan of Iconium, far from having proceeded to take up duties in his own church at Iconium, simply took over the church of Attaleia and left his own flock in Iconium without leadership. Consequently, the patriarch removed him from all metropolitan functions until he should present himself before the synod where he would be judged and removed in accordance with canon law.[248] In 1394 we have an example of a metropolitan taking over another seat illegally. In this case it is the metropolitan of Seleuceia, either unable or unwilling to enter his own church, who manufactured false letters from the Christian community of Attaleia saying that the latter were without leadership. His deception, however, was discovered only after he had set out to take over the church of Attaleia.[249]

THE CONGREGATIONS

Up to this point the examination of the synodal acta has proceeded from the point of view of the structure of the church, its property, and its clerics. But what, if anything, do the acta say about the congregations themselves? Do they give any indication or hint on the fate of the Greek Christian populations in the various areas? Generally speaking, they are not so specifically informative on the members of the communities as they are on the clergy. The acta, however, are indicative of the overall fate and general types of experiences among the Christians. The general impression they give is one of a great decline in the numbers of the Christians of Asia Minor, though the information is scanty at best. One of the acta dated 1387 and concerned with the metropolitan seat of Ephesus relates that

every city and every land were wasted by the foreigners and were entirely obliterated. And if some of these were ever cities it is not even ascertainable from names, while other are recognizable from some few traces, having very few Christian inhabitants.[250]

A synodal decision of about 1315 mentions the metropolitanate of Syllaion and the archbishopric of Leontopolis as inhabited by a "very few Christian folk."[251] Another document of 1387 relates that the metropolitan of Attaleia and Perge had a very small congregation,[252] and a

---

[247] *Ibid.*, 536.
[248] *Ibid.*, II, 89.
[249] *Ibid.*, 205–206.
[250] *Ibid.*, 104. This is also reflected in a document of 1318 relative to Melitene and Celtzine. *Ibid.*, I, 82.
[251] *Ibid.*, I, 34.
[252] *Ibid.*, II, 93, " . . . τὸν ὀλίγον ἐκεῖ τοῦ κυρίου λαόν . . ."

similar document of 1397 again reveals the smallness of the Christian community in Attaleia and in Side as well.

> Since it had been captured long ago [there was] a scarcity of the faithful in [Side].[253]

Sizable congregations, however, remained in a number of cities throughout Anatolia. In 1315 the Christians of Amaseia wrote to the patriarch, petitioning for a metropolitan,

> because they find themselves in the midst of foreigners . . . and most necessarily need a guide and leader in those matters pleasing to God.[254]

The reason they need a spiritual leader emerges from a decree of 1317, by which time the Amaseians had not yet received a metropolitan because of the enmity of their Turkish master. This document says:

> The Christian congregation there, as many that is as remained and having remained were not seduced by the abusive and ruling foreigners, for a sufficient time was without a metropolitan and was deprived of a shepherd and of his teaching and aid. . . . But the Lord . . . sends shepherds to the greatest thrones, leaders of souls and affairs, so that thus what time has thrown down . . . He shall restore to the ancient form and honor by their aid and care.[255]

According to the text a number of the Christians who had remained in Amaseia were converted to Islam. The language of the document would seem to imply at least an active program of proselytization by the Muslims. The text emphasizes the importance of the leadership of the metropolitan in keeping the flock together and in restoring it to a healthy state.[256] The community was sufficiently strong and articulate to petition the patriarch continuously for a spiritual leader during the period of upheaval.

Continued occupation and rule of the Turks and isolation from Constantinople subjected the Christians to temptations to abandon their faith for that of the rulers, and often also subjected them to overt pressure to do so. A proceeding of 1387 relates that there remained only a few Christians in the city of Pontoheracleia. But few though they were, they were to have shepherding.

> Because as men, being seduced by the deception of life, they look out for only a few of those heavenly and immortal rewards. But also dwelling among the foreigners and associating with them constitute the greatest obstacle to salvation.[257]

The implications are obvious. The Christians, if left without leadership too long, will join the religion of their conquerors, as indeed many have already done. Thus, dwelling among the Turks and daily association with them eventually would lead to conversion. When the Christians of Gangra

[253] *Ibid.*, 276–277.
[254] *Ibid.*, I, 37.
[255] *Ibid.*, 69.
[256] *Ibid.*, 69–71.
[257] *Ibid.*, II, 103.

asked for a metropolitan in 1400–01, it was for similar reasons. As a result of the death of the metropolitan of Gangra,

all the Lord's people who are found there beseeched our humility by their own letters that I send to them a metropolitan and protector, because the foreigners abuse and endanger them on all sides concerning the most crucial matters [i.e., religion]. They have not the teaching and spiritual leadership of a protector (for people are on the whole wont to fall easily into evil rather than to be elevated to virtue, and these things are so especially when they are under the barbarians) and our humility deemed it necessary that such a church no longer be found without a shepherd, as there should arise to it from this not a small harm and damage.[258]

Here the language implies both voluntary apostasy and conversion under a certain amount of pressure, though the text is not very explicit. Similar disorders are implied by the acta for the churches of Sebasteia, Euchaita, Iconium, Mocissus, and Nazianzus in 1327.[259]

The most significant and informative of these documents in regard to the fate of the congregations of Anatolia, however, are two acta from about 1338 and 1340 addressed to the inhabitants of Nicaea. The first of these is the longest and most explicit.

The church of God, the common clinic of souls, opens its doors of salvation to all those returning from sin, and, providing the appropriate medicines looks after the salvation of all. It is essential not to forbid anyone, nor to disdain the salvation of him falling into denial [apostasy] for there is not, there is generally no sin which triumphs over God's philanthropia. And the Holy Scriptures bear many examples of those refraining from their former sins [and] showing a genuine return and repentance; among these [examples] is that of the prodigal, that of the whore, that of the robber, that of the Ninevites, that of Manasses who prepared the people to worship idols for forty years, rebelling from the Creator. He rejects none, nor does God turn away, for He has an unbounded sea of philanthropia, if only we should genuinely repent and fall at his feet, and weep, and beseech His goodness. Since the attack of the Ismaelites prevailed over us by God's permission as a result of the multitude of our sins, and they having captured and enslaved many of our own and violently forced them and dragged them along alas! so that they took up their evil and godlessness; and to those having fallen into such a depth of evil occurred a realization [that] they were evil and [this] aroused them to seek the ways of the Christians again. But another thought came to them, and they hesitate and wish to learn for certain whether they will not fail utterly or shall achieve their salvation. The church of God pledges itself to all such and gives definite information; that it [the church] will heal and cure and number among the side of the Christians again those taking up the true belief in God and [those] removing [themselves] *from the evil of the Muslims into which they fell*. Nor shall they find any obstacle to the salvation of their own souls because of the failure, as it is said, which occurred to them. But as many of these who will show their repentence openly and freely so that they choose to suffer for the faith in God, these will bind on the crown of martyrdom (an exact proof of this is the great martyr of Christ, Jacob the Persian). As many as wish to live in secret practicing and keeping in their heart the Christian way, because of the fear of punishments against them, these also

---

[258] *Ibid.*, 491.
[259] *Ibid.*, I, 143–144.

shall attain salvation. Only, they shall try as much as possible to keep the commands of God. And this present letter of the church of God became an assurance concerning this.[260]

The second of the letters, though somewhat shorter, deals with the same subject.

[To] the clerics, the consecrated, the monks, and all the remaining Christian congregation being found in Nicaea, our . . . beloved Children in the Lord. We beseech, for all of you, the peace and compassion of God, freedom from troubles, and every other good and salvation from almighty God. We are unable to say how much we suffer and are grieved on your behalf and on behalf of all other Christians under the barbarians. Be informed, thence, that we do not intermit supplicating and beseeching God night and day so that He might transform the storm (brought against our race because of the multitude of sins) into a clear sky and turn back the evils upon the enemies, which we are confident, will not remain long. . . . Simply have care that you serve God by your good works and a life pleasing to God. For if the enemies rule you, be you the masters of your own souls and mind(s), and of your choice [which] is to guard over the good or not to guard [it]. But as we learned from the judge, you preserve and guard your Christian situation, in which I pray that you remain firm and unshakable, so that you may gain the promised good rewards God prepared for those who love him with their soul, and [that] you will observe his commands of salvation, the grace of which shall preserve you.[261]

The first of these pastoral letters is concerned with the Islamization of many of the inhabitants of Nicaea. It says that the Turks forced them to convert to Islam,

And they [Turks] having captured and enslaved many of our own and violently forced them and dragged them along, alas! so that they took up their evil and godlessness.

This is also implied more generally in some of the documents described previously and seems to indicate that conversion under duress, far from being unknown during the Turkish conquests of the fourteenth century, was certainly one of the many factors working for the diminution of the Christian communities. These Christians, who have apostatized to Islam at the bidding of their conquerors, are concerned with their salvation and have referred the matter to the patriarch in Constantinople. His solicitous and sympathetic reply offered the petitioners salvation if they would reject Islam. There were two possible roads to salvation from their apostasy; martyrdom or crypto-Christianity. To those who were brave enough to renounce Islam openly was to be awarded the matryr's crown, as had been the case of the Persian martyr Jacob. The others, who were afraid to die, were to be accounted as within the fold of the church again if they practiced their Christiantity in secret and to the best of their ability in these conditions.

[260] *Ibid.*, 183–184.
[261] *Ibid.*, 197–198.

As many as wish to live in secret practicing and keeping in their heart the Christian way, because of the fear of punishments against them, these shall also attain salvation.[262]

In the second letter to the Nicaeans, dated about 1340, the patriarch commends the Nicaeans for successfully preserving their christianity. Again there seems to be a hint at crypto-Christianity in the sentence,

For if the enemies rule you, be you the masters of your souls and mind(s), and of your choice.

The religious pressure to convert is apparent in other accounts of the situation in fourteenth-century Bithynia, and crypto-Christianity and neo-martyrdom, though poorly known, nevertheless existed in the Ottoman period. The process of religious conversion in northwest Asia Minor which emerges from the synodal acta finds striking confirmation in the letters that the absentee metropolitan Theophanes (d. 1381) sent to his flock in Nicaea,[263] and explicitly in the annals of the earliest Turkish chronicles.[264]

Matthew of Ephesus—A Case Study

Actual on-the-spot reports of the situation in Asia Minor by priests who had churches there are, unfortunately, rare. A notable exception is

[262] On Jacob, F. Halkin, *Bibliotheca hagiographica graeca* (Brussels, 1957), I, 252. There is a considerable literature of unequal value on the phenomenon of Crypto-Christianity. Arnakis, Ὀθωμανοί, pp. 188–189. I. K. Voyiatzides, " Ἐκτουρκισμὸς καὶ ἐξισλαμισμὸς τῶν Ἑλλήνων," in Ἱστορικαὶ Μελέται (Thessalonike, 1933), pp. 3–60. N. E. Meliores, Οἱ Κρυπτοχριστιανοί (Athens, 1962). N. Andriotes, Κρυπτοχριστιανικὴ Φιλολογία (Thessalonike, 1953). Hasluck, "The Crypto-Christians of Trebizond," *J.H.S.*, XLI (1921), 199–202. R. M. Dawkins, "The Crypto-Christians of Turkey," *Byzantion*, VIII (1933), 247–275. Gordlevski, *Izbrannye Soch.*, III, 37–44, 326–334. R. Janin, "Musulmans malgré eux: les Stavriotes," *E.O.*, no. 97 (1912), pp. 495–505. A. D. Mordtmann, *Anatolien. Skizzen und Reisebriefe aus Kleinasien (1850–1859)*, ed. F. Babinger (Hannover, 1925), *passim*. M. Deffner, " Πέντε ἑβδομάδες παρὰ τοῖς ἀρνησιθρήσκοις ἐν Ὄφει," Ἑστία, no. 87 (1877), pp. 547 ff. K. Lameras, Ἡ περὶ Μικρᾶς Ἀσίας καὶ τῶν ἐν αὐτῇ Κρυπτοχριστιανῶν (Athens, 1921). S. Antonopoulos, Μικρὰ Ἀσία (Athens, 1907), pp. 57–72. Istor Pontion, " Αἱ ἐξισλαμίσεις ἐν Πόντῳ καὶ οἱ Κλωστοί," Π.Φ., I (1936), 3–6. Phikas, " Ἀπὸ ἕνα χειρόγραφο τοῦ 1886 γύρω ἀπ' τοὺς Κρυπτοχριστιανούς," Π.Ε., XI (1960), 5647. P. Triantaphyllides, " Οἱ Κλωστοί," Π.Ε., II (1951), 967, 1032. P. Sallapasides, " Περὶ τῶν ἄλλοτε ἐν Τουρκίᾳ κρυπτοχριστιανῶν," Π.Φ., II (1937), 280; " Ἐπεισόδια ἀπὸ τὴν ζωὴν τῶν κρυφῶν τῆς Ἀργυρουπόλεως," Π.Φ., II (1937), 372–373. M. Metalleides, " Ἀπὸ τὴν ζωὴν τῶν Κλωστῶν. Μιὰ μικρὴ ἱστορία," Π.Φ., II (1937), 196–197. P. Melanophrydes and X. Xenitas, " Οἱ Κλωστοί," Π.Ε., II (1951), 1193. P. Melanophrudes, " Ὁ Χρῆστον (ἀπὸ τὴ ζωὴ τῶν Κρυφοχριστιανῶν Κλωστῶν)," Π.Ε., V (1954), 2640. Ph. Ktenides, " Οἱ Κρυπτοχριστιανοὶ τοῦ Πόντου," Π.Ε., V (1954), 2664–2666, 2710–2712, 2743–2745.

[263] Theophanes Nicaenus, *P.G.*, CL, 287–325.

[264] Ashïkpashazade-Ali, pp. 23 ff, 41–42, 43. Ashïkpashazade-Kreutel, pp. 46, 48, 67–70. Anonymous-Giese, pp. 18–19, 23. They describe extensive conversions of Greeks in Nicaea, regions of Yalova, Taraklï-yenidjesi, Goynuk, and Modreni. For the details of these conversions see chapter v below. Here I refer to them only to confirm the general reliability of the synodal acta on the diminution and absorption of the Christian community throughout Asia Minor. When Theodora, daughter of Cantacuzene, journeyed to Bithynia after her marriage to Orhan (1345), she found many Greeks converted to Islam. She endeavored to dissuade them and she herself resisted the efforts of the Turks to convert her, Cantacuzene, II, 588–589.

the case of Matthew, metropolitan of Ephesus. Though less spectacular than the account Gregory Palamas, metropolitan of Thessalonike, left of his captivity in Bithynia and his visit to the Ottoman capital at Bursa, the information that Matthew records is of greater significance for the actual fate of the ecclesiastical establishment in Asia Minor. His account of personal experiences as metropolitan of Ephesus specifically confirms what the synodal acta imply more generally. First, it is interesting to note that the acta mention no metropolitan of Ephesus in the years 1315 through 1329, and it is quite probable that this church seat was unoccupied because of the conditions prevailing during the aftermath of the conquest.[265] We have already noted the numerous references to troubled times and vacant seats particularly in the acta between 1315 and 1318. Matthew first appears as metropolitan of Ephesus in a synodal document dated December 2, 1329, and all the protocols of the Constantinopolitan synod thereafter (until June, 1339) mention a metropolitan of Ephesus.[266] This would indicate, almost certainly, that during these ten years he was not able to occupy the metropolitan seat of Ephesus but remained mostly in Constantinople, hence his presence at all the synods. Sometime between 1331 and 1337 Matthew actually moved to the ecclesiastical seat of Brysis in Thrace, which he received as an epidosis. Though he retained his title of metropolitan of Ephesus, he still was unable to enter his legitimate church in Asia Minor, and as a result was cut off from his revenues.[267] It was not until sometime between June, 1339 and February, 1340[268] that Matthew finally made his way to his church in Ephesus. Thus, it would seem that a metropolitan had not actually set foot in Ephesus from the time the city was taken (1304) until the entrance of Matthew some thirty-five years later! This, as we have seen above, was a situation roughly parallel to that in many of the Anatolian metropolitanates in the first quarter of the fourteenth century, at the time when the Turkish emirates were expanding and liquidating the last remains of Byzantine control in Asia Minor. Matthew held the metropolitanate of Ephesus until May or June, 1351, when he was removed as an adherent to the heresy of Barlaam and Acindynus.[269] Of particular interest, for the status of the church and the Christians of Anatolia, among his writings are the "Prayer Pronounced upon Our Entrance into Ephesus" and three letters written from Ephesus to a friend or friends in Constantinople in which he narrates his experiences at Ephesus.

With his opening prayer (delivered upon arrival at Ephesus) Matthew beseeches God to endow him with the same power that he gave to the Holy

---

[265] Matthew of Ephesus-Treu, p. 3.

[266] *Ibid.*, p. 4. Miklosich et Müller, I, 149, 151, 155, 164, 170, 178, 179, 190, 193. It is not possible to say when he first occupied the throne.

[267] Matthew of Ephesus-Treu, pp. 37–38, gives the contents of this unpublished letter.

[268] Dölger, *Regesten*, no. 2837.

[269] Matthew of Ephesus-Treu, pp. 8–10. He had previously been a Palamite.

Apostles, "whom You sent to the foreign nations."[270] He asks to be "armed" with the cross so that he "might trample these serpents and pass safely from their deadly harm."[271] He calls upon God to halt His wrath, to free the Christians from the heavy yoke of slavery, and to repel their oppressive overseers. His trip from Constantinople had been strenuous, studded with obstacles all along the way; fear of pirates on the seas between Chios and Clazomenae, dangerous itineraries through forests and mountains between Clazomenae and Ephesus, and recalcitrant Turkish authorities. Though he found Smyrna a large city, its harbor was filled with pirate ships and the city had undergone a drastic ethnographic change.

> Accordingly we lamented, adding laments upon laments, and became as some Aristeides in calamity. But we did not cry simply over a city, as did he, hurled down by earthquake, nor over the sight of statues, but over the expulsion of Christians and the colonization of foreign nations from the extremities of the earth.[272]

Umur Beg, ruler of Smyrna, refused to grant Matthew an audience, declined to accept the correspondence that the Byzantine emperor had sent to him through Matthew and, more importantly, refused to allow the metropolitan to continue his journey to Ephesus.[273] Faced with the prospect of returning to Constantinople, Matthew decided that it would be the lesser of two evils to try and remain in Anatolia.

> And to take the road back seemed suspect, lest we be ambushed along the road by our enemies, or [even] if we should overcome this ambush we would [only] escape to run into many accusations that we were not hindered by the barbarians but that we had it in mind to return home. And the affairs of the bishops whom we appointed there were also very distressing. The unfortunate ones found some [temporary] abode and will halt there for some time, for neither have they in the meanwhile been permitted to see their churches.[274]

Faced by these customary difficulties of the Anatolian clergy, Matthew heeded the advice of a Chiote, bribed Umur Beg, and finally received permission to go to Ephesus.[275] In Ephesus he had an audience with Khidir Beg, brother of Umur, presented him with gifts, and requested the return of the metropolitan church, house, and properties. But the request was unheeded, and Matthew received words rather than deeds for his efforts. With the onset of the summer heat and dust storms, Matthew fell violently ill and despaired of life, as there were no doctors to treat him. After a miraculous recovery, the undaunted metropolitan once more pursued the question of the metropolitan possessions with Khidir Beg. The Turkish prince refused to return anything; the metropolitan

---

[270] *Ibid.*, p. 51.

[271] *Ibid.*

[272] *Ibid.*, p. 53.

[273] *Ibid.*, "οὐδὲ μέντοι συγχωρῶν ἀπιέναι διὰ τῆς αὐτοῦ χώρας εἴς γε τὴν Ἔφεσον . . ."

[274] *Ibid.*, pp. 53–54.

[275] *Ibid.*, p. 54.

church had been converted to a mosque [276] and the metropolitan residence had also been given to the Muslim religious men. As for the metropolitan lands:

Concerning the fields and other property he made some very funny defence. That since he had seized them with his own sword it was not possible for any other to have them in preference to himself.[277]

The result was that Matthew had to persevere for a long time without receiving anything from Khidir in return for his gifts, not even "one day's provisions." At the end of these protracted negotiations and entreaties, Matthew had to relinquish all claim to the metropolitan cathedral, residence, and all properties, receiving instead a small house and a tiny piece of land.

And if this thing is funny, it also has the greatest charm, having appeared amid tragedy. For having removed some old woman, and she an Ismaelite, from her own house he put in there, o wonder! the exarch of Asia [metropolitan of Ephesus], and he gave such a gift, one might say, that if it were not worthy of the recipient, [at least] it was worthy of the giver (that I might say the opposite of what Diogenes said to Alexander). And he added to such a great benefaction a most small piece of land for cultivation, which being far from the city would constitute not a [source] of nourishment to its owner but [a source] of destruction.[278]

Matthew was thus reduced to a very meager economic existence aided by only six priests.[279]

Matthew describes, in his correspondence, the distressing plight of the Christians in Ephesus. His flock consisted mostly of prisoners and slaves (numbering in the thousands), among whom were many priests and monks. The house assigned to him served, he says, as a witness to his "confinement and bonds" rather than as a "home."

Thus are our affairs and thus do we enjoy this beautiful metropolitanate. But that which distresses us more than the other evils is that living nearby the great church [the great church of St. John now become a mosque] we see the Corybants leaping up on the roof, daily, shouting out aloud the utterances of their worship as loudly as they can. And upon whichever of the churches we happen, we are thrown aside like some hierarchs without cities and without metropolitanates.[280]

Through the relations between Orthodox prelate and Turkish prince were now regularized on the terms of the latter, the Muslim inhabitants of Ephesus were apparently not reconciled to the presence of a preaching hierarch and his priests.

---

[276] *Ibid.*, p. 55; " ὁ δὲ τὸν μὲν ναὸν οὔ φησιν ἡμῖν ἀποδώσειν ἅπαξ εἰς τὴν αὐτοῦ μεταστάντα θρησκείαν." On p. 52, however, there is a reference to the fact that not only was it used as a mosque, but also as a storehouse for grain.

[277] *Ibid.*, p. 55.

[278] *Ibid.*

[279] *Ibid.*, " ἐπὶ δὲ τούτοις καὶ ἱερεῖς τοὺς σύμπαντας ἕξ, οὓς ἡ τῆς 'Ασίας μητρόπολις καὶ οὐ πλείους αὐχεῖ." Khidir taxed them as well.

[280] *Ibid.*, p. 56.

For it was not sufficient for the lawless ones that they neither wish to turn over to us the authority over the great church and house and property belonging to it from the beginning, nor that authority which is considered [to belong] to authorities; nor are they sparing of curses and blasphemies against God and us, but they have plotted an evil scheme either to kill us or at any rate to make us flee and some such evil are they contriving. Attacking with rocks in the depth of the night when the first cocks are not yet crowing, they hurl stones against our roof, aiming at the bed where we lie. These rocks, smashing the roof tiles, often fall inside. All of them would have fallen [in] one after another if they had not fallen upon the wooden boards which support the tiles and halt their rage and free us from such mutilation.[281]

The local Muslims were particularly aggravated by religious discussions and confrontations with the metropolitan, but they abstained from overt violence because of the realization that Khidir did not countenance such acts.

Seeing these things, the accursed ones are athirst for blood, always giving reign to their whole desire to taste flesh and blood, and they would not have abstained if they did not see that their chieftain was not exceedingly permissive to their madness, nor easily joining the assault. Accordingly what they are able to effect, this they do in the previously mentioned fashion with rocks, throwing them at night.[282]

It is at once apparent that the conditions of the church and of the Christians in Ephesus and in the jurisdiction of its metropolitanate were very unfavorable. The journey to Ephesus alone was a real trial to Matthew and his retinue, full of dangers of all kinds. There was danger from pirates on the sea and fear of Turkish ambushes on land, hence they often traveled by night and over obscure and difficult paths. The "Prayer" of Matthew represents the general state of mind in which most of the clergy sent to Anatolia must have found themselves. Their "condemnation" or dispatch to Anatolia is compared to the sending out of the apostles among the pagans, a comparison that appears quite often in the synodal acta. Umur Beg refused at first to see Matthew or to permit him to pass through his lands, and it was only by giving expensive bribes that Matthew was permitted to go on to Ephesus. Matthew found that all of his bishops were not permitted to go to their churches.

On his arrival in Ephesus he found conditions there even more intolerable. Khidir Beg, Umur's brother, refused to restore to the metropolitan his cathedral church, official residence, and property. He mentions that in addition to having to pay certain taxes, he and his priests were thrown out of their churches and forced to watch the imam calling the Muslims to prayer from atop the former cathedral church. By way of recompence they were permitted to keep a small chapel as their church, and the house of an old Turkish woman as the metropolitan residence. The Turkish inhabitants, however, were hostile and threw rocks at their

[281] *Ibid.*, pp. 56–57.
[282] *Ibid.*, p. 57.

house during the nights. Interesting is Matthew's assertion that if Khidir Beg had not intervened the Turks would have either killed or driven out the clerics. This would seem to indicate a difference in the attitudes of the Turkish begs and of the average Turks towards the Christian church. One was somewhat more tolerant, the other more fanatic. This fanaticism seems to have been further sharpened and honed in theological discussions between Muslims and Christians. The conversion of churches into mosques, along with the seizure of church property, were characteristic of the Turkish conquest throughout, as we have seen in the acta. The Dusturname-i Enveri says a propos of Ephesus:

> The Aydinoğlu coming to Ayasoluk [Ephesus], having conquered it and its dependencies, made many churches into mosques.[283]

The metropolitan found even the sending of letters to Constantinople restricted, and one of his letters had been confiscated by the Turks.

Finally, he draws a brief but dismal picture of the Christian community. In Ephesus it consisted largely of Christian prisoners who had been taken as slaves by the Turks and Jews.[284] These prisoners seem to have been great in number and probably were for the most part not originally inhabitants of Ephesus. For when the Turkish emir Sasan took Ephesus (on condition of sparing the inhabitants), he transplated the majority to Thyraeum, while large numbers were massacred.[285] He also states that the Christians of Smyrna had been largely deported and replaced with Muslim colonists and that the city was in ruins.[286]

Conclusions

The Turkish conquests and settlement of Anatolia not only destroyed the effective political control of a Christian state, but they also effectively crushed the Orthodox church. The repetitive and destructive nature of the Turkish conquests seriously undermined the foundations of the church and corroded the superstructure. The conquerors reduced the church to extreme poverty by confiscating the vast majority of its properties, revenues, and church buildings. The spoils belonged to the victorious begs and sultans, who apportioned them to their followers and to the members of the Muslim "religious institution." The episcopal institution, the structural heart of the church, survived in such a decimated state that it become a passive cultural vehicle. By the fifteenth century, there survived only seventeen metropolitanates, one archbishopric, and three

---

[283] *Le Destan d'Umur*, p. 47. Ibn Battuta-Gibb, II, 444, also remarks on the conversion of the cathedral church into a mosque. Lemerle, *Aydin*, pp. 31–32, for other references. Ludolph of Suchem-Neumann, p. 332; "Est eciam ibi pulchra ecclesia marmorea in modum crucis et bene plumbo tecta, in qua Turci vendunt mercimonia et locum sepulchri s. Iohannis in quandam crypta christianis ostendunt pro pecuniis."

[284] On Jews in western Asia Minor, see chapter i.

[285] Pachymeres, II, 589. The treasures of the church were confiscated.

[286] Ibn Battuta-Gibb, II, 445.

bishoprics in an area that had at one time possessed over fifty metropolitanates and more than four-hundred bishoprics! The episcopal structure had formerly constituted a vast ecclesiastical bureaucracy parallel to the Byzantine governmental bureaucracy, which like the latter was also centered in Constantinople. The conditions of the Turkish conquest were such that the vastness and the Constantinopolitan centripetality of the ecclesiastical institution became severe liabilities to the continued existence and functioning of the church. Every metropolitan or bishop was ipso facto a potential political agent of the emperor in Constantinople, for the emperor was the head of the church as well as the principal foe of Islam. The episcopate, parallel as it was to the Byzantine provincial government, possessed a highly developed administrative apparatus with numerous personnel and specialized functions, the so-called officia.[287]

These hierarchs provided not only spiritual ministration to the flocks but also furnished many of the material services that today are associated with the state, namely, care for the orphans, the poor, the sick, the wayfaring stranger, and education. From early times the episcopate had been an integral part of the Byzantine juridical system, and with the passage of time and the Turkish conquests, the bishops' courts became the principal juridical institution of the Christians. This highly developed ecclesiastical administration demanded extensive personnel and revenues in order to carry out its spiritual, social, and material functions. The conquests destroyed irrevocably the essential economic basis of the Anatolian church, depriving metropolitans and bishops of their administrative staffs, eleemosynary institutions, and reducing them to the state of indigent clerics with purely spiritual functions. They could no longer compete with

[287] On the inseparability of church and state in contemporary Byzantine mentality (late fourteenth century), see the letter of the patriarch Anthony IV to Basil the ruler of Moscow, Miklosich et Müller, II, 190–191. The emperor's name is mentioned in every land, where there are Christians, by the patriarchs, metropolitans, and bishops. " καὶ ἐν παντὶ τόπῳ καὶ παρὰ πάντων πατριαρχῶν καὶ μητροπολιτῶν καὶ ἐπισκόπων μνημονεύεται τὸ ὄνομα τοῦ βασιλέως ἔνθα ὀνομάζοντο χριστιανοί, ὅπερ οὐδεὶς τῶν ἄλλων ἀρχόντων ἢ τοπάρχων ἔχει ποτέ."

It is not possible, says Anthony, for Christians to have a church without an emperor. They cannot be separated. " οὐκ ἔνι δυνατὸν εἰς τοὺς Χριστιανούς, ἐκκλησίαν ἔχειν καὶ βασιλέα οὐκ ἔχειν. ἡ γὰρ βασιλεία καὶ ἡ ἐκκλησία πολλὴν ἕνωσιν καὶ κοινωνίαν ἔχει, καὶ οὐκ ἔνι δυνατόν, ἀπ᾽ ἀλλήλων διαιρεθῆναι ... ὁ δὲ κράτιστος καὶ ἅγιός μου αὐτοκράτωρ, χάριτι θεοῦ, ἔνι ὀρθοδοξότατος καὶ πιστότατος καὶ πρόμαχος τῆς ἐκκλησίας καὶ δεφένστωρ καὶ ἐκδικητής, καὶ οὐκ ἔνι δυνατόν, ἀρχιερέα εἶναι τὸν μὴ μνημονεύοντα αὐτοῦ."

Such mentality would undoubtedly render the church politically suspect in the eyes of the Turks.

The *pentas* constituted the heart of the episcopal offices and administration. It included the *oiconomus* (administered the wealth of the church), *saccelarius*, *sceuophylax*, *chartophylax*, *sacceliou*. It also included other offices such as those of the *chartularioi* of his bureau, his legal adviser the *ecdicon*, and others. Beck, *Kirche und theologische Literatur*, pp. 98–120. Ahrweiler, "Smyrne," 103, indicates that the administrative system of the metropolitanate was similar to and nearly as extensive as that of the patriarchate (at least in the case of Smyrna). In the cartulary of Lembus she has found mention of 26 dignitaries who exercised their functions under the metropolitan of Smyrna, though only the first two *pentades* appear complete in the Lembus documents.

their Islamic counterparts who boasted new and magnificantly endowed mosques, medresses (schools), imarets (soup kitchens), hospitals, and so forth. The Islamic institutions were not only endowed with lands, buildings, and properties formerly belonging to the Christian community (the church in the fourteenth century was also subjected to a heavy tax burden), but also with large numbers of Christian serfs.[288] The same economic wealth that had served as the foundation of the Byzantine religious institution was appropriated by the Turks and became the economic basis of a victorious, aggressive Anatolian Islam.

Though the economic factor in the decline of the church was exceedingly important, it was not the only factor. The periodic upheavals (especially those of the eleventh and twelfth, the late thirteenth and fourteenth centuries) seriously disrupted the administration of the Anatolian church. Given the highly centralized character of the ecclesiastical bureaucracy and the lack of secular support from a Christian state, the repeated absence of metropolitans, bishops, and their administrative staffs could not but have serious reprecussions for the Christian communities. The lack of political uniformity, of political stability, and of peaceful conditions frequently made it difficult or impossible for the Christian hierarchs to go to their churches. In many instances the Turks expelled the clergy, at other times they prevented the metropolitans from entering their church seats. Consequently, the Greek communities were left leaderless for extensive periods of time. The fact that they were without the direction of their leaders (in some instances churches were without metropolitans or bishops for as long as thirty-five years) constituted a serious impairment to Christian esprit in the communities, hindered ordinations, and led to a general relaxation of their social cohesion and cultural bonds. The churches of Anatolia were thus cut loose from Constantinople and were like so many pilotless and rudderless vessels adrift in a violent and stormy sea.

The successive blows of the Turkish conquests subjected Byzantine society in Anatolia to a series of shocks that so loosened its social bonds that it was prepared for cultural transformation.

[288] On this see chapter v and Gökbilgin, *Edirne, passim.*

V. Conversion to Islam

The purpose of this chapter is to describe the processes and institutions that effected the religious transformation of Greek Byzantine society, to show how a Greek-speaking Christian populace became Muslim (and eventually Turkish-speaking).[1] The Turkish conquest and settlement of Anatolia had been a long and disruptive affair that had brought enslavement, flight, plague, and famine to much of the Christian populace, and the Byzantine state had suffered repeated catastrophes. The conquests reduced the church to a state of extreme penury, which in turn barred it from effective social and economic action. The crippling of the ecclesiastical administrative apparatus left the demoralized Christian communities leaderless in a period of great psychological and economic crisis. All these constituted negative factors in the cultural transformation of Anatolia, factors, nevertheless, crucial to the process for they undermined the foundations of Byzantine society.

There were, however, institutions and a psychology that constituted the positive forces remolding Anatolian society on a Muslim pattern. The first and foremost of these institutions was the Islamic state (or more properly speaking the Islamic states). The maxim *"cuius regio eius religio"* very conveniently characterizes the outcome of Christiano-Islamic conflict throughout the Middle Ages—in Syria, Egypt, North Africa, Spain, Sicily, and Crete. Where the Muslim political forces were victorious, Islam prevailed over Christianity. But in Spain, Sicily, and Crete, the political and military success of Christianity removed the Arabs, and Christianity once more replaced Islam. The religious developments of Anatolia are in consonance with this pattern of *cuius regio eius religio*. The Muslim state (or states) supported and favored Islam in every way, and Christianity was tolerated only as the religion of its second-class citizens. The sultans and officials built mosques, medresses, imarets, zawiyas, hospitals, caravansarays, and fountains for the Islamic associations and

---

[1] Strictly speaking the subject of this book is the Islamization of Byzantine society, for the crucial phase of the cultural transformation is the change from Christianity to Islam. Turkification of course followed, and affected many of those who remained Christian, see chapter vii.

endowed them with lands, serfs, and revenues.[2] Consequently, the ulemas and dervishes had the economic wherewithal to perform their spiritual functions with elegance and their socioeconomic tasks with great efficiency. The key economic institution underlying the vitality and effectiveness of Muslim expression was the *wakf* (pl. *awkaf*), the economic endowment of religious and social foundations. Just as an economic institution reflected the decline of Christianity (the grant known as κατὰ λόγον ἐπιδόσεως, bestowed upon declining churches), so the wakf constitutes the economic form par excellence which testifies to the spread of Islam: the histories of κατὰ λόγον ἐπιδόσεως and wakf contain a substantial part of the history of Christian decline and Muslim expansion.[3]

A brief glance at the endowments of religious and social institutions in thirteenth-century Anatolia will amply illustrate the nature of the wakf and will demonstrate the implication of such an economic institution in the competition between Islam and Christianity. The great Seljuk emir Djalal al-Din Karatay, a Greek slave by origin, built and endowed a caravansaray forty kilometers east of Kayseri, a medresse (religious school) in Konya, and a *dar as-suleha* (rest home for the pious) in Antalya.[4] The officials and personnel necessary for the functioning of the foundations, and the purposes that the caravansaray, medresse, and rest house served required a considerable financial outlay. The caravansaray, as we learn from the wakf register, was staffed by a *mütevelli* (administrator), *müsrif*, *nazĭr*, *imam* (for the mosque in the caravansaray), *müezzin*, *muzif* (looked after the travelers and their food), *havayici* (administered provisions and the storehouse), *hani* (looked after the animals), *baytar* (veterinarian), *atlĭ emini*, and the cook. There were provisions for a hospital, for a *hammam* (bath) and attendant, for the shoeing of horses. Most important, each traveler, whether Muslim, Christian, or Jew, was to receive (free of charge) one okka of meat and one pot of food per day. The income necessary for

[2] For the activities of Seljuk officials in endowing religious foundations, Vryonis, "Seljuk Gulams and Ottoman Devshirmes," *Der Islam*, XLI (1965), 237–239.

[3] The history of the wakf in early Islam is obscure. Many have compared it to and derived it from the Byzantine *piae causae* that existed in the Levant at the time of the Arab conquests. Heffening, "Waqf," EI₁. Köprülü, "Vakĭf müessesesinin hukukî mahiyeti ve tarhî tekâmülü," *V.D.*, II (1942), 1–36, with a French precis at the end of the volume. Schacht "Early Doctrines on Waqf," *Fuad Köprülü Armağani* (Istanbul, 1953), pp. 443–452. M. Granič, "L'Acte de fondation d'un monastère dans les provinces grecques du Bas-Empire au Vᵉ et au VIᵉ siècle," *Mélanges Charles Diehl* (Paris, 1930), I, 101–106. Cahen, "Réflexions sur le waqf ancien," *S.I.*, XIV (1961), 37–56, argues for a non-Byzantine origin.

It is fortunate that a number of Anatolian wakf documents from the Seljuk, beylik, and Ottoman periods have survived. They contain material to complement the ecclesiastical documents that describe the state of the church, for the wakf literature reveals flourishing Muslim religious and social life and institutions. Remarkable for the wealth of detail which they contain are the documents from the Seljuk and beylik eras. O. Turan, "Mubarizeddin"; "Semseddin"; "Karatay." Temir, *Cacaoğlu*. Uzunçarşĭlı, "Nigde'de Karamanoğlu Ali Bey vakfiyesi," *V.D.*, II (1948), 45–69. H. A. Erzi, "Bursa'da Ishaki dervişlerine mahsus zaviyenin vakfiyesi," *V.D.*, II (1942), 423–428.

[4] For the texts and rich contents see the works of Turan cited above, n. 3.

the support of the caravansaray came primarily from the Christian villages of Sarahor and Likandon, which were to pay one-fifth of their produce to the administration of the caravansaray.[5]

The Seljuk official Er-Tokush, also of gulam origin, endowed a medresse (1224) in the village of Agros in the region of Borlu, a caravansaray in the same region at Dadil, and a mosque in Antalya. These foundations drew their financial sustenance from the Christian village of Agros (which had been conquered only two decades previously), and from the village of Pambuklu.[6]

The wakf of Shams al-Din Altun-Aba (of gulam origin), which provided for a medresse in Konya and a caravansaray at Arkït (between Ilgin and Akshehir), is the most instructive in regard to the functioning of Muslim religious schools. The expenditures included the following items:

mütevelli	400 silver dinars/year
nazïr	300 silver dinars/year
muderris	800 silver dinars/year
mu'it	240 silver dinars/year
15 students	
10 dinars/month/student	150 silver dinars/month
20 novices	
5 dinars/month/student	100 silver dinars/month
Hanefi imam to perform namaz	200 silver dinars/year
müezzin	100 silver dinars/year
ferrash (custodian)	60 silver dinars/year
books for library	100 silver dinars/year
(talebes who read in medresse—38?)	

One-fifth of the income from an eighteen-room khan at Yenibağche (outside Konya) was set aside to defray the yearly expenses for converts to Islam. It was to provide for the teaching of the Koran and prayers, the performance of circumcision, provision of shoes, clothes, and food to Christians, Jews, and pagans who apostatized to Islam.[7] The wakf's revenues came from three villages (two of which, Saraydjik and Arkïthanï-Arkït, were Christian), a number of shops, and a khan.[8]

---

[5] Turan, "Karatay," pp. 17–68. Salaries included the following:

müshrif	500 dirhems/yr.	and	50 mudd grain
nazïr	360 dirhems/yr.		24 mudd grain
imam	200 dirhems/yr.		24 mudd grain
müezzin	150 dirhems/yr.		24 mudd grain
muzif	200 dirhems/yr.		24 mudd grain
havayici	200 dirhems/yr.		24 mudd grain
hani	200 dirhems/yr.		24 mudd grain
baytar	100 dirhems/yr.		24 mudd grain
hamamci	120 dirhems/yr.		24 mudd grain
atlï emini	100 dirhems/yr.		24 mudd grain

[6] Turan, "Mubarizeddin," pp. 423–426.
[7] This important text is discussed below.
[8] Turan, "Semseddin," pp. 201–207, 211.

More extensive than all these, however, were the arrangements that the Seljuk emir Nur al-Din Djadjaoğlu of Kirshehir made in 1272. He endowed: in Kirshehir a medresse, mosque, *kanekah* (dervish cloister), *zawiya, mekteb, dar as-suleha,* a turbe for himself, and a turbe for his sister; in Kayseri, a mosque; in Iskilib, a medresse; in Talimeğini, a medresse and mosque; in Sultanyüği (Eskishehir) he built a mosque and khan, and repaired seventeen mosques and one zawiya. The lands and villages of the wakf were very numerous and included Armenian, Greek, and Jewish inhabitants as well as converts.[9]

Most illustrative of the process by which Muslim institutions expropriated and exploited the lands, manpower, and revenues formerly belonging to Christian institutions is the situation in the district of Trebizond during the early sixteenth century. The district had the following registered population and revenues.

	Muslim	*Christian*
199 villages,		
13,730 hearths	1,094	12,632
1,543 hearths—hass of mirliva	200	1,343
6,381 hearths—ziamet and timar	530	5,851
2,453 hearths—timars for Trebizond	206	2,246
1,092 hearths—timars for Azebs	42	1,050
2,263 Sultan Selim Validesi awkaf	120	2,143

Incomes		
Hass of the sultan	759,378	akches
Hass of the mirliva	188,245	
Zeamet and timar	582,200	
Timars of castle of Trebizond	196,400	
Timars of Azebs of Trebizond	89,700	
Yavuz Selim Validesi, Huseyn Ağa, Mahmud Ağa awkaf	342,938	
	2,158,861	akches[10]

The utilization of Christian manpower and revenues to support the provincial military and political structure in the district is obvious. But of immediate interest is the use of these resources to support the Muslim foundations. The documents mention four major awkaf in Trebizond:

Yavuz Sultan Selim Validesi Imaret—114,760 akches yearly (mostly local).

Fatih Sultan Muhammad awkaf—Muhammad converted the church of Chrysocephalus into a mosque (known as Ayasofya Manastiri), and it had a monthly revenue of 1,208 akches.

Hazinedar Huseyin Ağa awkaf—yearly income of 2,660 akches, including moneys from a monastery.

Kapi agasi Mahmud Ağa awkaf—yearly income of 9,310 akches, including revenue from a monastery.[11]

[9] Temir, *Cacaoğlu*, pp. 101–141, 287–299.
[10] Gökbilgin, "XVI. Yüzyil başlarinda Trabzon livasi ve doğu Karadeniz bölgesi," *Belleten*, XXVI (1962), 320–321.
[11] *Ibid.*, pp. 308–309.

Most of the revenues and manpower upon which the foundations relied in Trebizond came from the Christian community. The foundations, however, drew very extensively upon the Christians from various regions within the general district of Trebizond:

In the nahiye of Akcheabad the imaret of Yavuz Sultan Selim Validesi drew 150,997 akches and 1,830 souls from 1,655 hearths (80 Muslims and 1,575 Christian) in 21 villages.

In the nahiye of Yomra the imaret of Gülbahar of Trebizond had the income from the village of Hodj (48 hearths, 18 bashtina).

In the village of Hortokop (31 hearths, 4 mücerred, 4 bive, 6 bashtina; all Christian) in the nahiye of Madjka, a portion of the income had formerly belonged to the monasteries of Chrysocephalus, Ayia Sophia, and Ayios Phocas. But the Turks converted the monastic revenues into timar incomes.

The village of Smarohsa (nahiye of Madjka) was previously in part a monastic property. But this too was converted into timar.

The revenues of the village of Mesarya (nahiye of Madjka) were formerly incomes for the monasteries of Sumela, Soskayastos, Ayokos, and Alabene. These were converted into timar.

In the village of Istilaho (nahiyet) former monastic properties became timar.

The incomes of the monasteries of Ayios Phocas, Ayios Yoryis, Isfelyar and the property of Despina Khatun in the village of Shira (nahiye of Madjka) were converted into timar by order of the sultan.

The imaret of Yavuz Sultan Selim Validesi in Trebizond drew 56,507 akches and 634 souls from five villages in the nahiye of Madjka (542 hearths: 40 Muslim and 502 Christian).

The sultan converted large numbers of monastic properties into timar in the nahiye of Surmene.[12]

These Ottoman documents thus demonstrate that not only were Christian population, lands, and incomes put to work for Islam by means of the wakf, but that ecclesiastical property was confiscated on a large scale and utilized to support the military institution.

The wakf, by harnessing much of the land, manpower, and revenues of Anatolia to Islamic institutions, enabled the latter to achieve preeminence at the expense of Christianity. The above examples of the burgeoning of mosques, medresses, caravansarays, and other institutions, in Konya, Kayseri, Antalya, Agros, Arkit, Kirşhehir, Iskilib, and Trebizond contrast sharply with the economic decline of the metropolitanates and bishoprics in the same areas which is so obvious by the early fourteenth and fifteenth century. This parallel development is visible throughout Anatolia.[13]

Economic and political institutions alone, however, do not fully explain the success of Islam. The mentality of the men who created the institutions (as indeed of the whole of Muslim society) enters the picture, as does the psychology of the conquered Christians. To begin with the former, one must ask the question: Did there exist a missionizing zeal in the Muslim

[12] *Ibid.*, pp. 310–320.
[13] Vryonis, "Gulams," pp. 237–239.

society of Anatolia? A consideration of this question on purely legal and theoretical grounds, based on the traditional Muslim provision for the toleration of "people with a revealed scripture," can do no more than provide the broader context for examination of the problem. Generally the Seljuk, emirate, and Ottoman rulers observed this legal form and tolerated the non-Muslim religious institutions (at the same time one should realize that there were occasional violations, and that these were significant in terms of conversion). The letter of the law, however, did not ipso facto restrain the desire for conversion on the part of Muslims, whether dervishes, ulemas, laymen, or princes. Thus, theoretically, a Muslim could observe the tolerance of Christianity and yet also desire and work for the conversion of Christians. A second trend, which partly obscures the problem, is that some Islamists have often tended to argue by historical analogy from classical Islam. Since the Arabs of the seventh century were primarily interested in exploiting conquests for their own benefit, and because mass conversion would have threatened them with certain economic loss, they did not encourage conversion.

This argument from Islamic law (the toleration of the *ahl al-kitab*) and from classical Islamic history (the desire of the Arabs to enjoy, undisturbed and undiminished, the fruits of the conquest) has been adduced as proof that conversionary enthusiasm was absent from Turkish Islam. Usually, it is alleged, the Christians converted because of the material benefits, the higher civilization and culture of the Turks, and their greater moral virtues and justice. Arguments based on Islamic law, however, are frequently devoid of historical reality in the later period of Islamic history, and to apply the conditions of the first Islamic century to the Turkish period altogether ignores historical development. By the time of the arrival of the first Seljuks in Anatolia, the religious war between Byzantium and Islam had run a course of four centuries. The appearance of the Turks heightened and extended this religious war for another four centuries in the very heartland of Byzantium. The fervor of the Turkish ghazi was in part sustained by religious inspiration. The development of religious institutions (such as the dervish brotherhoods), which were not present at the time of the Arab conquests, added further religious ardor and conversionary motivation to Muslim society in Anatolia. Thus large numbers of Muslims must have felt that the conversion of Christians was highly desirable. This aggressive outlook on Greek Christianity subsided somewhat with the conquest of Constantinople in 1453, but it still colored the Muslim mentality as is evident in the account that the sixteenth-century Ottoman historian Sa'd al-Din gives of the conquest of the Byzantine capital.

That wide region, that strong and lofty city, from being the land of hostility [dar-ul-harb], became the city where money is coined [dar-uz-zarb]; and from being the nest of the owl of errors, was turned into the capital of glory and honor.

Through the noble efforts of the Mohammedan Sultan, for the evil-voiced clash of the bells of the shameless misbelievers was substituted the Moslem call to prayer, the sweet five-times-repeated chant of the Paracletic Faith of the glorious rites; and the ears of the people of the Djihad were filled with the melody of the ezan. The churches which were within the city were emptied of their vile idols, and cleansed from their filthy and idolatrous impurities; and by the defacement of their images, and the erection of the Islamic mihrabs and pulpits, many monasteries and chapels became the envy of the Gardens of Paradise. The temples of the misbelievers were turned into the mosques of the pious, and the rays of the light of Islam drove away the hosts of darkness from the place so long the abode of the despicable infidels, and the streaks of the dawn of the Faith dispelled the lurid darkness of oppression, for the word, irresistible as destiny, of the fortunate sultan became supreme in the governance of this new dominion. . . . On the first Friday [after the capture] prayers were recited in Aya-Sofia, and in the sultan's glorious name was the Mohammedan Khutba [Friday prayer containing the name of the sovereign] read. Thus, that ancient edifice was illumined with the rays of the Orthodox Faith, and perfumed with the breath of the odours of the Noble Law; and as the hearts of the Muvahhidin [those who testify to the Unity of God] were filled with joy at the erection of the emblems of the Faith, so that most desirable of shrines, that lofty mosque, that heart-pleasing temple, was full of the people of Islam; and its delight-reflecting interior, by being burnished with the Declaration of the Unity, became brilliant as a polished mirror.[14]

There is no indication that the Muslim rulers attempted to halt the conversions of Christians in Anatolia, and so it may be that satisfaction of a missionizing zeal may have outweighed losses from the head tax. Indeed, the conquests, commerce, and spoils of an entire empire may have served to soften the loss of such a considerable source of revenue as the *djizye*.

Contemporary observers report that the Turks anticipated and greatly rejoiced at the conversions of Christian subjects and prisoners of war. Though they generally observed their subjects' status, they did a great deal to make conversion attractive, as Schiltberger reports in the chapter entitled "How a Christian becomes an Infidel."

It is also to be noted how a Christian, from the beginning, becomes an Infidel. When a Christian wants to become in Infidel, he must before all men raise a finger, and say the words: "La il lach illallach"; Machmet is his true messenger. And when he says this, they take him to the high priest; then he must repeat the above written words before the priest, and must deny the Christian faith, and when he has done that, they put on him a new dress, and the priest binds a new kerchief on his head; and this they do that it may be seen he is an infidel, because Christians wear blue kerchiefs, and the Jews, yellow kerchiefs, on the head. Then the priest asks all the people to put on their armour, and who has to ride, rides; also all the priests who are in the neighborhood. And when the people come, they put him on a horse, and then the common people must ride before him, and the priests go behind him, with trumpets, cymbals and fifes, and two priests ride near him; and so they lead him about in the town; and the Infidels cry with a loud voice and praise Machmet, and the two priests say to him these words: "Thary wirdur, Messe

[14] Reproduced in P. Sherrard, *Constantinople. Iconography of a Sacred City* (London, 1965), p. 130.

chulidur, Maria cara baschidur, Machmet kassuldur'': which is as much as to say; There is one God, and the Messiah his servant, Mary his maid, and Machmet his chief messenger. After they have led him everywhere in the city, from one street to another, then they lead him into the temple and circumcise him. If he is poor, they make a large collection and give it to him, and the great lords shew particular honor to him, and make him rich; this they do, that Christians may be more willing to be converted to their faith. If it is a woman who wants to change her religion, she is also taken to the high priest, and must say the above words. The priest than takes the woman's girdle, cuts it in two, and makes of it a cross; on this, the woman must stamp three times, deny the Christian faith, and must say the other words above written.[15]

The great extent of religious syncretism in Anatolian volksreligion is in part to be explained by the desire of the dervishes to convert the Christians. This current of syncretism was so powerful that it served political ends in the case of the great socioreligious rising unleashed by Badr al-Din, Bürklüdje Mustafa, and Torlak Hu-Kemal in western Asia Minor (1416). Badr al-Din and his followers, preaching the communistic doctrine of the community of property, attracted the poor and the socially discontented to their standards, and also made a strong appeal to the Christians by preaching religious equality.[16] Prior to the rebellion, Badr al-Din had visited Chios where he conversed with the Genoese ruler and the Christian religious men. Consequently, two priests and five monks became converts and the people received Badr al-Din as the second Messiah. Both he and Bürklüdje Mustafa preached the toleration of Christianity and went even further by declaring the Christian and Muslim religions to be equally valid. Borklüdje, who was also in frequent contact with the Chiotes, sent to inform them of his belief that no one who was not in

---

[15] Schiltberger-Neumann, pp. 130–132. Schiltberger-Hakluyt, pp. 74–75.

[16] The family history of Badr al-Din is a concrete example of the symbiosis between Christians and Muslims, which intermarriage brought. The sheikh's father, Israil, married the daughter of the Greek commander of a Thracian fort. She converted to Islam, received the name Meleke, and became the mother of Badr al-Din. Israil first settled in the Thracian town of Samavna where he confiscated a Christian church and converted it into his residence. Following Meleke's conversion, 100 of her relatives became apostates to Islam and henceforth served Israil. Badr al-Din himself married a Christian slave, Gazila, in Egypt, who bore him a son, Ismail. Ismail in turn married the Christian Harmana (whose father was Armenian), the niece of a Christian priest from Ainus whom Badr al-Din had converted to Islam. Their son, Halil, composed the biography of his grandfather Badr al-Din, Kissling, "Das Menaqybname Scheich Bedr ed-Din's, des Sohnes des Richters von Samavna," *Z.D.M.G.*, C (1950), 114–116, 140–164. See also Babinger, "Schejch Bedr ed-din, der Sohn des Richters von Simaw, ein Beitrag zur Geschichte des Sektenwesens im Altosmanischen Reich," *Der Islam*, XI (1921), 1–106; *Die Vita (menaqybname) des Schejch Bedr ed-din Mahmud, gen. Ibn Qadi Samauna, von Chalil b. Isma'il b. Schejch Bedr ed-Din Mahmud, I. Teil: Urtext nach der einzig erhaltenen Handschrift im Revolutions-Museum zu Istanbul (Sammlung Muallim Cevdet Nr. 228)* (Leipzig, 1943). M. Serefeddin, "Simawne Kadisi oğlu Seyh Bedreddine dair bir kitap," *T.M.*, III (1935), 233–256. Gölpinarlı, Simavna Kadisioğlu Seyh Bedreddin (Istanbul, 1966): Gölpinarli and I. Sungurbey, *Halil bin İsmail bin Seyh Bedrüddin Mahmûd Simavna Kadisioğlu Seyh Bedreddin Manâkĭbĭ* (Istanbul, 1967). E. Werner, "Haresie, Klassenkampf und religiose Toleranz in einer islamisch-christlieben Kontaktzone, Bedr ed-din und Burkluce Mustafa," *Zeitschrift für Geschichtswissenschaft*, XII (1964), 255–276.

harmony with Christianity could attain salvation. Any Muslim who denied the efficacy of the Christian faith, he stated, was himself godless.[17]

The historical events indubitably exercised a profound influence on the psychology of the Christians. They had experienced and witnessed the defeat of Byzantium and they were now the subjects of military conquerors who professed an alien faith. Undoubtedly some saw in this fact a proof of Islam's validity. Others were prepared for assimilation by the preaching of dervishes and ulemas, and by the religious syncretism that tended to equate Islamic practices and saints with those of the Christians. In any case strong economic and social motivations were ever present. Converts would escape the onerous tax of the djizye, and their agricultural tax would be lightened. Others might hope for administrative positions and lands.[18] Conversion entailed entrance to the favored religious group and removed the discriminatory status attributed to Christianity. There is also evidence that the hedonism attendant upon polygamy and concubinage appealed to some converts.[19] Through conversion seems to have occurred

---

[17] Babinger, "Bedr ed-din," pp. 53, 64–67. Ducas, pp. 111–115. Kissling, "Badr al-Din ibn Kadi Samawna," EI₂. H. I. Cotsonis, "Aus der Endzeit von Byzanz: Burkludsche Mustafa, ein Marytrer für die Koexistenz zwischen Islam und Christentum," B.Z., L (1957), 397–404. Bombaci, Storia, pp. 304, 306, describes Badr al-Din as one who attempted to harmonize Islam with Christianity. The translation of the Mevlud (recitation of the birth of Muhammad) into Serbian, Albanian, and Greek also points to the direction of syncretism. These "Christianizing" currents were evident in the city of Bursa during the latter half of the fourteenth century at which time a preacher declared Christ to be no less a prophet than Muhammad. The sermon aroused a tumult in which the people sided with the preacher. It was this event that inspired the Ottoman poet Sulayman Chelebi to compose his poem on the birth of Muhammud. Sulayman, scandalized by this doctrine of prophetic equality, gave preeminence to Muhammad in his poem. But even so the poem was imbued with a certain Christian spirit and was translated into the Balkan languages. Wittek, "De la défaite d'Ankara à la prise de Constantinople (un demi-siècle d'histoire ottomane)," R.E.I., XII (1938), 30–32. W. Björkman, "Sulaiman Celebi," EI₁. I. Engelke, Suleyman Tschelebis Lobgedicht auf die Geburt des Propheten (Halle, 1926). The Mevlidi Sherif by Suleyman Chelebi, trans. F. Lyman (London, 1943). E. J. W. Gibb, History of Ottoman Poetry (London, 1900), I, 232 ff. Bartholomaeus Georgieuiz, Kidrić, p. 15, recounts the attempt of his Turkish master to convert him to Islam, and the argument of the Turkish master reveals a Turkish Islam heavily syncretized with Christianity. The Turk urges Bartholomaeus to convert and promises to reward him by putting the Christian in charge over all his horses when he goes to war. Bartholomaeus replies that he cannot deny God. The Turk attempts to overcome the austere religious scruples of his slave by remarking that the Turks believe in three books (Torah, Gospels, Koran) and in three prophets (Moses, Christ, Muhammad). Bartholomaeus counters with the question, why then do you not believe in Christ as the true prophet? The Turk reaffirms the belief of Muslims in Christ as a true prophet. The rejoinder of Bartholomeus is, "how can one impose such an affliction as to circumcize a baptized Christian?" The Turk makes the reply that all his own coreligionists are baptized. The work of F. W. Hasluck, Christianity and Islam under the Sultans, vols. I–II (Oxford, 1929), is a veritable mine of information on this religious syncretism in both the Balkans and Anatolia.

[18] Goitein, "Evidence on the Muslim Poll Tax from non-Muslim Sources. A Genizeh Study," J.E.S.H.O., VI (1963), 278–295. This is graphically evident from the account that Bartholomaeus gives of the attempt of his Turkish master to convert him. For a specific case of mass conversion arising from oppressive taxation in the district of Erzerum, 1643. F. Macler, "Erzereum ou topographie de la Haute Arménie," J.A., 11th ser., XII (1919), 177.

[19] On all the motives see chapter vi.

largely under these impulses, there is both Muslim and Christian evidence that forced conversion was far from insignificant.[20] The letters of the fourteenth-century Calecas to the inhabitants of Nicaea reveal not only forced conversions and crypto-Christianity but also they refer to the phenomenon of neo-martyrdom. This latter phenomenon is mentioned one century later in the "Pastoral Letter on the Fall of Constantinople" which Gennadius Scholarius delivered to the congregation in Constantinople after he had become the first patriarch of Turkish Constantinople.

No one may doubt [in regard to those who live in the midst of the barbarians and who suffer evil on behalf of the faith] that they are "new" Mercurioi, Procopioi, and Georges, if indeed they are not even greater than those predecessors inasmuch as they are also braver. . . . For these present confessors [of Christianity] bear with marvellous patience the unspeakable daily bitternesses from the barbarians which arise simply because of their Christian name. Nor do they hesitate to live with these [bitternesses] and they have no hope for escape . . . neither do they waver from the love of Jesus by the process of apostasy which God has reasonably allowed.[21]

This neo martyrology included no less a person than the famous Theodore Gabras, the virtual ruler of Trebizond, who, about 1098, was captured by the Turk Amir Ali (Amiralis) in the regions of Paipert-Erzerum. His captor tried, without success, to force the conversion of Gabras. Gabras was first layed out on the snow, face down, and beaten on the back. He remained steadfast, however, so his captors then proceeded to dismember him alive, severing his tongue, plucking out his eyes, and then removing the scalp, limbs, and other parts. His remains were burned and the Amir Ali had a golden drinking cup fashioned from his skull.[22]

[20] On this see the references (throughout the book) to the Danishmendname, Ashĭk-pashazade, Balsamon, Cantacuzene, Theophanes Nicaenus and to the patriarchal documents. In the sixteenth century forced conversion was still extensive, *Hans Dern-schwam's Tagebuch einer Reise nach Konstantinopel und Kleinasien (1553/55)*, ed. F. Babinger (Munich and Leipzig, 1923), pp. 69, 73-74, 140, 142-143, 107.

[21] *Oeuvres complètes de Gémnade Scholarios*, L. Petit, X. A. Siderides, M. Jugie (Paris, 1928-1936), IV, 219 (hereafter cited as Gennadius Scholarius). Further on the neo-martyrs, P. V. Paschoe, Νικοδήμου τοῦ ῾Αγιορείτου, Νέον Μαρτυρολόγιον, 3d ed. (Athens, 1961). A. Vakalapoulos, Πηγὲς τῆς ἱστορίας τοῦ Νέου ῾Ελληνισμοῦ (Thessalonike, 1965), pp. 281–286. Laurent, "Le pseudo-Michel d'Andrinople ou le néomartyr Michel Mavroeides," *E.O.*, XXXVIII (1939), 31-34; "Encore le néomartry Michel Mavroeides," *E.O.*, XXXVIII (1939), 371-379. S. M. Vitti, "῾Ο νεομάρτυρας Μάρκος Κυριακόπουλος ποῦ ἀποκεφαλίστηκε στὴ Σμύρνη τὸ 1643(μία Δυτικὴ πηγή)," M.X., X (1963), 89-103. S. Petrides, "Le néo-martyr Michael Mauroeides et son office," *E.O.*, XV (1911), 333-334. Demetrius Cydones in Vakalopoulos, πηγές, p. 92, also refers to forced conversion in the fourteenth century, " Τῶν δ᾽ οἰκητόρων ταῖς μὲν ψυχαῖς ἐλυμήναντο, τὸν μὲν ἀλαθῆ θεὸν ἀναγκάσαντες ἀγνοῆσαι, τῶν δὲ παρ᾽ αὐτοῖς μεταδεδωκότες μιαρῶν μυστηρίων."

[22] Between 1115 and 1140 Constantine Gabras arranged for the formal return of the martyr's skull to Trebizond where it became the focus of the neo-martyr's cult. Papadopoulos-Kerameus, " Συμβολαὶ εἰς τὴν ἱστορίαν Τραπεζοῦντος," *V.V.*, XII (1906), 132-137; *Ist. trap. imp.*, p. 59. Zonaras, III, 739.

More detailed is the account that appears, in the synaxarion, of the neomartyr Nicetas the Young. He and two Christian merchants set out from Ankara for Nyssa and arrived at their destination during the Muslim fast of Ramadan. When the Turks observed the Christians taking their meal inside the city, they were so outraged that they brought the Greeks before the governor. During the course of interrogation the three young men defended their actions, vigorously affirmed their Christianity, and cast aspersions on the religion of the prophet. The governor ordered them beaten about the face, and the judge who was present condemned them to death. En route to the place of execution the mob gathered and attacked them with stones, sticks, and knives. The executioners prepared the fire, over which they were to be burned, and then offered them the choice of apostasy or death. The terror of the coming ordeal weakened the resolve of the two merchants who at this point abjured Christianity and turned Muslim. Nicetas, however, loudly proclaimed his Christian faith and violently rejected Islam. The executioners next began the torture of the condemned man, beating him on the face, tearing out his hair, and wrenching out his limbs. Nicetas' aunt, a witness to the horrible spectacle, cried out and urged her nephew to save himself. Nicetas, unweakened in his resolve, began to anathematize Muhammad and so enraged the mob that some now jumped on the tormented victim while others urged the executioners to carry out the death sentence. Nicetas was hung by the feet, from a beam over the embers and roasted to death. His few remains were piously gathered by the Christians and eventually placed in the church of St. Gregory.[23]

These specific cases tend to confirm the assertion of Calecas, Scholarius,

---

[23] Delehaye, "Le martyre de Saint Nicetas le Jeune," *Mélanges offerts à M. Gustave Schlumberger* (Paris, 1924), I, 205–211. The date of the martyrdom is set within the limits of the reign of Andronicus II, 1282–1328. The text relates that it occurred in the reign of the "caliph" Mas'ud, the "Persian," clearly a reference to the Seljuk sultan of Rum. There were two monarchs with this name during the reign of Andronicus II: Mas'ud II, 1282–1304, and Masud III, 1307–08. Therefore the martyrdom is to be dated sometime between 1282–1304 or 1307–08. Of equal interest is the martyrdom of St. Michael, AS, Nov. IV, 671–676, captured at a young age by the Turks near Smyrna, sold as a slave in Egypt where he turned Muslim and became a soldier. He repented, professed Christianity publicly, was beheaded and burned. The martyrdom took place in the reign of Andronicus II. On forced conversion and the use of fire see Ducas, pp. 186–187 who recounts the apostasy of Michael Pylles. Pylles was a Greek from Ephesus who served as a secretary (he knew Greek and Turkish) in the palace of Murad II. Accused of intrigue he was bound, mercilessly tortured, placed before the fire and given the choice of apostasy or death by burning. Choosing the former, he denied Christianity, was circumcised, and was paraded through the streets. For the details of the martyrdom of a Chiote Catholic in Istanbul in 1465, E. Dalleggio, "Un néo-martyr à Constantinople, André de Chio (1465)," *Mémorial Louis Petit* (Bucharest, 1948), pp. 64–77. Of historical interest is the martyrdom in Adrianople of the Neo-Martyr George (d. 1437), a Christian soldier in the Ottoman army, Ch. Patrinellis, " Μία ἀνέκδοτη διήγηση γιὰ τὸν ἄγνωστο Νεομάρτυρα Γεώργιο (1437)," Ὀρθόδοξος Παρουσία, I (1964), 65–74. For the neo-martyrs after. 1453, Delehaye, "Greek Neo-martyrs," *The Constructive Quarterly*, IX (1921), 701–712 Dernschwam-Babinger, pp. 69, 111, on burning and neo-martyrs.

and others that neomartyrdom was a significant feature in the religious history of Anatolia from the eleventh century onward.

The conversionary process, set in motion by this wide variety of factors and conditions, was overpowering, and it spread to every part of Anatolia between the eleventh and fifteenth centuries (and continued in operation even afterward). Sources specifically mention conversion in the following districts, towns, and villages:[24]

Altïntash	Tokat
Susuz (Germiyan)	Mihalich
Tavas (Menteshe)	Egridir
Konya (Iconium)	Gemlik
Sis	Kocjaili
Meram	Bolu/Samsun
Yalova	Sinope
Taraklï-yenidjesi	Malatya
Goynuk	Karahisar
Modreni	Arapkir
Bursa	Cemiskezek
Nicaea	Cizre
Antioch	Sivas
Castamon	Erzerum
Sisiya-Comana	Diyarbekir
Yankoniya-Euchaita (Chorum)	Kemah
Seveverek	Paipert
Georgia	Nigde
Pontoheracleia	Beğshehir
Amaseia/Gangra	Karaman
Sebasteia	Zulkadiriye
Mocissus	Kutahya
Nazianzus	Manyas
Trebizond	Biledjik
Marash	Sarahor
Lefke	Likandon
Kayseri	Agros
Rize	Saraydjik
Cikar	Arkit
Mirokalo	District of Kirshehir-Iskilip
Ksanos	Menohort
Vanak	Zavandos
Giresun	

Scholarius' writings bear extensive testimony to the large-scale conversions that were emptying the Christian ranks. In his fervent exhortation to conclude union with the Latins at the Council of Florence, Scholarius described the pitiful state and afflictions of the Greek Christians who were under Turkish rule or else threatened by imminent conquest: sieges, massacres, enslavement, famine, taking away of children, dishonoring of priests, and above all conversion to Islam, both voluntary

[24] For the references to these see chapter iii and chapter v.

and involuntary. Because of all these, he continues, ecclesiastical union must be concluded or else the consequences will be fatal to Christianity in the East.

And these very things must happen to the Christians on whatever part of the earth they live and are under the rule of the barbarians; everywhere the reverence for Christ will be utterly destroyed. And I believe that in a few years there will arrive for all Christians that deluge, and impiety shall occupy all and all shall be enslaved to the barbarians.[25]

Muslim Institutions: Tasawwuf

Many scholars have pointed to the fact that the conquest of and immigration into Antolia by the Turkish tribes were accompanied by the entrance and appearance of a number of important Islamic organizations and brotherhoods. Actually the Ottoman chronicler Ashikpashazade had made this observation as far back as the fifteenth century when he grouped them into four separate categories.

And also in this Rum [Anatolia] there are four bands who are among the strangers and travellers: One of them [are] the Ghaziyan-i Rum, one the Akhiyan-i Rum, one the Abdalan-i Rum and one the Bahdjiyan-i Rum. [26]

Though these four associations have been the subject of a host of learned studies, scholars are in complete agreement on only one thing—namely, that our knowledge about them far from being exact and precise is rather general, and the relations of the various groups to one another are even more vague and difficult to establish. It is true, however, that they adhered to the futuwwa and tasawwuf ideals in one form or another. Adherence to the futuwwa distinguished the akhis whereas allegiance to sufi ideals characterized the abdals (dervishes). Both groups, however, shared to some extent in the tasawwuf and futuwwa ideologies respectively, and all four associations played an important role in establishing a Muslim society in Anatolia. The nature and character of, first, Anatolian sufism and, second, of the Anatolian futuwwa were highly complex and made up of many divergent elements.

Sufism (tasawwuf) had its origin in the ascetic movement of the Umayyad period when asceticism arose as a protest against the worldiness of the contemporary society. The element of mystical love transformed this asceticism from a withdrawal (in protest against worldliness) into mysticism, a transformation that marked the beginnings of sufism. Because of its emotional approach to religion and the fact that man could know God directly through mystical love, sufism became the most popular form of Islam, in contrast to the cold, learned, and seemingly

---

[25] Gennadius Scholarius, I, 303. For other references to conversion in Scholarius' works, I, 286, III, 250, 384. For the evolution in his attitudes on union with the Latin church, C. J. G. Turner, "George-Gennadius Scholarius and the Union of Florence," *The Journal of Theological Studies*, XVIII (1967), 83–103.

[26] Ashikpashazade-Ali, p. 201.

incomprehensible orthodox form of sunni theology and religious law. This theosophical element, eventually compounded by pantheism, reached an extreme development in the figure of al-Halladj whom the Orthodox theologians condemned to be executed (921 or 922) for identifying himself with God. By the end of the tenth century, sufism had become a distinct way of religious life and thought and in the eleventh century spread throughout the Islamic lands. Because of its immense popularity and rapid spread, it incurred the suspicion and wrath of the ulemas and this in turn resulted in sufi apologetics. Important in sufi apologetics were Qushairi and especially al-Ghazzali who attempted to reconcile sufism with the more formal type of Islamic religious expression. Because of this successful attempt at apologetics, the less extreme elements or groups henceforth found a place within the framework of orthodox Islam.[27]

There was thus one development within sufism, centered in Baghdad, which stood in fairly close relationship to sunni Islam. But a second tendency within sufism, centering in Khurasan (and existing elsewhere as well), went in the direction of extreme attitudes. Three important elements in particular, which have been characterized as antinomian, penetrated the sufi movement in Khurasan, and all three appear in the sufi movement of Anatolia. The Malamatiyya (from the Arabic word malama meaning blame), were a group of nonconformists in the sense that they believed the mere discharge of duties entailed by the sharia was at very best hypocrisy and especially if done so ostentatiously. They avoided ostentation, even in their nonconformity, so as to evade the odium of insincerity. They were known as Malamatiyya because of the fact that they were willing to incur blame for nonobservance of the external aspects of Islamic ritual. A second feature that went against the grain of the orthodox sunni was the important role of al-Halladj in Khurasani sufism as the "martyr of mystical love." The sunnis could not countenance this as it was the orthodox ulema who had been responsible for his execution and also because of his extreme theosophical doctrines and claims. Halladji sufism attained important proportions among the Turks of Khurasan and affected the greatest of the eastern Turkish mystic poets Ahmad Yasawi. The third important antinomian element in Khurasani sufism was that of the Batiniyya which called for the allegorical interpretation of the Koran. The doctrine of the Batiniyya and the links with the family of Ali were important points of similarity and agreement between the sufis and shiites, though these two groups were often hostile on other matters.[28] All these factors are important, for it was in the region of Khurasan that the invading and migrating Turks came into contact with Islam and many

---

[27] A. J. Arberry, *Sufism, an Account of the Mystics of Islam* (London, 1950), *passim.* H. A. R. Gibb, *Mohammedanism* (New York, 1955), pp. 99–109.

[28] Gibb and Bowen, *Islamic Society and the West* (Oxford, 1951), I_1, 2.

became associated with the ghazi branch of the futuwwa and their religious leaders, the so-called babas, came under heavy Khurasani sufi influence.[29]

After the transformation of asceticism into mysticism and the elaboration of the latter into the sufism of the eleventh century, the next great development of sufism was the foundation and spread of the great dervish orders over the Islamic world. The great orders grew out of smaller independent groups of disciples who voluntarily formed around some prominent mystic personality. A simple initiation ceremony for the new disciples was added, and the disciples lived with the sheikh or pir until they in turn went out to preach their master's way (*tariqa*). Upon the master's death his tomb became the object of special veneration on the part of his disciples, and it became the center of the new tariqa or order to which all the newly founded monasteries (*ribat, zawiya,* or *kanekah*) paid allegiance. Though the various dervish orders that arose differed among themselves in many respects, the most significant external differences were in the matter of the ritual (*dhikr*) and in their attitudes toward the ordinary observances of orthodox Islam. There were also important variations, as will appear in Anatolia, between the orders that were essentially urban and those brotherhoods that were predominantly rural.[30] The membership of the dervish associations generally included the dervishes themselves, who withdrew to the monasteries where they were entirely engaged in religious life, and the lay brethren who though they participated in the religious ceremonies of the monasteries were engaged in secular occupations by which they earned their daily bread. The growth and spread of these orders reflected the fact that men found an emotional religion more satisfying than the cold, prosaic, orthodox Islam. Further, the dervish orders spread at a time when the Islamic world was disintegrating politically, and the instability of conditions must have produced a certain anxiety among men. Finally, the latitudinarian character of dervish religiosity opened the gates of conversion to pagan Turks and Christians alike.

By the twelfth and thirteenth centuries a number of important orders had been founded in Asia, Egypt, and North Africa. These included the Qadiriyya (an urban association founded near Baghdad), the Suhrawardiyya, the Badawiyya and Shadhiliyya (founded in Egypt), the Yasawiyya (the first Turkish mystical brotherhood), and the Kalandariyya in the eastern Islamic lands.[31] The dervish orders which played so significant a

---

[29] *Ibid.*

[30] Gibb, *Mohammedanism*, pp. 117–119. Köprülü, "Anadoluda Islamiyet," *Edebiyat Fakültesi Mecmuasï*, II (1922), 388. For other general literature on the dervish orders: Kissling, "Das islamische Derwischenwesen," *Scientia*, XCIV (Sept., 1955), 230–235; "Die Wunder der Derwische," *Z.D.M.G.*, CVII (1957), 348–361; "Die islamischen Derwischorden," *Zeitschrift für Religions- und Geistesgeschichte*, XII (1960), 1–16. V. Mirmiroglu, Οἱ Δερβίσσαι (Athens, 1940).

[31] Gibb, *Mohammedanism*, pp. 120–122. Arberry, *Sufism*, pp. 84–88.

role in Anatolian developments from the thirteenth through fifteenth centuries were in part actually founded in Anatolia (Mawlawiyya and Bektashiyya), and in part founded and developed in other Islamic lands (Kazaruniyya, Kalandariyya, Rifa'iyya). In both cases the influx of holy men fleeing the Mongol invasions in Khurasan and seeking refuge in Anatolia greatly stimulated the founding and evolution of the dervish brotherhoods.

The Turks themselves, during their settlement and passage through Khurasan and the northern fringes of the Islamic lands, had been subject to strong currents of Sufi influence. Very important in this respect had been Ahmad Yasawi the founder of the first Turkish dervish tariqa. Though his life is obscured by much legend, it seems that Yasawi was born in Sairam, Chinese Turkestan, and, eventually coming west, studied with the famous mystic and jurist Yusuf Hamdani at Bukhara. Yasawi played a very important role, perhaps even a decisive one, in the Islamization of the Turks. Previously, the newcomers had been subject to a wide variety of religious influences, but Yasawi took the sufism that he found and adapted it for his people in a Turkish context and in the Turkish language. Various legends number his disciples from 12,000 to 99,000, and his influence spread eastward to the Kirghiz in Turkestan, to the Turkish peoples in the north around the Volga, and to the west into Anatolia.[32]

Among the dervish orders that came into Anatolia in the thirteenth and fourteenth centuries was that of the Rifa'iyya, founded in Irak in the twelfth century. Originally, its founder seems to have preached doctrines of poverty, abstinence, nonresistance to injury, and the early adherents were generally unwilling to kill or give pain to any living creature, including even lice and locusts.[33] But the beliefs and practices of the order seem to have undergone a drastic transformation following the Mongol invasions, probably due to the penetration of shaman influences. After this transformation, the fraternity, which later came to be known as that

[32] Köprülü, *Turk edebiyatǐnda ilk mutassavǐflar* (Istanbul, 1919) (hereafter cited as Köprülü, *Mutassavǐflar*). There are two extensive precis of this fundamental work, in French: L. Bouvat, "Les premiers mystiques dans la litterature turque," *Revue du Monde musulman*, XLIII (1921), 239–249; Th. Menzel, in *Körösi Csoma Archivium*, II₄, 281–310. Toğan, "Yeseviliğe dair bazi yeni malumat," *Fuad Köprülü Armagani* (Istanbul, 1953), pp. 523–529. Gordlevski, "Choğa Ahmed Jasevi," *Festschrift Georg Jacob* (Leipzig, 1932), pp. 57–67, on his shrine in the city of Turkestan (formerly Jasy). Köprülü had formerly considered the Yasawis Orthodox, but in *Les origines de l'empire ottoman* (Paris, 1935), pp. 118–119 (hereafter cited as Köprülü, *Origines*), he altered his opinion and considered them quite heterodox. On the element of the Turkish shaman see Köprülü, *Influence du chamanisme turco-mongol* (Istanbul, 1929), p. 16 (hereafter cited as Köprülü, *Chamanisme*). Babinger, "Der Islam in Kleinasien," *Z.D.M.G.*, I (1922), 126–152. Menzel, "Die ältesten türkischen Mystiker," *Z.D.M.G.*, LXXIX (1925), 269–289.

[33] By way of illustration, it is reported that al-Rifa'i permitted his wife to belabor him with a metal poker, though his friends and disciples collected 500 dinars to make it possible for him to divorce her by returning her marriage gift. *New Shorter Encyclopedia of Islam*, pp. 475–476.

of the "Howling Dervishes," was characterized by marvelous and sensational feats such as riding lions, sitting in heated ovens, stabbing and burning themselves, fire-eating, and other such accomplishments.[34] Another tariqa, which came to Anatolia from Persia, was that of the Kazaruniyya or Ishakiyya. The association was founded in Kazarun, a province of Shiraz, by Shaikh Abu Ishak b. Shahsiyar Kazaruni (963–1033), descendant of a family of fire-worshipers who had been converted to Islam only in the time of his father. Kazaruni was a fervent missionary who, according to his biography, converted 24,000 fire-worshipers and Jews to Islam, and his order eventually spread to India, Persia, China, and Anatolia. Though tradition says that Kazaruni himself sent disciples into Anatolia to fight the Christians, there is no contemporary evidence for the presence of the Kazaruniyya there until the fourteenth century. These Kazarunis were characterized above all by their militant missionary spirit and ghazi mentality, and by their role in the djihad. Accordingly, the Kazaruniyya played a very important role in Ottoman history in the fifteenth century. Though it was primarily urban-oriented, it evidently had great influence among the Turkmens and in the organization of the djihad.[35]

A great number, perhaps even the majority, of the dervishes fleeing Turkestan, Bukhara, and Khwarazm to Asia Minor were of the so-called Kalandariyya.[36] This order, which seems to have originated in Central Asia and to have been under some Indian influence, first came into Arab lands in the eleventh century. The movement was inspired, to a certain degree, by the teachings of the Malamatiyya, but the Kalandars differed from the adherents of the latter in that they went out of their way to draw blame upon themselves for not conforming to the outward and customary practices of orthodox Islam. One could perhaps describe them as "ostentatious" Malamatis. Thus they shaved their eyebrows and beards, wore strange clothing, led an errant life, living off the charity of the local

[34] Gibb and Bowen, *Islamic Society*, I₂, 196. Köprülü, *Mutassaviflar*, pp. 228 ff. *New Shorter Encyclopedia of Islam*, pp. 475–476.

[35] Köprülü, "Abū Ishāq Kāzerūnī und die Ishāqī Derwische in Anatolien," *Der Islam*, XIX (1930), 18–26. W. Caskel, *Der Islam*, XIX (1930), 284 ff. A. J. Arberry "The Biography of Shaikh Abū Ishāq al-Kāzarūnī," *Oriens*, III (1950), 163. Wittek, "Kâzerûnî," *I.A. New Shorter Encyclopedia of Islam*, "Kāzerūnī." F. Meier, *Die Vita des Scheich Abu Ishaq al-Kazaruni* in *Bibliotheca Islamica*, XIV (Istanbul, 1943). Köprülü, *Origines*, p. 116.

[36] Köprülü, "Anadoluda Islamiyet," *passim*. Theodore Spandugino, *De la origine deli imperatori ottomani, ordini de la corte, forma del guerreggiare loro, religione, rite, et costumi de la natione*, ed. C. Sathas in *Documents inédits relatifs à l'histoire de la Grèce au moyen age* (Paris, 1890), IX, 247 (hereafter cited as Spandugino-Sathas), describes them as follows in the sixteenth century: "Li Calenderi si lassano crescer la barba, et tengone etiamdio li capelli longi, vanno vestiti di sacco, overo alcuno di gabeniccio, et alcuni di pelle di castrato con le pelo di fuora; questi, intra li altri lore religiosi, usano manco la lussuria, et portano apiccati ale loro orecchie, che sono forate, certi anelli di ferro, et altri anelli de ferro alla pelle del membro genitale, per non lussuriare; portano etiam ferri intorno al cello et le braccie. Questi sono piu honorati et reputati, et tenuti in maggior existimation di santita che tutti li altri."

populations. They had no (or very few) zawiyas and wandered about in bands accompanied by flags, drums, and strange music. Their greatest appeal, generally, was to members of the lower and uneducated classes. Their doctrine of disregard for formal religious observances led to great laxity and immorality in their behavior. They were of major importance in the historical development of Asia Minor, for it was the Kalandars, or dervishes like them but called by other names, who had such great influence among the Turkmen babas in causing them to rebel against the Seljuk government and also in exciting them to the djihad on the frontiers against the Christians. The penetration of the Kalandars into Asia Minor was accompanied by the appearance of another heterodox group, that of the Haydariyya, who likewise had their major appeal among the tribesmen in the villages and plains.[37]

The evolution of these tariqas and the continuous emergence of new branches by the fifteenth and sixteenth centuries were truly phenomenal. There were the Zayniyya and the Badraddiniyya;[38] from the Chalvatiyya emerged the Shabaniyya, Rushaniyya and Gulshaniyya;[39] from the Bayramiyya the 'Isawiyya, Himmatiyya, Tannsuwiyya, and Shamsiyya.[40]

Though a number of the above groups played significant roles in the history of the period, certainly the most famous and widespread of the dervish brotherhoods within the Ottoman Empire came to be those of the Bektashis and Mawlawis, the former originally a "rural" order, the latter

---

[37] Gibb and Bowen, *Islamic Society*, I₂, 188. J. K. Birge, *The Bektashi Order of Dervishes* (London, 1937), p. 38. Köprülü, *Mutassaviflar*, pp. 66–67; "Anadoluda Islamiyet," 290 ff. Babinger, "Kalandariya," *Shorter Encyclopedia of Islam*, and also *I.A.*; Der Islam, XI (1921), 94–95. Köprülü, *Origines*, pp. 118–119. Köprülü had promised a systematic monograph on this important and interesting subject. In general the connections and relations of the Turkmen babas, Yasawiyya, Haydariyya, Kalandariyya, need to be clarified by further research. This need is brought out by the vagueness in the various scholarly treatments of that most important social and religious phenomenon, the revolt of Baba Ishaq of Amasya in 1239. Köprülü, *Origines*, pp. 118, 122, maintains that the Babais originated in the Yasawiyya and Kalandariyya and that these Babais are the Abdal-i-Rum, representing a melange of heterodox brotherhoods such as those mentioned above and also the traditions of the Anatolian tribesmen. These dervishes, distinguished in the sources by the title *abdal*, accompanied the Ottoman sultans in their conquests and spread Islam far and wide. On the revolt of the Babais one may consult Köprülü, "Anadoluda Islamiyet," pp. 302–305; *Mutassaviflar*, pp. 232–234; *Origines*, pp. 58–59. Ibn Bibi-Duda, pp. 216 ff. Cahen, "Babai," EI₂.

[38] Kissling, "Einiges über den Zejnîje-Orden im Osmanischen Reich," *Der Islam*, XXXIX (1964), 143–179; "Das Menaqybname Scheich Bedr ed-Din's des Sohnes des Richters von Samavna," *Z.D.M.G.*, C (1950), 112–176; "Badr al-Din b. Kadi Samawna," EI₂. Babinger, "Schejch Bedr el-din, der Sohn des Richters von Simaw, ein Beitrag zur Geschichte des Sektenwesens im altosmanischen Reich," *Der Islam*, XI (1921), 1–106. Spandugino-Sathas, pp. 247–248. Babinger, "Das Grabmal des Schejchs Bedr al-Din zu Serres," *Der Islam*, XVII (1928), 100–102.

[39] Kissling, "Ša'bân Velî und die Ša'bânijje," *Serta Monacensia. Franz Babinger zum 15. Januar 1951 als Festgruss dargebracht* (Leiden, 1952), pp. 86–109.

[40] Kissling, "Zum Geschichte des Derwischenordens der Bajramijje," *Südost Forschungen*, XV (1956), 237–267; "Aq Şems-ed-Din. Ein türkischer Heiligen aus der Endzeit von Byzanz," *B.Z.*, XLIV (1951), 322–333. B. Lewis, "Bayramiyya," EI₂. Gölpinarlï, "Bayramiye," *I.A.*

an urban one.[41] The earliest written version of the life of Hadji Bektash, spiritual founder of the Bektashis, goes back only to the beginning of the fifteenth century and is very heavily encrusted with tradition and legends, added to enhance the origins of the order.[42] Consequently, it is only with the aid of scattered references, from earlier sources, that the history or biography of Hadji Bektash can be controlled, though it is obvious that the Vilayetname contains a historical kernel going back to the thirteenth century. This early portion of the work is of greater interest for the insight into Bektashi mentality and outlook in the fifteenth century rather than for the facts of Bektash's life.[43] It is a colorful mixture of selections from the history and legends of the shiites, embellished with miracles of the Khurasani holy men and details from the background of Hadji Bektash himself. His *silsile* or genealogy is traced from Muhammad the prophet, through Ali, as is fitting for the founder of a sufi order, and eventually he is made the son and heir of the ruler of Nishapur.[44] According to the tradition, after being educated by Lokman Perende and initiated into dervish life by Ahmad Yasawi (an anachronism), the latter sent Hadji Bektash to Rum (Anatolia).[45] The Vilayetname relates that the 57,000 dervishes of Rum gathered to block his entrance, so Bektash changed into a dove,[46] flew to heaven, and then landed at Suludja Kara Öyük near Kirshehir.[47] The remainder of his life in Anatolia was spent in wandering over various parts, winning disciples and converts, and performing spectacular miracles. He entered into contact with many sectors of Anatolian society, including the pagan nomads, Muslims, and Christians.

[41] Still the best discussion of the dervish movement in Asia Minor during the period of the Seljuks and Beyliks is that of Gordlevskii, *Izbrannye Soch.*, I, 197–214, and also, 219–225.

[42] R. Tschudi, "Bektashiyya," EI₂. E. Gross, *Das Vilayetname des Hadji Bektash*, edited in *Türkische Bibliotheque*, XXV (1927), 204 (hereafter cited as Vilayetname-Gross). This latter includes translations of only a portion of the text. See Gölpinarlï, *Vilayetname* (Istanbul, 1958). Köprülü, "Bektaş," *I.A.* G. Jacob, *Beiträge zur Kenntnis des Derwisch-Ordens der Bektaschis*, in *Türkische Bibliothek*, vol. IX (1908). K. Samancïgïl, *Bektaşilik tarihi* (Istanbul, 1945).

[43] Vilayetname-Gross, p. 202. The composite nature of this part of the work is quite obvious, for the fifteenth-century compiler or editor has not bothered to integrate and unify this portion of the biography.

[44] Vilayetname-Gross, pp. 10–13. This latter detail is typical of the oriental holy man's life, i.e., the young prince who gives up his throne for the religious life, and is as old or older than the story of Buddha. The Vilayetname, having manufactured the necessary genealogy, provides Hadji Bektash with desirable spiritual affiliations to famous Sufis. But this is done in a very confused fashion, as he is variously provided with the famous Ahmad Yasawi, who certainly died before Hadjii Bektash was born, and then with Lokman Perende (a disciple of Yasawi). This effort on the part of the biographers is understandable, and actually there is some truth in it if one takes the story symbolically. For Hadji Bektash, born in Khurasan, must certainly have come under the influence of the mysticism preached earlier by Ahmad Yasawi.

[45] Vilayetname-Gross, pp. 15–33.

[46] See Köprülü, *Chamanisme*, passim, for this phenomenon of changing into the form of a bird, which he asserts to be of Shaman origin.

[47] Vilayetname-Gross, pp. 36–39.

Among the more famous disciples that the Vilayetname claims for Hadji Bektash are the Turkish poet Yunus Emre[48] and Akhi Evran.[49]

Actually much of the narrative in the Vilayetname is legendary, but one cannot fail to recognize the historical kernel in it nor to perceive in many of the fantastic stories a symbolic or cultural truth. Hadji Bektash did actually come to Anatolia from Khurasan in the thirteenth century,[50] where he came to be connected with the great movement of the Turkmen babas.[51] He was a disciple of the famous Baba Ishaq who unleashed the bloody revolt of the Turkmen tribes which fatally weakened the Seljuk state of Konya on the eve of the Mongol invasion.[52] More important for the fate of Byzantine civilization, Bektash was highly successful in winning followers and was eventually recognized as one of the principal holy men in Anatolia. Though he himself probably did not found an actual dervish fraternity, by the fourteenth century the Bektashi order had a formal existence.[53] Subsequently, the brotherhood underwent two marked changes: first, in the early fifteenth century heavy Hurufi influence (the latter were spreading over all Anatolia and were extremely influential with Muhammad II),[54] and second, in the early sixteenth century Balïm Sultan, known as the second founder of the order, introduced certain new practices (including celibacy).[55]

[48] Vilayetname-Gross, pp. 78–79. Birge, *Bektashi*, pp. 53–54, feels this to be correct historically.

[49] Vilayetname-Gross, pp. 82–89, this seems to be a fabrication. His link to the person of Osman and to the early Ottoman conquests in Bithynia is very probably mythical, *ibid.*, p. 138. His miracles are many and varied. He causes stones to talk and raises the dead, *ibid.*, p. 121; Predicts the execution of the beg of Kayseri, *ibid.*, p. 124; Saves ships and men from sinking at sea, *ibid.*, pp. 127–128. On his way to the Holy Places he turns lions into stone and is greeted by fish in the rivers, *ibid.*, pp. 35–36. One of his spectacular feats is related in a story that further illustrates the competition and rivalry of the holy men for religious leadership among the dervishes of Anatolia. Seyid Muhammad Harran of Akshehir went forth to meet Hadji Bektash and to impress him with his own great religious powers. He rode astride a lion with a serpent as a whip and accompanied by 300 mollahs. Hadji Bektash, not to be outdone, spread his prayer rug over a stone, commanded the stone to walk and thus confronted his rival. He explained to the latter that while anyone could make an animal walk, it was not the same thing as causing a stone to move! Birge, *Bektashi*, p. 39.

[50] Birge, *Bektashi*, pp. 41–43. He is mentioned as a contemporary and rival of Djalal al-Din Rumi, Eflaki-Huart, I, 296–297. He also appears in a wakf document of 1295 as already dead, and again in 1297. A wakf document of 1306 mentions the town of Hadji Bektash.

[51] Eflaki-Huart, I, 296–297. Tschudi, "Bektashiyya," EI₂. Cahen, "Babai," EI₂. Köprülü, "Bektas," *I.A.*

[52] Birge, *Bektashi*, pp. 43–44. Köprülü, "Les origines du Bektachisme," *Actes du Congrès international d'histoire des religions* (Paris, 1925), II, 407 (hereafter cited as Köprülü, "Bektachisme,") who corrects a translation of Huart in Eflaki-Huart, I, 296–297, that described Hadji Bektash as Rasul Allah, to read "the disciple of Rasul Allah." Also Ashïkpashazade-Ali, p. 201, records in the fifteenth century that when Hadji Bektash came to Anatolia he became a disciple of Baba Ilyas or Baba Ishaq.

[53] Tschudi, "Bektashiya," EI₂. Birge, *Bektashi*, p. 50. Gibb and Bowen, *Islamic Society*, I₂, 190 ff., however, maintain that it was not until the fifteenth century that it became a formally organized order.

[54] Birge, *Bektashi*, pp. 58–62, 148 ff.

[55] *Ibid.*, p. 56. He was born at Dimotika of a Christian mother and a Bektashi father. This recalls the series of mixed marriages in the family of Badr al-Din.

Bektashi doctrine is a conglomeration of widely varying doctrines and influences, and hence it has been very difficult to give it a strict and clear-cut definition. Because of the influence of so many different religious groups from whom elements were absorbed into the order, its practices and beliefs were extremely disparate. Thirteenth-century Anatolia, the seed bed in which the Bektashis sprouted, was overrun by Kalandar and Haydari dervishes (both of which were batini), and Baba Ishaq the pir of Hadji Bektash was probably himself a Kalandar.[56] Consequently, the Bektashis were markedly heterodox from the beginning, and this heterodoxy was greatly strengthened in the fifteenth century by Hurufi penetration. The Bektashis were strongly shiite in their tendencies, acknowledging the twelve imams, revering Ali and his sons during Muharrem. They observed the practice of *tevella* and *teberra* (friends of the friends of Ali, and enemies of his enemies). There were also definite traces of old shaman traditions that the Turkmen tribes conserved through their babas.[57] Perhaps the participation of unveiled women in the Bektashi ceremonial is a reflection of shaman holdovers. The sema, or ritual dance, and the hymns of the Bektashis have been compared to the ecstatic dances of the shamans and to their incantations, while the sacrifice of animals, especially oxen, is possibly another such old tradition.[58] Many of the miracles of the Bektashi saints are formed on old traditions, especially the miracles in which the holy man takes the form of a flying bird. The shaving of the beard, while at the same time allowing the mustache to grow long, was probably a holdover from such shaman practices.[59] On the other hand, there are many doctrines and practices that are similar to those of the Christians, though in some cases this would not necessarily imply a Christian origin. It is difficult, however, to avoid the conclusion that similar practices and doctrines existed because of the entrance of Christians into the order, and because of close relations between Bektashis and Christians.[60] Christian baptism is paralleled, as a cleansing of sins, by the

---

[56] Köprülü, "Bektachisme," pp. 398, 404.

[57] Köprülü sees in these babas nothing more than the old Qazogan under a thin veneer of heretical Islam. A. Inan, "Müslüman Türklerde Şamanism kalïntïlarï," *Ilahiyat Fakültesi Dergisi*, I₄ (1952), 19–30. P. N. Boratav, "Vestiges oguz dans la tradition bektaşi," *Akten des XXIV internationalen Orientalisten-Kongresses* (Munich, 1957), pp. 382–385.

[58] The Christians had also long practiced animal sacrifice, see chapter vii. Justinian is said to have performed animal sacrifice upon completion of St. Sophia, Th. Preger, *Scriptores Originum Constantinopolitanarum* (Leipzig, 1901), I, 104.

[59] Birge, *Bektashi*, pp. 213–214.

[60] Köprülü, "Bektachisme," p. 463, had been the most active opponent of this idea. He maintained that many of these elements, especially among the Bektashi Kïzïlbash, go back to pre-Christian practices in Anatolia. But this of course says nothing, for in effect most of Christian folk practice is itself pre-Christian. G. Jacob has emphasized the pre-Muslim elements, "Die Bektaschijje in ihrem Verhältnis zu verwandten Erscheinungen," *Abhand. der philos.-philolog. Kl. der Kön. Bayer. Akad. der Wiss.*, XXIV (Munich, 1909), 1–53; Jacob, "Fortleben von antiken Mysterien und Altchristlichem im Islam," *Der Islam*, II (1911), 232–234, He too is not always convincing. Kissling, "Eine bektasitische Version der Legende von den zwei Erzsündern," *Z.D.M.G.*, XCIX (1945/49),

Bektashi practice of ablution with its accompanying formulas before the aynicem. Chrism is parallel to the Bektashi annointing with rose water and the accompanying ceremony. The Holy Eucharist of the Christians as a symbol of Christ's death is similar to the use of wine and bread in the aynicem in memory of Huseyn's death, in either case only the initiate partaking in the rite. Both among Bektashis and Christians there were celibate and married priests and babas. Christian confession and penitence were similar to the Bektashi practice of *baş okutmak*, while Christian excommunication was not unlike the Bektashi *düşkünlük*.[61] Other items are more obviously incidental or accidental parallels that the Bektashis employed to good propaganda advantage among the Christians. They equated the twelve imams with the twelve apostles; the virgin birth of Christ with that of Balîm Sultan, the second founder of the order. They considered Hadji Bektash a reincarnation of St. Charalambus. As the Christians had a Trinity, so did the Bektashis, consisting of God, Muhammad, and Ali.[62] And, of course, Bektashi mysticism as was true of most Islamic mystical orders, ultimately derived much of its mystical doctrine from Neoplatonism in which the Godhead created the world by emanating from itself: It is obvious how ecletic and syncretistic Bektashism was, and how accommodating and latitudinarian it was. This syncretism, which so facilitated the conversion from Christianity to Islam, recalls the religious syncretism that had accelerated the transition from paganism to Christianity a thousand years earlier in Anatolia.

Because of the great variety of doctrines Bektashism embraced, one would expect to find a strong element of proselytization in the history of the brotherhood. This was certainly characteristic of many of the orders in Khurasan, particularly of the Kazaruniyya and the Yasawiyya, both of which are represented as having converted large numbers of Zoroastrians, Jews, and pagan Turks. The conditions of Anatolian society in the thirteenth and fourteenth centuries were similar, no doubt, to those of Khurassan in certain respects. Both areas were the scenes of upheaval brought on by continued strife, wars, destruction, and the entrance of new ethnic groups, the Turks, who were either pagan or superficially Islamized. Both regions also possessed considerable non-Muslim populations, Anatolia more so than Khurasan. The societies in Khurasan and Anatolia received severe external shocks, shocks that undermined the validity of the old religious and social values of the non-Muslims and prepared the way for the penetration of new ways. Obviously these were

---

181–210, traces the origins of certain motifs in Bektashi legends to Anatolian Byzantine cultural circles. On this syncretizing and popular character see K. E. Müller, *Kulturhistorische Studien zur Genese Pseudo-islamischer Sektengebilde in Vorderasien* (Wiesbaden, 1967)· E. Krohn, "Vorislamisches in einigen islamischen Sekten und Derwischerden," *Ethnologische Studien*, I (1931), 295–345.

[61] Birge, *Bektashi*, p. 216.

[62] *Ibid.*, pp. 217–218.

areas in which conditions were rife for the work and activity of religious missionaries. It was the dynamic, though heterodox and often heretical, dervish orders rather than the conservative, static sunni ulema, who propagated most aggressively the new "values" in these areas in a language and form that readily communicated with the masses. This missionary spirit is to be found in the Vilayetname of Hadji Bektash, wherein he and his disciples are seen actively proselytizing: Muslims adhere to their "way" rather than to the other religious "ways"; pagans are converted to Islam and enter their dervish order; finally, Christians are likewise converted by the Bektashis as adherents to their particular religious fraternity. The last part of the Vilayetname, in which the sending out of Hadji Bektash's disciples is described, clearly illustrates this missionary aspect of Bektashism.

The most notable of the Muslims whom Hadji Bektash allegedly converts into a follower of his "way" in the Vilayetname is the famous poet Yunus Emre.[63] Though he "converted" other Muslims to the "way" (such as the "robber" of Germiyan),[64] his missionary activity, and that of his disciples, is more significant among the pagans and Christian infidels than among the Muslims. Indeed, the biography of Hadji Bektash attributes successful missionary activity to him even before he left Khurasan to come to Anatolia. This is elaborated in the comparatively long incident of the attempted conquest and conversion of the district of Bedakhshan.[65] This Bedakhshan episode, occurring in the early period of

[63] See Vilayetname-Gross, pp. 39–40, for the Bektashi view of Tapdïk Emre's adherence to Bektashism. See also A. Gölpinarlï, *Yunus Emre ve tassavuf* (Istanbul, 1961). M. T. Açaroğlu, "Yunus Emre için bir bibliyografya denemesi," *Kitap Belleten*, IV (Ekim, 1963), 8–10. Yunus Emre is portrayed, in the Vilayetname, as a farmer in the village of Sarïköy to the north of Sivrihisar in the region of the Sakaria River. He comes to Hadji Bektash as a result of a great drought because of which the fields yielded no grain that particular year. So Yunus Emre decided to load up his oxen with wild plums, journey to Suludja Kara Öyük, and attempt to trade the plums for wheat at the establishment of Hadji Bektash. On his arrival he presented the plums to Hadji Bektash and then remained with him for a few days, after which he decided to take leave of his host. Hadji Bektash offered his guest a certain amount of wheat or a blessing for each plum. Emre, inasmuch as he had a family, said he would prefer the wheat, whereupon Hadji Bektash raised his offer to two blessings per plum and finally to ten. But his guest persisted in collecting the wheat, which he loaded on the oxen and then set out for home. As soon as he had left Suludja Kara Öyük, however, he repented his choice and returned to Hadji Bektash in an effort to exchange the wheat for the religious blessing. Bektash declared that it was too late and that if he still desired the blessing he would have to go to Tapdïk Emre in order, finally, to attain it. For the next forty years Yunus Emre is said to have remained in the service of Tapdïk Emre cutting and hauling wood. At the end of this period he received the religious blessing of Hadji Bektash and then became a great poet. Vilayetname-Gross, pp. 78–80. Köprülü, *Mutasavvïflar, passim,* denies that Yunus Emre was a disciple of Hadji Bektash, asserting that it was later Bektashi legend that appropriated the poet. But Birge, *Bektashi,* pp. 53–55, and Gölpinarli, *Yunus Emre hayatï* (Istanbul, 1936), pp. 11 ff., argue for the genuineness of the tradition.

[64] Ibn Battuta-Gibb, II, 424, refers to the beg of Germiyan and his followers as nothing more than bandits who infest the roads. In another episode of the Vilayetname-Gross, pp. 94–95, occurs the conversion to Bektashism of the bandit of Germiyan, whose descendants came to be known as the Bostandjï Babaoğullari.

[65] Vilayetname-Gross, pp. 21–28.

Hadji Bektash's biography, is largely mythical and highly anachronistic. It is the spirit that the biography reflects, rather than the accuracy or inaccuracy of the factual content, which is significant, for it is a missionary and proselytizing zeal that incorporated this incident into the Vilayetname sometime between the thirteenth and the early fifteenth century. The incorporation of the Bedakhshan story into the body of the Vilayetname in this period reflects an important historical fact. At this time the Bektashi order was very much concerned with missionary activities and, consequently, in the telling and composition of Bektash's early life, the compilers felt it imperative that he should have performed important conversions while still living in the province of Khurasan.

In the next conversionary incident there are again anachronistic and legendary elements intertwined with historical fact. Inasmuch as the event occurred in the period after Hadji Bektash had come into Anatolia, there is less of the mythical and more of the historical than there was in the Bedakhshan narrative. In this particular incident of the Vilayetname, Hadji Bektash decided to send his disciple Djan Baba to a large tribe of pagan Tatars under Kelü Khan camping in the vicinity of Erzindjan in easternmost Asia Minor. The Tatars, finally convinced of the great religious power of Islam, began to discuss the possibility of becoming converts, and after a final demonstration of the true faith, they converted. The Tatar begs held a council of war and decided that as they had now become Muslims, they could not war on their fellow Muslims in Anatolia. Desiring to convert other lands and people to the new religion by war and conquest, they invaded the land of Kelü Khan's father, but when he refused to accept the new religion they decided to petition the Seljuk sultan 'Ala' al-Din for lands. To this purpose Kelü Khan sent a letter to the sultan, informing him that as he had become a Muslim he could not return to his father's land, and, consequently, the sultan should give him land with both summer and winter pastures (the letter also informed 'Ala' al-Din of Kelü Khan's conquest of Bagdad!). The sultan ceded to the Tatars the districts between Sivas and Kayseri (as summer pastures) and those between Chorum and Ankara (as winter grounds). The grant included the stipulations that the Tatars could never transgress these set boundaries, that they were to be obedient to the law of the land, and that they were to perform military service for the sultans.[66]

---

[66] *Ibid.*, pp. 66–69. These Tatars being pagan, Hadji Bektash had instructed Djan Baba to inform their leader Kelü Khan that they could not enter the land of Rum if they did not first accept Islam. The Tatar khan, on receiving Djan Baba and his message, had him boiled in a kettle for three days. But as the victim emerged unhurt the Tatars then ordered him to be burned alive. The dervish challenged the religious head of the Tatars to undergo the trial with him, and though the Tatar was afraid, yet he could not let the challenge go unheeded. So both were immersed in the fire and remained there for three days. At the end of this period Djan Baba emerged from the flames unharmed but all that had remained of the Tatar was a finger which Djan Baba had kept in his own hand. Upon showing the finger to Kelü Khan, the dervish remarked that had the unfortunate holy man entrusted him with his heart rather than with his finger he would

The Vilayetname remarks that the sultan and the Seljuk nobles were overjoyed at Hadji Bektash's success in settling such a difficult problem for them. So they presented him with many gifts and henceforth whenever 'Ala' al-Din was in need or in difficulty he sought the advice of Hadji Bektash. Not satisfied with the Herculean labors that the compilers of the Vilayetname had heaped upon the holy man, they add that it was through the latter's miracles that 'Ala' al-Din was able to conquer western Anatolia.[67] The relationship of the Tatars with Bektash and his establishment, after the former had entered and settled in Anatolia, continued to be a close one. Twice a year the Tatar begs and people of rank, before their departure for the summer pastures and after their entrance into the winter quarters, went to the tekke of Hadji Bektash. They brought with them as offerings numerous livestock, remained in the tekke as guests for a few days, and then went on their way.[68] Even though the Tatars had been converted to Islam they had persisted in many of their old religious practices and beliefs. The most flagrant example of this, and certainly the most offensive to the Islamic community, was the fact that the Tatars had not abandoned their idols. Consequently, after a number of years had passed (Kelü Khan had died and been succeeded by another Khan), Bektash sent Huva Ata, one of his disciples, to destroy the Tatar idols. After overcoming initial difficulties and Tatar reluctance, he succeeded in persuading the nomads to abandon their idols and messengers were then sent among the Tatars ordering them to burn their idols. Huva Ata remained among the Tatars instructing them in Islam and finally died among them. His grave, according to the Vilayetname, was in the town of Balï Sheikh at the foot of Denek Daǧï to the east of Ankara.[69]

Certain anachronistic elements are immediately apparent in the narrative of the entrance into Anatolia and conversion to Islam of these

---

have still been alive. The khan's wife devised a final plan by which the spiritual strength and powers of the dervish and hence of the new religion would be tested. He would be given poison, and if he survived they would all accept Islam. Djan Baba drank the poison without any ill effect and the Tatars accepted Islam.

[67] Vilayetname-Gross, 70–71, an obvious anachronism.

[68] *Ibid.*, p. 71.

[69] *Ibid.*, pp. 71–73. The Tatars, unaware of Huva Ata's mission, received him with great hospitality and kindness as a disciple of Hadji Bektash. The guest remained with them for a year, attempting at first to identify the house of their idols and then to burn it and the idols. After having identified the idol house he waited until the khan of the Tatars had gone out to hunt before putting his plan into effect. He built a funeral pyre, burned the idols and their housing and then jumped into the flame. When the khan returned and inquired as to the meaning of these actions, Huva Ata replied that Islam did not tolerate the worship of idols, and if the idols had possessed any efficacy, the fire would not have consumed them but would have left them untouched, as it had left Huva Ata unharmed. On idolatry among Mongols and Tatars, see chapter iii. The continued and close connections of the Bektashis and these new converts is illustrated by other incidents in the Vilayetname (*ibid.*, p.121). Hadji Bektash settled a dispute between two Tatar fathers by bringing back to life the son of one killed by the son of the other. In *ibid.*, pp. 122–126, he intervenes with the Seljuk authorities at Kayseri on behalf of the son of one of the Tatar nobles.

Tatar tribesmen. But even so, both of these events have in fact a solid historical background. We know that in the thirteenth century Turkmen and Mongol tribes were settled in the vicinity of Ankara in considerable numbers,[70] and the disciples of Hadji Bektash had a very close and definite relationship with the emirates of western Asia Minor. It is highly probable that they participated in the Turkish advance into these areas or else they appeared in the areas soon after their conquest.[71] The great influence that Hadji Bektash and his followers enjoyed among the tribesmen is in keeping with the tradition of all that we know of the early history of the Bektashi order. All scholars have emphasized the "rural" character of the order and the fact that it exercised its influence predominantly among the tribes rather than in the urban centers during this early period. Of Hadji Bektash's five disciples mentioned at the end of the Vilayetname, only one is sent to an old established Muslim urban center—to Konya. The other four go to the Turkmen tribes on the western borders. Bektash was thus in the direct tradition of his own spiritual master, Baba Ishaq, who had acquired preeminence among the Anatolian Turkmens. The story of the Tatar conversion has an appreciable amount of highly probable and realistic detail. It represents the conversion of the Tatars as a gradual process in which the Tatars kept their idols for a considerable time and finally abandoned them with the greatest reluctance. The large number of specifics in the relationship between the dervish leader and his followers on the one hand, and the Tatar tribesmen on the other, would seem to imply that we are dealing here with an actual historical fact, the conversion of a large tribe of Tatars by the Bektashis. The Seljuk leaders would naturally attempt to maintain a friendly relationship with dervishes who had attained great influence among the troublesome tribes, for the lesson that Baba Ishaq had taught them was not forgotten. The prestige that Hadji Bektash is depicted as enjoying with 'Ala' al-Din, though not factually correct, is nevertheless indicative of the prestige he and his followers enjoyed with later rulers.

Thus far Hadji Bektash and his followers appear as energetic missionaries among Muslims and pagans in Central Asia and Anatolia. One would expect to see them in a similar relationship with the Christians, especially in Anatolia during the thirteenth and fourteenth centuries.

---

[70] Köprülü, *Origines*, p. 53. For the nomadic settlements around Ankara see chapter iii. Anachronistic is the detail that these Tatars, having conquered Baghdad, petitioned the Seljuk sultan, 'Ala' al-Din, for lands in his kingdom. The death of this sultan (1237) took place some twenty years before the Mongol conquest of Baghdad in 1258. Similarly the assertion of the Vilayetname that Hadji Bektash played a major role in assisting 'Ala' al-Din to conquer western Asia Minor, i.e. such places as Germiyan, Denizli, Kutahya, Menteshe, is anachronistic. Some of these were conquered at the end of the thirteenth and the beginning of the fourteenth century.

[71] This is brought out in the short biographies of four of Hadji Bektash's successors, and also by the fact that already in 1321 the ruler of Germiyan had dedicated property to the zawiya of Hadjim Sultan, the disciple of Hadji Bektash. See Birge, *Bektashi*, p. 42.

Actually, incidents of contact with Christians do occur in the Vilayetname. The first of these took place during a journey of Hadji Bektash from Kayseri to Ürgüp. In the town of Sinassus he met a Christian woman who had just baked rye bread and was carrying it in a tray atop her head.[72] When she caught sight of Hadji Bektash she stopped and began to lament the poor quality of the bread and begged him to aid her. Bektash declared to her that henceforth the inhabitants of the town would continue to sow rye but that they would instead harvest wheat. He granted them a second miracle by which they would be able to make large loaves of small portions of flour. And that which he declared to them came true, says the Vilayetname, as a result of which the local inhabitants turned the site of the miracle into a pilgrimage shrine. There was an annual celebration held on the spot by the Christian inhabitants of Sinassus.[73] Though this incident does not expressly mention any conversion, it does point to a close relationship between the Christians of Sinassus and the order of Bektashis. Possibly he became a local "saint" to whom the Christians turned in time of need, and one whom they equated with a corresponding Christain saint.[74]

Of equal interest in the relations with the Christians is the case of the nameless monk in a Christian province not yet taken by the Turks, possibly in western Anatolia. This monk was allegedly a secret follower of Hadji Bektash. It so happened that the land in which the monk lived was visited by a severe drought and everyone was suffering from famine. The monk desired aid from Bektash—more specifically wheat. The latter was able to perceive the wish of the monk and so he ordered a disciple to load one of the pack animals with the grain and to take it to the monk.[75]

[72] On the town of Sinassus, which was still predominantly Greek at the time of the exchange of populations between Greece and Turkey in the twentieth century, I. S. Arkhelaou, Ἡ Σινασσός (Athens, 1899). R. M. Dawkins, *Modern Greek in Asia Minor* (Cambridge, 1916), p. 27. The population in 1905 seems to have been roughly, 3,000 Greeks and 1,000 Turks. The author visited Sinassus in the summer of 1959 and found that the abandoned Greek monastery (of the trogoldyte variety) of St. Nicholas had in its courtyard a tree to which were attached strips of clothing. These were placed there by families, whose members were ill, in the hope that the sick persons would be cured by the "Baba."

[73] Vilayetname-Gross, p. 43.

[74] See, for example, Hasluck, *Christianity and Islam*, II, 571. This aspect of Bektashi-Christian relations will be dealt with at a later point.

[75] Vilayetname-Gross, pp. 95–97. On the way this dervish encountered many people who were also suffering from the famine and who offered him large sums of money for some of the wheat. So as he went the dervish gave in to the condition of these people, and to their attractive financial offers, selling much of the wheat and replacing it with straw and dust. Finally arriving at his destination, he turned the load over to the monk who entertained him very hospitably. Impressed by the hospitality that an infidel tendered him, the dervish thought to himself that this monk would actually make a good Muslim. The monk divined the dervish's thought and informed him that he was already a Muslim, but he was afraid to be such a Muslim as the dervish, who had betrayed the trust of his master by selling some of the grain. The dervish suddenly realized that he was dealing with a holy man and became much distressed at his own conduct. By then it was time for church service and the Christians were entering the church. As soon as the service was over and the last Christian had left the church, the monk, accompanied by the

In another incident Hadji Bektash is said to visit a Christian monk on an island of "Frenkistan" once every year.[76] Yet another anecdote of the Vilayetname involves a certain Christian architect from the court of Murad I who was chosen by the sultan to build the turbe of Hadji Bektash, but while he was atop the new structure a sudden storm threw him down.[77] In desperation he appealed to the saint, was saved, converted to Islam, and entered the Bektashi tekke under the name of Sadik.[78]

These incidents of relations between Hadji Bektash and Christians are of interest not only because they indicate the existence of these relations and of conversions, but they illustrate another point. We have noted earlier the poverty of the Christian church in Anatolia as a result of the Turkish conquests. This poverty prevented the church from coming to the material aid and support of its congregations in times of great need. Now in two of the meetings between Christians and the dervish saint, the Christians are appealing for wheat, the staff of life, not for religious benefits (this was also the case with the poet Yunus Emre). The Bektashis, in the Vilayetname, appear as a group that dispenses charity and food to all the needy, with a guest house and kitchen by the side of the tekke at Suludja Kara Öyük to accommodate all such needy people. It is certainly true that this dervish fraternity along with others were able to furnish to Christians, as well as to Muslims, the charity and sustenance that the Christian church was no longer able to provide.

Aside from his personal contacts with Christians, Hadji Bektash allegedly dispatched a number of missionaries to Christian lands in order to convert them to Islam. The first of these was Sarï Saltïk, a shepherd, whom Bektash allegedly met on Mt. Arefat while on his way to the holy well of Zemzem. Sarï Saltïk joined Bektash and then went to Rum after his new pir had bestowed upon him a wooden sword, bow, seven arrows,

---

dervish, entered the church and closed the door securely behind him. He then lifted a stone slab, opened a door underneath it, and there came into view a beautiful room which they entered. There lay a bundle of fine clothing, a tall dervish cap, and in the mihrab a reading stand with a Koran. The monk, to the great amazement of the dervish, donned the clothing and dervish cap and prayed before the mihrab. Then he opened the Koran and began his recitation. Finally he prayed once more, passed his hand over his face, and informed the astonished dervish that he was himself a Bektashi dervish. The religious ceremony over, the monk-dervish removed the dervish garb and put on again his Christian garment. This curious anecdote is interesting from the point of view of culture, though it may have no basis in actual historical fact. The double religious sanctuary is well known in Anatolia, as are crypto-religious phenomena and the close relations of Muslim dervishes and Christian monks.

[76] Vilayetname-Gross, pp. 119–120. This probably refers to the Aegean isles. Firenk and Frenkistan are used frequently by Muslim authors of Anatolia to refer to Greeks and Greek territory.

[77] Vilayetname-Gross, p. 151, no. 2.

[78] Ibid., p. 152. On Christian architects and their connections with dervish orders and their conversions, see chapter iii. R.C.E.A., XII, 164–165. Eflaki-Huart, II, 3. Kissling, "Ša'bân Veli und die Ša'bânijje," Serta Monacensia (Leiden, 1952), p. 91.

and prayer rug. Saltïk and his accomplices proceeded to missionize in Georgia and the Dobrudja.[79]

The sending out of Djamal Seyid, Sarï Ismail, Hadjim Sultan, Rasul Baba, and Pirab Sultan, with which the Vilayetname closes, emphasizes above all the missionary activity of the order. Djamal Seyid went to the province of Altïntash (western Asia Minor) where many of the inhabitants became his followers. Hadjim Sultan received from the Beg of Germiyan the place of Susuz in the neighborhood of Ushak (which he was to retain upon slaying the dragon that infested the vicinity).[80] Sarï Ismail, in setting out for the area that Bektash assigned to him, hurled his cane into the air (according to his pir he was to settle where the cane landed). It happened that the stick came down onto the cupola of a Christian church in Tavas[81] in the province of Menteshe. The cane went through the dome, entered the church, and appeared in the form of a dragon to the monk who was inside the church reading the Gospels. The latter went out to greet the dervish, kissed his hand, and touched his face to Ismail's foot. Thereupon Ismail entered the Christian temple, transformed it into a beautiful dervish monastery, and converted the monk to Islam. In a second miracle, even more wondrous than the first one, Sarï Ismail took the form of a marvelous yellow falcon with a musical instrument around his neck and bells attached to his feet. The presence of such a strange bird did not long escape the notice of Zapun, the Christian prince of Tavas. In the meantime Ismail reverted to human form and appeared to the Christian inhabitants as Jesus. The Christian prince, his nobles and the people went to the dervish, greeted him and, at the latter's bidding, were converted to Islam. Thereafter Ismail settled in Tavas, took over the monastery of the monk (whom he had converted) as his tekke, and many of the town's inhabitants became dervishes.[82]

Rasul Baba was also sent to western Asia Minor to the region of Altïntash, a region ruled by a Christian prince and inhabited by Christians. No less resourceful and spectacular than his fellow dervish Sarï Ismail, he appeared as a golden deer to the Christian prince who was out on the hunt! The prince and his hunting party gave chase to the animal, which finally sought refuge under a church only recently built by the prince. Here Rasul Baba took the form of a dove, flew up and onto the church, came down once more and in a final transformation became a

---

[79] Vilayetname-Gross, pp. 73–77. Ibn Battuta-Gibb, II, 499–500 notes on his travels through the Dobrudja that he stopped in a town by the name of Baba Saltïk, which, he says, was named after an unorthodox religious man. Birge, *Bektashi*, pp. 51–52. Evliya Chelebi, von Hammer, I, ii, 245. Evilya Chelebi, *Seyahatname* I, 659; III, 366. Babinger, "Sarï Saltuk," EI₁.

[80] Vilayetname-Gross, p. 173. R. Tschudi, *Das Vilayetname des Hadschim Sultan*, in *Türkische Bibliotheque* XVIII (Berlin, 1914), 30.

[81] This is the former Greek bishopric of Tabai (plural accusative would be pronounced Tavas), Gelzer, *Ungedruckte Texte*, p. 555, and was a suffragant of the metropolitanate of Caria.

[82] Vilayetname-Gross, pp. 163–168.

human once again. The hunters, greatly astounded at this miracle, touched their faces to the feet of the dervish, who informed the Christians that he was Rasul Baba, sent hither by Hadji Bektash. He appropriated the new church as his residence and converted the Christians to Islam. He next journeyed to Hisardjik two days distant, and the inhabitants of that area also became his followers.[83] The sending of the Bektashi disciples to western Asia Minor where the emirs were conquering the last of the Greek lands, and even into the Balkans, in contrast to the fact that only one disciple was sent south to Konya (a nonborder area), is not without significance. It illustrates not only the missionary aspect of the order but also its "ghazi" associations.

Sarï Saltïk converted Christians not only in Georgia but in the Balkans as well. Djamal Seyid and Hadjim Sultan won followers in the districts of Altïntash and Germiyan, though the Vilayetname does not specifically state that they converted Christians to Islam. Yet there can be no doubt that many of their converts must have been Christians. But the narrative is quite definite in respect to the activities of Sarï Ismail and Rasul Baba, who converted large numbers of Christians to Islam in western Anatolia. Again there is much of the miraculous and fantastic in the stories of the conversions; nevertheless, they certainly represent what actually happened in the area. The town of Tavas, the center of Sarï Ismail's missionary activities, was formerly the Byzantine bishopric of Tabai, one of the many bishoprics that during this period disappeared from the episcopal lists. A chief characteristic of these miracles in the Vilayetname is the overt physical appropriation of Christian churches and monasteries, which are then turned into Muslim religious centers. This fact is supported not only by the testimony of the synodal acta, but also by a flood of contemporary sources (Pachymeres, Dusturname of Enver, Ibn Bibi, Aksaray, Ashïqpashazade).

Despite its semilegendary and wondrous character, the Vilayetname provides the historian with a crucial insight into the problem of cultural change in medieval Anatolia. The Bektashi tradition in the fifteenth century was inspired by a powerful missionizing element, the most essential content of which was the desire to save the souls of others by converting them to "the way." Beneath the thick incrustations of miraculous yellow falcons, golden deer, dragons, flying rugs, and the like, one becomes aware of Baktashi missionaries actively converting Christians in the recently conquered Byzantine domains of western Anatolia. The appropriation of monastic and other ecclesiastical buildings, and the conversions of monks, priests, and laymen, are all facts that we saw described by the Christian ecclesiastical sources. The only difference lies in the fact that the Byzantine description of the process emerges from administrative documents and is therefore couched in mundane, economic, and

[83] *Ibid.*, pp. 191–194.

bureaucratic language, whereas the Muslim account is the product of a wondrous mystic imagination. But the events that the patriarchal synod and the dervish hagiographer describe are one and the same: the cultural transformation of Asia Minor.

THE MAWLAWIS

Though the sources for the history of the Bektashis during the thirteenth and fourteenth centuries are semilegendary and so must be interpreted symbolically, this is not the case with the order of the Mawlawi dervishes. The detailed history of the latter during this period fortunately survives in the writings of Djalal al-Din Rumi and his followers, and the personalities, doctrines, and history of the order during this important era emerge in a somewhat more nearly historical fashion.[84] The Mawlawi writings and history parallel those of the Bektashis in a number of ways and so strengthen

[84] There is a considerable body of literature on the person of Rumi and on the order. The most recent critical studies on Rumi himself are those of H. Ritter, "Celaleddin Rumi," *I.A.*, pp. 53–59; "Philologika, XI. Maulana Galaladdin Rumi und sein Kreis," *Der Islam*, XXVI (1942), 116–158; "Mevlânâ Celâleddin Rûmî ve etrafîndakiler," *T.M.*, VII–VIII (1940–42), 268–281. A. J. Arberry, "Jalal al-Din Rumi," *Islamic Studies*, I (1962), 89–105. A. Gölpinarlï, Mevlana Celaleddin (Istanbul, 1951). B. Fürûzanfer, *Mevlâna Celâleddin*, trans. by N. Uzluk into Turkish (Istanbul, 1963). A. Iqbal, *The Life and Thought of Rumi* (Lahore, 1956). A. Schimmel, "The Symbolical Language of Maulânâ Jalâl al-Dîn Rûmî," *Studies in Islam*, I (1964), 26–40. Bausani, "Djalal al-Din Rumi," EI₂. H. Schaeder, "Die islamische Lehre vom Vollkommenen Menschen, ihre Herkunft und ihre dichterische Gestaltung," *Z.D.M.G.*, LXXIX (1925), 256, discusses the relation of Rumi to Ibn al-'Arabi. R. Nicholson, *Rumi, Poet and Mystic, 1207–1273* (London, 1950). A. Bausani, *Persia religiosa da zaratustra a Baha'u'llal* (Milan, 1959), pp. 251–286. M. Önder, *Mevlana und seine Mausoleum* (1959). Ritter, "Neue Literatur über Maulana Calaluddin Rumi und seinen Orden," *Oriens*, XIII–XIV (1960–61), 342–353.

I have referred to the following translations of Rumi's works; R. A. Nicholson, *The Mathnawi of Jalalu'ddin Rumi*, vols. I–VIII (London, 1925–1940). Arberry, *Discourses of Rumi* (London, 1961), a translation of the *Fîhi ma fîhi*. Nicholson, *Selected Poems from the Dîvanî Shamsi Tabrîz* (Cambridge, 1898). V. von Rosenzweig, *Auswahl aus den Diwanen des . . .* (Vienna, 1838). Gölpinarlï, *Mevlânâ Celâleddin. Mektuplar* (Istanbul, 1963). The contents of the letters are summarized by S. Yaltakaya in *T.M.*, VI (1939), 323–345. A special issue of *Konya halkevi kültür dergisi* (Istanbul, 1943), is devoted to Rumi. On the interesting problem of the use of Greek and Turkish in Rumi's poetry: R. Burguière and R. Mantran, "Quelques vers grecs du XIIIᵉ siècle en caractères arabes," *Byzantion*, XXII (1952), 63–80: S. Yaltakaya, "Mevlana'da türkçe kelimeler ve türkçe siirler," *T.M.*, IV (1934), 111–168.

The works of Gölpinarlï are of especial value. The author was himself, formerly, a dervish and so his writings have the added vitues that accrue from his personal circumstances. His book, *Mevlana'dan sonra Mevlevilik* (Istanbul, 1953), is a veritable mine of information on Mawlawi history, ritual, music, dress, etc. It is very conveniently summarized in his article, "Mevlevilik," *I.A.*, pp. 164–171. Further literature on the order and the writings of Sultan Walad include: Gölpinarlï, *Mevlevî âdâb ve erkân* (Istanbul, 1963). T. Yazïcï, "Mevlana devrinde sema'," *Şarkiyat Mecmuasï*, V (1964), 135–159. Uzluk, *Mevlevilikte resim, resimde Mevleviler* (Ankara, 1957). D. Margouliath, "Mawlawiya," *Shorter Encylcopedia of Islam*, p. 364. Ritter, "Der Reigen der 'Tanzenden Derwische'," *Zeitschrift für vergleichende Musikwissenschaft*, I (1933), 5–32. C. Haurt, *Les saints des derviches tourneurs* (Paris, 1918–1922), I–II. Uzluk, *Divani Sultan Veledin hayat ve eserleri* (Istanbul, 1941). Huart, "De la valeur historique des mémoires des derviches tourneurs," *J.A.*, XIX (1922), 308–317. G. Meyer, "Die griechische Verse im Rebabnama," *B.Z.*, IV (1895), 401–411. V. D. Smirnov, "Les vers dit 'Seljdouk' et le christianisme turc," *Actes du onzième congrès international des orientalistes à Paris 1897, troisième section* (Paris, 1899), pp. 142–157. M. Mansuroğlu, *Sultan Veled'in türkçe manzumeleri* (Istanbul

certain conclusions that were stated in regard to the former brotherhood. Two of the more striking parallels between the two tariqats lie in their active colonization of large parts of Anatolia and their great missionary fervor.

Djalal al-Din Rumi, around whose image, literary production, and mystical practices the Mawlawi order later coalesced, was, like so many other Anatolian holy men, an immigrant from the northeastern reaches of the Muslim world. During the thirteenth century the prosperity and patronage of the sultans in Konya served as powerful magnets in attracting religious men, especially after the Mongol conquests of Iran had begun. Hadji Bektash himself had come from Khurasan, as did many of the disciples of Rumi and his successors.[85] While still a young boy, Rumi left his native Balh in the company of his father Baha' al-Din Walad (a distinguished and learned member of the ulema) shortly before the Mongols conquered the town in 617 (1220–1). After peregrinations that led them as far as Mecca, Baha' al-Din and his son entered Anatolia (probably in 618), settling first in Erzindjan and Akshehir, and then moving south to Laranda within the Seljuk kingdom. Emir Musa, the governor of the town, built a medresse for Rumi's father and the latter remained some seven years in this town. It was at this time that the great Seljuk sultan 'Ala' al-Din invited the ulema from Balh to come to the Seljuk capital and to make it the permanent abode of his descendants. When Rumi accompanied his father to Konya, the city was just entering the period of its greatest splendor. In the preceding half century the sultans had succeeded in consolidating their kingdom and had by their studied, efforts made Konya one of the commercial, artisanal, and, eventually cultural centers in the Islamic world. Mosques, medresses, zawiyas, bazaars, and walls had been, and were still being, built in an effort to embellish the growing city. When the father and son arrived in Konya the sultan invited them to stay in the royal *tasthane* (vestiarium) but Baha' al-Din declined the ruler's hospitality on the grounds that,

> Imams are lodged in the medresses, the zawiyas are suitable for the dervishes, the sarays for the emirs, the caravansarays for the merchants, the chamber corners for the runud, the streets for the strangers.[86]

Consequently he took his retinue to the medresse of Altun Aba.

After the death of Baha' al-Din, Rumi succeeded his father as a preacher and deliverer of fatwas. But he also became the murid of a series of mystics,

---

1958). Gibb and Bowen, *Islamic Society*, I₂, 193–195. Köprülü, "Anadoluda Islamiyet," pp. 388 ff. S. Rymkiewicz, "Gazele Sultana Veleda," *Przeglad Orientalistyczny*, Nr. i (41) (1962), pp. 3–17. Ritter, "Die Mevlanafeier in Konya vom 11.–17. Dezember 1960," *Oriens*, XV (1962), 249–270.

[85] Eflaki-Huart, I, 1, 14, 45–46, 68–69, 113–114, 240–241; II, 3, 393, mentions that holy men and disciples of the Mawlawi Khalifs came from Balh, Tirmid, Tabriz, Merend, Bukhara, Turkestan, Djend, Khodjend, Samarqand. This phenomenon is also to be observed in connection with the Ottoman court in the fourteenth and fifteenth centuries.

[86] *Ibid.*, 22. This is indicative of the Islamic institutional patterns after which Anatolia was molded.

the most influential of whom was Shams al-Din, a dervish of Tabriz. The result was that Rumi developed into one of the greatest mystics in Islam and one of the most remarkable masters of poetic expression in the realm of religious mysticism. By the end of his life (1207–73) he had exercised a great influence upon the religious and cultural history of Konya, and the religious brotherhood that he inspired, the Mawlawi, was to have a profound effect on Anatolian society in the next few centuries. During Rumi's lifetime the force of his personality was such that he attracted a considerable following both inside Konya and in the environs.

Despite the fact that the Mawlawi tariqa and ritual were not formally organized and regulated until after Rumi's death, many of the elements of the order were present in his practices. They had begun to take definite form under Rumi's son and grandson, Sultan Walad (d. 1312) and Ulu Arif Chelebi (d. 1320?) at which time one of the salient characteristics of the Mawlawis came to be the sema' or musical and dancing performance by which the adepts attained spiritual ecstasy. The sema' was usually performed in the tekke after the Friday prayer. The dervishes gathered here with their guests for a common meal, the guests often including the leading members of the urban classes, after which the religious dance took place to the accompaniment of the flute, tambourine, rebab (a sort of guitar), and the keman (a crude violin-like instrument). Through this ritual, which the orthodox ulema violently attacked, the participants attained a spiritual union with God enabling them to see one of His attributes. The use of the dance and music, an aesthetic means of arousing human emotions, had great appeal to the individuals who were exposed to it.[87] Indeed, it was this appeal to the emotions, so

[87] The author had the occasion to hear a recorded performance of this type of music at the turbe of Rumi in Konya, July, 1959, and was indelibly impressed by its melancholy and beauty. The lines of Rumi (trans. A. Arberry, *Sufism* [London, 1950], p. 111)

"Hearken to this Reed forlorn,
Breathing, ever since 'twas torn
From its rushy bed, a strain
Of impassioned love and pain.
The secret of my song, though near,
None can see and none can hear.
Oh, for a friend to know the sign
And mingle all his soul with mine!
'Tis the flame of Love that fired me,
'Tis the wine of Love inspired me.
Wouldst though learn how lovers bleed,
Hearken, hearken to the Reed!"

express this sensation quite aptly. The sema' itself was prefaced by a reading before the assembly and by the performance of a flute solo. Then those of the dervishes and murids who were to participate actively arose and passed before the sheikh three times in saluting him. After the performance of the Sultan Walad devri, as this part of the ceremony was called, the leader of the dance (semazen bashï) came before the sheikh and then one by one the dervishes kissed the hand of the latter. In the ceremonial dancing that followed, the dervishes moved through four cycles during which time they attained ecstasy. This ended with the taksim. After the reading of the Koran and Mathnawi, the ceremony was concluded. For a remarkable example of the dancing phase of the Mawlawi sema' see plate on the fifth page of illustrations.

characteristic of dervish spirituality, which enabled the dervishes to attain such remarkable successes throughout the Seljuk and Ottoman periods. There were other heterodox elements characteristic of the Mawlawis, but Rumi, Sultan Walad, Arif Chelebi, and others of the Mawlawis were able to influence the sultans, the begs, and even the Mongols, so that they were not only protected from the ulema but they also acquired prestige, respectability, and wealth.

Among the upper classes who became devotees of Rumi and the order were Seljuk sultans and governors, Mongol officials, and emirs of the principalities arising on the ruins of the Seljuk state.[88] The fact that they were much more urban-oriented than many other orders strengthened their respectability in a period when there was considerable antagonism between certain groups within rural and urban societies. Aside from heterodox elements, the generally tolerant and eclectic attitudes of the order were no doubt critical factors in the spread of the Mawlawi way throughout the urban centers of Asia Minor. Socially the tariqa was very influential among the artisan and merchant classes, and many of the incidents recounted by Eflaki take place in the bazaars of Konya. This middle-class coloration seems to have been repugnant to certain of the aristocracy, as is evident in an incident occurring during a sema' which Rumi held in the presence of the pervane. The emir Kamal al-Din attempted to calumniate Rumi and his followers to the perwane as being common.

"The disciples of our Master are for the most part ordinary people and artisans; the learned men and people of merit frequent them rarely. Everywhere where there is a tailor, a cotton merchant, or a grocer, him does he accept as a disciple." Suddenly in the middle of the concert our Master (Rumi) uttered such a roar that all swooned. He said: "Miserable one! Was not our Mansur a carder of cotton? Sheikh Abu Bakir Bukhari, was he not a weaver? And that other perfect man, was he not a merchant of glassware?"[89]

Rumi very much resembled Socrates in that he constantly associated with the people of the bazaar, among his favorite haunts having been the caravansaray of the sugar merchants and the cotton bazaar.[90] His followers included merchants, butchers, bakers, tailors, carpenters, painters, goldsmiths,[91] and even prostitutes.[92] The urban lower classes

[88] Eflaki-Huart, I, 24, 80, 98, 167–168, 208, 299; II, 10–11, 14–15, 182–183, 195–197, 272–273, 312–313, 373, 384, 392–393.

[89] *Ibid.*, 117.

[90] *Ibid.*, 75; II, 118–119.

[91] *Ibid.*, 336–337. Rumi, in passing by a goldsmith's shop, was inspired by the musical tic-tac of the workers' hammers to perform his dance on the spot. Also, *ibid.*, II, 198–199, for a similarly inspired sema' in the quarter of the goldsmiths. See the plates in Uzluk, *Mevlevilikte resim, resimde Mevleviler* (Ankara, 1957).

[92] Eflaki-Huart, I, 185–186. In the caravansaray of Diya al-Din there was a female harpist, Ta'ous, who on encountering Rumi became his disciple, and she became so eminent that all the huris of Konya became her followers. Prostitution seems to have been an integral part of life in the caravanasarays, if we may judge by this incident and

similarly gravitated to the order.[93] At times, however, the Mawlawi were at odds with the Akhis, representatives of the ulema, and with some of the other dervish associations. Often the cadis attacked the use of the sema' by the Mawlawis, or competed with them for the favor of the power-ful government officials and the sultans.[94] On a few occasions there were serious difficulties with certain of the akhis over the possession of property,[95] and there was also rivalry of a sort with other dervish orders for the allegiance of the Konyiote populace. For example, when Tadj al-Din, the son of Ahmad al-Rifa'i, came to Konya with a band of Rifa'i dervishes, their remarkable feats soon attracted large numbers from all classes in the city, much to the annoyance of Rumi.[96] Nevertheless, the evidence suggests that the relations of the Mawlawis with cadis, akhis, and other dervishes were more often of an amicable nature and that many of the representatives of the first two groups became disciples of the Mawlawis. The cadis of Amaseia and Sivas became followers of Rumi. Large numbers of the akhi-runud in Konya, Paipert, Sivas, and Akshehir were disciples, and the Mawlawis established friendly connections with a Kalandar tekke in Konya.[97]

Just as the tariqa of Mawlana spread among many classes of Anatolian society, so did it likewise penetrate Anatolia geographically. Though Rumi had a few followers in Amasya, Sivas, and Meram, his activities centered on Konya.[98] It was thanks to the efforts of his son, Sultan Walad, and his grandson, Amir Arif, that the order underwent a very rapid geographical expansion. Sultan Walad is said to have filled Anatolia with

the one that follows. *Ibid.*, II, 70–71. In the caravansaray of Sahib Isfahani were a noto-rious prostitute and her female slaves. When Rumi passed through the khan she and her slaves prostrated themselves before the master, and the prostitute gave up her shameful life to become a disciple. One of the aristocrats of Konya reproached Rumi for his association with the prostitutes of the cabarets. The master justified the life of the pros-titutes in remarking that without the burden that the prostitutes bear, the purity and chastity of honest women would be vanquished by the concupiscence of men.

[93] *Ibid.*, I, 123-124; II, 14, 210. The people often turned to the order in times of calamity, drought, invasions, etc. *Ibid.*, 270–271.

[94] *Ibid.*, I, 103, 119, 128; II, 86.

[95] *Ibid.*, II, 237–239, when the emir Tadj al-Din decided to give the tekke of Ziya al-Din to the Mawlawis, Akhi Ahmad the leader of the runud intervened and attempted to dislodge the brotherhood; also II, 293. *Ibid.*, II, 307, Akhi Mustafa forbade the order to perform the sema' in his house. For an analysis of the relations of the akhis and Mawlawis, Cahen, "Sur les traces des premiers Akhis," *Fuad Köprülü Armağani* (Istanbul, 1953), pp. 81–91.

[96] Eflaki-Huart, II, 203–205. Their marvelous feats were more than Rumi could offer to the sensation seekers of Konya. They walked in fire, put hot irons in the mouth, swallowed serpents, sweat blood, washed with boiling oil, practiced such legerdemain as making sugar, changing wax into laudanum, etc. When Rumi's mother finally went to the medresse of Karatay to see the performance, Rumi was so beside himself with jealous outrage that he punished his mother by inflicting an illness upon her. *Ibid.*, I, 296-297, also records the meeting between Rumi and a disciple of Hadji Bektash.

[97] *Ibid.*, I, 305-307; II, 61, 241, 309, 326-327, 346, 361. Most of the Akhis of Konya became disciples of Sultan Walad. This indicates that the Mawlawis and akhis were not such intractable foes as has been stated in the past. On the association of the two, Gölpinarlĭ, "Mevlevilik," *I.A.*

[98] Eflaki-Huart, I, 83, 107, 109.

his lieutenants,[99] while Arif, through his indefatigable travels and labors, founded zawiyas throughout the peninsula.[100] By the mid-fourteenth century the order was a vital social factor, established in most of Muslim Anatolia and playing an important role among all classes in the towns. Here the influence of the Mawlawis spread not only among the Muslims but also among the dhimmis upon whom the combination of Muslim proselytizing ardor, religious tolerance, and syncretism had a marked effect. This missionizing spirit appears prominently in the biographies of the Mawlawi Khalifs which Eflaki compiled in the middle of the fourteenth century.[101] Djalal al-Din evidently considered himself divinely ordained to missionize among the Christians of Anatolia.

> The Most High reserved great favors for the inhabitants of Asia Minor, who by the prayer of the Great Veridique [Abu Bakir], and [by] those of the Muslim community are the object of the greatest mercy. The region of Asia Minor is the best of the climes, but its inhabitants are ignorant of mystical love. . . . He [God] has withdrawn us [Rumi] from Khurasan to send us to Asia Minor, and has given our successors a domicile in this pure land so that we may spread generously the philosophical stone of our mysteries over the coinage of its inhabitants' existence. [This] in such a manner that we may transform them alchemically and they will become confidants of the world of gnosis and companions of the entire world's mystiques. . . . You [God] removed me from Khurasan in order to lead me to the land of the Greeks so that I might mingle with them and lead them to the good doctrine.[102]

His enthusiasm was such, remarks Eflaki, that Rumi converted 18,000 infidels during his lifetime, and, the author continues, the dervishes persisted in their work of conversion right down to his own day.[103] The tolerance toward, and the free association with, other religious groups were characteristics that also facilitated the conversionary efforts of the Mawlawis. Rumi and members of the order were in frequent contact and indulged in religious discussions with Christian priests, monks, and Jewish rabbis. Both Rumi and his grandson were close friends with the

---

[99] *Ibid.*, II, 263.

[100] For these see *ibid.*, *passim*. Arif had followers and zawiyas in the vilayet of Danishmend, Menteshe, Sivas, Ladik, Tavas, Afyon Karahisar, Tokat, Akshehir, Erzerum, Kavala, Nigde, Amasya, Alaiya, Antalya, Beğshehir, Kayseri, Castamon, Eğridir, Kutahya, Birgi, Laranda, and Paipert. He had close ties with the Germiyan, Ashraf, Aydin, and even Karaman dynasties. There were disciples in such distant regions as Tabriz, Sultaniyya, and Merend.

[101] The missionary spirit discernible in the writings of Eflaki parallels that found in the Vilayetname of Hadji Bektash and in the Danishmendname. But the Menaqib al-Arifin, in sharp contrast to the Vilayetname, was the composition of a fourteenth-century contemporary and was based on observed historical events, many of which are independently confirmed by inscriptions, chronicles, and other sources.

[102] Eflaki-Huart, I, 190. Rumi remarks that he had to utilize music and the dance to appeal to the Anatolians. "Lorsque nous vîmes qu'ils n'inclinaient en aucune manière vers la voie de Dieu, et qu'ils restaient privés des mystères divins, nous insinuâmes ces idées par la voie gracieuse du concert spirituel et de la poésie cadencée, choses conformes au goût des humains; car les habitants de l'Asie Mineure sont des gens de plaisir et soumis à l'influence de la planète Vénus."

[103] *Ibid.*, II, 111-112.

learned abbot of the Greek monastery of "Plato" (St. Chariton) in the district of Konya, and very often they retired there for meditation and conversation with the monks.[104] Disciples of the order visited Christian monks as far away as Constantinople,[105] and, conversely, Christians frequently sought out the leader of the order in Konya.[106] Thus the relations of the dervishes and Christians were friendly and relaxed.[107]

The missionary spirit of the Menaqib al-Arifin, as indeed of the Mawlawi order, emerges most clearly in individual cases of converted dhimmis recounted therein. One is not surprised that the Mawlawis attained such a marked success among the Christians of the towns, for the Christians formed a numerous element, and the brotherhood concentrated its efforts in these areas. Furthermore the dervishes worked under favorable political, social, and economic circumstances, whereas the moral and emotional bonds connecting the Greek Christians with emperor and patriarch in Constantinople had been destroyed or largely corroded. Thus the dervishes often found these Christians quite receptive to their preaching.[108] The most striking and detailed written account of a conversion which has survived is that of Thiryanus 'Ala' al-Din. The reason

---

[104] *Ibid.*, I, 261; II, 67-68, 358. The close association of the abbot with Rumi recalls the relations of Badr al-Din with the monks of Chios. It was also the sight (the Christian monastery) of some of the miracles that Rumi worked. In the nineteenth and twentieth centuries there were three churches and a small mosque within the monastic complex. The Christians of the monastery reported a legend according to which the mosque was built by the Muslims in honor of St. Chariton when he saved Rumi's son from a death fall in the hills surrounding the monastery. This miracle was celebrated, prior to World War I, by an annual gift of oil from the dervishes to the monastery. The leader of the Mawlawis spent one night each year in prayer at this mosque. See Hasluck, *Christianity and Islam*, II, 373-374. There is a photograph of the monastery in Hasluck, "Christianity and Islam under the Sultans at Konia," *Annual of the British School at Athens*, vol. XIX (1912-1913). The church of Sille seems to have had a similar relation with the Mawlawis. For the monastery of St. Chariton, see the recent archaeological study of Eyice, "Konya ile Sille arasında Ak manastır, Menākib al-'Arifin'deki Deyr-i Eflatun," *Sarkiyat Mecmuası*, vol. VI (1966), 135-160.

[105] Eflaki-Huart, I, 105-106. One devotee was ordered to seek forgiveness from a "Frankish" holy man in the "West," I, 78.

[106] *Ibid.*, I, 107-108, 184.

[107] See A. J. Arberry, *Discourses of Rumi* (London, 1961), pp. 134-136 (hereafter cited as Arberry, *Discourses*), for a discussion between Rumi and a Christian on the divinity of Christ. Rumi always prostrated himself before those who greeted him, even if they were infidels, remarks Eflaki-Huart, I, 119. He did so seven times before the Armenian butcher Tenik. Eflaki-Huart, I, 194, he bowed his head thirty-three times in greeting a Christian monk from Constantinople who came to visit him. In keeping with this broad-mindedness, Rumi criticizes a Muslim preacher who in one of his sermons praised God for not having created him and his congregation infidels. Rumi sarcastically remarked that indeed the preacher was of greater worth than an infidel, by one-sixth of a dram! Eflaki-Huart, I, 108. In Arberry, *Discourses*, p. 214, he states that "love for the Creator is latent in all the world and in all men, be they Magians, Jews, or Christians." This again recalls the preachings of Badr al-Din.

[108] Eflaki-Huart, I, 262-263. Rumi remarks that it was easier to convert seventy infidel Greeks than to purify a certain muderris in the medresse of the cotton merchants. Though perhaps this story is more indicative of the obstinacy of the muderris, this receptivity is reflected in other anecdotes. Arberry, *Discourses*, pp. 108-109.

"The Master said: I must go to Toqat, for that region is warm. Although the climate of Antalya is warm, there the majority of the people are Rumis and do not understand

that Elfaki has gone to some trouble to record the particulars is that Thiryanus became one of the more important members of the order.[109] One day the Master, accompanied by his followers, was on his way from the gate of the Horse Bazaar to the tomb of his father when he perceived a crowd of excited people. Upon catching sight of Rumi a few of the spectators hurriedly appealed to him to intercede on behalf of a young Greek who had just slain someone. As Rumi advanced, the police retreated and he spread his mantle about the young dhimmi indicating that the latter was henceforth under his personal protection. When the police prefect reported the affair to the sultan, the latter gave in to Mawlana. He justified his acquiescence as follows: because Rumi had intervened (with the Mongols) on behalf of the whole town he could also intervene on behalf of one individual, even though he was a Greek and a murderer. The companions led Thiryanus to the bath and then brought him to the medresse to pronounce the act of faith before the Master. He was circumcised and so became a Muslim. The ceremony was followed by the performance of a sema', and it is interesting to note that Rumi gave him a new name.

"What is your name?" asked the Master. "Thiryanus," replied the young man. "Henceforth," said Djalal al-Din Rumi, "you shall be called 'Ala' al-Din Thiryanus."[110]

---

our language; though even amongst the Rumis there are people who do understand it. I was speaking one day amongst a group of people, and a party of non-Muslims was present. In the middle of my address they began to weep and to register emotion and ecstasy.

"Someone asked: What do they understand and what do they know? Only one Muslim in a thousand understands this kind of talk. What did they understand, that they should weep?

"The Master answered: It is not necessary that they should understand the inner spirit of these words. The root of the matter is the words themselves, and that they do understand. After all, every one acknowledges the Oneness of God, and He is the Creator and Provider, that He controls every thing, that to Him all things shall return, and that it is He who punishes and forgives. When anyone hears these words, which are a description and commemoration of God, a universal commotion and ecstatic passion supervenes, since out of these words comes the scent of their Beloved and their Quest.

"Though the ways are various, the goal is one. Do you not see that there are many roads to the Kaaba? For some the road is from Rum, for some from Syria, for some from Persia, for some from China, for some by sea from India and Yemen. So if you consider the roads, the variety is great and the divergence infinite; but when you consider the goal, they are all of one accord and one . . . . Once they have arrived there, that disputation and war and diversity touching the roads—this man saying to that man, 'You are false, you are an infidel,' and the other replying in kind—once they have arrived at the Kaaba, it is realized that that warfare was concerning the roads only, and that their goal was one."

Also in R. A. Nicholson, *The Mathnawi of Jalalu'ddin Rumi* (London, 1937), VII, 202–203. Nicholson maintains that Rumi here does not refer to the Greeks but to Anatolians. Though it is true that the epithet Rumi is occasionally employed to designate people of Anatolia, most frequently it means Greeks. It is thus used in Eflaki, Ibn Bibi, Marwazi, Evliya Chelebi, etc. The Armenian is usually called Armen, and the Turk either Turk or Muslim.

[109] Eflaki-Huart, I, 206, 244–247, 325, 365.

[110] *Ibid.*, 245. According to *ibid.*, 365, Rumi had appeared to Thiryanus in a dream even before this confrontation.

This convert became so renowned for his "knowledge" that the cadis and muderris' of Konya were reduced to silence in his presence. The story of Thiryanus is doubly significant for not only is it the most detailed case of conversion in the Menaqib al-Arifin, but it demonstrates how the Mawlawis helped construct a Muslim society in Anatolia. An individual who had committed a crime was rehabilitated and transformed into a useful member of the Muslim community.

The conversion of the Greek painter 'Ayn al-Dawla Rumi[111] was, in contrast to that of Thiryanus, accomplished by intellectual persuasion.

Kalo-Yani the painter and 'Ayn al-Dawla were two Greek painters who were beyond compare in this art and in that of representing figures. They became disciples of the Master.[112] One day Kalo-Yani said: "In Constantinople a picture of Jesus has been painted that is beyond compare. The painters from throughout the world have gone there but have not been able to reproduce similar figures." 'Ayn al-Dawla, moved by an intense desire to see this painting, set out and for one year remained in the great monastery of Constantinople (where it was kept) in the service of the monks. One night, when he found a favorable opportunity, he took the painting under his arm and left. After arriving in Konya he went to visit the Master: "Where were you?" asked the latter. He told of the adventures of the painting. "Let us see this charming painting," said the Master. "It must be very beautiful and gracious." After having contemplated it for some time, he continued: "These two beautiful figures complain bitterly of you. They say: 'He is not proper in his love for us. He is a false lover.' " "How is that?" replied the painter. "They say: 'We never sleep or eat, we are awake at night and fast during the day, while 'Ayn al-Dawla has abandoned us.' " "It is absolutely impossible," said the painter, "for them to sleep and eat. They are not able to speak, for they are figures without soul." "You, who are a figure with a soul,' " replied the Master, "you who are so richly talented in the arts, you who have been created by a Creator whose work includes the universe, Adam, and everything on the earth and in the skies, are you allowed to abandon Him and to fall enamored of a painting without soul and mind? What can result from these non-conscious figures? What profit can you derive from them?" Immediately the painter repented and . . . was converted to Islam.[113]

Rumi's conversion of a Greek architect reflects on other factors and motives that often facilitated the abandoning of the old religion and the acceptance of the new.

One day . . . a Greek architect constructed a chimney in the house of the Master. The friends, by way of joking, said to him: "Since Islam is the best religion, why do you not become a Muslim . . . ?" He replied: "I have been a follower of Christ for fifty years. I fear Him and would be ashamed to abandon His religion." The Master suddenly entered and spoke: "The mystery of faith is fear. Whosoever fears God, even though he be a Christian, is religious not irreligious." After having pronounced these words, he disappeared. The Christian architect was converted, and become a disciple and sincere friend as well.[114]

[111] *Ibid.*, 333, describes him as a second Manes in the art of painting; a painter who would have been able to say to Manes, "You remain powerless before my talents."

[112] This passage implies that though Kalo Yani remained a Christian he became a disciple of Rumi.

[113] Eflaki-Huart, II, 69–70.

[114] *Ibid.*, 2–3.

Perhaps the explanation for the architect's conversion is to be found in his frequent association with the members of the order and a certain economic motivation.[115]

The significance of dervish activity among the Christian artisans and laborers of the towns is further illustrated by another incident from the pages of the Menaqib al-Arifin. After a sema' that Rumi had conducted before the notables of Konya, he made his way through the streets of the city with his companions when he heard music issuing from a tavern. He halted and began once more to perform his dance and gyrations. The runud came out of the tavern and fell at the feet of the Master who then removed his clothing and donated it to his audience. On the next day, adds Eflaki, these Armenians came to the medresse of Rumi, converted to Islam, and became disciples who henceforth held performances of the mystical dance.[116] The Greek laborers of Konya were no doubt also responsive to the charms of Mawlana. The conversion of monks and priests was of critical importance, as they were the very bulwark of the Christian element against the eroding process of Islamization. Eflaki speaks of the conversion of monks in the districts of Sis, Meram, Konya, and other areas,[117] and of Jewish rabbis.[118]

The most eloquent testimonial to the great influence Rumi and his successors obtained over the Anatolian Christians, however, is the account Eflaki gives of Rumi's funeral.

After they had brought forth the body on the litter, all the grandees and people bared their heads. Men, women, and children were present, and such a tumult arose that it resembled the great resurrection. Everyone wept, and most of the men marched, crying out, tearing their clothes and the body denuded. The members of the different communities and nations were present, Christians, Jews, Greeks, Arabs, Turks, etc. They marched ahead, each holding aloft their sacred books. Conforming to their customs, they read verses from the Psalms, Pentateuch, and Gospel, and uttered funereal lamentations. The Muslims were not able to push them back with blows of the cudgel and the flat of the sword. It was impossible to halt this gathering. An immense tumult arose, the news of which came to the great sultan and to the pervane, his minister. They summoned the chiefs of the monks and priests and demanded of them what connection this event might have with them, since this sovereign of religion was the director and obeyed imam of the Muslims. They answered: "In seeing him we have comprehended the true nature of Jesus, of Moses, and of all the prophets. In him we have found the same guidance as that of the perfect prophets about which we have read in our books. If you Muslims say that our Master is the Muhammad of his epoch, we recognize

---

[115] There are other cases, *ibid.*, II, 208, 275–276, of association between Greek builders and workers with the Mawlawi order. *Ibid.*, I, 23–24, the anonymous butcher and baker who were commissioned to furnish provisions for the dervishes became disciples, no doubt, because of economic factors. The Greek domestics of the order were probably similarly converted.

[116] *Ibid.*, II, 13–14. *Ibid.*, I, 289, a drunk Christian enters the dance of Rumi.

[117] *Ibid.*, I, 65, 84, 106–108. In some cases a type of religious syncretism rather than true conversion took place.

[118] *Ibid.*, II, 9, 111–112.

him similarly as the Moses and Jesus of our times. Just as you are his sincere friends, we also are one thousand times over his servers and disciples. It is thus that he has said: 'Seventy-two sects hear their own mysteries from us. We are like unto a flute which, in a sole mode, is in accord with two-hundred religions.'

"Our master is the sun of truth who has shone upon mortals and has accorded them his favors. All the world loves the sun, which illumines the abodes of all." Another Greek priest remarked: "Our master is as bread, which is indispensable to all the world. Has a hungry man ever been seen to flee far from bread? And you, do you know who he was?" All the grandees were silent, not articulating one word. However, on the other side the readers of the Koran softly read wondrous verses. There arose a mournful and woeful murmur. The pleasant-voiced muezzins called out the prayer of the resurrection. Twenty groups of excellent chanters recited the funeral chants which our Master had himself previously composed.[119]

This indicates quite clearly that a powerful process of religious syncretism was in dynamic motion by which Christians and Jews were accommodating themselves to this particular Muslim religious fraternity. This very syncretism and mutual accommodation of dervishes and Christians would eventually result in the absorption of a great many Christians through conversion. Half a century later (c. 1320) at the funeral of Rumi's grandson, Amir Arif, the same great commotion took place and many Christians "rent the girdle of negation . . ." and became Muslims.[120]

The Mawlawi *Menaqib al-Arifin*, in contrast to the Bektashi Vilayetname, records specific historical acts in the cultural transformation of the Greek Christian population and supplies a further and most important confirmation of the ecclesiastical acta from the fourteenth-century patriarchal synod.

By the time of Seljuk decline in the second half of the thirteenth century, large numbers of dervishes had come into Anatolia and had become firmly established, thanks to the support of both government and populace. The rise of the independent beyliks and their expansion against the Greeks in the west and north provided the dervishes with new horizons, as they joined in close association with the various emirs during or just after the conquests. The emirs welcomed them as important colonizing elements in the newly conquered Christian lands for a variety of reasons.[121] The newly conquered lands were in an unsettled state as a result of the raids and conquest. Portions of the indigenous population had perished or

[119] *Ibid.*, 96–97. B. Fürûzanfer, *Mevlâna Celâleddin*, trans. F. Uzluk (Istanbul, 1963), pp. 153–154.

[120] Eflaki-Huart, II, 410. A miracle occurred at the coffin which was instrumental in the conversions. The miracle, which had to do with the feet of the defunct, was of a type which one would expect to find in Christian hagiography.

[121] The importance of the dervishes as colonizing elements in Asia Minor is treated in great detail by Ö. Barkan, "Osmanlı imparatorluğunda bir iskân ve kolonizasyon metodu olarak vakîflar ve temlikler. I Istilâ devirlerinin kolonizatör türk dervşileri ve zaviyeler," *V.D.*, II (1942), 279–386. There is a French precis at the end of the volume, pp. 59–65. The study is based primarily on the early Ottoman chronicles and, more importantly, on the wakf registers of the Ottoman period. These latter contain considerable information on the period of the Beyliks prior to their absorption by the Ottomans.

fled and cultivation of the land in many cases was interrupted. A large proportion of the new settlers were nomadic tribesmen who often presented problems of administrative control. Then there were the indigenous Christians who had remained in the conquered lands. When the dervishes came the emirs bestowed upon them lands, tax exemptions, Christian serfs, and often built tekkes for them. The dervishes, as a result, were instrumental in bringing large areas of land under cultivation once more. They built mills, planted fruit trees, performed police functions, and assured the safety of roads and communications. They also acquired great influence over many of the recalcitrant tribesmen, and by their aggressive policies of spreading Islam converted the majority of the Christian villagers and townsmen.

It is not mere coincidence that the first great expansion of the Mawlawis manifested itself during the leadership of Sultan Walad (d. 1312) and Amir Arif (1312–20), for this was the period in which many of the beyliks were firmly established. Arif gave his personal blessing to the conquests that the dynasty of Aydin undertook,[122] and there was close contact with the dynasts and lands of Menteshe, Germiyan, Ashraf, Djandaroğullari, Saruhan, Alaiya, Antalya, Ladik, Afyon, Karahisar, Kütahya, and many others.[123] The emirs made grants of land and revenues and built zawiyas for the Mawlawis in these regions. In the towns they soon attracted the ruling class and the akhi-rind groups, but even though they were primarily an urban order, they also had important connections with the tribal groups on the borders.[124] Because of the concern with the Ottomans in the pages of the early Ottoman chroniclers, this phenomenon of dervish colonization in northwestern Anatolia is somewhat more visible. The sultans were intimately associated with these holy men throughout the fourteenth and fifteenth centuries. One of Osman's personal advisers, and simultaneously his father-in-law, was the dervish sheikh Edebali; the dervish Kumral Dede, a murid of the latter, was likewise within the immediate circle of Osman.[125] In the reign of Orhan the dynasty became closely affiliated with the dervish order of the Ebulfeva when Geyikli Baba blessed the dynasty.[126] According to the traditional

[122] Eflaki-Huart, II, 391–393.

[123] Ibid., II, 316–317, 327, 331, 343–344, 350, 367, 373–374, 381, 384, 389–393, 396, 380. Babinger, "Sarukhan," EI₁.

[124] Both the Karamanids and the ghazis of the western Udj under Muhammad Beğ were in close relations with the Mawlawis, Eflaki-Huart, II, 10, 11, 373–374.

[125] Ashïkpashazade-Ali, pp. 6–8. Ashïkpashazad-Kreutal, pp. 25–26. Neshri-Köymen, I, 80–83.

[126] The dervish, allegedly a murid of Baba Ilyas (Barkan says he was a Yasawi), planted a poplar by the door of Orhan's court and stated that so long as the tree should stand, the family of Osman would enjoy the benedictions of the dervishes. Orhan built a turbe over the grave of Geyikli Baba, a teke and a Friday mosque. In the fifteenth century it was still known as the Geyikli Baba Zaviyesi and five times daily the blessings of the dervishes for the dynasty were recited therein. Ashïkpashazade-Ali, pp. 46–47. Ashïpashazade-Kreutel, pp. 72–74.

accounts a close tie developed between the Bektashi order and the Ottoman military forces under Orhan and Murad I,[127] and if this is legendary for so early a period, the close connections of the order with the Janissaries in later times is an established fact. Murad II apparently joined a dervish fraternity, and certain dervishes were very important in the intimate circles of Muhammad II.[128] As the conquest of northwestern Anatolia progressed, dervishes settled down in the new Ottoman domains in large numbers. When Balïkesri and Karasï were taken, "the district of Karasï was filled with holy men."[129] Subsequent to his conquest of Bursa, Orhan sought out dervish colonists and soon discovered that many of them had already settled in the villages of Keshish Daği in the district of Aynegöl.[130] During his reign many dervishes from Khurasan, Balh, and Bukhara settled in and around Bursa.[131] Following this settlement of holy men, one can observe the customary relations between sultan and dervishes wherein the latter received lands, tekkes, and villages. Osman bestowed a village upon the dervish Kumral Dede; Orhan offered Geyikli Baba the town of Aynegöl, but interestingly enough the dervish requested instead some unoccupied hills; Murad I built a tekke for the dervish Postinpush in Yenishehir; Bayazid erected a zawiya for the Ishaki or Kazaruni fraternity in Bursa.[132] These isolated instances are representative of a much more widespread phenomenon of dervish colonization which becomes fully evident only in the wakf registers of the fifteenth and sixteenth centuries. According to the documents of the reign of Sulayman I, the zawiyas of Asia Minor were distributed in the following manner,[133] see top of p. 394.

[127] Ashïkpashazade-Ali, pp. 201–202. Anonymous-Giese, p. 22.

[128] Ashïkpashazade-Ali, pp. 148–149. Ashïkpashazade-Kreutel, p. 209. In the very attack on Constantinople, it was the counsel of a dervish which prevailed over that of Djandarlï and so led to the final capture of the city. See Kissling, "Aq Şems-ed-Din. Ein turkischer Heiliger aus der Endzeit von Byzanz," *B.Z.*, XXXXIV (1951), 322–333. On the anti-dervish stand of Muhammad I, Kissling, "Einiges über den Zejnije-Orden im Osmanischen Reich," *Der Islam*, XXXIX (1964), 164–165.

[129] Ashïpkashazade-Ali, pp. 46. Ashïkpashazade-Kreutel, p. 72.

[130] Ashïkpashazade-Ali, pp. 46–47. Ashïkpashazade-Kreutel, pp. 72–74. It was from this group that Geyikli Baba came.

[131] Barkan, "Türk dervişleri," 290. In some cases the dervishes seem to have founded the zawiyas in the border regions that, though deserted by the Christians, had not yet been assimilated by the Ottomans. Such was the dervish zawiya that Osman encountered near the Sangarius en route to attack Taraklï-yenidjesi. Neshri-Köymen, I, 91. Of interest is the fact that Sheikh Muhammad Kushteri, who is said to have introduced the Chinese shadow theater (Karagöz) into Asia Minor emigrated from Iran to Bursa. He died in the latter city in 1399–1400, R. Mantran, "Les inscriptions turques de Brousse," *Oriens*, XII (1959), 158–159.

[132] Ashïkpashazade-Ali, pp. 4–8, 47, 64. Ashïkpashazade-Kretuel, pp. 25–26, 74, 86, 96. The Karamanids, at the other end of Asia Minor, were doing the same thing, M. Z. Oral, "Konyada Ebu Ishak Kazeruni Zaviyesi," *Anit*, vol. I, no. 7 (August, 1949), pp. 3–8; no. 8 Eylul (1949), pp. 12–14.

[133] Barkan, "Türk dervişleri," 301. These figures include a considerable number of akhi zawiyas. For the establishment of Bayramiyya, Chalvatiyya, Shabaniyya, Zayniyya tekkes in Amasya, Castamon, Balïkesri, Kutahya, Bursa, Konya, Egridir, see the various works of Kissling cited above, especially nn. 36, 37, 38. The study of Gökbilgin," XVI.

Vilayet of Anadolu	622
Vilayet of Karaman	272
Vilayet of Rum	205
Diyarbekir	57
Zulkadiriye	14
	1,170

The continuous activities of the dervishes in the newly conquered regions of western Anatolia had a marked effect on the Christian communities. Just as they had accomplished extensive conversions in central Anatolia, so the dervishes now attained considerable success throughout western Asia Minor as champions of Islam. In fact so successful were they that when the western traveler Ludolph von Suchem passed through these regions in the mid-fourteenth century, he remarked that the Turks as a people were in part Christian renegades.[134] At times the dervishes were able to convert entire villages in a relatively short time. Such was the case with Yalova and the surrounding districts during Osman's reign, where the populace was persuaded to accept Islam as a result of a miracle that a dervish performed.[135] Similarly the Christians in the regions of Tarakli-yenidjesi, Goynuk, and Modreni apostatized at sometime in the reign of Orhan.[136] Dervish missionaries are said to have converted the Christians of Tabai (Tavas) and Altintash,[137] and it was probably the dervishes who were responsible for the apostasy of extensive Christian elements in Pontoheracleia, Amaseia, Gangra, Sebasteia, Euchaita, Iconium, Mocissus, Nazianzus, Nicaea, and Castamon.[138] But even in those areas where the Christians retained their religion for longer periods, the establishment of the numerous dervish zawiyas constituted important centers from which religious propaganda constantly radiated. This in turn, gradually had its effect on many of the local Christians.[139] As has

---

yüzyil başlarinda Trabzon livasï ve doğu Karadeniz bölgesi," *Belleten*, XXVI (1962), 295, indicates that the dervish establishments must have been far more numerous. The documents that he has here studied show that there were 1,275 dervish houses in the eyalet of Rum (northeastern Asia Minor) in the early sixteenth century. There were only 93 djamii and 216 mesdjids (smaller mosques).

[134] Ludolph of Suchem-Neumann, pp. 375–376. "Et sunt christiani ad legem Magumeti se habentes ex parte." A variant reads, "non tamen de genere Sarracenorum, sed potius christianorum renegatorum."

[135] Anonymous-Giese, pp. 18–19. The turbe of the dervish was still to be seen near the warm baths of Yalova in the late fifteenth century.

[136] *Ibid.*, p. 23.

[137] Vilayetname-Gross, *passim.*

[138] Miklosich et Müller, I, 69, 103, 143, 183–184; II, 491. A sixteenth-century author refers to the mass Islamization of the majority of the villages in southwest Anatolia which occurred at an earlier time, Vakalopoulos, Ἱστορία, II₁, 47, no. 1, " . . . ἐξέκλιναν καὶ ἠχρειώθησαν ἐκ πολλοῦ," On the word ἀχρεῖος (and variants) denoting apostate, see the following: Tietze, *Oriens*, X (1957), 378. Vakalopoulos, Ἱστορία, II₁, 45, no. 1. Köprülü, "Din tarihimize ait notlar: I: Ahïryan kelimesi hakkïnda. XVII inci asïrda Trakyada hïristiyan Türkler," *Hayat Mecmuasï*, VI (1929), 42–43.

[139] Gökbilgin, "Trabzon," pp. 321–324, 331–332. A slow process of Islamization is

already been mentioned, most of the zawiyas received grants of Christian serfs along with the lands the beys and sultans gave them. These Christians, or gilman-i vakfi as they were called in Ottoman times,[140] were in constant association with the dervishes, a circumstance that eventually brought about the Islamization of many, as is clearly illustrated in the case of the zawiya of Sheih Ak Bïyïk Dede on Karïs Daǧï in the district of Bursa.[141] In a document from the Bursa awkaf defter of the sixteenth century, the kullar of the zawiya are listed on p. 396.[142] Three of the individuals who appear in this list, Mustafa, Davud, and Yusuf, are converts to Islam, as the kunya veled-i 'Abdullah shows, and Nusuh is possibly the son of the convert Yusuf.[143] It is quite probable that

---

discernible during the early sixteenth century in the districts of Rize, Hemsin, and Giresun, which had compact Christian populations.

	Christian hearths	Hearths of Converts
Rize	215	2
Cikar	8	2
Mirokalo	36	3
Ksanos	67	8
Menohort	40	30
Vanak	49	2
Zavandos	30	7
Giresun		5

[140] Barkan, "Türk dervişleri," p. 303. For examples of these Greek serfs, *ibid.*, pp. 327, 352, 353, in the wakfs of Umur Pasha of Aydin and of certain zawiyas in the district of Bursa. P. 352, gives the names of the Christians attached to the wakf.

Yâni veled-i Kosta
Kodja Kosh
veled-i Yorgi
Mihal veled-i O
Yorgi birader-i O
Yakub veled-i Yusuf
Manol birader-i O
Korsh veled-i Yorgi Makri
Kiryako birader-i O
Bürak veled-i Mihal
Mihal veled-i Somuncu Kosta
Yorgi birader-i O
Atranos veled-i Todor

Ibid., p. 327, Kiryazï ve Yâni evlâdïndan Bazarlu ve 'Aleksi ve Kosta ve Yâni veled-i Bazarlu ve Kara Göz birâder-i 'Aleksi veled-i Yâni ve Hosh veled-i O. Of interest is the use of Turkish names by Greek Christians. On these serfs, or *ortakçïlar*, see the studies of Barkan, "XV ve XVIinci asïrlarda osmanlï imparatorluǧunda toprak işçiliginin organizasiyonu şekilleri. A. Kulluklar ve ortakçï kullar. B. Bursa ve Biga civarïndaki kulluklar. C. Rumelindeki kulluklar ve ortakçï kullar," *Iktisat Fakültesi Mecmuasï*, I (1939), 29-74, 198-245, 397-447.

[141] Ak Bïyïk Dede lived near Yenishehir in the reign of Murad I and preached against the unchastity and pederasty that prevailed among the Muslim religious leaders of Bursa. Anonymous-Giese, pp. 35-36. Murad I apparently endowed his zawiya with lands. Barkan, "Türk dervişler," p. 351.

[142] Barkan, "Türk dervişler," p. 351.

[143] *Ibid.*, pp. 303-304, on the fact that many dervishes had the kunya veled-i 'Abdullah. The kunyas veled-i 'Abdülhâlik and veled-i 'Abdülkerim might also indicate conversion in the case of the document concerning the zawiya of Sheikh Ak Bïyïk. Some of the dervish zawiyas were founded on the ruins of Christian churches, *ibid.*, p. 335. See also Turan, "Şemseddin," p. 205.

(Gulam-i vakf)	Yusuf veled-i 'Abdullah
(Gulam-i vakf)	Davud veled-i 'Abdallah
	Nasuh veled-i Yusuf
	Mustafa veled-i 'Abdullah
	'Abdülkerim veled-i 'Abdülhâlik
	Salih birâder O
	Haydar birâder O
	Mehmed birâder O
(Atîk)	Ismail 'Abdullah
(Dervish)	Ahmed veled-i Isa
(Dervish)	Pîri veled-i O
(Dervish)	Seydi 'Ali birâder O
(Dervish)	Ṣa'ban veled-i Abdülkerim
(Dervish)	Ca'fer veled-i Sinan
(Dervish)	Ömer veled-i O

among the remaining individuals there are some who are descendants of Christians who at some time in the fourteenth and fifteenth centuries were converted. This document illustrates not only the process by which the Greek serfs attached to the zawiyas were converted but also how many, eventually, became dervishes in the convents. This is similar to the fate of the two villages of Saraydjik and Arkït which were attached to the medresse of Altun Aba in Konya. During the thirteenth century the villages were inhabited by Christians, but by the sixteenth century the inhabitants were Muslim.[144] It is highly likely that Christian serfs attached to wakf lands of other institutions (mosques, hospitals, and so forth) were similarly absorbed in the course of time.

Muslim Institutions: Futuwwa

In his description of the "travelers" in Anatolia Ashïkpashazade makes mention not only of the abdalan-i Rum (dervishes) but also of the akhiyan-i Rum (the akhis and rinds).[145] The akhi groups, which came to play an extraordinarily important role in the economic and political life of Anatolia in the thirteenth and fourteenth centuries, were organizations that paid allegiance to the concept of the futuwwa, an ideal which by this period had undergone a long and rather obscure development.[146] As an ideology, futuwwa seems to go back in its origins to certain early

[144] Mantran, "Brousse," pp. 118–121. Umur Beg specified that the revenues for the awkaf are to be collected by his (white) slave Khoskadem ibn 'Abdullah and then by his sons and descendants. Umur Beg, on his death in 1461, left an extensive wakf donation in support of the mosque which he built in Bursa. Among the items which he left were his fields, below Bursa, with their infidels; his villages in the district of Bursa with their infidels; his mill and gardens with their infidels at Isa Viran near Inegöl; his lands, gardens, and infidels at Tekfur Pinar. When Muhammad I took the Byzantine village of Darïdjalar he gave it in wakf to an imaret (soup kitchen for the poor), Ashïkpashazade-Ali, pp. 93–94. Ashïkpashazade-Kreutel, p. 133.

[145] See above in this chapter.

[146] The literature on this difficult subject is extensive. The most important studies are those of Taeschner, "Futuwwa-Studien," *Islamica*, V (1932), 285–333; "Die islamischen Futuwwabünde. Das Problem ihrer Entstehung und die Grundlinien ihrer Geschichte," *Z.D.M.G.*, LXXXVII (1939), 6–49; "Der Anteil des Sufismus an der Formung des

Arab ideals centering on the concept of the young man (fata, pl. fityan) and the virtues of nobility, generosity, bravery, and so on, which were expected of him. After the great Arab conquests, this concept was received by the Persian aristocracy who found it similar to their ideal of virtue, and sufism likewise took over the futuwwa ideal from the Arab ghazis. The mystics, however, transformed it by establishing as the ideal of human virtue altruism—putting one's fellow man over one's self. More important than the origin and spread of futuwwa as an ethical ideal was the social and historical development of futuwwa in the form of associations of young men in the Islamic towns. In contrast to the evolution of the ethical concept that possibly goes back to early Arab traditions, the history of the futuwwa associations very probably originates in the institutional forms of the pre-Islamic Near East.[147] When the Arabs expanded into these areas, they found in existence urban corporations of various sorts, and these associations seem to have adopted, at least in theory if not in practice, the Arab moral concept of the fata-futuwwa. These organizations, however, did not always follow the altruistic interpretation of the futuwwa which the sufis enjoined and gave themselves up to a loose life characterized by eating, drinking, sexual immorality, stealing. In the period between the ninth and twelfth centuries these associations of fityan became very unruly in the towns and frequently attempted to assert themselves as political factors in opposition to central authority. The chronicles of the period, seemingly unfavorable to them, brand them *ayyarun* (robbers, vagabonds). Inasmuch as they were spread throughout the lands of the caliphate and their power was great, the Caliph Nasir (1180–1225) made efforts to reform the futuwwa and to bring it under his immediate control so as to strengthen his own power.[148]

Futuwwaideals," *Der Islam*, XXIX (1937), 43–74; "Futuwwa, eine gemeinschaftbildende Idee im mittelalterlichen Orient und ihre verschiedenen Erscheinungsformen," *Schweizerisches Archiv für Volkskunde*, LII (1956), 122–158. An informative study of the futuwwa literature is the work of Gölpinarlï, "Islam ve Türk ellerinde Fütüvvet teşkilatï ve kaynaklarï," *Istanbul üniversitesi Iktisat Mecmuasï*, vol. II (1948–50). There is a shorter French version in the French edition of the periodical, "Les organisations de la Futuvvet dans les pays musulmans et turcs et ses origines," pp. 5–49. Taeschner, "Akhi," EI₂.

[147] L. Massignon, "La 'Futuwwa', ou pacte d'honneur artisanal' entre les travailleurs musulmans au Moyen Age," *La nouvelle Clio*, IV (1952), 171 ff., derives them from the guilds of the Sassanid capital at Ctesiphon. Taeschner traces their origins to the societies of the Greek and Persian cities. Cahen suggests the possible connections between these futuwwa groups and the Byzantine demes and circus factions, "Ahdath," EI₂; "Mouvements et organisations populaires dans les villes de l'Asie musulmane au Moyen Age: milices et associations de Foutouwwa," *Recueils de la Société Jean Bodin*, VII (1955), 285, 288; "Zur Geschichte der städtischen Gesellschaft im islamischen Orient des Mittelalters," *Saeculum*, IX (1958), 59–67. It is very probable that the Byzantine neaniai (youths), that is to say the members of the circus factions, are at the base of the fityan and ahdath groups of the Islamic towns. Vryonis, "Byzantine Circus Factions and Islamic Futuwwa Organizations (neaniai, fityan, ahdath)," *B.Z.*, LVIII (1965), 46–59.

[148] G. Salinger, "Was the Futuwa an Oriental Form of Chivalry?" *Proceedings of the American Philosophical Society*, vol. XCIV, no. 5 (Oct., 1950), pp. 481–493. P. Kahle, "Die Futuwwa-Bündnisse des Kalifen en-Nasir," *Festschrift Georg Jacob* (Leipzig, 1932), pp. 112–127.

In his reform, and even before, there is an indication that the influence of the sufis in the futuwwa increased considerably, a factor of some significance inasmuch as it foreshadows the close association of futuwwa associations and dervish orders in Asia Minor.

The futuwwa in Anatolia was represented among at least three groups: the association of ghazis engaged in fighting the Christians; the Seljuk court; the urban groups often referred to as akhis or runud. With the first of these, the ghazis, we are not concerned here. As for the second, the Seljuk court, Ibn Bibi relates that the caliph Nasir in 1215–16 invested the sultan Kaykaus with the symbols of the futuwwa, but it is not possible to determine whether the akhis developed from the court futuwwa or whether they developed independently. It is this akhi form of the futuwwa which was most important for the history of the towns in Asia Minor, the ghazis having been concerned more with the border regions.[149] The term akhi in thirteenth- and fourteenth-century Anatolia is frequently used to designate a prominent individual[150] in the affairs of a town, who is also the leader of the rinds (runud). These runud consisted largely of unmarried young men from the artisan classes[151] as well as idle youth. By extension of the term, akhi seems to have been used to denote not only the head of this group but the group itself.[152] In the period between the decline of the Seljuk state and the establishment of the Ottomans, the akhi-runud appear as important factors in the political life of the Anatolian

[149] Again it is the works of Taeschner which are at the basis of the study of the Futuwwa in Asia Minor, "Akhi," EI₂; "Zwei Gazels von Gülşehri," in *Fuad Köprülü Armağani* (Istanbul, 1953), pp. 479–485; "Futuwwa, eine gemeinschaftbildende Idee im mittelalterlichen Orient und ihre verschiedenen Erscheinungformen," *Schweizerisches Archiv für Volkskunde*, LII (1956), 144–151; *Gülschechris Mesnevi auf Achi Evran den Heiligen von Kirschehir und Patron der türkischen Zünfte* (Wiesbaden, 1955), *Abhandlungen für die Kunde des Abendlnades*, XXXI, 3; *Der anatolische Dichter Nasiri (1300) und sein Futuvvetname* (Leipzig, 1944); "Legendbildung um Achi Evran, dem Heiligen von Kirsehir," *Festschrift Friedrich Giese* (Leipzig, 1941), pp. 61–71; "Das anatolische Achitum des 13.–14. Jahrhunderts und seine Beziehung zu Mevlânâ Celâleddin Rumi," *VI. Türk tarih kongresi. Ankara 20–26 Ekim 1961* (Ankara, 1967), pp. 230–234; "Das Futuvvetkapitel in Gülşehris altosmanischer Bearbeitung von Attars Mantiq ut-tair," *Sitz. der Preus. Akad. der Wiss.* vol. XXVI (1932); "Beiträge zur Geschichte der Achis in Anatolien (14–15 Jht.)," *Islamica*, IV (1929), 1–47. Cahen, "Sur les traces des premiers achis," *Fuad Köprülü Armağani* (Istanbul, 1953), pp. 81–91. N. Cagatay, "Futuvvet-Ahi müessessesinin mensei meselesi," *Ilahiyat Fakültesi Dergisi*, I₁ (1952), 59–69; I₂, 61–84.

[150] He is often, but not always, well off financially from his economic endeavors either in commerce, the crafts, or agriculture. Akhi Ahmad Shah of Tabriz was a silk merchant, Eflaki-Huart, II, 350–351. Akhi Amir Ahmad was one of the wealthy of Paipert, Eflaki-Huart, I, 305–307. Akhi Muzaffar al-Din of Ab-i Garm became prosperous from farming, Eflaki-Huart, II, 349. Akhi Ahmad Shah of Konya was one of the wealthiest men of the city and gave gifts to the Mongol Djaitu in 1291, Eflaki-Huart, II, 112–114. Cahen, "Achis," pp. 81–91.

[151] The associations in the early fourteenth century seem to have cut across guilds, so that members of more than one guild might be members of a given akhi group, Ibn Battuta-Gibb, II, 420.

[152] According to Deny, "Fütüwwet-name et romans de chevalerie turcs," *J.A.*, XI (1920), 182 ff., the term akhi is of Turkish rather than Arab origin, and means noble, generous. The akhis existed in Iran before their appearance in Asia Minor according to Taeschner, "Futuwwa," p. 145. But see Cahen, "Achis," *passim*.

towns. In this they are strongly reminiscent of the Islamic ahdath and ayyarun, and of the sixth-century Byzantine circus factions-neaniai and eleventh-century guilds.[153] The akhis and runud were armed, very often even in ceremonies that took place in their hospices, and government officials frequently employed them as troops.[154] They took an active, sometimes decisive, part not only in internal political intrigues,[155] but also in "foreign" affairs.[156] As conditions progressively degenerated in Asia Minor in the latter half of the thirteenth and in the early fourteenth century, there are indications that the akhis took over political control in a number of towns. Ibn Battuta was conscious of this development and so commented.

It is one of the customs in this land that in any part of it where there is no sultan, it is the Akhi who acts as governor; it is he who gives horses and robes to the visitors and shows hospitality to him in the measure of his means, and his manner of command and prohibition and riding out [with a retinue] is the same as that of the prince.[157]

Their hospices and organized life resembled, somewhat, the exterior aspect of dervish practices and life. Again it is Ibn Battuta who is the keenest observer of the tekke organization of the akhis.

Account of the Young Akhis (Akhiyya). The singular akhiyya is akhi, pronounced like the word akh [brother] with the possessive pronoun of the first person singular. They exist in all the lands of the Turkmens of al-Rūm, in every district, city, and village. Nowhere in the world are there to be found any to compare with them in solicitude for strangers, and in ardour to serve food and satisfy wants, to restrain the hands of the tyrannous, and to kill the agents of police and those ruffians who join with them. An Akhi, in their idiom, is a man whom the assembled members of his trade, together with others of the young unmarried men and those who have adopted the celibate life, choose to be their leader. That is [what is called] al-futuwwa also. The Akhi builds a hospice and furnishes it with rugs, lamps, and what other equipment it requires. His associates work during the day

---

[153] On the Byzantine guilds and their political activities, Vryonis, "Byzantine Δημοκρατία and the Guilds in the Eleventh Century," *D.O.P.*, XVII (1963), 289–314.

[154] Ibn Battuta-Gibb, II, 427, remarks that all of the akhis of Ladik (Denizli) appeared in arms during the parade that he witnessed. In Attaleia, II, 421, when he first entered an akhi hostel, Ibn Battuta noticed that many of the young men carried knives. When the runud of Sivas drew their swords in a social disturbance, the governor had to restore order by recourse not only to government troops but he also employed the armed runud of Konya and Kayseri, Eflaki-Huart, II, 317–320.

[155] The runud leaders of Akshehir and Ab-i Germ were promised fiefs (iqtas) and other gifts by the Pervane Abu Bakir in return for their armed support, Ibn Bibi-Duda, pp. 241–243, 247.

[156] The akhis and runud of Konya assisted Djimri and the Karamanids in the capture of Konya and joined their armies, Ibn Bibi-Duda, pp. 311, 313. The akhi Ahmad Shah undertook to negotiate with the Mongol Djaitu when he appeared before Konya in 1291, Eflaki-Huart, II, 112–114.

[157] Ibn Battuta-Gibb II, 434. Such seems to have been the case, at one time or another, in Konya, Paipert, Aksaray, Nigde, Kayseri, Ankara, and no doubt elsewhere as well. Eflaki-Huart, I, 305–307; II, 306–309. Ibn Battuta-Gibb, II, 433, 434. Neshri-Köymen, I, 190. On Ankara see Taeschner, "War Murad I Grossmeister oder Mitglied des Achibunds?" *Oriens*, VI (1952), 23–31.

to gain their livelihood, and after the afternoon prayer they bring him their collective earnings; with this they buy fruit, food, and the other things needed for consumption of the hospice. If, during that day, a traveller alights at the town, they give him lodging with them; what they have purchased serves for their hospitality to him and he remains with them until his departure. If no newcomer arrives, they assemble themselves to partake of the food, and after eating they sing and dance. On the morrow they disperse to their occupations, and after the afternoon prayer they bring their collective earning to their leader. The members are called fityān, and their leader, as we have said, is the Akhī. Nowhere in the world have I seen men more chivalrous in conduct than they are. The people of Shīrāz and of Isfahān can compare with them in their conduct, but these are more affectionate to the wayfarer and show him more honor and kindness.[158]

When Ibn Battuta journeyed through Anatolia he found free and generous hospitality at these akhi convents throughout the length and breadth of the peninsula, and it is obvious from this alone that the akhi brotherhood was at the height of its political and economic existence.[159] According to the futuwwa literature that appeared in Anatolia during the late thirteenth and the fourteenth century, there was a twofold division of the akhis. According to the one they were divided into kavli and sayfi— akhis of the word and those of the sword. Only the latter were full members, the former being attached in some less rigid form.[160] The second division, separated according to yiğit (novice), akhi, and sheikh, is of interest because it probably indicates the association of dervishes with the akhis. Prior to their appearance in Asia Minor the futuwwa organizations had come increasingly under sufi influence. In some cases they modeled themselves after the dervish orders in corporations, and dervish sheikhs appeared as members of futuwwa groups, on occasion taking over their direction. In Anatolia, too, the sufis had a great effect on the akhi brotherhood. In the anecdotes that Eflaki relates one learns that the akhis in Konya, Ab-i Germ (Ilgin), Laranda, Seyid Abad, Akshehir, Paipert, Sivas, and in the Udj regions had an intimate relationship with the Mawlawi order. Very often this was ceremonially manifested by the Mawlawi leaders who journeyed to these towns and performed the dervish ritual in the abodes of the leading akhis and was no doubt rein- forced by the presence of Mawlawi tekkes in these towns.[161] The influence

---

[158] Ibn Battuta-Gibb, II, 418–420.

[159] *Ibid.*, 420–465, mentions them in Antalya, Burdur, Gül Hisar, Ladik (Denizli), Tavas, Milas (Mylasa), Barjin, Konya, Aksaray, Nigde, Kayseri, Sivas, Gümüshhane, Erzindjan, Erzerum, Birgi, Tire, Manisa (ad Sipylum), Balīkesri, Bursa, Kurluk, Kawiye (Geyve), Yaniya (Taraklī-yenidjesi), Mudurnu, Bolu, outside of Castamon. Eflaki-Huart, I, 305–307; II, 61–62, 323, 350–351, 370–371, 402, adds Seyid Abad, Laranda, Paipert, Tabriz, and the border regions (Udj). Ibn Bibi-Duda, pp. 241–243, mentions them in Akshehir and Abi-Germ (Ilgin), and Neshri-Köymen, I, 190, in Ankara.

[160] Taeschner, "Futuwwa," pp. 147–148. Ibn Battuta's repeated reference to the fact that they were armed with knives and swords seems to explain the description of sayfi.

[161] Eflaki-Huart, I, 305–307; II, 61–62, 112–114, 323, 326–327, 349, 370–371. The governor of Akshehir attempted to expel the Mawlawi Amir Arif from the city because the emirs, Akhi Musa, and the runud supported him. This indicates that Amir Arif was a real political force. There are also instances of enmity between some of the akhis of

of the dervishes was no doubt responsible for the altruistic aspect of Anatolian futuwwa and for some of the semireligious mentality that the akhi ritual displayed. On the other hand their antinomian tendencies are reminiscent of the ayyarun in Mesopotamia.

What effect, if any, did these akhi corporations have on the indigenous Christian populations of the Anatolian towns? The importance of the Greek and Armenian elements in the towns, in the commerce, and in the crafts of Asia Minor is apparent from the incidental remarks of Marco Polo and Ibn Battuta. Thus one may assume that in such a city as Ladik (Denizli), where most of the artisans were Greeks and where there was an extensive guild organization, the akhi association probably had a strong effect on the Christians.[162] Again, in a city such as Erzindjan, which in Ibn Battuta's time was mostly Armenian, there was an association of the fityan under an akhi,[163] which likewise must have influenced the Armenian artisans. The critical question is, however, whether there is any detailed evidence that definitely states that the akhi-runud corporations cut across denominational lines. Their urban character and the strong dervish influence would certainly suggest the probability that these corporations were not rigid and denominationally exclusive. Three incidental bits of information would tend to confirm the proposition that these Anatolian associations included Greeks and Armenians. First there is a Greek inscription from the district of Konya which mentions a Greek akhi.[164] Second, Eflaki records that among the runud of Konya and Sivas there were Armenians.[165] It is true that this is very meager evidence, but nevertheless it is significant and would indicate that these associations definitely penetrated all regligious groups. Thus one can assume that the akhi-runud played an important role in the absorption of the Christian urban populace of Anatolia into the Islamic world by penetrating the economic organizations and proletariat of the towns. It is probable that for a while Greek and Armenian runud[166] maintained their original

---

Konya and the Mawlawis. Such was the case when Akhi Ahmad disputed the possession of a tekke with the Mawlawi leader Husam al-Din (Eflaki-Huart, II, 237–241). But in this case it is significant that many of the akhis took the side of the Mawlawis against Akhi Ahmad, and after the death of the latter, his son and the runud became devotees of the Mawlawis. There was a similarly hostile encounter between Akhi Mustafa, who obtained control of Konya, and the Mawlawi Sultan Walad who was supported by the aristocrats of Konya, Eflaki-Huart, II, 306–309. Taeschner, "Türk ahiliği ve ahilik müessesenin Mevlevilikle münasebetine dair," *Mevlana Güldestesi* (Istanbul, 1964), pp. 5–7.

[162] Ibn Battuta-Gibb, II, 425, 427. He describes the prominence of the Greeks in the textile manufactures and a procession of the town guilds. For similar economic activity and organization in Ladik (Laodiceia) during late antiquity, T. Broughton, *Asia Minor*, *passim*.

[163] Ibn Battuta-Gibb, II, 437–438. The craftsmen here were probably largely Armenian.

[164] Taeschner, "Beiträge," *Islamica*, IV, 20. Hasluck, *Christianity and Islam*, II, 383.

[165] Eflaki-Huart, II, 14, 317–320.

[166] There is perhaps some difficulty in distinguishing between the specific and generic uses of runud.

religious affiliations to Christianity, but with the passage of time they were converted to Islam. The Islamic environment made it inevitable, a fact accelerated by the influence of the dervishes in the organization. In the first incident recounted by Eflaki (above), it was Djalal al-Din Rumi himself who converted to Islam the Armenian runud who were enjoying themselves in the tavern. The influence of the Mawlawis in converting Greek craftesmen in Konya has already been discussed.

Conclusions

With the removal of Byzantine control from Anatolia, Christian society had to readapt itself to a Muslim government and culture. Traditionally this reorientation should have taken place within its ecclesiastical institutions. But these latter were reduced to impotence by the nature of the Turkish conquest and so the Christian communities succumbed to the forces of Islam. The various Turkish states and society that arose on Anatolian soil were imitations of those in the older Islamic lands, and various historical circumstances caused a continuous migration of Muslim ulemas and dervishes to settle in Anatolia. The sultans confiscated the vast majority of Christian lands, revenues, and buildings and bestowed them upon their Muslim secular and religious followers. Consequently, mosques, medresses, tekkes, hospitals, and the like spread across Anatolia, often in the very buildings and on the same lands formerly belonging to the Greek church. These institutions (staffed by zealous missionaries) and Muslim society (itself religiously aggressive) easily absorbed the dejected and abandoned Christians.

VI. *The Loss of Byzantine Asia Minor and the Byzantine World*

Causes and Effects of the Loss

The loss of Anatolia to the Turks was an unmitigated disaster for the empire because, with the consummation of the Turkish conquest, the process by which Islam had begun to devour Byzantium in the seventh century was once more set in motion. In any consideration purporting to deal with Byzantine decline in Asia Minor, it is necessary to consider the reasons for the loss of this great peninsula and the effects this loss produced. Throughout most of the four centuries in which the Turks were actively conquering the area, it was a combination of internal and external factors which resulted in the defeat of the Byzantines. In the eleventh century the strife of the Byzantine bureaucratic class with the magnate-military aristocrats of the provinces (especially in Anatolia) was the critical development. Not only did it paralyze Byzantine political life with its endless intrigues and rebellions but it destroyed the Anatolian armies and brought in the Turkmens as mercenary troops. Simultaneously, the transplanting of Armenian populations to the eastern themes of Byzantine Anatolia in the face of the Seljuk invasions caused further difficulties. These Armenians were frequently hostile to the Byzantine government and to their Greek and Syrian neighbors in the new homeland. Political resentment was compounded by religious antagonism. The Armenian church had not subscribed to the council of Chalcedon and so was in the same category with the Coptic and Jacobite churches. Byzantium faced a situation in eleventh-century Anatolia which resembled somewhat the situation of the Syro-Egyptian provinces on the eve of the Arab conquest in the seventh century. Throughout the eleventh century, the Byzantine government and church attempted to force ecclesiastical union upon Armenians and Syrians. This religious and political animosity of Greeks, Armenians, and Syrians in the districts of eastern Asia Minor completed the disorganization of the Byzantine regions just at the crucial moment when the Turkish pressure was building to a climax. Greek troops occasionally had as much to fear from the Armenian soldiery as they had to dread from the Turks themselves, and many Armenians joined the invading Turks. Something approaching an undeclared state of war had come to prevail between the two groups.

The internal disintegration coincided with an increasing complication of Byzantine foreign relations. It is true that the Normans who established themselves in Sicily and southern Italy were not as numerous as the Turkmens who poured into Anatolia, but their political expectations and desires were far more ambitious in the beginning. Guiscard's followers were not nomadic tribesmen in search merely of booty and pasture lands, rather they hoped to capture Constantinople itself and to take over the empire. They were a much more dangerous threat to the seat of the empire than were the Turkish invaders in the eleventh and twelfth centuries. The Balkan provinces were similarly consumed by the devastating raids of Patzinaks and Uzes and then splintered by the foundation and growth of Balkan states.

Henceforth foreign pressures on the empire from these three directions would be unrelenting. The Byzantines found themselves burdened with the maintenance of a three-front defense which demanded larger military forces and expenditures than previously had been the case. As the need for manpower and money suddenly expanded, the human and financial resources drastically contracted. The emperors of the twelfth century had to develop their policies against this background of increasing foreign pressure and decreasing internal stamina. The fate of Byzantine Anatolia in the twelfth century was partially determined by this situation. So long as Alexius Comnenus had to confront the nomads of the Balkans and especially the Norman danger in western Greece, there was nothing that he could do against the Turks of Anatolia. When, however, the Normans were defeated, Alexius turned his attention to the Anatolian situation and with the aid of the First Crusaders managed to rescue important provinces in Anatolia from the Turks. John II in particular concentrated his attention on the Turkish wars and so was able to stabilize the reconquest that his father had effected. Manuel I, however, became so involved with western affairs that he relaxed the Greek efforts in Asia Minor much to the great advantage of the sultan of Konya. When he died, the Byzantine provinces in Anatolia rapidly disintegrated in a bewildering succession of rebellions, Turkish raids, and Armenian separatism. It was, paradoxically, the success of the Westerners in taking Constantinople which prolonged Greek rule in western Asia Minor throughout the thirteenth century, because with their expulsion from Constantinople, the Greeks were forced to devote more attention to Anatolian affairs. But the concept of the empire was inseparably associated with Constantinople and so the efforts of the Lascarids in Bithynia had as their ultimate goal the reconquest of the city. This in turn necessitated increasing involvement with Balkan reconquests and Latin crusades. With the reentry of

Michael VIII in Constantinople, Byzantine Anatolia was once more relegated to a position of secondary consideration. Not only was it neglected but its ability and will to resist the Turks were systematically undermined in a fashion recalling the events of the eleventh century.

While Byzantine efforts oscillated between Asia Minor and the Balkans, the Turkish invaders concentrated their efforts on Asia Minor, first consolidating their gains, and then expelling Greek authority from the coastal regions. At the same time, the numbers of Turkmen tribes increased steadily as they wandered into Anatolia where they frequently settled on the borders. The numbers of the Muslim population were increased by the emigration of Arabs, Persians, and Turks from the Middle East, but especially by the steadily mounting tide of religious conversions.

Given the geographical extent of Byzantine political interests and pretensions, it becomes clear that Byzantine resources were not sufficient to maintain the empire's former pride; the loss of Anatolia made it impossible.

Byzantium was first reduced to a power of the second order by this loss. Though the magnificent ceremonies of the past were frequently observed at the court and in the capital, they were meaningless forms which in no way obscured the newer and grimmer reality: the empire was simply one of a number of smaller Balkan states. This loss of Anatolia ultimately resulted in the fall of Constantinople and the destruction of the Byzantine Empire.

The Turkish conquest of Asia Minor deprived the empire of the major sources of its manpower. As the most populous eastern province of first the Roman and then the Byzantine Empire, it became the principal military recruiting ground after the loss of much of the Balkans to the Slavs in the seventh century. The Anatolian Greek and Armenian soldiery had formed the basis of those armies that had halted the Arab advances in the seventh and eighth centuries and then had carried the struggle into Syria. The martial pride and glory of these Anatolians are reflected in the history of the Anatolian aristocratic families, in the legends perpetuated in the *Digenes Acritas*, and in other popular literature. The naval levies of the Anatolian maritime districts were also of considerable importance, and it is perhaps no accident that Byzantium became dependent upon Venetian naval power only after the battle of Manzikert.

The events of the eleventh century would have resulted in the degradation of Byzantium to inferior political status on economic grounds alone. The Turkish raids and occupation had, by the reign of Nicephorus III (1078–81), completely deprived Constantinople of the rich Anatolian tax incomes.[1] Following the partial reconquests of the Comnenoi, strenuous

[1] Bryennius, 129. " τῆς γὰρ τῶν χρημάτων ἐπεισροῆς τῶν ἀπὸ τῆς Ἀσίας χορηγουμένων τοῖς ταμείοις ἀποφυγούσης ἐκ τοῦ τῆς Ἀσίας ἀπάσης κατακυριεῦσαι τοὺς Τούρκους."

efforts to recolonize western Anatolia were undertaken in order that revenues for the treasury might be forthcoming. But the constant Turkish raids seriously hampered both the recolonization and tax production. The disturbance and then the loss of Anatolia in the eleventh century coincide with the further and precipitous debasement of the Byzantine gold coinage in the reigns of Michael VII and Nicephorus III.[2] This numismatic decline is, no doubt, partially a reflection of the economic loss that Byzantium sustained as a result of the Turkish occupation of the peninsula. Anatolia had also constituted the richest agricultural and pastoral domain of the empire prior to its loss. Its grain, fruit, and live-stock were important not only for the provisioning of the capital but also essential to the Crimean Chersonese, and occasionally to Egypt. The mines, local crafts, commerce, and industries were also productive, and the economic wealth of Anatolia was the essential basis that underlay the temporary eclat of thirteenth-century Nicaea and Konya. Of all the Byzantine provinces, none could compare with Anatolia as a source of economic wealth. Politically and militarily Anatolia had served as an immense buffer protecting Constantinople from militant Islam. The defeat at Manzikert at once removed the buffer and brought the traditional foe to the doorstep of the capital. The Turkish conquest was almost as disastrous for the Greek church as it was for the empire. The church lost a great portion of its flock and witnessed the reduction of its most impor-tant metropolitanates and bishoprics. The great Anatolian monastic centers largely disappeared, and the church was pauperized, losing most of its revenues and properties to the Turks.

The Turkish domination was equally fateful for the Greek population of the peninsula, which was in large part Islamized and Turkified. The Arab historian Ibn Khaldun, who pondered the complex questions of cultural change, extrapolated certain "laws" from historical events that would seem to be relevant. One should not imply that the events in Anatolia are here being established by this "law" of Ibn Khaldun, but the events do seem to coincide with Ibn Khaldun's generalizations. "The vanquished," he stated, "always want to imitate the victor in his distinctive mark(s), his dress, his occupation, and all his other conditions and customs."[3] Further, "a nation that has been defeated and comes under the rule of another nation will quickly perish."[4] Ibn Khaldun observed that conquered peoples frequently imitated the religion, language, dress, weapons, mounts, and customs of the conquerors. The conquered are motivated by a variety of factors in so doing, for they assume that the victors have conquered because of their perfection, because of the superiority of their customs and manners. Thus the fact of military and

[2] See chapter ii.
[3] Ibn Khaldun-Rosenthal, I, 299.
[4] *Ibid.*, I, 300.

political victory imbues the social and cultural forms of the conquerors with a charisma and an appeal that are taken away from the comparable forms of the vanquished. The Arab historian clearly perceived the validity of the familiar maxim, *cuius regio eius religio*, "The common people follow the religion of the ruler."[5] Ibn Khaldun's law of religious change was closely paralleled by those of linguistic change.

The dialects of the urban population follow the language of the nation or race that has control of [the cities in question] or has founded them.[6]

This apathy and dejection are illustrated by the conversation that supposedly transpired between Orhan and the Christian representative of Bursa after the city had capitulated and when the sultan inquired why it was that the Greeks had finally surrendered. The answer of the Greek was a combination of historical specifics and philosophical generalities. He remarked that whereas the Turkish power increased daily that of the Greeks declined. In addition Osman had constructed forts in the environs, had taken over the villages, and so the Greeks could not provision themselves, and even though the Greek governor had money for supplies and troops, he refused to spend it. Consequently, the walls of Bursa had become a prison for the starving and dying Christians. Finally, the Greek reflected, the world is full of changes and it was such a change that overtook the Greeks.[7] Thus the Greeks were assimilated largely by Islamization which was accompanied by Turkification, and even those of the urban Christians who were not converted were Turkified linguistically according to the "law" of Ibn Khaldun.[8] Those of the Greek Christians who remained in isolated villages seem to have been more successful in preserving the Greek language.

The historical memories of the Christians often died hard. For example the Christians of Melitene and other cities anxiously awaited the arrival of John II and his armies;[9] the monks of the troglodyte monastic communities appear to have preserved the memory of the Greek emperors;[10] the memory of John IV Vatatzes remained alive among the Greek peasants

---

[5] *Ibid.*, I, 300. It is much the same thing that Ricolde-Cydones, *P.G.*, CLIV, 1105, states, " Πρῶτόν ἐστι τὸ τὸν Μαχούμετ ἐκείνοις εἰπεῖν ἐπὶ τοσοῦτον διαμενεῖν τὸν νόμον αὐτοῦ, ἔφ' ὅσον ἂν αὐτοῖς διαμείνῃ καὶ ἡ ἐν τοῖς ὅπλοις ἰσχύς, καὶ ἡ πρόσκαιρος δυναστεία."

[6] Ibn Khaldun-Rosenthal, II, 305.

[7] Ashïkpashazade-Kreutel, pp. 54–55. Ashïkpashazade-Ali, pp. 29–30.

[8] Here I refer to the so-called Karamanli Christians who spoke Turkish rather than Greek, but who wrote it in the Greek alphabet. For a more detailed discussion of the Karamanlidhes, see chapter vii. The change of customs and manners of dress are also noted among the Armenians by Nerses in the twelfth century, Nerses, *R.H.C.*, *D.A.*, I, 597–599. There existed among the Armenians the equivalent of the Orthodox Karamanlidhes, that is to say Turkish-speaking Christians who wrote Turkish in the Armenian alphabet and belonged to the Armenian church.

[9] Michael the Syrian, III, 249.

[10] Bees, *Die Inschriftenaufzeichnung des Kodex Sinaiticus Graecus 508 (976) und die Maria-Spilaötissa-Klosterkirche bei Sille (Lykaonien), mit Exkursen zur Geschichte der Seldschuken-Türken* (Berlin, 1922), *passim*.

of the Maeandrian regions as late as the nineteenth century.[11] Finally, it is interesting that the first manuscript of the epic *Digenes Acritas* was discovered in Anatolia during the nineteenth century, and that much of Byzantine folklore survived there.[12] But Turkish Islam, by virtue of its political and social superiority, gradually corroded these sentiments. The conquest had not only created a respect for Turkish customs among the inhabitants, but it induced an apathy that, Ibn Khaldun says,

comes over people when they lose control of their own affairs and, through enslavement, become the instruments of others and dependent upon them. Hope diminishes and weakens.[13]

The Anatolian Christians were isolated from the heartbeat and mainstream of their culture, and as time passed historical memories became increasingly dimmer. Thus the Greek Christians succumbed to cultural change.

One other effect of the Anatolian loss on the Byzantines was that henceforth more consideration was given to the European domains. By the time of George Gemisthus Pletho, the Peloponese was so important that he made it the center of his proposed reforms.[14] It now became the center of Greek feeling, and the pendulum of history swung back to its starting point. The long historical process that had spread Hellenism eastward to Asia Minor, Egypt, and Syria, and had then begun to recede with the Arab conquests, was now completely reversed.

Byzantine Reflections on and Reactions to the Loss of Anatolia

Contemporary Byzantine literature partially reflects the trauma that the loss of Anatolia inflicted on Byzantine civilization. This literature was largely the product of historians and chroniclers, though more revealing as to the extent of the trauma are the writings of *belle-lettristes* and theologians whose professional aim was not that of recording the empire's history. Literary reflection on the loss of Anatolia was very often subsumed under the literature of decay and decline, so that frequently this body of

[11] A. Heisenberg, "Kaiser Johannes Batatzes der Barmherzige. Eine mittelgriechische Legende," *B.Z.* (1905), pp. 160–233.

[12] Ioannides, Ἔπος μεσαιωνικὸν ἐκ τοῦ χειρογράφου Τραπεζοῦντος ὁ Βασίλειος Διγένης Ἀκρίτης ὁ Καππαδόκης (Constantinople, 1889).

[13] Ibn Khaldun-Rosenthal, I, 300–301. Apostasy and desertion to the enemy for personal gain and betterment are phenomena that led to the same result. Metochites, *Miscellanea philosophica et historica*, ed. Ch. G. Müller and Th. Kiessling (Leipzig, 1821), pp. 405–412 (hereafter cited as Metochites, *Miscellanea*). Metochites blames men for believing in providence only when affairs prosper. If, however, this arrangement of events is upset by tyche, then the naive belief in providence is overturned and the belief in God collapses. Metochites, along with Ibn Khaldun, remarks that political misfortune seriously undermines religious belief and affiliation. For a graphic illustration of this dispondency in Asia Minor see the anecdote that Pachymeres, II, 596, relates about the inhabitants of the Greek village of Eligmoi.

[14] Lampros, Π.Π., III, 246 ff.

literature referred to Asia Minor as well as to the empire in general.[15] Genres of literature that became increasingly frequent were the θρῆνοι (laments) and λόγοι (discourses purporting to explain the origin of the many evils plaguing the empire). In many ways the most striking reflection of the disturbance that the loss of Asia Minor caused in the Byzantine world is presented by the writings of the Byzantine official and intellectual Theodore Metochites.[16] Though he was not born an Anatolian, Metochites spent a portion of the formative years of his life in Anatolia and retained a strong attachment to these eastern regions. As an important official, Metochites was keenly aware of the disasters afflicting the empire, and his writings are frequently concerned with the causes and effects of decay. He often integrates his thoughts about the loss of Asia Minor with his more general considerations on Byzantine bad times. Thus the reasons that he assigns to Byzantine decline are valid also for western Anatolia.

Though Metochites sees certain immediate causes for the fall from greatness, such as dissension, envy, stupidity, luxury, abuse of religious life, and the like,[17] his writings are permeated by the concept of tyche. It is tyche, rather than the Christian God, who guides the affairs of men and this tyche is blind and arbitrary. The lives of men, nations, and lands, are governed by inconstancy, uncertainty, oscillations, and the only certainty in life is this very uncertainty.[18] Metochites soliloquizes upon the inconstancy of the history of various states in chapter 110 which,

[15] There is now a substantial literature that deals with Byzantine reflections on decline. For a general orientation see C. J. G. Turner, "Pages from the Byzantine Philosophy of History," *B.Z.*, LVII (1964), 346–373, who separates the Byzantine authors into two camps: first, those who explain Byzantine decline within the traditional framework of the Byzantine Weltanschaung. This "monastic" interpretation relates prosperity to virtue and decline to sin. Thus ecclesiastical authors and the historians Ducas and Sphrantzes belong to this first group. Second the authors such as Chalcocondyles, Critobulus, and Metochites, who were indifferent to dogmatic Christianity and believed that an arbitrary, impersonal force, Tyche, governed history. Beck, *Vorsehung und Vorherbestimmung in der theologischen Litertur der Byzantinern*, vol. CXIV of *Orientalia Christiana Analecta* (Rome, 1937), and *Theodores Metochites, die Krise des byzantinischen Weltbildes im 14. Jahrhundert* (Munich, 1952), discusses both types of historical interpretation in great detail. Other literature on the subject includes: I. Ševčenko, "The Decline of Byzantium Seen through the Eyes of its Intellectuals," *D.O.P.*, XV (1961), 167–186; Zoras, "Orientations idéologiques et politiques avant et après la chute de Constantinople," in *Le cinq-centiéme anniversaire de la prise de Constantinople, l'Hellénisme contemporaine* (Athens, 1953), 103–124; E. von Ivanka, "Der Fall Konstantinopels und das byzantinische Geschichtsdenken," *J.Ö.B.G.*, III (1954), 19–34; Dölger, "Politische und geistige Strömungen im sterbenden Byzanz," *J.Ö.B.G.*, III (1954), 3–18.

[16] Beck, *Metochites*, *passim*, presents an interesting analysis of Metochites' writings as they reflect the crisis of the "Byzantine Soul" during the decline. For further bibliography on the life and writings of Metochites, Ševčenko, *La vie intellectuelle et politique á Byzance sous les premiers Paléologues. Études sur la polémique entre Théodore Métochite et Nicéphore Choumnos* (Brussels, 1962). Also H. Hunger, "Der Ἠθικός des Theodores Metochites," Πεπραγμένα τοῦ Θ´ διεθνοῦς βυζαντινολογικοῦ συνεδρίου, III (Athens, 1958), 141–158.

[17] Metochites, *Miscellanea*, p. 231. All virtues, wisdom, nobility, harmony, civil grace, noble outlook, law-abiding men, great men, have departed from the empire.

[18] Beck, *Metochites*, pp. 100 ff. The historical and aetiological mentality of Metochites is often more akin to that of the pagan Greeks than to that of the Christian Byzantines. See his description of the undulating curves of human prosperity and misfortune, *Miscellanea*, pp. 184–195, 570–574.

appropriately, deals with the "Scythians." Nations that formerly ruled over others were then enslaved in their turn:

> This was formerly the case with the Assyrians who, having failed, passed under the Persians, the Persians and all their subjects under the Macedonians, and the Macedonians under the Romans. And these events constantly occur in an alternating fashion according to chance of both time and tyche. Nor is there anything constant in human affairs nor unchangingly eternal. Just as there is in an individual man, or in whatever animal, birth, progress toward the prime, the prime, afterward decay, and finally destruction and death, thus is it also in human affairs, politics, and despotisms. These are to be seen in constant flux and change, in no way remaining constant, but coming into being, advancing, little by little decaying and changing into the opposite state, coming to an end and dying.[19]

It is this reversal of fortune common to all states which has overtaken Byzantium in the east and west.[20] Among the more immediate causes for the defeat of Byzantium and the victory of the Turks, Metochites lists the superior virtue of the latter. The Scythians, Metochites relates, were from time immemorial a great and unsubjugated race. That is not to say that some of them were never at any time under foreign rule, rather the entire race was never under one rule. They are a numerous and bellicose people, prone to wars with foreigners and with one another. In ancient times they crossed the Danube, plundered Thrace, and passing through the Ionian regions they overran Italy, the Celtic lands, Spain, and crossed over into Libya. In more recent times these Scythians have enslaved most of Asia, Babylon, Assyria, and the lands as far as India.

Methochites explains why the Scythians throughout their history have remained unconquered (both Alexander and Xerxes, and all those down to Metochites' day who attempted to subjugate them failed). It is because they have lived a type of life entirely different from that of the rest of mankind, a manner of existence that foreign peoples cannot assail and destroy. Though the Scythians live together in a society as do all other men, they live a beastly life, unpracticed in any contrivance and productivity. The Scythians neither dwell in cities, nor safeguard their lives with walled enclosures, nor do they live in rural villages. They know not the care of crafts, commerce, the cultivation of fields and gardens, and they are not familiar with the customs of men from normal societies. They wander constantly, not merely to one land in summer and to another in winter, but to other lands as well. They move about in search of water, and pasture, remaining largely under the open skies. If they need protection against winter, they erect felt huts on a circular framework of little sticks, and these huts, which they carry about on wagons, satisfy their

---

[19] Metochites, *Miscellanea*, pp. 725–726. Beck, *Metochites*, p. 86, though the empire is approaching its end it is not to be a cosmic, eschatological catastrophe.

[20] Metochites, *Miscellanea*, p. 792. E. Trapp, *Manuel II. Palaiologos. Dialoge mit einem "Perser"* (Vienna, 1966), pp. 56–57 ff. (hereafter cited as Manuel Palaeologus-Trapp).

needs for housing. Their cuisine is simple and devoid of lavish gastro-
nomical preparations. They eat the flesh and milk from their flocks and
also wild animals and fowl that they hunt. They warm a little meat over
the flames and without any further preparation eat it, doing so only to
discharge the inescapable demands of the body. It is in this manner, Metochites relates, that the Scythians were from the beginning accustomed to a
light, simple, unburdened life, naturally avoiding twisted reasoning,
knavery, trials, arguments, contradictions of speech, court pleadings,
slander, and so on. They have no elected judges, orators, assessors of laws,
interpreters of dogmas, distorters, professors and perverters of speech in
advocacies and accusations, contests of wordiness, such as are customary
among Greeks and other barbarians. Because of the simplicity of their life
and its freedom from material concern, the Scythians have led a more just
life than many other peoples. As support for his assertion, Metochites
refers to the poet Homer, who also alludes to these qualities and
virtues.[21]

The Περὶ Σκυθῶν of Metochites is of considerable interest inasmuch as it
appears, on first glance, to be an objective evaluation of the superior
qualities of the Turks, their moral virtues arising from the simplicity of
their life. In fact, however, Metochites is praising the "noble savage"
(so familiar in the literature of more modern times), who living close to
nature is free of the artificialities of urban life which so pervert human
character. An even closer look at the Περὶ Σκυθῶν indicates that it is a
stereotype piece that goes back to classical Greek and Roman literature,
the best known of this genre, Tacitus' *Germania*, immediately coming to
mind. Tacitus idealized the low state of development among the Germanic
barbarians in order to hurl his literary shafts at conditions in Roman
society which he found disagreeable and undesirable. Methochites
similarly converted Scythian barbarity into a state of moral purity
so that using it as a foil he might attack the shortcomings of his
own society. He admits that he has "lifted" the material for this
chapter on the Scythians from Herodotus, Diodorus, Dionysius, Aelian,
and Homer.[22] The chapter is, accordingly, a "scissors and paste"
product taken from ancient authors and then applied to the Turks.
The terms "Scythian," as Metochites employs it, refers to all the
Germanic peoples of the early medieval period as well as to the
Turks and Mongols. In short it is synonymous with "nomad" and therefore with a way of life, rather than with any ethnic group. His observations
on nomadic life are vastly oversimplified and ignore the fact that nomadic
groups are possessed of certain crafts, do indulge in commerce and marginal agriculture, often live in close symbiotic relationship with sedentary
groups. It further oversimplifies the phenomenon of the Turkish conquest,

[21] Metochites, *Miscellanea*, pp. 732–733.
[22] *Ibid.*, pp. 733–734.

which was after all not exclusively a nomadic affair. Had the Seljuks and Ottomans never developed beyond the nomadic state, they could never have erected the political structures that were the Seljuk sultanate and the Ottoman Empire. In addition, these states had all the trappings of society—cities, guilds, elaborate court ceremonial, teachers and students of law, judges, theologians, and so forth. The parallel between Metochites and Tacitus on this one point is striking. They are both moralizing and use the noble savage as a literary device to this end. One can hardly imagine Tacitus, the *arbiter elegantiae*, or Metochites, a leading intellectual and commissioner of the most splendid monument of art in the Palaeologan period, adopting the crude life that each pretended to admire.[23]

It is in chapters 37 to 40 of the *Miscellanea* that Methochites laments the separation by the Turks[24] of Anatolia from the empire. Chapter 37 introduces the theme of the general disaster that has overtaken the empire. The affliction is so great, says Metochites, that it is beyond his ability to describe it. The old days were a golden age in which the empire stretched from Britain to the Euphrates and from the Danube to Ethiopia. Now it is reduced to very slight proportions in both east and west, and lies a helpless victim of the malignity and beastliness of neighbors. The empire is like a large oak that has fallen, and enemies are gathering its wood almost effortlessly. It has been humiliated, and the dogmas and mysteries of Christ are being extinguished by the impious enemies who have defiled and trampled them underfoot. Those peoples who were formerly contemptible, and who were permitted to exist by Roman generosity, now have become arrogant and violent and prevail over the Byzantines. Because of the extent to which the Byzantines have exchanged that former glory for dishonor, they are objects of reproach and laughter not only to the Muslims but to the Christians as well. Metochites expresses the belief that his contemporaries would find a happier existence if only they were unaware of the great national prosperity of past times, but who could be ignorant of such a thing, he rejoins. Who could be so unperceiving as to fail to notice the ancient remains that time amasses? He concludes,

[23] One generation later Alexius Macrembolites transposed the theme of the noble savage into the familiar monastic idiom when he explained Turkish success and Byzantine failure by the greater moral virtue of the former, Ševčenko, "Alexios Makrembolites and his 'Dialgoue between the Rich and the Poor', *Z.R.V.I.*, VI (1960), 196–197 (hereafter cited as Ševčenko, "Markembolites,"). The patriarch Athanasius had adumbrated the same theme, R. Guilland, "La correspondance inédite d'Athanase, patriarche de Constantinople (1289–1293, 1304–1310)," *Mélanges Charles Diehl* (Paris, 1930), I, 121–140. In both cases the Turks serve as moral strawmen, for the primary theme is the sinful state of the Greeks.

[24] Metochites, *Miscellanea*, pp. 230–258. These four chapters have the following titles: No. 37 "Laments on the Diminution of the Affairs of the Romans and on the Transformation of that Great Prosperity." No. 38 "Laments on the Evils of the Roman Empire in the East." No. 39 "Additional Laments on these same things; It is not Possible to Compare all those (Lands) in (Asia Minor) with the Roman (Lands) Elsewhere." No. 40 "Additional Laments on these same Things, and Because the Estate of the Monks Prospered more (in the East) than anywhere else."

accordingly, that the Byzantines are left only with the contemplation of their ancient glory.[25]

In Methochites' eyes the loss of Anatolia was not only a disaster for the state, but it was a tearing personal tragedy. The sadness it inspired he compared to the grief one experiences at the death of a close relative, for to Metochites Anatolia was his "nourishing" mother.

O most beautiful Ionia, most beautiful Lydia, Aeolia, Phrygia, and Hellespont, [lands] with which I became familiar and in which I dwelt most pleasantly and in every manner from a tender age! I have now been left a mournful exile, pouring out tears and lamentations at great length in the manner of sepulchral sacrifices. O my dearly beloved cities, plains, mountains, glens, river streams, groves, meadows, [who are the] origins of every pleasantness to those acquainted with you, to those who view you, and to those who in any way experience you, as I did miserable one! I who tarried so long among you, and having been vitally endowed by residence and training among you (residence and training which produce every mild and upright disposition in the soul), now am I greatly pained in my recollection of you, my heart melts instantly as do [my] very thoughts, and I am unable to breathe, and live only with difficulty .... O my most beloved concord and administration of that life and of human institutions, [which arrange] public affairs, private business and [provide] men with social grace, noble customs, and all things of value .... O subtleties of manifold arts! O careful professions of every type which bring fulfillment to all that comes into being! O cultivations of earth, valued crafts, and origins of all livelihoods, which best effect prosperity and all cultivation of natural fertility! O churches and monasteries, and communities of all piety and customs of faith, priestliness, and people .... There is no other [land] like it [Asia Minor] to be contemplated anywhere else. I do not speak here of other nations and states, but not even in our own lands, [lands] of the Roman Empire]. From the beginning of time and throughout time it was the most beautiful [land], the most perfect in the virtues and happiness of human life, and the noblest in these very Christian matters, the most beautiful and magnificent in our Roman Empire .... Woe to us who now remain! It [Anatolia] has departed from the Roman state! O this destitution! O this loss! We live in a few remnants and members of life and body (formerly so great and beautiful), as though the majority and most vital members have been severed. And we continue to live in shame and derision, wholly incapable in the means of existence and life.[26]

In the following chapter (39), Methochites continues the lament, repeating the theme of his "orphaned" state and the mental and spiritual despondency that it has effected within him. Though he has traveled throughout the empire's domains and to more foreign lands than most of his contemporaries, he has seen no region so fair as Asia Minor. In this chapter Metochites extols the economic vitality and prosperity of Anatolia by comparing its wealth and natural resources with those of the empire's European provinces.

And what are all of these others ... I mean those lands of this empire which are in the other, western regions, [in comparison] with all those [of the east]? Or how can the former be akin to the latter .... I speak of luxuries and ornaments,

[25] *Ibid.*, pp. 230–237.
[26] *Ibid.*, pp. 238–241.

provisions from all types of arts, indeed professions of all sorts, every commercial necessity arising from all points for those generally desiring them and for those who especially use them, or [necessarily] all those things which are by nature indispensable, or freely beyond necessity, as is fitting to those who prosper in every well-being, success, and luxury of life. These are in no way lacking, neither those things which are produced entirely locally, nor all those items which come from all points through commerce [and which are] customary for human life and use, both necessities and luxuries. And all these were no less available to those in the fields and villages who live by agriculture than they were to those who live gracefully in city buildings. For there [Asia Minor] rather do the countrymen live comfortably, prospering greatly in farming, gardening, and animal husbandry. They prosper more than do other races of men, or rather, I should say, than do the others of our race [in the west], or than do some city dwellers to whom it was allotted to have houses in the west, and who have a better fate than do the many. It is not possible to compare the affairs of one [east] with those of the other [west], neither their houses, nor possessions, nor their type of life, nor their pursuits, nor their customs.[27]

Metochites' life (1269-70/1332) was virtually coterminous with that process and period in which the Turks expelled Greek rule from practically all of western Anatolia (Nicomedia fell to the Turks in 1337 and Philadelpheia in 1390). The miserable efforts of Byzantine arms against the Turks had gravely depressed the Christians of Ionia. The flight of numerous Anatolian refugees to Constantinople and Thrace no doubt intensified the demoralization of the inhabitants in the capital itself with the result that the laments of Metochites on the loss of Anatolia were probably in keeping with the emotional state of a large segment of Constantinopolitan society itself. Hence these dirges represent something more than an individual reaction. They display the state of mind that prevailed among the defeat-weary Greeks on the eve of the Turkish invasions of Europe. Metochites realized that without Anatolia, Constantinople had come to be an enormous head without the body that was necessary to sustain it.

Almost sixty years after the death of Metochites, an imperial prince was forced to help Sultan Bayazid I to capture the last independent Byzantine city in western Anatolia, Philadelpheia. As a Turkish vassal, Manuel Palaeologus was also summoned by his Turkish overlord to participate in the campaigns against the Turkish principalities of north-central Asia Minor. This experience left an indelible impression on Manuel and is gloomily reflected in his writings. Aside from the lengthy religious discourses that he composed (the product of debate with the Muslim muderris of Ankara), Manuel wrote a number of letters to friends about what he saw and experienced in Anatolia. These letters describe the desolation of a formerly prosperous land. The inhabitants who had managed to survive death at the hands of the invading armies have fled to the safety of mountain peaks, caves, and forests; food is scarce; roads are

[27] *Ibid.*, pp. 246–248.

unsafe and infested with bandits.[28] More impressive, however, is that the country Manuel traversed was entirely foreign to him, though it had at one time been Greek and Christian.

The plain in which we are now [encamped] had some name when it prospered and was inhabited and ruled by Rhomaioi. Now that I seek to learn that name, I am ignorantly inquiring after wolf's wings, as the saying goes, for there is no one to teach it to me. There are many cities to be seen here, but they have no inhabitants, by which inhabitants towns are ornamented and without which [inhabitants] one could not call them cities. The majority of the cities remain a miserable sight to those whose ancestors formerly inhabited them. Not even their names survive as a result of their previous ruin. Upon inquiring as to the names of the cities, whenever those to whom I addressed the inquiry would reply, "we call them by those names" (for time obliterated their names) I am instantly distressed, but I lament in silence still being in control of my senses.[29]

Manuel had seen, and recorded, the devastation and the cultural transformation that occurred in these as well as in other parts of Anatolia.[30] The change was so drastic that even the place names had largely changed.[31] When Manuel journeyed through Anatolia, the process of Turkification and Islamization had been going on for three centuries and was largely complete. His lament is inspired by these facts.

Metochites and Manuel Palaeologus were, of course, not the only literary figures to express themselves on the related subjects of the loss of Anatolia and the empire's decline. The bulk of this material may be conveniently divided into two artificial categories: the category in which the explanation for the misfortune is primarily religious; that in which the authors speak in terms predominantly historical and philosophical. Often the historians and *belle lettristes*, while not disavowing the role of providence in their historical analyses, are nevertheless much concerned with manmade causes or laws of history that are not immediately inspired by Christian doctrine. Conversely, the religious documents and the writings

---

[28] Legrand, *Lettres de l'empereur Manuel Paléologue* (Amsterdam, 1962), pp. 22, 28, 30–31 (hereafter cited as Manuel Palaeologus, *Lettres*). In a letter to Cydones, Manuel describes a formerly inhabited area that is now deserted. All have fled or perished. In addition, the Christian soldiers in the sultan's army have taken the opportunity to settle all old scores with the Turks by slaying the Muslim religious leaders whenever they come upon them, p. 22. " Καὶ, τὸ δὴ σχετλιώτερον, ὃς ἐν τοῖς τῶν Περσῶν ἱερεύσι σεμνός, εἰρήσθω δὲ καὶ ἐπίτριπτος, μαυλωνᾶς ὀνομάζεται. Οἷς οὖν ἡ σεμνοτάτη αὕτη προσηγορία οὐδὲν πλέον παρὰ τῶν ὁμοφύλων ἐγένετο ἢ παρὰ τῶν Τριβαλῶν καὶ Μυσῶν καὶ Ἰλλυριῶν, οἳ, δίκην ἀνθ' ὧν πόρρωθεν ὑπὸ τοῦ ἔθνους πεπόνθασιν οἰόμενοι λαμβάνειν καὶ τὸν Χριστὸν βοῶντες ἐπεκδικεῖν, κτείνουσι μὲν τοὺς παρατυχόντας πάντας ἑξῆς." On Manuel's Anatolian sojurn, Hunger, *Byzantinisehe Geisteswelt von Konstantin dem Grossen bis zum Fall Konstantinopels* (Baden-Baden, 1958), pp. 282–286.

[29] Manuel Palaeologus, *Lettres*, pp. 22–23.

[30] *Ibid.*, p. 23, he describes the runied state of Pompeiopolis. " Ἀκούεις τὴν Πομπηΐου, τὴν καλὴν καὶ θαυμαστὴν καὶ μεγάλην, μᾶλλον δὲ τὴν ποτε τοιαύτην οὖσαν (νῦν γὰρ μόγις λείψανα ταύτης φαίνεται)." The lands of the "satrap" Peitzas south of Sinope and Aminsus are also relatively uninhabited, p. 24, " ὁμόρου δεσπόζοντα γῆς τε Σινώπῃ καὶ Ἀμινσῷ ὡς δὲ καὶ πολιχνίων καὶ εὐαριθμήτων ἀνδρῶν."

[31] *Ibid.*,

of the churchmen and of the other historians and chroniclers are oriented much more toward religious explanation.

In spite of the Constantinopolitan orientation of much of the former type of literature, the loss of Anatolia was such a severe blow that the historians devoted considerable attention to it. Indeed many of these authors were either born in Asia Minor or else spent considerable time there.[32] It is largely because of their concern with events in Anatolia that the modern historian can dare to attempt a reconstruction of the decline of Byzantine civilization. The historians of the eleventh century were aware that the strife of the bureaucrats and generals had caused the loss of Asia Minor to the Turks. One century later Nicetas Choniates described at length the civil wars in western Asia Minor which destroyed the law, order, and prosperity that Alexius and John Comnenus had created by their Herculean efforts. He noted also the complications of Byzantium's "two-front" war in the east and west.[33] Pachymeres composed a history that is modern in its social, economic, religious, and political analyses of the events that prepared Bithynia for the final Ottoman conquest.[34] These authors realized that the political conquest of the Turks insured the cultural triumph of Islam and the decline of Byzantine civilization.[35] Manuel Palaeologus chose, appropriately, the funeral oration he delivered over the bier of his brother Theodore as an opportunity to explain that Islam was conquering not only the bodies but also the souls of many Greeks.

I say that those Christians who desert to our impious enemies are clearly mad, rather they do worse than those who have lost their wits. For the latter, even if they thrust the sword against themselves, neither harm their souls nor receive the hatred of those who see them, but rather their mercy. However, sober men must have great hatred for the former because these willingly contaminate their souls through their perceptory senses. They desire to find that for which they originally went over to the enemies of the faith, namely wealth, glory, and all those things which are pleasant in this life. It is impossible for them to attain these things if they do not please those to whom they deserted. And they cannot please them [Turks] if they do not do all these things in which they [Turks] rejoice, viz. to live generally in the barbarian manner and willingly to defile their souls with lawless deeds . . . . Those who think that they will obtain a very good place among the impious [Turks] are quickly puffed up like a bright bubble, and then they burst very quickly and their empty thought amounts to nothing in the end. Reasonably.

[32] The family of Michael Attaliates was probably from Attaleia. Anna Comnena's family was from Castamon. Nicetas Choniates, whose history contains interesting details on the events in the environs of Chonae, was born and raised there. The Anatolian Cecaumenus, though not a historian, relates a number of interesting things about this eastern province. Pachymeres and Gregoras were born in Nicaea and Pontic Heracleia respectively. Though Metochites and Acropolites were not born in Asia Minor, they spent considerable time there in their youth.

[33] Nicetas Choniates, pp. 340, 466, 657.

[34] See chapter iii.

[35] Anna Comnena, III, 205; Balsamon in Rhalles and Potles, II, 498, and Nicephorus Gregoras, I, 379, III, 509, were aware that a racial amalgamation was taking place between the Muslim and Christian populations in Anatolia.

If they should be sluggish in [executing] the desire [of the Turks], they become suspect and are soon despised . . . and they are disregarded, is it not so? If they readily accede to those things which the barbarians might desire, and the barbarians wish them to adopt the [Turkish] laws and customs and to destroy unsparingly the race [of the Greeks], they [the deserters] are justly despised because of the cruelty to the race, because of the change of character and life. They do not obtain praise from the [Turks] since they appear so unscrupulous in whatever one might wish. Because of this they are not trusted and remain in secondary positions. Suitably. How can he, who has easily trampled underfoot the customs with which he was raised, maintain strictly those which he has recently accepted? And he who is also manifestly evil to his race and to himself . . . ? How shall he who is evil to himself be useful to another . . . ? If we consider this matter more carefully, such a person becomes hateful to his own conscience. How would he not be so to all? But why do I talk about these things when I have not yet demonstrated the most important point? They do not preserve inviolate their confession and faith in Christ. Why? Because in arraying themselves with Christ they promise their highest love to Him and enmity to the demons. Then they do the opposite. Rather, more accurately, it is necessary to describe and indicate the extent of the evil. Desiring to live with the Muslims who are the enemies of the faith, and sharing in their projects against us, they struggle against the Saviour who has given the faith and they clearly war against Him. . . .

Among those things which they do is to declare Muhammad a prophet. That abominable one has proclaimed, to those races which he had beguiled and constrained, victory over us.[36]

For disillusioned Christians who bore witness to the defeat in Asia Minor, the Turkish conquest provided the impetus for socially and religiously motivated conversion.

Though these authors dealt in the facts and language of immediate and specific causation, they did not refrain from more comprehensive

[36] Manuel Palaeologus, edited in Lampros, Π.Π., III, 46–49. Richldo-Cydones, *P.G.*, CLIV, 1105, gives an interesting paragraph on this subject. " Ἰστέον δὲ τέτταρας εἶναι μοίρας τῶν κατεχόντων τὴν πλάνην τοῦ Μωάμεθ· πρώτη μοῖρα τῶν τὸν Σαρρακηνισμὸν ὑπελθόντων διὰ τοῦ ξίφους, ὡς εἴρηται· οἱ καὶ νῦν τὴν ἑαυτῶν γινώσκοντες πλάνην, ἐξωμόσαντο ἂν αὐτόν, εἰ μὴ τὸ ξίφος ἐδειλίων. Ἄλλη μοίρά ἐστι τῶν ὑπὸ τοῦ διαβόλου ἠπατημένων, πιστευόντων ἀληθῆ εἶναι τὰ ψευδῆ. Τρίτη μοῖρα τῶν μὴ βουλομένων ἀποστῆναι τῆς πλάνης τῶν προγόνων αὐτῶν, ἀλλὰ λεγόντων κρατεῖν ἃ κατεῖχον καὶ οἱ πατέρες αὐτῶν· ὧν ἀφίστανται μᾶλλον, οἳ ἀντὶ τῆς εἰδωλολατρείας, ᾗ πρότερον κατείχοντο, τὴν τοῦ Μωάμεθ αἵρεσιν, ὡς ἂν ἧττον πονηράν, ἀναμφιβόλως προείλοντο. Τέταρτον μέρος ἐστὶ τῶν . διὰ τὸ ἄνετον τῆς ὁδοῦ, καὶ τὸ τῶν γυναικῶν πλῆθος, καὶ τὰ ἄλλα ἐνδόσιμα, μᾶλλον τὴν ἐν τούτοις ἀκαθαρσίαν τῆς ἀϊδιότητος τοῦ μέλλοντος αἰῶνος. Καὶ τούτοις εἰσὶ σύμφωνες οἱ παρὰ τοῖς Σαρρακηνοῖς σοφώτεροι λεγόμενοι, καὶ γραμμάτων ἐπιστήμονες ὄντες. Οὐ γὰρ πιστεύουσι τὸν νόμον ἐκείνων ἀληθῆ εἶναι, ἢ ἀγαθὸν ἁπλῶς· ἀλλ' ἡ σφοδρότης τῶν ἡδονῶν καταπαύει τὴν κρίσιν τοῦ λόγου, ὥς φησιν ὁ σοφός· ὥσπερ καὶ πολλοὶ γραμμάτων ἔμπειροι παρὰ τοῖς Χριστιανοῖς οὐ φυλάττουσι τὸν τοῦ Εὐαγγελίου νόμον, καίτοι πιστεύοντες ἀληθῆ εἶναι καὶ ἀγαθόν· μᾶλλον δὲ τὴν ὁδὸν μιμοῦνται τοῦ Ἀλκοράνου, καίτοι πιστεύοντες ἐπ' ἀληθείας ἐκεῖνον πεπλᾶσθαι. Καὶ τούτου σημεῖον ἐν ἀμφοτέροις· μετατιθεμένων γάρ τινων Σαρρακηνῶν εἰς Χριστιανούς, καὶ Χριστιανῶν τινων γινομένων Σαρρακηνῶν. ὁ μὲν Χριστιανὸς οὐδέποτ' ἂν ἐν τῷ θανάτῳ γένοιτο Σαρρακηνός, ἀλλ' ἐν τῇ ζωῇ, ὁ Σαρρακηνὸς ἐν τῷ θανάτῳ μᾶλλον γίνεται Χριστιανὸς ἢ ἐν τῇ ζωῇ. Ἑκάτερος ἄρα Χριστιανὸς αἱρεῖται μᾶλλον ἀποθανεῖν ἢ Σαρρακηνός· εἰ μή που τῇ προειρημένῃ βίᾳ ἀφέλκοιτο." John Cantacuzene, *P.G.*, CLIV, 552, touches upon the theme of sexual hedonism as a motive for conversion.

speculation as to the reasons for the great reversal of fortune. Time, fortune, fate, bring both prosperity and disaster, situations that have been experienced by all peoples in a recurrent manner. Though it would be an easy matter to stress unduly this non-Christian element in the attempts of the Byzantine historians and literary figures to explain the disastrous course of their history, one is nevertheless impressed by the presence of this classical element.

The more usual explanation for the Turkish conquest of Anatolia was a purely religious one, God had sent the Turks to chastise the Greeks for their sins. Attaliates relates that when the Turks first invaded the provinces inhabited by the Armenians and Syrians, the Greeks reasoned that the invasions were a punishment sent by God for the heresy of those peoples. When, however, the Turks entered the Greek portion of Anatolia the Greeks changed their minds and decided it was their own sins that had caused the invasions.[37] Conversely, Michael the Syrian declared that God had sent the Turks to punish the Greeks for their religious persecution of the Monophysite Christians of eastern Anatolia.[38] Even many Turks seem to have considered their victories over the Greeks as having been due to the wickedness of the latter and God's desire to punish them.[39] The monk Christodoulus (who along with the other monks had to flee the monasteries of Asia Minor), declared the invasions to be the ἐστιλβωμένη ῥομφαία, the μάχαιρα κυρίου, and that the sins of the Christians had created the prosperity of Agarenes.[40] The synodal documents of the late thirteenth, fourteenth, and fifteenth centuries, which refer to the sad condition of the Christian communities within the Turkish emirates, explain these conditions in a similar fashion. There were also ideas among some that the coming of the Turks foretold the days of antichrist and the end of the world.[41]

[37] Attaliates, 140–141. Scylitzes, II, 686–687. Schiltberger-Neumann, p. 133.
[38] Michael the Syrian, III, 154.
[39] Schiltberger-Hakluyt, pp. 76–78. Schiltberger-Neumann, pp. 133–134.
[40] Miklosich et Müller, VI, 61–62.
[41] See chapter iv, and Pachymeres, II, 581–583. Also the unpublished discourse of Alexius Macrembolites in Sabbaiticus Gr. no. 417 which begins on fol. 14v. and is entitled, " τοῦ αὐτοῦ λόγος β'. Ἀπόδειξις ὅτι διὰ τὰς ἁμαρτίας ἡμῶν εἰς προνομὴν καὶ αἰχμαλωσίαν τοῖς ἔθνεσιν ἐξεδόθημεν κτλ." Of similar interest is the discourse attributed by some to Manuel Palaeologus in Vaticanus Gr. no. 1107, " Λόγοι πρὸς τοὺς σακνδαλιζομένους ἐπὶ τῇ εὐπραγίᾳ τῶν ἀσεβῶν." B.D. Papoulia, Ursprung und Wesen der "Knabenlese" im osmanischen Reich (Munich, 1963), pp. 102–103. A. Argyriou, " Ἰωσὴφ τοῦ Βρυεννίου μετά τινος Ἰσμαηλίτου διάλεξις," Ε.Ε.Β.Σ.,XXXV, (1966/67), 141–195. Macrembolites attributed the decline in part to the exploitation of the poor by the rich, Ševčenko, "Macrembolites," pp. 189, 198. Scholarius blamed it on sin, especially simony, L. Petit, X. A. Siderides, M. Jugie, Oeuvres complètes de Georges (Gennade) Scholarius (Paris, 1930), III, 250. " Ἐπὶ πᾶσι ἀναμφισβητήτως πιστεύσατε μὴ'ἂν ἄλλως τὴν βασιλείαν ἡμῶν καὶ τὴν ἐκκλησίαν εἰς τοσαύτην πενίαν καὶ συμφορῶν βυθὸν ἐμπεσεῖν καὶ τὰς τῶν Χριστιανῶν πόλεις καὶ χώρας καὶ σώματα καὶ ψυχὰς εἰς τὴν Μωάμεθ μεταστῆναι δυσσέβειαν, εἰ μή τι περὶ τὴν πίστιν ἐξημαρτάνομεν." Immediately relevant is the letter that Philotheus, metropolitan of Heracleia, wrote to his flock, S. Triantaphylles and A. Grappoutes, Συλλογὴ ἑλληνικῶν ἀνεκδότων (Venice, 1874), p. 43.

One of the better known texts of religious causation is chapter 47 from the work *Seven Times Seven Chapters* of the Byzantine preacher Joseph Bryennius entitled, "Some causes of the Pains which afflict us."[42] Bryennius, like so many moralizing preachers throughout history, bemoaned the fact that the morals of his own time were far below those of the "olden days," and so God had punished the Christians through the Turks.[43]

> If one who views the chastisements inflicted upon us by God is astonished and perplexed, let him consider not only these but our wickedness as well and then he will be amazed that we have not been struck by thunderbolts. For there is no form of evil which we do not anxiously pursue through all of life.[44]

Bryennius complains of violent irregularities in religious life. Some are baptized by single immersion, others by triple immersion. Many Christians do not know how, or simply refuse, to make the sign of the Cross. Priests perform ordinations, administer communion, and remit sins all for cash payment. They live with their wives before marriage, and the monks cohabit with the nuns. There is no blasphemy that Christians do not employ.

> We grumble at God whenever it rains and whenever it does not rain; because he creates summer heat or cold weather; because he gives wealth to some and allows others to be poor; because the south wind rises; because a great north wind blows, and we simply appoint ourselves irreconcilable judges of God.[45]

The mortality of the laity is not superior to that of the clergy.

> Not only men, but the race of women also, are not ashamed to sleep as nakedly as when they were born. They give over immature daughters to corruption. They dress their wives in men's clothing. We are not ashamed to celebrate the holy days

---

" Κατανόησον ἄνθρωπε, εἰ βούλει μαθεῖν τὸ δίκαιον καὶ ἴσον τῆς τοῦ Θεοῦ κρίσεως, καὶ πῶς τοὺς ἁμαρτάνοντας τὰ αὐτὰ καὶ μὴ μετανοοῦντας, ὁμοίως κολάζει. Ἴδε ποῦ εἰσι αἱ περιφανεῖς τῆς Κυζίκου πόλεις, ἵνα ἀπὸ τῶν γειτονούντων ἡμῖν ἄρξωμαι. Ποῦ αἱ τῆς Βηθυνίας ἡ μεγάλη φημὶ Νίκαια καὶ Προῦσα, Νικομήδεια καὶ Χαλκιδών, τὰ πάλαι τῆς ἐκκλησίας καὶ τῆς βασιλείας τῶν Χριστιανῶν ἐγκαλλωπίσματα ; Ποῦ αἱ κατὰ τὸν Ἀστακηνὸν Κόλπον, καὶ τὰ ἐπέκεινα τῆς Προποντίδος καὶ τοῦ Εὐξείνου Πόντου, Παφλαγονία καὶ Ἀρμενία, Καππαδοκία, Παλαιστίνη καὶ Συρία ; Ὅλαι μυριάδες πόλεων καὶ χωρῶν, ὧν οἱ χριστιανῶν βασιλεῖς πρὸ χρόνων ὀλίγων ἐκράτουν, ἵνα μὴ δόξωμεν τὰ πόρρω λέγειν. Οὐχ αἱ αὐταὶ ἀνομίαι καὶ τὸ ἀμετανόητον τὰ μὲν τελείως ἠφάνησαν, τὰ δὲ τοῖς ἀσεβέσιν ἐχθροῖς παρέδωκεν ; "

[42] The text, translation, and commentary were published in L. Oeconomos, "L'état intellectuel et moral des Byzantins vers le milieu du XIVᵉ sièlce d'après une page de Joseph Bryennios," *Mélanges Charles Diehl* (Paris, 1930), I, 225–233. On Bryennius, N. Tomadakes, Ἰωσὴφ Βρυέννιος in Σύλλαβος βυζαντινῶν μελετῶν καὶ κειμένων (Athens, 1961), pp. 489–611, especially pp. 527–545; " Ἰωσὴφ τοῦ Βρυεννίου ἀνέκδοτα ἔργα κρητικά," Ε.Ε.Β.Σ., XIX (1949), 130–154; " Ἁγιορειτικοὶ κώδικες τῶν ἔργων Ἰωσὴφ Βρυεννίου," Ε.Ε.Β.Σ., XXXII (1963), 26–39. Beck, *Kirche und theologische Literatur*, pp. 749–750. P. Meyer, "Des Joseph Bryennius Schriften, Leben und Bildung," *B.Z.*, V (1896), 74–111.

[43] Tomadakis, Σύλλαβος, p. 536.

[44] Oeconomos, "L'état," 227. Though Bryennius evidently composed the text with Crete in mind, the contents reflect conditions throughout the empire as well, Tomadakis, Σύλλαβος, p. 527, no. 1.

[45] Oeconomos, "L'état," p. 227.

of the feasts with flutes, dances, all satanic songs, carousels, drunkenesses, and other shameful customs.[46]

The low moral level is matched by widespread crass superstition. These superstitious practices are often remnants from the life of pagan antiquity: future events are predicted by the movements of icons; omens are taken from greetings and farewells, and in the taking of auguries the cries of domestic fowl and flights of ravens are observed; people deceive themselves in believing, like astrologers, that hours, fates, chances, the zodiac, planets, control life; they believe in the Nereids of the sea and spirits that inhabit the land. Some burn incense before fig trees, cucumber plants, and house plants; others greet the new moon and worship it; calends are celebrated, the amulets of March are worn, wreaths are placed on houses in May, and the jumping over of fires is practiced.

Spells are our refuge in the fertility of fields, health, and increase of flocks, fortune in the hunts, fruitfulness of the vineyards. The pursuit of sin grows and the flight of virtue accelerates.[47]

Society has come apart at the seams and is disintegrating.

Our rulers are unjust, those who oversee our affairs are rapacious, the judges accept gifts, the mediators are liars, the city dwellers are deceivers, the rustics are unintelligible, and all are useless. Our virgins are more shameless than prostitutes, the widows more curious than they ought to be, the married women disdain and keep not faith, the young men are licentious and the aged drunkards. The nuns (have) insulted their calling, the priests have forgotten God, the monks have strayed from the straight road.... Many of us live in gluttony, drunkenness, fornication, adultery, foulness, licentiousness, hatred, rivalry, jealousy, envy, and theft. We have become arrogant, braggart, avaricious, selfish, ungrateful, disobedient, irreconcilable.... It is these things and others like them which bring down upon us the chastisements of God.[48]

Though the two categories of explanations or causes of the reversal of Byzantine affairs were diametrically opposed, they frequently had one element in common. The decline need not be final and irreversible. Pletho and Bessarion could still consider seriously the problem of saving the situation with new schemes. The former suggested the founding of a new Greek state along Platonic lines in the Peloponese, whereas the latter proposed that Byzantine youths should be sent to the West to study Western technology.[49] Even for those who saw causation as completely

[46] *Ibid.* On sexual immorality as the cause of the empire's downfall, Koukoules, " Τὰ οὐ φωνητὰ τῶν Βυζαντινῶν , " 'Αθηνᾶ, LVI (1952), 90.

[47] Oeconomos, "L'état," p. 228.

[48] *Ibid.*

[49] Lampros, Π.Π., III, 246–265; IV, 32–45. Bessarion's plan calls to mind the efforts of the Balkan, Muslim, and Far Eastern peoples to westernize in the nineteenth and twentieth centuries. The Greeks who would go to the West were to study primarily Western mechanics, metallurgy, weapons-making, and shipbuilding, and secondarily the production of glass, silk, wool, and dyes. See A. G. Keller, "A Byzantine Admirer of 'Western' Progress; Cardinal Bessarion," *The Cambridge Historical Journal*, XI (1953–55), 343–348. See Cydenes' exhoration to the Byzantines to shake off their apathy and to halt the Turkish advance by a greater display of vigor, A. Vakalopoules, Πηγὲς τῆς ἱστορίας τοῦ νέου Ἑλληνισμοῦ (Thessalonike, 1965), I, 91–93.

in the hands of God there was some hope. Charitonymus Ermonymus exhorted the "remnants of the Rhomaioi" not to despair over their misfortune, for such misfortune is experienced, has been experienced in the past, and will continue to be experienced in the future by many others. But by contemplating their errors and mistakes, by correcting them, and by coming closer to God, from whom the Greeks have strayed, their fortunes will be reversed and they shall once more prosper. "Thus it is that a small town becomes a large city, and a large city is preserved."[50] Ermonymus has simply extended one line of logic implicit in the religious category of causation. If decline has been brought by sin, it could be reversed by abandoning sin and embracing the life of virtue. Thus the outlook of the Byzantines was not ultimately and irrevocably fatalistic.[51] This is remarkable when one considers the desperation of the state in the fifteenth century.

Religious Polemic

One genre of Greek literature which specifically concerned itself with these problems was religious polemic. Great disasters, especially those of a political and military nature, cause crises in the established order and frequently call into question the values of institutions of that order. The history of the ancient and medieval worlds is replete with such upheavals. The Roman conquest of Spain and Gaul resulted in the Latinization of these areas. The Spanish reconquest of the Iberian peninsula from the Arabs brought with it the obliteration of Islam and Arabic. In a similar fashion the Arab expansion was eventually followed by the practical extinction not only of Christianity in North Africa, Egypt, and the Levant, but of the Greek, Coptic, Syriac, and Berber tongues in those areas. As even the most cursory readings of Augustine and Orosius will reveal, the members of the defeated society nearly always found themselves faced with the perplexing problem of explaining the sudden change and reversal of fortune. If their religion were indeed the one true religion, why did God abandon them? In the medieval world, where exclusive, monolithic religious systems dominated society, political disaster invariably stimulated religious explanation and rationalization, as has already been made clear. In pagan times political defeat did not necessarily entail an eclipse of the religious values and systems of the defeated, and so for example, Greek paganism was not destroyed by the Roman conquest. But Christianity and Islam, though historically tolerant of each other (because of the facts of history and existence), were both conscious of their exclusive, "true," and unique nature. The political defeat of one or the other necessarily required a religious explanation, for political victory of a Muslim

[50] Lampros, II.II., IV, 271–273.
[51] See n. 108 below. A. Bryer, "The Great Idea," *History Today*, XV (1965), 159–168. On p. 159 he translates part of a folk song from the regions of Trebizond on the fall of Constantinople, "If Romania is lost now, she will flower once more and bear fruit."

or Byzantine state would seem to imply the "truth" of Islam or Christianity.

Byzantium had come to feel the military force of Islam at a comparatively early date. Though it had managed to survive the almost fatal onslaught of the seventh century, it had remained on the defense until the ninth century. This preoccupation with the advance of Islam was reflected in Byzantine society and in its international relations. Gradually the West was abandoned politically, and eventually Byzantine chroniclers and historians restricted their coverage of events in a manner that increasingly neglected the West and concentrated on the East. The genre of religious polemic between Christianity and Islam was directly stimulated by the Muslim conquest of Christian lands within which Muslims and Christians came to live side by side. It has been pointed out that Syria and the adjacent regions had, because of their mixed religious configuration, seen considerable religious polemic in Byzantine times prior to the Arab conquest. Not only was there religious controversy among such diverse religious groups as Orthodox, Monophysites, Nestorians, Jews, and pagans, but there was also a cultural polemic of a type as a result of the revival of local cultures.[52]

It was in these areas and under these circumstances that the intellectuals of the Byzantine church inaugurated the genre of religious polemic with Islam. At its origin this literature centers on the names of the Orthodox theologians John of Damascus and Theodore Abu Qurra, both born in Muslim lands and, as is well known, the family of the former was associated with official service to the caliphs. Theodore was born in the polyglot city of Edessa, and wrote in Greek, Syriac, and Arabic. He was eventually appointed bishop of Harran in northern Mesopotamia, a city that included within its confines pagans (Sabaeans), Manichaeans, Jews, Muslims Melkites, Jacobites, and Nestorians. Though the authenticity of the chapter on Islam in John of Damascus' περὶ αἱρέσεων is highly doubtful, the older traditional Byzantine polemic with the various Christian sects is first expanded to include Islam by John and his successor Theodore Abu Qurra.[53] This early polemic, which was important not only in the general

[52] A. Abel, "La polémique damascenienne et son influence sur les origines de la théologie musulmane," *L'élaboration de l'Islam* (Paris, 1961), pp. 62–63 (hereafter cited as Abel, "Polémique damascenienne").

[53] *Ibid.*, 64–73; Abel, "Le chapitre CI du Livre des Hérésies de Jean Damascene: son inauthenticité," *S.I.*, XIX (1963), 5–25. I. Dick, "Un continuateur arabe de saint Jean Damascène: Théodore Abuqara, évéque melkite de Harran. La personne et son milieu," *Proche Orient Chrétien*, XII (1962), 209–223. G. Graff, *Geschichte der christlichen arabischen Literatur* (Vatican, 1947), II, 7–11, for further bibliography on Abu Qurra., J. Meyenderff, "Byzantine Views of Islam," *D.O.P.*, XVIII (1964), 113–132. W. Eichner, "Die Nachrichten über den Islam bei den Byzantinern," *Der Islam*, XXIII (1936), 136–137. Dvornik, *Les légendes de Constantin et de Méthode vues de Byzance* (Prague, 1933), pp. 104–108. Manuel Palaeologus-Trapp, 11*–28*. C. Guterbock, *Der Islam im Lichte der byzantinischen Polemik* (Berlin, 1912), pp. 10–16. For polemic in Islamic lands, M. Steinschneider, *Polemische und apologetische Literatur in Arabischer Sprache, zwischen Muslimen, Christen, und Juden, nebst Anhängen verwandten Inhalts* (Leipzig, 1877). M. Perlmann, *Samau'al*

formation of Greek theological argument but also in the rise of Muslim polemic and theology, did not rest upon a detailed knowledge of the Koran. The Christians at this early date had to defend themselves against Muslim attacks on the dogmas of the incarnation and the Trinity, in which attacks the Arabs denied the divinity of Christ and alleged that the doctrine of the Trinity was proof that the Christians were polytheists. The Orthodox dealt with the charges by retorting that the Muslim God must, in consequence of the denial of Christ's incarnation and of the Trinity, be lifeless and without reason.[54] Then they proceeded to strike at the basis of Islam by the assertion that the Koran was not a revealed book and that Muhammad was a pseudoprophet. Neither, they contended, was predicted or mentioned in the Old or New Testament and therefore there was no prophecy as there had been in the case of Christ. To this charge they appended the "immorality" of Muslim ethics. Thus this early religious debate was based on the more apparent aspects and characteristics of the two religions rather than upon any detailed and systematic knowledge arrived at through a careful study of the religious scriptures. Anti-Muslim religious disputation made its initial appearance within the empire in the writings of the ninth-century author Nicetas of Byzantium,[55] who opened a new path to Greek authors by dealing with the Koran in some detail and by presenting numerous translated passages from the Arabic.[56] As the most detailed analysis of the Koran, the writings of Nicetas became an important source for later Byzantine writings on the subject.[57]

The threat of a victorious and militant Islam reappeared at the end of the eleventh century when the Turks entered Anatolia. The political forces of Islam at that time entered Greek lands proper and began also to take away the "flocks" of the church. As Islam moved westward so did the concern with religious polemic. The new social and political

---

al-Maghribī. Ifḥām al-Yahūd (New York, 1964). Cahen, "Note sur l'accueil des Chrétiens d'Orient à l'Islam," *Revue de l'histoire des religions*, CLXVI (1964), 51–58. Abel, "La signification apologétique et politique des apocalypses islamo-chrétiennes au Moyen Age," *Proceedings of the Twenty-Second Congress of Orientalists*, II (Leiden, 1957), 533–536. D. Sourdel, "Un pamphlet musulman anonyme d'époque 'abbāside contre les chrétiens," *R.E.I.*, XXXIV (1966), 1–34.

[54] Abel, "Polémique damascènienne," p. 65.

[55] Beck, *Kirche und theologische Literatur*, pp. 530–531. Guterbock, *Polemik*, pp. 24–33. Eichner, "Nachrichten," p. 138. Abel, "La lettre polémique d'Arethas' à l'émir de Damas," *Byzantion*, XXIV (1956), p. 354 (hereafter cited as Abel, "La lettre,").

[56] In his principal polemical work, Ἀνατροπὴ τῆς παρὰ τοῦ Ἄραβος Μωάμετ πλαστογραφηθείσης βίβλου, *P.G.*, CV, 669–806, Nicetas examined the Koran at length. In the first seventeen chapters, he dealt with suras 2–18; in chapter eighteen, with the remaining suras. In chapters nineteen through thirty, he took individual points of Islamic doctrine and placed them opposite their corresponding Christian doctrine. On pp. 808–841, are edited two further polemical works of Nicetas, letters composed in the name of Michael III in answer to Muslim correspondents.

[57] Eichner, "Nachrichten," pp. 133–134. For later polemic prior to the eleventh century, Abel, "La lettre," 354 ff.

realities facing Byzantium induced an efflorescence of religious explanation as the Orthodox Christians saw their empire devoured by the Turks.
Not only lowly monks but even atticizing emperors turned their pens to
the task of explaining the reasons for Christianity's misfortune. The form
and content of these literary efforts went back to the traditions of earlier
times, and especially to the writings of the ninth-century Nicetas. There
were, however, certain new elements that characterized their arguments,
elements that had less to do with content than with the general tone. It
should be noted, parenthetically, that one of the most important literary
contributions to this renewed literary defense against Islam was of Latin
origin, the *Improbatio Alcorani* of the Florentine Dominican Ricoldo da
Monte Croce (d. 1320).[58] Ricoldo, after a pilgrimage to Jerusalem, went
onto Baghdad where he studied Arabic with a view to translating the
Koran into Latin. During his stay in the Mesopotamian city he had the
opportunity to hear and participate in religious discussions with prominent
Muslim theologians with the result that Ricoldo acquired a comparatively
detailed knowledge of the Islamic doctrines, the sects, and the Koran.
When the prominent Byzantine Latinist Demetrius Cydones translated
Ricoldo's *Improbatio Alcorani* into Greek between 1354 and 1360, he
provided Byzantine polemicists with a fresh arsenal of details and
arguments. One decade later the emperor John VI Cantacuzene relied
heavily on the Cydones translation of Ricoldo in composing his own
defense of Christianity and attack upon Islam. Manuel II Palaeologus
was in turn partially influenced by the latter's treatise and thereby
indirectly by Ricoldo.

This second phase of Graeco-Islamic polemic (post-eleventh century)
was often characterized by a tone of immediacy and realism. Though it
continually involved the well-established categories of disputation, these
were placed in realistic surroundings and were pursued at greater length.
This literature was not primarily a theoretical intellectual exercise
abstractly and disinterestedly composed in the isolation of monastic
scriptorium and imperial library, because much of it arose as a result of
immediate contact and debate between Muslims and Christians. Two of
the texts are associated with the eastern Anatolian towns of Melitene and
Edessa, both of which were early surrounded and conquered by the
Turks.[59] Cantauzene allegedly composed his treatise at the instigation of a

---

[58] Eichner, "Nachrichten," pp. 139–140. Beck, *Kirche und theologische Literatur*, pp. 732,
734, 736. On Ricoldo, U. Monneret de Villard, *Le studio dell'Islam in Europe nel XIIe e nel
XIII secolo* (Vatican, 1944), *passim*. Manuel Palaeologus-Trapp, 35*–44*.

[59] The Δάλεξις μετὰ Σαρακηνοῦ φιλοσόφου περὶ πίστεως ἐν τῇ Μελιτηνῆς ascribed to
Euthymius Zigabenus in *P.G.*, CXXXI, 19–38, seems to be of a later period, Beck,
Kirche und theologische Literatur, p. 614. The Ἔλεγχος Ἀγαρηνοῦ of Bartholomaeus of
Edessa," *P.G.*, CIV, 1384–1448, has been variously dated to the ninth, twelfth, and
thirteenth centuries: Beck, *Kirche und theologische Literatur*, p. 531, dates it to the ninth
century; Guterbock, *Polemik*, pp. 22 ff., says it is not before 1100 on the basis of late
philological forms; Eichner, "Nachrichten," p. 137, dates it to the thirteenth century

Muslim converted to Christianity, Meletius by name. Meletius, formerly a member of the Ottoman court circles, had aroused considerable concern among the Turks as a result of his apostasy to Christianity. Consequently, one of the Muslims, Shams al-Din Isfahani, wrote to Meletius beseeching him to return to the sultan's court and to Islam.[60] The religious debate on the relative merits of the two religions and the reasons for Islam's victory doubtlessly remained very lively in the period between the eleventh and fifteenth centuries and even afterward.[61] We are told by a Muslim chronicle, for example, that the Greek beğlerbeğ of the Seljuk sultan 'Izz al-Din took a perverse stand against the Muslim emirs because of his Christian fanaticism and attempted to surround the sultan with his own men in order to remove him from the influence of his Muslim advisers. While at Filubad, the sultan's pleasure palace, the Christian official is reported to have taunted the Muslim Badi al-Din with the remark, "I understand that your caliph has been killed" (in reference to the fall of Baghdad to the Mongols). The Muslim promptly replied that this should not seem strange to one in whose religion God (Christ) was "hanged"![62]

Further incidentals in regard to this polemic that transpired between Christian priests and Muslim religious men emerge from the accounts of Eflaki and the synodal documents of the fourteenth century. Matthew, the fourteenth-century metropolitan of Ephesus, complains that his religious discussions with the Muslims of Ephesus aroused the animosity of the Turks and resulted in his being stoned.

And they have no reason from us for such audacities [stoning] except that the heralds of [their] error who are considered to be their priests think that they have been deprived of their religion as we priests related to them the most holy worship and put forward the holy dogma and preached Christ the Son of God and true God. This appears exceedingly abominable to them, and we dispatch the cross as some frightful whip against the demons and those who are no less then demons.

---

because the text mentions the use of hashish by dervishes. Certainly philological evidence would seem to preclude a ninth-century date. The author uses ἄλογον, σουλτάνον, Ζεκχέτης, φορακίδες-φουκαράδες, Μουσουλμάνοι, καμῆλι, πηγάδι, ἐτζάκισαν, ὅτις for ὅτι, etc. The title sultan came into widespread use during the eleventh century. Φορακίδες would seem to be a metathesized form of φουκαράδες the fakirs or dervishes, also a later religious phenemenon. The Byzantine authors generally referred to Muslims as Agarenes, not Mousoulmanoi. Also the forms καμῆλι, πηγάδι, ἐτζάκισαν, etc. would possibly indicate a later date. The text would seem to be from the twelfth century for Bartholomaeus speaks of Μορατίνου- Nur al-Din of Aleppo. See the comments of Manuel Palaeologus-Trapp, 32*–34*, who dates it prior to 1146, the date of the sack of Edessa by the Muslims.

[60] John Cantacuzene, P.G., CLIV, 372–377.

[61] See for example the interesting disputation between Panayiotakis Mamonas and Vani Effendi which transpired in the seventeenth century, I. Sakkelion, " Παναγιωτάκη τοῦ Μαμονᾶ τοῦ χρηματίσαντος μεγάλου ἑρμηνέως, πρώτου χριστιανοῦ, τῆς τῶν Ὀθωμανῶν βασιλείας διάλεξις μετά τινος Βανλῆ ἐφένδη Μουσουλμάνου, διδασκάλου τῶν Τούρκων."Δ.Ι.Ε.Ε., III (1889), 235–273. See also the exposition of the Christian faith which Gennadius made before the sultan, Petit, Siderides, Jugie, Oeuvres, III, 435 ff.

[62] Aksaray-Gençosman, p. 145.

And if we undertake to come to words, we refute them as silly concerning the prophet himself and in [their] laws and legislation. We freely declare that all their [religious beliefs] are of use only to the eternal fire and worm.

Seeing these things, the accursed ones always cry out, giving way to [their] entire desire, to taste flesh and blood, and they would not have abstained if they had not seen that their chieftain was not at all permissive to their madness, not easily joining [the assault]. Accordingly what they are able to do, this they dare to do in the previously mentioned manner with rocks, throwing them at night.[63]

The intensity with which both sides pursued questions and discussions appears most clearly, perhaps, in the account that Gregory Palamas, archbishop of Thessalonike, gives of his captivity by and sojourn among the Turks in Bithynia.[64] The prelate was captured by a Turkish naval attack on the ship that was carrying him through the Hellespont in the year 1354. The Turks held him and his companions for ransom and in the course of his captivity Palamas traveled through the towns of Lampsacus, Pegae, Bursa, and Iznik. He relates that during the course of his peregrinations he was constantly accompanied by Turkish guards except when the procession reached some town and then he was allowed to dwell among the local Christian population. But during the time when he was actually traveling, Palamas and his Turkish escort engaged in continuous discussions of a very interesting sort.

If one had time to record the questions which they [the Turkish guards] addressed to us and the answers which we made to them and their agreement with them, and generally all the conversations on the road, it would be exceedingly sweet to Christian ears.[65]

This polemical curiosity was not restricted to the Turkish soldiers who accompanied the archbishop, for no sooner did the captives arrive at Lampsacus than the Turkish governor of the town arranged a religious debate.[66] The Greeks also flocked to the archbishop to relate their problems and woes and especially, say Palamas, to ask why it was that God had so

[63] Matthew of Ephesus-Treu, p. 57.

[64] G. Georgiades-Arnakes, "Gregory Palamas among the Turks and Documents of his Captivity as Historical Sources," *Speculum*, XXVI (1951), 104–118; "Gregory Palamas, the χιόνες and the Fall of Gallipoli," *Byzantion*, XXII (1952), 305–312. Wittek, "Χίονες" *Byzantion*, XXI (1951), 421–423. Meyendorff, "Grecs, Turcs, et Juifs en Asie Mineure au XIVᵉ siècle," *B.F.*, I (1966), 211–217. The texts are printed in the following studies. The most detailed account is that which Palamas recorded in his letter to the Thessalonicans, Lampros-Dyobouniotes, " Γρηγορίου Παλαμᾶ ἐπιστολὴ πρὸς Θεσσαλονι-κεῖς," *N.E.*, XVI (1922), 3–21 (hereafter cited as Palamas, "Thessalonicans"). A shorter version is to be found in his letter to David Monachus the Dishypatos, M. Treu, " ᾿Επισ-τολὴ Γρηγορίου τοῦ Παλαμᾶ πρὸς Δαυὶδ μοναχὸν τὸν Δισύπατον," Δ.Ι.Ε.Ε.Ε., III (1889), 227–234. The text of the controversy between Palamas and the Chiones which Taronites recorded is edited by Sakellion, " Γρηγορίου Θεσσαλονίκης τοῦ Παλαμᾶ ἀνέκδοτος διάλεξις," Σωτήρ, XV (1892), 236–246 (hereafter cited as Palamas-Taronites).

[65] Lampros-Dyobouniotes, p. 14.

[66] *Ibid.* p. 10. The Greeks asserted that Palamas' captivity, as indeed the subjugation of the Greeks, proved that the Turks enjoyed God's favor. " τὴν αἰχμαλωσίαν ἡμῶν προφέρ-ειν, ὡς τι σημεῖον τῆς περὶ τὸ σέβας οὐκ ἀσφαλείας. Μεγαλαυχοῦσι γὰρ τὸ δυσσεβὲς καὶ θεομισὲς καὶ παμμίαρον τοῦτο γένος, ὡς ὑπὸ τῆς σφῶν θεοφιλείας ἐπικρατοῦντες ῾Ρωμαίων."

completely abandoned the Christians.[67] From Lampsacus, Palamas and his Turkish escort made their way to Pegae and Bursa where once more he ministered to the demoralized local Christians. En route from Bursa to Iznik the party halted at a mountain village where the sultan happened to be staying. Once more Islam and Christianity became the subject of special discussion when the sultan's son, Ismail, invited the archbishop to break bread with him on the grass. Though the conversations were interrupted by rain and eventually by their departure from the village, they were renewed on a grander scale when the sultan's Christian physician, Taronites, spoke of the archbishop's learning and eloquence to the ruler. The sultan then set a debate between Palamas and his own theologians, a group of Jews known as Chiones who had apostatized to Islam. The course of the dispute seems to have excited the Turks and especially the Chiones who in the end struck Palamas in the eye, much to the displeasure of the Turks who had participated in the debate.[68] The last polemical episode Palamas describes occurred in Nicaea. Here the prelate happened to witness a Turkish funeral procession at the eastern gate of the city and picked this inappropriate moment to engage the Muslim danishmend, who was presiding over the funeral, in religious discussions. The conversations were terminated when, after a considerable crowd of Turks and Greeks had gathered, the Greek audience noticed that the Turks were angered at the turn of the debate and the aggressiveness of Palamas. They motioned to the archbishop to put an end to the talks and so the assembly dispersed.

The experiences of Palamas in Bithynia one generation after its conquest illuminate an important chapter in the history of the struggle between Islam and Christianity in Anatolia. Greeks and Turks incessantly discussed and disputed the meaning of the history that had unfolded in Anatolia. Both the Christians and Muslims of Bithynia plied Palamas with queries as to the religious significance of the Turkish conquest.

One must assume that this dispute between the Christian and Muslim points of view continued in Anatolia far beyond the departure of Palamas from his Turkish captivity. The last great polemic on Anatolian soil which has survived in written form took place between Manuel

---

[67] Lampros-Dyobouniotes, p. 11. " τῶν δὲ πλειόνων, τὴν αἰτίαν ἀπαιτούντων τῆς περὶ τὸ ἡμέτερον γένος παρὰ Θεοῦ τοσαύτης ἐγκαταλείψεως." On the anxiety of the Christians and their reliance upon the clergy for assurances, see the interesting incident from the Saltukname in Turan, "L'Islamisation dans la Turquie du moyen age," S.I., X (1959), 145. A Greek priest of Amaseia, in projecting the reasons of the Turkish victories was asked if the Turks would enter Paradise. He replied that they would simply gaze at it from outside the gates. But a young Greek rejoined that he could not believe that the Turks, who had already chased the Greeks from their hearths, would remain content to gaze in through the gates and see the Greeks in possession of Paradise.

[68] The treatment of Palamas at the hands of the Turks seems to have varied greatly. When he was first captured, he was cruelly treated by Orhan's son, who also threw the prelate's works into the sea and had him deprived of his clothing, R. Guilland, *Essai sur Nicéphore Grégoras. L'homme et l'oeuvre* (Paris, 1926), pp. 46, 236.

Palaeologus and the muderris of Ankara while Manuel was performing military service in the army of Bayazid in 1390–1391.[69] The background of the principals in this debate, and the languages that they utilized, are of interest in that they symbolize the whole process of transformation in Asia Minor. The muderris and his sons were recent immigrants to Anatolia from the Islamic heartlands, and Manuel was of course from Constantinople. As the latter spoke only Greek, and the former spoke Persian, Arabic, and Turkish, the debate had to be carried on through an interpreter. Fittingly, the interpreter was a young Anatolian Greek, born of Christian parents, who had recently converted to Islam. As he was bilingual (speaking both Greek and Turkish), it was through his linguistic mediation that the debate progressed.[70] But the muderris and his sons did not fully trust the new convert, who still felt some affection for the religion of his parents.[71] So at difficult points in the debate the muderris would consult with his sons in a language other than Turkish, thus cutting off the interpreter. The three parties to the debate present the historian-spectator with a still-shot, an isolated and microcosmic view, of the long complex process by which Anatolia was culturally transformed. Manuel represents the defeated and exhausted forces of Byzantine Hellenism which had previously Hellenized Asia Minor, and the muderris symbolizes the newly arrived and victorious forces of Islamic civilization which are assimilating Anatolia. The interpreter, a Greek Christian by birth and a Muslim by choice, individualizes in concrete form the process of change. He is in a sense not only bilingual but almost "bireligious." Only he is able to bring the two forces together in the debate by virtue of his split cultural personality. As time progresses, however, his descendants will forget Greek and become completely alienated from Christianity.

What was the nature of these debates and which were the favored themes? The polemical literature was remarkably consistent in its choice of topics. The authenticity of the revelations in the Bible or Koran was vigorously contested, but no less intensely debated were the contents of religious doctrine, ethical commands, and ritual practices. And, of course, the less spiritual fact of the Turkish conquest demanded explanation.[72]

In discussing the revelations of the respective scriptures, the Christians enjoyed a certain forensic advantage because of the fact that the Muslims accepted in principle the validity of the Old and New Testaments, whereas the Christians did not accept the revealed character of the Koran. The most systematic effort to disprove the divine inspiration of the Koran, that of Ricoldo-Cydones, commences by asserting this very fact. The

---

[69] Manuel Palaeologus-Trapp, *passim.*

[70] *Ibid.,* p. 23.

[71] *Ibid.,* p. 79, " . . . ὁ τηνικαῦτα ἑρμηνεὺς (Χριστιανῶν δὲ ἦν βλάστη καὶ τὰ γονέων ἠγάπα καὶ τῇ γνώμῃ τούτοις προσέκειτο, εἰ καὶ μὴ καθόσον προσῆκε)."

[72] Eichner, "Nachrichten," pp. 144–162, 197–244, gives a convenient and detailed summary of these categories.

Koran is not the law of God precisely because the Muslims accept both the Old and New Testaments, neither of which foretells Muhammad's revelation. And, the polemicist continues, this is proved by further considerations. The Koran differs in literary form, being written in verse, from other divinely revealed texts. Its contents too are at variance with the essentials of God's law and even with the teachings of the philosophers on virtue, for Muhammad said noting of virtue but concerned himself with war and rapine. The Koran is not only self-contradictory, illogical, and devoid of proper order and arrangement, but it contains falsehoods. For these reasons, Ricoldo-Cydones concludes, the Koran is not truly a revealed book.[73] The Christian theologians dwelt in particular upon the proposition that Muhammad's revelation was not satisfactorily witnessed, as had been that of Christ. The coming of Christ had been prophesied in the Old Testament and it had been witnessed by the numerous miracles of the New Testament and by the Evangelists. These miracles, as essentials to the witnessing of divine revelations, continued long after Christ's sojurn on earth. The very spread of Christianity by the apostles and the gift of tongues, the miracles wrought at the graves of the martyrs, all present valid testimonial to Christian revelation.[74] Contrastingly, Muhammad's mission was not only unmentioned in the Jewish and Christian scriptures, it was not reliably witnessed either by individuals or by miracles. Thus when Palamas engaged in controversy with the danishmend of Nicaea, the latter put to his Christian opponent a much repeated question. Since Muslims honor all the prophets (Christ included) and the four books that have come down from God, why do the Christians not accept Muhammad and the Koran?[75] Palamas, and the other Greek polemicists as well, inevitably replied that nothing can be accepted without proof or witnesses, and this proof can be of two categories, proof from Muhammad's works and proof from reliable individuals. Both were lacking. Muhammad did not resurrect the dead, heal the sick, or halt the winds and waves, as Christ had. And the few miracles that the Muslims alleged were not satisfactorily witnessed. Who saw Gabriel convey God's revelation to Muhammad as the latter slept? Even if the angel had actually appeared to Muhammad with the revelation of God, it was the angel rather than Muhammad who was the real prophet. And was it not strange that though the Muslims required "twelve" witnesses to the taking of a legal wife, yet they accepted Muhammad's miraculous leap to heaven on the sole testimony of Fatima?[76]

[73] *P.G.*, CLIV, 1052–1112.
[74] Euthymius Zigabenus, *P.G.*, CXXXI, 33; John Cantacuzene, *P.G.*, CLIV, 392–433, 500, 512–513, 517.
[75] Lampros-Dyobouniotes, p. 16.
[76] Nicetas Choniates, *P.G.*, CXL, 108. Euthymius Zigabenus, *P.G.*, CXXXI, 333. Bartholomaeus of Edessa, *P.G.*, CIV, 1389–1393, 1418, contains the most violent attack on the question of witnesses and miracles. The acerbity is sufficient to demonstrate that Bartholomaeus either did not compose this work in a Muslim-held city or else that he

The danishmend, confronted with the argument that Muhammad's coming had not been prophesied in the Bible, resorted to the customary weapon of defense from the arsenal of traditional Islamic polemic. The prophecies relevant to Muhammad in these earlier scriptures had been excised by the Christians and the Gospels corrupted, and finally why had Muhammad come, if not as the seal of prophecy?[77] The Christian answer was the Muhammad had come to deceive. Christ had warned that though prophecy had come to an end with John, there would be pseudoprophets. The alleged corruption of the Gospels was disproved by the mere fact that though the Gospels exist in many tongues and among many heretics such as Nestorians and Jacobites, their contents are everywhere the same. They have not even deleted the hateful names of Judas and Pontius Pilate, therefore they would not have removed the name of Muhammad had it been in the text originally. Furthermore, how could Nestorians and Jacobites, who are enemies, have come to any kind of agreement, especially to corrupt the texts?[78] The basic argument of the Christians in regard to Muhammad and the Koran was that they were both false because they were unprophesied and unwitnessed.

Doctrinally, the opponents were most absorbed by the concept of God, which involved the questions of Christological and Trinitarian theology. Here the Christians were most frequently defending their religion against the Muslim charges of polytheism. By the mystical doctrine of the Trinity, it was charged, the Christians had given God associates. And if they could associate two with God, why not three, four, or more? Moreover, the argument continued, Christ was a man and not divine, for how could God fit into and be born from the womb of woman? What does the incarnation avail Christians? Could not God have saved man in some other fashion? The Byzantine replies to these attacks were a curious mixture

---

kept the document private. Thus, on p. 1388, he describes the "pseudo-prophet" Muhammad with excessive venom, " Λοιπὸν διὰ τί αὐτὸν προφήτην καὶ ἀπόστολον Θεοῦ καλεῖς λάγνον ὄντα, καὶ τοιοῦτον παμμίαρον, καὶ ληστήν, καὶ ἄδικον, καὶ φονέα, καὶ ἄρπαγα ; Φράσον μοι, τί ἑρμηνεύεται προφητεία, καὶ ἀπόστολος." His attempted miracles are ridiculous, Bartholomaeus, *P.G.*, CIV, 1432–1433; Euthymius Zigabenus, *P.G.*, CXXX, 1358. Finally, Muhammad attempts to cover up his lack of miracles and witnesses with the assertion that he has come to give the law not through miracles but by the sword, John Cantacuzene, *P.G.*, CLIV, 544. " Ἐγὼ οὐκ ἦλθον διὰ θαυμάτων δοῦναι τὸν νόμον, ἀλλὰ διὰ σπάθης καὶ ξίφους. Καὶ οἱ μὴ ὑποκύψαντες τῷ ἡμετέρῳ νόμῳ, ὅς ἐστι παρὰ θεοῦ, θανάτῳ ἀποθανέτωσαν, ἢ φόρους διδότωσαν."

[77] Lampros-Dyobouniotes, p. 17. In Euthymius Zigabenus, *P.G.*, CXXXI, 33, and Bartholomaeus, *P.G.*, CIV, 1384, the Muslims charge that the Christians hid the Gospel and wrote another one. In Nicetas Choniates, *P.G.*, CXL, 117, the Saracen states that Daniel and Christ foretold the coming of Muhammad. John Cantacuzene, *P.G.*, CLIV, 540. A further extension of this argument was that the Old and New Testaments were no longer necessary as everything good in them had been incorporated into the Koran, Ricoldo-Cydones, *P.G.*, CLIV, 1148.

[78] Lampros-Dyobouniotes, pp. 17–18. Euthymius Zigabenus, *P.G.*, CXXX, 1344. Nicetas Choniates. *P.G.*, CXL, 116. Ricoldo-Cydones, *P.G.*, CLIV, 1053–1055. John Cantacuzene, *P.G.*, CLIV, 541–544.

of clever philological arguments and propositions attained as a result of faulty translation from the Arabic of the Koran. First, the prophets who spoke of Christ referred to Him as the Son of God, as God, and as One who would be incarnate. Second, the Muslims themselves accepted the fact that Jesus is the λόγος and πνεῦμα of God and that these are in God. For to argue the contrary is to say that God is ἄλογος and ἄπνους (thoughtless and breathless), and this would reduce God to dead matter. Therefore the spirit and the logos have always been with God. And Christ, as being born of the Virgin, is also man, as the prophets prophesied. How his birth came about is a mystery, but to deny God's incarnation as an impossibility is to admit that God is not omnipotent. God became incarnate in order to save man, and it is useless to inquire why He did not seek to save man in some other manner for this is beyond the comprehension of man.[79] In the process of upholding the incarnation and the Trinity, the Christian polemicists brought against the Muslims the countercharge that they worshiped a material God, a God who was ἄλογος and ἄπνους. Here it would seem they combined their conclusions from the arguments on the Trinity with a mistranslation of the epithet of Allah, samad, in Sura 112 to prove their point. Samad in this Koranic passage refers to God *eternal*, but inasmuch as the term also had the meaning of "not hollow," or "solid," the Greek translator rendered it as ὁλόσφυρος, compact, solid.[80] In short, the Greeks argued that the denial of the Trinity and the incarnation reduced God to pure matter and divested Him of His omnipotence.

Other doctrines (free will, prophetic history, angels, demons, eschatology,) exercised the theologians of both camps but perhaps not as extensively as matters concerning ethical and ritual commands. The outward manifestations of religious difference were more immediately obvious than were doctrinal subtleties. In those regions where Muslims and Christians lived side by side, differences of this nature were constantly and saliently evident. The Christian argument fastened upon the ethical teachings of Muhammad and the Koran, charging the Muslims with following a religion that not only condoned the life of the "lascivious and murderer," but one that also purported to give divine sanction for such a life. How could a religion that permitted man to acquire four wives and

---

[79] Euthymius Zigabenus, *P.G.*, CXXX, 1337. "'Αλλ' ἐπεὶ Ἰσοῦν Χριστὸν λέγετε Λόγον τοῦ Θεοῦ, καὶ πνεῦμα αὐτοῦ, συνομολογεῖτε καὶ ἄκοντες ὅτι ὁ Λόγος τοῦ Θεοῦ καὶ τὸ Πνεῦμα αὐτοῦ ἐν τῷ Θεῷ εἰσιν. Ὁ γὰρ Λόγος τοῦ Θεοῦ καὶ τὸ Πνεῦμα αὐτοῦ ἀχώριστά εἰσι τοῦ οὗ εἰσιν, ἵνα μὴ ἄλογος καὶ ἄπνους ὑπολειφθῆ. Εἰδὲ ἐν τῷ Θεῷ ἐστιν ὁ Λόγος αὐτοῦ, δηλονότι καὶ Θεός ἐστι. Καὶ λοιπὸν ὁ Χριστός, ὡς μὲν Λόγος τοῦ Θεοῦ, Θεός ἐστιν, ὡς δὲ ἐκ Παρθένου γεννηθείς, ἄνθρωπός ἐστι." John Cantacuzene, P.G., CLIV, 392, 440–492. For variations, Euthymius Zigabenus, *P.G.*, CXXXI, 21–33. God could not have intervened directly to save man, for satan would have boasted of it. The incarnation is analogous to the rays of the sun which though they enter a deep well are no less rays of the sun.

[80] See Eichner, "Nachrichten," pp. 159–161.

innumerable concubines be considered moral?[81] The unrestrained hedonism of Muslim life was, to the Christians, manifested in a variety of ways. Not only were "sodomic" practices allowed[82] and the defloration of virgins and the custom of prostitution[83] but wives were easily and frequently divorced. The immorality in such "easy" divorce was compounded, in the eyes of the Christians, by the fact that should the husband wish to remarry the wife, he could not do so until she had been taken in wedlock by another man. Thus the law of divorce and remarriage involved further and "legalized" adultery.[84] This was not to be wondered at, for Muhammad himself was a fornicator who used aphrodisiacs,[85] a pseudo-prophet who manufactured a revelation ordering his companion Zayd to relinquish his beautiful wife so that Muhammad could marry her.[86] The very hedonistic and physical character of Muhammad's teaching was sufficient to indicate to Byzantines that it was a false teaching.[87]

In addition, there is no sin which is so unendurable among prophets as

[81] Ricoldo-Cydones, *P.G.*, CLIV, 1065. John Cantacuzene, *P.G.*, CLIV, 548, 549. How can he who preaches many wives be from God? Further on p. 552, if a man is to be given many women in paradise because of his good life on earth, then it follows that women should enjoy the same rewards because man and woman are of one nature and they shall be judged in the same manner. Therefore, according to the foolish preaching of Muhammad, it follows that a woman who has lived a good life should be rewarded with many men! But, Cantacuzene continues, this is obviously nonsense. For God's reward to the righteous does not consist of banquets, baths, and women (which are the end·of sin and orgy), but of εὐφροσύνη and ἀγαλλίασις. Nicetas Choniates, *P.G.*, CXL, 140. Euthymius Zigabenus, *P.G.*, CXXX, 1349, " "Ω τῆς ἀνυπερβλήτου καὶ χοιρώδους ἢ κυνώδους ἀκολασίας." Bartholomaeus, *P.G.*, CIV, 1388.

[82] Euthymius Zigabenus, *P.G.*, CXXX, 1349. " Αἱ γυναῖκες ὑμῶν ναετὸς ὑμῶν. Εἰσέλθετε εἰς τοὺς ναετοὺς ὑμῶν, ὅθεν βούλεσθαι· καὶ συνέλθετε ταῖς ψυχαῖς ὑμῶν. τουτέστι, πᾶσι ἐπιθυμίαν τῶν ψυχῶν ὑμῶν πληρώσατε, καὶ χρήσασθαι ταῖς γυναιξὶν ὑμῶν ἀμφοτέρωθεν. Τὶ τῆς ἀκαθαρσίας ταύτης ἀσελγέστερον καὶ μιαρώτερον ; " Ricoldo-Cydones, *P.G.*, CLIV, 1045. " Δοκεῖ δὲ συγχωρεῖν καὶ τὰ σοδομιτικὰ ἔν τε ἀνδράσι καὶ γυναιξίν, ἐν τῷ περὶ τῆς βοὸς κεφαλαίῳ."

[83] John Cantacuzene, *P.G.*, CLIV, 545.

[84] Nicetas Choniates, *P.G.*, CXL, 112. Euthymius Zigabenus, *P.G.*, CXXX, 1349. Ricoldo-Cydones, *P.G.*, CLIV, 1081, " Δύναται γὰρ Σαρρακηνὸς ἐκβάλλειν τὴν ἑαυτοῦ γυναῖκα, καὶ πάλιν αὐτῇ καταλλάτεσθαι, ὁσάκις ἂν τούτῳ ἀρέσκῃ· οὕτω μέντοι, ὅτι μετὰ τὴν τρίτην ἐκβολὴν μὴ δύνασθαι αὐτὴν εἰσδέχεσθαι, πλὴν εἰ μή τις ἕτερος σαρκικῶς αὐτὴν γνοίη, μὴ οὖσαν ἐν τοῖς ἐμμήνοις. Εἰ δὲ ταύτην γνοίη μὴ ἱκανῶς ἐντεταμένῳ αἰδοίῳ, ἀνάγκη περαιτέρω γνῶναι ταύτην, ἱκανῶς ἐντεταμένῳ τῷ μέλει. Ὅθεν ὅταν βούλωνται καταλλάτεσθαι ταῖς ἑαυτῶν γυναιξί, τίμημα διδόασι τυφλῷ τινι, ἢ ἑτέρῳ εὐτελεῖ προσώπῳ, συνεσομένῳ τοιαύτῃ γυναικί, καὶ μετὰ ταῦτα μαρτυρήσοντι δημοσία, καὶ ἐροῦντι βούλεσθαι ταύτην ἐκβαλεῖν. Οὖ γενομένου, ὁ πρῶτος δύναται καταλλάτειν αὐτὴν ἑαυτῷ. Ἐνίοτε δὲ τοσοῦτον ἀρέσκουσιν αὐταῖς οἱ δεύτεροι, ὥστε λέγειν αὐτὰς μὴ δύνασθαι ἐκείνων χωρίζεσθαι· καὶ τότε ὁ πρῶτος ἀποβαλὼν τὸ τίμημα καὶ τὴν γυναῖκα, ἐκπίπτει τῆς ἑαυτοῦ ἐλπίδος."

[85] Bartholomaeus, *P.G.*, CIV, 1388. " Καὶ ταῦτα διὰ γυναῖκας, καὶ δι' ἄκρατον μίξιν ἐξεωνήσατο βοτάνια συμβαλλόμενα ταῦτα εἰς πορνείαν ἄσχετον, ὡς μὴ ὅλως κόρον ἔχων τῆς τοιαύτης ἐπιθυμίας."

[86] Nicetas Choniates, *P.G.*, CXL, 105-108. Ricoldo-Cydones, *P.G.*, CLIV, 1077, 1113

[87] Euthymius Zigabenus, *P.G.*, CXXX, 1353. Nicetas Choniates, *P.G.*, CXL, 112-113, 128. The Jews and Christians will become fuel for the fires of hell and the Samaritans will be forced to remove the excrement of Muslims from paradise. Paradise, in which the Muslims are to enjoy women and the physical pleasures, is traversed by four rivers of water, milk, honey, and wine.

licentiousness and depravity, because, as says Hieronymus, the Holy Spirit will not touch the prophetic hearts during erotic acts.[88]

The philosophers had stated that man, when involved in carnal acts, cannot think. And so it was that many learned Muslims and Christians accepted Islam by reason of the hedonistic intensity of these acts that defeated their reason.[89] Since Muhammad pronounced his law as a man who was enslaved by the carnal knowledge of his wives, it followed that the Koran is entirely senseless.[90]

For as Aristotle said, in the fourth book of the Ethics and in the twelfth of the Metaphysics, life of the mind is the noblest. The gluttonous and aphrodisiacal [life] is the basest, for it becomes an obstacle to the good of the mind.[91]

Muhammad had cleverly utilized this hedonism in his teachings to convert men to Islam and to keep them in his religion despite their reason.[92]

Muhammad also preaches a religion of violence, not one of peace. He admonishes the Muslims to kill the Christians because God will reward them in heaven for this religious murder.[93] In the Koran the Muslims are admonished to slay all those Christians who do not pay a tax to the Muslims. But is it possible, inquire the Christian theologians, that God would be pleased with the one-fifth of the booty and spoils taken in wars and in the slaying of men? Obviously God who is just and merciful could never demand such a tribute.[94] Muhammad, whose religion encourages conversion by the sword and the slaying of Christians, is obviously not preaching the commands of God but of Satan, who has armed him with the sword. Hence the false religion he has created has inaugurated the third great period of the persecution of the Christian church. The first era was that between the Crucifixion and Constantine's conversion, and the second was coterminous with the Arian, Sabellian, Macedonian, and other heresies the Church Fathers successfully combatted.[95] In illustrating the "murderous" character of Islam, John Cantacuzene made a rather interesting but perhaps irrelevant observation.

What could be worse than such cruelty and misanthropy when they murder the innocent? For whenever the Muslims go to war and one of them falls in battle, they do not blame themselves, as causers of the war, but each one slaughters as many men as he can over the dead body. The more he slays the more does he

[88] Ricoldo-Cydones, *P.G.*, CLIV, 1077.

[89] Ricoldo-Cydones, *P.G.*, CLIV, 1105. " ἀλλ' ἡ σφοδρότης τῶν ἡδονῶν καταπαύει τὴν κρίσιν τοῦ λόγου, ὥς φησιν ὁ σοφός."

[90] Ricoldo-Cydones, *P.G.*, CLIV, 1077.

[91] Ricoldo-Cydones, *P.G.*, CLIV, 1084.

[92] John Cantacuzene, *P.G.*, CLIV, 552. " Ὁ γὰρ δηλωθεὶς Μωάμεθ τὰ πρὸς χάριν καὶ τέρψιν τῶν ἀνθρώπων ἐσπούδασε καὶ ἐδίδαξεν, ἵνα διὰ τῆς ἡδονῆς ἐπισπάσηται τὸ πλῆθος τῶν ἀφρόνων." Ricoldo-Cydones, *P.G.*, CLIV, 1105. " Ἰστέον δὲ τέτταρας μοίρας τῶν κατεχόντων τὴν πλάνην τοῦ Μωάμεθ . . . Τέταρτον μέρος ἐστὶ τῶν διὰ τὸ ἄνετον τῆς ὁδοῦ, καὶ τὸ τῶν γυναικῶν πλῆθος, καὶ τὰ ἄλλα ἐνδόσιμα, μᾶλλον τὴν ἐν τούτοις ἀκαθαρσίαν τῆς ἀϊδιότητος τοῦ μέλλοντος αἰῶνος ἠγάπησαν."

[93] Euthymius Zigabenus, *P.G.*, CXXX, 1352. Nicetas Choniates, *P.G.*, CXL, 17. Ricoldo-Cydones, *P.G.*, CLIV, 1045, 1080.

[94] Ricoldo-Cydones, *P.G.*, CLIV, 1112.

[95] Ricoldo-Cydones, *P.G.*, CLIV, 1104-1105, 1037-1040.

reckon it to be of aid to the soul of the dead man. If, however, he who wishes to aid the soul of the dead has no captives, he buys Christians if he can find any. And these he slays over the dead body or over the latter's grave. How can he who preaches such things be of God?[96]

This would seem to be a reference not to Islamic practice but rather to a type of custom that may have been associated with nomadic peoples of the Asiatic steppe and a practice already described in the pages of Herodotus dealing with the Scythians. Perhaps Cantacuzene, who was intimately associated with the Turks throughout his career, had seen such ceremonies among the Turkish troops he had borrowed from the sultan during the civil wars of the fourteenth century.

In the realm of cult and ritual, the Muslims most frequently attacked the Christian "worship" of the Holy Cross and icons as idolatrous, and also raised the question why the Christians did not practice circumcision inasmuch as Jesus was circumcised and the practice was enjoined by the Old Testament. As a result of the iconoclastic controversy, the Orthodox arsenal was well supplied with defenses against the charges of idolatry. Christians worshiped only Christ as God, and the Cross was honored, not as wood, but because it was graced by the passion of Christ. Having thus shared in divine grace because of the Crucifixion, the Cross has miraculous powers.[97] John Cantacuzene used the argument by analogy: the Cross is comparable to the rod of Moses, which he used to rend asunder the Red Sea in order to save the Jews. Christ used the Cross to free man from the bitter slavery of the devil. When the Jews came to Marra and found the water bitter, God showed Moses a stick and he put it in the water and it became sweet. Similarly Jesus sweetened the bitterness, which the devil brought to the world, by means of the Cross.[98]

In a similar manner the Christians do not worship the religious images but rather reverence them much as the ancients did the statues of the Roman emperors. By so reverencing the statues the Romans did honor to the emperors. In addition the images brought to the mind of the beholder the sufferings of Christ and the deeds of the saints in general.[99] The Christian disputants were not satisfied to remain on the defensive in the face of charges of idolatry. They seized upon the Muslim reverence for the Kaaba as proof of the fact that it was the Saracens rather than the Christians who were guilty of idolatry. The Byzantines argued that the Kaaba was a remnant of Arab paganism, indeed a head of Aphrodite, and that the Muslims performed ceremonies about the Kaaba foolishly believing that either Abraham had copulated with Agar on the stone or

[96] John Cantacuzene, *P.G.*, CLIV, 545. For human sacrifice among the Turks see chapter iii.

[97] Nicetas Choniates, *P.G.*, CXL, 120–121.

[98] John Cantacuzene, *P.G.*, CLIV, 525–529. Manuel Palaeologus-Trapp, dialogue no. 10 defends reverence of the Cross.

[99] John Cantacuzene, *P.G.*, CLIV, 529–532. Euthymius Zigabenus, *P.G.*, CXXXI, 26. Manuel Palaeologus-Trapp, chap. 20, defends the images.

else that he had tied his camel there when he was about to sacrifice Isaac.[100] As for the practice of circumcision, it had been enjoined upon the Jews so that they might be distinguished from the Egyptians during their stay in Egypt, and it was also a measure intended to abate their sexual lust. God did not order the circumcision of the Jews in order that they might attain Orthodox faith, for thus women would have been excluded. When Christ came, the law of circumcision was discarded, and He gave baptism as the means of attaining Orthodox belief and salvation. The proof of it is that both men and women are baptized whereas only the former had been circumcised. At any rate, the mere fact that the Jews practiced circumcision was not sufficient to prove that it was religiously obligatory, because if one accepted this proposition, then it would follow that one must subscribe to all religious practices and beliefs of the Jews and therefore to Judaism.[101]

Muslim ritual was considered to be legalistic and hypocritical and it was frequently, though often incorrectly, ridiculed. At Ramadan the Muslims are forbidden to eat or drink during the day, and yet at night they are free to stuff themselves and to copulate with their wives. What kind of fasting is this? In performing ablutions before the prayer, the "believer" must wash his πρωκτόν with finger and water, and then with the same finger he must wash his mouth. If he has drunk wine, he must be careful that none of the wine has spilled on his clothing. If the clothing has been soiled by wine, it must be washed. Bartholomaeus of Edessa, the most virulent of the polemicists, jeers, "The pithos is full of wine, but on the outside it is washed!"[102]

The most convincing argument of the superiority of Islam, at least in the eyes of the Turkish advocates and of many of the Greeks in Anatolia, was the indisputable fact that the forces of Islam had triumphed over the Anatolian Christians militarily. Thus this historical event was repeatedly brought forward by the Turks whenever they engaged in polemic. The Christian reply was the obvious one: God had not favored the Turks because of His greater love for them. He had merely delivered the Christians to chastisement at the hands of the Turks much as one punishes an errant but beloved son. Even from the point of view of military and political prowess, the Christians alleged, it was not strictly accurate to say that the Muslims were superior to the Christians, for the majority of the Christians had not taken up arms against Islam. If they should do such a thing, the webs of spiders would prove more effective a restraining force than Muslim arms.[103]

[100] Nicetas Choniates, *P.G.,* CXL, 109. Euthymius Zigabenus, *P.G.,* CXXX, 1340–1341.

[101] John Cantacuzene, *P.G.,* CLIV, 533–537. Palamas-Taronites, p. 145.

[102] Bartholomaeus, *P.G.,* CIV, 1405, 1393, 1408–1409. Euthymius Zigabenus, *P.G.,* CXXX, 1349.

[103] John Cantacuzene, *P.G.,* CLIV. 648–649. Lampros-Dyobouniotes, pp. 10–11, 19. Manuel Palaeologus-Trapp, *passim.*

Clearly, the discussions carried on between the two sides in Anatolia were very lively, though often conducted on the basis of mistranslations and a poor knowledge of the details of the opponent's religion. There has been no systematic attempt here to disengage the fact from the fiction and error in the debates, but the principal concern has been to indicate the views the Christians, primarily, and the Muslims, secondarily, had of one another. Seldom does it occur that opponents in strife attempt to comprehend or succeed in understanding the position of each other.[104]

The composition of these polemical treatises represents only one measure Byzantine society adopted in the face of the Muslim threat. It might appear that the composition of polemics and the spread of their contents among the Christians were insignificant in the struggle with Islam and simply represent another instance of Byzantine archaism and ineffectiveness. The mass conversions in Anatolia would apparently justify such an evaluation of polemic as a defense against the inroads of Islam. But this polemic did serve an important function in that it provided a simple and credible rationalization for Christian low fortunes, and thus furnished an important emotional basis for the partial survival of Christianity in Asia Minor, and for its mass survival in the Balkans.

Folklore

A rather sizable body of prophetic and astrological lore, which arose during the last centuries of Byzantium, served, as did religious polemic, to comfort the Greeks. It prophesied the fall of the Byzantine Empire but also the eventual liberation of the Greeks. Typical of this superstitious outlook is the development of legends associated with the great bronze equestrian statue of the emperor Justinian in the Augustaeum. The mounted emperor held in his left hand the globus crucifix and his right hand was outstretched in the direction of the east. Procopius not only describes the statue but reports the interpretation of its symbolism, current in the sixth century: the orb signified the world, the cross symbolized the faith by which Justinian held world dominion, and his right hand was raised to stay the advance of the barbarians from the east.[105] After the disappearance of the Sassanid state the symbolism of the outstretched hand was reinterpreted to refer to the Muslim empire.[106] By the fourteenth

---

[104] For an analysis of the Byzantine errors see Eichner, "Nachrichten," *passim*. The exhortation of Ricoldo-Cydones, *P.G.*, CLIV, 1048, is particularly revealing in this respect. Chap. 2 is devoted to the tactic that is to be followed in controversy with a Muslim. The Muslims are curious to hear something about the faith of the Christians, but the Christians must avoid supplying them with information. It is always easier to start by attacking the falseness of the Muslim faith than to begin by proving the truth of Christianity.

[105] Procopius, *Buildings*, I. ii. 1–12, see also the comments in Procopius of Caesareia, *Buildings*, H. B. Dewing and G. Downey (London and Cambridge, 1954), pp. 395–398. In a later version, T. Preger, *Scriptores originum Constantinopolitarum* (Leipzig, 1907), II, 159, his hand is raised against the Persians.

[106] Vasiliev, "Quelques remarques sur les voyageurs du Moyen Age à Constantinople,"

century, at a time when the Turks had crossed from Asia into Europe, the fall of the globe (or apple as it came to be called) from the statue's hand was interpreted as an unmistakable sign that the Greeks had lost their political power to the Turks.[107]

In the fifteenth and sixteenth centuries this lore had become centered on the Turkish conquest of Constantinople and the future expulsion of the Turks for which the Greeks fervently hoped.[108] The most popular element

---

Mélanges Charles Diehl (Paris, 1930), I, 295, in the account of the twelfth-century al-Harawi, the globe is a talisman that prevents Greeks and Arabs from invading the lands of one another. On books of predictions relating to military success of Greeks and Arabs in the tenth century, Liudprand of Cremona, *Legatio*, xxxix. In the eighth century the statue was thought to protect the city against the plague, Michael the Syrian, III, 7. Khitrovo, *Itinéraires russes*, I, 228. De Clavijo-Le Strange, p. 72.

[107] *Mandeville's Travels*, ed. and trans. M. Letts (London, 1953), II, 232–233. "E, deutant celle eglyse est lymage Iustinien l'empereur, et est ycelui ymage de cuyure doret et est a cheual couronne. Et souloit tenir une pomme doree en sa main, mais elle est piece a cheute hors. Et dist on que ce signifie se que empereur a perdu grand partie de sa terre et de sa seigneurie. Car il souloit estre empereur des Romains, de Gresce, de toute Asia la meilleur, de toute la terre de Surie, de la terre de Iudee, en la quelle est Iherusalem, et de la terre degypte, darabie et de Persie. Mais il a tout perdu fors Gresce et le pays qui se tient seulement. Et aucuns ont cuidie pluseurs foiz a remectre la pomme en sa main, mais elle ne se voult tenir. Celle pomme signifie la seigneurie que il auoit sur le monde, qui est ront. Et lautre main il tient leuee contre orient en signe de mancier les malfaiteurs." Schiltberger-Neumann, p. 137, "Das pild hat vor zeiten einen guldin apffel in der hand gehapt und hat bedut, daz er ein gewaltiger kaiser ist gewesen über cristen und über heiden. Aber nun hat er des gewalts nit mer, so ist och der apffel füder." On the damage that the statue suffered and the repairs in 1317 which may have had something to do with the fall of the "apple," Nicephorus Gregoras, I, 275–277. The legend of the red apple, qïzïl elma, was adopted by the Turks for whom it symbolized political dominion of the infidel. See the following literature: W. Heffening, *Die türkischen transkriptionstexte aus den Bartholomaeus Georgievits aus den Jahren 1544–1548. Ein Beitrag zur historischen Grammatik des Osmanisch-türkischen, Abhandlungen für die Kunde des Morgenlandes*, vol. XXVII, no. 2 (Leipzig, 1942), pp. 22–37. Dawkins, "The Red Apple,"Ἀρχεῖον τοῦ θρακικοῦ λαογραφικοῦ καὶ γλωσσικοῦ θησαυροῦ, ἐπίμετρον ΣΤ' τόμου (1941), pp. 401–406. E. Rossi, "La leggenda turco-bizantina del Pomo Rosso," *Studi bizantini e neoellenici*, V (1937), 542–553. P. E. Schramm, *Sphaira Globus Reischsapfel. Wanderung und Wandlung eines Herrschaftszeichens von Cesar bis zu Elisebeth II. Ein Beitrag zum "Nachleben" der Antike* (Stuttgart, 1958). Turan, "The Idea of World Domination among the Medieval Turks," *S.I.*, IV (1955), 89. J. Deny, "Les pseudo-prophéties concernant les Turcs au XVIᵉ siècle," *R.E.I.*, X (1936), 201–220. A. Fischer, "Qyzyl elma die Stadt (das Land) der Sehnsucht der Osmanen," *Z.D.M.G.*, LXXIV (1920), 170–175. Babinger, "Qïzïl Elma," *Der Islam*, XII (1922), 109–111. C. Brockelmann, *Die Welt des Islams*, V (1917), 283–285. N. Polites, παραδόσεις, I, 22; II, 658–674.

[108] G. Megas, La prise de Constantinople dans la poésie et la tradition populaire," *Le cinq-centième anniversaire de la prise de Constantinople, L'Hellénisme Contemporain* (Athens, 1953), pp. 125–133. C. Mango, "The Legend of Leo the Wise," *Z.R.V.I.*, VI (1960), 59–94. B. Knös, "Les oracles de Léon le Sage. D'aprés un livre d'oracles byzantins illustrés récemment découvert," Ἀφιέρωμα Μ. Τριανταφυλλίδη (Thessalonike, 1960), pp. 155–188. A. Komines, "Παρατηρήσεις εἰς τοὺς χρησμοὺς Λέοντος τοῦ Σοφοῦ," Ε.Ε.Β.Σ., XXX (1960–61), 398–412. E. Trapp, "Vulgärorackel aus wiener Handschriften," Ἀκροθίνια *H. Hunger* (Vienna, 1964), pp. 83–120. J. Nicolaides, *Les livres de divination* (Paris, 1884), published a Karamanlidhico version of some of this prophetic literature. Lampros, "Μονῳδίαι καὶ θρῆνοι ἐπὶ τῇ ἀλώσει τῆς Κωνσταντινουπόλεως," *N.E.*, XIX (1925), 93–123. Bees " Ἀνακοίνωσις περὶ τοῦ ἱστορημένου χρησμολογίου τῆς κρατικῆς βιβλιοθήκης τοῦ Βερολίνου (Codex Graecusfol. 62–297) καὶ τοῦ θρύλου τοῦ Μαρμαρωμένου Βασιλιᾶ," *B.N.J.*, XIII (1937), 203–244 λς'. I. Dujčev, "La conquête turque et al prise de Constantinople dans la litterature slave contemporaine," *B.S.*, XVII (1956), 304–309. Vacalopoules, Ἱστορία II₁, 156, and H. Carney and J. Nicolaides, *Folkore*

in these legends, an element common to the whole Greek world, was the story of the petrified emperor, ὁ μαρμαρωμένος βασιλιᾶς. According to versions of this legend an angel intervened during the final battle of May 29, 1453, to save the emperor Constantine as he was fighting the Turks who had surrounded him. The angel took him from the battle to an underground cavern near the Golden Gate in the western regions of Constantinople. Here he would remain in a petrified state (or asleep) until God should again send the angel. At this time God's messenger would arouse the emperor, return his sword to him, and the emperor would then issue forth with his army. He would enter Constantinople through the Golden Gate and give chase to the Turks as far as the Red Apple Tree where he would massacre them. The legend of the final mass in St. Sophia and the fate of the great altar was similarly widespread. In this story the Turks broke into St. Sophia just prior to the consecration during the divine liturgy, at which point the priest disappeared into the walls of the church. The interrupted liturgy will, however, be completed when the Greeks retake the city, at which time the priest will emerge from his hiding place to consummate the liturgy. The altar, which sank into the sea of Marmara, will also return to the church at this time.

These legends, though they gave no immediate impetus to historical action, became a vital part of the Greek "world of ideas" that, along with the religious polemics, helped to sustain the subjugated Greeks. It is interesting that much of this lore passed into Turkish popular beliefs, including the element that provided for a Greek reconquest and expulsion of the Turks from Constantinople. The reappearance of the last emperor and the reconquest of Constantinople were central themes in what was to become the μεγάλη ἰδέα, for these particular legends invariably ended with the positive avowal that possession of the empire would return to the Greeks. Romania would once more bloom!

Governmental Measures

Faced with the mass conversions of the Anatolian Greeks and also with the entrance of large numbers of Turkish Muslims into Anatolia, the Byzantine state and church undertook various acts to hold the religious allegiance of the Greeks and even partially to alter that of the Turks. In spite of the fact that the issue of religious affiliation was basically decided by political and military realities, the emperors and churchmen resorted to various measures to salvage Christianity. They did not passively acquiesce in the cultural transformation that the Turkish

---

de Constantinople (Paris, 1894), pp. 47–49, on the interpretation of an inscription supposedly by Genadius Scholarius, which predicted the defeat of the Turks and liberation of Constantinople by the Ξανθὸν Γένος, the Blond Race. For the ideas on the end of the world, Vasiliev, "Medieval Ideas of the End of the World," *Byzantion*, XVI (1942–43), 462–502. P. Alexander, "Historiens byzantins et croyances éschatologiques," *Actes du XIIᵉ Congrès d'Études byznatins* (Belgrade, 1964), II, 1–8.

conquest of the peninsula had set into motion. Some measures that they undertook were far more important than the mere literature of polemics. Inasmuch as religion was the most pervasive and cohesive force in the life of society, the emperors made every effort to preserve the structure of the church in Asia Minor, because now that Byzantine political authority had been largely removed, only the church could maintain the Christian society of Asia Minor. Hence the emperors, beginning with Alexius Comnenus, made every effort to save the ecclesiastical structure in the eastern provinces. Often this involved the maintenance of a large portion of the episcopal administration in Constantinople over long periods of time until conditions were such that metropolitans and bishops might be able to reenter their Anatolian seats. At other times, a Manuel Comnenus could force the Turks to allow the reentry of the bishops.[109]

The hierarchs thereafter became the leaders of the Christian communities, not only maintaining the connections of the subject Christians with the cultural center of the Greek world, but also serving as mediators between the new Turkish rulers and the Christians. It was the bishops and metropolitans who endeavored to boost the morale of the conquered Christians and to lead them. In the letters of Matthew of Ephesus and Gregory Palamas, one sees the anxiety with which the Greeks appealed to these clergymen for comfort and explanations. A possible explanation, though one that I hesitate to offer here, for the rather strange proliferation of Anatolian metropolitanates in the notitiae episcopatum of Isaac Angelus, Andronicus II Palaeologus, Andronicus III Palaeologus, and the others, is that it was a governmental measure partly intended to strengthen the Anatolian church when it began to decline. As the Muslim conversionary inroads commenced, the emperors possibly felt that more hierarchs were needed to halt the conversion of the Christians.[110] But by the late fourteenth and the fifteenth century, it was obvious that Christianity had lost the struggle, as the majority of the Christians had apostatized and Constantinople as well fell to the Turks; in any case, fiscal poverty made such a policy unfeasible. Thus in the fifteenth century the church gave up an extensive number of Anatolian metropolitanates and bishoprics, retaining only seventeen metropolitanates and three bishoprics.[111]

Within the Christian communities there were certain factors that helped to strengthen the resistance to assimilation. There was, throughout the whole period, a certain Christian element in the Seljuk and Ottoman courts which in one way or another alleviated the position of the Greeks. Christian wives and mothers of Seljuk sultans are in evidence, as are

---

[109] Rhalles and Potles, II, 388–391; III, 156. Euthymius Tornices, Papadopoulos-Kerameus, pp. 182–183. For details see chapters iii and iv.

[110] On the notitiae see chapter iv.

[111] See chapter iv.

Christian women in the Ottoman household.[112] Also, Greek Christians often played a significant role in the administration and on many occasions exercised influence on behalf of their coreligionists. The reign of 'Izz al-Din, the half-Greek sultan, seems to represent a period of Seljuk history wherein the Christian elements had gained extensive political influence. As the maternal uncles of the sutan seemed to be running the political affairs of the state, the Turkmens plotted to kill the sultan and to replace him with his brother who had been born of a Turkish mother.[113] Other influential Greeks in Seljuk court circles were evident during the thirteenth century. A recently published inscription from the Cappadocian cave church of St. George is of particular interest. The church was dedicated at the expense of the emir kyr Basil Yiakoupes and the lady Thamar. Basil was obviously a court official and Thamar possibly a Georgian lady of the sultan's harem. Because of their position and wealth they undertook the expenses of the dedication of the church.[114] The Greek hetaereiarch Maurozomes and the Christian physician of Orhan, Taronites, extended their hospitality and influence on behalf of the captive Palamas, and other Anatolian Christians helped to pay the ransoms of Palamas' retinue.[115] Theodora, the daughter of John Cantacuzene given in marriage to Orhan, not only resisted religious conversion but exercised her power and wealth on behalf of the Greek poor and ransomed the captured Greeks. It is interesting that the Byzantine princess made successful efforts in persuading Greeks converted to Islam to return to Christianity. It may be that she was dealing with the phenomenon of crypto-Christianity inasmuch as relapse from Islam was punishable by death. This likelihood is strengthened when one notes that the Greek patriarch, only a few years earlier, wrote to the Greeks of Bithynia justifying their crypto-Christiantiy as a practice by which they could retain their Christianity and their lives, and Theophanes the metropolitan of Nicaea refers to the same situation at the end of the fourteenth century.[116]

---

[112] Nicetas Choniates, 690. Pachymeres, I, 130–132. See chapter iii.

[113] Aksaray-Gençosman, p. 145. Ibn Bibi-Duda, p. 265. William of Rubruque-Wyngaert, p. 330–331. When he fled to Constantinople he was brought by the metropolitan of Pisidia. He took part in the patriarchal liturgy of St. Sophia, was an intimate of the patriarch, embraced the icons, etc. Pachymeres, I, 130–132, 174, 263–268; Nicephorus Gregoras, I, 95. The killing of the vizier Gabras in the late twelfth century and the parading of his head on a lance during the feast of the Cross in Sebasteia, seems to indicate the same type of animosity over the presence of Greeks in the administration, Bar Hebraeus, I, 330, and chapter iii above.

[114] N. and M. Thierry, *Nouvelles églises rupestres de Cappadoce* (Paris, 1963), p. 202. Basil wears the garb of a Muslim official. The fresco that produces the figures of both Basil and Thamar thus presents us with an example of contemporary Seljuk court costume.

[115] Lampros-Dyobouniotes, pp. 11, 13, *passim*.

[116] John Cantacuzene, II, 588–589. "ἀλλὰ καὶ πολλοὺς τῶν πρὸς τὴν ἀσέβειαν ὑπαχθέντων ἀνακαλέσατο λόγοις πείθουσα πρὸς τὴν αἵρεσιν τῆς ἀληθείας. οὕτω δὲ περὶ τὴν πίστιν ἀσφαλῶς πολιτευσαμένη καὶ τόγε εἰς αὐτὴν ἧκον ὑπὲρ αὐτῆς προκινδυνεύσασα πολλάκις, οὐδὲ τῶν ἄλλων ἀγαθῶν ἡμέλει, ἀλλὰ πάσῃ τρυφῇ καὶ πολυτελείᾳ χαίρειν εἰποῦσα, τὰ ὄντα τοῖς πένησι διεδίδου, καὶ πολλοὺς τῶν ἐπὶ δουλείᾳ παρὰ τῶν βαρβάρων ἀποδιδομένων ἐρρύετο, χρυσίον αὐτὴ παρέχουσα,

Another measure to which the emperors resorted in their desire to safeguard the allegiance of the Christian population was simply physical removal of the populace of certain areas to Byzantine territory. The practice seems to have been of significant extent in the eleventh and twelfth centuries when the Comnenoi transplanted Greeks from the Turkish-held regions of Philomelium, Bourtzes, Iconium, and Neocaesareia.[117] This, of course, meant the weakening of the Byzantine character of these particular areas, and even though the transferred population would not succumb to Islamization, the regions they had abandoned would be more easily Islamized.

As early as the twelfth century, and continuing throughout the centuries until the fall of Constantinople, considerable numbers of Christianized Turks served in the Byzantine armies. Their military qualities made of them highly desirable additions to the empire's military strength, and we see them in the armies of Alexius I, John II, and Manuel I, and, by the thirteenth and fourteenth centuries, the Tourkopouloi had become standard contingents of the Byzantine armies.[118] The Tourkopouloi, sons of those Turks who had sought service with the emperors and had embraced Christianity, were generally settled in the European provinces and especially in the regions of the Vardar River. The emperors made efforts, thus, to convert at least that segment of the Anatolian Turks who had sought service with the Byzantines. After his Anatolian reconquests, Alexius Comnenus received Scaliarius, Elchanes, and most of the other Turkish emirs of the western Anatolian coast in Constantinople and had them baptized. He is reported to have entertained the desire of converting all the Turks of Anatolia.[119] The concept of converting the barbarians was an old imperial idea that now became a necessity. When John Comnenus captured the Muslim city of Biza'a near Aleppo the cadi and 400 of the inhabitants were induced to convert to Christianity.[120] At a later date the sultans Ghiyath al-Din and 'Izz al-Din were baptized, as were also the son and granddaughter of the latter.[121] By the last half of the twelfth century, the extent of apostasy from Islam was sufficient to be reflected

---

καὶ πᾶσι σωτηρίας ἦν λιμὴν τοῖς δυστυχοῦσι 'Ρωμαίων καὶ δεδουλωμένοις ὑπὸ τῶν βαρβάρων κατὰ συγχώρησιν θεοῦ."Miklosich et Müller, II, 394–395, a patriarchal document of 1400 refers to the death (sometime previously) of Theodore after she had returned to Constantinople and donned the monastic habit. " 'Η ἀοίδιμος καὶ μακαρῖτις ἐκείνη καὶ ἁγία μου βασιλίς, ἡ δέσποινα τῆς 'Ανατολῆς, κυρὰ Θεοδοσία μοναχὴ ἡ Καντακουζινή, εἰς τὴν τῆς 'Ανατολῆς ἀρχήν τε καὶ αὐθεντείαν ἔτι εὑρισκομένη."

[117] Anna Comnena, III, 29, 200–203. Cinnamus, 21, 41–42, 63.

[118] Anna Comnena, II, 30, 202. John Comnenus captured large numbers of them at Castamon, and Turks of Gangra joined his army, Nicetas Choniates, 27, 33–34; Cinnamus 9, 15; Theodore Ptochoprodromus, P.G., CXXXIII, 1376. Manuel I also had Christianized Turks in his army at the battle of Myriocephalum. The sultan's troops continually called out to them to desert. Nicetas Choniates, 243; Cinnamus, 272.

[119] Anna Comnena, II, 81.

[120] Abu'l-Feda, R.H.C., H.O., I, 24.

[121] Goerge Acropolites, I, 14. George Pachymeres, I, 263–268; II, 591, 609–613.

in the synodal proceedings and in the commentaries on canon law regarding baptism. During the ceremony of official conversion, the newly converted were required to recite a formula of abjuration of Islam which rejected the Muslim God as being ὁλόσφυρος.[122] The converts found this rejection of God ὁλόσφυρος a stumbling block and Manuel Comnenus intervened vigorously with the ecclesiastical authorities in an effort to remove the word from the formula of abjuration.[123] Balsamon relates that numerous Agarenes came to Constantinople who alleged that they did not need to be baptized as they had already received baptism in Anatolia.[124]

The Turks who were Christianized were undoubtedly much smaller in number than the Christians who were Islamized, and they were primarily soldiers who were eventually settled in Europe.[125] Had the political fortunes of Anatolia been otherwise, it is highly probable that Byzantine missionaries would have had the success the dervishes enjoyed.[126]

[122] This formula is edited in *P.G.*, CXL, 123-136, after the *Thesaurus Orthodoxae Fidei* attributed to Nicetas Choniates. The convert is to repeat the abjuration through an interpreter, p. 123. See also E. Montet, "Un riteul d'abjuration des musulmans dans l'Église grecque," *Revue de l'histoire des religions*, LIII (1906), 145-163, who gives text and translation of such a formula probably of the ninth century. The earliest manuscript came from the regions of Trebizond in the latter half of the thirteenth century.

[123] Nicetas Choniates, 278-284. Bones, " Ὁ Θεσσαλονίκης Εὐστάθιος καὶ οἱ δύο 'τόμοι' τοῦ αὐτοκράτορος Μανουὴλ Α' Κομνηνοῦ (1143/80) ὑπὲρ τῶν εἰς τὴν Χριστιανικὴν 'Ορθοδοξίαν μεθισταμένων Μωαμεθανῶν." Ε.Ε.Β.Σ., ΧΙΧ (1949), 162-169.

[124] For his comments, Rhalles and Potles, II, 498. Also chapter iii.

[125] Some of the more prominent Turks converted to Christianity were the following John Axouchus, a Turk taken at Nicaea by the Crusaders, who rose to power under John Comnenus (Nicetas Choniates, 14; Cinnamus, 6; Theodore Scutariotes-Sathas, p. 188-189). Poupakes, a "Rhomaios" of "Persian" origin (Cinnamus, 48). Prosuh, though a Turk by birth, was a Greek by education and rearing (Cinnamus, 73). John Ises was "Πέρσης μὲν τὸ γένος τροφῆς δὲ καὶ διαίτης μεταλαχὼν 'Ρωμαϊκῆς" (Cinnamus, 238). There were many others, Cinnamus, 129, 298; Nicetas Choniates, 542; Theodore Scutariotes-Sathas, p. 545; Pachymeres, I, 329; Cantacuzene, II, 488. Manuel Palaeologus-Trapp, p. 247, mentions that conversions of Turks were still frequent in his day, "εἶδον γὰρ ἐγὼ πολλοὺς τῆς ὑμετέρας θρησκείας, οἳ τῷ ἡμετέρῳ προσεληλ-. ύθασι δόγματι ὑπὲρ μὲν τούτου τὰς ψυχὰς προέσθαι προθυμουμένους."

[126] On the converted Turks and Turkopouloi in Byzantium and the Balkans see the following. G. Moravcsik, *Byzantinoturcica*, 2d ed (Berlin, 1958). Janin, "Les Turcs Vardariotes," *E.O.*, no. 160 (1960), pp. 437-439. Laurent, "Perses, Turcs asiatiques ou Turcs hongrois," *Sbornik v' pamet na Petr Nikov* (Sofia, 1940), pp. 275-279; "Une famille turque au service de Byzance, les Melkites," *B.Z.*, XLIX (1956), 349-368; "Les bulles métriques dans la sigillographie byzantine," 'Ελληνικά, V (1932), 142-143, on the body of μουρτάτοι in the imperial guard which consisted of Turkish converts to Christianity, hence the name murtatoi. Grégoire, "De Marsile à Andernas ou l'Islam et Byzance dans l'epopée française," in *Miscellanea Giovanni Mercati* (Vatican, 1956), III, 452-456, on the ἀτζουπάδες. Wittek, "La descendance chrétienne de la dynastie Seldjuk en Macédoine," *E.O.*, XXXIII (1934), 409-412. G. Konidares, " Ἡ πρώτη μνεία τῆς ἐπισκοπῆς Βαρδαριωτῶν Τούρκων ὑπὸ τὸν Θεσσαλονίκης," Θεολογία, XXIII (1952), 87-94, 236-238.

On the origins of the Gagaus in the eastern Balkans: W. Zajaczkowksi, "Gagauz," EI₂. Wittek, "Les Gagaouzes-Les gens de Kaykāūs," *Rocznik Orientalny*, XVII (1951-52), 12-24; "Yazicioglu Ali on the Christian Turks of the Dobrudja," *B.S.O.A.S.*, XIV, (1952), 639-668. G. Balaščev, " Ὁ αὐτοκράτωρ Μιχαὴλ Η' ὁ Παλαιολόγος καὶ τὸ ἱδρυθὲν τῇ συνδρομῇ αὐτοῦ κράτος τῶν 'Ογούζων παρὰ τὴν δυτικὴν ἀκτὴν τοῦ

Despite the various measures, systematic and otherwise, which the Byzantines undertook to preserve Anatolian Christianity, Islam's political victory was the ultimate and decisive factor. The charge of Muslim Polemicists that the Turks had triumphed because of the superiority of Islam over Christianity as a religion had a pragmatic veracity that was far more powerful than any purely theological or philosophical argument.

Εὐξείνου," *III Congrès international d'études byzantines* (Sofia, 1930). P. Mutafčiev," Die angebliche Einwanderung von Seldschuk-Türken in die Dobrudscha im XIII Jahrhundert," *Spisanie na Bulgarskata Akademiia na Naukite i Izkustva*, LXVI, *Kloni istor.-philolog.* (1943), 1–129. H. Duda, "Zeitgenössische islamische Quellen und das Oguzname des Jazyǧyoglu Alï zur angeblichen Besiedlung der Dobrudscha im 13. Jhd. n. Chr.," pp. 131–145, in the same journal. R. Tschudi, "Die Bekehrung des Kaighusuz," *Schweizerisches Archiv für Volkeskunde*, XLVII (1951), 203–207.

According to the apocryphal literature, when the Greeks retake Constantinople and destroy the Turkish empire, one-third of the Turks will be slain, one-third driven out, and one-third converted to Christianity. V. Istrin, *Otkrovenie Mefodiia Patarskago i apokrificheskiia videniia Daniila v vizantiiskoi i slaviano-russkoi literaturakh* (Moscow, 1897), II, 141.

VII. The Byzantine Residue in Turkish Anatolia

The process by which Turkish Islam had absorbed the majority of the Christian population in Asia Minor effaced the Byzantine exterior of Anatolian society. But as this process had not been complete, there survived a significant and visible Byzantine residue in Turkish Anatolia. Beyond the direct survival of this manifestly Byzantine element, there was a less visible Byzantine ingredient that went into the constitution of the new Turkish society. As with all historical cases of assimilation, the Islamized Byzantine population brought with it a great part of its popular culture and consequently "Byzantinized," partially, the emerging society on the folk level. Inasmuch as the formal culture was Islamic and the language Turkish, this Byzantine ingredient is not immediately apparent, but a detailed examination of Anatolian society reveals its presence in all major aspects of life. There will be no attempt to investigate the absorption of Byzantine culture in all its details, for such an effort is not yet possible. Scholarship still lacks the necessary studies on each aspect of this phenomenon, and the body of folklore, language, economic, and religious history is indeed vast. This final chapter, however, will explore, cursorily, all these in order to point out the nature of the Byzantine residue, both visible and invisible.

The Physical Residue

Approximately four centuries after the battle of Manzikert, a Greek monk lamented the stark decline of the Byzantine church in Anatolia.

> And neither is a metropolitan to be found in the metropolitanates, nor an archbishop in the archbishoprics, nor a bishop in the bishoprics, nor priest in church, nor monk in monastery or pious foundation or cell, nor other Christian layman in castle or land.
>
> Fifty-one metropolitanates and eighteen archbishoprics and four hundred seventy-eight bishoprics are desolate.[1]

This statement, with the notitia episcopatum to which it was appended, illustrates most clearly the colossal scale of the cultural transformation in Asia Minor. Of a total of seventy-two metropolitanates subordinate to the

[1] Gelzer, *Notitiae Episcopatum*, pp. 630–631; chapter v above for the complete quote.

Constantinopolitan patriarchate, only seventeen survived in Anatolia, and there remained but three bishoprics. In the eleventh century, before the cultural change had begun, there had been approximately forty-seven Anatolian metropolitan seats, and in the *diatyposis* attributed to Leo VI there had been 374 bishoprics.[2] Only a fragment of the Greek Christian population survived in the fifteenth century.

This Greek ecclesiastical document strongly corroborates the early Ottoman tax registers from Anatolia. These registers, of a comprehensive nature, were compiled for the collection of the hearth tax. Though these statistics are not completely accurate (slaves are not mentioned), nevertheless they are an important index as to the relative proportion of Christians and Muslims in early sixteenth-century Anatolia.[3]

Number of Hearths[4]

Provinces	Muslims	Christians	Jews	Hearth total	x	5
Anadolu	517,813	8,511	271	526,595		2,632,975
Karaman	134,452	3,172	...	137,579		687,895
Zülkadriye	64,102	2,631	...	66,733		333,665
Diyarbekir	70,858	11,938	288	83,084		415,420
Rum	116,772	51,662	...	168,434		842,170
Hearths	903,997	77,869	559	982,425		
Population	4,519,985	389,345	2,795			

Of the total registered hearths (982,425), 903,997 or 92 percent were Muslim, 77,869 or 7.9 percent were Christian, and 559 were Jewish. Though these figures are not exact, they give a good idea of the over-whelming Muslim nature of Anatolia in the early sixteenth century. It is significant that the region in which the proportion and number of Christian hearths were highest was that of Rum, containing 116,772 (69.3 percent) Muslim hearths and 51,662 (30.7 percent) Christian hearths. A sampling of tax registers of some of the Anatolian towns will perhaps illustrate this important fact somewhat more adequately (p. 446). Sivas was still a predominantly Christian town (Armenian and Greek), and Tokat was almost evenly divided, whereas in the towns of central and western Anatolia the Muslim element was preponderant.

The evidence as to the extent of remaining Christian populations in

[2] *Ibid.*, pp. 549–559.
[3] On the importance and limitation of early Ottoman tax figures as indices of population, Ö. L. Barkan, "Essai," pp. 9–36, which repeats the findings in his earlier works on the subject: "Tarihi demografi araṣtïrmalarï ve osmanlï tarihi," *T.M.*, X (1951–53), 1–26 (hereafter cited as Barkan, "Araṣtïrmalarï"); "Türkiyede imparatorluk devirlerinin büyük nüfus ve arazi tahrirleri ve hakana mahsus istatistik defterleri," *Iktisat Fakültesi Mecmuasï*, II₁ (1940), 1–19; "Quelques observations sur l'organisation économique et sociale des villes ottomans des XVIe et XVIIe siècles," *Recueils de la société Jean Bodin*, VII (1955), 289–311.
[4] Barkan, "Essai," table 1.

Hearths: 1520–30[5]

Towns	Muslim	Christian	Jewish	Total
Bursa	6,165	69	117	6,351
Ankara	2,399	279	28	2,706
Tokat	818	701		1,519
Konya	1,092	22		1,114
Sivas	261	750		1,011

the fifteenth and sixteenth centuries contrasts greatly with the testimony of the twelfth- and thirteenth-century sources which indicated that the Christians were probably still the majority. The continuing upheaval, conquest, tribal migrations, and conversions attained a climactic intensity in the two hundred years separating these two groups of documents of the mid-thirteenth and mid-fifteenth centuries.[6] The critical transformation of the population, prepared by the events of the eleventh and twelfth centuries was consummated in the late thirteenth, the fourteenth, and the early fifteenth century. But the absorptive process had been a long one, stretching over four hundred years. In the course of this interaction both groups influenced each other and both bore the marks of the experience.

But important numbers of Christians did survive throughout the centuries of Ottoman rule and in the nineteenth century constituted a minority of considerable importance. Though there are no exact census reports for the nineteenth century, again there are sets of figures that give some idea as to the number and proportion of Christians, Muslims, and Jews (see chart on opposite page). Of the estimated 12,254,459 inhabitants, 9,676,714 (78.96 percent) were Muslim, and 2,350,272 (19.2 percent) were Christian.[7] The Greek Orthodox element amounted to 1,016,722 or 8.3 percent. In these statistics the Muslim element again appears preponderant,[8] but the percentage of Christians has almost tripled when

[5] *Ibid.*, tables 4 and 7. There are some discrepancies in the tables, as for instance in the population of Ankara. But for the correct figures see the Turkish version of this work, "Araştīrmalarī," table 4. This overwhelming Muslim proportion in many of the Anatolian towns is also suggested by the comments of Evilya Chelebi on the number of Muslim and Christian quarters in the towns that he visited. See below for the causes that led to the survival of a higher proportion of Greek-speakers in Pontus.

[6] That tribal migration into Anatolia continued in the sixteenth century seems to be suggested by the statistics in *ibid.*, table 5. The tax hearths of the province of Anadolu in 1520–35 (A) and 1570 (B) show marked increase in nomads:

1520–30	1570–80
72,268	116,219

It is possible that this increase is due not only to arrival of new tribal groups, or to more efficient tax registers, but also to a general and natural increase of population. At the same time, there is evidence for the transplanting of Greeks and Armenians from Anatolia to the Balkans, G. D. Galabov and H. W. Duda, *Die Protokollbücher des Kadiamtes Sofia* (Munich, 1960), p. 144, a firman dated 1618–19 fixes the djizye of Greeks and Armenians from Anatolia settled in the district of Sofia.

[7] Reproduced in Taeschner, "Anadolu," EI₂, who has taken it from the monumental collection of V. Cuinet, *Turquie d'Asie. Géographie administrative. Statistique descriptive et raisonnée de l'Asie Mineure*, vols. I–IV (Paris, 1890–95).

[8] The 9,676,714 Muslims includes not only Turks but also a sizable Kurdish minority and lesser groups of Arabs and Circassians.

	Muslims (*Shi'ites and Yazidis)	Greek and Syr. Orthodox	Armen. Gregorian	Armen. Catholic	Armen. Protest.	Other Catholics (Uniate and Latin)	Non-Uniate Jacobites Chaldaeans and Nestorians	Jews	Copts	Gypsies	Others (Foreigners)	Total
k. Adalar (Ist.)	2,990	5,010	1,300	300	—	903	—	—	—	—	—	10,503
w. Adana	158,000 *56,000	67,100	69,300	11,550	16,600	4,539	—	—	—	16,050	4,400	403,539
w. Ankara	763,119	34,009	83,063	8,784	2,451	—	—	478	—	997	—	892,901
k. Antākya (Hal.)	46,000	1,000	2,084	2,500	—	6,500	4,500	266	—	—	—	62,850
w. Aydin (Izmir)	1,093,334	208,283	14,103	737	265	1,177	—	22,516	—	—	56,062	1,396,477
k. 'Ayntāb (Hal.)	65,085	4,000	2,046	2,000	—	6,500	5,906	857	—	—	594	86,988
k. Beykoz (Ist.)	5,444	2,150	1,900	—	—	—	—	—	—	—	—	9,494
i.s. Bighā	106,583	17,585	1,636	—	60	92	—	2,988	—	—	494	129,438
w. Bitlis	254,000 *3,863	210	125,600	3,840	1,950	2,600	6,190	—	372	—	—	398,625
w. Diyār Bakr	328,644 *6,000	14,240	57,890	10,170	11,069	206	38,974	1,269	—	3,000	—	471,462
w. Erzerum	500,782	3,725	120,273	12,022	2,672	—	—	6	16	—	6,206	645,702
k. Gebze (Ist.)	14,000	5,100	—	—	—	—	—	—	—	—	150	19,250
w. Khudāwendigār (Brusa)	1,296,593	230,711	85,354	3,033	604	4,146	3,000	3,225	—	—	—	1,626,839
k. Iskenderūn (Hal.)	12,500	1,000	1,142	1,500	—	—	—	42	—	—	7,319	23,330
i.s. Izmid	129,715	40,795	46,308	390	1,937	—	—	2,500	—	1,115	—	222,760
n. Kadiköy (Ist.)	9,374	8,137	10,480	200	100	—	—	450	—	290	3,180	32,211
n. Kafilḍja (Ist.)	16,796	3,387	4,080	—	—	—	—	120	—	—	800	25,183
k. Kartal (Ist.)	10,870	5,000	2,200	180	—	—	—	—	—	—	50	18,300
w. Kastamoni	992,679	21,507	2,617	30	—	—	—	—	2,079	—	—	1,018,912
k. Kilis (Hal.)	73,520	1,000	1,547	1,300	—	2,774	3,000	747	—	—	—	83,888
w. Konya	989,200	73,000	9,700	—	—	—	—	600	400	15,000	100	1,088,000
w. Ma'muret al-'Aziz (Kharpūt)	322,366 *182,580	650	61,983	1,675	6,060	—	—	—	—	—	—	575,314
s. Mar'ash (Hal.)	134,438	5,505	1,850	2,463	7,806	18,505	8,918	368	—	—	—	179,853
w. Sivas	559,680 *279,834	76,068	129,523	10,477	30,433	—	—	—	—	—	—	1,086,015
k. Shile (Ist.)	15,750	3,200	800	—	—	—	—	—	—	—	—	19,750
w. Tirabzon	806,700	193,000	44,100	2,300	800	400	—	400	—	—	—	1,047,700
s. Urfa (Hal.)	122,665	5,060	2,000	2,437	2,000	2,738	6,218	367	—	—	—	143,485
n. Üskūdar (Ist.)	71,210	12,180	15,800	250	250	—	—	5,100	—	700	200	105,690
w. Van	241,000 *5,400	—	79,000	708	290	6,002	92,000	5,000	—	600	—	430,000
Total	9,676,714 (9,143,037+ *533,677)	1,042,612	977,679	79,749	85,347	56,179	168,706	47,299	2,867	37,752	79,555	12,254,459

compared to the figures of the early sixteenth century (when the ratio was 92 percent to 7.9 percent). How is this rather significant change to be explained? The Ottoman sultans practiced the policy of transplanting populations, and Balkan Greeks and other Christians were on occasion settled in Asia Minor, but there was also an important migratory current of Greeks from the Aegean isles as well as from other regions. The lush riverine valleys of western Anatolia offered greater economic opportunity for many of these islanders, and as they were only a few miles away many Greeks emigrated to Asia Minor during the centuries of Ottoman rule. In this manner began a movement that reversed the exodus of Greeks from western Anatolia occasioned by the Turkish invasion of the eleventh and fourteenth centuries. Many of these Christians gradually made their way inland as merchants, a movement that received considerable impetus with the building of the railroads in the latter half of the nineteenth century.[9] Aside from these external factors, the Ottoman unification and pacification of Anatolia, and Muhammad the Conqueror's regularization of the church's status after the destruction of the Byzantine Empire, brought more felicitous conditions for the remaining Christian communities in Anatolia. Not only did Asia Minor benefit from unified political rule but the Christians, protected (by the millet system) from further shrinkage of their communities, were henceforth effectively united with the spiritual and hierarchical head of the church in Constantinople. Accordingly, one sees an increase in the number of Christian hearths by the end of the sixteenth century.[10] Because a large number of the Anatolian Orthodox Christians spoke Turkish rather than Greek in the nineteenth century when Cuinet gathered his statistics, many have declared these Orthodox Christians (the so-called Karamanlidhes) to be of Turkish rather than of Greek origin.[11]

The Greek-speaking Christians who lived in Anatolia prior to the exchange of populations in 1923 were of two types. There were the Greek-speakers who were descended from the Byzantine population resident in Asia Minor prior to the Turkish conquest, and there was a second group of Greek-speakers who came to Asia Minor after the Ottoman conquest. These latter were heavily settled on the western coastal and riverine regions, their main center being Izmir (Smyrna).[12] Of the regions in which Greek-speaking populations (descended from Byzantine times)

[9] Ramsay, *Geography*, pp. 25–26. Cuinet, *Turquie, passim*. V. Sphyroaeras, "Μετανασ-τεύσεις καὶ ἐποικισμοὶ Κυκλαδιτῶν εἰς Σμύρνην κατὰ τὴν Τουρκοκρατίαν," *M.X.*, X (1963), 164–199.

[10] Barkan, "Essai," table 5, shows a marked increase of Christian hearths in the province of Anadolu (western Asia Minor) from 8,511 hearths in 1520–30 to 20,264 in 1570–80. Again one must note that perhaps this rise is due to a variety of factors rather than to any single cause.

[11] See below for a more detailed discussion of the origin of the Karamanli Christians.

[12] Though there is no definitive account of the later Greek migrations and settlements, one may consult with profit the articles in the following Greek periodicals: Ξενοφάνης, Ἀρχεῖον Πόντου, Μικρασιατικὰ Χρονικά, Ποντιακὴ Ἑστία.

survived into the nineteenth century, Pontus was the single most important. The Graecophone element survived in considerable numbers throughout the towns and villages located between Rize in the east and Cerasus in the west,[13] Trebizond, Oenoe, Samsun (Amisus), and Gümüshhane constituting the principal centers. The Greek mining communities of the Pontus region, especially Gümüshhane, were actively colonizing other mining sites such as Ak Dağ, Bulgar Maden, Bereketli Maden, farther to the south, and when the mining industry began to decline about 1870 in Gümüshhane, they colonized elsewhere as well. A second area in which Greek-speakers were to be found was the region south of Pontus and north of Cappadocia and centered in Shebin-Karahisar.[14] A third group of Hellenophones were those Dawkins studied

[13] The best survey of this second category of Greek-speaking "Byzantines" is the remarkable work of R. M. Dawkins, *Modern Greek in Asia Minor* (Cambridge, 1916); "Modern Greek in Asia Minor," *J.H.S.*, XXX (1910), 109–132, 267–291; "Notes on the Study of Modern Greek of Pontus," *Byzantion*, VI (1931), 389–400. The work by Archbishop Chrysanthos, Ἡ ἐκκλησία Τραπεζοῦντος, Α.Π., vols. IV–V (1936), is monumental. The Greek language and history of Pontus have attracted considerable attention. H. Kiepert, "Die Verbreitung der griechischen Sprache im pontischen Kustengebirge," *Zeitschrift der Gesellschaft für Erdkunde*, XXV (1890), 317–333. Ξενοφάνης, III (1906), 470–481, lists 102 of these Greek-speaking villages. P. Triantaphylides, Ἡ ἐν Πόντῳ ἑλληνική φυλή, ἤτοι τὰ Ποντιακά (Athens, 1866), gives, among other important data, a history of the Greek-speaking towns and villages and the approximate number of the Greeks. Papamichalopoulos, Περιήγησις εἰς τὸν Πόντον (Athens, 1903). The collective enterprise of F. Cumont, J. Anderson, H. Grégoire, *Studia Pontica*, vols. I–III (1903–10), is also valuable. Other philological studies include the following: G. N. Hatzidakis, "Analogien Bildungen im pontischen Dialect," *Indogermanische Forschungen*, XXXI (1912–13), 245–250; D. E. Oeconomides, *Lautlehre des Pontischen* (Leipzig, 1908); Hatzidakis, "Περὶ τῆς Ποντικῆς διαλέκτου καὶ ἰδίᾳ περὶ τῶν ἐν αὐτῇ ἀναλογικῶν σχηματισμῶν," in his Φιλολογικαὶ Ἐρεῦναι (Athens, 1911), 1–35; A. A. Papadopoulos, "Συμβολὴ εἰς τὴν ἔρευναν τῆς ποντικῆς διαλέκτου," Ἀθηνᾶ, XLV (1934), 15 ff. More detailed studies on towns and villages in the Pontus area include: N. E. Lampadarios, Περὶ Ἀμισοῦ καὶ περὶ τοῦ Πόντου ἐν γένει," Ξενοφάνης, I (1896), 172–190, 218–240, 264–272, who discusses, among other things, the reasons for the longevity of Greek in Pontus; Anonymous, "Περὶ Σάντας," Ξενοφάνης, V (1908), 363–364; "Περὶ Κοτυώρων ('Ορδοῦ)," Ξενοφάνης, II (1905), 561–565; "Ἡ Κρώμνα," Ξενοφάνης, V (1908), 341–348; K. Spyrantes, "Περὶ τῆς παρὰ τὴν Τραπεζοῦντα κειμένης κωμοπόλεως Σάντας," Ξενοφάνης, I (1897), 446–453; "Ὁ Ἅγιος Γεώργιος ὁ Περιστερεώτας," Ξενοφάνης, III (1906), 568–569. On the decline of the Greek Christian population of Cerasus as a result of periodic raids and devastations, K. Paulides, " Ὀλίγα τινὰ περὶ τῆς πόλεως Κερασοῦντος," Ξενοφάνης, IV (1906), 10–28. Cerasus was the seat of a Greek metropolitan until 1703, at which time the metropolitanate of Cerasus was abandoned and the church was placed under the metropolitan of Trebizond. In the early twentieth century, with a population of 14,000, it was said to have about 1,200 Greek, 1,000 Turkish, and 300 Armenian families.

[14] Identified by Ramsay, *Geography*, pp. 57, 267, with Coloneia. Dawkins, *Greek*, pp. 9–10. Cumont, *Pontica*, I, 794. Triantaphylides, Ποντιακά, pp. 117–119, lists the villages of Anastos, Kamishli, in the regions of Ali Yara with 35 houses. In the regions of Nicopolis, Paltzana, 50 houses; Karakereviz, 30; Feilere, Esola and Kalatzouk, 50; (Ispahan-melesi, 40 and Hahavla, 30, were the only two villages that were Turkish-speaking, whereas Alisher had both Greek and Turkish-speaking Christians), Kahya Tepe, 8; Eski Köy and Keltzana, 30; Katochorion, 35; Litzasa and Asartzoukh, 130; Litzasan, Koinuk, 45; Agadjik, 40; Kegilik, 70; Hatzi Köy, 50; Aloutcha and Abu Deresi, 25; Eskidje, 30; Supah, 60; Kok Köy, 20. In the regions of Coloneia (Koilisari) there were 4 villages; Mouseli and Ameli, 30; Hasantamih and Havzul, 40. On the following page Triataphylides lists villages in Chaldia, Neocaesareia, Erzerum, Kars, and Paipert. See also S. Zumpulides, " Ἡ Ἐπαρχία Κολωνίας," Ξενοφάνης, VII (1910), 273 ff.

in the twenty Cappadocian villages located about the regions of Nigde and Kayseri.[15] These villages, in the area of the famous troglodyte ecclesiastical and monastic communities of the Byzantine empire, retained lively memories of and associations with the Byzantine past.[16] Slightly to the southeast was a fourth area consisting of six villages, the most important of which was Pharasa.[17] The three remaining regions wherein Byzantine Greek-speaking populations had survived as late as the nineteenth century were Sille (a small town very near Konya), Livisi (on the Lycian coast), and Gölde (near Coula and Philadelpheia).[18]

Unfortunately, the systematic study of the Anatolian Greek dialects began comparatively late, so that we do not know whether the above list is satisfactory. The facts indicate that the Byzantine Greek-speaking element that survived to the nineteenth century was most numerous in the Pontic or north Asia Minor regions. This coincides with the general information from the Ottoman tax registers showing the spread of the Christian population, which was most numerous in this area. Why did

[15] Dawkins, *Greek*, pp. 10–30. See I. S. Archelaos, Ἡ Σινασσός (Athens, 1899). I. Sarantides, Σινασσός (Athens, 1899). A. M. Levides, Αἱ ἐν μονολίθοις μοναὶ τῆς Καππαδοκίας καὶ Λυκαονίας (Constantinople, 1899). B. A. Moustakides, "Καππαδοκικά," Παρνασσός, XV (1892), 368–379, 445–458, 600–615. S. Krinopoulos, Τὰ Φερτέκαινα ἀπὸ ἐθνολογικὴν καὶ φιλολογικὴν ἄποψιν ἐξεταζόμενα (Athens, 1899). S. Pharasopoulos, Σύλατα, κτλ (Athens, 1895). N. S. Rizos, Καππαδοκικά, ἤτοι κτλ (Constantinople, 1865). de Lagarde, *Neugriechisches aus Kleinasien*, *Abh. der kön. Gesell. der Wiss. zu Göttingen*, XXXIII (Göttingen, 1886). Kyrillos (as Kyrillos VI patriarch from 1813–18), Ἱστορικὴ περιγραφὴ τοῦ ἐν Βιέννῃ προεκδοθέντος χωρογραφικοῦ πίνακος τῆς μεγάλης ἀρχισατραπίας Ἰκονίου (1815). S. Kholopoulos, " Ἱστορία Ζήλης ἢ Σύλατας," Ξενοφάνης II (1905), 322 ff. S. Basileiadou, "Συλλογὴ λέξεων λαϊκῶν ἐν Ζήλῃ Ἰκονίου τῆς Μικρᾶς Ἀσίας," Ξενοφάνης, I (1896), 190, 285, 382, 430, 479; continued by S. Kholopoulos in Ξενοφάνης IV (1907), 469–480. P. Karolides, Γλωσσάριον συγκριτικὸν Ἑλληνοκαππαδοκικῶν λέξεων ἤτοι ἡ ἐν Καππαδοκίᾳ λαλουμένη Ἑλληνικὴ διάλεκτος καὶ τὰ ἐν αὐτῇ σωζόμενα ἴχνη τῆς ἀρχαίας Καππαδοκικῆς γλώσσης (Smyrna, 1885). N. Levides, "Περὶ τῶν ὀνομασίων κωμῶν, πόλεων καὶ κωμοπόλεων τῆς Καππαδοκίας," Ξενοφάνης, V (1908), 182–188. Anonymous, "Τὰ ἤθη καὶ τὰ ἔθιμα τὸ ἐπτάγγελμα ἡ ἐνδυμασία τῶν ἐν ἀποκέντροις Καισαρείας Καππαδοκίας οἰκούντων Ὀρθοδόξων Χριστιανῶν," Ξενοφάνης, I (1897), 365–382. S. Panteleimonides, "Περὶ τῶν Κελλιβάρων (Κέλβερι)," Ξενοφάνης, I (1904), 511–513. I. Balabanes, " Ἡ καμπάνα τοῦ χωρίου μου," Παρνασσός, XI (1888), 316–334, on Aravanion. S. Cholopoulos, "Μονογραφικὴ ἱστορία Ζήλης ἢ Σύλατας," Ξενοφάνης, II (1905), 92–96, 205–210, 284–288, 322–327, 342–344. O. Makroas, " Ἡ Μαλακόπη," Ξενοφάνης, IV (1907), 408–431. C. Felekes, "Τοπογραφία μεταλλείου Βουλγὰρ τῆς ἐπαρχίας Χαλδίας," Ξενοφάνης, IV (1907), 344–351.

[16] The estimated populations of these villages are collected in Dawkins, *Greek*, pp. 10 ff.

[17] *Ibid.*, pp. 30–35, again for the population figures. Grégoire, "Rapport sur un voyage d'exploration dans le Pont et en Cappadoce," *Bulletin de Correspondance Hellénique*, XXXIII (1909), 142 ff. on the dialect of Pharasa. N. P. Andriotes, Τὸ γλωσσικὸ ἰδίωμα τῶν Φαράσων (Athens, 1948). B. Phebes, "Συντακτικαὶ παρατηρήσεις εἰς τὸ γλωσσικὸν ἰδίωμα Φαράσων," Ε.Ε.Β.Σ., XVIII (1948), 173–191.

[18] Dawkins, *Greek*, pp. 35–38. The "Byzantine" pedigree of the Greek-speakers of the environs of Bursa and Nicomedia is debated by I. C. Charitonides, "Περὶ τῆς Λιβισιανῆς διαλέκτου " (Trebizond, 1911). M. I. Mousaios, Βατταρισμοί, ἤτοί λεξιλόγιον τῆς Λειβησιανῆς διαλέκτου (Athens, 1880), written by a local schoolmaster with the object of "correcting" barbarisms of the local Greek. I. Koukoules, "Τὰ Νέα Μύλασα," Ξενοφάνης, III (1906), 448–459; "Τὰ Μύλασα," Ξενοφάνης, II (1905), 234–240, 456–464. Anonymous (Εἰς Λύκιος), "Περὶ Λυκίας καὶ Λυκίων. Περὶ Μάκρης καὶ Λειβισίου," Ξενοφάνης, I (1904), 86–93.

both the Greek language and Greek Christianity put up a stronger resistance to Islamization and Turkification in Pontus than elsewhere? It has often been "explained" by the reason that the Hellenic colonization and settlement in classical times were more intensive there than elsewhere in Asia Minor. But certainly ancient Greek emigration and colonization were no more intense in Pontus than in western Anatolia, and the twenty Greek-speaking villages of Cappadocia were far removed from this ancient coastal Hellenism. One must search for another explanation.

The Turks did not conquer the Empire of Trebizond until 1461, and so in contrast with most of Anatolia it remained free of Muslim domination for a much longer period. It was spared the disruption and social upheaval attendant upon so much of the Turkish conquest throughout Anatolia. Its church remained protected by a Christian ruler, enjoyed the possession of wealth and estates, and was regularly administered and maintained at a time when the church in the rest of Asia Minor had been dispossessed of its land, deprived of its administration, and generally crushed. When the Turkish conquest did come to Trebizond it was a relatively rapid affair, and though the Greek ruler and many of the aristocrats were taken away, the inhabitants of the kingdom were incorporated into the already well-developed Ottoman system with far less upheaval than had been the case in many other Anatolian areas. Consequently, the conquest of Trebizond was a simple, unprolonged event. The conquest did not destroy the bonds of cultural and social unity of the region,[19] and the Christians to the south of the Trebizondine empire had, though under Muslim domination, almost continuous contact with and access to a thriving Christian and Greek society. The city of Philadelpheia (where Greek was still evidently spoken in Ottoman times) and Gölde similarly represent a small isolated enclave that managed to defend itself against Turkish domination until 1390. Perhaps the reason for the relatively long survival of Greek here is also explicable on similar historical grounds. Sille (a rallying point for Greeks in the Seljuk period) and Livisi represent isolated cases for which there seems to be no apparent explanation. The twenty-six villages of Cappadocia and Pharasa possibly maintained their dialects because of partial isolation (the former were separated from Kayseri by Mt. Argaeus) and the absence of significant Turkish settlements at an early date. This is, of course, a hypothetical explanation. It has been noted, however, that Greek began to decline in those Cappadocian villages that were near large Muslim towns, such as Nigde, or where Turks began to settle in the villages in number, or, finally, where the men of the villages began to abandon this isolation to seek work in the towns. It would seem, then, the existence of a large number of Greek-speaking Christians in Pontus during Ottoman times is

[19] This theory was advanced as early as 1896 by N. E. Lampadarios, "Ἀμισοῦ," pp. 236–237.

in large part due to political facts, and in Cappadocia to geographical isolation.

A large proportion of the Greek Orthodox population of nineteenth-century Anatolia (the so-called Karamanlidhes) was Turkophone. These Christians very often knew no Greek (save those who had relearned it as a result of the new Greek schools founded in many of the communities)[20] but wrote Turkish with the Greek alphabet. They were comparatively numerous in many parts of the peninsula and the term "Karamanlidhes" evidently came to be applied to them because so many of them were from the domains that formerly belonged to the Turkmen dynasty of the Karamanids. They were to be found in the regions of Adana, Ankara, Aydin, Kayseri, Khudavendigiar, Castamon, Konya, Sivas, as well as in other localities.[21] The origins of this group of Christians came to be the

[20] S. B. Zervoudakis, "Διανοητικὴ ἀναγέννησις ἐν Καισαρίᾳ τῆς Καππαδοκίας," Ξενοφάνης, I (1904), 74–85, on the founding of the gymnasium at the monastery of Τίμιος Πρόδρομος at Zendjidere in the last quarter of the nineteenth century. Also, "Συμβολαὶ εἰς τὴν ἱστορίαν τῆς ἐκπαιδεύσεως ἐν Μικρᾷ Ἀσίᾳ," Ξενοφάνης, II (1905), 120–124, 181–187, 211–216, 304–310, 345–351, 421–424, 465–472.

[21] Material on the Turkophone communities of Asia Minor is widely scattered in periodical literature that is not easily accessible. The bibliography that follows does not pretend to completeness, but will serve as a useful guide. For the Turkophone Christians of Bithynia, G. Pachtikos, "Ἐντυπώσεις," Ξενοφάνης, III (1905), 134–141, 150–163, 212–225. For the central Anatolian plateau, I. P., " Ἡ ἐπαρχία Ἀγκύρας," Ξενοφάνης, IV (1907), 157–161; M. M. Moyseides, "Συμβολαὶ εἰς τὴν ἱστορίαν τῆς ἀνθυπατικῆς Γαλατίας, Μονογραφία περὶ Ἀγκύρας," Ξενοφάνης, II (1905), 158–172, 241–253, 270–279, 294–304, 369–379, 414–420, 433–437. For Kars and the Caucasus, E. Muratchanides, "Οἱ ἐν Κὰρς Ἕλληνες," Ξενοφάνης, V (1908), 364–365.

The accounts of various Anatolian Greeks and European travelers testify to the prevalence of the Turkish language among large numbers of Greek Orthodox Christians; A. A. Gabrielides, "Περὶ τῆς ἐπαρχίας Νεοκαισαρείας ἰδίᾳ δὲ τῆς Θεοδωρουπόλεως (Σαφρανπόλεως) καὶ τοῦ Παρθενίου," Ξενοφάνης, I (1904), 130–131, the Orthodox Christians (3,000) of Castamon, Tosia, Gangra (1,000), Tuht (500), Karata (Kerede) (200), Djai Djuna (250) were largely Turkophones. P. Paulides, " Ἡ ἐπαρχία Νεοκαισαρείας," Ξενοφάνης, IV (1906), 94–96, 125–136, for Orthodox Turkophone communities in northern Asia Minor. In the mid-nineteenth century, prior to the foundation of the Greek schools in Isparta, the Greek Orthodox Christians (some 1,000 families) spoke Turkish, G. Sakkares, " Ἡ Σπάρτη τῆς Πισιδίας," Ξενοφάνης, I (1897), 356–362; "Πισιδικά," Ξενοφάνης, V (1908), 348–351. K. Iatrides, " Ἤθη καὶ ἔθιμα ἐν Ἀνατολῇ, παιδίαι ἐν Βουρδουρίῳ τῆς Πισιδίας," Ξενοφάνης, IV (1906), 68–79, 362–374, 503–510, 433–464. De Planhol, Nomadisme, passim. The 1,600 families of Orthodox Christians in Nevshehir were Turkish-speaking and the 600 families of Indje Su had as their mother tongue Turkish, A. Ioannides, " Ὁδοιπορικαὶ σημειώσεις," Ξενοφάνης, I (1897), 323–324. But there were Greek-speakers in both places, Ξενοφάνης, II (1905), 230–233. Probably there were numerous cases of bilingualism, especially after the revival of the schools. The Orthodox inhabitants (about 1,000 in number) of the island Nis in the lake by Eğridir were entirely Turkophone at the end of the nineteenth century, F. Sarre, Reise in Kleinasien (Berlin, 1896), pp. 149–150. Similarly Turkophone in large part were the Orthodox Christian inhabitants of Chonae, Denizli, Philadelpheia (Alashehir), Zafranbolu, Amasra, and Caesareia, R. Chandler, Travels in Asia Minor and Greece (Oxford, 1825), I, 277, 299, 311–312; A. D. Mordtmann, Anatolien, ed. F. Babinger (Hannover, 1925), pp. 95, 255, 492. B. A. Moustakides, "Καππαδοκικά," p. 455, remarked that in traveling from Nicomedia via Ankara to Kayseri one usually encountered Turkophone, rather than Greekophone, Christians. The 900 Orthodox families of Kutahya in 1905 were Turkophone, Ch. Simeonides, "Τὸ Κοτύαιον," Ξενοφάνης, III (1905), 121, 123. On the Turkophone Orthodox in Bithynia, G. Iosephides, "Περί τινων πόλεων καὶ κωμῶν τῆς Βιθυνίας," Ξενοφάνης, II (1905), 509–513; III (1906), 236–237; IV

subject of debate after World War I not only in historical but even in diplomatic and political circles as well. According to some the Karamanlidhes were of Greek origin but had in the course of their existence in Ottoman Anatolia been linguistically Turkified.[22] Others asserted that the Karamanli Christians were descendants of Turkish soldiers whom the Byzantine emperors had settled in Anatolia throughout the period of Byzantine history preceding the great invasions of the eleventh century.[23] There were also those who supported this latter theory on the basis of the allegedly "pure" character of the Turkish spoken by the Karamanlidhes.[24]

The Turkish-speaking Greek Christians appear for the first time in a Latin report presented to the council of Basle in 1437 on the state of the Eastern church. The author of this text remarks that in many parts of Anatolia some of the clergy, including bishops and archbishops, not only wear the garments of the Turkish infidels but also speak their language. Only the liturgy, gospels, and epistles were read in Greek: the sermons, however, were delivered in Turkish.[25] Shortly thereafter Gennadius Scholarius, the first patriarch in Ottoman Constantinople, drew up the Greek confession of faith in Greek, which was then translated into Turkish (but written in the Greek alphabet).[26] Gian-Maria Angiolello

---

(1907), 535–544; V (1902), 206–209; VII (1910), 15–19. M. Moesides, "Βιθυνιακαὶ σελίδες," Ξενοφάνης, III (1906), 421–422. For the district of Philadelpheia (Alashehir), G. Iosephides, "Περί τινων πόλεων καὶ κωμῶν τῆς ἐπαρχίας Φιλαδελφείας," Ξενοφάνης, III (1906), 424. For Orthodox Christians in Cilicia, M. Georgiades, "Περὶ τῆς Κιλικίας Καθόλου καὶ 'Αδάνων," Ξενοφάνης, I (1896), 273–281. "Περὶ τοῦ νομοῦ 'Αδάνων," Ξενοφάνης, IV (1907), 496–499. See the remarks of William of Tyre, III, 19; Bar Hebraeus, I, 280, 449–450, Michael the Syrian, III, 319, the Armenian Thoros slew 10,000 of these Greeks. Wilbrandus de Oldenborg, *Peregrinatio*, ed. J. C. M. Laurent in *Peregrinatores medii aevi quatuor* (Leipzig, 1873), p. 174. Nerses of Lampron, *R.H.C., D.A.*, I, 596. On Attaleia, " 'Η πυρκαϊὰ τῆς 'Ατταλείας," Ξενοφάνης, I (1904), 566–567; "Περιγραφὴ τῆς πόλεως 'Ατταλείας," Ξενοφάνης, V (1908), 244–259.

[22] Taeschner, "Anadolu," EI₂.

[23] J. Eckmann, "Einige gerundiale Konstruktionen im Karamanischen," *Jean Deny Armağani* (Ankara, 1958), 77. For further bibliography, G. Jaeschke, "Die Türkisch-Orthodoxe Kirche," *Der Islam*, XXXIX (1964), 95–129.

[24] Jaeschke, "Kirche," pp. 96–98. Hamdullah Subhi asserts that he learned many such old Turkish words from the Turkophone Orthodox women of Attaleia in 1923. Cami Baykurt, who first proposed the Turkish origin of the Karamanlidhes, *Osmanlï ülkesinde Hïristiyan Türkler*, 2d ed. (Istanbul, 1932), was an organizer of the Turkish League for the defense of Izmir against Greek claims.

[25] S. Lampros, " 'Υπόμνημα περὶ τῶν 'Ελληνικῶν χωρῶν καὶ ἐκκλησιῶν κατὰ τὸν δέκατον πέμπτον αἰῶνα," *N.E.*, VII (1910), 366, "Notandum est, quod in multis partibus Turcie reperiuntur clerici, episcopi et arciepiscopi, qui portant vestimenta infidelium et locuntur linguam ipsorum et nihil aliud sciunt in grece proferre nisi missam cantare et evangelium et epistolas. Alias autem orationes multi dicunt in linguam Turcorum." On the liturgy among the Karamanlidhes see now the interesting article of R. Clogg, "The Publication and Distribution of Karamanli Texts by the British and Foreign Bible Society before 1850, I," *The Journal of Ecclesiastical History*, XIX (1968), 57–81.

[26] S. A. Chudaverdoglu-Theodotus, " 'Η τουρκόφωνος ἑλληνικὴ φιλολογία 1453–1924," *Ε.Ε.Β.Σ.*, VII (1930), 299–300. Among the versions of the text is that published in *P.G.*, CLX, 333–352. In a sense this does not belong to the later phenomenon of Karamanli literature.

remarked that the fifteenth-century Greek inhabitants of Meram (outskirts of Konya) spoke Turkish (with some exceptions), and that their liturgical books were written in Turkish and Arabic script.[27] These Turkophone Christians of the Greek church are first referred to as "Karamanos" in the travel account of Hans Dernschwamm (1553–55) who encountered them in the Yedikule quarter of Istanbul and described them as a Christian folk of the Greek faith whom Selim I had transplanted from Karaman. He noted that they were a numerous people, that they knew no Greek, but he did not know whether their original language was Turkish.[28] Other travelers observed and commented on their presence thereafter, including the famous Turkish traveler Evliya Chelebi.[29] These Orthodox Christians of Anatolia began to found Greek schools in the nineteenth century in an effort to revive a knowledge of Greek.[30] It is interesting that with the Graeco-Turkish war of 1919–1921, the complexities of the minority problem brought the question of the origin of the Turkish-speaking Anatolian Orthodox Christians into the political and diplomatic spheres, and that at this time the Kemalist government momentarily considered a project for a Turkish Orthodox church under the direction of the Anatolian priest Papa Eftim Karahisaridhes.[31]

By the early eighteenth century, there had come into existence a printed Karamanli literature that, though Turkish, was written in the Greek alphabet. This literature consisted largely of translations into Turkish of the Old and New Testaments, the Apostles, Apodeipnon, various other liturgical texts, hagiography, and other religious writings. There were in addition books of a nonreligious nature concerning such subjects as

[27] Babinger, *Mahomet II le conquérant et son temps 1432–1481* (Paris, 1954), p. 401.

[28] *Hans Dernschwam's Tagebuch einer Reise nach Konstantinopel und Kleinasien (1553/55)*, ed. F. Babinger (Munich-Leipzig, 1923), p. 52. "Nicht weit von abstander burg, so Giedicula genant, an einem oeden orth der stadt, wont ein cristen volkh, nent man Caramanos, aus dem landt Caramania, an Persia gelegen, seind cristen, haben den krichischen glauben. Und ire mes halten sy auff krikisch und vorstehen doch nicht krikisch. Ir sprach ist turkisch. Nit weiss ich, ab sy anfenglisch turkische sprach gehapt haben. Des jeczigen turkischen kaysers vatter Slinua sol dis volkh her gen Constantinapol gefurt haben, als er die selbigen lender bekriegt. Scheint ein gros stark volkh sein. Die Weyber haben lange, spiczige, weysse und auch von farben huthe auff, also ungerarlich gestaltt wie ein bapstkron. Und wan sy ausgehen, so decken sy ein dunn durchsichtigs thuch daruber bis uber die bruste."

[29] Evliya Chelebi, *Seyahatnamesi, Anadolu, Suriye, Hicaz (1671–1672)* (Istanbul, 1935), IX, 288.

[30] G. Sakkares, "Ἡ Σπάρτη τῆς Πισιδίας," Ξενοφάνης, I (1897), 362. S. B. Zervoudakes, "Διανοητικὴ ἀναγέννησις ἐν Καισαρίᾳ τῆς Καππαδοκίας," Ξενοφάνης, I (1904), 74–85, describes the founding and functioning of the gymnasium in the monastery of Timios Prodromos in Zendjidere, Cappadocia, during the last quarter of the nineteenth century. See also the general remarks of Dawkins, *Greek, passim.*

[31] For the confusing details and motives, Jaeschke, "Kirche," pp. 95-129; H. J. Psomaides, "The Ecumenical Patriarchate under the Turkish Republic: The First Ten Years," *Balkan Studies*, II, (1961), 50 ff.; *The Eastern Question: The Last Phrase, a Study in Greek-Turkish Diplomacy* (Thessalonike, 1968), pp. 91–92 and *passim*. T. Ergene, *Istiklal harbinde Türk Ortodoksları* (Istanbul, 1951), is, according to Psomaides, the work of Papa Eftim himself.

mathematics, geography, astronomy, physics, and Greek chrestomathies and lexica. The Karamanlidhes also printed a newspaper in Istanbul.[32]

Inasmuch as the question of the historical origins of the Karamanlidhes is intimately related to the subject of the "Byzantine Residue" in Anatolia, a brief investigation of the problem is necessary. The theory of their Turkish origin appeared in a developed form immediately after World War I when the partition of Turkey seemed imminent. The connection of this theory with the political circumstances that so threatened Turkey at that time, especially from Greek claims in Asia Minor, is unmistakably clear. The author of this explanation, Cami Baykurt, was general secretary of the League for the Defence of Ottoman Rights in Izmir in 1918–1919. In his writings Cami Baykurt, as did certain other Turkish authors,[33] expounded the Turkish origins of the Karamanlidhes on historical, linguistic, and other grounds. Baykurt alleged that the Turkish language (and it was, he said, purer Turkish than that spoken by many Muslim Turks)[34] and the Turkish customs of the Turkophone Christians were due to the fact that they were descendants of Turkish soldiers whom the Byzantine emperors had settled in Anatolia prior to the Seljuk invasions. Here they were converted to Christianity, and because of Seljuk and Ottoman religious tolerance, they were permitted to retain the Christian religion.[35]

Neither the alleged historical nor linguistico-cultural arguments advanced by this theory provide satisfactory explanations of the Karamanlidhes phenomenon, a phenomenon, incidentally, which is by no means unique and restricted to the history of Turkish Anatolia. Though the linguistic problem must be solved by the philologists and there is no attempt to pronounce judgment on this specialized question here, still

---

[32] On their literature and language see the following works: Jaeschke, "Kirche," pp. 99–101 gives a short but succinct sketch of this literature with useful bibliography, Chudaverdoglu-Theodotos, "Τουρκόφωνος,"pp. 306–307; S. Salaville and E. Dalleggio. *Karamanlidika 1584–1850*, vol. I (Athens, 1958), is the first volume of a comprehensive descriptive catalog of printed Karamanli literature. See the review of Eyice, *Belleten*, XXVI (1962), 369–374. F. Halkin, "Accoolouthies gréco-turques à l'usage des grecs turcophones d'Asie Mineure," in *Mémorial Louis Petit* (Bucharest, 1948), pp. 194–202. E. Photiades, " Τουρκόφωνα ἑλληνικὰ βιβλία," *Ἑλληνικά*, IV (1931), 493–495. G. Arbanitakes, *Les reliques d'un monde disparu* (Athens, 1930), is a catalog of Karamanli manuscripts to be found in Athens. Eckmann, "Die karamanische Literatur," in *Philologiae Turcicae Fundamenta* (Wiesbaden, 1964), II, 819–834. Huart, "Notice sur trois ouvrages en turc d'Anqara imprimés en caractères grecs," *J.A.*, 9ᵉ ser., XVI (1900), 459–477. G. Hazai, "Über den osmanisch-türkischen Abschnitt des dreisprachigen Sprachführers von Saloniki," *Ural-altaische Jahrbücher*, XXXIII (1961), 66–72.

[33] The arguments of Cami were repeated in a series of articles by Izzet Ulvi, which appeared in the journal *Hakimiyet-i Milliye*, under the title "Anadolu'da Hiristiyan Türkler," For translated excerpts, Jaeschke, "Kriche," pp. 110–111.

[34] "Jaschke, "Kirche," p. 96, n. 9a.

[35] *Ibid.*, pp. 110–111, Izzet Ulvi gave a variant explanation. These Karamanlidhes were descendants of the indigenous "Turanian" inhabitants of Anatolia who had lived in the peninsula at least as early as 4,000 years ago. Under Byzantine rule, he says, they adopted Christianity but retained their language. Cami Baykurt developed his thesis at length in *Osmanli Ülkesinde Hïristiyan Türkler*, 2d ed. (Istanbul, 1932).

one is struck by the comments of the seventeenth-century traveler Evliya Chelebi who also noticed the cultural peculiarities of the Karamanlidhes. When he visited Antalya he recorded the fact that the Christians spoke only Turkish.

And there are four quarters of Greek infidels. But the infidels know absolutely no Greek. They speak erroneous Turkish.[36]

Soon after Antalya, Evliya's itinerary brought him to the coastal town of Alaiya where he observed the same condition.

There was, from olden times, an infidel Greek quarter. There are altogether 300 [who pay] the haradj. They know absolutely no Greek but know erroneous Turkish.[37]

To Evliya these Turkish-speaking Christians appeared as Greeks who spoke no Greek.[38] It is interesting to note his observation that they spoke an "erroneous" form of Turkish, a form that evidently distinguished them linguistically from their Turkish Muslim neighbors.[39] Evliya, in contrast to Baykurt, considered the Turkish of the Karamanlidhes in seventeenth-century Antalya and Alaiya to be anything but "pure."

More important is that the sources do not indicate that Turks were settled as military colonists on any significant scale in Byzantine Anatolia prior to the battle of Manzikert. It is remarkable how often articles and

[36] Evliya Chelebi, IX, 288, ". . . ve dördü Urum keferesi mahallesidir Amma keferesi asla ürumca bilmezler Batĭl Türk lisanĭ üzre kelimat iderler."

[37] *Ibid.*, p. 297, "Amma kadim eyyamdan beru Urum keferesi bir mahalledir Cümle üç yüz haracdĭr Amma asla Urum lisanĭ bilmiyüb batĭl Türk lisanĭ bilürler."

[38] We have an affirmation of the Greek origin of these Karamanlidhes from a Greek traveler of the late sixteenth century. Jacob Meloites, from the Dodecanesian island of Patmos, composed in 1588 an account of his journeys throughout the Middle East and Europe, and in so doing left us some precious notes on south and west Anatolia. He specifically mentions three Turkophone Christian communities, in Isparta, Attaleia, and Kula. S. Papageorgiou, " Ὁδοιπορικὸν ᾽Ιακώβου Μηλοΐτη," Παρνασσός (1882), 635, "Καὶ εἰς τὴν χώρα τὴν ᾽Ατάλια ἔστι πολλοὶ χριστιανοὶ Ἕλληνες, ἀλλὰ οὐ γινώσκουσι γλῶσσα ἑλληνικήν· μόνον τούρκικη γλῶσσα· καὶ ὑπάρχουσι καλοὶ χριστιανοὶ καὶ γραμματισμένοι, γράμματα ἑλληνικά, τυπογραφία ἐκ τῆς Βενετήας. Καὶ ἐκ τῆς ᾽Ατάλιας ἔσω τῆς στερεᾶς δύο καὶ ἥμισυ ἡμέρας εἰς χώρα ὀνομάζεται Σπαρτά· καὶ εἰς τὰ Σπαρτὰ πολλοὶ χριστιανοὶ Ἕλληνες· οὐ γινώσκουσι γλῶσσα ἑλληνική." Isparta still had many Christians when Lucas visited it in the early eithteenth century. *Voyage du Sieur Paul Lucas, fait par ordre du roi dans la Grece, l'Asie Mineure, la Macedoine et l'Afrique* (Amsterdam, 1714), I, 247–248 (hereafter cited as Lucas, 1714). P. 636, " . . . εἰς Κοῦλα. Πολλοὶ χριστιανοὶ Ἕλληνες· οὐ γινώσκουν γλῶσσα ἑλληνική· πάντες τεχνίτες, ποιοῦσι ταπέδικα· " Meloites, like Evliya, considers these Christians to be of Greek origin, for he refers to them not only as Christians but as Greeks (the use of Hellenes is most interesting). The testimony of the Greek and Turkish sources thus corroborate each other and both consider these Turkophone Christians as Greeks (Rum, Ellenes). As of the seventeenth century, there were no Jews or Armenians in Muğla, only Turks and Greeks. Evliya Chelebi, IX, 202.

[39] My colleague Prof. Janos Eckmann kindly informed me that even today the Turkish of the Karamanlidhes differs from that of the ordinary Turkish-speaker. On peculiarities and characteristics, Eckmann, "Einige gerundiale Konstrukionen in Karamanischen," *Jean Deny Armağani* (Ankara, 1958), pp. 77–83; "Anadolu Karamanli agĭzlarĭna ait araştĭrmalar I. Phonetica." *Dil ve tarih-cografya fakültesi dergisi*, VIII (Ankara, 1950), 165–200. J. Deny, "Le gerondif en-(y)isin, d'après les écrits du moine Ioanni Hierotheos en turc des Grecs-orthodoxes turcophones d'Anatolie," *K.C.A.*, III (1941), 119–128.

books refer to this supposed large-scale "Turkish colonization" by the emperors. If there was such a colonization of Turks, the contemporary histories, chronicles, and other documents certainly passed over it in silence. There was large-scale colonization in Anatolia prior to the eleventh century, but mostly of Slavs. The Turks were most often settled in Europe, especially in the Vardar regions.[40] If indeed Turks had been settled in Anatolia during this earlier period, they would probably not have survived the process of Hellenization and Christianization. This is what happened to the Slavs and other smaller groups settled in Anatolia by the Byzantines. There is no indication that Slavic-speakers from the Byzantine period survived in Ottoman Anatolia, rather they had been Hellenized. The basic languages that survived into the Ottoman period were Greek and Armenian. One must assume that in this Hellenic Christian environment most ethnic groups would have been largely assimilated.

It would seem more likely that the Karamanlidhes were in origin largely Greek-speaking Christians of Byzantine Anatolia, who in the course of Seljuk and Ottoman rule were Turkified linguistically, abandoned the use of Greek, and adopted a number of Turkish customs and practices. There are many parallel cases that would support such an assertion. That the vanquished very often abandoned their language for that of the conqueror and also imitated many of the victor's customs were already apparent to Ibn Khaldun in the fifteenth century.[41] The process by which Turkish replaced Greek as the spoken language of these Christian communities was still alive in the late nineteenth and the early twentieth century, so that the philologists turned their attention to it, described it, and thus we have some knowledge of it. Social, political, and economic reasons most frequently require the conquered to acquire some knowledge of the language of their rulers. They must do this in order to carry on and facilitate the business of everyday existence. The language of government, administration, courts, tax collection, and commerce was most often, though not exclusively, Turkish. Conversion to Islam led to Turkification, and since the majority converted to the new religion, they also became Turkophone. There is also some evidence that the Turks occasionally insisted upon the use of Turkish in the thirteenth century.[42] The cities, as the political and religious centers of the Turks, no doubt became principal centers from which the process of Turkification radiated. Those villages that were geographically nearby or else closely bound economically to the cities were strongly affected in matters of language. In those villages where

[40] This is repeated in the useless study of L. Vrooman, "The Pre-Ottoman Conquest of Asia Minor," *Muslim World*, XXI (1941), 249–256. Yinanc, *Fethi, passim.* makes similar assertions, all of them based on misquoted and misunderstood sources, most of these sources being quoted from other secondary works.

[41] See chapter vi.

[42] Ibn Bibi-Duda, pp. 313, 345.

the ruling Turks settled, the same phenomenon was to be observed. Even in villages that had no Turkish settlers and were geographically isolated Turkish was often introduced by Christians who, emigrating to Istanbul, Kayseri, and other towns, in order to find work, returned to their provincial homes to retire. The change was usually manifested in the local Greek speech by a saturation of Turkish lexicographical material and syntactical forms. The villagers might become bilingual for varying periods of time until at some critical point Turkish would replace Greek as the language of the house and family. Then a generation would appear for which the mother tongue would be Turkish and Greek would be relegated to a secondary position. Finally, the process would be consummated when the last old men and women of the village who remembered a few words and phrases of Greek would pass away.

All these conditions for and stages of the decline of Greek and the victory of Turkish have been recorded in nineteenth- and twentieth-century Anatolia. In the Cappadocian villages of Andaval (an all Christian village of about 2,000 inhabitants in the early twentieth century) and Limna (about 2,000 Christians and 650 Turks), the Christians had spoken Greek up to the latter part of the last century by which time Turkish had almost completely replaced Greek (by 1884 in Andaval, and by 1880 in Limna).[43] Similarly the Greek-speaking miners from Pontus who colonized Bereketli Maden in the Taurus eventually abandoned Greek for Turkish.[44] By 1891 all that remained of Greek in the village of Gölde was a scant fifteen words, and these were recited by an old woman to the German philologist K. Buresch.[45] At Isparta, before the founding of the Greek schools, the number of Greek-speakers could be counted on the fingers.[46] Even in the regions of Pontus, where the Greek-speaking tradition had been strongest, Turkisms in the language were frequent, and the closer the villages were to the periphery of the area, the more readily did they succumb to Turkish.[47] There were other areas in which the retreat of Greek, though not at the final stage of disappearance, was well along the way. In the Cappadocian villages of Semendere, Ulağadj, Fertek, as a result of increases in the number of Turks or of contacts with the outside world, Greek had been, lexicographically and syntactically, heavily permeated by Turkish, and linguistic Turkification of the inhabitants was far advanced.[48] In other Cappadocian Graecophone

[43] Dawkins, Greek, p. 11. Rizos, Καππαδοκικά (Constantinople, 1856). Archelaos, Σινασσός, p. 126. Karolides, Γλωσσάριον, p. 37. Moustakides, Καππαδοκικά, pp. 455–456.

[44] Balabanes, Μικρασιατικά (Athens, 1891), pp. 134–139.

[45] Dawkins, Greek, p. 38. K. Buresch in Wochenschrift für Philologie, IX (1892), 1387.

[46] Sakkares, " Ἡ Σπάρτη τῆς Πισιδίας," Ξενοφάνης, I (1897), 362.

[47] Triantaphylides, Ποντιακά, pp. 142–143. Dawkins, "Notes on the Study of the Modern Greek of Pontus," Byzantion, VI (1931), 396.

[48] Dawkins, Greek, pp. 13–18. Moustakides, Καππαδοκικά, pp. 455–457.

villages such as Ghurzono and Aravanion, which had no Turkish population, the existence of the language was secure. But because of proximity to Nigde, the main arteries of communication and the movements of trade, Greek experienced a certain corruption, ensuing from Turkish linguistic borrowings.[49] Pharasa, where previously Turkish had not been understood, became bilingual as a result of the influx of some Turkish settlers, but Greek remained the principal language of the Christians.[50] In Sille, outside of Konya, Turkish had also been unknown, but with the appearance of a sizable Turkish population in the nineteenth century, the position of Greek became precarious.[51] As far west as Bithynia, the same process was observable in the village of Saridagounion where the Greek of the 1,500 Christians was heavily contaminated.[52]

The process by which Greek-speaking communities could abandon their language for Turkish is amply illustrated by these recorded instances from the last century of Ottoman history.[53] No doubt the process was one that did not suddenly begin in the nineteenth century, that very period of extraordinary awakening and consciousness when strenuous efforts were made to teach the Karamanlidhes Greek anew through the extensive program of founding schools. The retreat of Greek before the progress of Turkish was constant throughout the long centuries of Seljuk and Ottoman rule in Asia Minor.[54]

The actual process of linguistic Turkification, so apparent to observers in the nineteenth century, is not the only evidence indicative of a Greek origin for the Karamanlidhes. There are many parallels among other cultural groups in which their language was replaced by the language of the ruling class. In Anatolia itself large numbers of Armenian Christians became Turkophone and often wrote Turkish in the Armenian script.[55] In Syria, where Arabic replaced Syriac at an earlier date, the former Syriac-speaking population utilized the Syriac alphabet to write Arabic (Karshuni). The Copts of Egypt too were Arabized in language so that they eventually retained Coptic only as a liturgical language, and on occasion used the Coptic alphabet to write Arabic. Moving to the northern

---

[49] Dawkins, *Greek*, pp. 17–18.

[50] *Ibid.*, pp. 30–34.

[51] *Ibid.*, p. 36; C. Niebuhr, *Reisebeschreibung* (1837), III, 126 ff.

[52] G. Paschalides, " 'Ανακοίνωσις περὶ πόλεών τινων τῆς Βιθυνίας," Ξενοφάνης, I (1896), 284.

[53] The ancient geographer Strabo gives a parallel description of the victory of Greek over the Anatolian languages, see chapter i.

[54] Perhaps the earliest example is that in Nicetas Choniates, 50, in which the Greek Christians of the isles in the lakes began to associate intimately with the neighboring Turks."ᾤκουν μὲν οὖν ταύτας τηνικάδε καιροῦ Χριστιανῶν ἐσμοί, οἳ καὶ διὰ λέμβων καὶ ἀκατίων τοῖς Ἰκονιεῦσι Τούρκοις ἐπιμιγνύμενοι οὐ μόνον τὴν πρὸς ἀλλήλους φιλίαν ἐντεῦθεν ἐκράτυναν ἀλλὰ καὶ τοῖς ἐπιτηδεύμασιν αὐτῶν ἐν πλείοσι προσεσχήκασιν. ἀμέλει καὶ ὡς ὁμοροῦσι αὐτοῖς προστιθέμενοι Ῥωμαίους ὡς ἐχθροὺς ὑπεβλέποντο· οὕτω χρόνῳ κρατυνθὲν ἔθος γένους καὶ θρησκείας ἐστὶν ἰσχυρότερον."

[55] Von Harff, von Groote, p. 201, and n. 793, chapter iii above.

shore of the Mediterranean, once more, the Greek populations were subjected to the same cultural transformation in southern Italy. Here they were absorbed by the Latin element and the Greek language underwent the same obliteration that it did in Asia Minor. Many of these Greeks in southern Italy eventually wrote Italian utilizing the Greek alphabet.[56] In many ways the history of medieval Spain, as a border region where the forces of Christianity and Islam clashed, presents an interesting parallel with Anatolia. By the reign of the Umayyad 'Abd al-Rahman II (822–852) extensive numbers of the population had apostatized to Islam, and a significant portion that had not become Muslim had been Arabized culturally. This latter class, known as the Mozarabs (Arabic, *musta'rib*, he who adopts the language and customs of the Arabs), accommodated itself to Arab language, literature, and manner of life. They seemed to prefer Arabic literature to the Latin writings of the Church Fathers, had the Bible translated into Arabic, often bore Muslim names, maintained harems, practiced circumcision, and so forth.[57] The many parallels between the Mozarabs and Karamanlidhes in matters of imitation of language and customs of the conqueror further reinforces the probability that the Karamanlidhes were Greek in origin. Had events in Anatolia followed the pattern of a Christian *reconquista* as occurred in Spain, the phenomenon of linguistic change from Greek to Turkish would probably have reversed itself. The Spanish *reconquista* terminated the process of linguistic Arabization before it could remove Spanish. The Karamanlidhes, like the Mozarabs who imitated the Arabs, often had Turkish names,[58]

[56] G. N. Sola, "Spigolature di Codici Greci Siciliani," *Archivio Storico per la Sicilia orientali*, XXV (1929), 408–412. G. Schiro, " Ἡ βυζαντινὴ λογοτεχνία τῆς Σικελίας καὶ τῆς κάτω Ἰταλίας," Ἑλληνικά, XVII (1962), 182. On the state of the Greek communities in the fourteenth century, J. Gay, "Notes sur la conservation du rite grec dans la Calabre et dans la terre d'Otrante au XIVᵉ siècle; listes de monastères basiliens (d'après les archives du Vatican)," *B.Z.*, IV (1895), 59–66. G. Rohlfs, *Neue Beiträge zur Kenntnis der unteritalienischen Grätzität*, Bay. Akad. d. Wiss. Phil.-Hist. Kl. Sitz. (1962). G. Morosi. "L'elemento Greco nei dialetti dell' Italia meridionale," *Archivio Glottologico Italiano*. XII, (1890–92), 76–96. A. Guillou, "La Lucanie byzantine," *Byzantion*, XXXV (1965), 119–149; "Inchiesta sulla popolazione greca della Sicilia e della Calabria nel Medio Evo," *Rivista Storica Italiana*, LXXV (1963), 53–68. M.-H. Laurent and J. Guillou, *Le 'Liber Visitationis' d'Athanase Chalkéopoulos (1457–1458)* (Vatican, 1960).

[57] P. Hitti, *History of the Arabs* (New York, 1951), pp. 515, 530, 545, 551. E. Levi-Provencal and L. P. Harvey, "Aljamia," EI₂. G. Levi Della Vida, "I Mozarabi tra Occidente e Islam," *L'Occidente e l'Islam nell'alto medicevo* (Spoleto, 1965), II, 667–695, with a good bibliography. Levi-Provencal, *Histoire de l'Espagne musulmane*, (Paris, 1950–53), I, 233; III, 214–226, 233–240. F. J. Simonet, *Historia de los Mozarabes de Espana* (Madrid, 1897–1903). A. G. Palencia, *Los Mozarabes de Toledo en los siglos XII y XIII* (Madrid, 1926–30). I. de la Cagigas, *Los Mozarabes* (Madrid, 1947–48). H. Peres, "Les éléments éthniques de l'Espagne musulmane et la langue arabe, au V–XI siècle," in *Études d'orientalisme dediées à la mémoire de Lévi-Provençal* (Paris, 1962), II, 717–731, especially 725 on Islamization and Arabization of Christians.

[58] Anatolian Greeks with Turkish names appear as early as the thirteenth century. Thierry, *Nouvelles Eglises*, pp. 202–206, published dedicatory inscriptions from the church of St. George not far from Gelveri which included the name Georgios Yiag(oupes). Turkish names, titles, and double Greek-Turkish names were in use in the empire of Trebizond. The emperor Andronicus' two brothers had Greek and Turkish names, and

and imitated Turkish customs in dress, in amusements, and in other ways.[59]

The scant historical sources and evidence from the period of the eleventh through the fifteenth centuries would also support the probability that the Karamanli Christians were formerly Graceophone and that Greek was the principal language of the peninsula on the eve of the invasions. The cities of Ankara, Neocaesareia, Attaleia, Iconium, and Amaseia, whose Orthodox Christian population in the eighteenth and nineteenth centuries was largely Turkophone, were inhabited by Greek-speaking Christians in the earlier periods. In 1391 the translator for the religious debate between Manuel Palaeologus and the Ancyrene muderris was a bilingual inhabitant who had been converted to Islam. At the time Neocaesareia was besieged by the emperor John II Comnenus, the Turkish defenders had the inhabitants of the city compose a letter to the attackers in Greek. Many of the inhabitants of Attaleia in the thirteenth century also spoke Greek, and the Danishmendname refers to Greek-speakers in Amaseia and Comana Pontica.[60] Also indicative of the fact that Greek was the principal language of Anatolia prior to Turkification is the phenomenon that the children of mixed marriages, as well as converts to Islam, were very frequently Greek-speaking or bilingual. Thus large numbers of *mixovarvaroi* in the Seljuk armies of the twelfth century were both Greek-speaking and Turkish-speaking. The Turkish troops who attempted to defend Chios against the counteroffensive of Alexius I also knew Greek.[61] The geographical spread of Greek in this early Turkish period is often reflected in the administration of the various Turkish principalities. The Danishmendids minted a coinage that often utilized Greek inscriptions. The Seljuks, Ottomans, and house of Aydin, who ruled over large numbers of Greeks and had to deal with Greek states, all had Greek chanceries in their administration. John Cantacuzene remarks that the Ottomans

---

there was even a partial Turkification of court titles. Panaretus-Lampsides, pp. 64–66, 72, 75–76. Greek Christians with Turkish or Turko-Greek names also appear in the monastic documents of Vazelon, T. Uspenski and V. Beneševič, *Vazelonskie Akty* (Leningrad, 1927), pp. 10, 17. The spread of Turkish names among the Greek Christians of both Anatolia and the Balkans was extensive. See the following for references to them in Turkish documents: M. Koman, "Anadolu Hiristiyanlarda Islam ve Türk adları," *Konya*, III, 180–183; Konyalï, *Aksehir*, pp. 540 ff.

[59] Nicephorus Gregoras, III, 555, reports that even in fourteenth-century Constantinople, the Greek youths were adopting "Perisan" and Latin dress. The adoption of Muslim clothing, customs, and titles (as well as those of the Latins) was apparently strong among the Armenians of eastern Anatolia and Cilicia in the twelfth century, Nerses of Lampron, *R.H.C., D.A.*, I, 597 ff. De Clavijo-Le Strange, p. 115, for Turkish influence on Trebizondine cavalry and weapons. For the adoption of Turkish style archery contests in Constantinople see the traveler, Brocquière-Schefer, p. 158.

[60] Bar Hebraeus, I, 306. Manuel Palaeologus, *P.G.*, CLVI, 121–122. A. J. Arberry, *Discourses of Rumi* (London, 1961), pp. 108–109. Danishmendname-Melikoff, I, 212, 315; II, 26, 129.

[61] Anna Comnena, II, 111–112; III, 205. *Gesta Francorum*, pp. 101, 107. The converted Greeks in parts of Pontus continued to speak Greek, as did the converts of Crete.

themselves were familiar with the Greek language.[62] Greek religious and funerary inscriptions are frequent in Anatolia as late as the end of the thirteenth century and continue in many regions, sporadically, until the fifteenth century. But by the eighteenth and nineteenth centuries these inscriptions are often in Turkish inscribed with Greek characters.[63] In many ways one of the most striking testimonials to the importance of Greek in part of thirteenth-century Anatolia are the Greek verses in the Rebab-name of Sultan Walad, the son of Djalal al-Din Rumi. He obviously composed these verses for the benefit of Greek-speakers and these Graeco-phones must still have been comparatively numerous in thirteenth- and early fourteenth-century Konya. Again, this would indicate that although Konya was Turkish-speaking in the nineteenth century, it had been Greek-speaking prior to the twelfth century.[64] Finally, Greek has left important philological traces, via loan words, in both the Turkish Hochsprache and the Turkish dialects of Anatolia.[65]

[62] See chapter iii, nn. 536-538. To the bibliography there, one may consult further, Lampros, " Ἑλληνικὰ δημόσια γράμματα τοῦ Σουλτάνου Βαγιαζὶτ Β', N.E. V (1908), 155–189; "'Ορκος τῶν Μουσουλμάνων πρὸς Χριστιανούς," N.E., XV (1921), 363–366. A. Bombaci, "Il liber graecus, un cartolario veneziano comprendere inediti documenti ottomani in greco (1481–1504)," Westostliche Abhandlungen (Wiesbaden, 1954), pp. 301–302. John Cantacuzene, P.G., CLIV, " βαρβάρους ὄντας, καὶ τῆς τῶν Ἑλλήνων σοφίας, οὐ μὴν γὰρ γλώττης ἀμοίρους σχεδόν . . ."

[63] Bees, Die Inschriftenaufzeichnung des Kodex Sinaiticus Graecus, 508 (976) und die Maria Spiläotissa Klosterkirche bei Sille (Lykaonien), mit Exkursen zur Geschichte der Seldschuken-Türken (Berlin, 1922), passim. Thierry, Églises nouvelles, passim. De Jerphanion, Cappadoce, passim. On Karamanli inscriptions the recent article of E. Hatzidake is most interesting, " Χρισ-τιανικὲς ἐπιγραφὲς Μικρᾶς 'Ασίας καὶ Πόντου," M.X., VIII (1959), 1–48.

[64] For the phenomenon of the Greek verses, written in the Arabic script, G. Meyer, "Die griechischen Verse im Rababnama," B.Z., IV (1895), 401–411. "Divan-i Sultan Veled'den," Konya, VI, 376–378. P. Burguière and R. Mantran, "Quelques vers grecs du XIIIe siècle en caractères arabes," Byzantion, XXII (1952), 63–80.

[65] This question will be examined in somewhat more detail in relation to Turkish cultural borrowings from the Greek Christians in Anatolia. The most important contribution is that of A. Tietze, "Griechische Lehnwörter im anatolischen Türkischen," Oriens, VIII (1955), 204–257 (hereafter cited as Tietze, "Anat. Türkisch). In this study Tietze was the first to isolate the loan words in the spoken dialects of Anatolia (in contradistinction to loan words in the Hochsprache). He based his study on the lexicographical material collected in Anatolia by the Linguistic Society from the spoken language, which material evidently excluded recognizable Greek words. Therefore the study of Tietze represents those words that were absorbed and Turkified in appearance. This is of great significance for the study of the Byzantine cultural influence in Turkish Anatolia. The 303 words that Tietze has here compiled exclude, however, loan words that were also in the Hochsprache, as well as certain other categories. For the nautical terms borrowed by Turkish from the Greek, H. and R. Kahane and A. Tietze, The Lingua Franca in the Levant (Urbana, 1958) (hereafter cited as Kahane and Tietze, Lingua Franca). Other works include Tietze, "Griechischen Lehnwörter im anatolischen Türkisch, Actes du Xe Congrès inernational d'études Byzantines (Istanbul, 1957), pp. 295–296 (hereafter cited as Tietze, "Griech. Lehnwörter"), of the 32,000 words in the Turkish Dialectical Dictionary Tietze found about 1,000 that had passed into Turkish via Greek. Also his "Einige weitere greichische Lehnwörter," Nemeth Armağni (Ankara, 1962), pp. 373–388 (hereafter cited as "Einige weitere"). E. Mpoga, " Τὰ εἰς τὴν τουρκικήν, περσικήν καὶ ἀραβικὴν δάνεια τῆς 'Ελληνικῆς," 'Αθηνᾶ, LV (1951), 67–113. Andriotes, " Οἱ ἀμοιβαῖες γλωσσικὲς ἐπιδράσεις 'Ελλήνων καὶ Τούρκων," Μορφές IV (1950), 558 ff. A. A. Papadopoulos, "Τὰ ἐκ τῆς ἑλληνικῆς δάνεια τῆς Τουρκικῆς," 'Αθηνᾶ, XLIV (1933), 3–27. Meyer, Türkische Studien, I. Die griechischen und romanischen Bestandtheile im Wortschatze des Osmanische-Turkischen. Sitz. der kon. Akad. der Wiss., Phil.-Hist. Cl., CXXVIII (Vienna, 1893) (hereafter cited as Meyer, Türk. Studien).

The rupestrian churches of Cappadocia, *Voyage du Sieur Paul Lucas* (Amsterdam, 1714), p. 129.

Interior view of Sultan Khan caravansaray, K. Erdmann, *Das anatolische Karavansaray des 13. Jahrhunderts* (Berlin, 1961), pl. 119 (courtesy Verlag Gebr. Mann).

Exterior view of Saad al-Din Khan caravansaray, K. Erdmann, *Das anatolische Karavansaray des 13. Jahrhunderts* (Berlin, 1961), pl. 184 (courtesy Verlag Gebr. Mann).

View of Seyid Ghazi Tekke from the south showing the use of a formerly Christian basilica (left), alongside the türbe (center) and the mosque (right). *Monumenta Asiae Minoris Antiqua*, vol. V, C. W. M. Cox and A. Cameron, pl. 10 (courtesy The Manchester University Press).

Tahtadji women from Chibuk Khan, E. Petersen and F. von Luschan, *Reisen im südwestlichen Kleinasien*, vol. II, *Reisen in Lykien Milyas und Kibyratis* (Vienna, 1889), pp. 200–201 (Druck und Verlag von Carl Gerold's Sohn).

A Bektashi sheikh with disciple, C. E. Arseven, *L'art turc* (Istanbul, 1939), fig. 448 (Devlet Basimevi).

Mawlawi dervishes participating in a sema', V. Minorsky, *The Chester Beatty Library. A Catalogue of the Turkish Manuscripts and Miniatures* (Dublin, 1958), pl. 42 (courtesy The Chester Beatty Library, Hodges Figgis and Co., Ltd.).

Danishmendid coinage (courtesy Dr. George Miles, Chief Curator, The American
Numismatic Society).

1. Malik Muhammad 1084–1136   4. Muhammad ibn Dhu'l Karnain 1161–1169
2. Dhu'l Nun   1143–1174   5. Muhammad ibn Dhu'l Karnain 1161–1169
3. Dhu'l Karnain   1152–1161   6. Malik Ismail   1164–1173

The former church of St. Amphilochius at Konya as a mosque, *The Annual of the British School at Athens*, XIX (1912–13), 123, fig. 1 (courtesy Macmillan and Co., Ltd., and British School at Athens).

Equestrian statue of Justinian I. *Jahrbuch des deutschen archäologishes Instituts*, XLVI (1931), 334, fig. 12 (courtesy Walter de Gruyter and Co.).

The threshing sledge, *Voyage du Sieur Paul Lucas* (Amsterdam, 1714), p. 182.

If the surviving Christians of nineteenth- and early twentieth-century Anatolia represent the visible physical Byzantine residue, a significant portion of the Muslim population in Anatolia, as the product of ethnic mixture, represents the "invisible" physical residue of this Byzantine past. The mass conversions, intermarriage, gulam-devshirme, and slave systems resulted in the fusion of the majority of the Byzantine population with the Turks and, consequently, made of the Turks a people with origins as mixed as those of the Greeks, Serbs, Armenians, and Bulgars.

Formal Institutions

Any attempt to estimate the Byzantine residue in the administrative, military, and fiscal institutions and practices of the Seljuks, Anatolian beyliks, and Ottomans is fraught with incredible difficulties. There is a paucity of source material, and the Byzantine and Turkish institutions of the period are still incompletely investigated even on the basis of this little material. The problem of institutional origins and influence is complicated by the very fact that the Byzantine and Ottoman Empires were similar in many respects. They were both polyglot, multisectarian, bureaucratic theocracies whose core consisted of Anatolia and the Balkans. Accordingly, the emperors and sultans faced many of the identical political, social, and economic problems and cultural phenomena. These problems, common to both empires, could not help but be reflected in the institutional and administrative apparatus, hence some of these institutions might, theoretically at any rate, have been independently inspired by the prevailing conditions without any question of direct influence or inheritance of institutions. In addition the Balkans, Asia Minor, the Levant, and Egypt had, since the conquests of Alexander, formed a common cultural area that, though it possessed strong local cultural variety, had nevertheless many common characteristics. When the Arabs conquered these areas they incorporated and adapted many of the political, economic, social, and cultural forms they found and which were common to the Balkans and Anatolia. The political and social structure they erected resembled that of the Byzantines in many respects. As the Arab conquest preserved much of Syrian and Egyptian society intact, the Byzantine forms were adopted. Many of the urban institutions of the Muslim cities developed from Byzantine models: the public baths,[66] marketplace and guild organization,[67] urban military and sportive organizations.[68] The Umayyad caliphs adopted or adapted items from the

[66] Von Grunebaum, "Die islamische Stadt," *Saeculum*, VI (1955), 138–139. In general, Vryonis, "Byzantium and Islam, Seventh-Seventeenth Century," *East European Quarterly*, II (1968), 205–240.

[67] Von Grunebaum, "Stadt," pp. 139, 144. G. Marçais, "Considérations sur les villes musulmanes et notamment sur le rôle du Mohtasib," *Recueils de la Société Jean Bodin*, VI₁ (1954), 260–261.

[68] Vryonis, "Byzantine Circus Factions and Islamic Futuwwa Organizations (Neaniai, Fityān, Ahdāth)," *B.Z.*, LVIII (1965), 46–59.

policies and administrative practices of the Byzantine emperors, in particular from the tax system and bureaucracy,[69] the concepts of monumental architecture,[70] and legislation by imperial rescript. Similarly, the Arabs copied the gold and copper coinage of the Byzantines, in the beginning imitating not only the weight standard but even the figures and inscriptions on the coins. The Byzantine standards of weight and volume, too, influenced those of the Arabs. It is of some interest that the Muslims acquired the Byzantine manner of sealing their documents with lead seals.[71]

In the field of religion the practice of endowing economically religious foundations, the wakf, may have been inspired by Christian practice,[72] and the development of Muslim theology was connected with Christian polemic.[73] In such everyday items as cuisine, domestic architecture, and dress, the Arabs absorbed a number of practices, perhaps even the custom of veiling women.[74] Most conspicuous of all were the intellectual borrowings, for Arab science, geography, grammar, medicine, philosophy, and musical theory were indebted to the Byzantines in varying degrees.[75]

As a result of the erection of the caliphate partially on Byzantine soil, the developing Islamic society incorporated many elements that were Byzantine. Thus when the Turks passed into the Muslim lands and were Islamized, they too were influenced by many of these institutions and practices Islam had absorbed from Byzantium. When they conquered the Byzantine Empire they brought many of these institutions (in a transformed state) with them, and they were often similar to the Byzantine institutions they encountered. The fourteenth-century tax official and chronicler Karim al-Din Mahmud of Aksaray illustrates his awareness of this phenomenon in his comment on the fiscal establishment in Seljuk Anatolia. He remarks that the tax books, which in the old days had been

[69] A. Grohmann, *Einführung und Chrestomathie zur arabischen Papyruskunde* (Prague, 1954); "Griechische und lateinische Verwaltungstermini im arabischen Aegypten," *Chronique d'Egypt*, nos. 13–14 (1932), pp. 275–284.

[70] Gibb, "Arab-Byzantine Relations under the Umayyad Caliphate," *D.O.P.*, XII (1958), 223–233.

[71] J. Walker, *A Catalogue of the Arab-Byzantine and Post-Reform Umaiyad Coins* (London, 1956). G. Miles, "A Byzantine Bronze Weight in the Name of Bisr b. Marwan," *Arabica*, IX (1962), 113–118; *A Byzantine Weight Validated by al-Walid* (New York, 1939).

[72] Köprülü, "Vakif müessesesinin hukuki mahiyeti ve tarihi tekamulu," *V.D.*, II (1942), 1–36.

[73] Abel, "Polémique damascènienne," pp. 61–85.

[74] Dozy, *Dictionnaire detaillé des noms des vêtements chez les Arabes* (Amsterdam, 1845), pp. 327 ff., derives feredje from φορεσιά. See also Procopius, *History of the Wars*, II, 8. 35, on the veiling of women in sixth century Antioch. On the continuity of cuisine, Koukoules, Βίος V, 1–205.

[75] F. Rosenthal, *Das Fortleben der Antike im Islam* (Zurich, 1965). Von Grunebaum, "Parallelism, Convergence, and Influence in the Relations of Arab and Byzantine Philosophy, Literature, and Piety," *D.O.P.*, XVIII (1964), 91–111; "Islam and Hellenism," in *Islam. Essays in the Nature and Growth of a Cultural Tradition* (Menasha, 1955), 159–167; "Greek Form Elements in the Arabian Nights," *J.A.O.S.*, LXII (1942), 286–292. M. Meyerhoff, *Von Alexandrien nach Baghdad, Sitz. der Preus. Akad. der Wiss., Phil.-hist. Kl.* (1930).

translated from Greek and Persian into Arabic, were in his own day
retranslated into Persian.[76] The consequence of all this was that the
Turks brought a number of institutions into Anatolia and the Balkans
which were in some way already familiar to the inhabitants.

Finally, there were certain customs and usages of the Byzantine
Christians the Turks adopted outright in Anatolia and in the Balkans. The
route by which the Turks might theoretically have adopted or imitated
Byzantine practices is therefore a threefold one: by direct adoption from
the Christian subject populations; by adoption of older Islamic practices
the Arabs themselves adopted when they conquered Syria and Egypt;
by reason of the fact that the Turks found similar problems in ruling the
Balkans and Anatolia, and therefore their solutions had to be similar to
those of the Byzantines. This last route might have therefore produced
similar institutions.

The Seljuks and Ottomans derived their political and military
establishments primarily from the Islamic world. Such institutions as the
sultanate, vezirate, iqta, gulam, and others, were part of the state
accoutrement the Turks acquired when they entered the Muslim world
in the tenth and eleventh centuries.[77] Yet the Seljuk and Ottoman
apparatus differed in many ways from contemporary Muslim states in
Egypt, Syria, and Persia,[78] because the Seljuks and Ottomans, in bringing
the traditional Muslim institutions with them (and combining therein
their own Turkish traditions), had to apply them to a Byzantine milieu, a
milieu in which the conquerors preserved certain local practices and often
absorbed portions of the local aristocracy and their modus operandi.
Though these Christians were culturally absorbed into Turkish Muslim
society, they left a distinct coloration in the new society as a result of the
absorptive process.[79] The Turkish institutions therefore represent a new
synthesis of these elements, Islamic, Turkish, and Byzantine.

[76] Aksaray-Gençosman, p. 154. This process is clearly reflected in the Rückwanderung
of certain Greek and Latin terms into Persian and Arabic, then into Turkish and finally
back into Greek. Meyer, *Türk. Studien, passim*. A. Maidhoff, "Rückwanderer aus den
islamitischen Sprachen im Neugriechischen (Smyrna und Umgebung)," *Glotta. Zeitschrift
für griechische und lateinische Sprache* X, (1920), 1–21.
[77] Köprülü took an essentially negative view on the question of Byzantine influences:
"Bizans müesseselerinin Osmanlï müesseselerine te'siri hakkïnda bazi mulahazalar,"
Türk hukuk ve iktisat tarihi mecmuasï, I (1931), 165–313 (hereafter cited as Köprülü, "Bizans."
Alcune osservazioni intorno all' influenza delle istituzioni bizantine sulle istituzioni ottomane (Rome,
1953); "Les institutions byzantines ont-elles joué un rôle dans la formation des institutions
ottomanes?" *Resumés des communications presentées au Congrès de Varsovie, 1933* (Warsaw,
1933), I, 297–302. For comments on this view, Taeschner, "Eine neue türkische Publikation zur Wirtschaftsgeschichte," *Orientalistische Literaturzeitung*, XXXVI (1933), 485–
486. Also Arnakes, 'Οθωμανοί pp. 101–107. Babinger, "Byzantinisch-osmanische Grenzstudien," *B.Z.*, XXX (1929-30), 414–415. The work of Uzunçarsïlï, *Osmanlï devleti
teskilatïna medhal* (Istanbul, 1941), is a particularly useful work on the traditional Islamic
elements in Ottoman institutions. My study, "The Byzantine Legacy and Ottoman
Forms," will soon appear in *D.O.P.*, XXIII.
[78] Taeschner, "Publikation," pp. 486–487.
[79] For Greek, Armenian, and Georgian nobles who passed to the side of the Turks:
Matthew of Edessa, pp. 195, 199, 205–206, 209–210; Danishmendname-Melikoff, I,

The Seljuk and Ottoman courts were, theoretically, open to Byzantine influence through four channels. There were occasionally sultans and princes who spent time by the side of Byzantine rulers in Constantinople and Nicaea.[80] Such, by way of example, were Kïlïdj II Arslan, his son Ghiyath al-Din Kaykhusraw, and 'Izz al-Din II Kaykaus, the latter two being half-Greeks, or mixovarvaroi. A second channel through which such influence might have penetrated into Turkish court life was marriage alliance. Numerous were the Seljuk, Danishmendid, emirate, and Ottoman rulers who took Christian wives: Kïlïdj II Arslan, Ghiyath al-Din I Kaykhusraw, 'Ala' al-Din Kaykubad. Ghiyath al-Din II Kaykhusraw had Greek, Georgian, and Turkmen wives. The Turkmen princes of northern Anatolia took Trebizondine princesses as wives, as did the dynasty of Uzun Hasan. The Ramazan and Karaman princes took Greek wives, and the Ottomans in particular satisfied their diplomatic and personal needs with Byzantine and Serbian princesses. Did and could women of the harem exercise influence on court life? They obviously did in terms of its everyday content, but it is harder to answer in regard to form. 'Izz al-Din II, whose mother was the daughter of a Greek priest, held a court that was run by his maternal uncles and their influence and Christian orientation were such that there was a sharp and dangerous split between Muslims and Christians in the dynastic politics of Konya. The Byzantine influence was quite strong at this court. He was not only baptized (Ramazan and Karaman princes were also baptized) but revered the holy icons and had close relations with the Greek hierarchy. When Orhan married the daughter of Cantacuzene, the Byzantine imperial ceremony of *prokypsis* was lavishly performed before the mixed Greek and Turkish party attending the celebrations. She herself refused to convert to Islam and actively aided the Christian community of Bithynia which was undergoing strong proselytizing pressures.

The presence of Christian aristocrats at the court (some of whom converted) certainly constituted natural links between Byzantine practices and Turkish courts. The three Gabras' who served as Seljuk vizirs, the nephew of John II Comnenus who married the daughter of Kïlïdj II

126, 128–129; Brosset-*Géorgie*, I, 331; Bar Hebraeus, I, 130, 265; Michael the Syrian III, 247; Nicetas Choniates, 48–49, 72, 245–246; Cinnamus, 56; Ibn Bibi-Duda pp. 38–41, 117–120, 330–331; Ashïkpashazade-Kreutel, pp. 31, 32, 46–48, 67–69. Ashïkpashazade-Ali, pp. 11–12, 23–24, 43–44.

For the Ottoman period: M. T. Gökbilgin, *XV–XVI asïrlarda Edirne ve Paşa livasï vakïflar-mülkler-mukataalar* (Istanbul, 1952), pp. 89, 93, 106–107, 151–152. R. Anhegger and H. Inalcik, *Kānūnnāme-i sultānī ber mūceb-i örf-i osmānī. II Mehmed ve II Bayezid devirlerine ait yasaknāme ve kānūnnāmeler* (Ankara, 1956), pp. 73–74. Babinger, "Beiträge zur Geschichte des Malqoč-Oglus," pp. 355–369, and "Eine Verfügung des Palaologen Chass Murad-Pasa," pp. 344–354, both reprinted in *Aufzätze und Abhandlungen zur Geschichte Südosteuropas und der Levante*, vol. I (Munich, 1962).

See also chapter iii above for greater detail. A number of titles were thereby incorporated into Turkish: effendi, despina, patrik, kira, archon, knez, voyvod, tekfur, etc.

[80] For greater details and sources on what follows see chapter iii.

Arslan and turned Muslim, the great emir Maurozomes in the thirteenth century (whose relative had married a sultan), the two uncles of 'Izz al-Din, Michael Palaeologus who waxed so powerful in his brief stay at Konya, and others too numerous to mention could have been instrumental in Seljuk contact with Byzantine forms and influences.

Finally there were the gulams or royal slaves, usually of Christian origin, who staffed the court, administration, and select military bodies. The question arises whether these gulams, usually taken at a young age and converted within a rigidly Islamic institution, really had a sufficiently Christian character to exercise any Byzantine influence on the empire's life. Undoubtedly most did not. Yet information from the fifteenth and sixteenth centuries indicates that some of these gulams had strong memories of their Christian past and often behaved in a manner that would be incomprehensible without taking this into account.[81]

The visits of Turkish sultans to the Byzantine court, intermarriage with Christian princesses, Christians or converts in high offices, and the gulam institution brought a very definite Christian atmosphere and element into the most intimate aspects of court life, but all this tells us nothing specific. Here and there one detects examples of a definite Turkish taste for the Byzantine court style. The sultan 'Izz al-Din II wore as symbols of the sultanic authority the ἐρυθροβαφὲς πέδιλον, the scarlet boot.[82] Turkish emirs of the realm had a special preference for Byzantine ceremonial robes in the eleventh and twelfth centuries, and the emir of Ankara, in a treaty with Alexius III Angelus, demanded as part of the terms forty silk garments of the type manufactured in Theban workshops for the emperor himself.[83] The gold and silk tissue of the sultan 'Ala' al-Din I Kaykubad in the museum of Lyon is according to some art historians done in a modified Byzantine style. A rare Seljuk coin of the twelfth century depicts the sultan in Byzantine imperial garb. Linguistically the Turkish terms *avlu* and *kiler* used to designate the sultan's court and pantries are of Byzantine origin.[84]

The evidence for Turkish military life, though uneven, is more considerable. Byzantine military practices had a certain influence on Turkish military life both in Anatolia and the Balkans. This influence arose from

---

[81] Vryonis, "Byzantine Legacy," *D.O.P.*, XXIII. Bartholomaeus Georgieuiz-Goughe, chapter entitled "Of the Unmerciful Tribute Exacted at the Christian Handes." Vacalopoulos, Ἱστορία, I₁, 163–164. Uzunçarşïlï, *Osmanlï devleti teşkilatïndan kapukulu ocaklarï* (Ankara, 1943), I, 19. L. Hadrovics, *Le peuple serbe et son église sous la domination turque* (Paris, 1947), pp. 48–50.

[82] Pachymeres, I, 131–132.

[83] Nicetas Choniates, 608–609. Attaliates, 277.

[84] Von Falke, *Kunstgeschichte der Seidenweberei*, I, Fig. 162. Inalcik, "Harir," EI₂, reproduces the silk of Lyon. *Victoria and Albert Museum, Brief Guide to Turkish woven Fabrics* (London, 1950), pp. 1–3. Effendi and despina appear as early as the thirteenth and fourteenth centuries, Eflaki-Huart, II, 430. Tietze, "Anat. Türkisch.," p. 224. Meyer, *Türk. Studien*, pp. 37, 44. Ibn Battuta-Gibb, II, 463. Dilger, *Untersuchungen zur Geschichte des osmanischen Hofzeremoniells im 15. und 16. Jahrhundert* (Munich, 1967), concentrates on those aspects of Ottoman court ceremony which have a specifically Islamic background.

the large number of renegades and Christians who at different times served in Turkish armies, and especially from the incorporation of sizable Christian contingents into the Turkish military apparatus. The Seljuk armies were, from early times in their Anatolian experience, of a highly diverse ethnic character. They included Turks, Arabs, Persians, Georgians, Armenians, Russians, Franks, and Greeks.[85] In short they were similar to the multinational armies of the caliphate and Byzantium. Armenian military contingents, led by Armenian patricians, served the Seljuks in the late eleventh and the early twelfth century in eastern Anatolia.[86] Nicephorus Gregoras relates that the sultans recruited military corps of Greek Christians from among the Greeks inhabiting the Seljuk domains and that these served under their own generals with their own uniforms. It was over these troops that Michael Palaeologus was appointed kondistabl when he fled to Konya.[87] The survival of Christian military groups and their incorporation into the Ottoman war machine are phenomena that have received considerable attention and have been correctly stressed as elements that helped make possible the rapid military conquests of the Ottomans who, without auxiliary manpower, would not have been sufficiently numerous to take and hold their vast empire. The body of Ottoman soldiers known as *martolos* was very probably of Byzantine provenance as is indicated not only by the word itself but by the fact that the first-mentioned martolos were Christians and Christians figured prominently in the body of martolos thereafter.[88] Early in the Bithynian conquests of Osman, Byzantine feudal lords joined the Ottoman armies, the most famous of them, Mikail Beğ, forming one of the longest-lived Muslim aristocratic dynasties.[89]

The incorporation of large numbers of Christian soldiery (*pronoiarioi*) raises the complicated question of the relationship between the Ottoman and Byzantine military fiefs, the *timar* and *pronoia*. In the fourteenth and fifteenth centuries the Turks established the timar as a basic military, fiscal, and administrative institution. In its essentials the Ottoman timar

[85] Ibn Bibi-Duda, pp. 97, 219–220, 223, 227–230, 333–334.

[86] Matthew of Edessa, pp. 199, 205–206, 209–210. They were still active in the Ottoman struggle against Timur in the fourteenth century. Timur recruited Cappadocian Armenans, Ducas, p. 62.

[87] Nicephorus Gregoras, I, 58. These troops were not only to wear Greek uniforms but were also to be armed in the Greek manner.

[88] Anhegger, "Martoloslar hakkïnda," *T.M.*, VII–VIII (1940–42), 282–320. M. Vasič, "Die Martolozen im osmanischen Reich," *Zeitschrift für Balkanologie*, II (1964), 172–189. See the treatments for the somewhat later period: Inalcik, "Stefan Duşan'dan osmanlï imperatorluğuna. XV asirda Rumeli'de hïristiyan sipahlier ve menşeleri," in *Fatih devri üzerinde tetkikler ve vesikalar* (Ankara, 1954), I, 137–209 (hereafter cited as Inalcik, "Stefan Duşan'dan); "Timariotes chrétiens en Albanie au XVᵉ siècle," *Mitteilungen des* österreichischen Staatsarchivs, IV (1952), 118–138; *Hicri 835 tarihli suret-i defter-i sancak-i Arvanid* (Ankara, 1954). Cvetkova, "Novye dannye o khirstianakhspakhiia na balkanskom poluostrove v period turetskova gospodstvo," *V.V.*, XIII (1958), 184–197.

[89] Inalcik, "Duşan'dan," pp. 141–142. Ashïkpashazade-Kreutel, pp. 31–37, 46, 48 ff., 52 ff. Asïkpashazade-Ali, pp. 11 ff., 24 ff.

was identical with the Byzantine pronoia. It was a revenue-producing grant, usually but not exclusively of land, the recipient of which, the *spahi*, was entitled to hold it in usufruct in return for military service. The basic difference between timar and pronoia was merely a function of the reverse fortunes of centralized authority in the Byzantine and Ottoman states. The sultan exercised strict control over these fiefs, whereas in Byzantium decentralization of imperial authority was reflected in the increasing passage of pronoia from the category of usufruct to that of dominium. It is of further interest that the Ottomans incorporated a number of the old Greek and Serbian pronoiarioi as Christian spahis, converting their pronoias into timars.[90] The Byzantine magnate-soldiers of Bithynia who joined the Ottomans were frequently allowed to retain their lands and castles, and the same seems to have occurred in certain other Anatolian regions (Paipert, Kutahya, Trebizond).[91] A number of tax practices associated with the old pronoia system were apparently incorporated when the Ottomans absorbed the Christian spahis into the timar establishment.[92]

It is very difficult to say whether all these facts are anything more than coincidence and that the timar somehow derives from the Byzantine pronoia. A brief glance at the Islamic nomenclature for such military grants, however, is not without importance. "Timar," of Persian origin, and "pronoia" have very similar meanings and underwent parallel semantological developments. They signify "care, providence, and finally a revenue granted by the ruler to the military and administrative officials for services rendered to the state." It seems that the Ottomans were the first of the Islamic peoples to employ the term with this last meaning. The Persians had previously used the Arabic term *iqta*, as did the Seljuks of Anatolia. With the appearance of the Mongols and rise of the Turkmen tribal confederations in eastern Anatolia, new terms, *tiyul* and *siyurgal*, appeared, but not timar.[93] Now this fact is of some interest if one keeps in mind the following. The Seljuks encountered Byzantine society at one stage of its development in the eleventh century, whereas the Ottomans of the fourteenth and fifteenth centuries encountered the same society at a later stage of development. The pronoia system was still in its infancy in the eleventh century, and the Seljuks did not encounter it within their Anatolian domains. The Ottomans expanded into Bithynia in the early fourteenth century, and then into the Balkans, by which time the pronoia system had spread over the entire Byzantine domains and over those of the

[90] Inalcik, "Dusan'dan," *passim*. Ostrogorsky, *Pour la féodalité byzantine* (Brussels, 1954,) p. 257.

[91] Inalcik, "Dusan'dan," *passim*.

[92] B. Cvetkova, "Influence exercée par certaines institutions de Byzance et des pays balkaniques du Moyen Age sur le systeme féodal ottoman," *Byzantino-Bulgarica*, I (1962), 237–257 (hereafter cited as Cvetkova, "Influence").

[93] W. Hinz, *Irans Aufstieg zum Nationalstaat im fünfzehnten Jahrhundert* (Berlin-Leipzig, 1936), p. 107.

South Slavs. This coincidence between the geographical diffusion of the pronoia institution and of the term "timar" is indeed striking and would reinforce the evidence for a hypothesis of the timar's Byzantine origin.[94]

Inasmuch as the various Turkish states had to deal with other Greek states and with a substantial Greek element within their own domains, they employed Greek scribes both in the provinces and the capital. Under the Seljuks these scribes constituted the *notaran-i divan-i saltanat* and a number of their documents have survived. These Christian secretaries continued in the palace service of the Ottoman sultans, and in the provinces played a prominent role in dressing the cadastral surveys for the fisc.[95]

The twelfth-century Danishmendid princes adopted the Byzantine manner of sealing official documents with lead seals. A seal of Dhu'l Karnain, Danishmendid prince of Melitene (1152–1161), which has survived, is a faithful imitation of Byzantine sigillographic patterns and traditions. On the obverse is the nimbate bust of St. Basil, rendered in the Byzantine fashion and with the Greek inscription [OA (γιος) B] A [CI]ΛΙΟΣ and on the reverse the Arab inscription

الواثق بالر

حيم ذو القرنين

The saints were a common device on the Byzantine seals of eastern Anatolia, and Basil was particularly appropriate as he was the patron of Caesareia, over which the Danishmendids ruled.[96]

---

[94] Deny, "Timar," EI₁, derived the timar from the Byzantine pronoia, as does Arnakis, 'Οθωμανοί pp. 103–104. Gordlevski, *Izbrannye Soch.*, pp. 101–103, and Köprülü," Bizans," pp. 219–240, in deriving the Ottoman timar from the Seljuk iqta, rely on the fifteenth-century Turkish text of Yazĭdjĭoğlu Ali rather than on the thirteenth-century Persian text of Ibn Bibi. Hence their conclusion is far from satisfactory, for where Ibn Bibi uses iqta, Yazĭdjĭoğlu has anachronistically used the term "timar" which was current in the fifteenth century. In addition, the Persian texts of Chahar Maqala, Nerchaky, and Ibn Bibi to which Köprülü referred in the note on p. 239 do not use "timar" as a terminus technicus to designate an iqta. My colleague Prof. Amin Banani, who very kindly examined the Persian texts, informs me that contrary to Köprülü's assertion, the word "timar" in these texts has the generic meaning of "surveillance, care." Uzunçarsĭlĭ, *Osmanlĭ devleti teşkilatĭna medhal* (Istanbul, 1941), pp. 123–124, also concludes, on the basis of a study of the texts, that the Seljuks of Rum used the term iqta, but not the term "timar," to designate a fief. V. P. Mutafčieva, "Sur le caractère du timar ottoman," *Acta Orientalia*, IX (1959), 55–61. Cvetkova, "Influence," p. 243. For the iqta, A. K. Lambton, "The Evolution of the Iqta' in Medieval Iran," *Iran*, V (1967), 41–50. Cahen, "L'évolution de l'iqta du IXe au XIIe siècle," *Annales*, VIII (1953), 25–52.

[95] See chapter ii for the details and bibliography. The thirteenth-century tetrevangelion in the Gennadius Library, MS Gr. 1.5, is signed by a protonotarius of Caesareia. Inalcik, "Ottoman Methods of Conquest," *S.I.*, II (1954), 111. The presence of Christian scribes recalls the activity of Greek, Coptic, and Persian scribes in the Umayyad administration.

[96] P. Casanova, "Numismatique des Danichmendites," *Revue Numismatique*, XIV (1896), 309–310. A photograph of the seal is to be seen in plate iii, 11, opposite p. 264. The Ottoman term sidjil, collection of judgments passed in court, is derived via Arabic from the Byzantine σιγίλλιον which in turn comes from the Latin sigillum, Meyer,

There is considerable evidence that the Byzantine fiscal traditions had considerable influence on the Turkish tax system both under the Seljuks and the Ottomans. The fiscal policies of the Seljuk and Ottoman sultans in newly conquered lands were largely motivated by the desire to restore order to these lands so the conquerors could enjoy their economic exploitation. Inasmuch as both Anatolia and the Balkans had possessed socioeconomic structures that were convenient for such exploitation, the conservative sultans adjusted these to their own needs. The tax forms that evolved in Anatolia, as also in the Balkans, were extremely varied and complex, including elements from the Islamic, Mongol, Byzantine, Armenian, and Slav tax systems. The Seljuks and Ottomans often preserved and continued tax practices they found, and consequently the early Ottoman Empire had no rigidly uniform tax structure. This conservative fiscal policy emerges from an incident Nicetas Choniates relates of the late twelfth century. At that time the sultan raided the two Greek comopoleis of Tantalus and Caria located on tributaries of the Maeander, kidnapped their population (about 5,000) and resettled them in the depopulated regions of Philomelium. He had them carefully guarded en route so that none might escape; he had a detailed register drawn up recording their number, possessions, livestock, and then gave them land and seed to plant. He bestowed upon these Greeks a five-year tax immunity with the provision that afterward they should pay exactly those taxes they had previously been accustomed to pay to the Byzantine emperors in their Byzantine habitat.[97]

The Ottoman tax system for western Anatolia and parts of the Balkans was very much influenced by the Byzantine model, and recent studies of the early Ottoman *tahrir defters* demonstrate the generally conservative Ottoman stance vis-à-vis the older tax structure and practices (*adet-i kadimiyye*), revealing a Turkish tax apparatus permeated with taxes of non-Turkish origin. When, after the conquest of a given area, an economic survey or *tahrir* was drawn up, the Turkish emin who supervised this important survey had the scribes (frequently Christians or renegades) note local tax practices and differences in tax rates. Then, after approval and adjustment by the sultan, these were included on the front page of the defter as the *kannunname* or fiscal law of the province.[98] The Ottoman absorption of Christian spahis and askers, as well as of the peasant

---

Turk. Studien, p. 70. The Turkish word "tomar," roll or roll of paper, comes ultimately from the Byzantine τομάριον with the sense of τόμος (χάρτου), skin covering, parchment, Meyer, Turk. Studien, p. 39.

[97] Nicetas Choniates, 655–657. When Muhammad II first appeared before the important Serbian city of Novobrdo he offered terms to the inhabitants which included the following provision, " ἐφ' οἶσπερ καὶ πρότερον, καὶ φόρους ἀποφέρειν οὓς καὶ τῷ σφῶν βασιλεῖ, τοῖς ἄλλοις ἅπασιν εἰρηνεύοντες." Critobuli Imbriotae de rebus per annos 1451–1467 a Mechemete II gestis, ed. B. Grecu (Bucharest, 1963), 185 (hereafter cited as Critobulus-Grecu).

[98] Inalcik, "Conquest," pp. 110–111.

communities subject to their exploitation, resulted in the simultaneous absorption of many of their tax practices.[99]

Halil Inalcik, in a daring study, has suggested that the basic agrarian tax structure of the Ottomans in western Anatolia and much of the Balkans was directly modeled on that of Byzantium. He sees this in the rates of taxation, in the manner the tax was assessed, in the categories of taxation, and finally in the *termini technici* themselves. The basic land tax in these regions centered about the *chift* (yoke). Chift was variously defined as the yoke of oxen that pulled the plow, a farm of the size that could be serviced by a yoke of oxen, or a plot of land that could be sown by four mud of seed. A *nim-chift* was a half-yoke or equivalent of land, a *chiftlü bennak* was less than half, and a *müjerred* included widows and agricultural workers. The taxes paid by these different categories were (in akches) 22, 11, 6 (or 9), 3 (or 6). The Byzantine tax units were quite similar. There was the ζευγάριον or *iugum* (yoke), usually defined as a yoke of oxen, or a piece of land that could be cultivated by a yoke. Below it was the βοϊδάτον, (one ox or half a ζευγάριον), and the ἀκτήμων or landless peasant. The *zeugaratos* paid one nomisma tax, the *boidatos* paid one half a nomisma, and the *aktemon* paid between one half and one sixth of a nomisma. In 1350 the Ottoman tax on a chift was 22 akches or approximately the equivalent of a nomisma or hyperperon.[100] The feudal rent included payments in kind and corvees that are frequently identical with their Byzantine equivalents and less frequently bear non-Turkish names. Particularly strong was the Byzantine influence in the domain of the Ottoman taxes known under the collective title of *avariz-i divaniye ve tekalif-i örfiye*, taxes the subjects paid to the state rather than to the feudal spahis.[101] A fleeting glance at the termini technici, which passed into Ottoman fiscal parlance from the various subject peoples, reinforces these other sources: *Angarya, irgadiyya, sinir, parik* (Greek); *Bennak, trngir* (Armenian); *Bashtina, gornina, pogaca* (Slavic).[102] The tax on maritime commerce, which the sultans of the

---

[99] Cahen, "Le régime de la terre et l'occupation turque en Anatolie," *Cahiers d'histoire mondiale*, II (1955), 95. Cvetkova, "Influence," *passim*. Hinz, "Das Steuerwesen Ostanatoliens," *Z.D.M.G.*, C (1950), 177–201.

[100] Inalcik, "The Problem of the Relationship between Byzantine and Ottoman Taxation," *Akten des XI. Internationalen Byzantinistenkongresses. München 1958* (Munich, 1960), pp. 237–242.

[101] Cvetkova, "Influence," pp. 243–257; *Izvunredni danutsi i durzavni povinnosti v bulgarskite zemi pod turska vlast* (Sofia, 1958); "Contribution à l'étude des impôts extraordinaires (avariz-i divaniye ve tekalif-i örfiye) en Bulgarie sous la domination turque. L'impôt nuzul," *Rocznik Orientalistyczny*, XXIII (1959), 57–65.

[102] Barthold and Hinz, "Die persische Inschrift an der Mauer der Manučehr-Moschee zu Ani," *Z.D.M.G.*, CI (1951), 268. Hinz, "Das Steuerwesen Ostanatoliens im 15. und 16. Jahrhundert," *Z.D.M.G.*, C (1950), 199–201, on irgadiyya in eastern Anatolia. Meyer, *Türk. Studien*, pp. 9, 39. Kahane and Tietze, *Lingua Franca*, p. 476. Turan, *Türkiye Selçuklulari hakkinda resmi vesikalar, metin, tercüme ve araştirmalari* (Ankara, 1958). Barkan, *XV ve XVI inci asirlarda osmanli imparatorluğunda zirai ekonominin hukuki ve mali esaslari* (Istanbul, 1945), I, 348. Inalcik, "Stefan Dušan'dan," pp. 171–177; "Osmanlilar'dan raiyyet rüsümü," *Belleten*, XXIII (1959), 588, 604. Cvetkova, "Influence," pp. 245, 254·

thirteenth and fifteenth centuries levied, was called, as in Byzantine times, "*commercium.*"[103]

An irrefutable, physical testimonial to the presence of influence from Byzantine political and economic institutions appears in the coinage of the Danishmendids, Mengüchekids, Saltukids, Ortokids, Seljuks, and Ottomans. The numismatic types and systems the mints of these various states employed often display a dual character, Byzantine and Muslim. The Byzantine influence on a portion of this Anatolian coinage is the last sign of vitality in a monetary system that would decline almost uninterruptedly until the fall of Constantinople. The numismatic borrowings from the Byzantine system had been frequent and significant from the time that the Germanic princes had imitated the solidus in the early medieval West. The gold and copper Islamic monetary arrangement had been modeled closely on the Byzantine solidus and folis. The Hungarians, South Slavs, and the Normans of Sicily and Antioch had also imitated the Byzantines in this respect.[104]

The Danishmendid princes issued series of coins that symbolized in a remarkable fashion the fusion of two different traditions. In a manner recalling the earliest hybrid Muslim coinage of the seventh century, the Danishmendids imitated the Byzantine bronze money of the tenth through twelfth centuries. The first type attributed to Malik Ghazi (1084–1136?) was a very obvious imitation of the so-called Anonymous bronze the Byzantine mints struck in such profuse quantity at the end of the tenth and in the eleventh century. The Turkish dynast issued similar bronzes with the frontal, cruciform-nimbate bust of Christ. The reverse, however, instead of reproducing the pious Christian formula, presented the following Greek inscription.

> ΟΜΕΓΑϽ
> ΑΜΝΡΑ which is, Ο ΜΕΓΑϹ ΑΜΗΡΑϹ ΑΜΗΡ ΓΑΖΗ
> ΑΜΡΓ
> -Ζ-

The second bronze type attributed to this prince was again exclusively inscribed in Greek.

> Ο ΜΜΕΛΗΚΙϹ ΠΑϹΗS ΡѠΜΑΝΙΑϹ (Ο ΜΕΓΑϹ ΜΕΛΗΚΙϹ ΠΑϹΗϹ
> ΡѠΜΑΝΙΑϹ)
> ΚΑΙΑΝΑΤΟΛΗϹ ΜΑΧΑΜΑΤΗϹ (ΚΑΙ ΑΝΑΤΟΛΗϹ ΜΑΧΑΜΑΤΗϹ)

This type has no figure of Christ, but often has a cross at the beginning of

---

[103] Lampros, " Ἡ ἑλληνικὴ ὡς ἐπίσημος γλῶσσα τῶν Σουλτάνων," *N.E.*, V (1908), 51. Brocquière-Schefer, p. 104.

[104] A. Engel, *Recherches sur la numismatique et la sigillographie des Normands de Sicile et d'Italie* (Paris, 1882). G. Schlumberger, *Numismatique de l'Orient latin* (Paris, 1878).

the inscription.[105] Dhu'l Nun (1143–74) introduced a truly bilingual coinage for his dominions the obverse of which bore the circular Greek inscription OMEMPAC ΔANOUNHC and in the center in Arabic عماد الدين. The reverse was likewise bilingual. OVIC TỐ MEΛHK MAXAMATH.[106]

بن الملك

محمد

Dhu'l Karnain (1152–61) not only maintained the bilingual inscriptions but also added a portrait that may have been copied from coins of ancient Parthia or Characene which were still circulating. The bearded portrait on the obverse carried the circular Greek inscription INΔIKTIⲰNOC ΔEYTEPIC (A.D. 1154) whereas the reverse was bilingual. O MEΓAC AMHPAC ΔOVΛXAPNAIN

الواثق

ذو القرنين بن

107عين الدولة

Other coins with purely Arabic inscriptions nevertheless display Byzantine religious and numismatic iconographic influence. The coinage of Malik Ismail (1164–73?) reproduced from Byzantine models depicts Christ seated on the throne. Muhammad (1161–69) employed the figure of Christ with his hand on the head of the ruler (the latter a Byzantine imperial type), and also the equestrian figure of St. George slaying the dragon.[108]

The Turkish dynasties of the Ortokids, Zangids, and Saltukids of eastern Anatolia and northern Syria also imitated the regal and religious motifs on Byzantine coins. The Seljuk coinage of the twelfth century included certain Byzantine types, though these seem to disappear from the coinage of the thirteenth century.[109] Finally the Ottoman silver coin,

---

[105] Casanova, "Numismatique," pp. 211–221, pl. iii, 1–4. He attributes examples of the second type to Malik Muhammad (1134–42) on the basis of an Arab countermark that he read as نب, a name supposedly adopted by Malik Muhammad to distinguish him from his father. For comparisons of type one with the Byzantine anonymous bronze, consult, A. Bellinger, *The Anonymous Byzantine Bronze Coinage* (New York, 1928).

[106] Casanova, "Numismatique," pp. 219–224, pl. iii, 6.

[107] *Ibid.*, pp. 306–309, pl. iii, 10.

[108] *Ibid.*, pp. 229–230, 310, pl. iv, 4, 6, 1, 2, 3; XII (1894), 311–314. The bust on the coinage of Yagï Basan (1142–64) with the diadem is very reminiscent of the diademed profiles of the tremissus and semissus of earlier Byzantine coinage.

[109] I examined a number of these Ortokid, Zangid, Saltukid, and Seljuk pieces in the collection of the American Numismatic Society through the courtesy of Dr. George Miles. Of the Seljuk pieces, one of the reign of Kaykhusraw I (1192(?)–96, 1204–11) depicts a bust of a ruler with Byzantine cross and crown, whereas the reverse bears an Arabic inscription. A second piece, also of copper, displays a standing ruler, again attired in Byzantine fashion and holding a tall cross in his left hand. On the extreme right is another figure holding the cross. A third example portrays a Byzantine type on the obverse with an Arabic inscription on the reverse. This piece, however, might be a Turkish restrike of an eleventh-century Byzantine coin already in circulation in Anatolia when the Turks came. For a Mengüchekid coin of the Byzantine type, Casanova, "Numismatique," XIV (1896), 312, pl. iv, 10, 11. In general see I. Ghalib Edhem, *Catalogue des monnaies*

the akche, apparently bears some relation to the Byzantine silver aspron, in regard to both weight and nomenclature.[110]

Economic Life

The economic life of the Seljuks and Ottomans, except for the nomadic sector, was very heavily indebted to the economic forces and forms of the Christian populations. The influence of the Christians is everywhere obvious in agriculture, crafts, commerce, and maritime life. The importance of these Christians in the agricultural domain arises from the very obvious fact that the bulk of the Turks who came to Anatolia in the early years were nomads and as such they practiced a marginal agriculture or in some cases no agriculture whatever. The basic farming stock of Seljuk Anatolia up to the mid-thirteenth century consisted of Greek, Armenian, and Syrian peasants.[111] After the thirteenth century, the majority of these farmers converted to Islam and these converts, with the sedentarized nomads, came to constitute the Turkish farming population of most of Anatolia. The policies of colonization which the sultans pursued in the twelfth century clearly indicate the almost exclusive predominance of Christians in the category of peasant farmers. Without going into all the details of this colonization, one sees the various Seljuk and Danishmendid rulers kidnapping large masses of Christian farmers not only from the Byzantine and Armenian held domains, but even from one another's kingdoms. There were numerous military campaigns between the Seljuks and Danishmendids in which the one attempted to coerce the other to relinquish these kidnapped Christian farming populations. We have already examined one specific instance in which the sultan took away 5,000 Greek farmers and brought them to Philomelium. Frequently,

---

turcomanes, Beni Ortok, Beni Zengui, Frou' Atabeqyeh et Meliks ayoubites de Maiyafarikin (Constantinople, 1894), pp. 7, 30, 31, pl. i, 6; pl. ii, 32. The former depicts Christ seated on a throne, the latter depicts the Virgin standing and blessing the emperor with her right hand. A. Tevhid, *Meskukat-i kadime islamiye katalogu*, vol. IV (Istanbul, 1321), pl. ii, 92; pl. iii, 120; pl. vii, 90. The first shows the emperor standing and holding a double cross in the left hand, while to the right is a figure also holding a cross. The latter two coins portray imperial busts.

[110] The question of the origin of the akche standard is, however, not entirely clear. On the similarity, Hinz, "Hyperper und Asper. Zur vorosmanischen Währungskunde," *Der Islam*, XXXIX (1964), 79–89. It is quite possible that akche is thus a direct translation of the Greek ἄσπρον, Arnakis, 'Οθωμανοί, p. 107. The Ottomans first struck imitations of Venetian gold ducats and then struck their first Islamic gold on the same weight standard, Babinger, *Reliquienschacher am Osmanenhof im XV. Jahrhundert. Zugleich ein Beitrag zur Geschichte der osmanischen Goldprägung unter Mehmed II. dem Eroberer. Bay. Akad. der hiss., Phil.-hist. Kl. Sitz. Jahr., 1964, Heft 2* (Munich, 1956). Other numismatic terms that passed into Turkish from Greek are ὀβολός and φλουρί from the Italian fiorina, Meyer, *Türk. Studien*, p. 63. Neshri-Köymen, I, 132. The dynasts of the emirates in western Anatolia also imitated Italian coinage, J. Karabacek, "Gigliato des jonischen Turkomanenfürsten Omar-beg," *Numismatische Zeitschrift*, II (1870), 525–538; "Gigliato des karischen Turkomanenfürsten Urchan-bej," *Numismatische Zeitschrift*, IX (1877), 200–215.

[111] See chapter iii for what follows.

however, the numbers involved were much larger. The importance of the more highly developed Byzantine agriculture is obvious in the occasional reliance of the thirteenth-century Seljuks upon grain imports from the kingdom of Nicaea.[112]

As the tribesmen settled down on the land, or even established a symbiotic relationship with the agrarian populations, and as the Muslim urban elements took up estates and farming (as a result of iqta grants or otherwise), they came into contact with a milieu whose agricultural forms were Byzantine. Beside the few specific references to this Greek farming population in contemporary accounts and the general historical assumptions, the Greek influence becomes readily apparent in the significant substratum of Greek loan words in the spoken Anatolian of modern Turkey. In a series of remarkable philological studies, Andreas Tietze has uncovered a very important Greek lexicographical stratum in the Turkish *kaba dil* of Anatolia which deals with agricultural and rural life.[113] This philological evidence indicating a strong Byzantine influence on Turkish rural life, and which consequently corrects the earlier assumption of the philologist Gustave Meyer that Byzantine influence on the Turks was restricted to urban and commercial life, reinforces the evidence of the historical texts. Tietze includes over 200 such loan words (without exhausting the subject) in the following categories: house, household furniture and items, food, bread, eating utensils, containers, farm tools, the wagon and its parts, earth and field, plants and parts of the plant, irrigation, birds, bees, and animals.[114] One may, therefore, conclude

---

[112] Nicephorus Gregoras, I, 42–43.

[113] Tietze, "Anat. Türkisch.," *passim*. For the Byzantine usage of some of these, Koukoules, Βίος, V, 256, 264. Also the texts in S. Eustratiadou, " Ἡ ἐν Φιλαδελφείᾳ μονὴ τῆς Ὑπεραγίας Θεοτόκου τῆς Κοτεινῆς," Ἑλληνικά, III (1930), 317–339.

[114] Tietze, "Anat. Türkisch.," *passim*. Of these, forty-nine have to do with plants, forty-eight with containers and tools. Some of this lexicographical material is detailed and highly specialized as in the words having to do with the farmer's wagon: akson, apsĭt, avsĭt, zĭvgar, kĭravat, iremas; or with agriculture: valta, vol, gangel, engebe, longoz, melank, evlek, endeme, temen, küpren, güpür, prasit, ṣervele, koraf, horyat, anavalĭ, bocurgat, anadot, dikel, dikran, düǧen, girifteri, korepi, mekel, iskelit. The düǧen, δουκάνη, τυκάνη, is particularly characteristic. It was the primary threshing tool in the Balkans and Asia Minor. Lucas, 1714, I, 181–182. "Leur manière de battre le bled est aussi toute differente de la nôtre. Ils prennent deux grosses planches épaisses de quatre doigts, garnies de pierres à fusil tranchantes. Ils les font passer par dessus le bled en gerbes, ce qui separe en un moment les épics d'avec la paille. Ce sont ordinairement des boeufs qui tirent ces sortes de machines: & l'on voit le plus souvent dessus des hommes & des enfans pour les rendre plus pesantes." The same instrument, along with the plow is described by other observers. Dernschwam-Babinger, pp. 27, 182–183, 184, 198, 253, who refers to the düǧen as ikyna (τυκάνη). Planhol. *Nomadisme*, pl. xxiii. The author witnessed the threshing at Sinassus in 1959 in which the Turkish farmers utilized this very same instrument. On the term düǧen and the instrument in modern Turkey, H. Z. Koṣay, "Turkiye halkının maddî kültürüne dair araştırmalar," *Türk etnografya dergisi*, I (1956), 25–26, and pls. iv–v. Eustathius, Koukoules, Εὐσταθίου τὰ λαογραφικά (Athens, 1950), I, 260–261, refers to the τυκάνη as an agricultural instrument that was used both in his own day and in antiquity. *Eustathii archiepiscopi thessalonicensis commentarii ad Homeri Iliadem* (Leipzig, 1829), III, 198, " καὶ ἡ παρὰ τοῖς παλαιοῖς καὶ εἰσέτι δὲ νῦν τυκάνη, ἥ φασιν ἀλοῶσιν."

The τυκάνη was also known as τρίβολος and as tribulum in the ancient Greek and

that Byzantine agrarian practices and techniques determined Turkish agricultural life in Anatolia.

In many areas the Byzantine urban population lived on as Christians or as converts to Islam and so had a considerable effect on the economic life of the Seljuk and Ottoman towns. The incidental appearance of Christian craftsmen and laborers in the sources coincides with the survival of a Greek lexicographical stratum in the Turkish language which has to do with this economic activity. <u>Indicative of this is that Greek terms denoting weights, measures, and dates have survived in Turkish.</u>[115] Both the texts and the loan words strongly affirm the importance of the Greeks in the making of textiles. The importance of Anatolian textiles in Roman and Byzantine times was considerable. The Greek weavers, spinners, and tailors of Bithynia, Denizli, Konya, Kayseri, Sivas, and other areas, in the thirteenth and fourteenth centuries and even later were famous for their silks, carpets, cottons, and other fine fabrics.[116] Accordingly, the Turks often borrowed Greek words for the tools, instruments, materials, and finished products.[117] The same types of borrowings are to be seen for the crafts and arts of the caulkers,[118] jewelers, potters,[119]

Roman authors. The edict of Diocletian uses the term τρίβολος ξύλινος, T. Mommsen and H. Blumner, *Der Maximaltarif des Diocletian* (Berlin, 1958), pp. 33, 141. The *Palatine Anthology*, VI, 104, speaks more specifically, . . . καὶ τριβόλους ὀξεῖς ἀχυρότριβας . . . Varro, *De lingua latina*, V, 21, "Hinc in messi tritura, quod tum frumentum teritur, et tribulum, qui teritur." The Latin dictionary defines tribulum in the following manner: "A threshing sledge, consisting of a wooden platform studded underneath with sharp pieces of flint or with iron teeth." On the tribolum in antiquity, K. D. White, *Agricultural Implements of the Roman World* (Cambridge, 1967), pp. 152–156, 191. My colleague Prof. Gregory Sifakis informs me that in Crete this threshing sledge is called βολόσυρος.

[115] οὐγγία-önge, ounce; πιθαμή-pitemi, measurement of either 25 cm or 50 cm; κύλινδρος-kelender, about two okes; λίτρα-litra, pound; χοινίκι-sinik, 1/8 of a kile of grain; ὀβολός-obolos, weight of three carats. Önge seems to have attained very widespread usage throughout Anatolia, Tietze, "Anat. Türkisch.," p. 234. Designations of season and time include april, yanar (January), ünüs (June), gireği (Sunday), kalendeas (first of month). In what follows the lexicographical material is taken primarily from the works of Tietze and Meyer, and secondarily from the collections of Mpogas and Papadopoulos.

[116] For the medieval references to this textile industry, see nn. 570–573 in chapter iii.

[117] Hans Dernschwam-Babinger, p. 186, observed that Greeks were the principal workers in the making of the famous Angora wool cloth, camlet. "Die zamlot, wie obstat, seindt von obstandeten gaisheren gespunnen. Haben nur krichn (Greeks) gesehen, die sy wyrkhen, waschen, syeden und wasser drikehn under ainer pres." Greek words for the tools, materials, and finished products passed into Turkish, Tietze, "Anat. Türkisch.," *passim*. These include, arahti, andi, istar, köleter, gugula, roka, üsküle, tulup, üskül, penevrenk, menevrek, erpeden, dimi, kavadi, kepe, haba, kukula, keküle, bolka, savan, fermene, alefi, alafa, alça, tilpitiri, galik, podime, takunya.

[118] For the crafts in Byzantium, Koukoules, Βίος III₁, *passim*. Turkish loan words include kalafat, kofter.

[119] Ashïkpashazade-Ali, pp. 11–12. Ashïkpashazade-Kreutel, p. 32, the Christians of Biledjik specialized in the manufacture of cups that they sold at the weekly fairs of Eskishehir. There is a reference to a lively commerce in pottery in this area already in Byzantine times, Nicholas Mesarites-Heisenberg, II, 44. See also Otto-Dorn, *Das islamisch Iznik* (Berlin, 1941); *Turkische Keramik* (Ankara, 1961); Erdmann, "Neue Arbeiten zur Turkischen Keramik," *Ars Orientalia*, V (1963), 191–219. The Christians continued to participate in the manufacture of the famous Ottoman tiles, Evliya Chelebi, *Seyahatnamesi*, IX, 19, "Çinici kefereler mahallesi . . ." C. Nomikos, Χριστιανικὰ κεραρουργήματα

metalworkers, miners,[120] painters,[121] musicians,[122] and doctors.[123] The indigenous traditions and elements were prominent in the crafts of the architect, carpenter, stonemason, and painter.[124] Dervish literature, Arab inscriptions, even stone markings of the masons reveal the activity of these Christians. The traces they have left in Turkish include the names of tools, of building materials, and of the various parts of the building.[125]

(Alexandria, 1924); Ἡ λεγομένη Ῥοδιακὴ ἀγγειοπλαστική (Alexandria, 1919). There are examples of specifically Armenian tiles in the Armenian patriarchate of Jerusalem, the Benaki Museum in Athens, and the Victoria and Albert Museum. Though the style of Ottoman tiles does not seem to betray any Christian stylistic influence, there seems to have been some continuity in technique, H. H. von den Osten, *The Alĭşar Hüyük Seasons of 1930-32, Part III* (Chicago, 1937), p. 205. T. Öz, *Turkish Ceramics* (Ankara, 1954), p. 44. For Islamic influence on Byzantine pottery, D. T. Rice, "Late Byzantine Pottery at Dumbarton Oaks," *D.O.P.*, XX (1966), 207–233.

Turkish loan words from the Greek include, fĭka, kavata, gavanoz, kanata, kilinder, patĭr, çukala.

[120] See nn. 574–576 in chapter iii. Also, R. Ettinghausen, E. Akurgal, C. Mango, *Treasures of Turkey*, pp. 167–168. M. von Berchem and J. Strzygowski, *Amida* (Heidelburg, 1910), pp. 120–128, 348–354. H. Buchthal, "A Note on Islamic Enameled Metalwork and its Influence on the Latin West," *Ars Islamica*, XI–XIII (1946), 198. O. von Falke, "Kupferzellenschmelz im Orient und in Byzanz," *Monatshefte für Kunstwissenschaft*, II (1909), 32 ff. L. A. Meyer, *Saracenic Heraldry* (Oxford, 1933), p. 102. Timur carried off many of these Christian metalworkers to Samarcand, de Clavijo-Le Strange, p. 288.

Loan words from Greek include, serma, helkek, halkin, helki, mermer, uskurun, sumpara, magnitis, istubedz, muhan.

[121] See nn. 566–567 in chapter iii. The word indal (picture) passed into Turkish from Greek.

[122] See n. 542, chapter iii. Loan words are dumban, çambuna, horos, sirto (type of circular dance). The circular form of dance in the Balkans is very ancient, being mentioned by Homer, *Illiad* Σ′ 593 ff., and appears in Greek vase painting and in the genre of terra cotta (see pls. iii and iv in Koukoules, Βίος, IV). The syrtos is described as an ancient religious dance in an inscription at the temple of Apollo at Ptoon in Boeotia in the years 37–41. Representation of the dance also appears on the obelisk of Theodosius II in the Constantinopolitan Hippodrome, Koukoules, Βίος, V, 207–222.

[123] See nn. 568–569 in chapter iii. Loan words from Greek are panukla, kulendž, sekires, ispazmos, tifos, hĭrĭzma, salya, iskelet, medire, hulya.

[124] The Greek ἐργάτης-ĭrgat became widespread in Turkish.

[125] See nn. 558–565 of chapter iii. Vayra, tĭrpane, cĭmbĭt, sakur, padar, pedavra, pur, halik, keremit, tuğla, duger, tolos, falak, palater, bodrum, temel. For the Byzantine usage of many of these terms, Koukoules, Βίος, IV, 261, 272, 285. One of the most prominent external features of the old Turkish houses, many of which are still to be seen in certain of the older quarters of Istanbul today, notably around Aghia Sophia, is the extension of a portion of the second story so that it will protrude out and over the first floor. This is a feature to be seen in a number of towns and the more prominent rural establishments in the Balkans and Anatolia. This feature was known in late Roman times, and perhaps earlier, as the solarium and in the Byzantine period as the heliakon or tablaton or exostes. It was intended to give the inhabitants of the house more sunlight and a better view. It was such a prominent characteristic in Byzantine domestic architecture that very often the sunlight was blocked from the streets of the towns by the solaria projecting from either side of the street. As a result Byzantine legislation is replete with laws governing this aspect of building and "civic planning." The heliaka are mentioned in the Theodosian code, in the legislation of Leo VI, and in the Hexabiblos of Harmenopoulos, etc. Koukoules, Βίος, IV, 290–292. The survival of Greek words that denote household items corresponds to the fact that in the beginning the nomad Turks had a very simple "household." Dernschwam-Babinger, pp. 181–182. "Item, wie man in Turkhej sehen mag an den zerschlaifften verprentten krichischen dorfern, seind die bej der cristen zeitten all von stainen und khot gemawert gewest, jeczundt ist es alles stainhauffen ubereinander. So bauen die t(urken) nichs, haben khain holcz, behelffen sich

The commercial life of the Anatolian Greeks, Armenians, and Syrians suffered temporary disruptions in periods of turmoil, but with the reestablishment of order the Christians returned to their enterprises. With the gradual stabilization of conditions in the twelfth century, the Greek merchants of Konya and Pousgousae reappear in the caravan trade between Konya and Constantinople, between Konya and Cilicia-Cyprus, and between northern Anatolia and Cappadocia.[126] In the east Armenians and Syrians reacted similarly to stabilized conditions, and there exists an archaeological monument testifying to their activity, a caravansaray built by a Christian merchant with inscriptions in Syriac, Armenian, and Arabic.[127] What of Byzantine commercial institutions as distinct from merchants? One of the most important Byzantine commercial institutions to be absorbed in the economic life of Seljuks and Ottomans was the Byzantine commercial-religious panegyris, which Martin Nilsson has convincingly derived from the Greek panegyris of pagan times. At the onset of the Seljuk invasions, the panegyris was a widespread and deeply rooted institution in both the Balkans and Anatolia. These fairs were discontinued in many areas because of the destruction of the initial conquests, but they eventually revived and by the late twelfth century, Turkish merchants were participating in the great commercial fair of the Archangel Michael at Chonae. From this time, and especially in the Ottoman Empire somewhat later, the panegyris remained a very important commercial institution.[128] The very word, as *panayïr*, passed into Turkish with numerous other commercial loan words. One of these was the term "commercium," in Turkish *gümrük* or *komerk*. In a commercial treaty between the ruler of Cyprus and the sultan of Konya in the thirteenth century (negotiated by a Greek of Konya), there is the provision that the old Byzantine tax, commercium, shall be paid on goods

---

in den gemewern under der erden, oben mit erden uberschut, also nider, das man daruber gehn mag, und die thuren also nider, das ein ros nicht hinein mag, welche thur ein wenig hoch ist. Ist fwr das viech und die turkhen selbs, dorumb ire heuser lautter stelle sein, haben khain keller, stuben, khamer, glassen fenster noch schlejmen fenster, khainen hausroth, wider schussel, teller, khandel, glesser, trinkgeschir, bethgewandt, tisch noch benkhe, dorumb sy auff der erden siczen und ligen, wie das viech von armut wegen. Das nu ir hoffart in stetten auch ist; wan er mir ein altten tebich vermag under zu braitten dungt er sich ein hern sein. Zw dem essen bedarff er khains tischtuchs noch handtuchs, dan ir essen das maiste von zorba ader suppenden ding ist, sawer gesotten und gesalczen, gerunnen milich, die man in allen dorffern findt. Dorumb das krigsvolkh alles loffel an dem gurttel tregt."

[126] Lampros, "Γλῶσσα," p. 51. Delehaye, "Le martyre de St. Nicétas le Jeune," *Mélanges G. Schlumberger* (Paris, 1924), I, 208. For other texts see nn. 473–474, chapter iii and *passim*.

[127] Erdmann, *Das anatolische Karavansaray des 13. Jahrhunderts* (Berlin, 1961), I, 63–67. Bar Hebraeus, I, 454.

[128] Michael Acominatus-Lampros, I, 56. Papadopoulos-Kerameus, *Ist. trap. imp.*, p. 65. R. Brundschvig, "Coup d'oeil sur l'histoire des foires à travers l'Islam," *Recueils de la Société Jean Bodin*, V (1953), 65–72.

coming into Anatolia. Bertrandon de la Brocquière commented that the Ottomans levied "komerk" on traffic passing through the Dardanelles in the early fifteenth century.[129]

The guild system of fourteenth-century Anatolia, and of a later period in the Balkans, included guilds that were exclusively Muslim, those that were exclusively Christian, and those that were interdenominational. To what degree Christian guild regulations were preserved and passed on to the Turkish system it is difficult to say. But the existence of purely Christian and mixed guilds, as well as of guilds the chiefs of which were Christians or converts, were conditions strongly favoring continuity in guild regulations and organization.[130] In the Anatolian towns, during the thirteenth and fourteenth centuries, the craftsmen had associations that were in addition penetrated by the Islamic ideology of futuwwa. These futuwwa groups (akhis) were probably an Islamic elaboration and version of the older Byzantine faction—neaniai—that dominated urban life in the sixth-century Levantine towns. Consequently, the Anatolian guild-futuwwa complex possibly reflects both a direct and an indirect Byzantine influence. All this points to strong similarities in Byzantine and Seljuk-Ottoman urban life and towns.[131]

The influence of the Greeks (and later of the Italians) on maritime life is relatively better attested in the written sources, though the early period is very inadequately documented. The Turks, coming from a landbound central Asiatic region and engaged primarily in pastoral life, had had very little experience with the sea. When between the eleventh and fifteenth centuries their migrations and conquests had made them masters of the Anatolian and Balkan peninsulas, they became exposed to the Black, Aegean, and Mediterranean seas, areas where their Greek subjects had enjoyed a long, unbroken tradition of seafaring, already celebrated in the Homeric epic and continuing to the present day. In Byzantine times Anatolia with its Pontic, Aegean, and Mediterranean harbors had figured very prominently in the history of overseas commerce and naval warfare. The thematic organization of the seventh through eleventh centuries had created a class of sailors who were not only responsible for manning the Byzantine provincial fleets, but also for building them. It was from the Anatolian Greeks that the Turks first learned the crafts of the shipbuilder, sailor, navigator, and fisherman. Apparently the

---

[129] See n. 102 above. Meyer, *Türk. Studien*, pp. 62–63. Darrouzès, "Lettres de 1453," *R.E.B.*, XXII (1964), 72–127, for precious materials indicating the continuity of Greek merchants and officials and their practices.

[130] Ibn Battuta-Gibb, II, 425, 427, 437–438. Eflaki-Huart, II, 14, 317–320. Hasluck, *Christianity and Islam*, II, 383. See chapter v.

[131] J. Cvijić, *La péninsule balkanique* (Paris, 1918), pp. 191–206. Mantran, *Istanbul dans la seconde moitié du XVIIᵉ siècle. Essai d'histoire institutionelle, économique et sociale* (Paris, 1962), *passim*, but especially pp. 419, 449, 497–498. Grégoire, "Les veilleurs de nuit à Trebizonde, *B.Z.*, XVIII (1909), 490 ff. Taeschner, "Das bosnische Zunftwesen zur Türkenzeit (1463 bs 1878)," *B.Z.*, XLIV (1951), 557–559.

Italian influence did not make itself directly felt before the fifteenth century.[132]

Within two decades of the battle of Manzikert (1071) a formidable Turkish maritime principality under the leadership of a certain Tzachas had appeared at Smyrna. But his ships were built and probably manned by Smyrniote Christians. A contemporary of his, Abu'l-Kasim, also had ships built in the old Byzantine shipyards, upon the capture of Cius, by the local Christians.[133] More specific information on Christian participation in Turkish maritime life comes only from Ottoman documents of the fifteenth century. A tahrir for Gallipoli, 1474, records that there were three *djemaats* of Greeks at this important Ottoman naval base: one of rowers, one of arbaletiers, and one of 95 Greeks for the repair and building of ships. Christians and renegades remained important throughout the long history of Ottoman naval enterprise.[134] Byzantine naval life has left an indelible impression in the Turkish language by virtue of the large number of termini technici which passed from Greek (and Italian) into Turkish. As the Byzantines managed to hold most of the Anatolian littoral through much of the twelfth century, and because Turkish exposure to the sea remained comparatively restricted for much of the thirteenth century, these loan words are limited at this early time.[135] By the sixteenth and seventeenth centuries, when the sources became more plentiful, the number of Greek loan words became more numerous, though it is to be supposed that many of these words were already employed in Turkish at an earlier time. The terminology includes words referring to the winds, seas, coastal geography, port, dockyard, types of boats, ropes, provisions, fishing, instruments, signals, rigging, and other words referring to naval life.[136]

Folk Culture

In matters of cuisine the conquerors undoubtedly absorbed some items from the conquered, but the problem is again obscured by a similarity in Byzantine and Islamic cuisine which probably existed before the appearance of the Turks. The Danishmendname gives descriptions of Christian feasts but unfortunately they are not complete.[137] Turkmen

[132] For an excellent and convenient survey of the development of naval power and life see Kahane and Tietze, *Lingua Franca*, pp. 1–45. On Byzantine maritime life, Koukoules, ínoς, V, 331–386. Ahrweiler, *Byzance et la mer* (Paris, 1966).

[133] Anna Comnena, II, 68–69, 110–114. Tzachas himself had been raised at the Byzantine court, a fact that would further his knowledge of Byzantine traditions. In fact there is much about Tzachas which puts him in line with Byzantine rather than with Seljuk traditions.

[134] Inalcik, "Gelibolu," EI₂. Mantran, *Istanbul*, pp. 487 ff.

[135] Kahane and Tietze, *Lingua Franca*, nos. 750, 791, 801, 841. Ibn Bibi-Duda, p. 283. Lampros, "Γλῶσσα," p. 51.

[136] Kahane and Tietze, *Lingua Franca*, pp. 16, 20–22, 32–35. The compilation lists over 150 words but excludes by and large ichthylological material. For maritime loan words in the Anatolian dialects, Tietze, "Anat. Türkisch," *passim*.

[137] Danishmendname-Melikoff, I, 30.

cuisine, as described by Brocquière, was a very simple affair consisting primarily of the produce of their flocks—meat, milk, yogurt, butter, cheese supplemented by millet or other grains, fruit, honey, eggs, and a type of unleavened wafer (prepared on a portable hot iron in the manner of our own pancakes) in place of bread.[138] The preparation of the unleavened cake was quite different from the baking of bread, and indeed the oven (*furnus*) of the Armenians and Greeks was conspicuously absent. It is significant that the Anatolian Turkish terminology for bread and its preparation has many words of Byzantine origin.[139]

Much of the later elaborate Turkish cuisine was foreign to the Turkmen nomads and belonged to a sedentary cuisine already common to the eastern Mediterranean world since Roman times if not earlier. A brief perusal of the pages of Athenaeus' *Deipnosophistae* will confirm the assertion, and therein the gastronomer will notice not only stuffed leaves but also the various oriental sweets. There is great similarity between Turkish sweets and those enjoyed by the Byzantines. The basic ingredients for these deserts were usually dough, sesame, wheat, nuts, honey, and various fruits. Thus the equivalents of the Turks börek, halva, baklava, and other delicacies are to be found in various Byzantine and classical texts. The Byzantine παστίλλα seems to have covered a variety of sweets, usually made of boiled wheat and honey, or crushed nuts and honey, or sesame and honey, or similar mixtures.[140] Another Byzantine favorite was the so-called κοπτή or κοπτόν (κοπτοπλακοῦς) that was the same as the Turkish baklava. This delicacy was known to Athenaeus who gives us the recipe. It was, he says, made of leaves of dough, between which were placed crushed nuts with honey, sesame, pepper, and poppy seed.[141] The börek are paralleled as early as the second century of the Christian

---

[138] Brocquière-Schefer, pp. 89, 91–92.

[139] Tietze, "Anat. Türkisch.," *passim*. Loan words that deal with baking of bread include, zĭmarĭ, külür, meze, meleksi, sisre, pinavut, senedi. On further lexicographical material that has to do with bread and baking in modern Turkish, H. Z. Koşay, "Türkiye halkĭnĭn maddĭ kültürüne dair araştĭrmalar II," *Türk etnografya dergisi*, II (1957), 7–28, and pls. ii–iii. For the unleavened bread in Seljuk times, M. Z. Oral, "Selçuk devri yemekleri ve ekmekleri," *Türk etnografya dergisi*, I (1956), 74–75. Travelers observed specifically Christian practices attendant upon making of bread in modern Anatolia among Turkish women, most striking of which was the marking of the cross on the unbaked loaf, see n. 173.

[140] John Chrysostom was attacked by his enemies for eating it after receiving communion. Byzantines ate it at weddings to increase fertility. It seems to be the equivalent of the Turkish susam halva. Koukoules, Βίος, V, 114–116.

[141] Athenaeus, XIV, 647–648. Koukoules, Βίος, V, 116. Tietze, "Einige Weitere," pp. 373–388, on παστίλλα, παστίλος, which passed into Turkish as a loan word. Von Hammer, *Geschichte des osmanischen Reiches* (Pest, 1827), I, 220, noted that Philadelpheia (Alashehir), famous in his own day for its halva (Honiggebäcke), had specialized in honey cakes when the Persian emperor Xerxes passed through the city in the fifth century. Herodotus, VII, 31, "... παρὰ Καλλάτηβον πόλιν ἐν τῇ ἄνδρες δημιοεργοὶ μέλι ἐκ μυρίκης τε καὶ πυροῦ ποιεῦσι." On the identification of Kallatebos with the latter Philadelpheia, see the article on "Kallatebos" in *P.W.* For the recipe of this type of halva in the sixteenth century, Dernschwam-Babinger, p. 125. "Inder andern ist ein solch weys confect, so man halwa nent, von mandeln, honig und ay weys."

era and throughout the Byzantine world by the πλακοῦντας ἐντυρίτας which Artemidorus and the medieval lexicographers mention.[142] Such dishes as the cheese μυζήθρα (*mizitra* in Turkish), cured meat παστόν (*pasdirma* in Turkish) were known to the Byzantines, and the roasting of meat on the spit, or shishkebab, was ancient in the Mediterranean area.[143]

As might be expected, the preparation of seafood and the art of wine-making were Christian specialities.[144] The Danishmendname illustrates the difficulty Muslim rulers had in suppressing the use of wine among the new converts,[145] and in the thirteenth century, Cappadocia, thanks to the Christian vineyards, was famous for its wines. Muhammad II paused long enough in Beğshehir, in the course of his Anatolian compaigns, to taste the wines of the Greek and Armenian inhabitants. Dernschwam in his journey through Anatolia during the sixteenth century constantly had recourse to the Greeks for his supply of wine.[146] Anatolian Turkish has, as a result of the Greek influence, borrowed a number of Greek words that are concerned with the cultivation of the vine.[147]

Christian religious and family practices left important traces in the Muslim society that emerged in Anatolia. The extensive intermarriage that took place not only between Christian women and Muslims but even between male converts or Christian men and Muslim women resulted in the introduction of many Christian features in Muslim family life and popular religious usage.[148] The large-scale conversions had very much the same effect with the result that the new Islam of Anatolia bore witness to the incomplete Islamization of the Christians.[149] The Anatolia in which

---

[142] Koukoules, Βίος, V, 118.

[143] H. Omont, *Evangiles avec peintures byzantines du XIe siècle* (Paris, n.d.), I, pl. 82 depicts the roasting of meat on the spit. Koukoules, Βίος, I, 50, 62, 65. Meyer, *Türk. Studien*, p. 57.

[144] Tietze, "Anat. Türkisch.," *passim*. Meyer, *Türk. Studien, passim*.

[145] Danishmendname-Melikoff, I, 380.

[146] Babinger, *Mahomet*, p. 399. Hans Dernschwam-Babinger, pp. 164, 166, 167, 191, 196, 213, 236. "Nindert in khainem turkischen dorff hot man wein gefunden, allein von der strossen in krichischen dorffern hot man in 1, 2 meilen darnach gesandt und bestelt." In Nicaea the Greeks and Armenians had to hide their wine barrels in the ground out of fear of the Turkish soldiers.

[147] Tietze, "Anat. Türkisch.," passim. The loan words include ombal, cingil, gevle, gilime, gilavadar, kilimaç, cambit, cubur, fitye, herek. Brocquière-Schefer, pp. 125–126, describes the making of a confection from nuts and grape, the Byzantine and modern Greek moustalevria.

[148] See nns. 246–251, 498–510 in chapter iii. Balsamon, Rhalles and Potles, I, 271–272; II, 473, refers to Georgian women married to Turks, and in II, 498, he specifically connects the adoption of Christian practices by the Turks to their Christian wives. He also refers to the fact that the twelfth-century patriarch of Alexandria was complaining because Orthodox women were marrying Muslims. The practice was widespread in the Ottoman Balkans, where western travelers referred to it as kabin (kepin-lease). See N. J. Pantazopoulos, *Church and Law in the Balkan Peninsula during the Ottoman Rule* (Thessaloniki, 1967), pp. 94–102.

[149] The Danishmendname-Melikoff, I, 380 gives a classic illustration. This same pattern is illustrated by the Greeks converted to Islam in Macedonia who were known as Vallahades. They preserved some of their churches; they celebrated feast days such

the Turks had settled had been one of the first regions to be Christianized and by the eleventh century every aspect of life was cast within a Christian mold and framework. Inasmuch as the economic and social life with which the Turks came into contact bore the Christian stamp, it was inevitable that this too would leave Christian coloration. As Islam vouchsafed both Christ and the Virgin a special place, this no doubt facilitated religious borrowing and syncretism at a popular level.

One would look in vain for any widespread Byzantine influence on the formal religious life of the Seljuk and Ottoman Turks because Islam had long since evolved into a highly structured, articulate, and unbending religious system. It is rather in the more vibrant aspect of Islam, popular Islam or volksreligion, that one must seek out this Christian influence. Hasluck opened the door to this intriguing subject in a memorable work that, unfortunately, has seen no systematic continuation. The persistence of popular religiosity within all formal religious structures is, of course, a well-known phenomenon, and yet, when one pauses to examine the details, he is invariably amazed by their freshness and vitality as well as by their grotesqueness. Such is the power of folk religion that the formal religious institution either acknowledges it openly or pretends to ignore it and thus absorbs it because it cannot eliminate it. This was characteristic of both the Christian church and Islam. Christian practices, beliefs, and forms, which are at the basis of a rather substantial portion of popular Turkish Islam, entered Islam as a result of conversions, intermarriage, everyday contact of Muslim and Christian in a cycle of life regulated by ancient custom, and through the religious syncretism of the popular dervish orders.

This borrowing was physically manifested and symbolized by the large scale appropriation of the church and monastic buildings themselves. The process was a widespread one, both geographically and chronologically. The history of the churches of Constantinople is better documented than that of perhaps any other region that came under Turkish domination. Only one church (St. Mary of the Mongols) from the myriad that existed in the Byzantine period remained in the hands of the Orthodox in modern times. The conquerors confiscated or otherwise removed all others from the possession of the Christians during the course of their centuries-long rule. So it was throughout Anatolia that they converted

as that of the healing saints Cosmas and Damianos, calling in Orthodox priests to celebrate in the church and to cross the women's heads with oil from the saints' lamp. Hasluck, *Christianity and Islam under the Sultans* (Oxford, 1929), I, 8. The same phenonenon was observed among Armenian converts in 1776 in eastern Anatolia, H. Barsegh and V. Sargisian, *Vijakagrakan nor tesutiun me i nbast Ankakh Hayastani* (Venice, 1919). The Armenian priest Boghos Mherian traveled among villages of Islamized and Turkified Armenians who opened a church to him and all about came to attend the service, which caused the frightened priest to flee. I am indebted for this reference to the kindness of my colleague Prof. Richard Hovanissian. For similar behavior on the part of Bulgarian Muslims, C. Vakarelski, "Altertumlich Elemente in Lebensweise und Kultur der bulgarischen Mohammedaner," *Zeitschrift für Balkanologie*, IV (1966), 149–172.

churches into mosques, turbes, dervish tekkes, or sometimes into store-houses and into other secular buildings.[150] Of course, the mere borrowing of these physical structures does not necessarily mean that the Muslims took over anything more than the buildings. But in many instances the Muslims appropriated characteristics and peculiarities attendant upon a particular Christian sanctuary along with the building itself. This resulted, not infrequently, in a syncretization of the old and new elements, particularly at the lower levels of society. This transferral of Christian practice, associated with a church converted to a mosque, was usually intensified or facilitated whenever conversion and intermarriage occurred.

This is apparent in the Muslim and Christian practice of equating saints of one religion with those of the other religion.[151] The best known equation of a Muslim with a Christian saint revolves about the figure of Khidr. As early as the fourteenth century, John Cantacuzene noted that the Turks worshiped St. George in the figure of Khidir Elias,[152] and at Elvan Chelebi, east of Chorum, he was associated with St. Theodore. In both cases he has been identified with equestrian, military, dragon slayers.[153] In Konya the Muslims reverenced St. Amphilochius under the guise of Plato or Eflatun, and elsewhere they identified Sarï Saltïk with St. Nicholas, and St. Charalambos with Hadji Bektash.[154] A religious ceremony held in honor of Hadji Bektash by the Greek Christians of Sinassus is recorded in the fifteenth century,[155] and in the nineteenth century local Christians believed that the tomb of Hadji Bektash near Kïrshehir was the tomb of St. Charalambos.[156] Often the sanctuaries that were relinquished to Islam retained a certain Christian holiness.[157] The Muslims of fifteenth-century Konya attributed miracles to the tomb of St. Amphilochius. At the extremes of Anatolia—at Edessa in the east and at Yalova in the west—the survival of the holy went back through the Byzantine era to pagan times; the famous hot springs of Yalova were in antiquity dedicated to Apollo, in the Byzantine days to St. Michael, and under the Turks they were resanctified by the burial of a dervish; at Edessa the sacred fish in the fountain of the mosque of Abraham continue a pre-Turkish tradition.[158]

[150] See nn. 357–363 in chapter iii, and see chapter iv, *passim*. Hasluck, *Christianity and Islam*, I, 3–118.

[151] Hasluck, *Christianity and Islam*, I, 17, 48–53; II, 363–367, 432–433, 568–586. Gordlevski, *Izbrannye Soch.*, I, 321–361.

[152] John Cantacuzene, *P.G.*, CLIV, 512. Hans Dernschwam-Babinger, p. 205.

[153] Hasluck, *Christianity and Islam*, I, 48–49, 320–336.

[154] *Ibid.*, I, 17; II, 364, 432–433, 571–572. Babinger, "Byzantinisch-osmanisch Grenzstudien," *Z.D.M.G.*, LXXVI (1922), 126 ff.

[155] Vilayetname-Gross, p. 43.

[156] Hasluck, *Christianity and Islam*, II, 572.

[157] In Constantinople, the doors of St. Sophia, said by the Christians to have been constructed from the wood of Noah's ark, were objects of Muslim veneration. The sacred well was believed by the Turks to cure heart ailments, and the sweating column was also believed to have curative powers, Hasluck, *Christianity and Islam*, I, 10.

[158] *Ibid.*, 207, 244–245.

The belief in the efficacy of Christian religious power was apparently rather widespread in Muslim Anatolia, and Christian saints and sanctuaries were thought to be possessed of both evil and beneficial magic. Certain Christian churches, converted to mosques, were found to be hostile to the Muslims, and their hostility was variously manifested. In St. John (Kĭzĭl Avlĭ) of Pergamum, it was said, the doorway continuously turned northward and the minaret fell. On the church of St. Sophia in the same town a cross appeared after its conversion into a Muslim sanctuary. In Thyateira (Akhisar) the Muslims attributed the collapse of a minaret to the "anti-Muslim influence" resident in the Turkified church. The Turks abandoned the church of St. Amphilochius in Konya and the Friday Mosque of Antalya (both Turkified edifices) when it was discovered that Muslims died upon entering them.[159] But other Christian sanctuaries and saints were possessed of beneficial powers that Muslims could utilize. The cults of the saints which developed so profusely throughout Byzantine Anatolia constituted the truly vital element in Anatolian Christianity, and it was to the saints that the local Christian populations had appealed in times of distress. It would seem that the influence of these local saints was particularly strong among the Turks in the "medicinal" realm. In the thirteenth century the emir of Sivas sent his wife, who was possessed by demons, to be cured by the prayers of the Christians. Upon her arrival in Trebizond she went to the monastery of St. Phocas and to the tomb of St. Athanasius where she was healed.[160] Schiltberger records in the late fourteenth century that Turks participated in a pilgrimage to a church in Ankara because of a stone inscribed with a cross which had healing powers.[161] The visitation of Christian shrines famed for their cures was a living tradition among Anatolian Muslims even in the nineteenth and twentieth centuries. Turks went to the church of St. Michael of Tepedjik of Bithynia for the cure of madness, to St. Photine of Izmir for ailments of the eyes, and to the Virgin of Sumela of Trebizond for relief from a wide assortment of misfortunes. In 1908 with the incidence of cholera the Turks of Ürgüp requested that the Christians parade the body of St. John Roussos through the Turkish quarter. During the course of the procession the Turkish women are reported to have deposited costly kerchiefs on the bier of the saint as a propitiatory offering.[162]

---

[159] *Ibid.*, 20–23. Murad sacrificed a ram before St. Demetrius of Thessalonike, Ducas, p. 201.

[160] Papadolpoulos-Kerameus, " Συμβολαὶ εἰς τὴν ἱστορίαν Τραπεζοῦντος," *V.V.* XII (1906), 141.

[161] Schiltberger-Neumann, p. 95. "In der stat sint vil cristen, die halten ermenischen globen. Und haben in ir kirchen ein crütz, daz schait tag und nacht. Dar in gond haiden kirch ferten und das crutz haissent sie den liechten stein. Es wollten och die heiden einvart genumen haben und woltens in iren tempel gefurt haben, und welcher das angriff der erkrumet an den henden."

[162] Hasluck, *Christianity and Islam*, I, 65–69.

The partial survival of Christian cults in Anatolian Islam is reflected in the appearance of double sanctuaries, sanctuaries that Christians and Muslims either formally shared or else visited. Such an ambiguous shrine was Ziyaret Kilise at Mamasun Tekke near Nevshehir in the nineteenth century. In this sanctuary, at which both Greeks and Turks worshiped St. Mamas, there were nine icons and a holy altar in the east end at which an itinerant Christian priest officiated. In the south wall was a mihrab for the benefit of the Muslims. The relics of St. Mamas in the possession of this sanctuary, of which the custodian was a dervish, are said to have effected miracles for both Christians and Muslims.[163] Similar was the Muslim turbe of Ghazi Shehid Mustafa and his son at Araplı near Bendereğli (Heracleia Pontica). The Christians considered it to be the tomb of St. Theodore Stratelates and one of his associates, and made the pilgrimage to the shrine bringing offerings of money and candles. One of the earliest of these mixed sanctuaries was the monastic complex around the church of St. Chariton near Konya. There existed a mosque, side by side with the churches of St. Chariton, St. Amphilochius, St. Sabbas, and the Virgin, which according to tradition was founded on the spot where St. Chariton interceded to save the son of Djalal al-Din Rumi from a fall. This is very probably the "monastery of St. Plato" that Rumi and his followers visited in the thirteenth century in order to meditate and to converse with the Greek monks.[164] In the fifteenth century the church of St. Amphilochius, converted into a mosque, was the object of pilgrimage for both Greeks and Turks.[165]

Of the important Christian practices that Muslims appropriated, the sources frequently mention that of baptism (in Turkish *vaftiz*). The Muslims of Anatolia had adopted baptism as early as the twelfth century, at which time the Byzantine canon lawyer Balsamon commented on the invalidity of such baptism.

In the days of the most holy patriarch, lord Loukas, Agarenes appeared before the synod. Upon being requested to receive baptism they replied that they had already been baptized in their own lands. On their being asked how, they answered that it is the custom for all the infants of the Agarenes to be baptized by Orthodox priests. But they [and their explanation] were not accepted. For they heard that the baptism which the unbelievers demanded from the Christians was not demanded by reason of good disposition and Orthodox purpose but for healing of the body. For the Agarenes suppose that their children will be possessed of demons and will smell like dogs if they do not receive Christian baptism. Accordingly they do not invoke baptism as a cathartic of all spiritual sordidness and as the provider of holy light and sanctification, but rather as a remedy or magical charm. Some of these [Agarenes] said they had Orthodox mothers and

[163] For details and bibliography, *ibid.*, 43–44; II, 759–761.
[164] *Ibid.*, I, 56. Eflaki-Huart, I, 261; II, 67, 358.
[165] Hasluck, *Christianity and Islam*, I, 17.

it was as a result of their [mothers'] care that they were baptized by Orthodox priests.[166]

Balsamon's testimony is particularly valuable as it gives the historian a brief but incisive view of the process of cultural and religious syncretism. Baptism is declared to have been widely accepted by the Turks of Anatolia, and in some cases it was obviously due to the cultural influence Greek mothers brought into the Muslim household. The Turks valued the physical rather than the spiritual efficacy of the sacrament, a fact that probably reflects in part upon the manner in which the Christians also viewed baptism. No doubt the Christians themselves believed in the therapeutical effects of this particular sacrament. The case of the Seljuk sultan 'Izz al-Din in the mid-thirteenth century seems to have been quite similar to what Balsamon describes. Born of a Christian mother, the young sultan was baptized before he attained the throne.[167] Brocquère observed the same phenomenon in southern Anatolia among the Turkmen princes of Ramazan and Karaman, who were baptized in order to remove "the bad smell."[168] Baptism is also mentioned in relation to the syncretistic religious movement associated with the name of Badr al-Din in the fifteenth century.[169] De Busbecq indicates that the Muslims continued to baptize their children a century later,[170] and the practice was so common that

[166] Rhalles and Potles, II, 498. This is repeated by the fourteenth-century lawyer Constantine Harmenopoulos, P.G., CL, 125, " οἱ τῶν' Ἀγαρηνῶν παῖδες βαπτιζόμενοι παρὰ ὀρθοδόξων ἱερέων ἀκόντων, οὐκ εὐσεβεῖ διανοίᾳ τῶν προσαγόντων αὐτοῖς, ἀλλ' ὡς φαρμακείᾳ ἢ ἐπαοιδίᾳ χρωμένων, εἰ προσέλθοιεν ἀληθῶς τῇ πίστει, ἀναβαπτίζονται. Ταῦτα γὰρ συνοδικῶς ἀπεφάνθη, ὡς ὁ Βαλσαμὼν λέγει."

[167] Pachymeres, I, 131, 263–268. Nicephorus Gregoras, I, 95. P.G., CXL, 956. In Constantinople he took an active part in the liturgy, kissed the icons, etc. Both Ibn Bibi and Karim al-Din reflect the tension between the Christians and Muslims at Konya, as does also William of Rubruque. For the supposed baptism of Murad III as a preventive of epilepsy, Hasluck, Christianity and Islam, I, 34.

[168] Brocquiere-Schefer, p. 90, "Ramadan ... avoit est filz d'une femme crestienne laquelle l'avoit fait baptiser a la loy gregiesque pour luy enlever le flair et le senteur qu'ont ceulx qui ne sont point baptisiez," p. 115, "C'estoit un tresbeau prince (Karaman) de trente deux ans, et estoit bien obey en son pays. Il avoit este baptise en la loy gregesque pour oter le flair, aussy duquel la mere avoit este crestienne, comme on me dist." It is also mentioned by Joseph Bryennius, Τὰ εὑρεθέντα (Leipzig, 1768), II, 34; " ὅθεν καὶ τῶν 'Ισμαηλιτῶν οἱ Σατράπαι, καὶ οἱ πλείους τῶν 'Αρχόντων αὐτῶν, βαπτίζονται τυραννοῦντες τοὺς ἐν ταῖς χώραις αὐτῶν ἱερεῖς."

[169] Bartholomaeus Georgieuiz, the sixteenth-century Christian captive who lived for a number of years as a slave in Anatolia, recounts that among the blandishments that his Turkish master proffered so as to induce him to convert was the similarity of religious practices between Islam and Christianity. This included baptism by the Turks. F. Kidrič, Bartholomaeus Gjorgevic: Biographische und bibliographische Zusammenfassung (Vienna-Prague-Leipzig, 1920), p. 15. "Tum ille, nos saepius baptizamur, haec verba recitantes, bisem allah alrah man elrahim: id est, in nomine Dei et misercordiae et misericordiarum, nec hac parte a Christianis differimus, sed quia eos idolatros credimus servitiem in eos exercemus, ut acerbitate malorum a tali religione avocentur." My colleague, Andreas Tietze, has suggested that this very probably refers to Muslim ablutions rather than to baptism. See nn. 16–17 in chapter v.

[170] Hasluck, Christianity and Islam, I, 32. In canon law of the seventeenth century it is related that Muslims baptized their children as prophylactic measures against ψεῖρα, faulty circumcision, and body smell. Koukoules, Βίος, IV, 55, "διὰ νὰ μηδὲν ψειριάζουν καὶ νὰ μηδὲν κακοπαθοῦν εἰς τὴν περιτομὴν καὶ διὰ νὰ μηδὲ βρωμῇ τὸ κορμὶ αὐτῶν."

Greek canon law forbade priests to baptize the children of the Turks under pain of defrocking.[171] The potency of immersion in the Christian manner survived among the Turkish inhabitants of Ladik (Laodiceia Combusta) in an Islamized version. These Muslims, who according to their own traditions were descended from the ancient Christian population, bathed their children in an ʿαγίασμα just outside of the town in order to prevent their offspring from becoming Christians.[172]

Among other Christian objects to which Turks frequently had recourse were the cross and the icons. To a stone decorated with the cross in Eldjik of Galatia they attributed curative powers. Cases have been recorded wherein the cross was used as a prophylactic device on buildings that were being built, and on bread dough before it was placed in the oven.[173] A Karamanid prince made offerings to an icon of the Virgin of Corycus and was cured of blindness by rubbing, on his eyes, cotton that had been passed across the icon.[174] Muslims visited the icon of the Virgin at the monastery of Sumela (said to have been painted by St. Luke) in order to obtain relief from locusts and other vexations.[175] In the thirteenth century the sultan ʿIzz al-Din demonstrated his affection for the icons openly in Constantinople.[176] De Busbecq observed that the Turks did not go to sea until the Christian blessing of the waters had taken place at Epiphany.[177]

The performance of animal sacrifice, *thysia* or *kurban*, was common to both popular Islam and Christianity in Anatolia, but it is not absolutely clear whether they arose independently or the one derived from the other.

---

[171] Koukoules, Βίος, IV, 54, " ἱερεῦς ἐὰν δεχθῇ θυσίαν αἱρετικοῦ ἢ βαπτίσῃ Τούρκου παιδίον . . . καθαιρείσθω."

[172] Calder, *M.A.M.A.*, I, xv; "A Journey round the Proseilemmene," *Klio*, X (1910), 233 ff. On Turkish reverence for the agiasma, V. Deligianes, " Ἡ λαϊκὴ λατρεία τῶν Κουβουκλίων," M.X., VI (1955), 200–201.

[173] Hasluck, *Christianity and Islam*, I, 30–31, 206. E. Pears, *Turkey and its People* (London 1911), p. 79. Vakalopoulos, " Ἱστορικὲς παραδόσεις τῶν Ἑλλήνων προσφύγων τοῦ Σογιούτ," Πρόσφορα εἰς Στίλπωνα Π. Κυριακίδην (Thessalonike, 1953), p. 79. Matthew of Ephesus-Treu, p. 57, indicates that the Christians used it in an apotropaic manner against the Muslims.

[174] Machairas, *Chronique de Chypre*, ed. E. Miller and C. Sathas (Paris, 1882), II, 60, " Καὶ θέλει εἶσται βαρετὸν εἰς ἐκείνους ὁποῦ 'γρικοῦσιν νὰ 'ξηγηθῶ καταληπτῶς τὰ καθημερινὰ θαύματα τὰ πολομᾷ ἡ αὐτὴ εἰκόνα, καὶ πῶς εἰς τ' ὅρομαν τοῦ Καραμάνου τοῦ μεγάλου τοῦ κυροῦ τοῦ Μαχομὲτ Μπαχία, καὶ ἐτύφλωσέν τον καὶ ἔμεινεν στραβὸς ἡμέραις πολλαῖς καὶ ἐμολόγησεν πῶς μία ἀρχόντισσα ἁπαὶ τὸ Κουρίκος ἔδωκέν τον κατἄμματα καὶ ἐτύφλωσέν τον, καὶ ἦτον πληροφορία τῆς εἰκόνος τὰ φοβερὰ θαύματα· ἐσήκωσεν τὸ φουσάτον του καὶ ἐποῖκεν πολλὰς λαμπάδας κερένας χοντραῖς καὶ γ' καντήλαις ἀργυραῖς ὁποῦ 'κρέμουνταν ὁμπρός της, καὶ πολλαῖς γέρναις λάδιν καὶ ἐποῖκεν λυχναψίαν καὶ ἐψάλλαν ὅλη νύκτα· καὶ 'πισαυρίου ἐσυναλεῖψαν παντπάκιν ἁπαὶ τὴν εἰκόνα καὶ ἔβαλάν το εἰς τὰ 'μάτιά του καὶ παραῦτα ἐγίανεν. Καὶ πολλὰ ἄλλα θαύματα." For examples of the same practice among the Greek Christians of western Anatolia in the nineteenth and twentieth centuries, N. E. Meliores, " Ἱστορικὰ καὶ λαογραφικὰ τῶν Βουρλῶν σύμμικτα," *M.X.* VI (1955), 226–227. During the panegyris of August 15, the believers passed under the icons and rubbed bits of cotton on their eyes.

[175] Hasluck, *Christianity and Islam*, I, 66. J. Fallmereyer, *Fragmente aus dem Orient* (Stuttgart, 1877), p. 121.

[176] Nicephorus Gregoras, I, 95. For other examples of the acceptance of icons and their powers by Turks, Hasluck, *Christianity and Islam*, I, 41, 53–54.

[177] Hasluck, *Christianity and Islam*, II, 384–386.

The sacrifice of animals is of course a very obvious phenomenon in Islam, but it has also been observed among Greek and Armenian Christians. Rycaut noted it to be widespread in the seventeenth century.

When they [Greeks] lay the Foundation of a new Building, the Priest comes and blesses the Work and Workmen with Prayer, for which they have an Office in the Liturgy, which is very laudable and becoming Christians. But when the Priest is departed, the Workmen have another piece of their own Devotion to perform, which they do by killing a Cock, or a Sheep, the blood of which they bury under the first stone they lay: It is not always, but very frequently practised, in which they imagine that there is some lucky Magick or some spell to attract good fortune to the Threshold; they call it, θυσία, or Sacrifice, and therefore I believe that this is a piece of ancient Heathenism.[178]

In the late nineteenth century, Greek Christians of the village of Zele (Sylata) in Cappadocia sacrificed animals to St. Charalambos especially in time of illness.[179] Though the Greeks frequently referred to these sacrifices by the Turkish term "kurban," the sacrificial practices went back to Byzantine and pagan times as is evident from several factors. They frequently referred to these sacrifices by the ancient Greek terms θυσία and θάλι. The question of Christian borrowing from the Muslim kurban sacrifice is probably restricted to the philological aspect for the pagan sacrifice seems to have remained very lively and widespread in Byzantine times. One of the most spectacular examples of its existence in Byzantine Anatolia was the sacrifice of the fawn to St. Athenogenes at Pedachthoe on July 17. On that day the young animal and its mother passed before the altar of the monastery church of St. Athenogenes while the Gospels were being read. The fawn was sacrificed, cooked, and eaten by the congregation and thus the faithful celebrated the glory of the martyred saint.[180] In the miracula of St. Theodore Teron there is mention of oxen offered as sacrifices to the saint.[181] The pagan usage of animal sacrifice survived also in the Byzantine practice of slaughtering and roasting animals after the celebration of ecclesiastical festivals. The sixteenth canon of the synod of Carthage asked the emperor to put an end to this habit; the commentary of Balsamon indicates that it was widespread in the twelfth century, and it has survived to the present day.[182]

---

[178] P. Rycaut, *The Present State of the Greek and Armenian Churches Anno Christi 1678* (London, 1679), pp. 371–372.

[179] The phenomenon was recorded by S. Holopoulos, " Μονογραφική ἱστορία Ζήλης ἢ Συλάτας," Ξενοφάνης, II (1905), 206.

[180] Cumont, "L'archevêché de Pedachtoe et le sacrifice du faon," *Byzantion*, VI (1931), 521–533. Kyriakides, " Θυσία ἐλάφου ἐν νεοελληνικοῖς συναξαρίοις," Λαογραφία, VI (1917), 189–215.

[181] Sigalas, " Διασκευή," pp. 333–334.

[182] Koukoules, Βίος II₁, 8. Rhalles and Potles, III, 465–466. Hasluck, *Christianity and Islam*, I, 261, for further references to the sacrifice of cocks to the mine spirits by Greek miners, etc.

The liturgical sacrifice·in the Armenian church, known as *madag*, is also a survival from antiquity.[183]

Not only was animal sacrifice (of pagan origin) a widespread practice among the Anatolian Christians in the Byzantine period, but there is evidence that it passed, in its Byzantine form, into popular Islamic usage. Bartholomaeus Georgieuiz gives the following account of animal sacrifice as the Turks practised it in sixteenth-century Anatolia.

The manner of their sacrifice.

In the time of anye disease or peril, they promise in certaine places to sacrifice either a Shepe or Oxe; after that the vowed offering is not burned, like unto a beast killed and layed on the aulter, as the custome was among the Jewes, but after that the beast is slaine, the skinne, head feete, and fourthe parte of the flesh are geven unto the prest, an other part to poore people, and the thirde unto their neighbours. The killers of the sacrifice doe make readye the other fragments for the͞ selves and their compaynions to feede on. Neyther are they bound to performe the vow, if they have not bene delivered from the possessed disease or peril. For all things with them are done condytionallye I will geve if thou willte graunt. The lyke worshyppinge of God is observed among the Gretians, Armenians, and other realms in Asia imitating yet ͞y Christian religio͞.[184]

Bartholomaeus identifies this sacrificial custom as something specifically Christian, which Greeks and Armenians (as well as Turks) practised. More convincing than Bartholomaeus' opinion as to the Christian origin is the description he gives of the apportioning of the sacrificed beast's parts. The "priest" receives the skin, extremities, and a portion of the meat, an arrangement that follows very closely the practice of pagan Greek sacrifice. The priest's share (in Bartholomaeus' account) clearly matches the pagan δερματικόν as Greek sacrificial inscriptions of the fourth and third centuries of the pre-Christian era depict it. The priest who presided over pagan sacrifices was entitled to the skin, extremities, and portion of the flesh. It would seem highly probable, therefore, that the Turkish custom derived from the Byzantine, which in turn originated in pagan sacrifice.[185]

---

[183] J. Karst, *Sempadischer Kodex aus dem 13. Jahrhundert oder mittelarmenisches Rechtsbuch nach der venediger und der etschmiadziner Version unter Zuruckführung auf seine Quellen* (Strassburg 1905), I, 59: II, 38–39.

[184] Bartholomaeus Georgieuiz-Goughe under "The manner of their sacrifice."

[185] For the priest's share, the δερματικόν, in pagan antiquity see the Greek inscriptions of the pre-Christian era, E. Schwyzer, *Dialectorum Graecarum exempla epigraphica potiora* (Leipzig, 1923), nos. 168, 366, 695, 721, 728, 729, 808, 811. In all these cases the priest's portion generally corresponds to that which Bartholomaeus describes for the Turkish "priests". See especially the articles "Dermatikon," and "Opfer," in *P.W.* The Greeks of Pharasa in eastern Asia Minor still performed these sacrifices (kurbania) in the early twentieth century, D. Loucopoulos and D. Petropoulos, Ἡ λαϊκὴ λατρεία τῶν Φαράσων (Athens, 1949), pp. 21, 44–49. They observed the exact apportioning of the parts of the sacrificed beast as is observed among the Turks by Bartholomaeus, i.e., portions were given to the poor, the priest received the skin, head, feet and the right part, etc. In Pharasa they used the ancient Greek word θάλι (from θάλεια, banquet of the Gods), and employed candles, incense, and a crown of vines for the animal, which was also pelted with flowers. For sacrifice of animals by the Greek Christians of Thrace in the early part of the century, G. Megas, " Θυσία ταύρων καὶ κριῶν ἐν τῇ βορειοανατολικῇ Θράκῃ," Λαογραφία, III (1911), 148–171; Ζητήματα ἑλληνικῆς λαογραφίας (Athens, 1950), III, 27–29.

The belief in tree spirits and the religious association of trees in general were also common to both religious groups. The groves of cypress trees in the graveyards outside the great land walls of Istanbul are indications of Turkish reverence for these trees, and numerous Turkish superstitious beliefs have been associated with the funereal cypress. The same tree is inextricably associated with Greek cemeteries today. The association of the cypress with the cemetery and with the regions outside the Constantinopolitan walls was prevalent in Byzantine times.[186]

A definite case of pagan survival, which passed through the Christains to the Muslims, was the use of "medicinal" earth. The use of such earth from Chios, Cimolus, Eretreia, Lemnus, Melus, Samos, and Sinope was attested as early as Pliny and continued into the nineteenth century.[187] At each stage new users associated their own religious practices with the digging of the earth. Galen records that the excavation of the earth in Lemnus was preceded by a religious ceremony of the priestess of Artemis in which she sprinkled barley on the "excavation" site and executed other ceremonies, after which she sealed the earth with a likeness of the goddess. In the fifteenth century the terra Lemnia was stamped with the seal of Christ, and in the sixteenth century with Turkish letters. In this later period the earth's excavation proceeded on the feast day of the Metamorphosis (August 6) after a religious celebration in the church of the Saviour. Both Greeks and Turks participated in the celebration and the Turks sacrificed a sheep.

Turkish customs attendant upon marriage and birth, because of the long history of intermarriage in Anatolia, quite probably reflect the absorption of some Christian practice. In Byzantium, and among the Greek Christians of Chile (Pontus) and Burdur (Pisidia) in the nineteenth century, the bride was accompanied to the baths and special festivities took place on the night preceding the wedding night.[188] It is thus perhaps significant that in the Turkish of Chankiri the bridal bath prior to the wedding is referred to by the word *hirizma* which derives from the Greek χρῖσμα.[189] The invitations to the wedding, among Byzantines and Anatolian Greeks of later times, were entrusted to the καλεστής, whose duty it was to go from house to house and to indicate the invitation by leaving

[186] In the Archaeological Museum of Istanbul is an inscription, dated 860 which records the planting of cypress trees at the grave of an important Byzantine official, C. Mango. "The Funeral Tree." *Archaeology*, III (1950), 140–141. Procopius, *Buildings*, I, iii, 6. Thucydides relates, in the Periclean funeral oration, that the wood of the cypress was used for the coffin of the unknown dead.

[187] Pliny, *Natural History*, XXXV, 6. On the subject, Hasluck, *Christianity and Islam*, II 671–687.

[188] Koukoules, Βίος IV, 105. On Byzantine customs attendant upon birth, baptism, marriage, G. Spyridakis, Τὰ κατὰ τὴν γέννησιν, τὴν βάπτισιν καὶ τὸν γάμον ἔθιμα τῶν βυζαντινῶν ἐκ τῶν ἁγιολογικῶν πηγῶν (Athens, 1953). K. Iatrides, " ' Η μνηστεία ἐν Βουρδουρίῳ ἄλλοτε καὶ νῦν," Ξενοφάνης III (1905), 72–82, 165–171, 201–211, 272–278, 335–342.

[189] Tietze, "Anat. Türkisch.," p. 244, "das Bad der Braut in der Nacht vor der Hochzeitsnacht."

a piece of fruit, usually an apple or lemon. The practice and the word survived in the Turkish of the regions of Konya, Isparta, and Nigde, as *gelis*, *kelisçi*, and in the verb *kelis gezmek*, and so forth.[190] Common to both Christians and Muslims is the association of fruit with love, engagement, and marriage. From the time Paris awarded the apple to Aphrodite in the divine concourse of beauty, the connection between fruit and the fair sex has been constant in Greek custom.[191] The emperors of the eighth and ninth centuries chose their brides in a beauty contest by presenting an apple to the future imperial consort;[192] golden apples or pomegranates were part of the ceremonial connected with the empress' procession to and from the bath after the wedding.[193] As early as the fourth century and into the medieval epoch the groom was "showered" with apples when he came to take the bride from her parents' house.[194] Mention is also made of the presentation of the peach by the youth to the object of his affection.[195] In the Danishmendname, the Turkish epic, an episode occurs which bears on the role of fruit in such cases. Efromiya, the daughter of the Greek governor of Amasya, becomes enamored of the warrior Artuhi, a Greek convert to Islam, and to indicate her love she tossed an orange at his feet. It is possible that this is a Persian matrimonial practice, and yet the author of the poem attributes it to a Christian woman. Perhaps it is merely an example of cultural "confusion" and syncretism of two similar practices.[196]

John Cantacuzene describes a case of Turkish exposure to Byzantine court matrimonial ceremony, the *prokypsis*, at the wedding celebration that took place at Selymbria in the marriage of his daughter to Orhan.[197]

He ordered that a wooden prokypsis [stage] be built in the plain before the city of Selymbria, so that the emperor's daughter who was to be married, standing upon it, might be clearly seen by all. For it is thus the custom of emperors to do when their daughters are given in marriage . . . . On the next day the empress remained on the scenium with her other two daughters, while Theodora, who was to be married, ascended the prokypsis. Only the emperor was mounted on horse,

[190] Koukoules, Βίος IV, 92–93. Tietze, "Anat. Türkisch.," pp. 221–222, "herumziehen und zur Hochzeit einladen." Tietze also records the use of the Greek word σκούφια in the form of uskuf, in the districts of Burdur and Kïrshehir as signifying the head ornament of the bride; also κουκούλα as kukul at Gumushhane to mean bridal cap, 239–240, 227.

[191] Koukoules, Βίος IV, passim.

[192] Bréhier, *Les institutions de l'empire byzantin* (Paris, 1949), pp. 30–31.

[193] Koukoules, Βίος IV, 146. Constantine Porphyrogenitus, *De Caerimoniis*, I, 214–215.

[194] Koukoules, Βίος IV, 146.

[195] Nicetas Choniates, 192.

[196] For other such associations of love with the apple, the rose, and with fruit in general: Danishmendname-Melikoff, I, 169, 208; II, 101, 129. Eflaki-Huart, II, 7, 14–15. Nicetas Choniates, 183. Psellus-Sathas, *M.B.*, V, 321. Koukoules, Βίος, IV, 104. Eflaki-Huart, I, 353, mentions the custom of preparing sugared almonds for weddings, a practice also common at Greek weddings.

[197] For details on this ceremony, Koukoules, Βίος, IV, 134–136. Heisenberg, *Aus der Geschichte und Literatur der Palaeologenzeit, Sitz. der bayer. Akad. Phil-hist. Kl. Abhand.*, X (1920), 90, 92–93, 109. Andreeva, "Sur la cérémonie de la prokypsis," *Seminarium Kondakovianum*, I (1927), 157 ff.

and all the others were on foot. As the curtains were raised [the prokypsis was covered on all sides by silk clothes and gold brocades], the bride was displayed and lighted torches surrounded her which were held by eunuchs who, as they were on bended knee, were not visible. Trumpets, flutes, pipes, and all instruments invented for the pleasure of men played loudly. When these were silent the chanters sang encomia which had been composed for the bride by some learned men. When all these ceremonies, which it is incumbent upon the emperors to perform for marrying daughters, were completed, the emperor entertained for many days the army and all the officials of the Greeks and barbarians.[198]

This ceremony of prokypsis is an interesting example of Ottoman contact with Byzantine ceremonial which may have occurred in other areas of contact as well. But once again mere contact does not tell us anything specific about influence, and more study and research are necessary before the question will admit of precise statement.

Common practices that have to do with the birth and early care of the infant are to be found in the customs of the Greeks and Turks of Anatolia. It is quite possible that in this domain one does perceive holdovers from the Byzantine period as a result of the large-scale intermarriage with Christian women. The wet nurse of Sultan Walad, the son of Djalal al-Din Rumi, was referred to as *yeramana*. This would seem to come from the Greek "old mother" (in modern Greek παραμάννα).[199] The daughter of Rumi was named Meleke Hatun, but Eflaki reports that she was better known as Effendi-poulo, which in Greek signifies "child of the master."[200] In the district of Isparta the Greek word signifying womb has passed into the local Turkish vocabulary as *medire;* and νηνί, meaning a small child, has become *nini, ninni,* in the Turkish spoken about Malatya, Isparta, and Muğla.[201] Both Christians and Muslims in Anatolia practised the "salting" of the new-born child during the early twentieth century.[202] Salt was also employed in the rites attendant upon the birth of a child in Byzantine times, and it is mentioned as early as Galen. The first bathing of the infant took place in water containing salt because, it was believed, the salt water would repel evil spirits, and the belief arose that this would make the child beautiful as well. After the bath, salt was sprinkled on the body. It would seem that salt was put into the baptismal font as late as the sixteenth century because of its power to turn away malevolent spirits.[203]

[198] Cantacuzene, II, 587–588.

[199] Eflaki-Huart, II, 291.

[200] *Ibid.*, I, 429, "poulo" being the suffix denoting "offspring" or "child."

[201] Tietze, "Anat. Türkisch.," 233. For the latter word in Byzantine times, Koukoules, Βίος, IV, 29.

[202] P. Eleutheriou, " Πραγματεία περὶ τῶν ἤθων καὶ ἐθίμων τῆς κωμοπόλεως Λιβισίου κατὰ τοὺς παλαιοὺς χρόνους," Ξενοφάνης, IV (1907), 178. For the practices of tuzlamak and sulamak, O. Acïpayanlï, *Türkiyede doğumla ilgili adet ve inanmalarïn etnolojik etüdü* (Erzerum, 1961), pp. 56–57. I am indebted to the kindness of my colleague Andreas Tietze for this latter reference.

[203] Koukoules, Βίος IV, 28–29, 50.

Studies of the folklore and popular literature of the Anatolian Christians have indicated that a remembrance of the distant Byzantine past remained alive among these people in the twentieth century. This literature and lore narrate the heroic deeds of such historic individuals as Gabras (eleventh century), the piety of the emperor John Vatatzes (thirteenth century), the fall of Trebizond and Constantinople, and, of course, the exploits of the Byzantine hero Digenes Akrites.[204] It is somewhat symbolic of this lively memory that the first manuscript of the poem of Digenes to be found was the copy the Greek scholar Ioannides discovered in the Trebizondine monastery of Sumela in 1873, and that Greek songs from the Acritic cycle were alive among the Cappadocian Greeks in the nineteenth and twentieth centuries.[205] The question arises as to whether any of this epic material was assimilated into the folk literature of the conquering Turks. Ioannides noticed that in a Karamanlidhiko edition of the Turkish epic of Kör-oğlu one sees many of the same loves, struggles, and adventures that are to be found in the story of Digenes.[206] Though there seems to be no other reference to this Karamanlidhiko edition of Kör-oğlu (in Turkish but with the Greek script), it is of interest that the Christians read and were exposed to the Turkish epic. The research of Kyriakides seems to indicate that this Turkish epic was possibly influenced in certain parts by the Byzantine epic. The second part of the Anatolian version of the epic of Kör-oğlu includes the tale of his abduction of the beloved and his defense against the girl's powerful family. The details are very close to that part of the Digenes Acritas in which the Byzantine hero first abducts his beloved and then repulses the furious attack of her relatives. Kyriakides has pointed out that this episode in the second part of the Kör-oğlu epic is present in the Anatolian version of the poem but does not exist in the versions to be found in Adharbaydjan. Thus, on these two grounds, he has argued that the Turkish has been influenced by the Byzantine epic.[207] If more detailed research in the future should prove

[204] The literature on this subject is considerable and no attempt is made here to include anything but a sampling of it. A. S. Alektorides, " Ἄσματα Καππαδοκικά," Δ.Ι.Ε.Ε.Ε. I (1883), 712–728. Megas, " Παλαιὰ ἱστορικὰ τραγούδια τοῦ Πόντου," Λαογραφία, XVII (1957–58), 373–382. Lampsides, " Τὸ ἀκριτικὸν ἔπος καὶ τὸ ᾆσμα τοῦ Γαβρᾶ," Α.Π., XXIII (1959), 33–38. D. K. Papadopoulos, " Ποικίλα ᾆσματα τοῦ χωρίου Σταυρίν," Α.Π., XI (1941), 29, no. 4.

[205] Alektorides, " Ἄσματα," passim. S. Ioannides, Ὁ Βασίλειος Διγένης Ἀκρίτης (Constantinople, 1887).

[206] Ioannides, Βασίλειος, p. 26.

[207] Kyriakides, " Τὸ ἔπος τοῦ Διγενῆ καὶ τὸ Τουρκικὸν λαϊκὸν μυθιστόρημα τοῦ Κιόρογλου," Ἑλληνικά, XVII (1962), 252–260. "Eléments historiques byzantins dans le roman épique turc de Seyyid Battal," Byzantion, XI (1936), 563–570. Grégoire, "L'épopée byzantine et ses rapports avec l'épopée turque," Bulletin de la classe des lettres et des sciences morales et politiques de L'Académie Royale de Belgique 1931, vol. XVII (1932), no. 12, 5ᵉ ser., pp. 463 ff. T. Alangu, "Bizans ve Türk kahramanlık eposlarının cıkısı üzerine," Türk Dili, II (1953), 541–557. A. Bombaci, Storia della letteratura turca dall'antico impero all'odierna Turchia (Milan, 1956), pp. 209–225. F. Iz, "Dede Korkut," EI₂. E. Rossi, Il "Kitab-i Dedi Qorqut". Racconti epico-cavallereschi dei Turchi Oguz tradetti e annotati con "facsimile" del ms. vat. turco 102, Studi i Testi, CLIX (Vatican, 1952). P. N. Boratav,

this assertion to be valid, it would indicate that in the symbiosis of Turks and Greeks which followed the Turkish conquest of Anatolia both groups would have borrowed elements in each other's folk epics.

Conclusions

Turkish formal society in Anatolia bore essentially Islamic characteristics. The inseparable union of church and state, and their determination of all formal aspects of society, resulted in a state structure and cultural life that were Muslim. The sultanate, bureaucracy, Islamic church, literature, and much of art were Islamic. Byzantine society, on the other hand, had been intimately connected with the *basileia* and Orthodoxy, and the large-scale adoption of Byzantine formal institutions could only follow the adoption of the Byzantine style of theocracy, as was the case in Bulgaria and Serbia, or else it might occur when the neighboring society was still unformed and not affiliated with another developed church-state apparatus. Whatever elements of this Byzantine formal culture appear in Ottoman society must have entered indirectly via the culture of Islamic civilization.

This Turkish society, though Muslim in its formal expression, or *Hochkultur*, nevertheless was strongly Byzantine in its *Tiefkultur* or folk culture. This was the result of the fact that in the beginning the conquered subjects of the Turks were the Christian inhabitants of Anatolia. The economic life of the Seljuks and Ottomans was heavily determined by these Christian peasants and city dwellers. The Byzantine influence was particularly strong in agricultural and village life, but also in the cities with their craft and commercial traditions. In these urban traditions, however, there was a significant admixture of Islamic urban elements. The economic continuity of Byzantium had important repercussions as well in the Turkish tax structure and administration. Finally, this widespread absorption and partial survival of Christian populations had a marked effect in the spheres of Turkish family life, popular religious beliefs and practices.

What was the effect of Turkish conquests and institutions on this Byzantine society and culture? The demands of the Turkish political, fiscal, feudal, and religious institutions destroyed the economic as well as the political and social bases of Byzantine Hochkultur in Anatolia (and in the Balkans as well), and in so doing reduced this culture to an almost exclusively Volkskultur. Thus, in contrast to the Ottoman Turks who developed a rich formal literature, a classical music, and an impressive architecture, the formal literary production of their Christian subjects

"Dede Korkut hikayelerindeki tarihî olaylar ve kitabin te'lif tarihi," *T.M.*, XIII (1958), 31–62; "Kör-oğlu," *I.A.*, VI; *Halk hikayeleri ve halk hikayeçiliği* (Ankara, 1946); *Köroglu destanı* (Istanbul, 1931). A. Chodzko, *Specimens of the Popular Poetry of Persia as Found in the Adventures and Improvisations of Kurroglou, and in the Songs of the People Inhabiting the Shores of the Caspian Sea. Orally Collected with Notes* (London, 1842). Melikoff, "al-Battal," EI₂.

496

was penurious by comparison; their secular music was largely of a folk character, as was much of their art. The survival of the greatly weakened church and rise of the Phanariot class would provide a diluted version of the old Byzantine Hochkultur on a limited scale (more so in the Balkans than in Anatolia), but essentially the church was a strong crutch upon which the Christian folk culture partly rested. Most important, the Turkish conquests resulted in the absorption of the major portion of this Byzantine population via religious conversion and linguistic Turkification.

Consequently, the old Byzantine society played both an active and passive part in the history of Anatolia. Its absorption, on the plain of Hochkultur (language and formal religious affiliation) constituted its passive role. But this assimilated Byzantine society was a basic constitutive element in the popular culture of Turkish Anatolia and in those aspects of society that Islam did not rigidly control. In this respect Byzantine society exercised an active force in the historical process that unfolded in Asia Minor.

Recapitulation

The Turkish conquest of Asia Minor and the Islamization of the area's inhabitants constitute the last major stage in the history of Hellenism outside the Greek peninsula. The expansion of Greek cultural boundaries beyond Greece proper began at any early date, engulfed the Levant in Hellenistic times, and became deeply rooted during three centuries of Roman imperial rule. Consequently, the process of Hellenization, though superficial outside the major urban centers in Syria and Egypt, was thorough in much of urban and rural Anatolia by the sixth century of the Christian era. The geographical boundaries of this medieval Greek cultural world in the Levant were, thereafter, determined by military struggles with the various Islamic states. The Umayyad Empire caused the first major contraction of Byzantine political and cultural boundaries by the conquests of the seventh century, but after the loss of Syria and Egypt, the Byzantine and Islamic empires attained an equilibrium within which a substantial portion of Anatolia remained Greek in language and religion. The invasions of the Muslim Turks in the eleventh century renewed the process of Muslim aggrandizement at the expense of the Greek Christian society, a process that was consummated in the fifteenth century. By this time the Turks had destroyed the empire of Constantinople and the Byzantinized Slavic states of the Balkans, and by the Islamization-Turkification of Anatolia had restricted the Greek world largely to the southern Balkans. The cycle of expansion and contraction, which had endured for more than two millennia, finally returned to the original point of departure.

This book, which focuses on this late phase of Greek retrenchment, attempts to describe the critical factors in the decline of medieval Hellenism and the concomitant process of Islamization in Anatolia. The basic conclusions may be stated in terms of seven interrelated theses:

1. Anatolian Hellenism, or the medieval Greek cultural element of Anatolia, was quantitatively and qualitatively significant during the Byzantine period. Thus, the Turkish conquest and Islamization of Asia Minor represent something more than a negative historical event, for the invaders had to subdue and absorb a vital society.

498

2. The Turks did not completely subdue the peninsula and subject it to political unification until the latter half of the fifteenth century.

3. The nature of the conquest and settlement caused major dislocation and destruction to Byzantine society. The Turkish conquest lasted almost four centuries, during which time the one unified, stable Byzantine administration was replaced by countless, smaller unstable political entities that were in an almost constant state of war with one another. Thus much of Anatolia was transformed into the scene of continuous military strife. This condition and Muslim hegemony exercised a corrosive action upon the bonds and sentiments that held the Christian communities together, thus preparing the members for religious conversion. Though there is evidence for extensive conversion of Christians in the earlier period, as of the mid-thirteenth century the Christians of Anatolia still constituted a large bulk of the populace, perhaps even the majority.

4. The political and historical events of the Turkish conquests in Asia Minor destroyed the Greek church as an effective social, economic, and religious institution. Given the fact that religion permeated and formed practically every aspect of medieval society, the sharp decline of the church was an unqualified disaster in the disappearance of the Byzantine character of Asia Minor.

5. Christian society, which had been subjected to such disruption and dislocation in the wake of the Turkish invasions, was isolated from the heartbeat of its own culture in Constantinople and deprived of ecclesiastical leadership in the provinces. Thus it was ripe for absorption into the new Islamic society. This was largely the work of Islamic institutions supported by the political and economic favor of the various Turkish principalities. These Muslim institutions (based securely on the economic possessions and revenues formerly belonging to the Christian church), most important of which were the dervish orders, consummated the cultural transformation by converting the Christians to Islam.

6. The great military disasters induced a considerable variety of aetiological rationalization among the Anatolian Christians. To some the military conquests of the Turks proved the religious superiority of Islam over Christianity. Others saw in the Byzantine defeats either divine chastisement of an errant society, the chiliasitic end of human history, or an impersonal tyche that arbitrarily raised and abased empires. Many, whether of religious or secular historical persuasion, contented themselves with the prospect that the enslavement of the Greeks would, after a passage of time, be followed by the resurrection of the Greek Christian empire.

7. Byzantine culture in Anatolia, though effaced on the level of formal culture by Islamic Hochkultur, exercised a determinant role in much of Turkish folk culture or Tiefkultur.

At this point one must note an apparent paradox. Though both Anatolia and the Balkans were conquered and subjected to centuries of Turkish rule, the Balkans, unlike Anatolia, remained predominantly Christian. On first glance, one sees that the Turkish presence in the Balkans lasted approximately four centuries whereas in Anatolia it endured for nine centuries. Thus one might suppose that Islamization in Anatolia was more extensive because the transforming forces were at work for a much longer period. But this does not seem to be the real explanation because the mass Islamization of the Anatolian Christians had already transpired by the fifteenth century, and the proportion of the Christian population to that of the Muslims in Anatolia remained relatively constant thereafter (though by the nineteenth century the proportion of Christians had increased). The answer to the question lies in a combination of factors. The Turkish conquest of the Balkans, beginning in 1354 and culminating in the reign of Muhammad II, was not nearly so prolonged or repeated a process as it was in Anatolia, and Turkish colonization (particularly of Turkmens) was not as heavy as it had been in Anatolia. The conquests and colonization were effected by one strongly centralized government that made every effort to restore order in the conquered provinces and to enforce obedience among the Turkmens, so that the state might reap the maximum fruits of an economically productive empire. Of great significance was the fact that the Balkan Christian communities were not cut off from the leadership and discipline of their ecclesiastical institution for a prolonged period. Muhammad, shortly after the conquest of Constantinople reconstituted the Greek patriarchate as the head of all the Orthodox Christians within the Balkan and Anatolian provinces of his empire. Thus the partriarchate, and therefore the Orthodox church, enjoyed a more regularized and uniform position in Turkish lands than had been the case prior to 1454. Up until Muhammad destroyed the Byzantine Empire, the patriarch and the church were associated with the foes of the Turkish states, and hence the clerics and properties of the church in Turkish lands were a legitimate prey for the Turks. Despite all these more favorable circumstances, Balkan Christians did apostatize to Islam in large numbers, both before and after 1453.

The last great cultural transformations in the Mediterranean basin occurred, simultaneously, at its western and eastern extremities, the two border regions between Christianity and Islam. In each case political-military events determined the cultural evolution of the Iberian and Anatolian peninsulas. The Spanish *reconquista* not only removed the Islamic political state but resulted in the Christianization and Hispanization of the populace. The Turkish conquest led to the Islamization and Turkification of the Anatolian populations and to the destruction of the Byzantine Empire. The disappearance of Greek in Anatolia and of Arabic in Spain was accompanied by the effort to write Spanish in the Arabic script and Turkish in the Greek alphabet. The role of refugees from both areas was particularly important in the struggle between Islam and Christianity in the Mediterranean during the fifteenth and sixteenth centuries. Greek refugees fled the Turkish conquests and established themselves in Italy and the West where they often spurred Western rulers to institute crusades for the purpose of destroying the Ottoman Empire. Spanish Muslims and Jews, embittered by their fate in Spain, migrated to the Ottoman Empire where they heightened the anti-Christian tenor of Ottoman expansion into central Europe.

Index